Belize
& Northern Guatemala

D1461440

Other Travellers' Wildlife Guides

Costa Rica
Ecuador
Peru

Belize
& Northern Guatemala

by Les Beletsky

Illustrated by:
David Dennis, David Beadle, Priscilla Barrett, Colin Newman,
and John Myers

Contributors:
Filadelpho Chablé, Simon Comerford, Richard Francis, Brian
Helmuth, Jon Lyon, and Briana Timmerman

ARRIS BOOKS
An imprint of Arris Publishing Ltd
Gloucestershire

First published in Great Britain 2005 by

Arris Books
An imprint of Arris Publishing Ltd
12 Main Street
Adlestrop
Moreton-in-Marsh
Gloucestershire GL56 0YN
www.arrisbooks.com

ISBN 1 84437 045 3

Printed and bound in China

To request our complete catalogue, please call us at **01608 659328**,
visit our web site at: **www.arrisbooks.com**, or e-mail us at:
info@arrisbooks.com.

CONTENTS

Plate Key Symbols and Codes

Explanation of habitat symbols:

 = Lowland wet forest.

 = Lowland dry forest.

 = Highland forest and cloud forest. Includes middle elevation and higher elevation wet forests and cloud forests.

 = Forest edge and streamside. Some species typically are found along forest edges or near or along streams; these species prefer semi-open areas rather than dense, closed, interior parts of forests. Also included here: open woodlands, tree plantations, and shady gardens.

 = Pastureland, non-tree plantations, savannah (grassland with scattered trees and shrubs), gardens without shade trees, roadside. Species found in these habitats prefer very open areas.

= Freshwater. For species typically found in or near lakes, streams, rivers, marshes, swamps.

= Saltwater/marine. For species usually found in or near the ocean or ocean beaches.

Political Districts (see Maps 1 and 2, pages 5 and 9)

COROZAL District is Northern Belize (COR)
ORANGE WALK   District is Northwestern Belize (ORW)
BELIZE   District is Central Eastern Belize (BEL)
STANN CREEK   District is Southeastern Belize (STN)
CAYO   District is Western Belize (CAYO)
TOLEDO   District is Southern Belize (TOL)
CAYES   are Belize's coastal islands (CAYE)
PETÉN   District is Guatemala's nothern department, or province (PET)

PREFACE

T his book and others in the series are aimed at environmentally conscious travellers for whom some of the best parts of any trip are glimpses of animals in natural settings; at people who, when speaking of a journey, often remember days and locations by encountered wildlife: "That was where we watched the monkeys," and "That was the day we saw the snake eat the frog." The purpose of the book is to enhance enjoyment of a trip and enrich wildlife sightings by providing identifying information on several hundred of the most frequently encountered animals of Belize and north Guatemala (Tikal and the entire Petén Department, or province), along with up-to-date information on their ecology, behavior, and conservation. With color illustrations of about 150 fish and other marine animals, 80 species of amphibians and reptiles, 50 mammals, and more than 200 birds, this book truly includes almost all the animals visitors are likely to encounter.

The idea to write these books grew out of my own travel experiences and frustrations. First and foremost, I found that I could not locate a single book to take along on a trip that would help me identify all the types of animals that really interested me – birds and mammals, amphibians and reptiles. There are bird field guides, which I've used, but they are often large, heavy books, featuring information on every bird species in a given country or region. For Belize and Guatemala, for instance, regional bird guides detail more than a thousand species, most of which are rarely seen. If I wanted to be able to identify mammals, I needed to carry another book. For "herps" – amphibians and reptiles – I was a bit astonished to learn, no good, small book existed that might permit me to identify these animals during my travels. Thus, the idea: create a single guide book that travellers could carry to help them identify and learn about the different kinds of animals they were most likely to see.

Also, in my experience with guided tours, I've found that guides vary tremendously in their knowledge of wildlife. Many, of course, are fantastic sources of information on the ecology and behavior of animals. Some, however, know only about certain kinds of animals, birds, for instance. And many others, I found, knew precious little about wildlife, and what information they did tell their groups was often incorrect. For example, many guides in Central America, when asked the identity of any large lizard, respond that it is an "iguana." Well, there certainly are iguanas in Central America, but there are also many other types of lizards, and people interested in wildlife need some way to identify more common ones. This book will help.

Last, like most ecotravellers, I am concerned about the threats to many species as their natural habitats are damaged or destroyed by people; when I travelled, I wanted current information on the conservation statuses of animals that I encountered. This book provides the traveller with conservation information on Belize and Guatemala in general, and on many of the animal family groups pictured or discussed in the book.

A few administrative notes: because this book has an international audience, I present measurements in both metric and English system units. By now, you might think, the scientific classification of common animals would be pretty much established and unchanging; but you would be wrong. These days, what with new molecular methods to compare species, classifications of various animal groups that were first worked out during the 1800s and early 1900s are undergoing sometimes radical changes. Many bird groups, for instance, are being rearranged after comparative studies of their DNA. The research is so new that many biologists still argue about the results. I cannot guarantee that all the classifications that I use in the book are absolutely the last word on the subject, or that I have been wholly consistent in my classifications. However, for most users of this book, such minor transgressions are probably irrelevant.

Finally, let me say that I tried, in several sections of the book, to make the information I present at least mildly entertaining. So many books of this type are written in a dry, terse style. I thought a lighter touch was called for – after all, many of the book's readers will be on holiday, and should not have to plod through heavy material. When I anthropomorphize – provide plants and animals with human characteristics – I do so for fun; plants and insects, I feel fairly safe in saying, do not actually think and reason. Readers who decide that they do not appreciate my sense of humor may simply ignore those sections; remaining still should be a solid wildlife natural history guide.

I must acknowledge the help of a large number of people in producing this book. First, most of the information here comes from published sources, so I owe the authors of those books and scientific papers a great deal of credit. The source I probably consulted most often during this book's preparation was *Costa Rican Natural History*, edited by Daniel Janzen (see reference page for complete citations); a great deal of the general information I present on tropical mammals, for instance, comes from this source. I freely acknowledge my debt to Janzen and the large numbers of contributors to that great compendium of information on the plants and animals of Central America; without it, my job would have been much harder. Other good sources of information were *A Neotropical Companion: An Introduction to the Animals, Plants, and Ecosystems of the New World Tropics*, by J. C. Kricher, *Neotropical Rainforest Mammals: A Field Guide*, by L. H. Emmons, *A Guide to the Birds of Mexico and Northern Central America*, by S. N. G. Howell and S. Webb, *The Amphibians and Reptiles of the Yucatán Peninsula*, by J. C. Lee, and *Birds of the Mayas*, by A. L. Bowes, and I recommend all these books for those wanting to delve deeper into their particular subjects.

I would like to take this opportunity to thank the many people who provided information for or helped in the preparation of this book, including Jeanette Bider, Jeff Corwin, Peter Eltringham, Kevin Gould, Ellen Gryj, Dana Heller, Robert Horwich, Tony Garel, Rosanna Griffith, Douglas James, Ellen McCrae, Tom McDonald, Martin Meadows, Gordon Orians, Conrad Reining, Osmani Salas, Karen Shine, and David Whitacre. Both the Burke Museum and the Department of Zoology at the University of Washington provided me facilities during the book's preparation. Special thanks to Jon Lyon for contributing the section on Belize habitats, Simon Comerford and Filadelfo Chablé for writing about Guatemalan habitats, Brian Helmuth and Briana Timmerman for writing about marine life, Richard Francis as special fish consultant and for writing the marine life plate captions, the artists who drew the wonderful illustrations, Priscilla Barrett (mammals), David Beadle (birds), David Dennis (amphibians and reptiles), Colin Newman (marine life), and John Myers (plants). Glen Murphy and Mark Peck at the Royal Ontario Museum permitted generous use of materials for producing the bird plates.

Please let me know of any errors you find in this book. I am also interested in hearing your opinions on the book, suggestions for future editions, and of your experiences with wildlife during your travels. Write care of the publisher or e-mail: ecotravel8@aol.com

—Les Beletsky

Chapter 1

ECOTOURISM: TRAVEL FOR THE ENVIRONMENTALLY CONCERNED

- *What Ecotourism Is and Why It's Important*
- *The History of Ecotourism*
- *How Ecotourism Helps; Ecotravel Ethics*

What Ecotourism Is and Why It's Important

People have always travelled and probably they always will. Historical reasons for travelling are many and varied: to find food, to avoid seasonally harsh conditions, to emigrate to new regions in search of more or better farming or hunting lands, to explore, and even, with the advent of leisure time, just for the heck of it (travel for leisure's sake is the definition of tourism). For many people, travelling fulfills some deep need; there's something irreplaceably satisfying about journeying to a new place: the sense of being in completely novel situations and surroundings, seeing things never before encountered, engaging in new and different activities.

During the 1970s and 1980s there arose a new reason to travel, perhaps the first wholly new reason in hundreds of years: with a certain urgency, to see natural habitats and their harbored wildlife before they forever vanish from the surface of the Earth. Ecotourism or ecotravel is travel to destinations specifically to admire and enjoy wildlife and undeveloped, relatively undisturbed natural areas, as well as indigenous cultures. The development and increasing popularity of ecotourism is a clear outgrowth of escalating concern for conservation of the world's natural resources and biodiversity (the different types of animals, plants, and other life forms found within a region). Owing mainly to peoples' actions, animal species, plant species, and wild habitats are disappearing or deteriorating at an alarming rate. Because of the increasing emphasis on the importance of the natural environment by schools at all levels and the media's continuing exposure of environmental issues, people have enhanced appreciation of the natural world and increased awareness of environmental problems globally. They also have the very human desire to want to see undisturbed habitats and wild animals before they are gone, and those with the time and resources increasingly are doing so.

But that is not the entire story. The purpose of ecotravel is actually two-fold. Yes, people want to undertake exciting, challenging, educational trips to exotic locales – wet tropical forests, wind-blown deserts, high mountain passes, mid-ocean coral reefs – to enjoy the scenery, the animals, the nearby local cultures. But the second major goal of ecotourism is often as important: the travellers want to help conserve the very places – habitats and wildlife – that they visit. That is, through a portion of their tour cost and spending into the local economy of destination countries – paying for park admissions, engaging local guides, staying at local hotels, eating at local restaurants, using local transportation services, etc. – ecotourists help to preserve natural areas. Ecotourism helps because local people benefit economically as much or more by preserving habitats and wildlife for continuing use by ecotravellers than they could by 'harvesting' the habitats for short-term gain. Put another way, local people can sustain themselves better economically by participating in ecotourism than by, for instance, cutting down rainforests for lumber or hunting animals for meat or the pet trade.

Preservation of some of the world's remaining wild areas is important for a host of reasons. Aside from moral arguments – the acknowledgment that we share the Earth with millions of other species and have some obligation not to be the continuing agent of their decline and extinction – increasingly we understand that conservation is in our own best interests. The example most often cited is that botanists and pharmaceutical researchers each year discover another wonder drug or two whose base chemicals come from plants that live, for instance, only in tropical rainforest. Fully one-quarter of all drugs sold in the USA come from natural sources – plants and animals. About 50 important drugs now manufactured come from flowering plants found in rainforests, and, based on the number of plants that have yet to be cataloged and screened for their drug potential, researchers estimate that at least 300 more major drugs remain to be discovered. The implication is that if the globe's rainforests are soon destroyed, we will never discover these future wonder drugs, and so will never enjoy their benefits. Also, the developing concept of *biophilia*, if true, dictates that, for our own mental health, we need to preserve some of the wildness that remains in the world. Biophilia, the word recently coined by Harvard biologist E.O. Wilson, suggests that because people evolved amid rich and constant interactions with other species and in natural habitats, we have deeply ingrained, innate tendencies to affiliate with other species and actual physical need to experience, at some level, natural habitats. This instinctive, emotional attachment to wildness means that if we eliminate species and habitats, we will harm ourselves because we will lose things essential to our mental well-being.

The History of Ecotourism

Tourism is arguably now the world's largest industry, and ecotourism among its fastest growing segments. But mass ecotourism is a relatively new phenomenon, the word being coined only during the 1980s. In fact, as recently as the 1970s, tourism and the preservation of natural habitats were viewed largely as incompatible pursuits. One of the first and best examples of ecotourism lies in Africa. Some adventurers, of course, have always travelled to wild areas of the Earth, but the contemporary history of popular ecotourism probably traces to the East African nation of Kenya. Ecotourism, by one name or another, has traditionally been a mainstay industry in Kenya, land of African savanna and of charismatic, *flagship*, mammals such as elephants and giraffes, leopards and lions – species upon which to base an entire ecotourism industry.

During most of the European colonial period in East Africa, wildlife was plentiful. However, by the end of colonial rule, in the middle part of the 20th century, continued hunting pressures had severely reduced animal populations. Wildlife was killed with abandon for sport, for trade (elephant ivory, rhinoceros horn, etc.), and simply to clear land to pave way for agriculture and development. By the 1970s it was widely believed in newly independent Kenya that if hunting and poaching were not halted, many species of large mammals would soon be eliminated. The country outlawed hunting and trade in wildlife products, and many people engaged in such pursuits turned, instead, to ecotourism. Today, more than a half million people per year travel to Kenya to view its tremendous wildlife and spectacular scenery. Local people and businesses profit more by charging ecotourists to see live elephants and rhinoceroses in natural settings than they could by killing the animals for the ivory and horns they provide. Estimates were made in the 1970s that, based on the number of tourist arrivals each year in Kenya and the average amount of money they spent, each lion in one of Kenya's national parks was worth $27,000 annually (much more than the amount it would be worth to a poacher who killed it for its skin or organs), and each elephant herd was worth a stunning $610,000 (in today's dollars, they would be worth much more). Also, whereas some of Kenya's other industries, such as coffee production, vary considerably from year to year in their profitability, ecotourism has been a steady and growing source of revenue (and should continue to be so, as long as political stability is maintained). Thus, the local people have strong economic incentive to preserve and protect their natural resources.

Current popular ecotourist destinations include South Africa, Kenya and Tanzania in Africa; Nepal, Thailand, and China in Asia; Australia; and, in the Western Hemisphere, Mexico, Costa Rica, Puerto Rico, Ecuador, Chile, and the Amazon Basin. Probably between 125,000 and 150,000 people visit Belize each year as tourists. Guatemala has more than half a million visitors annually, with perhaps one in five making their way to northern Guatemala – the Petén District.

How Ecotourism Helps; Ecotravel Ethics

To the traveller, the benefits of ecotourism are substantial (exciting, adventurous trips to stunning wild areas; viewing never-before-seen wildlife); the disadvantages are minor (sometimes, less-than-deluxe transportation and accommodations that, to many ecotravellers, are actually an essential part of the experience). But what are the actual benefits of ecotourism to local economies and to helping preserve habitats and wildlife?

The pluses of ecotourism, in theory, are considerable:

(1) Ecotourism benefits visited sites in a number of ways. Most importantly from the visitor's point of view, through park admission fees, guide fees, etc., ecotourism generates money locally that can be used directly to manage and protect wild areas. Ecotourism allows local people to earn livings from areas they live in or near that have been set aside for ecological protection. Providing jobs and allowing local participation is important because people will not want to protect the sites, and may even be hostile toward them, if they formerly used the now-protected site (for farming or hunting, for instance) to support themselves but are

no longer allowed such use. Finally, most ecotour destinations are in rural areas, regions that ordinarily would not warrant much attention, much less development money, from central governments for services such as road building and maintenance. But all governments realize that a popular tourist site is a valuable commodity, one that it is smart to cater to and protect.

(2) Ecotourism benefits education and research. As people, both local and foreign, visit wild areas, they learn more about the sites – from books, from guides, from exhibits, and from their own observations. They come away with an enhanced appreciation of nature and ecology, an increased understanding of the need for preservation, and perhaps a greater likelihood to support conservation measures. Also, a percentage of ecotourist dollars are usually funnelled into research in ecology and conservation, work that will in the future lead to more and better conservation solutions.

(3) Ecotourism can also be an attractive development option for developing countries. Investment costs to develop small, relatively rustic ecotourist facilities are minor compared with the costs involved in trying to develop traditional tourist facilities, such as modern beach resorts. Also, it has been estimated that, at least in Central America, ecotourists spend more per person in the destination countries than any other kind of tourists.

A conscientious ecotraveller can take several steps to maximize his or her positive impact on visited areas. First and foremost, if travelling with a tour group, is to select an ecologically committed tour company. Basic guidelines for ecotourism have been established by various international conservation organizations. These are a set of ethics that tour operators should follow if they are truly concerned with conservation. Travellers wishing to adhere to ecotour ethics, before committing to a tour, should ascertain whether tour operators conform to the guidelines (or at least to some of them), and choose a company accordingly. Some tour operators in their brochures and sales pitches conspicuously trumpet their ecotour credentials and commitments. A large, glossy brochure that fails to mention how a company fulfills some of the ecotour ethics may indicate an operator that is not especially environmentally concerned. Resorts, lodges, and travel agencies that specialize in ecotourism can also be evaluated for their dedication to eco-ethics. Some travel guide books provide such ratings.

Basic ecotour guidelines, as put forth by the United Nations Environmental Program (UNEP), the World Conservation Union (IUCN), and the World Resources Institute (WRI), are that tours and tour operators should:

(1) Provide significant benefits for local residents; involve local communities in tour planning and implementation.
(2) Contribute to the sustainable management of natural resources.
(3) Incorporate environmental education for tourists and residents.
(4) Manage tours to minimize negative impacts on the environment and local culture.

For example, tour companies could:

(1) Make contributions to the parks or areas visited; support or sponsor small, local environmental projects.
(2) Provide employment to local residents as tour assistants, local guides, or local naturalists.
(3) Whenever possible, use local products, transportation, food, and locally

owned lodging and other services.

(4) Keep tour groups small to minimize negative impacts on visited sites; educate ecotourists about local cultures as well as habitats and wildlife.

(5) When possible, cooperate with researchers; for instance, Costa Rican researchers are now making good use of the elevated forest canopy walkways in tropical forests that several ecotourism facility operators have erected on their properties for the enjoyment and education of their guests.

Committed ecotravellers can also adhere to the ecotourism ethic by disturbing habitats and wildlife as little as possible (including fish and other coral reef wildlife, not to mention the coral reef itself!), by staying on trails, by being informed about the historical and present conservation concerns of destination countries, by respecting local cultures and rules, by declining to buy souvenirs made from threatened plants or animals, and even by actions as simple as picking up litter on trails.

Now, with some information on ecotourism in hand, we can move on to discuss Belize and northern Guatemala. The area covered in this book is shown below in Map 1.

Map 1 Districts of Belize, the Petén Department of Guatemala, and major cities and towns.

Chapter 2

BELIZE AND NORTHERN GUATEMALA: ECOTOURISM, GEOGRAPHY, HABITATS, PARKS, AND RESERVES

- *A Brief Eco-history of Belize and Northern Guatemala*
- *Geography and Climate*
- *Habitats*
  Tropical Forest: General Characteristics
  Forest Habitats and Common Vegetation
- *Parks, Reserves, and Other Eco-sites: Brief Descriptions and Getting Around*

A Brief Eco-history of Belize and Northern Guatemala

Belize

For many reasons, Belize is a wonderful place to visit. In fact, the list of positive reasons to do so is a good deal longer for this small Central American nation than for most other, comparable spots. Aside from the obvious – the country's scenic beauty coupled with the fun and adventure involved in exploring an exotic, tropical locale – Belize consistently offers ecotravellers interesting, full, and thought-provoking trips. Mainly this is because Belize was "discovered" only recently as an ecotourism destination and, therefore, is in the midst of developing the areas and sites that attract foreign visitors. The part of this process of interest to environmentally concerned travellers is that, by starting its ecotourism development later than some other countries, Belize is able to evaluate successful and unsuccessful programs elsewhere, to be able to copy the best, reject the worst, and innovate using the trial-and-error learning of others. If it does things right, Belize may avoid some ecotravel mistakes and build a solid, sustainable, nature tourism industry. (Many of the innovative conservation projects developed recently in Belize, ones that are commonly visited by ecotravellers, will be described later in this chapter and in Chapter 3.)

In addition to a rapidly developing conservation ethic and associated eco-logical attractions, Belize has many other features to recommend it. Belize is a quiet, peaceful, relatively safe, politically stable, democratically governed, English-speaking place. Small in size, Belize has a correspondingly small population (perhaps, in 1998, 250,000 people, half of whom live in six larger towns, three of which are located along the Caribbean Coast – see Map 1, p. 5) and hence, a low human population density. In fact, it is the most sparsely populated nation in Central America. The country's infrastructure (roads, bridges, hospitals, tourist facilities) may, in some regions or instances, leave a bit to be desired, but that is, of course, part of the fun and allure of serious ecotravel. For the most part, Belize is easily and fairly safely navigable – by bus, car, airplane, and boat. Infra-structure is slowly being upgraded, with financial help from the USA's Agency for International Development, the United Kingdom, Canada's International Development Agency, and the European Union (EU). Most of the local people you meet are very friendly and helpful. Importantly, and in contrast to many other Central American countries, most Belizeans seem now to be enjoying a moderately high rate of improvement in their standard of living. Education is compulsory to age 14, and the adult literacy rate is thought to be between 80% and 90%. The government has made good progress in providing electrical service and adequate health care to even fairly remote villages, and sanitation is improving.

The main attractions of Belize to foreign visitors are its tropical rainforests and associated wildlife, its good number of highly accessible yet lightly visited Mayan ruin sites, and its long barrier reef and associated small, tropical islands. Actually, this small country contains a richly varied set of habitats, many of which will be encountered in your travels (unless the sole purpose of a trip is beach sunbathing and coastal underwater exploration). There is the flat coastal plain along the Caribbean Sea, much of it masses of mangroves and swamps and wet coastal marshland. Flying into Belize City and looking downwards as the airplane descends, you see amazing, glistening colors – pastel greens, blues, oranges – as sunlight reflects off these varied aquatic habitats. Much of this area is accessible only by boat or air. The northern half of Belize, covered mainly by tropical deciduous forest, has many agricultural districts (sugarcane is the main crop). Much of the region around Belize City consists of grass savannah with stands of palmetto palms and pine trees – a very open, attractive, soothing-looking habitat. The southern half of Belize is divided fairly evenly between coastal low-elevation rainforest (where citrus fruits are increasingly grown in agricultural sections) and inland mountainous areas that include a striking, quite beautiful habitat – *tropical pine forest*. Most famously, Belize is the site of the Western Hemisphere's longest barrier reef. This tropical coral reef, alive with thousands of kinds of fish and other reef-associated organisms, and the many nearby small, sandy, palm-treed islands (*cayes*, pronounced *keys*), increasingly attract divers, snorkellers, reef aficionados, and beach denizens from around the globe.

Owing to its unique history, Belize has a fairly good conservation record. Many parts of the country have had, until recently, little road access and hence, relatively light development and exploitation. (As one USA government publica-tion on Belize puts it, "No roads exist to large tracts of potentially arable land and timber" – which is just fine for conservation and, to a lesser extent, for eco-tourism!) Much of the development in colonial times was centered on the coast, with limited inland agriculture and logging. The southern half of the country, encompassing the Maya Mountains and Mountain Pine Ridge areas (Map 2), was too remote and rugged to sustain much development. In addition, there is some historical inheritance from the British colonial system of a conservation ethic – in name if not in actual practice: the British at least established protected forest areas, but they also allowed within those areas extensive *consumptive* uses such as logging. The Belizeans themselves recognized the need for conservation, and their recognition was reflected in the very first set of laws they enacted upon their independence in 1981: two of the first five laws were environment-related. The end result of first British, then Belizean, rule is that, whereas many other Central American countries have only very small percentages of their forests remaining, between 65% and 70% of Belize is still covered by its native forest.

The high degree of preservation of Belize's forests, coupled with its increasing exposure to the world community by way of visits to the coast and cayes by beachgoers and divers, led to rapid growth in tourism from 1990 through 1994. Tourism slowed a bit and leveled off during the mid-1990s, when Belize acquired an only partly deserved reputation for being a fairly expensive place to travel. (Recently, a value added tax – VAT – has been slapped on many products and services, further raising prices.) Also, owing to a few instances of crimes being committed against tourists, particularly in the Belize City area, the country gained what is probably an unfair reputation as being dangerous. In truth, because Belize is a very small country, a few crimes easily become magnified out of proportion.

The present conservation and ecotourism outlook in Belize is this: it's a beautiful spot rich with rewards for adventurous travellers, but it's also a poor, developing country, with many of the typical attendant problems. Poverty is widespread and pressure is strong for rapid economic development – in the form of more agriculture, logging, industry; there is substantial and growing pollution resulting from development; and there is the usual corruption that favors poor conservation practices. But recognition of the need for conservation by governmental officials and by other Belizeans is growing. They realize the importance of conservation and the maintenance of pristine areas, as well as the current contributions and future potential such areas have for attracting foreign visitors and foreign investment, thereby providing jobs and helping the economy.

The government of Belize, even with good intentions and actions (a new cabinet-level tourism department, the Ministry of Tourism and the Environment, and the recent passage of major environmental legislation, the Belize Environmental Protection Act of 1992), can do only so much. The problem, of course, is extremely limited money. Even the best environmental laws are of limited value without funds to hire environmental managers, inspectors, enforcement people, and park personnel. The result is that many parks and reserves exist in name only – tracts of land slated to be protected, but, in reality, left open to exploitation – because there is no money available to define the areas and hire on-site wardens or protectors.

Because the government cannot do much conservation management, habitat protection, or ecotourism development by itself, "partnerships" with private agencies that seek the same goals have been developed. Some of these agencies are domestic or international non-profit environmental groups, whereas others are for-profit groups or local community associations. The biggest such "partnership" is probably the one established between the Belize government and the Belize Audubon Society.

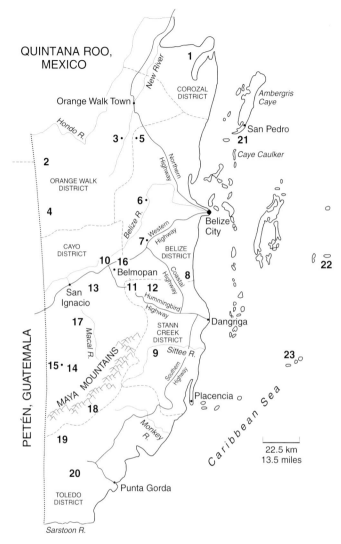

QUINTANA ROO,
MEXICO

COROZAL
DISTRICT

Orange Walk Town

Hondo R.

New River

Northern Highway

Ambergris Caye

San Pedro

Caye Caulker

ORANGE WALK
DISTRICT

Belize R.

Belize City

Western Highway

CAYO
DISTRICT

BELIZE
DISTRICT

Belmopan

San Ignacio

Coastal Highway

Hummingbird Highway

STANN
CREEK
DISTRICT

Sittee R.

Dangriga

PETÉN, GUATEMALA

Macal R.

MAYA MOUNTAINS

Southern Highway

Placencia

Caribbean Sea

Monkey R.

22.5 km
13.5 miles

TOLEDO
DISTRICT

Punta Gorda

Sarstoon R.

1 Shipstern Nature Reserve
2 Rio Bravo Conservation Area
3 Lamanai Archeological Reser ve
4 Chan Chich
5 Crooked Tree Wildlife Sanctuary
6 Community Baboon Sanctuary
7 Belize Zoo and Tropical Education Center
8 Gales Point
9 Cockscomb Basin Wildlife Sanctuary
   (Jaguar Sanctuary)
10 Guanacaste National Park
11 Blue Hole National Park
12 Five Blues Lake National Park

13 Tapir Mountain Nature Reserve
14 Chiquibul National Park
15 Caracol Archeological Reser ve
16 Monkey Bay Wildlife Sanctuary
    and Nature Reserve
17 Mountain Pine Ridge Forest Reserve
18 Bladen Branch Nature Reserve
19 Columbia River Forest Reserve
20 Blue Creek Field Station
21 Hol Chan Marine Reserve
22 Half Moon Caye National Monument
23 Glover's Reef

Map 2 Belize, showing locations of parks and reserves discussed in the book, as well as major highways, towns, and some larger rivers.

The Belize Audubon Society (BAS), formed in 1969, is Belize's pre-eminent environmental organization. Originally led mostly by foreign-born resort owners and managers, it is increasingly directed by native-born Belizeans. Almost from its inception, BAS provided technical advice on conservation matters to the Belize government, even helping to draft the plan for developing the national park system. In 1982, owing to past successful associations, the national government approached BAS with an important, mutually beneficial offer: to use their highly motivated conservation expertise to administer, manage, and protect six major national parks and wildlife sanctuaries. The government, in effect, turned the job of preservation of some vital parts of wild Belize over to people they trusted to do it right. Since 1984, BAS has operated Crooked Tree Wildlife Sanctuary, Cockscomb Basin Wildlife Sanctuary, Half Moon Caye Natural Monument, Guanacaste National Park, Blue Hole National Park, and Tapir Mountain Nature Reserve. The deal? From the fees collected at the parks' BAS administers, 70% goes to BAS for operations and management, 10% goes to the government, and 20% is placed in a trust fund the proceeds of which are slated eventually to be used for parks and other environmental programs. When you travel to Belize, contact the Belize Audubon Society for up-to-date information on the parks they administer (how to visit, where to go, what to see, where to stay, fees, etc.) as well as for other ecotourism information (The Belize Audubon Society, P.O. Box 1001, 12 Fort St., Belize City, Belize; phone: 501-2-35004; fax: 501-2-34985; www.belizeaudubon.org; e-mail: base@btl.net

One of the few acknowledged truths of ecotourism is that, if local people and communities of modest means are to accept and support local conservation measures and new nature reserves, they should be informed and consulted during all phases of the development process. For their continued support, local people should benefit economically from a park, reserve, or ecotourism facility, but local communities should also have a hand in the decision-making concerning the development and maintenance of ecotourism sites. Several ecotourism projects in Belize are at the forefront of this kind of three-way partnership between ecotourism, conservation, and community development. Several examples of such cooperation will be mentioned later in the chapter, in the parks section, and in Chapter 3. However, one pioneering venture deserves special attention: the Community Baboon Sanctuary, near Bermudian Landing. Located just 43 km (27 miles) from Belize City, this sanctuary is located along a 33 km (20 mile) length of the Belize River. The Community Baboon Sanctuary is a cooperative venture of private landowners (many of whom are subsistence farmers), conservationists and their organizations, and biological researchers. Their common aim is, by attracting and charging small fees to environmentally aware visitors, to preserve extensive forest habitat for a large population of wild primates (the so-called "baboons," actually Yucatán Black Howler Monkeys, Plate 73) and, coincidentally, for all the other wild animals and plants that inhabit the region.

Dr Robert Horwich, a biologist from the USA, was instrumental in establishing the sanctuary. He arrived in the area in 1981 to study the howler monkeys, and quickly became aware of the the shrinking populations of the species (which is limited to Belize, northern Guatemala, and Mexico's Yucatán region). The obvious cause: continued cutting and burning of the forest habitat in which the monkeys lived. In 1984 Horwich and colleagues approached villagers in the area with the idea of forming a cooperative wildlife sanctuary in which all participants might benefit: the local landowners would agree to preserve their remaining forested lands for the benefit of wildlife and to practice farming methods consistent with habitat preservation in return for help with farming, soil erosion control, healthy water management, and participation in ecotourism. Thus, the local people benefit by learning better farming practices, by helping to preserve wildlife and natural habitats, and, for some, by providing paid services (guided tours, restaurants, bed-and-breakfast-style accommodations) to visitors. The animals benefit because their living space is preserved, and researchers and ecotourists benefit because the animals and habitats are available for study and viewing.

Formally established in 1985 with only 11 landowners participating, the Community Baboon Sanctuary now includes lands owned by more than 100 families and involves about eight villages along approximately 32 km (20 miles) of the Belize River. Each participating landowner agrees to follow a customized plan for using their lands. The main agreement is to leave enough bits of forest standing, particularly along waterways and between properties, for howler monkeys and other wildlife to survive and prosper. Trees the animals feed in must be left standing and continuous bands of trees must be left intact so that the monkeys can travel in the trees from one place to another. The efforts are paying off: the sanctuary, which held perhaps 800 howler monkeys at its inception, now has an even larger population (more than 2000 individuals during the mid-1990s) – a population so healthy that monkeys are taken from this area for reintroduction to the Cockscomb Basin Wildlife Sanctuary in southern Belize. Sanctuary plans are eventually to extend its brand of habitat self-preservation to enough land to link the sanctuary with other reserves to the north (Crooked Tree Wildlife Sanctuary) and east.

The Baboon Sanctuary has four goals: conservation, education, research, and tourism. Visitors to the sanctuary, including many local school classes and travelling school groups from other countries, as well as tour groups and independent ecotravellers, are given guided tours during which wildlife and vegetation are pointed out and local culture discussed. A small museum describes local ecological communities and shows off some of the animals and plants found in the sanctuary. Researchers use the site to study the howler monkeys, as well as other species. Volunteers from around the world, living with local families, help to staff the sanctuary and assist the researchers. All-in-all, it's a successful – and by now much imitated – example of how mutually beneficial partnerships between local communities and conservationists, with the crucial ingredient of ecotourism thrown into the mix, can be established to preserve wildlife and habitats.

Guatemala

Guatemala is five times larger than Belize and has some spectacular natural scenery and other attractions for the ecotourist. Yet until recently, relatively few foreigners journeyed there to roam remote parts of the country. The reasons, of course, were the danger inherent in travelling in a state in the midst of long-term (36-year) civil war, combined with the war-associated lack of accommodations and other tourist-related services. Although fighting between rebel and government forces was sometimes light and sporadic for years, travelling for fun in a land where both sides in the conflict were periodically accused of atrocities and local people regularly "disappeared," was not to be done lightly. Furthermore, the very sites of greatest interest to ecotourists – remote, relatively pristine forested areas, were also the regions favored by the rebels as hideouts. (This fact of overlapping territorial interests was bad for ecotourism then, but good for conservation now: many forested areas that sheltered rebel forces for long periods escaped, at least until the present, the large-scale development, deforestation, and pollution that occurred in many other Central American states during the 1960s 1970s and 1980s.) With the changing world political scene during the early 1990s, a cease-fire was arranged and, following years of negotiating, peace was declared in 1996. As soon as active fighting ceased, the number of tourist visits to more remote parts of Guatemala increased; overall tourist arrivals currently hover at about 600,000 people per year. Many come for cultural tourism, including visits to isolated mountain villages and trips to one or more of the dozens of partly excavated Mayan archeological sites. But increasingly, people come to Guatemala as ecotourists – on organized tours or independently; a visit to northern Guatemala is often offered as a side trip on Belize tours.

I cover in this book only one section of Guatemala, the Petén, the largest province, or *departmento*, which comprises the northern third of the country. I have several reasons for including this region of Guatemala with Belize, and for not including more of the country. Belize and the Petén are adjacent (Map 1, p. 5), and many travellers to one side of the border also visit the other; many travellers to Belize also visit the unmatched Maya site at Tikal, located within the Petén; owing to fairly continuous habitat types along the border, much of the wildlife in Belize and the Petén is the same. Finally, the southern two-thirds of Guatemala, which consists predominantly of mountainous regions and a thin strip of low elevation Pacific coastal plain, is inhabited by a fauna largely different from that found in Belize.

The Petén is a huge, mostly lowland region (there are few sections with elevations greater than 500 to 600 m, 1600 to 2000 ft) which, owing to several factors, until recently held only a small human population and, as a result, has retained much of its original forest cover. Historically, the reasons include the hot, moist climate and the shortage of surface water over much of the region during the dry season, and the lack of roads. Another, more recent, reason for the intact survival of much of the Petén's forests is that, for many years, this remote region was a favored base for anti-government guerrilla armies. The result of this inadvertent protection is that the Petén's forests, together with adjacent areas of Belize and southern Mexico, comprise the largest unbroken tract of tropical forest north of the Brazilian Amazon. Biologists estimate that the region holds, for example, more than 450 species of birds (about 400 have been seen), at least 60 reptiles, and more than 800 tree species. Unfortunately, current economic and political forces in Guatemala, chiefly the ending of the civil war coupled with great poverty, joblessness, and overcrowding in other regions of the country, have led to a rapid increase in immigration to the Petén; and more people means more pressure for forest-clearing for agriculture and for industrial development. Several international conservation organizations are working together with local communities and with the Guatemalan government to establish and maintain a large Maya Biosphere Reserve in the Petén (on paper, the reserve has existed since 1990; making it a reality is another story). The need is to teach and encourage environment-friendly uses of the region's forests so that significant damage to the great expanse of forest can be slowed and, hopefully, halted (see Chapter 3).

The Petén is a fantastic region, worthy of extended exploration. But the jewel of the area, and, quite understandably, the most popular destination, is Tikal. Here, stunning Mayan temples and hundreds of other stone buildings and structures rise from the middle of the tropical forest (thousands of other structures are partly or wholly buried, awaiting excavation). Tikal, archeologists have discovered, was a powerful Mayan city, occupied by large numbers of people for about a thousand years, from at least 200 BC to AD 900. A few people visited the site during the 1800s and early 1900s but it was reachable only by horseback, and most of the ruins were hidden by jungle. During the early 1950s, an airstrip was built nearby, and so began detailed exploration, excavation by archeologists, partial restorations and, inevitably, visitation by tourists.

What exists at Tikal now is a large national park, only a small, central portion of which is occupied by the famous major ruins. The site is visited by people from all over the world. It is popular but large, so the tourist density at Tikal on any given day is usually manageable. During many months of the year, the place is still relatively deserted (during a recent September visit, I had the place virtually to myself). There are a few inexpensive restaurants in the entrance area, a few mid-priced hotels hidden amongst the trees, a campground, and a small museum. Strolling along the forest paths, emerging into clearing after clearing of magnificent stone ruins is a great experience, one that many people enjoy over a two- or even three-day period. And walking along the old, abandoned airstrip (which the tropical forest is rapidly reclaiming) in the early morning, birdwatching perhaps, and looking back toward the ruins, and seeing the high temples of the Great Plaza rising out above the misty forest canopy, is one of the truly unforgettable sights of world travel.

From an ecotravel perspective, however, it is not so much Tikal's historical stone structures that matter, but the setting: miles and miles of wide paths and slender trails through beautiful, highly protected tropical forest. And the site can be fairly said to be teeming with wildlife. About 350 bird species have been seen there, lizards abound along the forest trails and on the rocky ruins themselves, and larger mammals, including Jaguar, Ocelot, tapir, deer, and monkeys galore are frequently spotted. For some reason, animals that are rarely reported elsewhere are commonly seen at Tikal. Mention Tikal to one of the many biologists who have worked there or visited and, almost without exception, a smile will cross a face as he or she relates stories of the wonderful wildlife seen there. On a recent visit, for instance, I was surprised by a veritable herd of White-nosed Coatis, mid-sized raccoon-like mammals (Plate 78), perhaps 75 or 80 of them, moving through the forest only a few meters from the trail. Later, in one giant tree adjacent to an ancient temple, I saw perched at the same time several each of three large, colorful species: Keel-billed Toucans (Plate 48), Montezuma's Oropendolas (Plate 60), and Brown Jays (Plate 57). Quite simply, you don't see such fine, abundant wildlife in many other places.

As to specifics of travelling in Guatemela and, in particular, in the Petén, the people are friendly, transportation, most of it by minibus, boat, or airplane, is OK, accommodations are usually OK, and the prices are often a good bit lower than those found across the border in Belize. Getting to major ecotourism sites – Tikal, Ceibal, Uaxactún – is easy enough, whether with a group or alone. Of course, it always helps if you know a bit of Spanish. Yes, there is some crime. For instance, thieves occasionally stop tourist minibuses shuttling between Belize and Tikal. But these incidents are fairly rare; when they do occur, they are often magnified out of proportion. Travelling in the region is fairly safe – perhaps, as one travel book puts it "as safe as downtown Miami" – but perhaps that's not very reassuring. Travelling alone in the area, I've never had any problems.

In general, the conservation and ecotourism situation in the Petén today is this: the region recently emerged from three decades of civil war; it's still a poor area but it has a rich environment with large economic and tourism potential; and the area has both spectacular cultural and ecological attractions. The Guatemalans have a chance to preserve large chunks of their unspoiled habitats, and they have some interest in, and some governmental agencies and organizations charged with, doing so (CONAP, Guatemala's National Council for Protected Areas, operates all national parks and reserves except for the Biotopos; and CECON, the Center for Conservation Studies, which operates the Biotopos, the nature reserves). But, as in most other Central American countries, there is very little money available for active conservation. Parks and reserves have been established throughout Guatemala, but most of them, in relatively inaccessible areas, are parks in name only – lines drawn on maps; there are virtually no funds to survey, manage, and protect the sites. Increasingly, however, international conservation organizations show interest in and shower funds on this part of the world, on what is considered an international ecological treasure. The etablishment of the Maya Biosphere Reserve is the major, multi-faceted effort at preservation of the Petén's wild areas, and increased ecotourism is a major part of the plan (see Chapter 3).

Geography and Climate

Belize

Belize is a small, slender country that sits on the southeast side of the Yucatán Peninsula. With only 22,700 sq km (8866 sq miles) of area (which includes 689 sq km, or 266 sq miles, of offshore islands), Belize is slightly smaller than the USA's state of New Hampshire, slightly larger than Wales. On the map, Belize appears to be a small place stuck onto the much larger masses of Guatemala and Mexico (both of which, in the not-too-distant past, laid territorial claims to part or all of Belize). Belize is 280 km (174 miles) long and only 120 km (75 miles) wide at its broadest point. Its barrier reef, which runs along virtually the entire coast, lies about 25 km (15 miles) offshore. To its north Belize borders the Mexican state of Quintana Roo, to its west and south, Guatemala, and to the east, the Caribbean. The Hondo River traces the border with Quintana Roo, the border with Guatemala to the west is an arbitrary north–south line, and the southern border is the Sarstoon River. The population of about 250,000 is concentrated in six cities and larger towns: inland, the capital, Belmopan, and Orange Walk and San Ignacio; and on the coast, Belize City, the largest city, and Dangriga (formerly Stann Creek) and Punta Gorda (Map 2, p. 9).

Belize is usefully divided into three main parts: northern and southern mainland, and offshore cayes. The northern half of the mainland consists for the most part of low, flat habitats, generally not exceeding 100 m (330 ft) in elevation. The area includes coastal swamps, lagoons, flat plains and palm savannahs, and some inland flat areas and hills supporting semi-deciduous, broadleaf rainforest (Map 2). The southern half of the mainland includes a narrow (about 15 km, or 10 miles, wide), low-elevation coastal strip with marshes, savannahs, and some rainforest, and higher-elevation areas of evergreen forest and pine savannah associated with the Maya Mountains. The mountains form a crescent-shaped range that rises to high ridges and peaks at 700 to 900 m (2300 to 3000 ft), and includes Victoria Peak (1122 m, 3680 ft) and Doyle's Delight (about 1150 m, 3770 ft), the highest spots in the land. The Mayas extend from Belize into the Petén region of Guatemala. Belize's Mountain Pine Ridge, an area of particular scenic beauty and interest to ecotravellers, can be considered part of the northwestern section of the Maya Mountains. The offshore cayes consist of an assortment of tiny, small, and mid-sized islands fringed or covered with mangroves and palms. The most widely visited, and the only two with human colonies of any size, are Ambergris Caye (the larger, more commercialized site) and Caye Caulker (smaller, more low-key).

Belizean weather varies with location and time of year. The drier season runs from December through May or June (coinciding with the main tourist season), and the rainy season lasts from June through November (on average, in Belize City, there are about 16 rainy days in September or October, but only 4 or 5 rainy days in March or April). The amount of rainfall, surprisingly within such a small country, varies strongly with latitude. In the north, in the Corozal District, the average annual rainfall is only about 130 cm (51 in); moving southwards, to Belize City, the average is about 200 cm (79 in); and in the very southeast coastal corner, near Punta Gorda, the amount reaches 450 cm (177 in), or an average of about 1.2 cm (half an inch) a day. Temperatures (and humidity levels), except at higher elevations in the Maya Mountains and Mountain Pine Ridge region, are warmly, moistly, tropical: the *average daily* temperature in Belize City ranges from 23 °C (73 °F) in December through June to 31 °C (88 °F) in May through September. Average maximum temperatures, of course, are higher, and range into the mid-30s °C (mid-90s °F). High in the Mountain Pine Ridge, average daily lows are 17 °C (63 °F) in December, 22 °C (71 °F) in May; average highs are 26 °C (78°F) in December, 32 °C (90 °F) in May.

Guatemala

Guatemala has an area of 109,000 sq km (42,000 sq miles), with the Petén region accounting for fully a third of that: approximately 36,000 sq km (14,000 sq miles). Adding Belize to the Petén, the total area covered by this book is about 60,000 sq km (23,500 sq miles), approximately the size of the USA's West Virginia or Ireland.

The Petén consists almost completely of lowland habitats with the exception of the southwest corner of the Maya Mountains, which intrude from Belize into the Petén's eastern sector, and so provide some middle and higher elevation habitats (Map 3, p. 52). Lowlands, however, are the Petén's forte, most of the region being at between 150 and 225 m (500 to 750 ft) in altitude, with a topography of low rolling hills and ridges. Lowland habitats include large areas of intact rainforest, tropical savannah, as well as extensive wetlands that include many lakes and wooded swamps. The Petén's northern section, technically considered "tropical dry forest" habitat, is much dryer than the southern section.

The rainy season in the Petén lasts from May through November, with September and October often being particularly wet. Annual rainfall varies with year and location from 100 to 240 cm (40 to 95 in). Temperatures there are often higher than those found in the more coastally situated Belize, and hot, sweltering days of 35 °C (95 °F) are common. The humidity can be very high and bothersome, especially to non-natives; many a visitor from the north temperate zone has been found wandering the Petén, babbling about the wonders of air-conditioning.

Visitors to the tropics should keep in mind that, even during rainy parts of the year, seldom does it rain all day. A typical pattern along the Caribbean, for instance, is sunny mornings but afternoon showers. Also remember that, in contrast to temperate regions, where season largely determines temperature, in the tropics, elevation has the most important effect – the higher you are, the cooler you will be.

Habitats

Tropical Forest: General Characteristics

The most striking thing about many tropical forests is their high degree of species diversity. Temperate forests in Europe or North America often consist of only several tree species. The norm in many tropical forests is to find between 50 and 100 tree species (or more!) within the area of a few hectares or acres. In fact, sometimes after appreciating a specific tree and then looking around for another of the same species, one cannot easily be located. Ecologists say tropical areas have a much higher *species richness* than temperate regions – for plantlife, as well as for some animals such as insects and birds. The reasons for geographic differences in species richness are not well understood, but are an area of current research interest.

During first visits to tropical forests, people from Europe, North America, and other temperate-zone areas are usually impressed with the richly varied plant forms, many of which are not found in temperate regions. Although not every kind of tropical forest includes all of them, a number of highly typical plant forms and shapes are usually seen:

Tree shape and forest layering. Many tropical trees grow to great heights, straight trunks rising dramatically before branching. Tropical forests often appear layered, or *stratified*, and several more or less distinct layers of vegetation can sometimes be seen. A typical tropical forest has a surface herb layer (ground cover), a low shrub layer, one or more lower levels of shorter trees, and a higher, or *canopy*, tree layer (Figure 1). In reality, there are no formal layers – just various species of trees that grow to different, characteristic, maximum heights. Trees are sometimes referred to as *emergent*, lone, very tall trees that soar high above their neighbors (emergents are characteristic only of tropical forests); *canopy*, those present in the upper layer; *subcanopy*, in the next highest layers; or *understory*, short and baby trees (Figure 1). Many of the *crowns*, or high leafy sections, of tropical trees in the canopy are characteristically shaped, being short and very broad, resembling umbrellas (Figure 1).

Large-leaved understory plants. Tropical forests often have dense concentrations of large-leaved understory shrubs and herbs (Figures 1 and 2). Several plant families are usually represented: (1) Aroids, family Araceae, include plants such as *Dieffenbachia*, or dumb cane (Figure 9b), and climbers such as *Philodendron* (Figure 9a). (2) Marantas, family Marantaceae, including *Calathea insignis*, the rattlesnake plant, which is a herb whose flattened yellow flowers resemble a snake's

Figure 1 Exterior view of a typical tropical forest.

Figure 2 Interior view of a typical tropical forest.

rattle. (3) Heliconia (Figure 9e), family Heliconiaceae, which are large-leaved perennial herbs.

Tree roots. Any northerner visiting a tropical forest for the first time quickly stops in his or her tracks and stares at the bottoms of trees. The trunks of temperate zone trees may widen a bit at the base but they more or less descend straight into the ground. Not so in the tropics, where many trees are *buttressed*: roots emerge and descend from the lower section of the trunk and spread out around the tree before entering the ground (Figure 2). The buttresses appear as ridges attached to the sides of a trunk, ridges that in larger, older trees, are big and deep enough to hide a person (or a coiled snake!). The function of buttresses is believed to be tree support and, indeed, buttressed trees are highly wind resistant and difficult to take down. But whether increased support is the primary reason that buttressing evolved, well, that's an open question, one that plant biologists study and argue over. Another unusual root structure associated with the tropics is *stilt*, or *prop, roots*. These are roots that seem to raise the trunk of a tree off the ground. They come off the tree some distance from the bottom of the trunk and grow out and down, entering the ground at various distances from the trunk (Figure 2). Stilt roots are characteristic of trees, such as mangroves, that occur in habitats that are covered with water during parts of the year, and many palms. Aside from anchoring a tree, functions of stilt roots are controversial.

Climbers and stranglers. Tropical trees are often conspicuously loaded with hanging vines (Figures 1 and 2). Vines, also called *climbers, lianas*, and *bush-ropes*, are species from a number of plant families that spend their lives associated with trees. Some ascend or descend along a tree's trunk, perhaps loosely attached; others spread out within a tree's leafy canopy before descending toward the ground, free, from a branch. Vines are surprisingly strong and difficult to break; many older ones grow less flexible and more woody, sometime reaching the diameter of small trees. Common vines that climb trees from the ground up are philodendrons and those of the genus *Desmoncus* (or bayal), rattan-like vines used locally for basket-making. One group, known as strangler figs, (genus *Ficus*), begin their lives growing high on tree branches (that is, as epiphytes – see below), but their strong, woody roots grow down along a tree's trunk, attaching to and fusing with it, before entering the ground (Figure 8c). The "host" tree, surrounded by the fig, eventually dies and rots away, leaving a tall fig tree with a hollow center. The manner in which the strangler kills the host tree is not well understood.

Epiphytes. These are plants that grow on other plants (usually trees) but do not harm their "hosts" (Figure 2). They are not parasites – they do not burrow into the trees to suck out nutrients; they simply take up space on trunks and branches. (Ecologically, we would call the relationship between a tree and its epiphytes *commensal*: one party of the arrangement, the epiphyte, benefits – it gains growing space – and the other party, the tree, is unaffected.) How do epiphytes grow if they are not rooted in the host tree or the ground? Roots that grow along the tree's surface capture nutrients from the air – bits of dust, soil, and plant parts that breeze by. Eventually, by collecting debris, each epiphyte develops its own bit of soil, into which it is rooted. Epiphytes are especially numerous and diverse in middle and higher-elevation rainforests, where persistent cloud cover and mist provide them ideal growing conditions. Orchids, with their striking flowers that attract bees and wasps for pollination, are among the most famous kinds of epiphytes. Bromeliads (Figure 8d), restricted to the Americas, are common epiphytes with sharply pointed leaves that grow in a circular pattern, creating a central bucket, or *cistern*, in which collects rain water, dust, soil, and plant materials. Recent studies of bromeliads show that these cisterns function as small aquatic ecosystems, with a number of different animals – insects, worms, snails, among others – making use of them. Several groups of amphibians are known to spend parts of their life cycles in these small pools (some salamanders, for example, Plate 1), and a number of species of tiny birds nest in bromeliads. (Not all bromeliads are epiphytes; some grow on the ground as largish, spiny plants, such as pineapple; Figure 10c.) Other plants that grow as epiphytes are mosses and ferns.

Palms. The trees most closely associated with the tropics worldwide are palms. Seeing palm trees upon exiting a jet is a sure sign that a warm climate has been reached. In fact, it is temperature that probably limits palms mainly to tropical and sub-tropical regions. They grow from a single point at the top of their stems, and so are very sensitive to frost; if that part of the plant freezes, the plant dies. Almost everyone recognizes palms because, for trees, they have unusual forms: they have no branches, but all leaves (which are quite large and called *fronds*) emerge from the top of the single trunk; and their trunks are usually of about the same diameter from their bottoms to their tops. Many taller palms have stilt roots propping them up. Some palms have no trunks, but grow as small understory plants. Coconut palms, *Cocos nucifera*, found throughout the world's tropical beaches, occur along Belize's coast (Figure 10a), and a number of other palm species are quite common.

Forest Habitats and Common Vegetation

Belize (by Jon Lyon)

While Belize is in the tropical realm and much of the nation remains under a mixed hardwood forest cover, Belize lies in the *sub-tropical* belt due to its somewhat northerly latitude (15° to 19°N). This sub-tropical location means that there are greater temperature, rainfall, and humidity fluctuations than in more equatorial tropical forests. There are also strong differences in the amount of annual rainfall as one moves from north to south in Belize – a typical forest in the Toledo district receives almost three times more rain than a typical forest in Orange Walk. The forest habitats of Belize have characteristics that reflect these sub-tropical influences. Therefore, to say that Belize is covered with tropical rainforest is somewhat misleading. Many Belizean forests are not lush, well developed, high canopy rainforests. For example, in the northern and coastal parts of the nation there are many dry, broken canopy forests, mainly pine or pine-oak forests and savannah. These forests occur on sandy soils, contain relatively few plant species, and often are dominated by only a handful of tree species. Other forests occurring along lagoons and swamps and many high altitude forests in the Maya Mountains are also often scrubby, low canopy forests little resembling well developed classical rainforest.

Despite its small size, Belize supports a relatively diverse range of plants and forest habitats. It is home to an estimated 4000 species of flowering plants, including over 730 tree species and some 280 orchid species. Belizean forests also support a large variety of economically and historically important trees. Economically valuable trees have played, and continue to play, a vital role in the history and economy of the country.

A *forest habitat* refers to a specific assemblage of tree species and associated vegetation in a given area and the pattern of how those species are distributed.

a Orbigyna cohune (cohune palm)

b Astrocaryum mexicanum (warree palm)

c Acoelorrhaphe wrightii (pimenta palm, or palmetto)

d Chamaedorea elegans (xate)

Figure 3

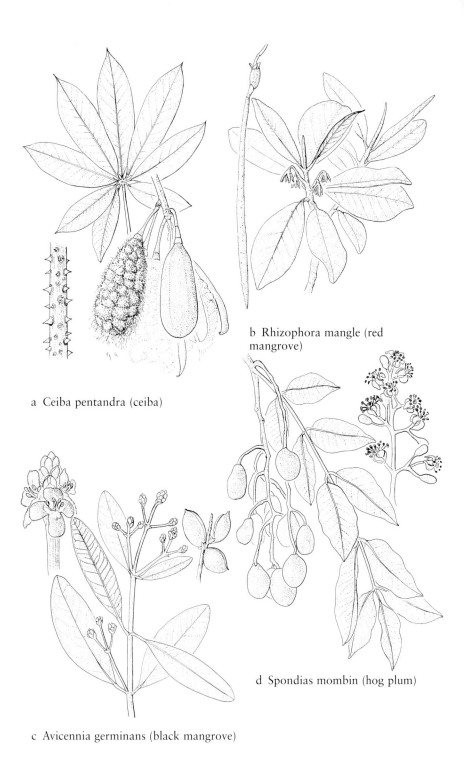

a Ceiba pentandra (ceiba)

b Rhizophora mangle (red mangrove)

c Avicennia germinans (black mangrove)

d Spondias mombin (hog plum)

Figure 4

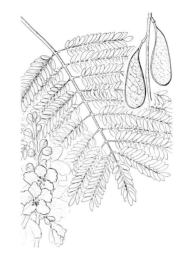

b Schizolobium parahybum
(quamwood)

a Enterolobium cyclocarpum (tubroos,
or guanacaste)

d Bursera simaruba (gumbo limbo)

c Cecropia obtusifolia (trumpet tree)

Figure 5

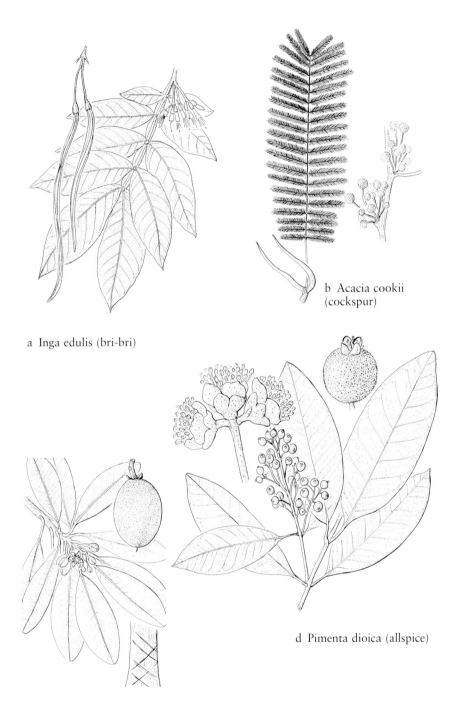

b Acacia cookii (cockspur)

a Inga edulis (bri-bri)

c Manilkara zapota (chicle, or sapodilla)

d Pimenta dioica (allspice)

Figure 6

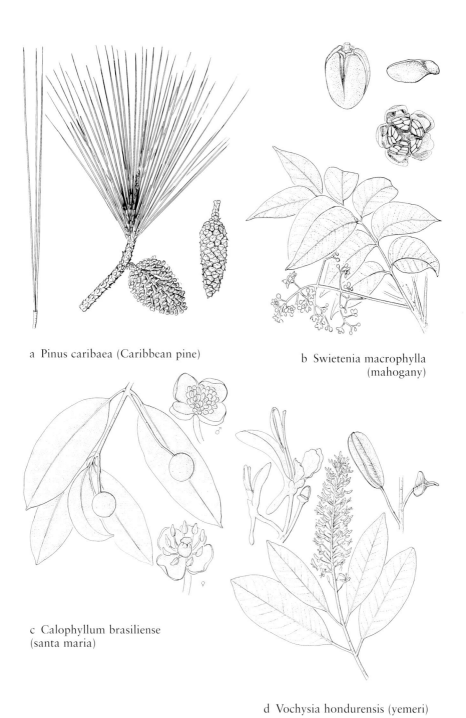

a Pinus caribaea (Caribbean pine)

b Swietenia macrophylla
   (mahogany)

c Calophyllum brasiliense
(santa maria)

d Vochysia hondurensis (yemeri)

Figure 7

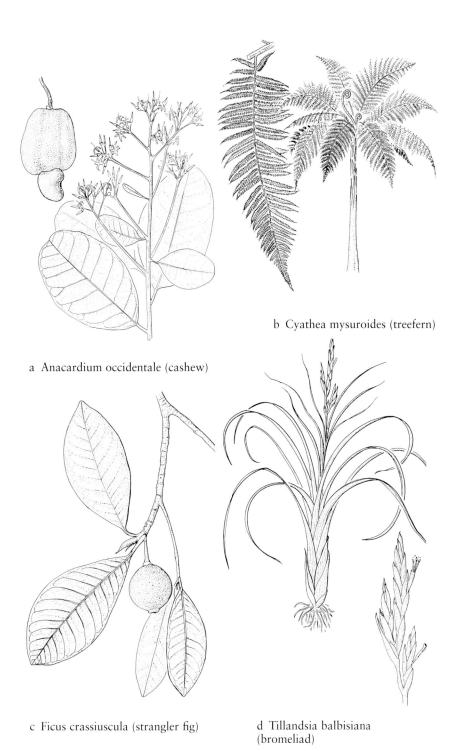

b Cyathea mysuroides (treefern)

a Anacardium occidentale (cashew)

c Ficus crassiuscula (strangler fig)

d Tillandsia balbisiana
   (bromeliad)

Figure 8

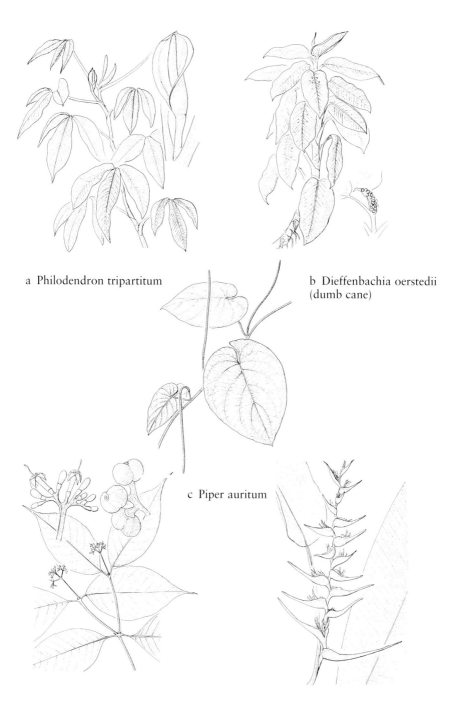

a Philodendron tripartitum

b Dieffenbachia oerstedii
   (dumb cane)

c Piper auritum

d Psychotria acuminata

e Heliconia latispatha

Figure 9

a Cocos nucifera (coconut palm) b Musa x paradisiaca (banana)

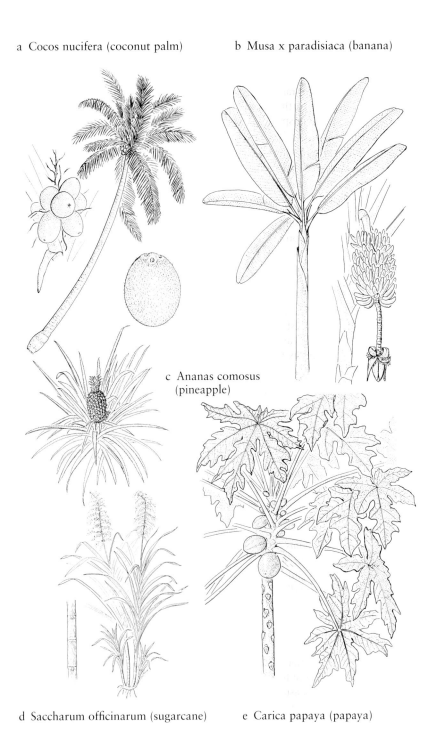

c Ananas comosus
(pineapple)

d Saccharum officinarum (sugarcane) e Carica papaya (papaya)

Figure 10

The location and extent of a given forest habitat depends on several factors, including geology, climate patterns, the type and quality of soil, seasonal rainfall, and topography. In Belize, rainfall and soils have a particularly strong influence on forest vegetation. For example, the limestone soils in Orange Walk that receive about 150 cm (60 in) of rain per year, support very different forests than the hilly, sandstone-shale soils in the Toledo District that receive over 400 cm (160 in) of rain per year. Another aspect of rainfall levels is that many forests in Belize experience a pronounced dry season from around February into April or May. During the dry season many forest trees in Belize are *deciduous* (shed their leaves) giving the forests a semi-deciduous and sub-tropical flavor.

Another key factor that has had an enormous impact on the forests of Belize is human activity. Due to both the extensive logging in the country for more than 300 years and agricultural activity, many of the forests in Belize have been modified and no longer resemble the undisturbed, mature forests of previous eras (although the Mayans probably altered the forests for centuries before European colonization). Many forests in the nation are *secondary forests* meaning they have been disturbed in the recent past, are not fully developed, and contain many species that grow only in disturbed areas. Mature undisturbed forests, often called *climax forests*, are less common in Belize and are generally found in remote regions.

In Belize, different forest types are commonly referred to as *ridges*. The word ridge refers only to forest type and not topography. For example, the most commonly used ridge terms are *pine ridge* (refers to pine or pine-oak forest and savannah), *broken ridge* (refers to mixed-hardwood, broken canopy forest), *high ridge* (refers to well developed, high canopy forest), and *cohune ridge* (refers to cohune palm forest).

The following are brief descriptions of some of the more distinctive and clearly identifiable forest types found in Belize, and the districts where they are found:

Coastal Forests – Corozal, Belize, Stann Creek, Toledo, Cayes

In Belize, *coastal forests* (or *littoral forests*) were originally found along virtually the entire 280 km of Caribbean coast, in fringes around some of the inland lagoons and watercourses, and on many cayes. There are two types:

Strand forests are found typically on beach sands, dunes, and levees that are at slightly higher elevations than the surrounding coastal landscape. In strand forests, the most common trees include coconut (*Cocos nucifera*) (Figure 10a), cocoplum (*Chrysobalanus icaco*), buttonwood (*Conocarpus erecta*), tea box (*Myrica cerifera*), sea grape (*Coccoloba uvifera*), and the exotics Norfolk Island pine (*Araucaria excelsa*) and cajeput (*Melaleuca quinquenervia*). In many instances, fruit trees such as cashew (*Anacardium occidentale*) (Figure 8a), and mango (*Mangifera indica*) may also be found planted in strand forest. Ground covers vary widely from bare sand to dense covers of a variety of shrub and herbaceous species.

Mangrove forests are also common in coastal Belize. Mangroves are defined as any group of woody plants growing in areas exposed to salt water, usually around bays, lagoons, and other protected coastal infoldings, and also on coastal cayes. Technically, they do not have to include species of mangrove trees, although most do. Most of Belize's coastal fringe is, or was at one time, occupied by mangroves. Mangroves now become much more common and more abundant as you move south along the Belizean coast. The main tree species found in the mangroves are red mangrove (*Rhizophora mangle*) (Figure 4b), buttonwood, white mangrove (*Laguncularia racemosa*), and black mangrove (*Avicennia germinans*) (Figure 4c).

Other coastal plant species include the sea grape, swamp caway (*Pterocarpus officinalis*), provision tree (*Pachira aquatica*), and marsh fern (*Acrostichum aureum*).

Northern Coastal Plain Forests – Corozal, Orange Walk, Belize, Cayo

Northern Belize is a relatively flat plain supporting semi-deciduous broadleaf forest, pine forest, and orchard savannah. Forests in this region receive from 130 to 200 cm (50 to 80 in) of rain per year and the elevation ranges from sea level to 40 m (130 ft). There are many forest types in northern Belize, but the following are commonly encountered and the most prevalent:

Pine Forest (or *Pine Ridge*). Pine ridge refers to pine, pine-oak, and palm-oak-palmetto forest and savannah. Pine ridge forests occur on lowland sandy soils along the coastal plain and in dry, sandy areas on the northern plains. The dominant species is the Honduran or Caribbean pine (*Pinus caribaea*) (Figure 7a). Other tree species associated with pine ridge are the calabash (*Cresentia cujete*), oaks (*Quercus* spp.), yaha (*Curatella americana*), craboo (*Byrsonima crassifolia*), and the palmetto palm (*Acoelorrhaphe wrightii*) (Figure 3c). In some areas there may be as many as 8500 palmetto palms per hectare (2.5 acres). Pine ridge areas not part of protected forest reserves are often deliberately burned during dry periods in an attempt to improve grazing for cattle and sometimes to attract deer for hunting.

Swamp Forest (or *Bajo*). The northern coastal plain has many inland, freshwater lagoons and waterways with *swamp forests* on their perimeters. These have wet soils throughout the year although they may dry out somewhat during the dry season. Swamp forests often have a low canopy (not over 12 m, 40 ft) with few emergent trees. Some of the more common species are the pokenoboy palm (*Bactris major*), give-and-take palm (*Chrysophila argentea*), cabbage palm (*Euterpe macrospadix*), wild grape (*Coccoloba belizensis*), copna (*Erythrina glauca*), provision tree (*Pachira aquatica*) and spiny bamboo (*Guadua spinosa*). Swamp forests are often very dense and form impenetrable thickets, especially where spiny bamboo is in abundance.

Another type of swamp forest is the *logwood thicket*. The logwood tree (*Haematoxylon campechianum*) is found in low, wet areas, especially along inland lagoons, in the northern plains of Belize. It often forms thick stands. The early history of Belize is largely based on the exploitation of the logwood tree. As early as the mid-1500s, the Spanish were cutting logwood along the Atlantic coasts of Guatemala, Honduras, and Mexico and shipping it to European ports. Logwood grows in abundance in low forests, swamps, and wet thickets on the eastern half of the northern plain of Belize. Swamp forests and logwood thickets are also common in the Petén of Guatemala. The logwood tree is usually small, 8 m (25 ft) or less, with a crooked, deeply fluted trunk.

The logwood tree contains a valuable dye which was much in demand in the European woolen industry. The dye was also used in the manufacturing of inks. The dye, known as *haematoxylon*, was extracted by mashing the logwood into small bits and boiling them in water. The extracted logwood dye was used as a basic fixing dye and depending on the additives used, colors ranging from yellow to black could be obtained.

Transitional Broadleaf Forest (or *Broken Ridge*). Transitional broadleaf forest is an intermediate stature forest with a canopy at less than 15 m (50 ft), although some emergents may reach up to 20 m (65 ft) or more. Many of the tree, shrub, and herb species found in the broken ridge are light-demanding species capable of rapid growth. Tree species typically found here include yemeri (*Vochysia hondurensis*) (Figure 7d), trumpet (*Cecropia peltata* and *C. palmata*) (Figure 5c), negrito (*Simarouba glauca*), white maya (*Miconia argentea),* wild cotton *(Cochlospermum vitifolium),* cowfoot (*Piper auritum*) (Figure 9c), nargusta (*Terminalia amazonia*), polewood (*Xylopia frutescens*), and bay cedar (*Guazuma ulmifolia*). A good example can be found on the Western Highway moving west towards Belmopan. The highway cuts through mangrove, pine ridge, broken ridge, and cohune ridge areas as it approaches the rich riparian gallery forests along the Belize River and Roaring Creek.

Cohune Palm Forest (or *Cohune Ridge*). The cohune palm (*Orbigyna cohune*) (Figure 3a) occurs throughout Belize from near sea level to about 600 m (2000 ft) and is one of the most abundant and distinctive trees in the nation. The cohune is prominent in many plant communities but is often the dominant species forming a plant association known as *cohune forest* or *cohune ridge*. The forest floor in these forests is often cluttered with fallen cohune fronds and nuts. The towering cohune fronds, some reaching up to 10 m (30 ft) long, also give the understory a cathedral-like quality. Despite the abundance of cohunes in the cohune forest, other tree species are common and attain canopy height including hogplum (*Spondias mombin*) (Figure 4d), tubroos (*Enterolobium cyclocarpum*) (Figure 5a), quamwood (*Schizolobium parahybum*) (Figure 5b), bucut (*Cassia grandis*), dogwood (*Lonchocarpus guatemalensis*), mampola (*Luehea seemanii*), and gumbo limbo (*Bursera simaruba*) (Figure 5d). Because of the fertile soils beneath cohune forests, many Belizean farmers use the cohune's presence as an indicator of rich, usable land for agriculture. Cohunes are also left on plantations and farms because of the difficulty in felling them with machetes or axes owing to their hard trunks. Cohunes are also commonly left in pastures as a source of year-round shade for cattle.

Broadleaved Hardwood Forest (or *High Ridge*). Closed canopy broadleaved forests cover large areas in northern and western regions of the northern coastal plain as well as in the Petén region of Guatemala and the southern part of the Yucatán in Mexico. Many *riparian* forests (forests along rivers and waterways, also called *riverine* or *gallery forests*) are broadleaved hardwood forests. Riparian forest composition overlaps with other forest types and is distinguished by the relative abundance of certain species and the seasonal dynamics of flooding. Trees along waterways must be adapted to seasonal patterns of flooding and drying out. Common riparian species include the bri-bri (*Inga edulis*) (Figure 6a), bullet tree (*Bucida buceras*), wild grape (*Coccoloba belizensis*), swamp dogwood (*Lonchocarpus hondurensis*), provision tree (*Pachira aquatica*), cabbage palm (*Euterpe macrospadix*), and many species of fig (*Ficus* spp.).

Bravo Hills – Orange Walk

The Bravo Hills region is located in northwestern Belize along the Mexican and Guatemalan borders. The region supports upland semi-deciduous broadleaf forest, or *high ridge*. Elevations range from near 20 m (65 ft) in the lowland areas up to 300 m (1000 ft) in the upland forests along the Guatemalan border and the region receives from 130 to 200 cm (50 to 80 in) of rain per year. The bulk of the Rio Bravo Conservation and Management Area lies in the Bravo Hills region. The forests of the Bravo Hills are dominated by broadleaf forests, but also include pine-oak savannah, transitional broadleaf forest, bajo, and cohune forest. Bravo

Hills forests are at higher elevations, occur on undulating plains and escarpments, and are less susceptible to widespread seasonal flooding than forests in the northern coastal plain. Some of the more common trees in the Bravo Hills include mahogany (*Swietenia macrophylla*) (Figure 7b), cedar (*Cedrela odorata*), chicle (*Manilkara zapota*) (Figure 6c), mylady (*Aspidosperma megalocarpon*), cojotone (*Stemmadenia donnell-smithii*), and bastard lime (*Trichilia havanensis*). The cohune palm (Figure 3a) is also prevalent in many areas. The Bravo Hills have a long history of timber extraction (mainly mahogany and cedar) and chicle exploitation.

Central Coastal Plain – Belize, Stann Creek

The Central Coastal Plain is a relatively small area of Belize situated south of the northern coastal plain, east of the Central Foothills, and north of the Maya Mountains. The area includes the Belize City peninsula, both Northern and Southern Lagoon, and south through the coastal areas of Stann Creek District. The area receives more rainfall than the northern coastal plain, and elevations range from sea level to only 20 m (65 ft). Much of the area is a flat coastal plain interlaced with an extensive network of lagoons and marshes. Similar to the northern coastal plain, the central plain supports extensive coastal forests, mangroves, saline marshes, pine forest and orchard savannah, and some broadleaved forests.

Central and Eastern Foothills – Stann Creek, Cayo, Toledo

The Central and Eastern Foothills are located in east-central Belize and are formed by ancient limestones that separate the Maya Mountains from the northern coastal plain. These hills form a distinct *karst* landscape (referring to limestone-supported topography) with hills typically protruding from a flat plain. Average annual rainfall across these regions ranges from 200 to 250 cm (80 to 100 in). Karst hills support unique forests owing to their soils, drainage, and location. Typical tree species found on karst hill forests include chicle (*Manilkara zapota*) (Figure 6c), ramón (*Brosimum alicastrum*), mammee ciruela (*Pouteria campechiana*), wild mammee (*Alseis yucatanensis*), turtlebone (*Inga stevensonii*), black poisonwood (*Metopium brownii*), and give-and-take palm (*Chrysophila argentea*).

Maya Mountains – Stann Creek, Cayo, Toledo

The Maya Mountains are an isolated mountain range that dominates the southern half of Belize and forms the highest and most rugged terrain in the country. Elevations in the mountains range from 120 m (390 ft) to about 1150 m (3770 ft). The region can be divided into two distinct categories: (1) The Mountain Pine Plateau region occupied by pine-oak savannah of the Mountain Pine Ridge; and (2) the mountainous broadleaf forests characteristic of the Maya Mountains proper.

Mountain Pine Ridge. The Mountain Pine Ridge is located in the west-central region of Belize north of the Maya Mountains. Although it makes up only about 3.4% of the country, it represents a unique habitat in Belize. The mountain pine ridge is highest in elevation in the east (900 m, or 2950 ft) and slopes down to its lowest point in the west (530 m, or 1740 ft). The region is characterized by the mountain pine (*Pinus oocarpa*) and tree species common in other "pine ridge" communities, with the addition of matapalo (*Clusia* spp.) and a few other species. Mountain pine, a valuable timber species, is a close relative of its more common cousin, the Caribbean pine, but is restricted to this region.

Maya Mountain Forests. Some of the most common tree species in the rugged Maya Mountain forests are the cohune (*Orbigyna cohune*) (Figure 3a), ironwood (*Dialium guianense*), mountain negrito (*Simarouba amara*), quamwood (*Schizolobium parahybum*) (Figure 5b), polewood (*Xylopia frutescens*), tree ferns (*Cyathea mysuroides; Hemitelia multiflora*) (Figure 8b), mountain trumpet (*Pourouma aspera*), and several species of melastome (*Miconia* spp.).

Western Uplands – Cayo
The Western Uplands region is covered primarily with semi-deciduous broadleaf forest with a few isolated pockets of pine shrubland. The region includes a northern area referred to as the Vaca Plateau, and a southern area called the Chiquibul Plateau. Elevations range from around 180 m (600 ft) in the northern portions of the uplands to some 700 m (2300 ft) in the southern uplands. Mean annual rainfall ranges from 150 to 200 cm (60 to 80 in). Common tree species found here include sapodilla (*Manilkara zapota*) (Figure 6c), ramón (*Brosimum alicastrum*), nargusta (*Terminalia amonzonia*), banak (*Virola koschnyi*), mountain cabbage palm (*Euterpe oleracea*), ironwood (*Dialium guianense*), and mapola (*Bombax ellipticum*). The landscape contains some very impressive karst formations including a host of large cave systems.

Southern Coastal Plain – Stann Creek, Toledo
The Southern Coastal Plain region extends from the central Stann Creek District southwards. The region is comprised of a coastal strip that drains the eastern flank of the Maya Mountains. Elevations range from sea level to some 30 m (100 ft), and the mean annual rainfall is 200 to 250 cm (80 to 100 in). Like the northern coastal plain, the southern plain contains a band of mangrove forests along the coast. However, the southern plain differs from the northern plain in that it contains relatively large inland expanses of pine forest and orchard savannah. Characteristic tree species include the Caribbean pine, cohune palm, and many others typical of the northern coastal plain.

Toledo Foothills and Lowlands – Cayo, Toledo
This is the southernmost region in Belize and is comprised of the southern Cayo and essentially the entire Toledo District. The region receives some of the highest rainfall in Belize; mean annual rainfalls typically are in the range of 250 cm (100 in) in the foothills to over 400 cm (160 in) in the lowlands. This is the only region in Belize that comes close to supporting tropical wet forests. Elevations range from about 300 m (1000 ft) in the foothills to sea level in the lowlands. Larger trees in the evergreen broadleaf forests top out at 30 m (100 ft) or more, and buttressed roots and epiphytes are very common.

The Toledo Foothills, the northern portion of the region, skirt along the southern face of the Maya Mountains. This area is comprised of hilly country in the north that fans out into the lowlands to the south. Characteristic tree species in these foothill areas include rosewood (*Dalbergia stevensonii*), banak (*Virola koschnyi*), santa maria (*Calophyllum brasiliense*) (Figure 7c), monkey apple (*Licania platypus*), and yemeri (*Vochysia hondurensis*) (Figure 7d). The Toledo Lowlands and swamps represent the extensive floodplains of the main rivers in the region. Common tree species in these flooded, lowland areas include banak (*Virola koschnyi*), waika chewstick (*Symphonia globulifera*), santa maria (*Calophyllum brasiliense*) (Figure 7c), rosewood (*Dalbsergia stevensonii*), caway (*Pterocarpus officinalis*), comfray palm (*Manicaria saccifera*), bastard lime (*Pterygota excelsa*), and ceiba (*Ceiba pentandra*) (Figure 4a).

Guatemala – The Petén (by Simon Comerford and Filadelpho Chablé)

The habitats of primary interest to ecotravellers in the Petén lie within the north-ernmost 40% of the province, protected within the Maya Biosphere Reserve (MBR; see p. 51), and that region is detailed here. Southern and central Petén habitats are of less interest because people have so altered those regions, for example, much of the central portion is now covered by cattle pastures. The types of forest found in the MBR vary with respect to species present and to local environmental conditions. Four forest types, defined mostly by the terrain over which they occur, are commonly recognized.

1. High dense forest on hillsides of moderate slope with a canopy height about 25 m (80 ft).

The dominant species here are: ramón (*Brosimum alicastrum*), leaves of which are used by local people as a source of forage for horses and mules in the forest and the seeds of which historically have been used to make tortillas in times of famine when corn harvests are poor; chicozapote (or chicle, *Manilkara zapota*) (Figure 6c), which grows up to 40 m (130 ft) and historically has been an important source of jobs in the Petén. This tree is instantly recognizable by the criss-cross pattern on the trunk, which arises from the cuts made by the *chicleros'* machetes to harvest the latex chewing gum base. The tree's bark is used medicinally to treat stomach ache and diarrhea.; cedro (*Cedrela odorata*), which historically, and still, has great economic importance as a commercial timber, and has whitish bark which is used medicinally to treat malaria and stomach aches; jobillo (*Astronium graveolens*), the aromatic leaves of which are used to treat skin rashes, and is used to make furniture and handicrafts; yaxnik (*Vitex gaumerii*), known primarily for the medicinal properties of its sap (used to treat insect bites and skin problems), and is sometimes used to make furniture; chile malache (*Trichilia glabra*) and chile chachalaca (*Allophylus* sp.), both smaller trees whose fruit is eaten by a variety of birds including curassows and chachalacas; and pimienta (or allspice, *Pimenta dioica*) (Figure 6d), a plant that grows, usually in clumps, to 25 m (80 ft) in height. It has smooth gray or brown bark, and its leaves, when crushed, smell of allspice and make an excellent tea which is used to treat colic and other digestive ailments. The fruits are collected from branches, dried in the sun or over a fire, and exported for spice production.

2. High dense forest on relatively flat terrain with good drainage.

The dominant species here are ramón (*Brosimum alicastrum*), chicozapote (*Manilkara zapota*), zapotillo (*Pouteria* sp.), silïún (*Pouteria amygdalina*), and can-isté (*Pouteria campechianum*), all of which bear fruits eaten by many species of forest animals including paca, deer, and armadillo; catalox (*Swartzia cubensis*), the fine-grained wood of which is used by artisans and the fruit of which is nibbled by parrots; pasak (*Simarouba glauca*), which has edible fruit and roots used medicinally to treat diarrhea; ceiba (*Ceiba pentandra*) (Figure 4a), the sacred tree of the Mayans, which has conical spines on its trunk when young, used to treat children with skin rashes. Individual ceibas are occasionally seen standing in isolation in pastures, but the best examples are seen at the Ceibal Archaeological Park and at the entrance to Tikal National Park. The tree is recognizable by its broad, tapering trunk with the branches emerging only at the top; caoba (or mahogany, *Swietenia macrophylla*) (Figure 7b), which is much sought after for its valuable orange-colored wood, and the bark of which is used locally to treat athlete's foot; chacaj colorado (or palo de jiote, broton, or indio desnudo, *Bursera simarouba*), evident by its red, peeling bark, which can be removed in paper-thin strips and is used locally to treat ulcers, fevers, and urinary infections. Its resin is used to soothe and heal burns caused by the resin of chechen negro trees, which are said to usually grow nearby; chechen negro (*Metopium browneii*), recognizable by the black spots on its leaves and bark, should be treated with caution and contact avoided because its resin causes severe burns; malerio colorado (*Aspidosperma megalocarpon*) and malerio blanco (*Aspidosperma stegomeris*), the strong timbers of which are used for posts to carry high-voltage electrical cables; son (*Alseis yucatensis*), which is used for roof frames; and copal (or pom, *Protium copal*), the aromatic resin of which has a long history of use as an incense at rituals, to fumigate houses and people to expel bad spirits, and to treat toothache and rheumatism.

3. Open high forest on level ground, with poor drainage and subject to long periods of flooding, with canopy height between 10 to 30 m (30 to 100 ft).

This type of forest is composed of species tolerant of seasonal flooding, the most common being pucté (*Bucida buceras*), commonly used as a parrot nesting tree and the timber of which is used in the construction of railway cars; pixoy (*Guazuma ulmifolia*), its bark used to treat stomach ailments; cericote (*Cordia dodecandra*), a valuable two-tone timber with fruits used to make preserves, bark used to treat coughs and influenza, and rough leaves used to clean pots and pans; and kanté (or madre cacao, *Gliricidia sepium*), the timber of which is used for stout corner posts in house construction, the leaves used as forage and to treat rashes, headaches, and sore eyes, and the flowers commonly eaten with eggs.

4. Low forest subject to flooding during wet season but to arid conditions during dry season, with a canopy height mostly between 5 and 8 m (16 to 26 ft).

The most common trees here are chicozapote (*Manilkara zapota*); chichipate (*Sweetia panamensis*), with bark used to treat diabetes; roble hippo (*Hippocratea sp*); and tinto (*Haematoxylon campechianum*), a small tree that grows here to 12 m (40 ft) and is very common in these *swamp forests*, or *bajos*. Tinto's value as a natural dye source played an important role in the Europeans' decision to colonize Belize, where it is known as logwood (see p. 30). These swamp forests are also known as *tintales*, for their high concentration of tinto trees. Orchids and bromeliads, common epiphytes most associated with these tropical forests, are especially common in swamp forest trees, particularly in tinto and a few others.

A distinctive feature of these Guatemalan forests (particularly types 1 and 2) are palms, some of which are seen as isolated trees in cattle pastures. Within high dense forest on hillsides, xate palm is common, growing up to 2 m (6.5 ft) in height and dependent on the shade and humidity provided by the canopy overhead. Xate palm is a local name for several species of the genus *Chamaedorea*, such as *C. elegans* (or xate hembra; Figure 3d) and *C. oblongata* (or xate jade). These species are harvested throughout the year by collectors, *xateros*, who stay in traditional camps in the forest. Normally two or three leaves are cut from each plant and then sold to a middleman who provisions the forest workers. The leaves are exported to European and American markets for use as green foliage in flower arrangements and for wreaths. Xate palm is important for providing income to families living in rural communities. Another palm of economic importance is corozo (*Orbigyna cohune*) (Figure 3a), which is common in certain forest and pasture areas. Its seeds provide an oil used as a substitute for coconut oil, as a salad or cooking oil, and in the manufacture of soap. In many rural communities, houses are thatched with fronds of guano (*Sabal morrisiana*), a palm commonly eaten in the form of palm heart, as are corozo, bayal (*Desmoncus lundellii*), and pacaya (*Chamaedorea* sp.). Sadly, when the growing part (the *apical meristem*) of these palms is extracted for eating, the trees die.

Parks, Reserves, and Other Eco-sites: Brief Descriptions and Getting Around

The parks and reserves described below were selected because they are the ones most often visited by ecotravellers or because they have a lot to offer ecotravellers. The animals profiled in the color plates are keyed to these parks in the following way: the profiles list the political districts (Corozal – COR, Orange Walk – ORW, Belize – BEL, Stann Creek – STN, Cayo – CAYO, Toledo – TOL, Cayes – CAYE, Petén – PET) in which each species is likely to be found, and the parks listed below are arranged by district. Park and district locations are shown in Map 2, p. 9, and Map 3, p. 52. If no special information on reaching parks and on wildlife viewing is provided for a particular park, readers may assume the site is fairly easy to reach and that wildlife can be seen simply by walking along trails, roads, beaches, etc. Tips on increasing the likelihood of seeing mammals, birds, reptiles, or amphibians are given in the introductions to each of those chapters.

Belize

In general, three of Belize's main roads – the Northern, Western, and Hummingbird Highways – are kept in sufficient repair to permit safe and relatively fast passage. The Southern Highway, running from Dangriga to Punta Gorda, historically has been a more adventurous thoroughfare, difficult to navigate in the rainy season, but it was being repaved during the writing of this book. Drive slowly, let the trucks and buses pass, and watch for potholes. Almost all secondary roads are unpaved, slowing driving times. As anywhere, condition of dirt and gravel roads varies tremendously, from OK to ones that require moving at a snail's pace. Standard sedans are fine for reaching sites in the Belize District or those right along the main highways, but four-wheel-drive vehicles, with their higher ground clearance, are recommended for remoter areas and for passage on dirt or gravel roads during wetter parts of the year.

Most directions in Belize are given by reference to the number of miles along the major highways a given destination is from Belize City, other towns, or main highway intersections. For example, the turnoff to the Community Baboon Sanctuary is given as Mile 14 on the Northern Highway. Some of the mile distances along the highways are marked, but most are not, so you have to keep your eye on your odometer (which may be calibrated in km instead of miles). When approaching a turnoff or park's locale, slow down, because the sign, if there is one, is probably small and inconspicuous. Usually there are no previous warning signs along the highway, just small signs at the intersections for important turns.

Taking buses between towns is easy. There are frequent school-bus-type buses that move along the main roads, and spiffier, scheduled express buses between the bigger towns. It is also possible to take local buses to many parks and reserves. For information on visiting parks, reserves, and other sites in Belize, contact:

The Belize Tourist Board, 83 N Front St, P.O. Box 325, Belize City, Belize; Belize phone: 501-2-77213/73255; in the USA: 421 Seventh Ave, Suite 1110, NY, NY 10001; phone: 1-212-563-6011; or 1-800-624-0686; in Europe: Bopserwaldstr. 40-G D-70184, Stuttgart, Germany; phone/fax: 49-711-233-947; e-mail: BTBB@btl.net.

Northern Belize: Corozal District

Shipstern Nature Reserve. A lightly visited reserve about an hour's dirt road drive northeast of Orange Walk town. Probably visited most often by birdwatchers. Has trails, including a botanical trail through a hardwood forest that passes by more than 100 tree species, a butterfly breeding center at the reserve headquarters, and a small visitors' center. More than 200 species of birds, many mammals (but no monkeys), 60 reptiles and amphibians, and 200 butterflies have been spotted there. Birds include Wood Stork, Great Egret, Reddish Egret, Roseate Spoonbill, Neotropical Cormorant, Black Catbird, and White-winged Dove. The large saltwater lagoon and mudflat areas are used extensively by migrant birds from North America. The reserve was established in 1987 within a large no-hunting zone, and is associated with a private Swiss agency, the International Tropical Conservation Foundation. (Area: about 9000 hectares, 22,000 acres. Elevation: sea level to 3 m, 10 ft. Habitats: broadleaf rainforest, savannah, mangroves, saltwater lagoon, and mudflats.)

Northwestern Belize: Orange Walk District

Rio Bravo Conservation Area. Located about an hour's drive southeast of Orange Walk town. A large reserve operated since 1988 by the Programme for Belize, a private, Belize-based, non-profit conservation organization (which the Massachusetts Audubon Society helped establish and fund in order to preserve Rio Bravo wintering habitat for North American migrant birds). In addition to fostering ecological and archeological research in the area, protecting their lands from illegal hunting and logging, and working with local people on sustainable agriculture projects (such as chicle production, growing orchids and houseplants, and logging), The Programme for Belize strongly promotes ecotourism. Visitors can stay for varying periods at the La Milpa Field Research Station, which can house about 30 people. Programs include guided tours of trails, jungle walks, visits to neighboring villages and to Maya sites on the property, and evening lectures on natural history, conservation, and sustainable development. (Programme for Belize, P.O. Box 749, Belize City, Belize; phone: 501-2-75616; e-mail: pfbel@btl.net) About 1000 people per year visit the reserve, including many students. Over 70 species of mammals, 350 birds, and about 250 trees have been noted there, as have Morelet's Crocodile and the threatened Central American River Turtle. (Area: at 93,000 hectares, 229,000 acres, Rio Bravo is the largest private reserve in Belize. Elevation: 5 to 240 m, 15 to 790 ft. Habitats: broadleaf rainforest, marsh forest, savannah.)

Lamanai Archeological Reserve. Located about 80 km (50 miles) northwest of Belize City, Lamanai (Lah-mahn-EYE) is one of Belize's largest and most easily accessible Mayan ceremonial centers; many organized ecotours stop there. More than 700 structures have been mapped at the site, and several large temples are partially or entirely excavated; a few are partly restored. The setting, along the banks of a large lagoon of the New River, is beautiful, and the forest trails that connect the ruins are often alive with wildlife – small lizards, birds, howler monkeys. There is road access to the site, but it is rough and often impassable during the rainy season. Most visitors arrive by boat via a very pleasant, scenic, 90-minute boat ride along the New River from Orange Walk town or other river access spots. The river is wide in some areas, narrow in others, lined with epiphyte-encrusted trees, and sometimes choked with flowering lily pads. Wildlife seen along the river typically includes turtles, Snail Kites, marsh birds, water birds, and bats roosting on trunks of riverside trees. (Area: about 380 hectares, 950 acres. Elevation: maximum 100 m, 330 ft. Habitats: broadleaf rainforest, river.)

Chan Chich. Chan Chich (chahn cheech) is a Mayan ceremonial site near the Guatemalan border that has been turned by its private owners into an unusual, upscale tourist site. It is reached via a three- or four-hour drive north and west of Belize City (or by a short flight from Belize City to tiny Gallon Jug airport). Luxurious thatch-roofed bungalows have been built smack in the middle of an ancient Mayan plaza. The site is surrounded by more than 90,000 hectares (220,000 acres) of forest, and is an excellent spot for wildlife viewing. There are about 14 km (9 miles) of trails and many small dirt roads to wander on foot or horseback. Birdwatchers, who have spotted more than 300 species in the area, adore the place. (Chan Chich Lodge, P. O. Box 37, Belize City, Belize; Belize phone: 501-2-75634; USA phone: 1-800-343-8009.)

Eastern Belize: Belize District

Crooked Tree Wildlife Sanctuary. Located about 55 km (35 miles) northwest of Belize City, this reserve was established in 1984 primarily for the protection of resident and migrant water-associated birds – ducks (waterfowl), cormorants, storks, herons, egrets, spoonbills, marsh birds, shorebirds, and Snail Kites. About 275 species of birds have been spotted there, as have many reptiles: several turtle species (including the threatened Central American River Turtle), lizards, and Morelet's Crocodile. Mammals in the area include howler monkeys and otters. Most of the interesting habitat is aquatic – lagoons, swamps, and waterways. But there is also an extensive trail system through and around the village of Crooked Tree, which is surrounded by the sanctuary. Trails along the lagoons and along sandy village lanes and tracks are ideal for birdwatching (vultures are common, as are several species of kingfishers, and Vermilion Flycatchers), and various hotels and local guides give nature tours by boat. Many people in the village of Crooked Tree try to make their living through ecotourism – operating restaurants, stores, small hotels, bed-and-breakfast lodgings, or boating and guide services. About 2500 people visit annually, but the place can be deserted during the off-season, April through October. The sanctuary is managed by the Belize Audubon Society (P.O. Box 1001, 12 Fort St., Belize City, Belize. phone: 501-2-35004; fax: 501-2-34985; e-mail: base@btl.net) with the cooperation of Crooked Tree Village. (Area: about 16,600 hectares, 41,000 acres. Elevation: 5 m, 15 ft. Habitats: freshwater lagoons and marshes, broadleaf rainforest, swamp forest, savannah.)

Community Baboon Sanctuary. Described in detail on p. 10. Located less than an hour's drive north and west of Belize City. Small visitors' center/museum, guided tours by local villagers, trails. More than 250 species of birds have been seen in the sanctuary; mammals there include Baird's Tapir, Jaguarundi, deer, and, of course, many troops of Black Howler Monkey (the *raison d'être* for the sanctuary); reptiles include Green Iguana, Morelet's Crocodile, and the Central American River Turtle. About 5000 people visit each year, including many school groups, both local and foreign; however, the place can be all but deserted during the off-season, April through October. (Area: about 5200 hectares, 13,000 acres. Elevation: about 25 m, 80 ft. Habitats: broadleaf rainforest, marsh, pastures/farmland.)

Belize Zoo and Tropical Education Center. Described in detail in Close-Up, p. 224. Not a reserve, but definitely an eco-attraction, and worth a visit. Located an hour's drive west of Belize City. (Phone: 501-8-13004.)

Gales Point. About a two-hour drive (or boat trip) from Belize City, Gales Point is a small village and mangrove-fringed peninsula whose main attraction is the surrounding lagoons. These waters are home to manatees (p. 221) and other kinds of wildlife, including many species of aquatic birds. The area includes a government-sanctioned manatee sanctuary. With government support, local people have formed a cooperative organization to operate the sanctuary. They profit economically by offering ecotourism services, such as boats, guides, and bed-and-breakfast style accommodations. There are also hotels in the area. (Area: up to 66,000 hectares, or 170,000 acres, of lagoons and public and private lands may eventually be part of a reserve.)

Southeastern Belize: Stann Creek District

Cockscomb Basin Wildlife Sanctuary (also known as the *Jaguar Sanctuary*). Located about an hour's drive (in dry weather) south of the coastal town of Dangriga (about 40 km, 25 miles, along the Southern Highway), beneath the Cockscomb Mountains, a conspicuous ridge of the Maya Mountains that supposedly resembles a cock's comb. Part of a larger Cockscomb Basin Forest Reserve, which was established in 1984 as a no-hunting area specifically for the protection of Jaguars, a healthy population of which lives there (Dr Alan Rabinowitz conducted Wildlife Conservation Society-sponsored research on Jaguars in the area and was instrumental in having the Belize government establish the sanctuary). The sanctuary, only a small part of the reserve, was set up in 1986 to foster conservation and ecotourism in the area. A good place to see Jaguar, except for the fact that they're mostly nocturnal and, unless you're really lucky, extremely difficult to catch sight of. But the sanctuary is a beautiful place, with at least 12 miles (20 km) of trails, perhaps the most extensive system in the country. Visitors with reservations can stay overnight in dormitory-style lodgings – a good thing, because the best wildlife sightings often occur during the late afternoon, early evening, and at dawn (although on a recent trip, I saw a host of great birds from 1:00 to 4:00 in the afternoon). The sanctuary is run by the Belize Audubon Society, which can be contacted about staying there (or write to Cockscomb Basin Wildlife Sanctuary, P.O. Box 90, Dangriga, Belize); many hotels in and around Dangriga and Placencia can arrange trips to the sanctuary, and it is on the itineraries of most professional ecotours of Belize. Wildlife includes an unknown (!) but extensive number of bird species (Scarlet Macaws are occasionally sighted); Baird's Tapir, a bunch of cats (Jaguar, Ocelot, Margay, Jaguarundi, Puma), Black Howler Monkeys transplanted recently from the Community Baboon Sanctuary, and what is estimated to be representatives of 70% of Belizean reptiles and amphibians (approximately 80 species). Don't miss this one! Note: A tiny village (nine families) of Mayan Indians was moved from within the sanctuary's borders when it was established. The new village, Maya Centre, is located at the entrance to the sanctuary. A few of the local people work for the sanctuary as wardens or guides, and the village operates a small crafts store where you turn off the main road and pay admission to the sanctuary. (Area: about 35,000 hectares, 87,000 acres. Elevation: approximately 100 to 600 m, 330 to 1960 ft. Habitats: broadleaf rainforest, pools, waterfalls, streams and rivers.)

Western Belize: Cayo District

Guanacaste National Park. Located two hours west of Belize City, near Belmopan. A small park along a main road, at the junction of the Belize River and Roaring Creek. The park preserves a large, old Guanacaste tree. There's a small visitors' center/museum and about 3 km (2 miles) of trail, mostly along the Belize River. More than 100 bird species have been recorded there. The park is administered by the Belize Audubon Society and, although small in size and in a populated area, it is visited frequently by local school classes and is considered to be "a symbol of the conservation ethic in Belize." It was established on Earth Day, 1990. (Area: 23 hectares, 58 acres. Elevation: about 40 m, 130 ft. Habitats: broadleaf rainforest, river.)

Blue Hole National Park. Located about 20 km (12 miles) southeast of Belmopan, along the Hummingbird Highway. The "blue hole" is a water-filled hole, actually a section of exposed underground river, about 100 m (330 ft) wide, and perhaps 30 m (100 ft) deep. The park is a popular swimming (in the blue hole) and picnicking site, and can be crowded on weekends. Aside from the cool water attraction, the park has a small network of trails (toucans, motmots, and jacamars are seen regularly), trail access to a large cavern (St Herman's Cave), and a small visitors' center. Established as a national park in 1986, Blue Hole is administered by the Belize Audubon Society. (Area: 230 hectares, 575 acres. Elevation: 60 to 200 m, 200 to 650 ft. Habitats: broadleaf rainforest, caves.)

Five Blues Lake National Park. Located about 35 km (22 miles) southeast of Belmopan, along the Hummingbird Highway. The lake, a 60-m (200-ft) deep sinkhole covering approximately 3 hectares (7.4 acres), supposedly changes colors among a host of shades of blue – hence, the name. There is a small visitors' center, a good trail network, and some caves. About 200 bird species have been seen in the park, as have more than 20 cave-roosting bat species. The park's access road is often in poor condition, and can be impassable during and after heavy rains. Established as a national park in 1991. (Area: 1720 hectares, 4250 acres. Elevation: 15 to 360 m, 50 to 1180 ft. Habitats: broadleaf rainforest, freshwater lagoon, caves.)

Tapir Mountain Nature Reserve. Located 18 km (11 miles) southwest of Belmopan, well off the Western Highway. Established as a nature reserve in 1986 to protect animals and plants characteristic of the northern foothills of the Maya Mountains. Because the site is relatively little developed and because the reserve is mostly for research and education, special permission from the Belize Audubon Society is needed to visit. About 130 bird species have been seen in the park, as have many mammals: Baird's Tapir, howler monkeys, peccaries, Paca, anteaters, deer, etc. (Area: 2728 hectares, 6741 acres. Elevation: about 30 to 280 m, 100 to 920 ft. Habitats: broadleaf rainforest.)

Chiquibul National Park and Caracol Archeological Reserve. This is a huge, remote site in the Maya Mountains along Belize's western border with Guatemala. Access is via a rough, frequently flooded dirt road; most visitors go with organized tour groups, as guests of local lodges, or with small groups put together by tour operators in San Ignacio. The national park was established in 1991, carved out of unlogged areas of the larger Chiquibul Forest Reserve; the Caracol site was added to the park in 1995. Caracol, archeologists believe, was a Mayan city that rivaled and, in time, conquered the magnificent Mayan center of Tikal, which is located 75 km (45 miles) away (straight line distance), across the border in northern Guatemala. Whereas much of Tikal has been wholly or partially excavated and restored, little work has yet been done with the Caracol site; work is ongoing. Most of the large temples and other structures are still hidden in the forest, but the sight of the partially buried stone masses erupting from the jungle floor is well worth seeing. Caracol represents a rare opportunity to visit a stunning set of jungle-cloaked Mayan ruins in the absence of tourist hordes – indeed, often in the absence of anyone. The surrounding forest is beautiful, and there are trails to explore. Also in the area, and accessible with knowledgeable local guides, is what is probably Central America's largest underground cave and tunnel system. Most of the national park is rather inaccessible, and the entire eastern half of it is considered a wilderness area. Guatemala recently declared its lands adjacent to the Belize park to be a protected biosphere reserve. (Area: 107,000 hectares, 265,000 acres. Elevation: most of the park is at between 400 and 800 m, 1300 to 2600 ft. Habitats: broadleaf rainforest.)

Monkey Bay Wildlife Sanctuary and Nature Reserve. Located about 50 km (30 miles) west and south of Belize City, along the Western Highway. The Monkey Bay Wildlife Sanctuary is a private, non-profit organization dedicated to conservation, environmental research and education, and vegetarian self-sufficiency. The sanctuary was established in 1990; the government of Belize gave the sanctuary an additional section of mostly inaccessible land, now called the Monkey Bay Nature Reserve (or National Park), to manage in 1992. The sanctuary has a field research station, education programs (including visiting overseas college courses), overnight accommodations, camping, trails, a meadow, an arboretum, river access, and good birding – more than 220 species have been seen there. More than 1000 people per year visit the sanctuary. (Area: sanctuary is 430 hectares, 1070 acres; adjacent wilderness nature reserve is 900 hectares, 2250 acres. Elevation: most of the sanctuary lies between 30 and 45 m, 100 to 150 ft. Habitats: broadleaf rainforest, pine savannah, meadow, river.)

Mountain Pine Ridge Forest Reserve. Located south and east of San Ignacio, along the northwest flank of the Maya Mountains. Access is via a rough, sometimes steep, dirt road south of the Western Highway; most visitors go with organized tour groups or small groups put together by tour operators in San Ignacio. This is a wonderful part of Belize, a cooler, higher-elevation site with an off-beat type of habitat: tropical pine forest. The topography is rolling forested hills, rocky hillsides, and mountains. The reserve was established in 1944; some of it is logged, and logging goes on to this day. The wildlife has not been well documented, but more than 150 bird species have been spotted there. Woodpeckers are common, as are Ocellated Turkeys and King Vultures; rare Orange-breasted Falcons can be reliably seen at some sites. There are trails and a camping area around the D'Silva Forest Station. Some of the lodges located within the reserve own large chunks of land with their own (often spectacular) trails. For instance, the Hidden Valley Inn (P.O. Box 170, Belmopan, Belize; Belize phone: 501-8-23320; USA phone: 1-800-334-7942) sits on 7300 hectares (18,000 acres) of privately owned land, with wonderful forested trails and jeep-tracks to hidden streams, wild overlooks, and high waterfalls (incuding one of the region's prime attractions, the Thousand-foot Falls, which is located on the property). The owners of Hidden Valley have designated the eastern third of the property as a nature reserve, the Hidden Valley Institute for Environmental Studies. Some of the region's other attractions are a number of impressive waterfalls, and caves such as the Rio Frio Cave – a limestone cavern through which the Rio On flows. This part of Belize is increasingly popular with tourists (about 3000 visit per year), but definitely worth a trip. Some of the hotels and lodges located within the reserve are pricey, but their stunning settings and trail systems make it money well spent. (Area: 51,000 hectares, 127,000 acres. Elevation: 120 to 1015 m, 400 to 3330 ft. Habitats: 80% tropical pine forest and pine savannah, 20% broadleaf rainforest, rivers, waterfalls, bogs.)

El Pilar Archeological Reserve for Maya Flora and Fauna. Mayan ruins in the reserve, located about 19 km (12 miles) north of San Ignacio, are presently being excavated and studied. This is still a lightly visited sight, but the plazas and 10 or more large pyramids are spread over a large forested area (including an adjacent site in Guatemala) and there are several nature trails. Good wildlife spot. Ask in San Ignacio for directions, guides, etc.

Southern Belize: Toledo District

Bladen Branch Nature Reserve. This large, remote, relatively pristine wilderness area, named for the Bladen River, is located in the Maya Mountains, northwest of Punta Gorda. The scenery is spectacular, the wildlife diverse. When I discussed Bladen with a long-time Belize resident who has led local birding tours for more than 15 years, his face lit up as he described the area – he had been there recently for the first time and could not wait to return. As of this publication date (late 1998), few ecotravellers make it to Bladen. There is still only poor road access, although there is a serviceable trail that knowledgeable local guides can find and follow. The site, as a wilderness nature reserve, is officially closed to tourists and open only to researchers. Some organized tours, with special permission, make it to Bladen. The area, a reserve since 1977 (there was scattered logging in the region through about 1970), received upgraded nature reserve status in 1990, and is designated now especially for wildlife conservation. From initial surveys, it is suspected that this region contains the most diverse assortment of reptiles and amphibians in Belize. One group of researchers recorded 194 bird species in the month they wandered the area; they spotted such mammals as Puma, Jaguar, Baird's Tapir, otter, deer, Paca, agouti, peccary, and spider monkey. Bladen is obviously worth the trip, but good luck getting there! (Area: 40,350 hectares, 99,670 acres. Elevation: 80 to 1000 m, 260 to 3270 ft. Habitats: broadleaf rainforest at a wide range of elevations, tropical pine forest, scrub thicket, savannah, caves, river.)

Columbia River Forest Reserve. This is a large, remote, hot and wet area located west of Punta Gorda, nestled against Belize's western border with Guatemala. Only the most intrepid ecotourists make it this far! There is wonderful scenery and wildlife-laden tropical forest at various elevations. The reserve functions to conserve the high degree of biodiversity in the area, to protect the watershed, and to try to create a sustainable hardwood timber industry in the area (which has a long history of logging). More than 225 bird species have so far been spotted here. About 15 Maya Indian farming villages surround the reserve. Access is usually by taking a bus from Punta Gorda to one of the villages (San Jose, San Pedro Columbia, San Miguel, Na Luum 'Ca, or Crique Jute), walking several hours to the reserve (perhaps with a local guide), then walking along logging tracks. A better road into the reserve is planned. (Area: about 42,000 hectares, 103,000 acres. Elevation: 275 to 820 m, 900 to 2700 ft. Habitats: broadleaf rainforest at a wide range of elevations, tropical pine savannah, caves, river.)

Blue Creek Field Station and Nature Reserve. Located an hour's drive west of Punta Gorda, this education-oriented student, researcher, and tourist field station is run by a private company, International Zoological Expeditions (210 Washington St, Sherborn, MA 01770 USA; phone: 800-548-5843 or 508-655-1461; e-mail: IZE2belize@aol.com). The station, with dormitory-style accommodations, hearty local cooking, research/classroom hut, and elevated rainforest canopy walkway and platforms (not for the faint-hearted) is situated on the banks of Blue Creek, which rises dramatically during heavy rains – meaning quite frequently. There are forest trails and caves to explore. Local guides from the adjacent Blue Creek Village can be engaged for trail or road walking tours in the area. The company, which also operates a second, marine-life-oriented field station on South Water Caye can, for a price, arrange pick-ups and drop-offs at Punta Gorda. (Area: 80 hectares, 200 acres. Elevation: maximum to 300 m, 1000 ft. Habitats: broadleaf rainforest, caves, river.)

Offshore Belize: The Cayes

Ambergris Caye and *Caye Caulker* are the two most heavily visited cayes, and the most developed. Ambergris, the most commercialized island (it has real hotels), is used by many organized tour groups as a base for water activities – snorkelling, diving, fishing. Off the southern end of Ambergris, about 6.4 km (4 miles) south-east of the island's town of San Pedro, is the *Hol Chan Marine Reserve* (Area: 1115 hectares, 2758 acres). The reserve, the most popular reef diving spot in Belize, is located along the northern part of the barrier reef. Also in the reserve are a lagoon with seagrass beds and seven small cayes with mangrove habitat. Hol Chan's office and visitor's center is located in San Pedro. About 26,000 tourists visit the reserve annually, almost all for diving or snorkelling.

Caye Caulker, with its two sand walkway-streets lined with dive shops, restaurants, and inexpensive guest houses, is smaller and more laid-back than Ambergris, with a reputation as a hippie hang-out. Some local residents have been trying for years to establish a multi-habitat marine sanctuary on the southern end of Caye Caulker, to be called the Siwa-ban Marine Reserve (*Siwa-ban* is the Mayan word for the Black Catbird (Plate 56), whose habitat the reserve would protect). One long-time resident has spotted about 140 species of birds on or near Caye Caulker, many of them using this dry bit of land as a migratory rest stop.

A second marine reserve has been established at *Glover's Reef* atoll, east of Dangriga. The reserve, established in 1993, partially to relieve overcrowding at the Hol Chan diving site, preserves a region of diverse reef types and fish spawning beds. Some consider the off-shore habitat at Glover's Reef Marine Reserve to harbor the finest coral reef animal community in the Caribbean. (Area: 32,900 hectares, 81,230 acres.) A number of small cayes have been designated as parks or bird sanctuaries. These include: Bird Caye, Doubloon Bank Caye, Little Guana Caye (Cayo Pájaros), Man-o-War Caye, and Little Monkey Caye. Some of these islands are important nesting areas for egrets, herons, Anhingas, cormorants, ibises, frigatebirds, and gulls. There are no tourist facilities on these cayes, but people make day trips from the mainland. Laughing Bird Caye, a small island (less than a hectare, about 2 acres) with coconut palms and mangroves, located east of Placencia, was designated as a national park in 1991. The site is used for day trip outings and for snorkeling and diving.

Half Moon Caye National Monument represents Belize's first site to be designated for wildlife protection – the British did it in 1928. The main wildlife to be protected is a nesting colony of Red-footed Boobies (p. 114) at the western end of the island (which can be observed from a viewing platform after hiking along a brushy trail) and a surprisingly diverse group of lizard species, including Green Iguana, Spiny-tailed Iguana, anoles, and geckos. (Area: the island is 18 hectares, 44 acres; the surrounding protected marine area, with 6.4 km (4 miles) of reef, is 3950 hectares, 9770 acres.)

Since 1972, the USA's Smithsonian Institution, National Museum of Natural History, has operated the Caribbean Coral Reef Ecosystem Field Research Station on *Carrie Bow Caye*, southeast of Dangriga. Over the years, researchers at the tiny island (Area: 0.4 hectares, or 1 acre) have studied reef, mangrove, seagrass, and plankton biology. Access to the island's field station is by permission of the USA's National Museum of Natural History. Good luck!

Guatemala

Driving in Guatemala's Petén is pure adventure; four-wheel-drive is recommended. The only good paved road in the region is the one from Flores/Santa Elena to Tikal (Map 3, p. 52). The unpaved road from Flores/Santa Elena to Sayaxché, used by many heavy trucks, is rough but OK. The partially paved roads from Flores/Santa Elena to Poptún and toward San Ignacio, Belize are usually passable. Most visitors take organized tours of the Petén, or leave the driving to locals – by taking tourist minibuses or regular buses. The Petén's tourist industry anywhere but in Flores or Tikal is still in its infancy, so the required infrastructure is rough or lacking; therefore, getting around on your own can be difficult.

For information on any of the parks or sites described here, you can contact the Guatemalan Institute of Tourism (Inguat) at: 7a Avenida 1–17, Zona 4, Centro Civico, Guatemala City, Guatemala; phone: 502-2-331-1333; fax: 502-2-331-8893; e-mail: inguat@geo2.poptel.org.uk Located off the central plaza in Flores is a clearing-house for information on tourism in the Petén, CINCAP (Center for Information on the Nature, Culture, and Handicrafts of the Petén).

Tikal National Park and World Heritage Site. Tikal is described in detail on p. 13. Most visitors to the area arrive by air, taking a flight from Guatemala City or Belize City to Flores, the small, attractive, cobble-streeted town on Lake Petén Itza that is the Petén's capital and that serves as a tourism hub for Tikal and the Petén. Adventure-seekers with healthy backs can take the 20-hour bus trip from Guatemala City. The site can also be reached via bus or minibus from San Ignacio, Belize. Minibus shuttle service leaves Flores several times a day for the one-hour ride to Tikal. (Area: the park area is 568 sq km, 222 sq miles; the ancient city of Tikal itself, inside the park, is 130 sq km, 50 sq miles. Elevation: about 150 to 600 m, 500 to 2000 ft. Habitat: broadleaf rainforest.) Another, smaller, Maya ruin site and village is Uaxactún, which is located 24 km (14 miles) north of Tikal, up a dirt road that begins from inside Tikal.

Maya Biosphere Reserve. This reserve is discussed in detail in Chapter 3. It includes nearly 40% of the Petén, about 14% of Guatemalan territory. Located within the huge, sparsely populated reserve are Tikal, Laguna del Tigre (Jaguar Lake), Sierra del Lacandon (Lacandon Mountain), El Mirador (The Lookout), and Río Azul (Blue River) National Parks, and El Zotz, Naachtun-Dos Lagunas, and Laguna del

Tigre-Río Escondido Nature Reserves (biotopos). Trips to some of these parks are for hardy people, as they can involve several days in heat and mud on foot or horseback. At least 350 species of birds occupy the region. In addition to visiting Mayan ruins, people travel to these parks and reserves for trekking through remote forests and wetlands, birdwatching, cave exploration, and river and lake trips, including white-water rafting. (Area: about 1.6 million hectares, 4 million acres. Elevation: about 100 to 1000 m, 330 to 3300 ft – the higher parts are in the Maya Mountains in eastern Petén. Habitats: broadleaf rainforest, seasonally flooded forest, lakes, rivers, wooded swamps and grassy and other wetlands.)

El Ceibal Archeological Park. Ceibal is an interesting, well kept Mayan ruin site with some partially restored structures and plazas within an area of about one sq km (0.5 sq miles); the *stelae* (tombstone-like stone sculptures with hieroglyph inscriptions) here are considered to be among the finest and best-preserved of a certain Maya period. The site is named for the Ceiba, the national tree of Guatemala. This is not a huge, developed, excavated site, as is Tikal. Limited trails around the site and up to it from the river landing are good for birdwatching; lizards abound along the trails and on the ruins. Most visitors arrive via a two-hour (60 km, or 35 miles), bone-jarring minibus ride from Flores to the river-edge town of Sayaxché, where boat transportation along the Passion River to Ceibal, about 30 km (18 miles) away, is available. There is also road access, but the road is usually in very bad condition. The site has a problem with theft of artifacts, so some of the stonework, for protection, has been moved to museums. (Area: there is, on paper, a large protected area, sometimes designated as a national park, of 17,612 sq km, 6875 sq miles surrounding the ruins. Elevation: the ruins are at about 220 m, 720 ft. Habitats: hilly rainforest, parkland, river.)

Cerro Cahui Nature Reserve (Biotopo). Located on the way to Tikal from Flores, a short hike off the main road, this nature reserve is near the northeastern edge of Lake Petén Itza. It has about 8 km (5 miles) of trails through semi-open rainforest and two nice lookouts with long views of the surrounding countryside. It was established recently to try to protect the Ocellated Turkey, Morelet's Crocodile, and Baird's Tapir, all of which occur in the area. Birding is good along the trails – plenty of toucans, trogons, cuckoos, and hummingbirds; lizards such as basilisks and whiptails are also common. One of the best parts of the trip is that, after a few hours hiking along the steamy trails, you can walk or drive a few more kilometers down the road and arrive for lunch or cool drinks at the Westin Camino Real Tikal Hotel, the fanciest place in the region. (Area: 650 hectares, 1600 acres.)

Finca Ixobel. Located near the village of Poptún, about 110 km (65 miles) south and east of Flores. This privately owned farm (finca) in the middle of extensive forest has become a popular ecotourism site, especially with the younger back-packing set. The farm has forest trails (multi-day guided hikes on foot or horse-back can be arranged), swimming, budget accommodations, camping, and good, homemade food.

Chapter 3

ENVIRONMENTAL THREATS AND CONSERVATION

- *Belize*
  Major Threats and Conservation Record
  Conservation Programs and Ecotourism
- *Northern Guatemala – the Petén District*
  History of the Petén
  Major Threats
  Conservation Programs and Ecotourism

Belize and northern Guatemala, although having very different recent histories, face some similar environmental threats. Belize has always been at peace, but Guatemala just recently emerged from almost 40 years of serious civil strife. Belize has a small population; Guatemala's is fairly large. But both are poor, developing countries with low *per capita* gross domestic products (1995: Belize, US$2750; Guatemala, $3300). In both, a small number of well-off citizens, together with large corporations, own most of the available land. Guatemala's large population has affected both countries because during the civil war, many thousands of Guatemalans crossed the border to seek refuge in Belize; some became permanent immigrants.

Belize

Major Threats and Conservation Record

The major threats to Belize's environment are deforestation, pollution from poor agricultural practices, and a small but growing human population that is mainly poor. Logging was about the only major economic activity in Belize through the early part of the 20th century. When the supply of accessible timber dropped off, people turned to sugarcane production, then, more recently, to citrus fruit, bananas, and to seafood harvesting.

Most would agree that, so far, given the nation's general lack of funds, Belize's conservation record is OK. More than a third (about 36%) of Belize is under environmental protection of one kind or another – parks, wildlife sanctuaries, nature reserves. However, the government has very little money to manage these lands or enforce environmental regulations there or elsewhere. Often one underpaid warden in a park or reserve is single-handedly responsible for enforcement over an enormous area. The result is that rules are widely flouted. For example, one important but usually ignored rule is that new farms and orchards carved out of forests should leave standing a belt of about 20 m (65 ft) of forest along all waterways. Cutting the forest right up to rivers and streams impedes animal movements, takes needed shade from the water, and allows agricultural pesticides to move directly into waterways.

Furthermore, although the attitude of the Belize government toward conservation is good, the attitude of most Belizeans is only so-so. The commonly voiced explanation is that people of limited means necessarily must worry more about today – obtaining food and shelter for their families – than about the country's or the world's future environmental state. Most care about conservation only when they can benefit economically from it, when it can make their lives better. But so far, such as in the case of conservation by ecotourism, only a small number of local people benefit and most of the profit "leaks" out of Belize, mostly flowing to North America and Europe (to tour operators and hotel owners). Even the best examples in Belize between ecotourism and local community participation – the Community Baboon Sanctuary and Crooked Tree Wildlife Sanctuary – often provide only meager incomes to participating villagers. The picture is slowly improving. The government now maintains a social investment fund (accumulated partly by the airport departure tax) to give grants and loans to people trying to improve their lives, for example, by building up their stakes in ecotourism by developing or upgrading tourist facilities. In the past, most of the committed environmentalists that controlled local conservation organizations and lobbied for environmental protections were resort owners and the like, well-off people who stood to profit greatly from increased tourism (and, as often as not, were North American and European expatriots). Now, with increasing frequency, native-born Belizeans in various professions understand the need for conservation and are sitting on the executive boards of these organizations.

Conservation Programs and Ecotourism

The outstanding feature of conservation in Belize is the success private organizations have had in developing and implementing programs. The government simply has no money for such projects, but private, mostly non-profit conservation organizations do, and they are very interested in working in Belize – a peaceful country with a stable government and with substantial remaining unspoiled habitats. Many of the organizations have already been mentioned in Chapter 2. The Belize Audubon Society has been instrumental in developing and managing many of Belize's parks and wildlife sanctuaries. The Community Baboon Sanctuary and Monkey Bay Wildlife Sanctuary are organizations that preserve large tracts of important habitats not far from Belize City. A Swiss foundation established the Shipstern Nature Reserve. Several organizations, some for-profit, some non-profit, promote ecotravel to Belize. The Program for Belize, among other projects, manages the Río Bravo Conservation Area, works with researchers and local people to develop a sustainable mahogany logging industry, and hosts travellers at its field station. Chan Chich Lodge, a favorite birdwatching destination, preserves the Mayan ruin site in which it is located. International Zoological Expeditions (IZE), through its Blue Creek field station, attracts ecotourists to southern Belize, and employs local villagers. Coral Cay Conservation Ltd, a British-based organization interested in conservation in coastal communities in developing nations, brings groups of paying volunteers to Belize's cayes (especially South Water Caye) to learn about and gather data on marine biology in general, and the coral reef in particular (Coral Cay Conservation, 154 Clapham Park Rd, London, SW4 7DE, UK; phone: 44-171-498-6248; www.coralcay.org; e-mail: ccc@coralcay.demon.co.uk)

Ecotourism in Belize expanded rapidly during the late 1980s and early 1990s. Most people came to visit the cayes for diving and snorkeling, but the number of people visiting mainland rainforests also increased. A good example is the Crooked Tree Wildlife Sanctuary. There were 25 visitors to the site in 1986, 558 in 1987, 1055 in 1988, 1529 in 1989, and about 2500 in 1990 and subsequent years. Of course, too much of a good thing – too many ecotravellers – can be bad. Belize's barrier reef, for instance, the country's biggest tourist draw, is experiencing some damage from over-use. The reef at Hol Chan Marine Reserve, where most diving occurs, is slightly damaged every time people touch it or stand on it. To counter such damage, and to try to disperse divers over a larger area of reef, Belize has established other marine reserves, such as the one at Glover's Reef. But that strategy, too, has problems. As tour and resort operators move quickly to capitalize on the burst of interest in offshore islands other than Ambergris Caye and Caye Caulker, rapid and unrestricted development occurs on more and more of the cayes. In one famous case, a foreign resort owner used explosives to blast holes in the reef so that his guests could have better access to other islands. (The barrier reef is not the only part of Belize's coastal ecology to be threatened: there is coastal erosion, land-based pollution, poorly planned jetty construction, and unregulated fishing and other harvesting of seafoods.)

Still, even with its many problems and lack of funds to address them, Belize is considered to be among the planet's most environmentally concerned countries. Belizeans have seen what uncontrolled development has done to their closest neighbors – the near total deforestation that occured over broad swaths of southern Mexico, Guatemala, and Honduras – and they do not want the same for their small, green nation. They made a good start by giving preservation status to large chunks of the country. Ecotourism is strongly and officially encouraged. Because tourism is the fastest growing sector of the Belizean economy, local people should increasingly see the benefits of preserving pristine habitats.

An exciting plan that many local conservationists are working on is to be able to link up existing preserves so that there is a continuous belt of highly protected, wild, green habitat running through Belize. Such a green *corridor*, or *greenway*, would provide a permanent path for movement of land animals (for their migrations and dispersals) that often are blocked or inhibited by roads, farms, and human settlements. Among such large reserves as Río Bravo Conservation Area and the Community Baboon Sanctuary in Belize's North, and Cockscomb Basin Wildlife Sanctuary and Bladen Branch Nature Reserve in the South, much of the corridor already exists. What is needed is to acquire some critical connecting pieces of land or obtain the owners' legal promises (easements) never to develop those parcels. When the corridor is in place, it can become part of the *Paseo Pantera* (Path of the Panther), the in-progress green corridor being put together by all of Central America to provide and forever preserve a continuous band of wild habitat from Mexico to Colombia. (The Maya Biosphere Reserve, in northern Guatemala, would also be part of the corridor.)

Belize also plans to create more land reserves – the future Siwa-ban reserve on Caye Caulker, for example – and, in all probability, more marine reserves. Belizeans have more than 65% of their rainforest habitat remaining and many residents want to keep it that way. They recently (1996) completed a detailed master conservation plan for the country. Conservation-minded citizens are working for more and better enforcement of existing enviromental laws. They are trying to involve more local people in conservation via education programs (for instance, an anti-litter campaign has helped reduce litter) and via increased local participation in ecotourism. Ultimately, it will be better education and an increased standard of living that will instill the conservation ethic. So let's say that Belize has made a good conservation start. Because it still has some relatively undisturbed habitats and good wildlife, and because it has the advantage of being able to evaluate recent development and conservation efforts of neighboring countries, Belize, with some motivation, help, and luck, has the chance to learn from others' mistakes and to do things better – to develop economically while still keeping its environmental house in good shape.

Northern Guatemala – the Petén District

History of the Petén

The main bit of the Petén's history relative to its current environmental and conservation status is that, as the result of a number of inter-related factors, the Petén contains Guatemala's and, indeed, the region's, largest remaining area of forest habitat – the largest stand of continuous virgin tropical rainforest north of the Amazon. In fact, the Petén holds what are essentially Guatemala's last pristine habitats. The Pacific coastal lowland forests have been mostly cleared for agriculture, and the central highlands are everywhere (except for the highest-elevation mountainous regions) dotted with small villages and their associated pastures and croplands.

Until about 1970, about 90% of the Petén, a vast area, was still covered with undisturbed rainforest. The reasons? First, it was a difficult place for people to live because much of the region is hot and steamy and there was little surface water available over wide swaths of the Petén (especially the northern half) during much of the year. Also, the region's soils generally are less-than-ideal for farming and there was little water to support extensive agriculture. With few people living there and, consequently, a low economic productivity, the Guatemalan government never had much reason to build or improve roads in the Petén; the lack of easy road access further inhibited people from moving there. To be sure, there was some use of the Petén's forests, but the main industries that developed (mainly extracting chicle, xate, and allspice from trees – see below) did little harm. Finally, for a major portion of the almost 40 years of civil war, the Petén was a dangerous place to live. The Sayaxché area, for instance, where travellers now routinely visit the Ceibal Archeological Park, was a particularly dangerous spot, where rebel guerillas held sway. (So, in an ironic way, Guatemala's civil war helped preserve its forests, but the war also had catastrophic effects on the country: more than 100,000 people were killed, and a government at war necessarily spent little money on educational and cultural programs, road-building, health care, or conservation.)

As a result of the Petén's unique history, through about 1970, the region's population was fairly low and stable – about 60,000 people lived there. But during the following 25 years, the Petén's population increased six-fold, to about 350,000 in 1997; and the projections are for a population of at least 400,000 by 2000 (if not many more – the region's growth rate in the mid-1990s approached 10% per year). The main reasons have to do with poverty, high population growth, and limited arable land in other parts of Guatemala, and the ending of the war. The Petén somehow acquired a reputation as a region where land could still be had for the asking, where crowding was nonexistent, and where, owing to increasing development, jobs were available. Roads put in during the 1970s and 1980s, as the government sought to profit from the area by opening it to oil exploration and logging, permitted easy immigration. With the increased safety in movement associated with the winding down of the war, people began to move to the Petén from Guatemala's other districts. Further, when the war ended and Guatemalan refugees from abroad – particularly those that fled to Mexico and Belize – returned home and had to be resettled, the Petén, with its large expanse of state-owned, undeveloped lands, was a logical place to look.

Major threats

The major environmental threat to the Petén is its rapid human population growth, and the pressure that growth puts on its forests; in other words, deforestation. When new people arrive, they clear land for homes, farms, and cattle pastures. Moreover, the operation of almost any industry – timber, agriculture, oil, factories – results in cleared or spoiled forest land, and causes pollution. Conservation organizations estimate that since 1970, about half of the Petén's virgin forest has been cut, burned, or otherwise destroyed, and that at the current rate of loss – about 300 square km (120 square miles) per year – it will all be gone by 2025. A secondary environmental threat, clearly related to the increased human population, is hunting. Soils are poor for farming, so for many poor people – most of the population – hunting and fishing are main food sources. Many game animals, including especially deer, Paca (tepezcuintle), and large birds such as Ocellated Turkey, are quickly disappearing over wide areas. Poaching is common in protected areas, even within Tikal National Park.

Conservation Programs and Ecotourism

All is not lost. Because of the unique nature of the Petén's forests, there is a huge amount of interest among the international conservation community in taking steps to preserve as much as possible of what remains. With the relative safety provided by the long cease-fire between government and rebel forces that was in effect through much of the early 1990s, conservation organizations moved into the Petén to assess the situation, make plans, and begin to implement those plans. With the official ending of Guatemala's civil war at very end of 1996, foreign governments – the USA, Europe, Japan – were poised to pour funds into Guatemala for national reconstruction, including conservation.

The major ongoing conservation effort in the Petén is the establishment and development of the *Maya Biosphere Reserve*. CONAP (Consejo Nacional de Areas Protegidas), Guatemala's National Council of Protected Areas, together with what is becoming an army of international conservation organizations, is working to preserve in pristine condition the most remote, unspoiled wilderness areas of the Petén, while working with local people to teach and encourage sustainable, ecologically sensitive yet economically profitable, use of other sections of the Petén. (*Sustainable* means using plants and animals in ways that are economically profitable for the local economy yet not ecologically harmful; the use, in other words, will not lead to significant ecosystem damage or to decline in biodiversity.)

The plan is simple – on paper. The Maya Biosphere Reserve (MBR), at about 1.6 million hectares (4 million acres), includes about 40% of the Petén (Map 3). It is divided into three zones that have varying degrees of environmental protection. *Core Zone* areas (784,000 hectares, or 1.9 million acres) are set aside for absolute protection of biodiversity. No human settlements are allowed, and only research and ecotourism are permitted. The core areas are the national parks and nature reserves (biotopos) located within the MBR. The *Multiple Use Zone* consists of sparsely settled areas that surround the core zone areas. Some oil and timber industry is allowed, as is sustainable use of forest resources by local people. The *Buffer Zone* is a 15-km (9 mile) wide band of land that separates the MBR from the southern part of the Petén, and in which all kinds of industrial and agricultural practices are allowed. If the buffer and multiple-use zones serve their intended purpose, then the core areas should remain pristine. The plan's success, of course, depends on local education and participation, and money being made available for education and enforcement.

Chores involved in implementing the huge, complex plan were doled out among a host of cooperating environmental organizations, including The Nature Conservancy, Conservation International, CARE/Guatemala, and others. Much of the financial backing and coordination is by the USA's Agency for International Development. I spoke to members of the Conservation International team, called ProPetén, so let me tell briefly of their part in the plan. ProPetén's main job, in the Multiple Use Zone, is to promote economic alternatives to forest-destroying livelihoods such as slash-and-burn farming, logging, and cattle ranching. Many of the small villages in the zone have traditionally supported themselves by extracting from the forests three natural products that are sold for export: *Chicle* (CHEE-clay), a base for chewing gum, is collected by cutting into the trunks of sapodilla (*Manilkara zapota*) trees (p. 24). Most trees heal from the cuts and are used repeatedly. *Xate* (ZAH-tay) is a leafy part of a palm tree (genus *Chamaedorea*) (p. 21) that is used in many flower arrangements. *Allspice* (Figure 6d, p. 24) is a cooking and fish-curing spice that comes from tree berries (*Pimenta dioica*) that are harvested and dried. ProPetén works with local people to develop these industries in ways that maximize profits but minimize harmful forest impact. For instance, they study how chicle-bearing trees respond to the gashing required to access the gum base, and try to develop new harvesting methods that are simple and inexpensive, yet minimize the negative impacts on the trees. Also, ProPetén works to help local villages develop small "cottage industries" that may eventually employ all or most people in a village. They have already assisted one village to create and market successfully to the international community a new product – a potpourri (a scented mixture of dried plant materials that many people place in drawers and other indoor areas to improve household odors) – made from sustainable rainforest products (including dried leaves, seeds, flowers, moss, and bark). In addition

CAMPECHE, MEXICO

1 Tikal National Park
2 Cerro Cahui Nature Reserve
3 El Ceibal Archeological P ark
4 Finca Ixobel
5 El Zotz Nature Reserve
6 Río Azul National Park
7 Naachtun-Dos Lagunas Nature Reserve
8 El Mirador National Park
9 Laguna del Tigre National Park
10 Laguna del Tigre-Río Escondido Nature Reserve
11 Sierra del Lacandon National Park

Map 3 The Petén Department, Guatemala, showing locations of parks and reserves discussed in the book, as well as selected towns and roads. The Maya Biosphere Reserve (shaded area) shows only the Core and Multiple Use Zones (see p. 51).

to such activities, ProPetén is involved in developing and marketing ecotourism in the Petén as another use of forests that is locally profitable yet minimally destructive.

Tourism in Guatemala is big business. Depending on whose statistics you accept, it is either the largest or second-largest (after coffee exports) source of income for the country. The number of foreign visitors, especially from North America and Europe, rose substantially as the civil war ended (from about 400,000 tourists in 1988 to about 550,000 in 1993, to more than 600,000 in 1995). Ecotourists make up an increasing percentage of the total. For decades, the Tikal area of the Petén has been an important tourist destination. But because the Tikal site can be significantly damaged by increased tourism, and because it would be sensible to involve more local people, in other regions, in profitable yet environmentally clean tourism, additional ecotourist destinations are being developed. For example, ProPetén has recently developed three new tour routes within the Maya Biosphere Reserve. They plan the routes and organize and work with villagers so that these local people have better "products" (guide, transportation, meal, and lodging services) to sell to travellers; they also help with promotion and international advertising. Two of the routes were already operating as I wrote this book: The *Scarlet Macaw Trail* (Ruta Guacamaya), a week-long trip by foot, boat, and minibus for hardy adventure-lovers through some of the last remaining good Scarlet Macaw-containing habitat left in Guatemala; and the *Mirador Trail* (Ruta Mirador), to the really remote El Mirador archeological site, which takes at least five days, and moves via foot, mule, and boat. For information, contact Conservation International (2501 M St., NW, Suite 200, Washington, DC, 20037; USA phone: 1-800-429-5660; e-mail: newmember@conservation.org).

Chapter 4

HOW TO USE THIS BOOK: ECOLOGY AND NATURAL HISTORY

- *What Is Natural History?*
- *What Is Ecology and What Are Ecological Interactions?*
- *How To Use This Book*
  Information Given in the Family Profiles
  Information Given in the Color Plate Sections

What Is Natural History?

The purpose of this book is to provide ecotravellers with sufficient information to identify many common animal species and to learn about them and the families of animals to which they belong. Information on the lives of animals is generally known as *natural history*, which is usually defined as the study of animals' natural habits, including especially their ecology, distribution, classification, and behavior. This kind of information is important to know for a variety of reasons: animal researchers need to know natural history as background on the species they study, and wildlife managers and conservationists need natural history information because their decisions about managing animal populations must be partially based on it. More relevant for the ecotraveller, natural history is simply interesting. People who appreciate animals typically like to watch them, touch them when appropriate, and know as much about them as they can.

What Is Ecology and What Are Ecological Interactions?

Ecology is the branch of the biological sciences that deals with the interactions between living things and their physical environment and with each other. *Animal ecology* is the study of the interactions of animals with each other, with plants, and with the physical environment. Broadly interpreted, these interactions take into account almost everything we find fascinating about animals –

what they eat, how they forage, how and when they breed, how they survive the rigors of extreme climates, why they are large or small, or dully or brightly colored, and many other facets of their lives.

An animal's life, in some ways, is the sum of its interactions with other animals – members of its own species and others – and with its environment. Of particular interest are the numerous and diverse ecological interactions that occur between different species. Most can be placed into one of several general categories, based on how two species affect each other when they interact; they can have positive, negative, or neutral (that is, no) effects on each other. The relationship terms below are used in the book to describe the natural history of various animals.

Competition is an ecological relationship in which neither of the interacting species benefits. Competition occurs when individuals of two species use the same resource – a certain type of food, nesting holes in trees, etc. – and that resource is in insufficient supply to meet all their needs. As a result, both species are less successful than they could be in the absence of the interaction (that is, if the other species were not present).

Predation is an ecological interaction in which one species, the *predator*, benefits, and the other species, the *prey*, is harmed. Most people think that a good example of a predator eating prey would be a mountain lion eating a deer, and they are correct; but predation also includes interactions in which the predator eats only part of its prey and the prey individual often survives. Thus, deer eat tree leaves and branches, and so, in a way, they can be considered predators on plant prey.

Parasitism, like predation, is a relationship between two species in which one benefits and one is harmed. The difference is that in a predatory relationship, one animal kills and eats the other, but in a parasitic one, the parasite feeds slowly on the "host" species and usually does not kill it. There are internal parasites, like protozoans and many kinds of worms, and external parasites, such as leeches, ticks, and mites.

Some of the most compelling of ecological relationships are *Mutualisms* – interactions in which both participants benefit. Plants and their pollinators engage in mutualistic interactions. A bee species, for instance, obtains a food resource, nectar or pollen, from a plant's flower; the plant it visits benefits because it is able to complete its reproductive cycle when the bee transports pollen to another plant. In Central America, a famous case of mutualism involves several species of acacias (p. 24) and the ants that live in them: the ants obtain food (the acacias produce nectar for them) and shelter from the acacias and in return, the ants defend the plants from plant-eating insects. Sometimes the species have interacted so long that they now cannot live without each other; theirs is an *obligate* mutualism. For instance, termites cannot by themselves digest wood. Rather, it is the single-celled animals, protozoans, that live in their gut that produce the digestive enzymes that digest wood. At this point in their evolutionary histories, neither the termites nor their internal helpers can live alone.

Commensalism is a relationship in which one species benefits but the other is not affected in any way. For example, epiphytes (p. 19), such as orchids and bromeliads, that grow on tree trunks and branches obtain from trees some shelf space to grow on, but, as far as anyone knows, neither hurt nor help the trees. A classic example of a commensal animal is the Remora, a fish that attaches itself with a suction cup on its head to a shark, then feeds on scraps of food the shark leaves behind. Remora are commensals, not parasites – they neither harm nor help sharks, but they benefit greatly by associating with sharks. Cattle egrets (p. 117) are commensals – these birds follow cattle, eating insects and other small animals that flush from cover as the cattle move about their pastures; the cattle, as far as we know, couldn't care one way or the other (unless they are concerned about that certain loss of dignity that occurs when the egrets perch not only near them, but on them as well.)

A term many people know that covers some of these ecological interactions is *symbiosis*, which means living together. Usually this term suggests that the two interacting species do not harm one another; therefore, mutualisms and commensalisms are the symbiotic relationships discussed here.

How To Use This Book

The information here on animals is divided into two sections: the *plates*, which include artists' color renderings of various species together with brief identifying and location information; and the *family profiles*, with natural history information on the families to which the pictured animals belong. The best way to identify and learn about Belizean and Guatemalan animals may be to scan the illustrations before a trip to become familiar with the kinds of animals you are likely to encounter. Then when you spot an animal, you may recognize its type or family, and can find the appropriate pictures and profiles quickly. In other words, it is more efficient, upon spotting a bird, to be thinking, "Gee, that looks like a flycatcher," and be able to flip to that part of the book, than to be thinking, "Gee, that bird is yellow" and then, to identify it, flipping through all the animal pictures, searching for yellow birds.

Information Given in the Family Profiles

Classification, Distribution, Morphology. The first paragraphs of each profile generally provide information on the family's classification (or *taxonomy*), geographic distribution, and *morphology* (shape, size, and coloring of the animals). Classification information is provided because it is how scientists separate animals into related groups and often it enhances our appreciation of animals to know these relationships. You may have been exposed to classification levels sometime during your education but if you are a bit rusty, a quick review may help: *Kingdom* Animalia: aside from the plant information, all the species detailed in the book are members of the animal kingdom. *Phylum* Chordata, *Subphylum* Vertebrata: most of the species in the book are vertebrates, animals with backbones (exceptions are the corals and other marine *invertebrate* animals discussed in Chapter 9). *Class*: the book covers several vertebrate classes such as Amphibia (amphibians), Reptilia (reptiles), Aves (birds), and Mammalia (mammals). *Order*: each class is divided into several orders, the animals in each order sharing many characteristics. For example, one of the mammal orders is Carnivora, the carnivores, which includes mammals with teeth specialized for meat-eating – dogs, cats, bears, raccoons, weasels. *Family*: Families of animals are subdivisions of each order that contain closely related species that are very similar in form, ecology, and behavior. The family Canidae, for instance, contains all the dog-like mammals – coyote, wolf, fox, dog. Animal family names end in "-dae;" subfamilies, subdivisions of families, end in "-nae." *Genus*: Further subdivisions; within each genus are grouped species that are very closely related – they are all considered to have evolved from a common ancestor. *Species*: the lowest classification level; all members of a species are similar enough to be able to breed and produce living fertile offspring.

Example: Classification of the Keel-billed Toucan (Plate 48c):

Kingdom: Animalia, with more than a million species
Phylum: Chordata, Subphylum Vertebrata, with about 40,000 species
Class: Aves (Birds), with about 9000 species
Order: Piciformes, with about 350 species; includes honeyguides, woodpeckers, barbets, and toucans
Family: Ramphastidae, with 55 species; includes barbets and toucans
Genus: *Ramphastos*, with 11 species; toucans
Species: *Ramphastos sulfuratus*; Keel-billed Toucan

Some of the family profiles in the book actually cover animal orders; others describe families or subfamilies.

Species' distributions vary tremendously. Some species are found only in very limited areas, whereas others range over several continents. Distributions can be described in a number of ways. An animal or group can be said to be *Old World* or *New World*; the former refers to the regions of the globe that Europeans knew of before Columbus – Europe, Asia, Africa; and the latter refers to the Western Hemisphere – North, Central, and South America. Belize and Guatemala fall within the part of the world called the *Neotropics* by biogeographers – scientists who study the geographic distributions of living things. A Neotropical species is one that occurs within southern Mexico, Central America, South America, and/or the Caribbean Islands. The terms *tropical*, *temperate*, and *arctic* refer to climate regions of the Earth; the boundaries of these zones are determined by lines of latitude (and ultimately, by the position of the sun with respect to the Earth's surface). The tropics, always warm, are the regions of the world that fall within the belt from 23.5° north latitude (the Tropic of Cancer) to 23.5° south latitude (the Tropic of Capricorn). The world's temperate zones, with more seasonal climates, extend from 23.5° North and South latitude to the Arctic and Antarctic Circles, at 66.5° North and South. Arctic regions, more or less always cold, extend from 66.5° North and South to the poles. The position of Belize and Guatemala with respect to these zones is shown in Map 4.

Several terms help define a species' distribution and describe how it attained its distribution:

Range. The particular geographic area occupied by a species.

Native or Indigenous. Occurring naturally in a particular place.

Introduced. Occurring in a particular place owing to peoples' intentional or unintentional assistance with transportation, usually from one continent to another; the opposite of native. For instance, pheasants were initially brought to North America from Europe/Asia for hunting, Europeans brought rabbits and foxes to Australia for sport, and the British brought European Starlings and House Sparrows to North America.

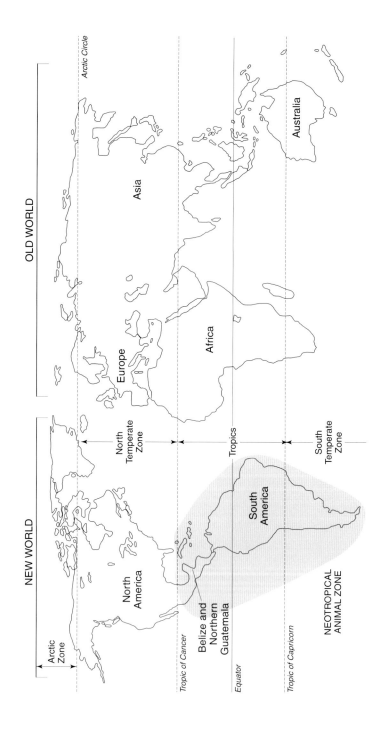

Map 4 Map of the Earth showing the positions of Belize and Guatemala; Old World and New World zones; tropical, temperate, and arctic regions; and the Neotropical animal life zone.

Endemic. A species, a genus, an entire family, etc. that is found in a particular place and nowhere else. Galápagos finches are endemic to the Galápagos Islands; nearly all the reptile and mammal species of Madagascar are endemics; all species are endemic to Earth (as far as we know).

Cosmopolitan. A species that is widely distributed throughout the world.

Ecology and Behavior. In these sections, I describe some of what is known about the basic activities pursued by each group. Much of the information relates to when and where animals are usually active, what they eat, and how they forage.

Activity Location – *Terrestrial* animals pursue life and food on the ground. *Arboreal* animals pursue life and food in trees or shrubs. Many arboreal animals have *prehensile* tails, long and muscular, which they can wrap around tree branches to support themselves as they hang to feed or to move about more efficiently. *Cursorial* refers to animals that are adapted for running along the ground.

Activity Time – *Nocturnal* means active at night. *Diurnal* means active during the day. *Crepuscular* refers to animals that are active at dusk and/or dawn.

Food Preferences – Although animal species can usually be assigned to one of the feeding categories below, most eat more than one type of food. Most frugivorous birds, for instance, also nibble on the occasional insect, and carnivorous mammals occasionally eat plant materials.

> *Herbivores* are predators that prey on plants.
> *Carnivores* are predators that prey on animals.
> *Insectivores* eat insects.
> *Granivores* eat seeds.
> *Frugivores* eat fruit.
> *Nectarivores* eat nectar.
> *Piscivores* eat fish.
> *Omnivores* eat a variety of things.
> *Detritivores*, such as vultures, eat dead stuff.

Breeding. In these sections, I present basics on each group's breeding particulars, including type of mating system, special breeding behaviors, durations of egg incubation or gestation (pregnancy), as well as information on nests, eggs, and young.

Mating Systems – A *monogamous* mating system is one in which one male and one female establish a pair-bond and contribute fairly evenly to each breeding effort. In polygamous systems, individuals of one of the sexes have more than one mate (that is, they have harems): in *polygynous* systems, one male mates with several females, and in *polyandrous* systems, one female mates with several males.

Condition of young at birth – *Altricial* young are born in a relatively undeveloped state, usually naked of fur or feathers, eyes closed, and unable to feed themselves, walk, or run from predators. *Precocial* young are born in a more developed state, eyes open, and soon able to walk and perhaps feed themselves.

Ecological Interactions. These sections describe what I think are intriguing ecological relationships. Groups that are often the subject of ecological research are the ones for which such relationships are more likely to be known.

Lore and Notes. These sections provide brief accounts of folklore associated with the profiled groups, and any other interesting bits and pieces of information about the profiled animals that do not fit elsewhere in the account.

Status. These sections comment on the conservation status of each group, including information on relative rarity or abundance, factors contributing to population declines, and special conservation measures that have been implemented. Because this book concentrates on animals that ecotravellers are most likely to see – that is, on more common ones – few of the profiled species are immediately threatened with extinction. The definitions of the terms that I use to describe degrees of threat to various species are these: *Endangered* species are known to be in imminent danger of extinction throughout their range, and are highly unlikely to survive unless strong conservation measures are taken; populations of endangered species generally are very small, so they are rarely seen. *Threatened* species are known to be undergoing rapid declines in the sizes of their populations; unless conservation measures are enacted, and the causes of the population declines identified and halted, these species are likely to move to endangered status in the near future. *Vulnerable to threat*, or *Near-threatened*, are species that, owing to their habitat requirements or limited distributions, and based on known patterns of habitat destruction, are highly likely to be threatened in the near future. For instance, a fairly common bird species that breeds mainly in coastal mangrove swamps might be considered vulnerable to threat if it is known that people are cutting mangroves at a high rate. Several organizations publish lists of threatened and endangered species.

Where appropriate, I also include threat classifications from the Convention on International Trade in Endangered Species (CITES) and the United States Endangered Species Act (USA ESA) classifications. CITES is a global cooperative agreement to protect threatened species on a worldwide scale by regulating international trade in wild animals and plants among the 130 or so participating countries. Regulated species are listed in CITES Appendices, with trade in those species being strictly regulated by required licenses and documents. CITES Appendix I lists endangered species; all trade in them is prohibited. Appendix II lists threatened/vulnerable species, those that are not yet endangered but may soon be; trade in them is strictly regulated. Appendix III lists species that are protected by laws of individual countries that have signed the CITES agreements. The USA's Endangered Species Act works in a similar way – by listing endangered and threatened species, and, among other provisions, strictly regulating trade in those animals.

Information Given in the Color Plate Sections

Pictures. Among amphibians, reptiles, and mammals, males and females of a species usually look alike, although often there are size differences. For many species of birds, however, the sexes differ in color pattern and even anatomical features. If only one individual is pictured, you may assume that male and female of that species look exactly or almost alike; when there are major sex differences, both male and female are depicted.

Name. I provide the common English name for each profiled species, the scientific, or Latin, name, and local names and their English translations, if known. A local name used in Belize is followed by "(Belize)." Other local names, mostly in Spanish, are used in Guatemala and often in parts of Belize. I did not attempt to list animal names used by local indigenous peoples.

ID. Here I provide brief descriptive information that, together with the pictures, will enable you to identify most of the animals you see. The lengths of reptiles and amphibians given in this book are *snout–vent lengths* (SVLs), the distance from the tip of the snout to the vent, unless I mention that the tail is included. The *vent* is the opening on their bellies that lies approximately where the rear limbs join the body, and through which sex occurs and wastes exit. Therefore, long tails of salamanders and lizards, for instance, are not included in the reported length measurements, and frogs' long legs are not included in theirs. I make an exception for snakes, for which in most cases I give total lengths. For mammals, measurements given are generally the lengths of the head and body, but do not include tails. Birds are measured from tip of bill to end of tail. For birds commonly seen flying, such as seabirds and hawks, I provide wing span (wingtip to wingtip) measurements, if known. For most of the passerine birds (see p. 109), I use to describe their sizes the terms *large* (more than 30 cm, 12 in, long); *mid-sized* (between 15 or 18 cm, 6 or 7 in, and 30 cm, 12 in); *small* (10 to 15 cm, 4 to 6 in); and *very small* (less than 10 cm, 4 in).

Habitat/Districts. In these sections I give the regions and habitat types in which each species occurs, symbols for the habitat types each species prefers, and the political districts where each species may be found. The districts listed for a particular species are (1) those in which the species is known to occur and also (2) those in which it probably occurs, based on the known range of the animal, the elevation and type of habitat it prefers, and the elevations and types of habitats known to be present in the various districts.

Explanation of habitat symbols:

 = Lowland wet forest.

 = Lowland dry forest.

 = Highland forest/cloud forest. Includes middle elevation and higher elevation wet forests and cloud forests.

 = Forest edge/streamside. Some species typically are found along forest edges or near or along streams; these species prefer semi-open areas rather than dense, closed, interior parts of forests. Also included here: open woodlands, tree plantations, and shady gardens.

 = Pastureland/non-tree plantations/savannahs (grassland with scattered trees, shrubs)/gardens without shade trees/roadside. Species found in these habitats prefer very open areas.

 = Freshwater. For species typically found in or near lakes, streams, rivers, marshes, swamps.

 = Saltwater/marine. For species usually found in or near the ocean or ocean beaches.

Political Districts (see Maps 1 and 2, pp. 5 and 9)

COROZAL District is Northern Belize (COR)
ORANGE WALK District is Northwestern Belize (ORW)
BELIZE District is Central Eastern Belize (BEL)
STANN CREEK District is Southeastern Belize (STN)

CAYO District is Western Belize (CAYO)
TOLEDO District is Southern Belize (TOL)
CAYES are Belize's coastal islands (CAYE)
PETÉN District is Guatemala's northern department, or province (PET)

Example

Plate 48

Keel-billed Toucan
Ramphastos sulfuratus
Bill Bird (Belize)
Tucán Piquiverde = green-billed
toucan
Pito Real

ID: A large, mostly black bird with yellow face and chest, yellowish green skin around eye, and that amazing, rainbow-colored (green-orange-blue) toucan's bill; to 51 cm (20 in).

HABITAT: Low and middle elevation forests; found in tree canopy in more open habitats such as forest edges, tree plantations, along rivers and streams.

DISTRICTS: COR, ORW, BEL, STN, CAYO, TOL, PET

Chapter 5

AMPHIBIANS

- *General Characteristics and Natural History*
- *Seeing Amphibians in Belize and Guatemala*
- *Family Profiles*
- *Environmental Close-up 1: Frog Population Declines: Amphibian Armageddon or Alarmist Absurdity?*

General Characteristics and Natural History

Amphibians arose during the mid part of the Paleozoic Era, 400 million years ago, developing from fish ancestors that had lungs and thus could breathe air. The word *amphibian* refers to an organism that can live in two worlds, and that is as good a definition of the amphibians as any: most stay in or near the water, but many spend at least portions of their lives on land. In addition to lungs, amphibians generally have wet, thin skins that aid in gas exchange (breathing). Amphibians were also the first animals to develop legs for walking on land, the basic design of which has remained remarkably constant for all other land vertebrates. Many have webbed feet that aid locomotion in the water.

Approximately 4500 species of living amphibians have been described. (Owing to their all-terrestrial existence, almost all reptiles, birds, and mammals living on Earth have been identified but, most experts agree, many more amphibians, with their aquatic ways, remain to be discovered.) They are separated into three groups. The *Salamanders* (Order Caudata, or "tailed" amphibians) comprise 450 species (only 5 or 6 in Belize/northern Guatemala), the mysterious *Caecilians* (sih-SIL-ians; Order Gymnophiona) number about 160 species, and the *Frogs* and *Toads* (Order Anura, "without tails") make up the remainder, and the bulk, of the group (with about 33 species in Belize/northern Guatemala).

Most amphibians live in the water during part of their lives. Typically, a juvenile stage is spent in the water and an adult stage on land. Because amphibians need to keep their skin wet, even when on land, generally they are mostly found in moist habitats – in marshes and swamps, around the periphery of bodies of water, in wet forests. Adults of most species return to the water to lay eggs, which must stay wet to develop. Some amphibians – toads and some salamanders – are entirely terrestrial, laying eggs on land in moist places.

Relatively little is known of the caecilians. They are confined to tropical forests of Africa, Southeast Asia, and Central and South America, the latter two locations being their principal home (there are no Sicilian caecilians). They are legless with slender bodies up to 40 cm (15 in) long and up to 2.5 cm (1 in) in diameter, with ringed creases along their lengths – resembling nothing so much as a cross between a snake and an earthworm (Plate 1). Their skin is studded with small scales. Caecilian eyes are tiny and most are blind as adults. For sensing their environment they possess a pair of small tentacles at the head end that are continually extended out of and then withdrawn into the body. They feed on worms and other small invertebrate animals – termites, beetles, etc. – that they find underground. Because they spend much of their lives beneath the ground, caecilians are very rarely seen by people. However, they commonly leave their burrows at night during rains, moving along the ground, presumably foraging. Occasionally they are found in meadows and forests under logs and rocks, or buried deep in the leaf litter. I remember finding one, apparently bloodied and dropped by a predator, on a dirt road in South America. It was the first one another biologist and myself had seen outside of photographs, and it took quite a while for us to decide just what it was (a mutant worm from outer space, our first guess, turned out to be incorrect). Caecilians do not lay eggs, but give birth to live young.

Salamanders, intriguingly, are not much interested in the tropics. They are an almost exclusively temperate zone group. In the tropics they usually inhabit moist, cool areas, such as middle and higher-elevation cloud forests. About 200 species are completely terrestrial. Females of these species lay eggs in moist places and then stay with the eggs, protecting them until hatching, sometimes coiling themselves around the eggs. *Newts* are a group of aquatic salamanders, usually with rough-textured skin, that generally lay their eggs singly on pond bottoms or on vegetation; other aquatic salamanders lay their eggs in large, jelly-covered clusters, which they attach to sticks or plants in the water. The aquatic salamanders do not protect their eggs.

Most species of frogs and toads live in tropical or semi-tropical areas but some groups are abundant in temperate zone latitudes. Frogs can be either mostly aquatic or mostly terrestrial; some live primarily in vegetation on land. A few species of frogs live in deserts by staying underground, remaining moist enough to survive. At the arrival of periodic rains, they climb to the surface and breed in temporary ponds, before scampering back underground. Eggs hatch and the froglets burrow underground before the ponds dry. *Toads* constitute a group of frogs that have relatively heavy, dry skin that reduces water loss, permitting them to live on land. Most frogs and toads leave their eggs to develop on their own, but a few guard nests or egg masses, and some species actually carry their eggs on their backs or in skin pouches. One Australian species swallows its eggs, which develop in its stomach; the young emerge through its mouth.

Frogs and toads are known for the vocal behavior of males, which during breeding periods call loudly from the edges of lakes and ponds or on land, attempting to attract females. Each species has a different type of call. Some species breed *explosively* in synchronous groups – on a single night thousands gather at forest ponds, where males call and compete for females and females choose from among available suitors. Many frogs, such as *bullfrogs*, fight fiercely for the best calling spots and over mates. Because frogs really have no weapons to fight with, such as teeth or sharp claws, size usually determines fight outcomes. Some species of frogs and toads have developed *satellite* strategies to obtain matings. Instead of staking out a calling spot and vocalizing themselves (which is energy-draining and risky because calling attracts predators), satellite males remain silent but stay furtively near calling males, and attempt to intercept and mate with approaching females. Smaller males are more likely to employ such "sneaky-mater" tactics.

All amphibians as adults are predatory carnivores – as far as it is known, there is not a vegetarian among them. Many animals eat amphibians, although it is not as easy as you might think. At first glance amphibians appear to be among the most defenseless of animals. Most are small, many are relatively slow, and their teeth and claws are not the types appropriate for aggressive defense. But a closer look reveals an array of ingenious defenses. Most, perhaps all, amphibians produce toxins in the skin, many of which are harmless to humans and so not very noticeable, but a few of which are quite poisonous and even lethal (see Close-Up, p. 105). These toxins deter predators. Most amphibians are cryptically colored, often being amazingly difficult for people, and presumably predators, to detect in their natural settings. The jumping locomotion of frogs probably evolved as an anti-predator strategy – it is a much more efficient way of escaping quickly through leaves, dense grass, thickets, or shrubby areas than are walking or running. Some frogs hiss loudly and inflate their throat sacs when approached, which presumably makes predators think twice about attacking. Last, some frogs give loud screams when grabbed, which are startling to predators and so create opportunities for escape.

In general, amphibians are under less direct threat from people than are other vertebrate groups, there being little commercial exploitation of the group (aside from certain peoples' inexplicable taste for the limbs of frogs). However, amphibians are very sensitive to habitat destruction and, particularly, to pollution, because aquatic eggs and larvae are very susceptible to toxic substances. Many amphibian populations have been noticeably declining in recent years, although the reasons are not entirely clear. Much research attention is currently focused on determining whether these reported population changes are real and significant and, if so, their causes. Not all ecologists agree on what is going on (see Close-Up, p. 77).

Seeing Amphibians in Belize and Guatemala

The amphibians of Belize and northern Guatemala have only recently been subjected to scientific surveys intended to determine which species exist and where. Although not all of those results are in, what is known is that the region supports a rich variety of species, many of which are observable, provided some effort is taken. First, an admonition: snakes have our respect, owing to the evil reputations of the venomous ones, but many people, with little knowledge of tropical amphibians, improperly do not show them the same respect. Skin secretions of some terrestrial frogs are highly toxic. The toxins can be dangerous if absorbed into the body through, for instance, a cut in your skin. The skin secretions of many frogs and salamanders, even if not harmful to humans, can sting badly. Take home message: when amphibians are located, enjoy them visually and leave their handling to experts.

With that warning in mind, here are the best ways to see amphibians. Look for them, of course, in moist habitats – wet forests, near bodies of water, in small pools and puddles, along streams. If you dare, and using your shoes, turn over rocks and logs in these habitats, or look through and under leaf litter. Most adult salamanders and most frogs are nocturnal, so a nightwalk with flashlight or head-lamp is often a good way to see amphibians. The best time is during a wet night (although not during torrential downpours), and especially during the rainy season, when most species breed. The calls of male frogs can be of assistance then in locating the little beasts.

Family Profiles

1. Salamanders

Salamanders are long, generally slender amphibians with four limbs. They loosely resemble lizards in body plan, but their skin is smooth and wet – both from the aquatic or moist locales that they inhabit and the skin secretions that keep their skin wet for breathing. Worldwide they number perhaps 450 species, most of them being found within temperate zone regions. The group's largest family, however, containing about half the known species, is well represented in the American tropics. This is the Family Plethodontidae, the lungless salamanders. All of the six salamanders that occur in Belize and northern Guatemala are members of this group. Being lungless, almost all gas exchange is through the moist skin (some occurs through the membranes of the mouth and throat). Most of the plethodontids are primarily terrestrial animals, inhabiting all but the very driest regions of Central America.

Plethodontid salamanders vary quite a bit in size and shape, from ones typi-cally only 3 cm (1 in) long to those 25 cm (10 in) long. Some have webbed hands and feet. Color patterns are often striking, and can vary within the same species between locations.

Salamanders are secretive and usually nocturnal in their activities; hence, unless searched for, they are only infrequently encountered.

Natural History

Ecology and Behavior

In contrast to frogs, with their vegetarian tadpole phase, all salamanders, both as juveniles and adults, are carnivores. They feed opportunistically, essentially snap-ping at and trying to ingest whatever squirms and will fit into their mouths – gen-erally, on land, insects and spiders, but also small frogs and other salamanders. Because studying salamanders in the wild is difficult, relatively little is known about what eats them, but the list includes snakes, salamanders, frogs, fish, and a few birds and mammals. Although most of the plethodontids are considered terres-trial, some are *semi-arboreal*, regularly climbing into trees and shrubs, and others are *semi-fossorial*, usually burrowing into the leaf litter or underneath rocks or logs.

Breeding

Salamanders are known for their complex mating behavior. Unlike frogs, sala-mander males do not call to advertise territories or attract mates, but males do fight each other for females. Losers employ various strategies to try to interfere with the winners' mating – either physically inserting themselves between a female and a courting male, or approaching the mating pair, which distracts the male, causing him to pause or stop.

How sperm gain access to eggs in terrestrial salamanders is different from the way one might expect. Following a courtship ritual, the male deposits a tiny, cone-shaped packet containing sperm, called a *spermatophore*, on the ground. The female maneuvers until she can pick it up with her *vent* (the opening on her belly that provides entry and exit for both reproductive and excretory systems), which permits the sperm to gain access to her reproductive tract. She can then store the sperm for many months, having it always available to fertilize her eggs.

In the terrestrial salamanders, females typically lay a clutch of eggs – for instance, a clutch of 63 eggs was found in a MEXICAN SALAMANDER (Plate 1) – under logs, moss, or rocks. Then they coil themselves around the eggs and stay with them, protecting them and keeping them moist with their skin secretions. Males have also been found protecting eggs in this way, but it appears to be mainly a female role. Egg care is apparently necessary; eggs not protected by an adult are unlikely to hatch. Eggs hatch in 4 to 5 months. The young emerge looking like miniature adults and must fend for themselves from the moment of birth. Growth proceeds very slowly, with many salamanders attaining sexual maturity only at 6 or more years of age.

Ecological Interactions
Salamanders are usually inconspicuous and hidden to casual observers. Actually, however, they are integral parts of the forest animal community, often being very abundant in good habitat. Therefore, they are one of the predominant predators on forest insects, acting to keep many bug populations in check.

In addition to hiding, running and, in some species, biting, to prevent themselves from becoming another animal's dinner, salamanders employ chemical weapons. All of them apparently have skin secretions that are sufficiently toxic or distasteful to render them unpalatable to most potential predators, and some of the secretions contain potent poisons. Unfortunately for the salamanders, a few predators, such as some snakes, have evolved immunity from the secretions' noxious effects.

Lore and Notes
Many salamanders apparently lead long lives, as do several other groups of cold-blooded animals. They have low metabolisms and they grow slowly in cool habitats, at times eating infrequently and going through long periods of inactivity. In captivity, some salamanders – for instance, one species from Japan – live more than 50 years. Many New World species have lifespans that commonly range up to 20 to 25 years.

Status
None of the plethodontid salamanders of Central America is thought to be rare or threatened; on the other hand, little is known of the biology of most of them. Several species of this group are threatened, however, in the USA, and three are endangered: DESERT SLENDER, SHENANDOAH, and TEXAS BLIND SALAMANDERS.

Profiles
Mexican Salamander, *Bolitoglossa mexicana*, Plate 1b
Rufescent Salamander, *Bolitoglossa rufescens*, Plate 1c

2. Toads

Scientists sometimes have trouble formally differentiating toads from frogs, but not so nonscientists, who usually know their toads: they are the frog-like animals with a rough, lumpy, wart-strewn appearance, not built for speed, that one finds on land. Actually, toads and frogs are both included in the amphibian group Anura; toads are a kind of frog. They have some special skeletal and reproductive traits that are used to set them apart (for instance, frogs lay eggs in jellied clusters, but toads lay them in jellied strings), but for our purposes, a modification of the common definition will do: toads are squat, short, terrestrial frogs with thick, relatively dry skins that prevent rapid water loss, short limbs, and glands that resemble warts spread over their bodies. A few families of frogs are called toads, but the predominant group, hugely successful, is the *true* toads, Family Bufonidae (*bufo* is Latin for "toad"), which spread naturally to all continents except Australia (and has been introduced by people to that continent; all the toads occurring in the USA are in this family). *Bufonids* usually have two prominent "warts" on each side of the neck or shoulder area, called *parotoids*. Often shades of olive or brown, toads vary in size, with the largest in Central America, the MARINE TOAD (Platee 1), being anywhere from 9 to 20 cm (3.5 to 8 in) long, and weighing in at up to 1200 g (2.5 lb). Worldwide there are perhaps 300 bufonid toad species; only three of them occur in Belize and northern Guatemala.

Natural History

Ecology and Behavior

Although their relatively heavy, dry skin (compared with that of other frogs) permits adult toads a permanently terrestrial existence, they experience some water loss through their skin, so unless they stay near water or in moist habitat, they dry out and die in just a few days. Many toads are primarily nocturnal, avoiding the sun and its drying heat by sheltering during the day under leaf litter, logs, or rocks, coming out to forage only after sundown. Toad tadpoles are vegetarians, feeding on green algae and bacteria in their aquatic habitats, but adult toads are all carnivorous, foraging for arthropods, mostly insects, amid the leaf litter. As one researcher defines the toad diet, "if it's bite-sized and animate it is food, no matter how noxious, toxic, or biting/stinging" (G. Zug 1983). Beetles and ants are frequent prey, as are small vertebrates such as small frogs, salamanders, and lizards.

Slow-moving toads (with their short legs they are capable of covering only very short distances per hop) have two methods to escape being eaten. They can be extremely hard to detect in their habitats, concealing themselves with their cryptic coloration and habit of slipping into crevices, under leaves, or actually burying themselves in the earth. Also, apparently quite effectively, they exude noxious fluids from their skin glands – the warts are actually a defense mechanism. If grabbed, a viscous, white fluid oozes from the warts. The fluid is very irritating to mucous membranes, such as those found in a predator's mouth and nose. Toads also have muscle control over the poison glands and some can squeeze them to spray the poison more than 30 cm (1 ft). Most predators that pick up a toad probably do not do it twice; peoples' four-legged pets that put toads into their mouths have been killed by the poisons. A few predators, however, such as raccoons and opossums, having learned their way around toad anatomy, avoid the warts on the back and legs by eating only the inside of the toad, entering through the mostly poison-gland-free belly.

Breeding

Many toads in Central America breed at any time of year (for example, MARINE TOADS), but often there are breeding surges when seasons change. Fertilization is external, which means that it happens outside of the animal, in water. To breed, males migrate to ponds and streams, calling to attract females. After appropriate mating maneuvers of both sexes, sperm are released by a male in a cloud into the water, followed by a female releasing her eggs into the cloud. The eggs are laid within jellied strings, the jelly protecting the eggs physically and also, because it contains toxins, discouraging consumption by potential predators. Depending on species and size, a female may lay from 100 to 25,000 eggs at a time. Eggs hatch in only a few days, releasing young in the larval feeding stage known commonly as *tadpoles*. They feed, grow, and develop, transforming themselves into *toadlets* after a few weeks, which then swarm up the banks and disappear into their terrestrial existences. Toads generally reach sexual maturity in a year or two, although the period before breeding is longer in some species.

Ecological Interactions
The MARINE TOAD, Central America's largest member of the Bufonid family, has somehow become semi-domesticated, and is now commonly found around human settlements at much higher densities than in wild areas. Adapting nicely to people's behavior, these toads will eat dog and cat food left outdoors for pets (which is quite a feat, given that most frogs will only eat live, moving prey). Because of their abundance around dwellings, they probably are the toad most likely to be seen by visitors to Belize and northern Guatemala.

Lore and Notes
The claim that a person will contract warts by handling toads is not true. Human warts are caused by viruses, not amphibians. The glands on toads' skin that resemble warts release noxious fluids to discourage predators. These fluids contain various poisons that, among other effects, cause increased blood pressure, blood vessel constriction, increased power of heartbeat, heart muscle tissue destruction, and hallucinations. Because these fluids minimally are irritants, a smart precaution is to avoid handling toads or, after such handling, make sure to wash your hands. Caustic irritation will result if the fluids are transferred from hands to eyes, nose or mouth. Some reports have it that voodoo practitioners in Haiti use the skin secretions of toads in their zombie-making concoctions.

Several hallucinogenic chemicals, which cause LSD-type effects when swallowed, have been isolated from the skin glands of Central American toads, for instance, from Marine Toads (Plate 1). Cultural historians suspect that these substances were known to the ancient Mayans and were used during religious and ceremonial occasions.

Status
A number of New World bufonid species are known to be threatened or endangered. Costa Rica's GOLDEN TOAD is considered highly endangered (CITES Appendix I and USA ESA listed) and may now be extinct. In fact, preservation of Golden Toads was one of the original reasons for the creation of the Monteverde Cloud Forest Reserve, one of Costa Rica's major ecotourism draws. The BLACK and HOUSTON TOADS of the USA and the SONORAN GREEN TOAD of Mexico and the USA are threatened, as are a few toads from Puerto Rico and Chile.

Profiles
Marine Toad, *Bufo marinus*, Plate 1d
Gulf Coast Toad, *Bufo valliceps*, Plate 2a

Rainforest Toad, *Bufo cambelli*, Plate 2b
Mexican Burrowing Toad, *Rhinophrynus dorsalis*, Plate 2c

3. Rainfrogs

The *rainfrogs*, Family Leptodactylidae, also known as the *tropical frogs*, constitute a large New World group that is distributed from southern North America to throughout most of South America and the Caribbean. Primarily frogs of low and middle elevations, they occupy many different types of habitats, but especially forests. Often they are the most abundant kind of amphibian found in a given habitat. Species are variously land-dwelling, aquatic, or arboreal. Only about eight of the more than 800 living species are represented in Belize and northern Guatemala.

Rainfrogs vary extensively in size and color patterns, so much so that a general description of the group is difficult. One distinctive trait is the greatly enlarged finger disks – little suction cups – characteristic of many, the better to get around their arboreal habitats. Sizes in Belize and northern Guatemala vary from small species that at their largest are only 2.5 to 3.5 cm (1 in) long, such as the MAYA RAINFROG (Plate 3), to the CENTRAL AMERICAN RAINFROG (Plate 3), which ranges up to 9 cm (3.5 in). Rainfrogs tend to be various shades of tan, beige, brown, gray, or pale yellow, often with dark markings such as bars or spots, particularly on the legs. Telling species apart by their markings is rendered more difficult because of the large amount of variation present within some species. For instance, in Costa Rica, one rainfrog species varies so extensively among individuals – even among those found in the same small area – in color, spotting pattern, and skin texture, that for many years even scientists were confused, repeatedly naming new species of rainfrogs although they were actually all the same species (the way a newcomer to Earth might mistakenly assign species status to each breed of domestic canine, which, although they look very different, are all of the same species of marginal intelligence that we call dogs). The explanation for such extreme variability in color schemes within a single species is unknown, but is suspected to have to do with the advantages each kind has in blending in with various types of surroundings on the forest floor.

Natural History

Ecology and Behavior

Rainfrogs in Belize and northern Guatemala are primarily terrestrial, encountered most often on the forest floor or in or adjacent to pools, ponds, or streams. Several small species typically coexist in the same area, making up a large portion of the "leaf litter amphibian community."

Many rainfrogs are known as ant specialists, but typically a variety of insects, other arthropods, and even small vertebrates, are included in the diet – mites, beetles, spiders, small lizards, and others. Rainfrogs are *sit-and-wait* predators. Some live in protective rock crevices or ground burrows, venturing out only to forage around the opening (or to breed), escaping back into the shelter at the first sign of trouble. Rainfrogs, especially the nocturnal ones, have reputations for being quite shy, which seems surprising for a night-active animal until one realizes that one of the chief predators on these frogs is also nocturnal – bats.

Breeding

These frogs breed in a variety of ways. One group (genus *Eleutherodactylus*) has become completely terrestrial in its breeding, females laying small clutches of eggs, often between 10 and 30, on land in moist sites. Embryos pass through a tadpole stage while still in the eggs, which hatch out fully formed but tiny froglets. Another group (genus *Leptodactylus*) deposits its eggs in foam nests, which are placed in pockets in the ground near water. Males use their hindfeet to whip into foam a concoction of air, water, mucous from the female, and semen. Tadpoles that hatch out from eggs within the foam are washed into nearby temporary ponds by rainwater (perhaps providing the common name for these frogs), later to emerge as fully developed frogs. Many rainfrogs breed at any time of year, but the ones that rely on rains to wash tadpoles into ponds often breed before heavy rains. Clutches vary in size from about 10 to several hundred eggs. Most rainfrogs reproduce at one year of age or younger.

Lore and Notes

Ancient American cultures such as the Mayans doubtless associated rainfrogs and other frogs with rain because these amphibians often appeared in large numbers in forests and ponds during heavy rains – when breeding occurs. The MAYA RAIN-FROG, *Eleutherodactylus chac*, is named for the Mayan rain god, Chac.

Rainfrogs, like most amphibians, secrete poisons of varying degrees of toxicity from skin glands to discourage predation. The SMOKY JUNGLE FROG, found over much of Central America, has a particularly potent poison, named leptodactylin, after the genus name, *Leptodactylus*. Its effects include blocking some neuromuscular activity and stimulating parts of the nervous system, particularly those that control blood vessels and hence, blood pressure. The secretions, very irritating to mucous membranes of the mouth, nose, and throat, presumably compel some predators to release the offending frog in their mouth (see Close-Up, p. 105).

Status

No rainfrogs of Belize and northern Guatemala are currently thought to be threatened, but as is the case with most amphibian groups, adequate monitoring on most species has yet to be done. Many rainfrogs of South America, particularly in Chile and Argentina, where a great number of species occur, are threatened or endangered, as are several from Jamaica and Puerto Rico.

Profiles

Broad-headed Rainfrog, *Eleutherodactylus laticeps*, Plate 2d
Maya Rainfrog, *Eleutherodactylus chac*, Plate 3a
Central American Rainfrog, *Eleutherodactylus rugulosus*, Plate 3b
Black-backed Frog, *Leptodactylus melanonotus*, Plate 3c
Tungara Frog, *Physalaemus pustulosus*, Plate 3d

4. Treefrogs

The *treefrogs*, Family Hylidae, are an intriguing array of animals that, somewhat anomalously for amphibians, but owing to big eyes and bright colors, have joined toucans, parrots and other glamorous celebrities to become poster animals for tropical forests. Rarely these days is a book, poster, or calendar printed with pictures of tropical animals that does not include at least one of a treefrog. There are about 700 species of *hylids* worldwide, with some 12 species occurring within Belize and northern Guatemala. They are distributed on all continents except Antarctica, but are most abundant and diverse in the American tropics. SPRING PEEPERS and CHORUS FROGS, their vocalizations familiar to so many North Americans, are hylids.

Most hylid treefrogs are small and elegantly slender-waisted. They have relatively large heads with long, rounded snouts, conspicuously large, bulging eyes, and long but skinny thighs and legs. Many have prominent, enlarged toe pads – sucking disks on the tips of their toes that permit them to cling to and climb tree leaves and branches. Most are between 3.5 and 8.5 cm long (1.5 to 3.5 in). Coloring is highly variable. Some are very cryptic, clad in greens and browns that produce virtual invisibility in their arboreal lodgings. Others, particularly ones that are poisonous, are brightly colored, presumably to warn away potential predators. For instance, the RED-EYED LEAF FROG (Plate 4), up to 7 cm (3 in) in length, is right out of a cartoon studio – bright leaf green above, with blue to purple sides, bright blue and green thighs, a white belly, orange hands and feet, and red eyes. Some species also have what biologists refer to as *flash* coloring – patches of bright blue, red, orange, or yellow on the hind legs or groin area that are concealed at rest but exposed as brilliant flashes of color when the frog moves. The purpose of flash coloring presumably is to startle predators as they attack, allowing a moment to escape.

Natural History

Ecology and Behavior
As their name suggests, most treefrogs are arboreal creatures, spending much of their time jumping and climbing among tree leaves and twigs. Although their skinny legs suggest weak muscles, they are good jumpers. Their adhesive toe pads allow them to climb even vertical surfaces. Some species are more ground-dwelling and some are fully aquatic. The majority are nocturnally active, passing the daylight hours sheltered in tree crevices or among the plants that grow on trees (epiphytes), especially bromeliads. They emerge at night to forage for insects, their predominant food, and to pursue their romantic interests. Most species have the ability to change their skin color rapidly, like chameleons.

Breeding
Even the most jaded observer of animal behavior would be forced to admit that treefrog reproduction has some unusual features. As in most amphibians, one or both of the non-adult life stages, eggs and/or larvae (tadpoles), occur in water, but not just in any pond or stream. Females of one group of species lay eggs only in what ecologists term *arboreal* water – small, stagnant puddles present in tree cavities, on logs, or at the center of bromeliads and other epiphytic plants that have central *cisterns*, or bucket areas, that always hold rainwater. The eggs hatch in a few days, releasing tiny tadpoles that feed and develop within these isolated, protected ponds, eventually turning into *froglets*.

Species from another group – now, tell me this isn't fascinating – attach their eggs to tree leaves over water and, as the eggs hatch, the tadpoles drop into the water below. For example, in the RED-EYED LEAF FROG, a male in a reproductive mood moves to a tree branch overlooking a temporary pond or puddle and proceeds to call. A female approaches the vocalizing male and, after appropriate behaviors, the male clings to the female's back in the mating position. The female, with the male on her back, then climbs down to the pond to soak up some water into her bladder. She climbs back up into the tree and deposits a clutch of 30 to 50 eggs onto leaves and releases water over them; the male deposits sperm onto the wetted eggs as the female releases them, and fertilization occurs then. She climbs down again with the male to get some more water and repeats the process, sometimes three to five times in a night. In species that typically deposit eggs over streams, the eggs are particularly large, so that the tadpoles that hatch out and drop into the moving water are large and powerful enough to stand up to the currents. A number of other breeding methods exist within the hylid family as well – this is currently a hot area of animal behavior research in Central America. Some species lay 2000 or more eggs per clutch. Eggs generally hatch in 2 to 6 days. Sexual maturity is reached usually at about a year of age. Breeding can be at any time of year.

Ecological Interactions

Why do treefrogs live on land and often breed at least partially away from water? Evolutionary biologists believe that the most likely reason that some groups of frogs, such as the hylids, have developed terrestrial behavior is not that terrestrial existences are inherently better than aquatic ones, but that terrestrial life means a great reduction in the loss of eggs and tadpoles to predators. The chief culprit driving such predator-avoidance is thought to be fish, which eat copious amounts of frog eggs and tadpoles – when they can reach them. Eggs laid on leaves are obviously out of fish range, as are eggs and tadpoles that develop in fishless ponds and small, ephemeral ponds and puddles. A study of the comparative distributions of Costa Rican fish and frogs provided evidence for the claim: above about 1500 m (5000 ft) in elevation there are no native fish but there is a large variety of stream-breeding treefrogs, which are distinctly rare below that elevation. This pattern suggests that where fish are present, treefrogs have evolved more terrestriality and its accompanying breeding away from streams; but where fish are absent, stream-breeding is less costly in terms of lost eggs and young, and so it continues. Avoiding fish predation by depositing eggs on land may be a good idea, but it is not without its own hazards: some snakes feed frequently on these egg clusters.

Lore and Notes

Treefrogs employ a number of methods to deter predation, including cryptic coloring that allows them to blend into their environments, rapid leaping (what must be, aside from flying or gliding, the most efficient way to move about quickly in trees), loud, startling screams or squalls emitted when grabbed by predators, and poisons. Some species are cryptic but not poisonous, some are brightly colored and poisonous, and some are both cryptically colored and poisonous. One hylid species produces in its skin secretions toxins that cause sneezing in people, even if they are not handling a frog, and that cause pain and paralysis when ingested or when penetrating the body via an open wound.

Status

No hylid treefrogs outside of Australia are positively known to be immediately threatened or endangered. However, for many New World species, there is currently insufficient information to determine population sizes and trends. Some Brazilian species are thought to be rare and, hence, vulnerable, as is the USA's PINE BARRENS TREEFROG. As far as it can be known, Belize and northern Guatemala treefrogs are not currently threatened.

Profiles

Red-eyed Leaf Frog, *Agalychnis callidryas*, Plate 4a
Morelet's Leaf Frog, *Agalychnis moreletti*, Plate 4b
Bromeliad Treefrog, *Hyla bromeliacia*, Plate 4c
Variegated Treefrog, *Hyla ebraccata*, Plate 4d

Red-footed Treefrog, *Hyla loquax*, Plate 5a
Yellow Treefrog, *Hyla microcephala*, Plate 5b
Cricket Treefrog, *Hyla picta*, Plate 5c
Pepper Treefrog, *Phrynohyas venulosa*, Plate 5d

Stauffer's Treefrog, *Scinax staufferi*, Plate 6a
Mexican Treefrog, *Smilisca baudinii*, Plate 6b
Blue-spotted Treefrog, *Smilisca cyanosticta*, Plate 6c
Casque-headed Treefrog, *Triprion petasatus*, Plate 6d

5. Other Frogs

There are a number of groups of frogs that, although not represented by many species in Belize and northern Guatemala, nonetheless are important members of the region's amphibian community and are often conspicuous to observant visitors. Frogs of the Family Ranidae are known as *true frogs* not because they are better frogs than any other but because they are the most common frogs of Europe, where the early classification of animals took place. Over 650 species strong, the true frogs now have a worldwide distribution, excepting Antarctica (the ones in Australia were introduced there by people); most are in Africa, 250 species occur in the New World, but in Belize and northern Guatemala there are only three. True frogs include many of what most people regard as typical frogs – green ones that spend most of their lives in water. Among frogs familiar to many North Americans, BULLFROGS and LEOPARD FROGS are members of the Ranidae. Typically *ranids* are streamlined, slim-wasted frogs with long legs, webbed back feet, and thin, smooth skin. They are usually shades of green. Size varies extensively. The RAINFOREST FROG (Plate 7), a typical true frog, reaches lengths of 11 cm (4.5 in), excluding the long legs, of course.

Frogs of the Family Centrolenidae, known as *glass frogs* owing to their transparent abdominal skin, are limited in their distributions to humid regions of the Americas from southern Mexico to Bolivia and northern Argentina. There are about 100 species in the group, only one of which occurs in Belize and northern Guatemala. These arboreal frogs are usually small, most in the range of 2.5 to 3.0 cm (an inch or so) long, and most come clad in a variety of greens, including lime, blue-green, and dark green. Various body organs and bones can be seen through the transparent skin of their bellies.

The *narrow-mouth toads*, Family Microhylidae, are a group of about 300 species that are distributed over large swaths of the southern hemisphere, including the Neotropics, sub-Saharan Africa, and Southeast Asia. They are highly variable in the way they look, and in their habits, also. Only two species occur in Belize and northern Guatemala. They are both small, squat frogs with small heads, pointed snouts, and fairly smooth skins.

Natural History

Ecology and Behavior
True frogs. These are aquatic frogs that are good swimmers and jumpers. With their webbed toes and long, muscular hind legs, they are built for speed on land or in water. This is fortunate for the frogs because most lack the poison glands in their skins that many other types of frogs use to deter predation. They have thin skin through which water evaporates rapidly and thus they tend to remain in or near the water, often spending much of their time around the margins of ponds

or floating in shallow water. Except during breeding seasons, they are active only during the day. True frogs feed mainly on bugs, but also on fish and smaller frogs. In turn, they are common food items for an array of beasts, such as wading birds, fish, turtles, and small mammals. Because they are such tasty morsels to so many predators, these frogs are very alert to their surroundings, attempting escape at the slightest movement or noise; the splashing heard as you walk along a pond or lakeshore is usually made by these frogs on the shore leaping into the water.

Glass frogs. Glass frogs are treefrogs of tropical moist forests. They are found along streams in lowland areas and all the way up to 3800 m (12,000 ft). Typically active during the day, glass frogs eat mainly insects, opportunistically taking whatever bugs they encounter. Males are highly territorial, defending sites to which, with their calls, they will attract females for mating. When another male intrudes into a resident's territory and will not leave, frog fights ensue.

Narrow-mouth Toads. These are terrestrial frogs that often spend large portions of the day hiding under the leaf litter or in ground holes or burrows. Much of their activity apparently is at night, when they roam the ground in search of their favorite foods – ants, termites and assorted other bugs. SHEEP FROGS (Plate 7) commonly appear at night on and along roads after heavy rains.

Breeding
True frogs. These frogs reproduce under what most would consider the standard amphibian plan. Eggs are released by the female into the water in ponds or streams, and are fertilized then by sperm released by the male. Eggs and tadpoles develop in the water. In some species, the jellied egg masses float, but in others, they are attached to the undersides of rocks in streams. Clutch size varies tremendously, but large females can release thousands of eggs. Sexual maturity occurs in from 1 to 4 years.

Glass frogs. Glass frog males call, attracting females to their territories. Females deposit their eggs on leaves that hang over puddles and temporary pools. Some species of glass frogs stay near their eggs, guarding them. Males have been observed to sit on eggs during the night and near them during the day. Eggs hatch in 8 to 20 days, the released tadpoles dropping into the water below. Often hatching occurs during heavy rain, which is thought to help increase the chances that tadpoles make it to the pools. Tadpoles develop in the pools, finally emerging as frogs.

Narrow-mouth Toads. Breeding occurs usually after the start of the rainy season, primarily in temporary pools – roadside ditch pools, small ponds, flooded pastures. Eggs are deposited into a pool and then fertilized. They hatch quickly, sometimes in only a few days, so that the tadpoles have time to develop and leave the pools before they dry.

Ecological Interactions
The way that biologists view how animals distribute themselves within an area has been partially worked out by thinking about how true frogs might arrange themselves in a pond. Predation is a major worry for many animals, including aquatic frogs, and it doubtless influences many aspects of their lives. Often, there is safety in numbers, the rationale being that, although a group is larger than a single animal and therefore more easily located by a predator, the chances of any one animal in the group being taken is low, and so associating with the group,

instead of striking out on one's own, is advantageous to an individual. But within the group, where should an individual frog, say one named Fred, position himself to minimize his chances of being eaten? Imagine a round pond around which frogs tread in the shallow water near shore or sun themselves on the bank. If the predator is a snake or a bird that for lunch will take one frog, the best place for Fred is between two other frogs, so that his left and right are "protected," the neighbor frogs there to be eaten first. To gain such advantageous positioning, clearly Fred's best move would be to find two frogs near each other and move into the gap between them. If such a strategy exists, then the neighboring frogs should move in turn, also trying to fit into small gaps. Eventually, all the frogs in the pond, if playing this game, should end up in a small heap, the best protected frogs at its center. And indeed, as any small child who hunts frogs will tell you, they are often found in tight groups at the edges of lakes and ponds. This *selfish herd* explanation for the formation of frog and other animal aggregations was first proposed about 30 years ago.

Lore and Notes

The true frogs have always provided a minor source of protein to people throughout the world – a bit revolting to this writer, but there's no accounting for national and ethnic taste. These frogs are often non-toxic, abundant, and large enough to make harvesting and preparation economically profitable. In much of Europe and parts of the USA, the long muscles of the rear legs, often dusted with flour and fried in butter, are eaten by otherwise civilized people. Tastes like chicken breast, so I gather. Some Mayan groups today include frog legs in their diet, particularly those of the RIO GRANDE LEOPARD FROG (Plate 7).

Status

As far as it is known, no species of true, glass, or microhylid frog are currently endangered in Belize, Guatemala, or other parts of the Americas. At least three species of true frogs are threatened in the USA. As is the case for many of the amphibia, relatively little is known about the sizes and health of the populations of many of these frogs; therefore, authoritative assurance that some are not endangered is impossible to provide.

Profiles

True Frogs

Rainforest Frog, *Rana vaillanti*, Plate 7a
Julian's Frog, *Rana juliani*, Plate 7b
Rio Grande Leopard Frog, *Rana berlandieri*, Plate 7c

Glass Frogs

Fleischmann's Glass Frog, *Hyalinobatrachium fleischmanni*, Plate 7d

Narrow-mouth Toads

Sheep Frog, *Hypopachus variolosus*, Plate 7e

Environmental Close-up 1
Frog Population Declines: Amphibian Armageddon or Alarmist Absurdity?

The Problem

Recently, there has been an outpouring of articles and stories about amphibians in the popular and scientific media, bearing titles such as *The Silence of the Frogs*, *Where Have All the Frogs Gone?*, *Why Are Frogs and Toads Croaking?*, *Playing it Safe or Crying Frog?*, and *Chicken Little or Nero's Fiddle?* What's stimulating all the silly titles? The issue traces back a few years, to 1989 to be precise, to a conference in Britain attended by many of the world's leading scientists who study reptiles and amphibians in the wild. Gabbing in the hallways of the convention center, as scientists will do, relating stories about their research and the respective species that they study, they noticed a common thread emerging: many of the populations of frogs, toads, and salamanders that had been monitored for at least several years seemed to be declining in numbers, often drastically. Where some species had been common 20 years before, they were now rare or near extinction. Suspecting that something important was afoot, the scientists met formally the next year in California to discuss the subject, compare notes, and try to reach some preliminary conclusions or, minimally, to phrase some preliminary questions. Such as:

1 Are amphibian populations really declining over a broad geographic area? Or are the stories just that – anecdotal accounts concerning a few isolated populations that, even if they are in decline, do not portend a general trend?
2 If amphibian population declines are, in fact, a general phenomenon, are they over and above those of other kinds of animals (many of which, after all, given the alarming rate of natural habitat destruction occurring over the globe, are also thought to be declining – albeit usually at a gentler pace than that ascribed to the amphibian drops); that is, is the amphibian decline a special case, happening for a reason unrelated to general loss of biodiversity? and
3 If there really is a generalized worldwide amphibian problem, why is it happening?

Most of the conferring scientists agreed that a widespread pattern of amphibian declines was indicated by available data: there were reports from the USA, Central America, the Amazon Basin, the Andes, Europe, and Australia. They speculated about two possible main causes. First, that habitat loss – continued destruction of tropical forests, etc. – was almost certainly contributing to general declines in population sizes of amphibians and other types of animals. That is, that amphibian declines could be at least partly attributed to worldwide biodiversity loss. Second, that owing to their biology, amphibians were doubtless more sensitive than other groups to pollution, especially acid rain (rain that is acidified by various atmospheric pollutants, chiefly from engine emissions, leading to lake and river water being more acidic). Amphibians are more vulnerable to this kind of pollution than, say, reptiles, because of their thin, wet skins, through which they breathe and through which polluting chemicals may gain entry to their bodies, and also owing to their highly exposed and so vulnerable early life stages – eggs and tadpoles in lakes, ponds, and streams. Changes in the acidity of their aquatic environments, or even changes in water temperature, are known to have dire consequences for egg and larval (tadpole) development – and therefore such changes could be the main culprits behind amphibian declines. Plainly, if their reproduction were compromised, population numbers would plunge precipitously. Although it sounded a bit far-fetched, some scientists also suggested that the increased bombardment of the Earth by ultraviolet (UV) light, a direct result of the thinning, protective atmospheric ozone layer, might likewise be taking a disproportionate toll on biologically vulnerable amphibians. (Indeed, recent studies have proved to the satisfaction of some, but not all, scientists that increased UV light in natural situations destroys frog eggs and can interact chemically with diseases and acid rain to increase amphibian mortality rates.)

The Controversy

As might be expected, not all herpetologists agree that pollution, UV light, or some other environmental factor is currently exerting lethal effects worldwide on frogs and salamanders. Some biologists point out that the amphibians they study in some of the world's most pristine environments, having little or no detectable pollution, also have experienced catastrophic population crashes. One of the prime examples is a Costa Rican resident, the Golden Toad. It had been monitored for many years in the same five breeding ponds at the Monteverde Cloud Forest Reserve, and until the late 1980s, more than 1500 adults had bred each year in the ponds; but from 1988 through 1990, fewer than 20 individuals could be found each year and the toad is now thought by many to be extinct. In total, populations of 20 of the approximately 50 frog species that inhabit the Cloud Forest Reserve crashed dramatically during the late 1980s and, as of 1996, still had not recovered. Pollution was probably not a factor, although UV light and weather could have had effects – average water temperature had risen a bit and there was a decrease in rainfall during the late 1980s.

Still other scientists, those who study natural size oscillations in animal populations, point out that science is aware of many animals whose populations cycle between scarcity and abundance. For instance, several small rodents of the arctic tundra, *voles* and *lemmings*, are famous for one year being at low population densities (a few per hectare or acre) but three or four years hence, being at very high densities (thousands per hectare or acre, so many that it's difficult to walk without stepping on them). These biologists point out that unless those sounding the alarm of amphibian declines can show that the declines are not part of natural cycles, it is too early to panic. Further, that the only way to know about possible natural population cycles is to monitor closely amphibian populations during long-term studies, which at present, are few and far between.

The side of the debate that takes the amphibian declines as established fact and suspects an *anthropogenic* cause (scientific jargon for *people-caused*), while agreeing that long-term studies are necessary, believes that it would be a grave mistake to wait for the conclusions of those studies, 10 or 20 years down the road, before decisions are reached about whether amphibians are declining on a broad scale and what to do about it – because at that point, they believe, it will be too late to do anything but record mass extinctions.

The Future

What will happen now is that the controversy will continue as long-term population studies are conducted. In one novel approach, current populations of frogs and toads in California's Yosemite National Park were compared with notes on their population sizes from a survey conducted in 1915; all seven native species were found to have declined, but the causes are unclear. A group of Australian researchers proposed in 1996 that the catastrophic declines in frogs in eastern Australian rainforests were caused by an unknown virus – a rapidly spreading, water-borne, epidemic. They further suspect that the same disease has spread over the past 15 or 20 years from continent to continent, perhaps in water transported with aquarium fish, and, in concert with pollution and other environmental stresses that make amphibians more vulnerable to diseases, may be responsible for the worldwide amphibian die-offs. This is a controversial idea and other scientists will have to test it before it is widely accepted as a correct explanation. However, recent work in Panama shows that many frogs there are dying of a protozoan disease, and findings from Central America and Australia prove a fungus is killing many frogs in those regions, supporting disease explanations for amphibian declines.

A major problem is that, even if the scientific consensus right now was that disease, fungi, pollution, and the increased incidence of UV light were harming amphibians around the world, the will and resources are currently lacking to do anything about it on the massive scale that conservation would require. Unless peoples' worldview changes, preservation of amphibians and reptiles, save special cases like *sea turtles* (p. 86), will always lag behind preservation efforts made on the behalf of the "cuddlies" – birds and mammals. The best hope is that the recent conservation emphasis on preserving entire ecosystems, rather than particular species, will eventually benefit the disappearing amphibians.

One positive element of the amphibian declines, if it can be called that, is that some scientists have suggested that if it is determined that amphibians are particularly sensitive to pollutants, then perhaps they can be used as indicators of environmental health: ecosystems with healthy amphibian populations could be deemed relatively healthy, those with declining amphibians could be targeted for hasty improvement. As one biologist phrased it, amphibians could be used as "yardsticks for ecosystem vitality," (R. B. Primack 1993) just as canaries in cages indicated to the coal miners who carried them something of vital importance about their environments.

Chapter 6

REPTILES

- *General Characteristics and Natural History*
- *Seeing Reptiles in Belize and Guatemala*
- *Family Profiles*
- *Environmental Close-up 2*
  Poisons and Potions in Snakes and Frogs

General Characteristics and Natural History

Most people journeying to Belize or Guatemala to experience tropical habitats and view exotic wildlife harbor ambivalent feelings toward reptiles. On one hand, almost all people react with surprise, fear, and rapid withdrawal when suddenly confronted with reptiles anywhere but the zoo (which is quite understandable, given the dangerous nature of some reptiles). But on the other hand, these creatures are fascinating to look at and contemplate – their threatening primitiveness, their very dinosaur-ness – and many have highly intriguing lifestyles. Most reptiles are harmless to people and, if discovered going about their daily business, are worth a look. Unfortunately, to avoid predation, most reptiles are inconspicuous both in their behavior and color patterns and often flee when alerted to people's presence; consequently most reptiles are never seen by people during a brief visit to a region. Exceptions are reptiles that achieve a great deal of safety by being very large – crocodiles and iguanas come immediately to mind. Also, some small lizards are very common along forest trails and stone ruins. But overall, you should expect to see relatively few reptile species during any brief trip to the Neotropics. Still, it is a good idea to keep a careful watch for them, remembering not to get too close to any that you find, and count yourself lucky for each one you see.

Reptiles have been around since the late portion of the Paleozoic Era, some 300 million years ago. Descendants of those first reptiles include 6000+ species that today inhabit most regions of the Earth, with a healthy contingent in the American tropics. Chief reptile traits, aside from being scary-looking, are that (1) their skin is covered with tough scales, which cuts down significantly on water loss from their body surface. The development of this trait permitted animals for the first time to remain for extended periods on dry land, and most of today's reptiles are completely terrestrial (whereas amphibians, which lack a tough skin, must always remain in or near the water or moist places, lest they dry out). (2) Their heart is divided into more chambers that increase efficiency of circulation over that of the amphibians, allowing for a high blood pressure and thus the sustained muscular activity required for land-living. (3) Some employ *oviparous* reproduction, placing their fertilized eggs in layers of tough membrane or in hard shells and then expelling the eggs to the external environment, where development of the embryos occurs; whereas others are *ovoviviparous* – eggs are not shell-encased or laid, but remain within the mother until "hatching," the young being born "live;" still others are *viviparous*, in which developing embryos are connected to mom via a type of placenta and derive nourishment from her until being born live. Most reptiles do not feed or protect their young, but desert their eggs after they are laid.

Reptile biologists usually recognize three major groups:

The *turtles* and *tortoises* (land turtles) constitute one reptile group, with about 240 species worldwide. Some turtles live wholly on land, the sea turtles live out their lives in the oceans (coming ashore only to lay eggs), but most turtles live in lakes and ponds. Although most eat plants, some are carnivorous. Turtles are easily distinguished by their unique body armor – tough plates that cover their back and belly, creating wrap-around shells into which head and limbs are retracted when danger looms.

The *crocodiles* and their relatives, large predatory carnivores that live along the shores of swamps, rivers, and estuaries, constitute a small second group of about 20 species.

Last, and currently positioned as the world's dominant reptiles, the 3000 *lizard* species and 3500 *snakes* comprise a third group (lizards and snakes have very similar skeletal traits, indicating a very close relationship).

Lizards walk on all four limbs, except for a few that are legless. Most are ground-dwelling animals, but many also climb when the need arises; a fair number spend much of their lives in trees. Almost all are capable of moving quite rapidly. Most lizards are insectivores, but some, especially larger ones, eat plants, and several prey on amphibians, other lizards, mammals, birds, and even fish. Lizards are hugely successful and are often the most abundant vertebrate animals within an area. Ecologists suspect that they owe this ecological success primarily to their ruthlessly efficient predation on insects and other small animals and low daily energy requirements.

Most Belizean and Guatemalan lizards are insectivores, also opportunistically taking other small animals such as spiders and mites. Lizards employ two main foraging strategies. Some, such as the small whiptail lizards, are *active searchers*. They move continually while looking for prey, for instance nosing about in the leaf litter of the forest floor. *Sit-and-wait* predators, highly camouflaged, remain motionless on the ground or on tree trunks or branches, waiting for prey to happen by. When they see a likely meal – a caterpillar, a beetle – they reach out to snatch it if it is close enough or dart out to chase it down.

Many lizards are territorial, defending territories from other members of their species with displays, such as bobbing up and down on their front legs and raising their head crests. Lizards are especially common in deserts and semi-deserts, but they are numerous in other habitats as well. They are active primarily during the day, except for many of the gecko species, which are nocturnal.

Snakes probably evolved from burrowing lizards, and all are limbless. Snakes are all carnivores, but their methods of capturing prey differ. Several groups of species have evolved glands that manufacture poisons, or *venom*, that is injected into prey through the teeth. The venom immobilizes and kills the prey, which is then swallowed whole. Other snakes pounce on and wrap themselves around their prey, constricting the prey until it suffocates. The majority of snakes are nonvenomous, seizing prey with their mouths and relying on their size and strong jaws to subdue it. Snakes generally rely on vision and smell to locate prey, although members of two families have thermal sensor organs on their heads that detect the heat of prey animals.

More snake species exist now than species of all other reptiles combined. This success is thought to be attributable to their ability to devour prey that is larger than their heads (their jaw bones are highly mobile, separating partially and moving around prey as it is swallowed). This unique ability provides snakes with two great advantages over other animals: because they eat large items, they have been able to reduce the frequency with which they need to search for and capture prey; and owing to this, they can spend long periods hidden and secluded, safe from predators. Like lizards, snakes use either active searching or sit-and-wait foraging strategies.

Snakes are themselves prey for hawks and other predatory birds, as well as for some mammals. While many snakes are quite conspicuous against a solid color, being decorated with bold and colorful skin patterns, against their normal backdrops, such as a leaf-strewn forest floor, they are highly camouflaged. They rely on their cryptic colorations, and sometimes on speed, to evade predators.

Mating systems and behaviors of snakes in the wild are not well known. In some, males during the breeding period remain in mating areas, where interested females tend to gather. Males may fight each other to gain the right to mate with a particular female. Male size seems to matter most in determining the outcomes of these fights. Males and females are known to engage in multiple matings with different individuals.

Seeing Reptiles in Belize and Guatemala

As with amphibians, many reptiles are difficult to observe. They spend most of their time concealed or still. Most do not vocalize like birds or frogs, so you cannot use sound to find them. The superb cryptic coloration of snakes, including venomous ones, makes a motionless snake a dangerous snake. Because of the difficulty people have of seeing snakes before getting very close to them, the rule for exploring any area known to harbor venomous snakes or any area for which you are unsure, is never, NEVER to place your hand or foot anywhere that you cannot see first. Do not climb rocks or trees, do not clamber over rocks where your hands or feet sink into holes or crevices; do not reach into bushes or trees. Walk carefully along trails and, although your attention understandably wanders as new sights and sounds are taken in, try to watch your feet and where you are going.

With safety in mind, if you want to see reptiles, there are a few ways to increase the chances. Knowing about activity periods helps. Lizards and most snakes are active during the day, but some snakes are active at night. Thus, a night walk with flashlights that is organized to find amphibians might also yield some reptile sightings. Weather is also important – snakes and lizards are often more active in sunny, warm weather. If all else fails, one may look for small snakes and lizards by carefully moving aside rocks and logs with a robust stick or with one's boots, although such adventures are not for the faint-hearted.

Some of Belize's parks are particularly good places to spot reptiles. Larger lizards such as iguanas and Jesus Christ lizards (p. 100) are abundant in many of the parks and reserves in the northern half of the country, such as the Community

Baboon Sanctuary and Crooked Tree Wildlife Sanctuary, and several species of smaller lizards are very common along trails in and around virtually all of the region's Mayan ruin sites, as well as on the ruins themselves. Happy hunting!

Family Profiles

1. Crocodilians

Remnants of the age when reptiles ruled the world, today's crocodilians (*alligators, caimans,* and *crocodiles*), when seen in the wild, generally inspire awe, respect, a bit of fear, and a great deal of curiosity. Recent classification schemes include a total of 23 species, distributed over most tropical and sub-tropical areas of the continents. Only two are found in Belize and northern Guatemala: The AMERICAN CROCODILE (Plate 8), which is the most widely distributed of the four New World crocodile species, and MORELET'S CROCODILE (Plate 8). There is a small population of American Crocodiles in southern Florida (USA), but mainly they range from Mexico, Central America and the Caribbean islands south to Colombia, Venezuela, Peru, and Ecuador. American Crocodiles can reach lengths of 7 m (21.5 ft), as large as any crocodilian species, but in the wild individuals over 4 m (13 ft) are now rare. American Crocodiles occur mostly in Belize's coastal areas, in both brackish and freshwater habitats such as river mouths and mangrove swamps, but sometimes spread up rivers farther inland. Morelet's Crocodile is found only in the Yucatán Peninsula region – southern Mexico, Belize, and Guatemala. These crocs are smaller than American crocs, most now obtaining lengths of no more than 2.5 m (8 ft). Morelet's Crocodiles inhabit inland freshwater sites in Belize and northern Guatemala, such as lagoons, marshy parts of lakes, and sluggish rivers. (A third, smaller, species, the CAIMAN, or SPECTACLED CAIMAN, probably the most abundant crocodilian in the New World, occupies Guatemala's Pacific coastal region.)

Generally, differences in coloring are not a good way to distinguish crocodilians – most are shades of brown or olive-brown. Anatomy and location are more useful clues. Snouts of alligators and caiman tend to be broad and rounded, whereas those of crocodiles are longer and more pointed. Also, in crocodiles, the fourth tooth of the lower jaw projects upwards outside the mouth and can be seen above the upper jaw. Morelet's and American Crocodiles can be distinguished by location and, where they might overlap in distribution, by the Morelet's wider snout and generally smaller size. Male crocodilians, in general, are larger than females of the same age.

Natural History

Ecology and Behavior

Although not amphibians, crocodilians are amphibious animals. They usually move slowly over land but in short bursts can cover ground rapidly. Most of their time, however, is spent in the water. They adore basking in the sunshine along the banks of rivers, streams, and ponds. Crocodilians in the water are largely hidden, resembling from above floating logs. This unassuming appearance allows them to move close to shore and seize animals that come to the water to drink. Crocodilians are meat-eaters. The foods taken depend on their age and size. Juveniles eat primarily aquatic insects and other small invertebrates such as snails, although young AMERICAN CROCODILES also feed on small aquatic and terrestrial vertebrates. Adult American Crocodiles, which often forage at night, specialize on fish and turtles.

American Crocodiles sometimes excavate burrows along waterways, into which they retreat to escape predators and, when water levels fall too low, to *estivate* (sleep until water conditions improve). Crocodilians may use vocal signals extensively in their behavior, in communicating with one another, but their sounds have been little-studied. It is known that juveniles give alarm calls when threatened, and that parents respond by quickly coming to their rescue.

One might guess that among such primitive reptiles, *parental care* would be absent – females would lay eggs, perhaps hide them, but at that point the eggs and hatchlings would be on their own. Surprisingly, however, crocodilians show varying degrees of parental care. Nests are guarded and one or both parents often help hatchlings free themselves from the nest. In some species, such as the AMERICAN ALLIGATOR, parents also carry hatchlings to the nearest water. Females may also remain with the young for up to two years, protecting them. This complex parental care in crocodilians is sometimes mentioned by scientists who study dinosaurs to support the idea that dinosaurs may have exhibited complex social and parental behaviors.

Crocodilians are long-lived animals, many surviving 60+ years in the wild and up to 90+ years in zoos.

Breeding
During courtship, male crocodilians often defend aquatic territories, giving displays with their tails – up-and-down and side-to-side movements – that probably serve both to defend the territory from other males and to court females. Typically the female makes the nest by scraping together grass, leaves, twigs, and sand or soil, into a pile near the water's edge. She then buries 20 to 30 eggs in the pile that she, and sometimes the male, guard for about 70 days until hatching. Nests of the AMERICAN CROCODILE are a bit different. The female digs a hole in sandy soil, deposits her eggs, then covers them with sand, which she packs down. She guards the nest and often helps the young emerge. As in the turtles and some lizards, the sex of developing crocodilians is determined largely by the temperature of the ground around the eggs: males develop at relatively high temperatures, females at lower temperatures (see p. 88). Crocodile young from a brood may remain together in the nest area for up to 18 months. Breeding seasons for crocodilians vary, with nesting observed during both wet and dry parts of the year; however, in the two species considered here, eggs are commonly laid in the Yucatán region from March through June.

Ecological Interactions
Somewhat surprisingly, crocodilians are prey for a number of animals. Young, very small crocodiles are eaten by a number of predators, including birds such as herons, storks, egrets and anhingas, and mammals such as raccoons and possibly foxes. Large adults apparently have only two enemies: people and large anaconda snakes. Slow-movers on land, crocodiles are sometimes killed by automobiles. Cases of cannibalism have been reported.

One of the more surprising mutualisms between species is the case of an African wading bird that actually picks and eats parasites and bits of food from among a basking crocodile's teeth. What is so interesting is that the cleaners are plainly potentially yummy prey for the crocs, yet the reptiles refrain from crunching them. Presumably when the mutualism began, the birds were not always so fortunate. It may be that long ago the birds began cleaning crocs on far less lethal sections of their anatomy.

Lore and Notes
Larger MORELET'S and, especially, AMERICAN CROCODILES are potentially dangerous to people, but they are not considered particularly aggressive species. Morelet's are usually inoffensive, most being below a size where they try to eat land mammals. There are few documented cases of American Crocodiles killing people. Some species *are* known to be aggressive, such as the NILE CROCODILE: In one famous, historical collecting trip, 444 large ones were shot randomly and opened; four had human remains in their stomachs. True, this number represents only 1% of the crocodile population, but still . . .

Owing to their predatory nature and large size, crocodilians play large roles in the history and folklore of many cultures, going back at least to ancient Egypt, where a crocodile-headed god was known as Sebek. The Egyptians apparently welcomed crocodiles into their canals, possibly as a defense from invaders. It may have been believed by Egyptians and other African peoples that crocodiles caused blindness, probably because the disease called river blindness results from infestation with a river-borne parasitic roundworm. To appease the crocodiles during canal construction, a virgin was sacrificed to the reptiles. Indeed, providing crocodiles with virgins seems to have been a fairly common practice among several cultures, showing a preoccupation with these animals. Even today, carvings of crocodiles are found among many relatively primitive peoples, from South America to Africa to Papua New Guinea. The ancient Olmecs of eastern Mexico also had a crocodile deity. Crocodile remains have been found at Mayan ruin sites in both southern Mexico (on the island of Cozumel, for instance) and in Belize, suggesting that these ancient groups made use of the large reptiles for food and/or ceremonially.

Status
Most crocodilian species worldwide were severely reduced in numbers during this century. Several were hunted almost to extinction for their skins. In the USA, hunting almost caused AMERICAN ALLIGATORS to become extinct. In 1961 hunting alligators was made illegal, but poaching continued. Thanks to the 1973 Endangered Species Act, which gave protection to the alligators, they have returned to most of the areas from which they were eliminated. Crocodile and alligator farms (with captive-bred stock) and ranches (wild-caught stock) in many areas of the world now permit skins to be harvested while wild animals are relatively unmolested. Many of the Latin American crocodilians were hunted heavily during the first half of the 20th century. MORELET'S CROCODILE, in particular, is one of the more endangered species, listed by CITES Appendix I and USA ESA. AMERICAN CROCODILES, considered by some agencies as vulnerable to threat, are also CITES Appendix I and USA ESA listed. Today, only the COMMON CAIMAN is hunted in large numbers, particularly in the Pantanal region of Brazil. All crocodilians are listed by the international CITES agreements, preventing or highly regulating trade in their skins or other parts, and their numbers have been steadily rising during the past 20 years. However, most of the 23 crocodilian species are still threatened or endangered.

Profiles
American Crocodile, *Crocodylus acutus*, Plate 8a
Morelet's Crocodile, *Crocodylus moreleti*, Plate 8b

2. Turtles

It is a shame that *turtles* in the wild are relatively rarely encountered reptiles (at least at close range) because they can be quite interesting to watch and they are generally innocuous and inoffensive. It is always a pleasant surprise stumbling across a turtle on land, perhaps laying eggs, or discovering a knot of them basking in the sunshine on rocks or logs in the middle of a pond. The 240 living turtle species are usually grouped into 12 families that can be divided into three types by their typical habitats. Two families comprise the *sea turtles*, ocean-going animals whose females come to shore only to lay eggs. The members of nine families, containing most of the species, live in freshwater habitats – lakes and ponds – except for the exclusively terrestrial *box turtles*. Finally, one family contains the *land tortoises*, which are completely terrestrial.

Turtles all basically look alike: bodies encased in tough shells (made up of two layers – an inner layer of bone and an outer layer of scale-like plates); four limbs, sometimes modified into flippers; highly mobile necks; toothless jaws; and small tails. This body plan must be among nature's best, because it has survived unchanged for a long time; according to fossils, turtles have looked more or less the same for at least 200 million years. Enclosing the body in heavy armor above and below apparently was an early solution to the problems vertebrates faced when they first moved onto land. It provides both rigid support when outside of buoyant water and a high level of protection from drying out and from predators.

Turtles come, for the most part, in a variety of browns, blacks and greens, with olive-greens predominating. They range in size from tiny terrapins a few inches long to 250-kg (550-lb) GALAPAGOS TORTOISES and giant LEATHERBACK SEA TURTLES (Plate 10) that are nearly 2 m (7 ft) long, 3.6 m (12 ft) across (flipper to flipper), and that weigh 550+ kg (1200+ lb). The Leatherbacks are probably the heaviest living reptiles. In many turtle species, females are larger than males.

Natural History

Ecology and Behavior
The diet of freshwater turtles changes as they develop. Early in life they are carnivorous, eating almost anything they can get their jaws on – snails, insects, fish, frogs, salamanders, reptiles. As they grow the diet of most changes to herbivory. Turtles are slow-moving on land, but they can retract their heads, tails, and limbs into their shells, rendering them almost impregnable to predators – unless they are swallowed whole, such as by crocodiles. Long-lived animals, individuals of many turtle species typically live 25 to 60 years in the wild. (GALAPAGOS TORTOISES routinely live 100 years, the record being 152 years.) Many turtle species grow throughout their lives.

Snapping turtles (Family Chelydridae; Plate 9) are large freshwater turtles with long tails, hooked, mean-looking jaws, and usually bad dispositions – they will bite people. They are found mainly in marshes, ponds, lakes, rivers, and streams. They are omnivorous, and often quite inconspicuous: sometimes algae grows on their backs, camouflaging them as they lunge at and snatch small animals that venture near. They remain predatory throughout their lives, even taking birds and small mammals, but they also eat aquatic vegetation.

Aquatic, or *pond*, turtles (Family Emydidae) occupy a variety of habitats. Some spend most of their time in lakes and ponds, but others leave the water frequently to bask in the sun during the day and to forage on land at night. Because they feed on land, they can occupy rivers that lack vegetation. FURROWED WOOD TURTLE and COMMON SLIDER are common pond turtles that are illustrated here (Plates 8, 9).

Semi-aquatic, *mud turtles* (Family Kinosternidae) are generally found in swamps, ponds, and slow streams, and only occasionally on land. Many appear to favor a diet of aquatic snails, but they have been also observed feeding on land. TABASCO MUD, WHITE-LIPPED MUD, and SCORPION MUD TURTLES from this family are illustrated here (Plate 9).

Sea turtles are large reptiles that live in the open oceans, with the result that, aside from their beach nesting habits, relatively little is known of their behavior. Their front legs have been modified into oar-like flippers, which propel them through the water. Although they need air to breathe, they can remain submerged for long periods. At first, all sea turtles were assumed to have similar diets, probably sea plants. But some observations of natural feeding, as well as examinations of stomach contents, reveal a variety of specializations. GREEN TURTLES (Plate 10) eat bottom-dwelling sea grasses and algae, HAWKSBILL TURTLES (Plate 10) eat bottom sponges, LOGGERHEAD TURTLES (Plate 10) feed predominantly on mollusks (snails, etc.) and crustaceans (crabs, etc.), and LEATHERBACK TURTLES (Plate 10), which may occur off the Belize coast, eat mostly jellyfish.

Breeding

Courtship in turtles can be quite complex. In some, the male swims backwards in front of the female, stroking her face with his clawed feet. In the tortoises, courtship seems to take the form of some between-the-sexes butting and nipping. All turtles lay their leathery eggs on land. The female digs a hole in the earth or sand, deposits the eggs into the hole, then covers them over and departs. It is up to the hatchlings to dig their way out of the nest and navigate to the nearest water. Many tropical turtles breed at any time of year.

Although the numbers of eggs laid per nest varies extensively among Central American freshwater turtles (from 1 to about 100), in general, these turtles, specialized for life in the tropics, lay small clutches, often only one to four eggs. The reason seems to be that, because of the continuous warm weather, they need not breed in haste like their northern cousins, putting all their eggs in one nest. The danger with a single nest is that if a predator finds it, a year's breeding is lost. Tropical turtles, by placing only one or a few eggs in each of several nests spread through the year, are less likely to have predators destroy their total annual breeding production. Also, it may pay to lay a few big eggs rather than many small ones because bigger hatchlings can run faster to the water and its comparative safety from predators.

All sea turtle species breed in much the same way. Mature males and females appear offshore during breeding periods (for example, GREENS, July to October; LOGGERHEADS, June through September). After mating, females alone come ashore on beaches, apparently the same ones on which they were born, to lay their eggs. Each female breeds probably every 2 to 4 years, laying from two to eight clutches of eggs in a season (each clutch being laid on a different day). All within about an hour, and usually at night, a female drags herself up the beach to a suitable spot above the high-tide line, digs a hole with her rear flippers (a half meter or more, 2 ft, deep), deposits about 100 golfball-sized eggs, covers them with sand, tamps the sand down, and heads back to the ocean. Sometimes females emerge from the sea alone, but often there are mass emergences, with hundreds of females nesting on a beach in a single night. Eggs incubate for about 2 months, then hatch simultaneously. The hatchlings dig themselves out of the sand and make a dash for the water (if tiny turtles can be said to be able to "dash"). Many terrestrial and ocean predators devour the hatchlings and it is thought that only between 2% and 5% survive their first few days of life. The young float on rafts of sea vegetation during their first year, feeding and growing, until they reach a size when they can, with some safety, migrate long distances through the world's oceans. When sexually mature, in various species from 7 to 20+ years later, they undertake reverse migrations, returning to their birth sites to breed.

Ecological Interactions
If turtles can make it through the dangerous juvenile stage, when they are small and soft enough for a variety of predators to take them, they enjoy very high year-to-year survival – up to 80% or more of an adult population usually survives from one year to the next. However, there is very high mortality in the egg and juvenile stages. Nests are not guarded, and many kinds of predators, such as crocodiles, lizards, and, especially, armadillos, dig up turtle eggs or eat the hatchlings. Although adult turtles have few predators because they are difficult to kill and eat, some turtles have additional defenses: Within the mud turtle family is a group known as *musk turtles*. When grabbed or handled they give off a musky smell from scent glands located on the sides of their bodies; in North America they are known as *stinkpots*.

There is an intriguing relationship between turtle reproduction and temperature that nicely illustrates the intimate and sometimes puzzling connections between animals and the physical environment. For many vertebrate animals, the sex of an individual is determined by the kinds of sex chromosomes it has. In people, if each cell has an X and a Y chromosome, the person is male, and if two Xs, female. In birds, it is the opposite. But in most turtles, it is not the chromosomes that matter, but the temperature at which an egg develops. The facts are these. In most turtles, eggs incubated at constant temperatures above 30 °C (86 °F) all develop as females, whereas those incubated at 24 to 28 °C (75 to 82 °F) become males. At 28 to 30 °C (82–86 °F), both males and females are produced. In some species, a second temperature threshold exists – eggs that develop below 24 °C (75 °F) again become females. (In the crocodiles and lizards, the situation reverses, with males developing at relatively high temperatures and females at low temperatures.) The exact way that temperature determines sex is not clear although it is suspected that temperature directly influences a turtle's developing brain. This method of sex determination is also mysterious for the basic reason that no one quite knows why it should exist; that is, is there some advantage of this system to the animals that we as yet fail to appreciate? Or is it simply a consequence of reptile structure and function, some fundamental constraint of their biology?

Lore and Notes
Turtles apparently were used by the ancient Mayans for both food and for religious/ceremonial purposes. Turtle remains from an array of species, often with markings that suggest cooking, were found at various archeological sites, including ones on Mexico's Yucatán Peninsula and in Guatemala's Petén region.

Identified remains include fragments of Central American River Turtles (Plate 8), Common Sliders (Plate 9), Furrowed Wood Turtles (Plate 8), mud turtles (Plate 9), and sea turtles such as Green Turtles (Plate 10). Several of these turtles are still eaten today by indigenous peoples.

Often there is some trans-Atlantic confusion over turtle names: Americans use the word *turtle* for many land species, whereas the British refer to them as *tortoises.*

Status

The ecology and status of populations of most freshwater and land turtle species are still poorly known, making it difficult to determine whether population numbers are stable or declining. However, it is mainly sea turtles, rather than freshwater or terrestrial turtles, that are exploited by people, and therefore that are most threatened. Sea turtle eggs are harvested for food in many parts of the world, including Belize, and adults are taken for meat (only some species) and for their skins. Many adults also die accidentally in fishing nets and collisions with boats. One of the sea turtles, the HAWKSBILL, is the chief provider of tortoiseshell, which is carved for decorative purposes. The Hawksbill is under international protection and is also legally protected in Belize, but some are still hunted. Other species of sea turtle – eggs and adults – are still eaten in Belize. All sea turtles are listed as endangered by CITES Appendix I.

Other than sea turtles, Belize and Guatemala's only endangered turtle may be the CENTRAL AMERICAN RIVER TURTLE (Plate 8; CITES Appendix II and USA ESA listed), known locally in Belize as the Hickatee. The species is the only surviving representative of a formerly widely distributed and diverse turtle family that traces back to the Jurassic Period, 195 million years ago. Unfortunately, Hickatees are still hunted for their meat throughout their limited range – in southern Mexico, Guatemela, and Belize. They make for particularly easy prey during dry seasons, when river levels fall. In northern Belize, a Hickatee is commonly the basis for Easter dinner. A Belizean law to protect this species was passed in 1993. There is still a short hunting season for these turtles, but there are restrictions on hunting, there are some large, completely protected areas set aside for them, and, increasingly, local villages are interested in protecting their populations.

Profiles

Central American River Turtle, *Dermatemys mawii*, Plate 8c
Furrowed Wood Turtle, *Rhinoclemmys areolata*, Plate 8d
Common Slider, *Trachemys scripta*, Plate 9a
Snapping Turtle, *Chelydra serpentina*, Plate 9b
Tabasco Mud Turtle, *Kinosternon acutum*, Plate 9c
White-lipped Mud Turtle, *Kinosternon leucostomum*, Plate 9d
Scorpion Mud Turtle, *Kinosternon scorpioides*, Plate 9e
Green Sea Turtle, *Chelonia mydas*, Plate 10a
Hawksbill Sea Turtle, *Eretmochelys imbricata*, Plate 10b
Loggerhead Sea Turtle, *Caretta caretta*, Plate 10c
Leatherback Sea Turtle, *Dermochelys coriacea*, Plate 10d

3. Colubrids: Your Regular, Everyday Snakes

All snakes, particularly tropical varieties, are thought by many people to be poisonous, and hence, to be avoided at all cost. This "reptile anxiety" is serious when it prevents people who are paying initial visits to tropical forests from enjoying the many splendors around them. The phobia is understandable because of the lethal nature of a small number of snake species, snakes' abilities to blend in with surroundings and to move and strike so rapidly, and the long history we have, dating back to the origins of the Bible and beyond, of evil snake stories and legends. It is much more than Western societies' legends that cause our fear of snakes. All people it seems, irrespective of geography or culture, recoil from images of snakes and regard the real thing as dangerous, indicating a long conflict over evolutionary time between snakes and people. The fact is, however, that everywhere except unfortunate Australia, the majority of snakes are not poisonous. Also, poisonous snakes in the American tropics tend to be nocturnal and secretive. Therefore, with a modicum of caution, visitors should be able to enjoy their days in Belize and Guatemala without worrying unduly about poisonous snakes, and, again with caution, be able to watch snakes that cross their paths. Many of them are beautiful organisms, fairly common, and worth a look.

The largest group of snakes are those of the Family Colubridae – the *colubrid* snakes. Most of these are nonpoisonous or, if venomous, dangerous only to small prey, such as lizards and rodents; in other words, they are only mildly venomous. This is a worldwide group comprising over 1500 species, including about three-quarters of the New World snakes. About 60 different species occur in Belize and Guatemala. Most of the snakes with which people have some familiarity, such as *water, brown, garter, whip, green, rat,* and *king snakes,* among a host of others, are colubrids, which have a wide variety of habits and lifestyles. It is not even possible to provide a general physical description of colubrid snakes because of the great variety of shapes and colors that specialize each for their respective lifestyles. Most people will not get close enough to notice, but an expert could identify colubrids by their anatomy: they have rows of teeth on the upper and lower jaws but they do not have hollow, venom-injecting fangs in front on the upper jaw.

Natural History

Ecology and Behavior

Because colubrids vary so much in their natural history, I will concentrate on the habits of the species illustrated (Plates 11, 12, 13), which are representative of several general types. You should keep in mind that many snakes have not been much studied in nature. Such research is difficult for several reasons. Most snake species are not plentiful in the wild – even members of healthy populations often are found only few and far between – making it difficult to locate and study simultaneously more than a few individuals. Snakes also spend long periods being inactive and they feed infrequently, which means that to collect enough observations, studies of behavior need to be of long duration.

Typical lifestyles of various colubrids are terrestrial, burrowing, arboreal, and aquatic. Arboreal snakes spend most of their time in trees and shrubs. *Vine snakes* (Plate 12), for instance, are slender, elegant, grayish, green, or brown snakes that inhabit dryer areas, feeding usually on lizards taken in trees. These snakes have a mild venom that helps subdue their victims. Their thin, long bodies look much like vines and if not moving, these snakes are very difficult to see. They rely on their camouflage for both hunting and protection: they freeze in place when alerted to danger. *Blunt-headed snakes* (Plate 12) are also arboreal. They possess exceptional heads – broad and squarish, relative to a long, thin body – and large, bulging eyes. They forage at night for small frogs and lizards that they locate in their special hunting preserve, at the very outer layer of leaves and branches of trees and shrubs. These light snakes, which are slightly sideways flattened, can move from branch to branch over open gaps that are half the length of their bodies. They hide during the day in trees.

The INDIGO SNAKE (Plate 11) is common throughout much of the American lowland tropics, inhabiting riverbeds, swamps, and marshes. It moves over the ground and sometimes through bushes or shallow water, searching for its varied prey, which includes small turtles, frogs, mammals, birds, fish, eggs, and even other snakes. These beige, brown, or greenish-brown snakes range up to 3 m (10 ft) in length. Having no venom, they simply grab prey with their strong jaws, hold it, and swallow it. Another common terrestrial snake is the MUSSURANA (Plate 11). It has a broad range in the Neotropics in wet and semi-dry lowland areas. Hunting nocturnally, Mussurana specialize on eating other snakes and, in fact, they even take the deadly FER-DE-LANCE (and are appreciated for this habit by knowledgable local people). Mussurana are also interesting because they subdue their prey with a combination of slow-acting venom and physical constriction.

Breeding
Relatively little is known of the breeding particulars of Central American colubrids. For the group as a whole, the best information is available for the North American garter snakes. In these snakes, group mating assemblages, or *mating balls*, occur on warm days in spring. Many males – dozens and sometimes hundreds – and a few females swarm together and mating occurs. Some males are successful in mating with one or more females, while others are not. Each female probably mates with several males, and DNA tests on snake babies indicate that a single brood may have more than one father. Some of the males within a mating ball actually mimic females by releasing female courtship pheromones, which distract other males from the real females; the mimics then obtain more matings themselves. In other colubrid species, monogamous mating seems to be the case. Males make prolonged searches for mates, perhaps using their chemical senses to detect female pheromones. Once a female is located, a male may spend several days courting her before mating occurs. Because larger female snakes lay more eggs per clutch, males, when given a choice, prefer to mate with larger females. The typical number of eggs per clutch varies from species to species, but some, such as the BLUNT-HEADED TREE SNAKE (Plate 12), lay small clutches of one to three eggs. Most snakes that lay eggs deposit them in a suitable location and depart; the parents provide no care of the eggs or young. A few snakes guard their eggs.

Ecological Interactions
(1) Body shape: Body shape of snakes nicely demonstrates how a single body scheme, in this case cylindrical and legless, can be modified superbly through evolution to cope with a variety of habitats and lifestyles. The colubrid *worm snakes* live primarily underground. Their bodies are for the most part uniformly round, like earthworms. The majority of colubrids are long and very thin, at least partly as an adaptation for speedy movement – they escape from predators by moving rapidly. This very light, slender body plan also permits many arboreal colubrids to cross broad gaps between tree branches. In contrast to the mainly slender colubrids, most of the *vipers* (see p. 93) are heavy-bodied and rely on their bites, rather than speed, for protection and hunting. Being mostly *sit-and-wait* predators, they move around a lot less than do the colubrids. Finally, *sea snakes*, which spend their time in the water, have flattened tails that help with aquatic propulsion. (N. G. Hairston 1994)

(2) Body temperature: Biologists who study snakes know that temperature regulates a snake's life, and is the key to understanding their ecology. Snakes are cold-blooded animals – they inhabit a world where the outside temperature governs their activity. Unlike birds and mammals, their body temperature is determined primarily by how much heat they obtain from the physical environment. Simply put, they can only be active when they gather sufficient warmth from the sun. They have some control over their body temperature, but it is behavioral rather than physiological – they can lie in the sun or retreat to shade to raise or lower their internal temperatures to within a good operating range, but only up to a point: snakes must "sit out" hours or days in which the air temperature is either too high or too low. This dependence on air temperature affects most aspects of snakes' lives, from date of birth, to food requirements, to the rapidity with which they can strike at prey. For instance, in cold weather, snakes are less successful at capturing prey (they move and strike more slowly) and have less time each day when the ambient temperature is within their operating range, and so within the range in which they can forage. On the other hand, their metabolisms are slower when they are cold, which means that they need less food to survive these periods. At lower temperatures, snakes also probably grow slower, reproduce less often, and live longer. (C. R. Peterson *et al.* 1993)

Lore and Notes

Snakes' limbless condition, their manner of movement, and the venomous nature of some of their number, have engendered for these intriguing reptiles almost universal hatred from people, stretching back thousands of years. Myths about the evil power and intentions of snakes are, as they say, legion. But one need go no further than the Old Testament, where the snake, of course, plays the pivotal role of Eve's corrupt enticer, responsible for people's expulsion from the Garden of Eden. The ensuing enhanced evil reputation of snakes came down through the ages essentially intact – so much so that even people who should have known better, such as Linnaeus, the 18th-century botanist who began the scientific system we currently use to name and categorize plants and animals, considered them an abomination. Linnaeus, lumping snakes with other reptiles and the amphibians, referred to them in his writings as "these foul and loathsome animals" that are "abhorrent because of their cold body, pale color, cartilaginous filthy skin, fierce aspect, calculating eye, offensive smell, harsh voice, squalid habitation and terrible venom." He concluded that, owing to their malevolence, "their Creator has not exerted His powers to make many of them."

Scientists who study the ancient Mayan civilization suspect that some larger colubrid snakes were considered good sources of animal protein. Remains of species such as Indigo and Tropical Rat Snakes (Plates 11, 13) have been found at Mayan sites such as Tikal.

Status

At this time, only one snake species that occurs in Belize or Guatemala is considered threatened, and that is a secretive animal of the highlands southeast of Guatemala City that spends much of its time underground, *Adelphicos daryi*, or DARY'S MIDDLE AMERICAN EARTH SNAKE. Most experts will concede, however, that little is known about the biology and population numbers of most snakes. Long-term studies are necessary to determine if population sizes are stable or changing. Because individual species of snakes normally are not found in great numbers, the truth is that it will always be difficult to tell when they are threatened. Worldwide, about 20 colubrids are listed as vulnerable, threatened, or endangered. The leading threats are habitat destruction and the introduction by people of exotic animals that prey on snakes at some point in their life cycles, such as fire ants, cane toads, cattle egrets, and armadillos. Considered a top priority now for research and conservation are the snakes of the West Indies. The islands of the Caribbean have hundreds of unique snake species, many of which appear to be declining rapidly in numbers – the result of habitat destruction and predation by mongooses, which were imported to the islands to control venomous snakes. The Belizean cayes hold several unique races of snakes that bear watching and perhaps special protection should they become threatened. For instance, there is a race of the GREEN-HEADED TREE SNAKE (Plate 12) that occurs only on Big Caye Bokel, off central Belize.

Profiles

Mussurana, *Clelia clelia*, Plate 11a
Brown Racer, *Dryadophis melanolomus*, Plate 11b
Indigo Snake, *Drymarchon corais*, Plate 11c
Speckled Racer, *Drymobius margaritiferus*, Plate 11d
Blunt-headed Tree Snake, *Imantodes cenchoa*, Plate 12a
Green Tree Snake, *Leptophis ahaetulla*, Plate 12b
Green-headed Tree Snake, *Leptophis mexicanus*, Plate 12c
Neotropical Vine Snake, *Oxybelis aeneus,* Plate 12d
Green Vine Snake, *Oxybelis fulgidus*, Plate 12e
Cat-eyed Snake, *Leptodeira frenata*, Plate 13a
Tropical Rat Snake, *Spilotes pullatus*, Plate 13b
Red Coffee Snake, *Ninia sebae*, Plate 13c
Neckband Snake, *Scaphiodontophis annulatus*, Plate 13d
Tropical Kingsnake, *Lampropeltis triangulum*, Plate 14a

4. Dangerous Snakes and Boas

In this section I group together what are usually considered the more dangerous snakes, those that are highly poisonous and large ones that kill by squeezing their prey. Few short-term visitors to Central America encounter a poisonous snake because most are well camouflaged, secretive in their habits, or nocturnal and, therefore, they are really outside the scope of this book. However, most people are extremely wary of snakes and want to be well-informed about them, just in case.

Vipers. Vipers, of the Family Viperidae, comprise most of the New World's poisonous snakes. Among all snakes they have the most highly developed venom-injection mechanisms: long, hollow fangs that inject poison into prey when they bite. The venom is often *neurotoxic*; that is it interferes with nerve function, causing paralysis of the limbs and then respiratory failure. Other venoms cause hemorrhaging both at the site of the bite and then internally, leading to cardiovascular shock and death. (The answer to the question of why venomous snakes are not harmed by their own venom is that they are immune.) Typically vipers coil prior to striking. They vary considerably in size, shape, color pattern, and lifestyle. Many of the *viperids* are referred to as *pit-vipers* because they have heat-sensitive "pits," or depressions, between their nostrils and eyes that are sensory organs. Pit-vipers occur from southern Canada to Argentina, as well as in the Old World. The familiar venomous snakes of North America are pit-vipers – rattlesnakes, copperheads, water moccasins – as are most of poisonous snakes of

Belize and Guatemala.

The deadly FER-DE-LANCE (Plate 15) is abundant essentially throughout Belize and northern Guatemala in lowland wet areas and at middle elevations in Belize's Mountain Pine Ridge. Most are shorter than the maximum length of 2.5 m (8 ft). They are slender snakes with lance- or spear-shaped heads (hence the name, which means "iron spear"). EYELASH VIPERS (Plate 15) are a kind of *palm viper*, common arboreal snakes of lowland areas. There are several species, all small (as long as 1 m, or 3 ft, but most are only half that long) with prehensile tails and large wide heads. Their color schemes vary extensively. The TROPICAL RAT-TLE SNAKE (Plate 14) probably occurs in most regions of Belize and northern Guatemala. Reaching lengths of 1.5 m (5 ft), they are heavy-bodied with slender necks and broad, triangular heads. The rattles consist of loosely interlocking segments of a horn-like material at the base of the tail. A new segment is added each time the snake sheds its skin.

Coral Snakes. The family Elapidae contains what are regarded as the world's deadliest snakes, the Old World *cobras* and *mambas*. In the Western Hemisphere, the group is represented by the coral snakes – small, often quite gaily attired in bands of red, yellow and black, and, unfortunately, possessed of a very powerful neurotoxic venom. Three coral snake species occur in Belize and northern Guatemala, one of which (Plate 14) is a fairly common terrestrial animal of the region's moist lowland areas and also of Mountain Pine Ridge. Coral snakes rarely grow longer than a meter (3 ft).

Boas. The Family Boidae, members of which kill by constriction, encompasses about 65 species that are distributed throughout the world's tropical and subtropical regions. They include the Old World *pythons* and the New World's *boas* and *anacondas*, the pythons and anacondas being the world's largest snakes. Only one boa species calls Belize and Guatemala home. The BOA CONSTRICTOR (Plate 14) occurs over a wide range of habitat types from sea level up to almost 1000 m (3300 ft). This boa reaches lengths of about 6 m (19 ft), but typical specimens are only 1.5 to 2.5 m (5 to 8 ft) long (on some of Belize's small coastal islands, boas are relatively small). They have shiny, smooth scales and a back pattern of dark, squarish shapes that provides good camouflage against an array of backgrounds.

Within a species male and female snakes usually look alike, although in many there are minor differences between the sexes in traits such as color patterns or the sizes of their scales.

Natural History

Ecology and Behavior
Vipers. FER-DE-LANCE as adults are terrestrial, but partially arboreal as juveniles. They inhabit moist forests but also some dryer areas. They eat mammals such as opossums, and birds. EYELASH VIPERS move through trees, along vines and twigs, searching when hungry for treefrogs, lizards, and mice. These snakes are often seen sunning themselves on leaves and branches. TROPICAL RATTLE-SNAKES are denizens of the forest floor and of more open areas. They eat primarily lizards, birds, and rodents. Like other pit-vipers (and some other snakes), they can sense the heat radiated by prey animals, which aids their foraging. Searching by heat detection probably works for both warm-blooded prey (birds, mammals) as well as cold-blooded (lizards, etc.), as long as the prey is at a higher temperature than its surroundings.

Coral Snakes. Coral snakes are usually secretive and difficult to study; consequently relatively little is known about their ecology and behavior in the wild. They apparently forage by crawling along slowly, intermittently poking their heads into the leaf litter. They eat lizards, amphibians including caecilians (p. 63), and small snakes, which they kill with their powerful venom. They are often found under rocks and logs.

Boas. Boas are mainly terrestrial but they are also good climbers, and young ones spend a good deal of time in trees. When foraging, boas apparently search for good places to wait for prey, such as in a mammal's burrow or in a tree, near fruit. The diet includes lizards, birds, and mammals, including domesticated varieties. Prey, recognized by visual, smell (chemical), or heat senses, is seized with the teeth after a rapid, open-mouth lunge. As it strikes, the boa also coils around the prey, lifting it from the ground, and then constricts, squeezing the prey. The prey cannot breathe and suffocates. When the prey stops moving, the boa swallows it whole, starting always with the head.

Breeding
Details of the breeding in the wild of most tropical snakes are not well known. Many of the vipers may follow the general system of North American rattlesnakes, which have been much studied. Males search for females. When one is located, perhaps by a pheromonal trail she lays down, the male accompanies and courts her for several days before mating occurs. Fighting between males for the same female is probably uncommon, because it is rare for two males to locate the same female at the same time. North American rattlers have distinct breeding periods, but many tropical vipers may breed at almost any time of year. Most snakes that lay eggs deposit the eggs in a suitable location and depart; the parents provide no care of the eggs or young. A few snakes guard their eggs.

Vipers. Most of the vipers give birth to live young. The FER-DE-LANCE has a reputation as a prolific breeder, females giving birth to between 20 and 70 young at a time. Each is about a third of a meter (one ft) long at birth, fully fanged with active poison glands, and dangerous. EYELASH VIPERS have clutches of up to 20 live young, and TROPICAL RATTLERS, 20 to 40.

Coral Snakes. Coral snakes lay eggs, up to 10 per clutch.

Boas. BOA CONSTRICTORS give birth to live young. Litters, born in the Belize region often during the rainy season, vary between 12 and 60. Each snakelet at birth is about half a meter (1.5 ft) long.

Ecological Interactions
Coral snakes hold a special place in snake biology studies because a number of nonvenomous or mildly venomous colubrid snakes (p. 89), as well as at least one caterpillar species, mimic the bright, striking coral snake color scheme – alternating bands of red, yellow (or white), and black. About 10 species of colubrid snakes in the Yucatán region (which includes Belize and northern Guatemala) imitate – to varying degrees – the color patterns of coral snakes (see Plates 13 and 14 for examples). The function of the mimicry apparently is to take advantage of the quite proper respect many predatory animals show toward the lethal coral snakes. Ever since this idea was first proposed more than a hundred years ago, the main argument against it has been that it implied either that the predators had to be first bitten by a coral snake to learn of their toxicity and then survive to generalize the experience to all snakes that look like coral snakes, or that the predators

were born with an innate fear of the coral snake color pattern. It has now been demonstrated experimentally that several bird predators on snakes (motmots, kiskadees, herons, and egrets) need *not* learn that a coral snake is dangerous by being bitten – they avoid these snakes instinctively from birth. Thus, many snakes have evolved as defensive mechanisms color schemes that mimic that of coral snakes. (However, some biologists argue that this explanation falls apart because, they say, the alternating color bands of the coral snake's body function as camouflage and *not* to warn predators away, and also because the snakes' mammalian predators lack color-vision and therefore could not make use of the patterns to avoid the mimics.)

Nonvenomous snakes also mimic some of the behavior of poisonous snakes, the most obvious example being that a good many snakes, when threatened, coil up and wiggle the tips of their tails, as do rattlesnakes and some other vipers.

Lore and Notes

These snakes are dangerous! Remember: Snakes, like traffic cops, lack a sense of humor. All of the venomous snakes discussed in this section, if encountered, should be given a wide berth. Watch them only from a distance. Very few visitors to Central America are bitten by poisonous snakes, even those that spend their days tramping through forests. (One tropical biologist, in fact, calculated that about 450,000 person-hours of field research were conducted at one Costa Rica biological research station without a single poisonous snake bite, and field biologists certainly have greater chances of coming into contact with snakes than average visitors. Ironically, the biologist in question reported his calculation after being bitten by a FER-DE-LANCE.) The biology of snake bites is an active area of study. Venomous snakes can bite without injecting any venom, and they can also vary the amount of venom injected – even if bitten, one does not necessarily receive a fatal dose. Within the same species, the toxicity of a snake's venom varies geographically, seasonally, and from individual to individual.

Vipers. Because of its aggressive nature, the FER-DE-LANCE is often said to be the most feared and dangerous of Central American snakes – when approached, it is more likely to bite than retreat. Stories abound attesting to the potency of the venom. One, out of Honduras, tells the sorry tale of a railway worker and his wife. The man, bitten by a Fer-de-lance at work, was brought home and ministered to by his wife. The venom killed the man two hours later and the wife the next day – she had scraped her finger the previous day while cooking, and the poison had entered through the open cut as she dressed his wound. These snakes killed so many sugarcane workers in Jamaica earlier this century that mongooses from the Old World were shipped to the island to kill them. They were somewhat successful, but unfortunately, the mongooses also killed many of the isle's nonvenomous snakes, not to mention domestic fowl. Also, unhappily for the mongooses, it turns out that the New World pit-vipers are a good deal faster striking than are cobras, their Old World nemeses. A documentary motion picture maker trying to film a mongoose killing a Fer-de-lance had several dead mongooses on his hands before obtaining the pictures he wanted. Somewhat amazingly, there is a colubrid snake, the MUSSURANA (Plate 11), that kills and eats the Fer-de-lance by first injecting it with its own considerably less potent venom and then by constricting it.

EYELASH VIPERS, although small, pack a potent venom and are a serious threat because of their arboreal habits and highly effective cryptic coloration. They move and coil themselves among a tree's leaves and branches. Some species of palm vipers have the habit of coiling their tails around a branch and hanging down, then turning their body in the air so that it is parallel to the ground, their head in a position to strike at a passing animal. Therefore, pushing through vegetation or clearing a path with a machete can be dangerous pursuits. The JUMP-ING VIPER (Plate 15), although possessing a weaker venom than many other vipers, is particularly scary and dreaded by local people: When threatened, these snakes sometimes jump nearly a meter (2 or 3 ft) into the air, and as they jump, they bite. TROPICAL RATTLESNAKES are usually more aggressive than North American rattlers, and their venom, stronger and faster-acting. For some reason, they do not always rattle when approached. If threatened, a Tropical Rattler will coil, raise its head high and, if necessary, attack.

Based on the frequency with which they are depicted on art and artifacts recovered at Mayan ruin sites, several viper species (especially the Fer-de-lance and Tropical Rattler) plainly were very important to the ancient Mayans.

Coral Snakes. These small, pretty snakes are rarely seen by people because of their secretive habits. Reports are that they are usually quite docile and seldom go out of their way to bite people. However, if threatened they give a scary defensive display: "the body is flattened and erratically snapped back and forth…the head… is swung from side to side with the mouth open, and any object that is contacted is bitten…the tail is coiled, elevated, and waved about" (H. Greene & R. Seib 1983). Their venom is very powerful and coral snakes have killed a good many incautious people.

Boas. Boa personalities appear to vary, but some are notoriously bad-tempered and aggressive. A BOA CONSTRICTOR may hiss loudly at people, draw its head back with its mouth open in a threat posture, and bite. They have large sharp teeth that can cause deep puncture wounds. Therefore, even though boas present no real threat to most people, keeping a respectful distance is advised.

Status

None of the vipers or coral snakes of Belize and Guatemala is considered threatened by people (for once, we can say that it's the other way around!). BOA CON-STRICTORS may be threatened in some regions of the Yucatán by habitat destruction and by capture for the pet trade; otherwise these boas seem to do well living near people and are still common in many parts of Belize and Guatemala, as well as in the rest of the American tropics. Several other boa species, particularly some island endemics, are endangered; all boas (and pythons) are CITES Appendix II listed.

Profiles

Coral Snake, *Micrurus diastema*, Plate 14b
Boa Constrictor, *Boa constrictor*, Plate 14c
Tropical Rattlesnake, *Crotalus durissus*, Plate 14d
Fer-de-lance, *Bothrops asper*, Plate 15a
Eyelash Viper, *Bothriechis schlegelii*, Plate 15b
Jumping Viper, *Atropoides nummifer*, Plate 15c
Rainforest Hognosed Pit-viper, *Porthidium nasutum*, Plate 15d

5. Geckos

Geckos are most interesting organisms because, of their own volition, they have become "house lizards" – probably the only self-domesticated reptile. The family,

Gekkonidae, is spread throughout tropical and sub-tropical areas the world over, 750 species strong. In many regions, geckos have invaded houses and buildings, becoming ubiquitous adornments of walls and ceilings. Ignored by residents, they move around dwellings chiefly at night, munching insects. To first-time visitors from northern climes, however, the way these harmless lizards always seem to position themselves on ceilings directly above one's sleeping area can be a bit disconcerting. Eight species occur in Belize and/or northern Guatemala.

Geckos are fairly small lizards, usually gray or brown, with large eyes. They have thin, soft skin covered usually with small, granular scales, often producing a slightly lumpy appearance, and big toes with well developed claws that allow them to cling to vertical surfaces and even upside-down on ceilings. The way geckos manage these feats has engendered over the years a fair amount of scientific detective work. Various forces have been implicated in explaining the gecko's anti-gravity performance, from the ability of their claws to dig into tiny irregularities on man-made surfaces, to their large toes acting as suction cups, to an adhesive quality of friction. The real explanation appears to lie in the series of miniscule hair-like structures on the bottom of the toes, which provide attachment to walls and ceilings by something akin to surface tension – the same property that allows some insects to walk on water.

Adult geckos mostly report in at only 5 to 10 cm (2 to 4 in) in length, tail excluded; tails can double the length. Because lizard tails frequently break off and regenerate (see p. 104), their length varies tremendously; gecko tails are particularly fragile. Lizards, therefore, are properly measured from the tip of their snouts to their *vent*, the urogenital opening on their bellies, usually located somewhere near to where their rear legs join their bodies. The geckos' 5 to 10 cm length, therefore, is their range of "SVLs," or snout–vent lengths.

Natural History

Ecology and Behavior

Although most lizards are active during the day and inactive at night, nearly all gecko species are nocturnal. In natural settings, they are primarily ground dwellers, but, as their behavior in buildings suggests, they are also excellent climbers. Geckos feed on arthropods, chiefly insects. In fact, it is their ravenous appetite for cockroaches and other insect undesirables that renders them welcome house guests in many parts of the world. Perhaps the only "negative" associated with house geckos is that, unlike the great majority of lizards, which keep quiet, geckos at night are avid little chirpers and squeakers. They communicate with each other with loud calls – surprisingly loud for such small animals. Various species sound different; the word *gecko* approximates the sound of calls from some African and Asian species.

Geckos are *sit-and-wait* predators; instead of wasting energy actively searching for prey that is usually highly alert and able to flee, they sit still for long periods, waiting for unsuspecting insects to venture a bit too near, then lunge, grab, and swallow.

Geckos rely chiefly on their *cryptic coloration* and their ability to flee rapidly for escape from predators, which include snakes during the day and snakes, owls, and bats at night. When cornered, geckos give threat displays; when seized, they give loud calls to distract predators, and bite. Should the gecko be seized by its tail, it breaks off easily, allowing the gecko time to escape, albeit tail-less; tails regenerate rapidly. Some geckos when seized also secrete thick, noxious fluids from their tails, which presumably discourages some predators.

Breeding
Geckos are egg-layers. Mating occurs after a round of courtship, which involves a male displaying to a female by waving his tail around, followed by some mutual nosing and nibbling. Clutches usually contain only a few eggs, but a female may lay several clutches per year. There is no parental care – after eggs are deposited, they and the tiny geckos that hatch from them are on their own.

Lore and Notes
One gecko species is Belize's only *endemic* reptile, found there and nowhere else. This is *Phyllodactylus insularis*, more familiarly known as the ISLAND LEAF-TOED GECKO (or BELIZEAN ATOLL GECKO), a small nocturnal lizard that roams the sandy ground and coconut palms on Half Moon Caye and a few other small offshore islands.

Indigenous peoples in parts of Central America regard some geckos, erroneously, as poisonous, as suggested by the common name given them: "escorpión."

The world's smallest reptile, at 4 cm (1.5 in) long, is a gecko, the CARIBBEAN DWARF GECKO. As reptile biologists like to say, it is shorter than its name.

Status
More than 25 gecko species are listed by conservation organizations as rare, vulnerable to threat, or endangered, but they are almost all restricted to the Old World. The MONITO GECKO, found only on Monito Island, off Puerto Rico, is endangered (USA ESA listed), as is Venezuela's PARAGUANAN GROUND GECKO. None of the geckos of Belize and northern Guatemala is currently threatened.

Profiles
Yucatán Banded Gecko, *Coleonyx elegans*, Plate 16a
Yellowbelly Gecko, *Phyllodactylus tuberculosus*, Plate 16b
Dwarf Gecko, *Sphaerodactylus glaucus*, Plate 16c
Central American Smooth Gecko, *Thecadactylus rapicaudus*, Plate 16d

6. Iguanids

The Iguanidae, a large family of lizards, has an almost exclusively New World distribution. There are more than 700 species, about 21 of which occur in Belize and/or northern Guatemala. Most of the lizards commonly encountered by ecotourists or that are on their viewing wish-lists, are members of this group. It includes the very abundant *anolis* lizards, the colorfully named Jesus Christ lizards, and the spectacular, dinosaur-like GREEN IGUANAS (Plate 17).

The *iguanids* are a rich and varied group of diverse habits and habitats. Many in the family are brightly colored and have adornments such as crests, spines, or throat fans. They range in size from tiny anolis lizards, or *anoles*, only a few centimeters in total length and a few grams in weight, to Green Iguanas, which are up to 2 m (6.5 ft) long. SPINY-TAILED IGUANAS (Plate 17), or Black Iguanas, range up to a meter (3 ft) in length and can weigh up to 1 kg (2 lb). The *basilisks*, or Jesus Christ lizards, likewise range up to 1 m (3 ft) long and can weigh more than 0.5 kg (1 lb). Most of the length in iguanid lizards resides in the long, thin tail; hence the paradoxically low weight for such long animals. The basilisk of

Belize and northern Guatemala, the STRIPED BASILISK (Plate 17), is usually fairly small, only 12 to 15 cm (5 to 6 in) long, minus the tail. *Spiny lizards* are a large group (80 species) of small to moderate-sized iguanids that range from southern Canada to Panama. The ones in Belize and northern Guatemala are usually 5 to 9 cm (2 to 3.5 in) long, excluding the tail. They are quite common in natural areas and also around human habitations. Scales on their backs are often overlapping and pointed, which yields a bristly appearance.

Natural History

Ecology and Behavior

Green Iguana. You won't mistake this animal; it's the large one resembling a dragon sitting in the tree near the river. They are common inhabitants of many Neotropical rainforests, in moist areas at low to middle elevations. Considered semi-arboreal, they spend most of their time in trees, usually along waterways. They don't move much, and when they do it's often in slow-motion. They are herbivores as adults, eating mainly leaves and twigs and, more occasionally, fruit; insects are favorites of youngsters. They are fun to discover, but boring to watch. When threatened, an iguana above a river will drop from its perch into the water, making its escape underwater; they are good swimmers. During their breeding season, males establish and defend mating territories on which live one to 4 females.

Spiny-tailed Iguana. These lizards are sometimes confused with GREEN IGUANA, but they are darker-colored, lack the Green's conspicuous head spines and crest, and are often found in dryer habitats, such as fields, farms, scrubland, dry woodlands, savannahs, and roadsides. Like Greens, they are semi-arboreal, spending considerable time in trees, feeding and basking; when chased on the ground, they often run to a tree and climb to escape. They also burrow into the ground and under rocks. Spiny-tails are territorial, each one defending its shelter and perch sites from all others. They are predominantly vegetarians, eating flowers, fruits, agricultural crops, but also the odd lizard or small mammal. Juvenile Spiny-tails eat insects and, in turn, are preyed upon by a variety of animals, including snakes, hawks, jays, skunks, and raccoons.

Basilisk. Basilisks are medium to large, active lizards commonly found along watercourses in lowland areas. Often they are very abundant – one study in Central America estimated their numbers to be more than 500 per hectare (200 per acre)! They are classified as terrestrial but are also semi-arboreal – possessed of a tendency to climb. They are omnivorous, eating a variety of invertebrate and vertebrate animals (especially hatchling lizards), some flowers, and a good deal of fruit. The name "Jesus Christ lizard" refers to their ability to run over the surface of ponds or streams, really skipping along, for distances up to 20 m (60 ft) or more. They do it in an upright posture, on their rear legs, further inviting the divine comparison. The trick is one of fluid dynamics: some of the force to support the lizard comes from resistance of the water when the large rear feet are slapped onto the surface; the rest of the upward force stems from the compression of the water that occurs as the lizard's feet move slightly downwards into the water (their feet move so rapidly up and down that they are actually pulled from below the surface before the water can close over them). Juveniles are better at water-running than are adults, which, when too heavy to be supported on the surface, escape predation by diving in and swimming underwater.

Anole. Anoles are small, often arboreal lizards. About 10 species are represented in Belize and northern Guatemala. Several are frequently encountered, but others, such as ones that live in the high canopy, are rarely seen. Some are ground dwellers, and others spend most of their time on tree trunks perched head toward the ground, visually searching for insect prey. The SILKY ANOLE (Plate 18) is commonly found in grass along roadsides; when startled, they align themselves on a blade of grass to try to appear inconspicuous. Anoles are known especially for their territorial behavior. Males defend territories on which one to three females may live. In some species males with territories spend up to half of each day defending their territories from males seeking to establish new territories. The defender will roam his territory, perhaps 30 sq m (325 sq ft), occasionally giving territorial advertisements – repeatedly displaying his extended throat sac, or *dewlap*, and performing *push-ups*, bobbing his head and body up and down. Trespassers that do not exit the territory are chased and even bitten. Anoles are chiefly sit-and-wait predators on insects and other small invertebrates. Anoles themselves, small and presumably tasty, are frequent prey for many birds (motmots, trogons, and others) and snakes.

Spiny Lizard. Most spiny lizard species in the wild are ground-dwelling or semi-arboreal, but around buildings they are climbers of fences, walls, and rooftops. Sit-and-wait predators, they eat mainly insects, and many also consume some plant materials.

Breeding
Green Iguana. Breeding occurs during the early part of the dry season. These large lizards lay clutches that probably average about 40 eggs. They are laid in burrows that are one to 2 m (3 to 6.5 ft) long, dug by the females. After laying her clutch, the female fills the burrow with dirt, giving the site a final packing down with her nose. It has been said that a female digging her nest burrow probably engages in the most vigorous activity performed by these sluggish reptiles.

Spiny-tailed Iguana. Female Spiny-tails annually lay a single clutch of between 12 and 88 eggs, older females producing more. Eggs are laid in burrows in open, sunny areas. They hatch in the Yucatán region from May through August.

Basilisk. Female Basilisks produce clutches of 2 to 18 eggs several times each year. Smaller, younger females, have fewer eggs per clutch. Eggs hatch in about 3 months. Hatchling lizards, weighing only 2 g, are wholly on their own; in one study, only about 15% of them survived the first few months of life.

Anole. Female Anoles lay small clutches of eggs throughout the year; an individual female may produce eggs every few weeks.

Spiny Lizard. In contrast to most iguanids, some spiny lizard species in Belize and northern Guatemala are *viviparous*, giving birth to live young once per year. Average brood size in one study was 6.

Ecological Interactions
Via interactions between the external environment and their nervous and hormonal systems, many iguanids have the novel ability to change their body color. Such color changes presumably are adaptations that allow them to be more cryptic, to blend into their surroundings, and hence, to be less detectable to and safer from predators. Also, alterations in color through the day may aid in temperature

regulation; lizards must obtain their body heat from the sun, and darker colors absorb more heat. Color changing is accomplished by moving pigment granules within individual skin cells either to a central clump (causing that color to diminish) or spreading them evenly about the cell (enhancing the color). It is now thought that the stimulus to change colors arises with the physiology of the animal rather than with the color of its surroundings. Spiny lizards change color with temperature or light intensity, some being very dark, even black, in the cool early morning and green at midday. Even the large SPINY-TAILED IGUANA has skin that lightens or darkens with changing temperature or activity levels. Anolis lizards also change color. North American species, particularly CAROLINA ANOLES (Carolina Fence Lizards), owing to their color-changing ways, are hawked in pet stores as "chameleons" even though the real chameleons are strictly Old World lizards.

Lore and Notes

The large iguanid lizards (GREEN IGUANA, SPINY-TAILED IGUANA) are not dangerous. They are not poisonous and they will not bite unless given no other choice. They are hunted by local people for invitation to the dinner table. Give them a try if the meat is offered; but it's an acquired taste. Their eggs are also eaten by present-day Mayan groups. Ancient Mayans also consumed these large lizards, as evidenced by the discovery of their remains around Mayan ruins. One theory is that, as Mayan populations increased in size about a thousand years ago, populations of local game animals (birds and mammals) became severely depleted, and so the Mayans turned to larger reptiles for meat.

Over parts of Central America, Spiny-tailed Iguana is thought to have great medicinal power, especially as an anti-impotence agent.

Status

None of the Belize or Guatemalan iguanids is currently considered threatened. Because SPINY-TAILED and GREEN IGUANAS are hunted for meat, they are scarce in some localities. Several iguanids of the Caribbean are endangered, such as the JAMAICAN GROUND IGUANA and VIRGIN ISLANDS (ANEGADA) ROCK IGUANA (both are USA ESA listed; all iguanas – that is, genus *Iguana* – are CITES Appendix II listed). At least three iguana species in the Galápagos Islands are threatened, and two iguanids in the USA are known to be endangered.

Profiles

Green Iguana, *Iguana iguana*, Plate 17a
Striped Basilisk, *Basiliscus vittatus*, Plate 17b
Spiny-tailed Iguana, *Ctenosaura similis*, Plate 17c
Big-headed Anole, *Anolis capito*, Plate 17d
Lesser Scaly Anole, *Anolis uniformis*, Plate 18a
Brown Anole, *Anolis sagrei*, Plate 18b
Silky Anole, *Anolis sericeus*, Plate 18c
Yellow-spotted Spiny Lizard, *Sceloporus chrysostictus*, Plate 18d

7. Skinks and Whiptails

The *skinks* are a large family (Scincidae, with about 1000 species) of small and medium-sized lizards with a worldwide distribution. Over the warmer parts of the globe, they occur just about everywhere. Skinks are easily recognized because they look different from other lizards, being slim-bodied with relatively short limbs, and smooth, shiny, roundish scales that combine to produce a satiny look. Many skinks are in the 5 to 9 cm (2 to 4 in) long range, not including the tail, which can easily double an adult's total length. (Lizards are measured by the distance from the tip of their *snout* to their *vent*, the urogenital opening on their bellies, usually located near to where their rear legs join their bodies – defined as their *snout-vent length*, or SVL; tails vary too much in length to be included as part of any accurate measure.) GROUND SKINKS and SHINY SKINKS (Plate 19), profiled here, are two of only four species that occur in Belize and northern Guatemala. They are common to rainforests at low to moderate elevations, and are especially prevalent in forest edge areas.

Whiptails, Family Tiidae, are a New World group of about 200 species, distributed throughout the Americas. Most are tropical residents, inhabiting most areas below 1500 m (5000 ft) in elevation. Although only six species occur in Belize and northern Guatemala, they are often quite abundant along trails, clearings, beaches, and roads, and, hence, are frequently conspicuous. Whiptails are small to medium-sized, slender lizards, known for their highly alert, active behavior. They have long, slender, whip-like tails, often twice the length of their bodies, which range from 7 to 12 cm (3 to 5 in) in length. Some whiptails are striped, others are striped and spotted.

Natural History

Ecology and Behavior

Skinks. Many skinks are terrestrial lizards, particularly appreciative of moist ground habitats such as sites near streams and springs, or of spending time under wet leaf litter. A few species are arboreal, and some are burrowers. Skink locomotion is surprising: They use their limbs to walk but when the need arises for speed, they locomote mainly by making rapid wriggling movements with their bodies, snake-fashion, with little leg assistance. Through evolutionary change, in fact, some species have lost limbs entirely, all movement currently being handled snake-fashion.

Skinks are day-active lizards, most activity in the tropics being confined to the morning hours; they spend the heat of midday in sheltered, insulated hiding places, such as deep beneath the leaf litter. Some skinks are sit-and-wait foragers, whereas others seek their food actively. They consume many kinds of insects, which they grab, crush with their jaws or beat against the ground, then swallow whole. Predators of skinks are snakes, larger lizards, birds, and mammals such as coati, armadillo, and opposum.

Skinks generally are not seen unless searched for. Most species are quite secretive, spending most of their time hidden under rocks, vegetation, leaf litter or, in the case of the SHINY SKINK, between stone slabs of Mayan ruins.

Whiptails. Whiptails actively search for their food, usually insects, but also small amphibians. Typically they forage by moving slowly along the ground, poking their nose into the leaf litter and under sticks and rocks. Although most are terrestrial, many also climb into lower vegetation to hunt. Whiptails have a characteristic gait, moving jerkily forward while rapidly turning their head from side to side.

Breeding

Skinks. Skinks are either egg-layers or live-bearers. GROUND SKINKS lay eggs, usually small clutches of one to three. They probably breed year round, with individual females laying several clutches annually.

Whiptails. Central American whiptails may breed throughout the year. They are egg-layers, females producing small clutches that average three to five eggs; individuals produce two or more clutches per year.

Ecological Interactions

Whiptails nicely demonstrate the ecological relationship known as *resource partitioning*. One study in Costa Rica, for instance, revealed three closely related whiptail lizards living in the same small region in happy coexistence, all very common and about the same size. At first glance, their mutual survival appears to violate one of the basic tenets of ecological theory, which posits that when two or more species are very similar in their habits, that is, if they occupy the same *niche*, then the best competitor will win out and the others will be driven to rarity and eventual extinction. The whiptails get around this rule by resource partitioning: although they coexist closely, each employs just a slightly different feeding behavior – differing in what, when, or where they eat; and that small amount of difference is sufficient to reduce competition to levels at which all three populations can thrive in the same locality.

Many lizards, including the skinks, whiptails, and geckos, have what many might regard as a self-defeating predator escape mechanism: they detach a large chunk of their bodies, leaving it behind for the predator to attack and eat while they make their escape. The process is known as *tail autotomy* – "self removal." Owing to some special anatomical features of the tail vertebrae, the tail is only tenuously attached to the rest of the body; when the animal is grasped forcefully by its tail, the tail breaks off easily. The shed tail then wriggles vigorously for awhile, diverting a predator's attention for the instant it takes the skink or whiptail to find shelter. A new tail grows quickly to replace the lost one.

Is autotomy successful as a lifesaving tactic? Most evolutionary biologists would argue that, of course it works, otherwise it could not have evolved to be part of lizards' present-day defensive strategy. But we have hard evidence, too. For instance, some snakes that have been caught and dissected have been found to have in their stomachs nothing but skinks – not whole bodies, just tails! Also, a very common finding when a field biologist surveys any population of small lizards (catching as many as possible in a given area to count and examine them) is that a hefty percentage, often 50% or more, have regenerating tails; this indicates that tail autotomy is common and successful in preventing predation.

Lore and Notes

Among the whiptails, a number of species exhibit what for vertebrate animals is an odd method of reproduction, one that is difficult for us to imagine. All individuals in these species are female; not a male among them. Yet they breed merrily away, by *parthenogenesis*. Females lay unfertilized eggs, which all develop as females that, barring mutations, are all genetically identical to mom. (Some fish also reproduce this way.) This hardly seems a happy state of affairs; many people would argue that something important is missing from such societies. It is likely that parthenogenetic species arise when individuals of two different but closely related, sexually-reproducing, "parent" species mate and, instead of having hybrid young that are sterile (a usual result, as when horses and donkeys mate to produce sterile mules), have young whose eggs can produce viable females.

Status

Skinks and whiptails of the Yucatán region, including Belize and northern Guatemala, as far as is known, are secure; none is presently considered threatened. As is the case for many reptiles and amphibians, however, many species have not been sufficiently monitored to ascertain the true health of populations. Many skinks of Australia and New Zealand regularly make lists of vulnerable and threatened animals and several Caribbean skinks and whiptails are endangered. In the USA, Florida's SAND SKINK (USA ESA listed) and the ORANGE-THROATED WHIPTAIL are considered vulnerable or threatened species.

Profiles

Ground Skink, *Sphenomorphus cherriei*, Plate 19a
Shiny Skink, *Mabuya brachypoda*, Plate 19b
Central American Whiptail, *Ameiva festiva*, Plate 19c
Barred Whiptail, *Ameiva undulata*, Plate 19d
Cozumel Whiptail, *Cnemidophorus cozumela*, Plate 19e

Environmental Close-up 2
Poisons and Potions in Snakes and Frogs

Even in the absence of extensive survey data, I feel safe in saying that the majority of people find reptiles and amphibians fascinating – either fascinating-interesting or fascinating-repulsive. In large measure, the great human feeling for these creatures, and their frequently evil reputations, is associated with the venoms and other poisons possessed by some of them. The thought that these relatively small animals with tiny, primitive brains can harm, even kill a person, unnerves us. Usually the more we know about something, the less we are afraid of it. In that vein, let's take a look at some of these animal poisons and the creatures that have them. Only recently have scientists, using sophisticated chemical analyses, isolated some of these substances, for instance in Neotropical amphibians, and determined their actual effects. (A main source for much of the information below was F. H. Pough *et al.* 1996.)

Amphibians

Many amphibians produce or accumulate chemical compounds in their skins that are defensive in nature: the presence of the chemicals discourages predators from eating the frog or salamander. Some of the compounds contain deadly poisons, while others simply produce unpleasant or irritating sensations in the mouth of the potential predator. Many of the poisonous substances found in frogs and salamanders were new to science and now bear the names of the animals in which they were discovered: *leptodactyline* was discovered in frogs of the genus *Leptodactylus* (p. 71), *physalaemin* was discovered in frogs of the genus *Physalaemus* (p. 71), and *bufotoxin* was discovered in toads, genus *Bufo* (p. 69).

The most famous of the toxic amphibians, which were relatively little-known to science until recently, are a family of spectacularly colored little ground and tree frogs known as *poison-dart frogs*. The family, Dendrobatidae, is comprised of about 115 species that are confined to tropical and sub-tropical Central America and northern South America (none is found as far north as Belize and the Petén). Usually quite small, most being less than 5 cm (2 in) long and many about half that, these frogs take on some brilliant hues. Some are shiny black overall with bright red, orange, green, or blue markings, while others are bright red, yellow or green. Not only are these amphibians easy to spot because they are colorful, most make little effort at concealment, being active during the day on low plants and on the ground. Plainly, they rely for safety on their skin toxins. Even large ants and large spiders avoid poison-dart frogs: In experiments in which ants or spiders that normally eat small frogs were presented in cages with either rainfrogs (p. 70) or poison-dart frogs, they attacked and consumed the rainfrogs, but attacked and rejected the poison-darts. Not all poison-dart frogs avoid predation. Some are taken by snakes immune to their poisons and some have been observed to be eaten by spiders, which avoid the skin by puncturing the body and sucking out the innards.

More than 200 toxic chemicals and compounds have been found in these small frogs. Researchers recently discovered that, in at least some of the poison-dart frogs, the poisons accumulate in the frogs' skin from their diet – the frogs eat ants and other small invertebrates that contain toxins known as *alkaloids*. Although chemists are only now isolating and naming the toxins, people have long known of the poisonous wallop packed by these forest creatures. The common name of the group comes from the practice by several indigenous South American peoples of using the poisons on their blow-gun darts, that is, as hunting tools. For instance, the Choco Indians of Colombia make use of a particularly poisonous yellow frog whose scientific name, *Phyllobates terribilis*, tells the story. They rub their darts on a frog's back – holding the frog carefully with leaves to avoid skin contact – transferring poison to the darts. The active ingredient here is *batrachotoxin*, 200 mg of which is considered a lethal human dose – and each frog has up to 10 times that amount in its skin! The poison, which can enter a body through a cut or kill if consumed, affects nerves and muscles, causing paralysis and, eventually, cessation of breathing. Fortunately for the people who use the poison to paralyze and kill animals they hunt, the heat of cooking breaks the poisons down into nontoxic substances.

Reptiles

Among the reptiles, snakes probably have the most interesting and elaborate mechanisms to hunt their prey and to deter their own predation. *Venoms*, produced by snakes and injected into prey animals or potential predators when the snakes bite, contain powerful mixtures of substances that can cause, among other effects, massive tissue destruction, paralysis, and even death. Venoms, generally defined as substances produced that have a role in subduing prey (thus, a frog's toxic skin secretion is not a venom), are usually manufactured in glands at the base of a snake's tooth. Compounds that can be found in various venoms include enzymes and other substances: *proteinases* (or *proteolytic* enzymes), which break down tissue proteins; *hyaluronidase*, which acts on tissues to speed the spread of venom; *phospholipases*, which break up cell membranes; *phosphatases*, which attack molecules involved with providing energy to an animal, and various *polypeptides* that block the transmission of the electrical signals between nerves and muscles. Blocking these signals in people or other mammals can quickly lead to death because the diaphragm, a muscle layer between chest cavity and abdomen whose correct functioning and movement is crucial for breathing, becomes paralyzed.

You might think that the function of a snake's venom is to immobilize and kill its prey. Well, that's right, but might there be other functions as well? The answer is yes, and the clue to another major function became evident when researchers isolated the proteinases and other enzymes in venoms that break down a prey animal's tissues. Breaking down tissue is the very definition of digestion. The venom injected into a prey animal actually starts digesting the beast before it is swallowed, and continues to speed digestion after swallowing. Snakes generally take relatively large prey – some routinely consume items that are a third of their own body weight. Capturing and killing such large prey would be much more dangerous without fast-acting venoms to immobilize the prey. But another problem snakes apparently overcome with their venom is how to digest such large items (which are swallowed whole) sufficiently fast to avoid excessive rotting and bacterial growth in their stomachs (which might sicken a snake or kill it). The digestive enzymes in venom are injected by fangs below a prey animal's skin – underneath, for instance, fur, feathers, or scales – and so can immediately begin digestion.

Various types of snakes generally are thought to have venoms that act in different ways. The coral snake family, Elapidae (p. 94), has venoms that produce mainly *neurotoxic* symptoms, such as paralysis and respiratory arrest. The viper family, Viperidae (p. 93), manufactures *hemotoxic* (or hemorrhagic or hemolytic) venoms that produce discoloration at the site of injection and hemorrhage, followed by cardiovascular shock and internal bleeding. But venoms are such complex mixtures of chemical substances that such easy classification-by-venom-type breaks down upon closer scrutiny: coral snake venom may also lead to internal bleeding and cardiovascular shock, and viper venom may produce paralysis and respiratory arrest. As pointed out recently by one snake biologist, many venoms appear to produce both neurotoxic and hemotoxic symptoms and, in any event, much of what we know about these effects comes from assessing snake-bitten humans; much more poorly known is how venoms act on snakes' natural prey (H. W. Greene 1997).

Chapter 7

BIRDS

- *Introduction*
- *Features of Tropical Birds*
- *Seeing Birds in Belize and Guatemala*
- *Family Profiles*
- *Environmental Close-up 3*
  Coffee Crops and Conservation

Introduction

Most of the vertebrate animals one sees on a visit to just about anywhere at or above the water's surface are birds, and Central America is no exception. Regardless of how the rest of a trip's wildlife-viewing progresses – how fortunate one is to observe mammals or reptiles or amphibians – birds will be seen frequently and in large numbers. The reasons for this pattern are that birds are, as opposed to those other terrestrial vertebrates, most often active during the day, visually conspicuous and, to put it nicely, usually far from quiet as they pursue their daily activities. But why are birds so much more conspicuous than other vertebrates? The answer lies in the essential nature of birds: they fly. The ability to fly is, so far, nature's premier anti-predator escape mechanism. Animals that can fly well are relatively less predation prone than those which cannot, and so they can be both reasonably conspicuous in their behavior and also reasonably certain of daily survival. Birds can fly quickly from dangerous situations, and, if you will, remain above the fray. Most flightless land vertebrates, tied to moving in or over the ground or on plants, are easy prey unless they are quiet, concealed, and careful or, alternatively, very large or fierce; many smaller ones, in fact, have evolved special defense mechanisms, such as poisons or nocturnal behavior.

A fringe benefit of birds being the most frequently encountered kind of vertebrate wildlife is that, for an ecotraveller's intents and purposes, birds are innocuous. Typically, the worst that can happen from any encounter is a soiled shirt. Contrast that with too-close, potentially dangerous meetings with certain reptiles (venomous snakes!), amphibians (frogs and salamanders with toxic skin secretions), and mammals (bears or big cats). Moreover, birds do not always depart with all due haste after being spotted, as is the wont of most other types of vertebrates. Again, their ability to fly and thus easily evade our grasp, permits many birds, when confronted with people, to behave leisurely and go about their business (albeit keeping one eye at all times on the strange-looking bipeds), allowing us extensive time to watch them. Not only are birds among the safest animals to observe and the most easily discovered and watched, but they are among the most beautiful. Experiences with Belize and Guatemala birds will almost certainly provide some of any trip's finest, most memorable naturalistic moments. A visitor who stumbles across a tree filled with a squawking flock of feeding parrots, for instance, is in for a stunning tropical treat.

General Characteristics of Birds

Birds are vertebrates that can fly. They began evolving from reptiles during the Jurassic Period of the Mesozoic Era, perhaps 150 million years ago, and saw explosive development of new species occur during the last 50 million years or so. The development of flight is the key factor behind birds' evolution, their historical spread throughout the globe, and their current ecological success and arguable dominant position among the world's land animals. Flight, as mentioned above, is a fantastic predator evasion technique, it permits birds to move over long distances in search of particular foods or habitats, and its development enabled vertebrates to explore and exploit an entirely new and vast theater of operations – the atmosphere.

At first glance, birds appear to be highly variable beasts, ranging in size and form from 135 kg (300 lb) ostriches to 4 kg (10 lb) eagles to 3 g (a tenth of an ounce) hummingbirds. Actually, however, when compared with other types of vertebrates, birds are remarkably standardized physically. The reason is that, whereas mammals or reptiles can be quite diverse in form and still function as mammals or reptiles (think how different in form are lizards, snakes, and turtles), if birds are going to fly, they more or less must look like birds, and have the forms and physiologies that birds have. The most important traits for flying are (1) feathers, which are unique to birds; (2) powerful wings, which are modified upper limbs; (3) hollow bones; (4) warm-bloodedness; and (5) efficient respiratory and circulatory systems. These characteristics combine to produce animals with two overarching traits – high power and low weight, which are the twin dictates that make for successful feathered flying machines. (The flying mammals, bats, also have these two traits.)

Classification of Birds

Bird classification is one of those areas of science that continually undergoes revision. Currently about 9000 separate species are recognized. They are divided into 28 to 30 orders, depending on whose classification scheme one follows, perhaps 170 families, and about 2040 genera. For purposes here, we can divide birds into *passerines* and *nonpasserines*. Passerine birds (Order Passeriformes) are the perching birds, with feet specialized to grasp and to perch on tree branches. They are mostly the small land birds with which we are most familiar – blackbirds, robins, wrens, finches, sparrows, etc. – and the group includes more than 50% of all bird species. The remainder of the birds – seabirds and shorebirds, ducks and geese, hawks and owls, parrots and woodpeckers, and a host of others – are divided among the other 20+ orders.

Features of Tropical Birds

The first thing to know about tropical birds is that they are exceedingly varied and diverse. There are many more species of birds in the tropics than in temperate or arctic regions. For instance, fewer than 700 bird species occur in North America north of Mexico, but about 3300 species occur in the Neotropics (Central and South America), most of those in the tropical regions. Tiny Belize is home to about 550 species, and northern Guatemala has at least 500. Many families of birds, such as the toucans, motmots, manakins, and cotingas, are *endemic* to the Neotropics – they occur nowhere else on Earth.

Many tropical birds rely for food on insects or seeds, but it is fruit-eating, or *frugivory*, that really distinguishes birds in the tropics. Frugivory has reached its zenith among tropical species, and the relationships between the birds that eat fruit and the plants that produce it exert powerful effects on the biology of both (see p. 170).

The mating systems of tropical birds range from typical, familiar *monogamy*, a male and a female pairing and cooperating to raise a brood of young, to *polygamy*, in which a single member of one sex mates with multiple members of the other, to the so-called *promiscuity* of manakins, some hummingbirds and others, in which males of the species gather in groups called *leks* to display and advertise for mates. Females attracted to the leks choose males to mate with and then depart to nest and raise their young themselves. The social systems of birds in the tropics are also quite variable. Many are *territorial*, aggressively defending parcels of real estate from other members of their species (*conspecifics*), typically during the breeding season, although some seem to exhibit year-round territoriality. Often it is a mated pair that keeps a territory, but in some species (some of the cotingas, jays, wrens, tanagers, and woodpeckers), small family groups stay together throughout the year, even engaging in *cooperative breeding* in which all members of the group assist with a single nest. A number of species, such as the oropendolas, stay in small colonial associations, and build their nests together in the same tree. Tropical birds often participate in *mixed-species foraging flocks*, spending nonbreeding periods travelling around a large territory or semi-nomadically in the company of many other species – searching, for example, for trees bearing ripe fruit. Some of these flocks contain primarily *insectivorous* birds, others primarily *granivores* (seedeaters), and still others typically follow swarms of army ants, feasting on the insects and other small animals that bolt from cover at the approach of the predatory ants.

Breeding seasons in the tropics tend to be longer than in other regions. The weather is more conducive to breeding for longer periods. Also, unlike many temperate zone birds, those in the tropics need not hurry through breeding efforts because, being resident all year, they do not face migration deadlines. Breeding in the tropics is closely tied to wet and dry seasons. Many Central American birds breed from April through August or September, timed to coincide with the greatest abundance of food for their offspring. April is usually when the months-long dry season ends, and spring showers bring heavy concentrations of insect life and ripening of fruit.

One notable aspect of bird breeding in the tropics that has long puzzled biologists is that clutches are usually small, most species typically laying two eggs per nest. Birds that breed in temperate zone areas usually have clutches of three to five eggs. Possible explanations are that (1) small broods attract fewer predators;

(2) because such a high percentage of nests in the tropics are destroyed by predators it is not worth putting too much energy and effort into any one nest; and (3) with more hours of daylight in northern areas, temperate zone birds have more time each day to gather food for larger numbers of growing nestlings.

Last, tropical birds include the most gorgeously attired birds, those with bright, flashy colors and vivid plumage patterns, with some of Central America's parrots, toucans, trogons, and tanagers, among others, claiming top honors. Why so many tropical birds possess highly colored bodies remains an area of ornithological debate.

Seeing Birds in Belize and Guatemala

Selected for illustration in the color plates are 211 species that are among the region's most frequently seen birds. The best way to spot these birds is to follow three easy steps:

1   Look for them at the correct time. Birds can be seen at any time of day, but they are often most active, and vocalize most frequently, during early morning and late afternoon, and so can be best detected and seen during these times.
2   Be quiet as you walk along trails or roads, and stop periodically to look around carefully. Not all birds are noisy, and some, even brightly colored ones, can be quite inconspicuous when they are directly above you, in a forest canopy. Trogons, for instance, beautiful medium-sized birds with green backs and bright red or yellow bellies, are notoriously difficult to see among branches and leaves.
3   BRING BINOCULARS on your trip. You would be surprised at the number of people who visit tropical areas with the purpose of viewing wildlife and don't bother to bring binoculars. They need not be an expensive pair, but binoculars are essential to bird viewing.

A surprise to many people during their first trip to a tropical rainforest is that hordes of birds are not immediately seen or heard upon entering a trail. During large portions of the day, in fact, the forest is mainly quiet, with few birds noticeably active. Birds are often present, but many are inconspicuous – small brownish birds near to the ground, and greenish, brownish, or grayish birds in the canopy. A frequent, at first discombobulating experience is that you will be walking along a trail, seeing few birds, and then, suddenly, a mixed foraging flock with up to 20 or more species swooshes into view, filling the trees around you at all levels – some hopping along the ground, some moving through the brush, some clinging to tree trunks, others in the canopy – more birds than you can easily count or identify – and then, just as suddenly, the flock is gone, moved on in its meandering path through the forest (see p. 166).

Most visitors to Belize spend at least a bit of time on the coastal islands, or cayes, and these are good places to spot seabirds and other kinds as well. It would be a shame to leave Central America without seeing at least some of its spectacular forest birds, such as macaws, toucans, trogons, and tanagers. If you have trouble locating such birds, ask people – tourguides, resort employees, park personnel – about good places to see them. One of the best times for birding in the region is late March and early April: broadleaf trees lose their leaves, migrant birds pass by on their trips northwards, and lakes and lagoons recede (such as at Crooked Tree Wildlife Sanctuary), concentrating wildlife.

Family Profiles

1. Seabirds

Along the Belizean coast, as along coasts almost everywhere, *seabirds*, many of them conspicuously large and abundant, reign as the dominant vertebrate animals of the land, air, and water's surface. Many seabirds in Belize commonly seen by visitors from northern temperate areas are very similar to species found back home, but some are members of groups restricted to the tropics and subtropics and, hence, should be of ecotraveller interest. A few of these birds will be seen by almost everyone. As a group seabirds are incredibly successful animals, present often at breeding and roosting colonies in enormous numbers. Their success surely is owing to their incredibly rich food resources – the fish and invertebrate animals (crabs, mollusks, insects, jellyfish) produced in the sea and on beaches and mudflats. Further, people's exploitation of marine and coastal areas has, in many cases, enhanced rather than hurt seabird populations. Many gull species, for instance, which make good use of human-altered landscapes and human activities, such as garbage dumps, agricultural fields, and fishing boats, are almost certainly more numerous today than at any time in the past.

Three birds treated here (Plate 20) are members of the Order Pelecaniformes: The BROWN BOOBY of the Family Sulidae (nine species worldwide, with two occuring in Belize), MAGNIFICENT FRIGATEBIRD of the Family Fregatidae (five species with mainly tropical distributions; only one occurs in Belize), and BROWN PELICAN, Family Pelecanidae (eight species worldwide, with two occurring in Belize). Two more species, the LAUGHING GULL and ROYAL TERN (Plate 20), are in Family Laridae (more than 80 species worldwide, with relatively few occuring in tropical climes), which is allied with the shorebirds, and is part of another order. *Boobies*, of which the Brown Booby is one of the most common, are large seabirds known for their sprawling, densely packed breeding colonies, spots of bright body coloring, and for plunging into the ocean from heights to pursue fish. They have tapered bodies, long, pointed wings, long tails, long, pointed bills, and, often, brightly colored feet. The Magnificent Frigatebird is a very large soaring bird, mostly black, with huge, pointed wings that span up to 2 m (6 ft) or more, and a long, forked, tail. Males have red throat pouches that they inflate, balloonlike, during courtship displays. Brown Pelicans are large heavy-bodied seabirds, and, owing to their big, saggy throat pouches, are perhaps among the most recognizable of birds. They have long wings, long necks, large heads, and long bills from which hang the flexible, fish-catching, pouches. Laughing Gulls are mid-sized seabirds with long, narrow wings and heavy bills; they are largely white and grayish, but adults' heads are black, or *hooded*, during the breeding season. Similarly, Royal Terns are mid-sized white and gray seabirds. They are also hooded during breeding, and they have long orange bills.

Natural History

Ecology and Behavior

Most seabirds feed mainly on fish, and have developed a variety of ways to catch them. Boobies, which also eat squid, plunge-dive from the air or surface dive to catch fish underwater. Sometimes they dive quite deeply, and they often take fish unawares from below, as they rise toward the surface. Frigatebirds feed on the wing, sometimes soaring effortlessly for hours at a time. They swoop low to catch flying fish that leap from the water (the fish leap when they are pursued by larger, predatory fish or dolphins), and also to pluck squid and jellyfish from the wave-tops. Although their lives are tied to the sea, frigatebirds cannot swim and rarely, if ever, enter the water voluntarily; with their very long, narrow wings, they have difficulty lifting off from the water. To rest, they land on remote islands, itself a problematic act in high winds. *Pelicans* eat fish almost exclusively. BROWN PELI-CANS, in addition to feeding as they swim along the water's surface, are the only pelicans that also plunge from the air, sometimes from considerable altitude, to dive for meals. While underwater, the throat sac is used as a net to scoop up fish (to 30 cm, 1 ft, long). Captured fish are quickly swallowed because the water in the sac with the fish usually weighs enough to prohibit the bird's lifting off again from the water. Pelicans, ungainly looking, nonetheless are excellent flyers, and can use air updrafts to soar high above in circles for hours. These are large, handsome birds; a flight of them, passing low and slow overhead on a beach, in perfect V-formation or in a single line, is a tremendous sight. Of special note is that adult pelicans, so far as it is known, are largely silent. *Gulls* and *terns* are highly gregarious seabirds – they feed, roost, and breed in groups. They feed on fish and other sealife that they snatch from shallow water, and on crabs and other invertebrates they find on mudflats and beaches. Also, they are not above visiting garbage dumps or following fishing boats to grab whatever goodies that fall or are thrown overboard.

Breeding

Seabirds usually breed in large colonies on small islands (where there are no mammal predators) or in isolated mainland areas that are relatively free of predators. Some breed on slopes, cliffs, or ledges (boobies), some in trees or on tops of shrubs (pelicans, frigatebirds), and some on the bare ground (gulls and terns, and also, if trees are unavailable, pelicans and frigatebirds). Most species are monogamous, mated males and females sharing in nest-building, incubation, and feeding young. In some groups, such as the pelicans, the male gathers sticks and stones for a nest, but the female carries out the actual construction (perhaps the male supervises). High year-to-year fidelity to mates, to breeding islands, and to particular nest sites is common. BROWN BOOBY females lay one or two eggs, which are incubated for about 45 days. Usually only a single chick survives to fledging age (one chick often pecks the other to death). MAGNIFICENT FRIGATEBIRDS lay a single egg that is incubated for about 55 days; male and female spell each other during incubation, taking shifts of up to 12 days. Young remain in and around the nest, dependent on the parents, for up to 6 months. BROWN PELICANS lay two or three eggs, which are incubated for 30 to 37 days; usually only one young is raised successfully. Gulls and terns typically lay one to three eggs, and both sexes incubate for 21 to 35 days; young fledge after 28 to 35 days at the nest. In most seabirds, young are fed when they push their bills into their parents' throats, in effect forcing the parents to regurgitate food stored in their *crops* – enlargements of the top portion of the esophagous. Seabirds reach sexual maturity slowly (in 2 to 5 years; 7+ years in frigatebirds) and live long lives (pelicans in the wild probably average 15 to 25 years, and some live 50+ years in zoos; frigatebirds and boobies live 20+ years in the wild).

Ecological Interactions

Frigatebirds are large, beautiful birds and are a treat to watch as they glide silently along coastal areas, but they have some highly questionable habits – in fact, patterns of behavior that among humans would be indictable offenses. Frigate-birds practice *kleptoparasitism*: they "parasitize" other seabirds, such as boobies, frequently chasing them in the air until they drop recently caught fish. The frigatebird then steals the fish, catching it in mid-air as it falls. Frigatebirds are also common predators on baby sea turtles (p. 86), scooping them from beaches as the reptiles make their post-hatching dashes to the ocean.

Lore and Notes

Boobies are sometimes called *gannets*, particularly by Europeans. The term *booby* apparently arose because the nesting and roosting birds seemed so bold and fear-less toward people, which was considered stupid. Actually, the fact that these birds bred on isolated islands and cliffs meant that they had few natural pred-ators, so had never developed, or had lost, fear responses to large mammals, such as people. Frigatebirds are also known as *man-of-war* birds, both names referring to warships, and to the birds' kleptoparasitism; they also steal nesting materials from other birds, furthering the image of avian pirates.

Status

The BROWN PELICAN is listed by USA ESA as endangered over parts of its range, but the species is still common in many areas. None of the other seabirds that occur along Belize's shores is considered threatened or endangered, and the ones profiled here are quite abundant. Some seabirds in other parts of the world are highly endangered. For example, for both the DALMATIAN PELICAN of Eurasia (CITES Appendix I listed) and the SPOT-BILLED PELICAN of India and Sri Lanka, only a few thousand breeding pairs remain. Also, ABBOT'S BOOBY (CITES Appen-dix I and USA ESA listed) is now limited to a single, small breeding population on the Indian Ocean's Christmas Island. The RED-FOOTED BOOBY breeds in Belize only on Half Moon Caye, a protected national site, where the booby colony is sev-eral thousand pairs strong. The boobies there are mostly white whereas the same species is usually brown or grayish in most other parts of the Caribbean.

Profiles

Brown Booby, *Sula leucogaster*, Plate 20a
Magnificent Frigatebird, *Fregata magnificens*, Plate 20b
Laughing Gull, *Larus atricilla*, Plate 20c
Royal Tern, *Sterna maxima*, Plate 20d
Brown Pelican, *Pelecanus occidentalis*, Plate 20e

2. Waterbirds

Included under the vague heading of *waterbirds* is a group of medium to large birds, all with distinctive, identifying bills, that make their livings in freshwater and coastal saltwater habitats. Visitors to Central American marsh or river areas are highly likely to encounter some of these species. Some, such as *cormorants* and *anhingas*, swim to catch fish, whereas others, *storks* and *ibises*, wade about in marshes, shallow water areas, and fields in search of a variety of foods. Cor-morants (Family Phalacrocoracidae) inhabit coasts and inland waterways over much of the world; there are 28 species, but only two occur in Belize and Guatemala. Anhingas (Family Anhingidae), closely related to cormorants, are fresh- and brackish-water birds mostly of tropical and sub-tropical regions; there are four species, one of which occurs in the covered region. Storks (Family Cicon-idae) are wading birds that occur worldwide in tropical and temperate regions;

there are 17 species, but only three occur in the New World, two of them in Belize and Guatemala. The 33 species of ibises and *spoonbills* (Family Threskiornthidae), also wading birds, are globally distributed; two ibises and a single spoonbill species occur in Belize and Guatemala.

Cormorants are medium-sized birds, usually black, with short legs, long tails, and longish bills with hooked tips. ANHINGAS (Plate 21) are similar to cormorants, blackish with long tails, but they have very long, thin necks and their bills are longer and end with sharp points. Storks are huge, ungainly looking – and so unmistakable – wading birds. Those in Belize and Guatemala are white with black or black-and-red heads; the head and neck area are featherless. Storks have very large, heavy bills. The JABIRU (Plate 21) is one of the largest of the world's storks, standing up to 1.5 m (5 ft) tall. Ibises and spoonbills resemble storks, but are smaller and have shorter necks. Most ibises are white, brown, or blackish, and in many, the head is bare of feathers. Ibis bills are long, thin, and curved downwards. Spoonbills are named for their straight, flat, spoon-shaped bills. The ROSEATE SPOONBILL (Plate 22), large, pink, and spoon-billed, must be one of the easiest birds on Earth to identify. In most of these waterbirds, the sexes are similar in plumage, but males are often a bit larger.

Natural History

Ecology and Behavior

Diving from the surface of lakes, rivers, lagoons, and coastal saltwater areas, OLIVACEOUS CORMORANTS (Plate 21) and ANHINGAS pursue fish underwater. Cormorants, which also take crustaceans, catch food in their bills; Anhingas, which also take young turtles, baby crocodiles, and snakes, use their sharply pointed bills to spear fish. Cormorants are social birds, foraging, roosting, and nesting in groups, but Anhingas are somewhat territorial, defending resting and feeding areas from other birds. Both anhingas and cormorants are known for standing on logs, trees, or other surfaces after diving and spreading their wings, presumably to dry them (they may also be warming their bodies in the sun following dives into cold water.) Storks feed by walking slowly through fields and marshy areas, looking for suitable prey, essentially anything that moves: small rodents, young birds, frogs, reptiles, fish, earthworms, mollusks, crustaceans, and insects. Food is grabbed with the tip of the bill and swallowed quickly. Storks can be found either alone or, if food is plentiful in an area, in groups. These birds are excellent flyers, often soaring high overhead for hours during hot afternoons. They are known to fly 80 km (50 miles) or more daily between roosting or nesting sites and feeding areas. Ibises are gregarious birds that insert their long bills into soft mud of marshes and shore areas and poke about for food – insects, snails, crabs, frogs, tadpoles. Apparently they feed by touch, not vision: whatever the bill contacts that feels like food is grabbed and swallowed. Spoonbills, likewise, are gregarious birds that feed in marsh or shallow-water habitats. They lower their bills into the water and sweep them around, stirring up the mud, then grab fish, frogs, snails, or crustaceans that touch their bills. Spoonbills are soaring birds, but ibises, although good flyers, do not soar.

Breeding

Most of these waterbirds breed in colonies of various sizes, although ANHINGAS sometimes breed alone, and JABIRUS usually do so. Mating is monogamous, with both male and female contributing to nest-building, incubation, and feeding offspring. Cormorants, which begin breeding when they are 3 or 4 years old, construct stick nests in trees or on ledges. Two to 4 eggs are incubated for about 4 weeks, and young fledge 5 to 8 weeks after hatching. Anhingas breed at 2 or 3 years of age. They have stick and leaf nests in trees or bushes. Three to five eggs are incubated for 4 to 5 weeks, and chicks fledge 5 weeks after hatching. Storks first breed when they are 3 to 5 years old. They build platforms of sticks in trees or on ledges. Sometimes they add new material each year, which results eventually in enormous nests. Two to four eggs are incubated for 4 to 5 weeks and chicks remain in the nest for 50 to 90 days after hatching. Ibises and spoonbills also make stick nests, mixed with green vegetation, in trees. Two to four eggs are incubated for about 3 weeks, and young fledge 6 to 7 weeks after hatching.

Lore and Notes

ANHINGAS are also known as *darters*, the name owing to the way the birds swiftly thrust their necks forward to spear fish. Because of their long necks, they are also called *snakebirds*. Cormorants were so common and conspicuous to early European mariners that they were given the name *Corvus marinus*, or "sea raven." (The word cormorant derives from the term corvus marinus.) Cormorants have been used for centuries in Japan, China, and Central Europe as fishing birds. A ring is placed around a cormorant's neck so that it cannot swallow its catch, and then, leashed or free, it is released into the water. When the bird returns or is reeled in, a fish is usually clenched in its bill.

Storks in folklore are generally assigned very positive personality traits. Europe's WHITE STORK, which nests on the roofs of buildings in villages, is highly respected by people and, because of its annual returns, is considered a symbol of continuity and reliability. Some Europeans believe that good luck will befall a family after a stork builds a nest on their house. A common legend, repeated by Aristotle, is that storks have such strong family ties that younger storks will feed older family members during their declining years.

Status

Most of the waterbirds considered here are widely or locally common in Belize and some range into northern Guatemala as well. JABIRUS are fairly rare in Belize and the species is considered threatened in Central America generally (CITES Appendix I listed even though not considered highly endangered); its likeness serves in several countries (most notably in Belize and Costa Rica) as a conservation symbol. WOOD STORKS, although still somewhat common in Belize and Guatemala, are threatened in other parts of their range, and are listed as endangered by USA ESA (there are small populations of Wood Storks in southeastern USA). Storks are declining because they are hunted for food over parts of their ranges (for instance, Jabiru are considered game birds in the Amazon Basin) and because nesting sites are disturbed by people. People still eat Wood Stork meat in parts of Belize and Guatemala. ROSEATE SPOONBILLS were almost eliminated in the southeastern USA in the late 19th and early 20th centuries when they were hunted to turn their pink wings into feather fans.

Profiles

Olivaceous Cormorant, *Phalacrocorax brasilianus*, Plate 21a
Anhinga, *Anhinga anhinga*, Plate 21b
Jabiru Stork, *Jabiru mycteria*, Plate 21c
Wood Stork, *Mycteria americana*, Plate 21d

Roseate Spoonbill, *Ajaia ajaja*, Plate 22a
White Ibis, *Eudocimus albus*, Plate 22b

3. Herons and Egrets

Herons and *egrets* are beautiful medium to large-sized wading birds that enjoy broad distributions throughout temperate and tropical regions of both hemispheres. Herons and egrets, together with the similar but quite elusive wading birds called *bitterns*, constitute the heron family, Ardeidae, which includes about 58 species. Sixteen species occur in Belize and/or northern Guatemala, most of which also breed there. Herons frequent all sorts of aquatic habitats: along rivers and streams, in marshes and swamps, and along lake and ocean shorelines. They are, in general, highly successful birds, and some of them are among the region's most conspicuous and commonly seen water birds. Why some in the family are called herons and some egrets, well, it's a mystery; but egrets are usually all white and tend to have longer *nuptial plumes* – special, long feathers – than the darker-colored herons.

Most herons and egrets are easy to identify. They are the tallish birds standing upright and still in shallow water or along the shore, staring intently into the water. They have slender bodies, long necks (often coiled when perched or still, producing a short-necked, hunched appearance), long, pointed bills, and long legs with long toes. In Central America they range in height from 0.3 to 1.3 m (1 to 4 ft). Most are attired in soft shades of gray, brown, blue, or green, and black and white. From afar most are not striking, but close-up, many are exquisitely marked with small colored patches of facial skin or broad areas of spots or streaks; the *tiger herons*, in particular, have strongly barred or streaked plumages. Some species during breeding seasons have a few very long feathers (nuptial plumes) trailing down their bodies from the head, neck, back, or chest. The sexes are generally alike in size and plumage, or nearly so. One exception to this general form is the BOAT-BILLED HERON (Plate 22), which, as its name implies, has an especially wide and thick bill.

Natural History

Ecology and Behavior

Herons and egrets walk about slowly and stealthily in shallow water and sometimes on land, searching for their prey, mostly small vertebrates, including fish, frogs, salamanders, and the occasional turtle, and small invertebrates like crabs. On land, they take mostly insects, but also other invertebrates and vertebrates such as small rodents. CATTLE EGRETS (Plate 23) have made a specialty of following grazing cattle and other large mammals, walking along and grabbing insects and small vertebrates that are flushed from their hiding places by the moving cattle. A typical pasture scene is a flock of these egrets intermixed with a cattle herd, with several of the white birds perched atop the unconcerned mammals. Many herons spend most of their foraging time as *sit-and-wait* predators, standing motionless in or adjacent to the water, waiting in ambush for unsuspecting prey to wander within striking distance. Then, in a flash, they shoot their long, pointed bills into the water to grab or spear the prey. They take anything edible that will fit into their mouths and down their throats, and then some. One particular heron that I recall grabbed a huge frog in its bill and spent the better part of a half hour trying to swallow it. Typically, the larger herons are easier to spot because they tend to stay out in the open while foraging and resting; smaller herons, easier prey for predators, tend to stay more hidden in dense vegetation in marshy areas. Most herons are day-active, but many of the subgroup known as *night herons* forage at least partly nocturnally. Also, the BOAT-BILLED HERON searches at night for prey along waterways. This bird's large bill may help it to catch prey in lower light levels, in which precise spearing with a finer bill would be difficult. Most herons are social birds, roosting and breeding in colonies, but some, such as the tiger herons, are predominantly solitary.

Breeding

Many herons breed in monogamous pairs within breeding colonies of various sizes. A few species are solitary nesters and some are less monogamous than others. Herons are known for their elaborate courtship displays and ceremonies, which continue through pair formation and nest-building. Generally nests are constructed by the female of a pair out of sticks procured and presented to her by the male. Nests are placed in trees or reeds, or on the ground. Both sexes incubate the three to seven eggs for 16 to 30 days, and both feed the kids for 35 to 50 days before the young can leave the nest and feed themselves. The young are *altricial* – born helpless; they are raised on regurgitated food from the parents. Many herons breed during wet seasons, but some do so all year.

Ecological interactions

Herons and egrets often lay more eggs than the number of chicks they can feed. For instance, many lay three eggs when there is sufficient food around to feed only two chicks. This is contrary to our usual view of nature, which we regard as having adjusted animal behavior through evolution so that behaviors are finely tuned to avoid waste. Here's what biologists suspect goes on: Females lay eggs one or two days apart, and start incubating before they finish laying all their eggs. The result is that chicks therefore hatch at intervals of one or more days and the chicks in a single nest are different ages, and so different sizes. In years of food shortage, the smallest chick dies because it cannot compete for food from the parents against its larger siblings, and also because, it has been discovered, the larger siblings attack it (behavior called *siblicide*). The habit of laying more eggs than can be reared as chicks may be an insurance game evolved by the birds to maximize their number of young: in many years, true, they waste the energy they invested to produce a third egg with little future, but in years of high food availability, all three chicks survive and prosper. Apparently, the chance to produce three surviving offspring is worth the risk of investing in three eggs even though the future of one is very uncertain.

The CATTLE EGRET is a common, successful, medium-sized white heron that, until recently, was confined to the Old World, where it made its living following herds of large mammals. What is so interesting about this species is that, whereas many of the animals that have recently crossed oceans and spread rapidly into new continents have done so as a result of people's intentional or unintentional machinations, these egrets did it themselves. Apparently the first ones to reach the New World were from Africa. Perhaps blown off-course by a storm, they first landed in northern South America in about 1877. Finding the New World to its liking, during the next decades the species spread far and wide, finding abundant food where tropical forests were cleared for cattle grazing. Cattle Egrets have now colonized much of northern South America, Central America, all the major Caribbean islands, and eastern and central North America, as far as the southern USA. We must assume that they have Chicago and New York City in their sights.

Lore and Notes

The story of the *phoenix*, a bird that dies or is burned but then rises again from the ashes, is one of the best-known bird myths of the Western world. One version, from about 2800 years ago, has it that one phoenix arrives from Arabia every 500 years. When it is old, it builds a nest of spices in which to die. From the remains a young phoenix emerges, which carries its parent's bones to the sun. Some authorities believe that the phoenix was a heron; in fact, the Egyptian hieroglyph for the phoenix appears to be a heron or egret.

Status

Some of Central America's herons and egrets are fairly rare, but they are not considered threatened species because they are more abundant in other parts of their ranges, outside the country. Two species of concern, that some authorities consider near-threatened, are the FASCIATED TIGER-HERON, which ranges from Costa Rica to Argentina and Brazil, and the colorful but secretive CHESTNUT-BELLIED HERON (or AGAMI HERON), with a distribution from southern Mexico to northern South America.

Profiles

Boat-billed Heron, *Cochlearius cochlearius*, Plate 22c
Bare-throated Tiger Heron, *Tigrisoma mexicanum*, Plate 22d
Little Blue Heron, *Egretta caerulea*, Plate 23a
Tricolored Heron, *Egretta tricolor*, Plate 23b
Snowy Egret, *Egretta thula*, Plate 23c
Cattle Egret, *Bubulcus ibis*, Plate 23d
Great Egret, *Casmerodius albus*, Plate 23e
Green Heron, *Butorides striatus*, Plate 24a
Yellow-crowned Night-Heron, *Nycticorax violaceus*, Plate 24b

4. Marsh and Stream Birds

Marsh and *stream birds* are small and medium-sized birds adapted to walk, feed, and breed in swamps, marshes, wet fields, and along streams. The chief characteristics permitting this lifestyle usually are long legs and very long toes that distribute the birds' weight, allowing them to walk among marsh plants and across floating vegetation without sinking. *Jacanas* (zha-SAH-nahs or hah-SAH-nahs; Family Jacanidae) are small and medium-sized birds with amazingly long toes and toenails that stalk about tropical marshes throughout the world. There are eight species; only one occurs in Belize and northern Guatemala, but it is found almost everywhere there is floating aquatic vegetation. The *rails* (Family Rallidae) are a large group of often secretive small and medium-sized swamp and dense vegetation birds, about 130 species strong. They inhabit most parts of the world save for polar regions. Twelve species occur in Belize and northern Guatemala, including rails, wood-rails, crakes, coots, and gallinules.

The NORTHERN JACANA (Plate 25), with incredibly long toes, has a drab brown and black body but a bright yellow bill and forehead. When their wings are spread during flight or displays, jacanas expose large patches of bright yellow, rendering them instantly conspicuous. Female jacanas are larger than males. GRAY-NECKED WOOD-RAILS (Plate 24) are brown, olive, and gray, with long necks, legs, and toes. Although most rails, like the wood-rail, are colored to blend into their suroundings, the PURPLE GALLINULE (Plate 24) is a strikingly colored bird, purple and green, with a reddish bill. Rails generally have short wings and tails. Males are often larger than females. RUDDY CRAKES (Plate 24) are small reddish-brown birds with gray heads.

Natural History

Ecology and Behavior
Jacanas are abundant birds of marshes, ponds, lakeshores, and wet fields. They walk along, often on top of lily pads and other floating plants, picking up insects, snails, small frogs and fish, and some vegetable matter such as seeds. Likewise, rails stalk through marshes, swamps, grassy shores, and wet grasslands, foraging for insects, small fish and frogs, bird eggs and chicks, and berries. Typically they move with a head-bobbing walk. Many rails are highly secretive, being heard but rarely seen moving about in marshes. PURPLE GALLINULES, brightly colored and less shy than many other rails, are usually easy to see as they forage singly or in small family groups. RUDDY CRAKES are very common birds found in marshes and other freshwater habitats, including roadside ditches and rain puddles. They eat mainly seeds, aquatic vegetation, and insects.

Breeding
NORTHERN JACANAS are one of three or four jacana species that employ *polyandrous* breeding, the rarest type of mating system among birds. In a breeding season, a female mates with several males, and the males then carry out most of the breeding chores. Males each defend small territories from other males, but each female has a larger territory that encompasses two to four male territories. Males build nests of floating, compacted aquatic vegetation. Following mating, the female lays three or four eggs in the nest, after which the male incubates them for 21 to 24 days and then cares for (leads and protects) the chicks. Young are dependent on the father for up to 3 to 4 months. Meanwhile, the female has mated with other males on her territory and provided each with a clutch of eggs to attend. (Predation on jacana nests is very common, PURPLE GALLINULES often being the culprits.) In rails such as wood-rails and gallinules, the sexes contribute more equally to the breeding effort. Male and female build well hidden nests in dense vegetation, sometimes a meter or two (several feet) off the ground, or floating nests of aquatic plants. Both sexes incubate the three to five or more eggs for 2.5 to 4 weeks and care for the young for 7 or 8 weeks until they are independent. RUDDY CRAKES build round grass nests; females lay three or four eggs per clutch.

Lore and Notes
Jacanas of Africa and Australia are also known as *lily-trotters* and *lotus-birds*. The word *jacana* is from a native Brazilian name for the bird.

Status
Although some of the region's rails are locally rare, most are not considered threatened or endangered because they are more numerous in other parts of their ranges. One species, the CLAPPER RAIL, which occurs in coastal saltmarshes of the southeastern USA, northern Mexico, the Yucatán, and northern Belize, is threatened in some areas (USA ESA listed). All four species profiled here are locally common or abundant. Throughout the world, a number of rail species are threatened or already endangered; several rare species of the New World are Venezuela's

PLAIN-FLANKED RAIL, Colombia's BOGOTA RAIL, and Brazil's RUFOUS-FACED CRAKE.

Profiles

Ruddy Crake, *Laterallus ruber*, Plate 24c
Gray-necked Wood-rail, *Aramides cajanea*, Plate 24d
Purple Gallinule, *Porphyrula martinica*, Plate 24e
Northern Jacana, *Jacana spinosa*, Plate 25a

5. Ducks

Members of the Family Anatidae are universally recognized as *ducks*. They are water-associated birds that are distributed throughout the world in habitats ranging from open seas to high mountain lakes. The family includes about 150 species of ducks, geese, and swans. Although an abundant, diverse group throughout temperate regions of the globe, ducks, or *waterfowl*, (*wildfowl* to the British), have only limited representation in most tropical areas. About 14 species occur in Belize and northern Guatemala, and only a fraction of those are local breeders; the remainder are migratory, only passing through or wintering in Central America. Only two ducks (Plate 25) are profiled here, the MUSCOVY DUCK, a bird of streams and ponds in lowland forests, and the BLACK-BELLIED WHISTLING DUCK, which frequents freshwater marshes, ponds, and lagoons. Also duck-like in appearance and habits is the SUNGREBE (Plate 25), a fairly common stream and river bird, a member of a separate, very small family of birds, the Heliornithidae. The Sungrebe is the only member of this family in the New World, enjoying a broad distribution from Mexico southwards to Brazil.

Ducks vary quite a bit in size and coloring, but all share the same major traits: duck bills, webbed toes, short tails, and long, slim necks. Plumage color and patterning vary, but there is a preponderance within the group of grays and browns, and black and white, although many species have at least small patches of bright color. In some species male and female look alike, but in others there is a high degree of difference between the sexes. The MUSCOVY DUCK is large, chunky in appearance, mostly black with white patches on its wings, and with bare patches of skin on its face; males are much larger than females. BLACK-BELLIED WHISTLING DUCKS are slender, medium-sized ducks, rust-colored with black bellies, and red bills and feet. The SUNGREBE is a brownish-olive and white bird with bold black and white stripes on its head and neck. It is distinguishable from the duck family by its long tail, short legs, and long, straight, non-duckish bill.

Natural History

Ecology and Behavior

Ducks are birds of wetlands, spending most of their time in or near the water. Many of the typical ducks are divided into *divers* and *dabblers*. Diving ducks plunge underwater for their food; dabblers, such as mallards, pintail, widgeon, and teal take food from the surface of the water or, maximally, put their heads down into the water to reach food at shallow depths. When they reach underwater, their rear quarters tip up into the air, providing the typical response of frustrated birdwatchers when queried about what they see on the water through their binoculars – "nothing but duck buttes." Ducks mostly eat aquatic plants or small fish, but some forage on land for seeds and other plant materials. The MUSCOVY DUCK, for instance, in addition to eating small fish and seeds of aquatic plants, feeds on terrestrial foods including crops such as corn, and insects. BLACK-BELLIED WHISTLING DUCKS eat seeds, leaves, and small invertebrates such as insects. This duck spends relatively little time in the water; it grazes on land, usually at night. During the day it roosts on riverbanks, or in trees adjacent to the water. The SUNGREBE, a highly specialized water bird and a nimble swimmer, can vary its profile in the water, riding high or partly submerged, only its head poking out from the water. Pairs establish territories along sections of stream or riverbank. They are consumers of insects, spiders, and small vertebrates such as frogs and lizards.

Breeding

Ducks place their nests on the ground in thick vegetation or in holes. Typically nests are lined with downy feathers that the female plucks from her own breast. In many of the ducks, females perform most of the breeding duties, including incubation of the two to 16 eggs and shepherding and protecting the ducklings. Some of these birds, however, particularly among the geese and swans, have lifelong marriages during which male and female share equally in breeding duties. The young are *precocial*, able to run, swim and feed themselves soon after they hatch. Both MUSCOVY and BLACK-BELLIED WHISTLING DUCKS most often nest in cavities. Females, after mating, incubate eggs and raise ducklings themselves. SUNGREBES are monogamous, both sexes helping to build the stick nest that is hidden in thick vegetation, and to incubate the two to four eggs.

Lore and Notes

Ducks, geese and swans have been objects of people's attention since ancient times, sometimes as cultural symbol (for instance, as a Chinese symbol of happiness), but chiefly as a food source. These birds typically have tasty flesh, are fairly large and so economical to hunt, and usually easier and less dangerous to catch than many other animals, particularly large mammals. Owing to their frequent use as food, several wild ducks and geese have been domesticated for thousands of years; Central America's native MUSCOVY DUCK, in fact, in its domesticated form is a common farmyard inhabitant in several parts of the world. Wild ducks also adjust well to the proximity of people, to the point of taking food from them – a practice that surviving artworks show has been occurring for at least 2000 years. Hunting ducks and geese for sport is also a long-practiced tradition. As a consequence of these long interactions between ducks and people, and the research on these animals stimulated by their use in agriculture and sport, a large amount of scientific information has been collected on the group; many of the ducks and geese are among the most well known of birds. The close association between ducks and people has even led to a long contractual agreement between certain individual ducks and the Walt Disney Company.

Status

None of the Belize and Guatemala ducks, neither the local breeders nor winter migrants, is currently threatened or endangered. A few species are now fairly rare, but they are more abundant in other parts of their ranges. The MUSCOVY DUCK, because of hunting pressures and habitat destruction, has had its populations much reduced throughout its broad range in the Neotropics, so that it is now common only in restricted areas. When these ducks were more common, local hunters would tether a female to a tree and then kill males that came a-courting; with this method, up to 50 males could be lured to their deaths in a single day.

Honduras regulates this species and the BLACK-BELLIED WHISTLING DUCK for conservation purposes (CITES Appendix III listed).

Profiles

Sungrebe, *Heliornis fulica*, Plate 25b
Black-bellied Whistling Duck, *Dendrocygna autumnalis*, Plate 25c
Muscovy Duck, *Cairina moschata*, Plate 25d

6. Shorebirds

Spotting *shorebirds* is usually a priority only for visitors to the Neotropics who are rabid birdwatchers. The reason for the usual lack of interest is that shorebirds are often very common, plain-looking brown birds that most people are familiar with from their beaches back home. Still, it is always a treat watching shorebirds in their tropical wintering areas as they forage in meadows, along streams, on mud-flats, and especially on the coasts, as they run along beaches, paralleling the surf, picking up food. Some of the small ones, such as SANDERLINGS (Plate 26), as one biologist wrote, resemble amusing wind-up toys as they spend hours running up and down the beach, chasing, and then being chased by, the outgoing and incoming surf (J. Strauch 1983). Shorebirds are often conspicuous and let them-selves be watched, as long as the watchers maintain some distance. When in large flying groups, shorebirds such as *sandpipers* provide some of the most compelling sights in bird-dom, as their flocks rise from sandbar or mudflat to fly low and fast over the surf, wheeling quickly and tightly in the air as if they were a single organ-ism, or as if each individual's nervous system was joined to the others'.

Shorebirds are traditionally placed along with the gulls in the avian order Charadriiformes. They are global in distribution and considered to be hugely suc-cessful birds – the primary reason being that the sandy beaches and mudflats on which they forage usually teem with their food. There are several families, four of which require mention. The sandpipers, Family Scolopacidae, are a worldwide group of approximately 85 species. About 25 species occur in Belize and northern Guatemala, some being quite abundant during much of the year, yet they are all migrants – none breeds in the country. *Plovers* (Family Charadriidae), with about 60 species, likewise have a worldwide distribution. Seven species occur in the cov-ered region, one of which breeds there; the others are migrants from breeding sites to the north. The broadly distributed Family Recurvirostridae consists of about seven species of *stilts* and *avocets*, two of which occur in Belize and north-ern Guatemala. Last, the family Aramidae contains a single species, the LIMPKIN (Plate 26), which occurs from the southeastern USA to Argentina.

All shorebirds, regardless of size, have a characteristic "look." They are usually drably colored birds (especially during the nonbreeding months), darker above, lighter below, with long, thin legs for wading through wet meadows, mud, sand, or surf. Depending on feeding habits, bill length varies from short to very long. Most of the Central American sandpipers range from 15 to 48 cm (6 to 19 in) long. They are generally slender birds with straight or curved bills of various lengths. Plovers, 15 to 30 cm (6 to 12 in) long, are small to medium-sized, thick-necked shorebirds with short tails and straight, relatively thick bills. They are mostly shades of gray and brown but some have bold color patterns such as a broad white or dark band on the head or chest. The BLACK-NECKED STILT (Plate 25), is a striking, mid-sized black and white bird with very long red legs and long, fine bill. Limpkins are largish brown birds with white spots and long, thin bills. The sexes look alike, or nearly so, in most of the shorebirds.

Natural History

Ecology and Behavior

Shorebirds typically are open-country birds, associated with coastlines and inland wetlands, grasslands, and pastures. Sandpipers and plovers are excellent flyers but they spend a lot of time on the ground, foraging and resting; when chased, they often seem to prefer running to flying away. Sandpipers pick their food up off the ground or use their bills to probe for it in mud or sand – they take insects and other small invertebrates, particularly crustaceans. They will also snatch bugs from the air as they walk and from the water's surface as they wade or swim. Larger, more land-dwelling shorebirds may also eat small reptiles and amphibians, and even small rodents; some of the plovers also eat seeds. Usually in small groups, BLACK-NECKED STILTS wade about in shallow fresh- and saltwater, using their bills to probe the mud for small insects, snails, and crustaceans. LIMPKINS inhabit marshes, ponds, swamps, and riversides; they eat mainly snails.

Many shorebirds, especially among the sandpipers, establish winter *feeding territories* along stretches of beach; they use the area for feeding for a few hours or for the day, defending it aggressively from other members of their species. Many of the sandpipers and plovers are gregarious birds, often seen in large groups, especially when they are travelling. Several species make long migrations over large expanses of open ocean, a good example being the AMERICAN GOLDEN-PLOVER, a migrant seen occasionally in Belize and Guatemala, which flies in autumn over the Western Atlantic, sometimes apparently nonstop from breeding grounds in northern Canada to Central and South America.

Breeding

Shorebirds breed in a variety of ways. Many species breed in monogamous pairs that defend small breeding territories. Others, however practice *polyandry*, the least common type of mating system among vertebrate animals, in which some females have more than one mate in a single breeding season. This type of breeding is exemplified by the SPOTTED SANDPIPER (Plate 26). In this species, the normal sex roles of breeding birds are reversed: the female establishes a territory on a lakeshore that she defends against other females. More than one male settles within the territory, either at the same time or sequentially during a breeding season. After mating, the female lays a clutch of eggs for each male. The males incubate their clutches and care for the young. Females may help care for some of the broods of young provided that there are no more unmated males to try to attract to the territory.

Most shorebird nests are simply small depressions in the ground in which eggs are placed; some of these *scrapes* are lined with shells, pebbles, grass, or leaves. Sandpipers lay two to four eggs per clutch, which are incubated, depending on species, by the male alone, the female alone, or by both parents, for 18 to 21 days. Plovers lay two to four eggs, which are incubated by both sexes for 24 to 28 days. BLACK-NECKED STILTS breed in small colonies. The scrape, into which four eggs are placed, is lined with vegetation. Both sexes incubate for 22 to 26 days. LIMPKINS build a nest of leaves and twigs, into which the female lays four to six eggs; both sexes incubate. Shorebird young are *precocial*, that is, soon after they hatch they are mobile, able to run from predators, and can feed themselves.

Parents usually stay with the young to guard them at least until they can fly, perhaps 3 to 5 weeks after hatching.

Lore and Notes

The manner in which flocks of thousands of birds, particularly shorebirds, fly in such closely regimented order, executing abrupt maneuvers with precise coordination, such as when all individuals turn together in a split second in the same direction, has puzzled biologists and engendered some research. The questions include: What is the stimulus for the flock to turn – is it one individual within the flock, a "leader," from which all the others take their "orders" and follow into turns? Or is it some stimulus from outside the flock that all members respond to in the same way? And how are the turns coordinated? Everything from "thought transference" to electromagnetic communication among the flock members has been advanced as an explanation. After studying films of DUNLIN, a North American sandpiper, flying and turning in large flocks, one biologist has suggested that the method birds within these flocks use to coordinate their turns is similar to how the people in a chorusline know the precise moment to raise their legs in sequence or how "the wave" in a sports stadium is coordinated. That is, one bird, perhaps one that has detected some danger, like a predatory falcon, starts a turn, and the other birds, seeing the start of the flock's turning, can then anticipate when it is their turn to make the turn – the result being a quick wave of turning coursing through the flock.

Limpkins apparently acquired their name because they walk as if with a limp.

Status

None of the plovers, sandpipers, or stilts of Belize or Guatemala is threatened or endangered, although one related shorebird, the DOUBLE-STRIPED THICK-KNEE, which occurs over the Pacific lowlands of Guatemala, is regulated by the country for conservation purposes (CITES Appendix III listed). A major goal for conservation of shorebirds is the need to preserve critical migratory stopover points – pieces of habitat, sometimes fairly small, that hundreds of thousands of shorebirds settle into mid-way during their long migrations to stock up on food. For instance, one famous few acres of coastal mudflats near Grays Harbor, Washington State, USA, is a popular, traditional stopover point for millions of shorebirds. Its destruction or use for any other activity could cause huge losses to the birds' populations. Fortunately, it has been deemed essential, and protected as part of a national wildlife refuge.

Profiles

Black-necked Stilt, *Himantopus mexicanus*, Plate 25e
Spotted Sandpiper, *Actitis macularia*, Plate 26a
Sanderling, *Calidris alba*, Plate 26b
Black-bellied Plover, *Pluvialis squatarola*, Plate 26c
Whimbrel, *Numenius phaeopus*, Plate 26d
Limpkin, *Aramus guarauna*, Plate 26e

7. Curassows, Quail, and Turkey

Large chickenlike birds strutting about the tropical forest floor or, somewhat to the surprise of visitors from temperate quarters, fluttering about in trees and running along high branches, are bound to be members of the *curassow* family. The family, Cracidae, contains not only the *curassows*, but their close relatives the *guans* and entertainingly named *chachalacas*. There are more than 40 species of *cracids*, which are limited in their distributions to warmer regions of the New World, most inhabiting moist forests at low and middle elevations. The curassow family is placed within the avian Order Galliformes, which also includes the *pheasants, quail, bobwhite, partridges*, and *turkeys* (and which, for want of a better term, even professional ornithologists refer to technically as the "chickenlike birds").

Curassows of Belize and Guatemala range in length from about 40 to 91 cm (16 to 36 in) – as large as small turkeys – and weigh up to 4 kg (9 lb). They have long legs and long, heavy toes. Many have conspicuous crests. The colors of their bodies are generally drab – gray, brown, olive, or black and white; some appear glossy in the right light. They typically have small patches of bright coloring such as yellow, red, or orange on parts of their bills, cheeks, or on a hanging throat sac, or *dewlap*. Male GREAT CURASSOWS (Plate 27), for instance, although all black above and white below, have a bright yellow "knob" on the top of their bill. Within the group, males are larger than females; the sexes are generally similar in coloring, except for the curassows, in which females are drabber than males. The OCELLATED TURKEY (Plate 28) is confined in its distribution to the Yucatán region, including northern Belize and northern Guatemala. It is a very large, brightly colored, ground-dwelling bird with a bare-skin blue head. The name arises with the eye-like images ("ocelli") adorning the birds' plumage.

Natural History

Ecology and Behavior

The guans and curassows are birds of the forests, but the chachalacas prefer forest edge areas and even clearings – more open areas, in other words. The guans and chachalacas are mostly arboreal birds, staying high in the treetops as they pursue their diet of fruit, young leaves, and treebuds, and the occasional frog or large insect. For such large birds in trees, they locomote with surprising grace, running quickly and carefully along branches. One's attention is sometimes drawn to them when they jump and flutter upwards from branch to branch until they are sufficiently in the clear to take flight. While guans and chachalacas will occasionally come down to the forest floor to feed on fallen fruit, GREAT CURAS-SOWS are terrestrial birds, more in the tradition of turkeys and pheasants. They stalk about on the forest floor, seeking fruit, seeds, and bugs. Paired off during the breeding season, birds of this family typically are found at other times of the year in small flocks of 10 to 20 individuals. Chachalaca males provide some of the most characteristic background sounds of tropical American forests. In the evening and especially during the early morning, males in groups rhythmically give their very loud calls, described variously as "cha-cha-LAW-ka" or "cha-cha-lac." OCELLATED TURKEYS, usually observed in small groups, are primarily birds of low elevation wet forests and clearings, but they are also found in open, brushy areas. They feed on seeds, berries, nuts, and insects.

Breeding

The curassows, guans, and chachalacas are monogamous breeders, the sexes sharing reproductive duties. Several of the species are known for producing loud whirring sounds with their wings during the breeding season, presumably during courtship displays. Male and female construct a simple, open nest of twigs and leaves, placed in vegetation or in a tree within several meters of the ground. Two to four eggs are incubated for 22 to 34 days. The young leave the nest soon after hatching to hide in the surrounding vegetation, where they are fed by the parents (in contrast to most of the chickenlike birds of the world, which feed themselves after hatching). Several days later, the fledglings can fly short distances. The family group remains together for a time, the male leading the family around the forest. OCELLATED TURKEYS place their seven to 18 eggs in a shallow scrape in a hidden place on the forest floor. The female only incubates for about 26 days. Young are born ready to leave the nest and feed themselves. Turkey nesting generally begins in April.

Ecological Interactions

In Central and South America, the curassows essentially take the ecological position of pheasants, which are only lightly represented in the Neotropics.

Status

A variety of factors converge to assure that the curassows will remain a problem group into the forseeable future. They are chiefly birds of the forests at a time when Neotropical forests are increasingly being cleared. They are desirable game birds, hunted by local people for food. In fact, as soon as new roads penetrate virgin forests in Central and South America, one of the first chores of settlers is to shoot curassows for their dinners. Unfortunately, curassows reproduce slowly, raising only small broods each year. Exacerbating the problem, their nests are often placed low enough in trees and vegetation to make them vulnerable to a variety of predators, including people. In the face of these unrelenting pressures on their populations, curassows are among the birds thought most likely to survive in the future only in protected areas, such as national parks. The HORNED GUAN, restricted to Guatemala and southern Mexico, is considered threatened or already endangered (CITES Appendix I and USA ESA listed), and several guan and curassow species of South America are currently on lists of endangered species. Owing to over-hunting and destruction of their forest habitats, OCELLATED TURKEYS are threatened throughout their range (CITES Appendix III listed by Belize, Guatemala, and Mexico). Protected areas of Belize and northern Guatemala (such as Tikal National Park and parts of Mountain Pine Ridge, where the turkeys are plentiful) are thought to provide the best chances for continued survival of the species.

Profiles

Plain Chachalaca, *Ortalis vetula*, Plate 27a
Crested Guan, *Penelope purpurascens*, Plate 27b
Great Curassow, *Crax rubra*, Plate 27c
Black-throated Bobwhite, *Colinus nigrogularis*, Plate 27d
Ocellated Turkey, *Agriocharis ocellata*, Plate 28a

8. Tinamous

The *tinamous* are an interesting group of secretive, chickenlike birds that are occasionally seen walking along forest trails. They apparently represent an ancient group of birds, most closely related not to chickens or pheasants but to the rheas of South America – large, flightless birds in the ostrich mold. The family, Tinamidae, with about 45 species, is confined in its distribution to the Neotropics, from Mexico to southern Chile and Argentina. Five species occur in Central America, Belize and northern Guatemala having four of them. They inhabit a variety of environments, including grasslands and thickets, but most commonly they are forest birds.

Tinamous are medium-sized birds, 23 to 45 cm (9 to 18 in) long, chunky-bodied, with fairly long necks, small heads, and slender bills. They have short legs and very short tails. The back part of a tinamou's body sometimes appears higher than it should be, a consequence of a dense concentration of rump feathers. Tinamous are attired in understated, protective colors – browns, grays, and olives; often the plumage is marked with dark spots or bars. Male and female look alike, with females being a little larger than males.

Natural History

Ecology and Behavior
Except for the GREAT TINAMOU (Plate 28), which sleeps in trees, tinamous are among the most terrestrial of birds, foraging, sleeping, and breeding on the ground. They are very poor flyers, doing so only when highly alarmed by a predator or surprised, and then only for short distances. They are better at running along the ground, the mode of locomotion ecologists call *cursorial*. The tinamou diet consists chiefly of fruit and seeds, but they also take insects such as caterpillars, beetles, and ants, and occasionally, small vertebrates such as mice. Some South American species dig to feed on roots and termites. Tinamous avoid being eaten themselves primarily by often staying still, easily blending in with surrounding vegetation, and by walking slowly and cautiously through the forest. If approached closely, tinamous will fly upwards in a burst of loud wing-beating and fly usually less than 50 m (160 ft) to a new hiding spot in the undergrowth, often colliding with trees and branches as they go. Tinamous are known for their songs, which are loud, pure-tone, melodious whistles, and which are some of the most characteristic sounds of Neotropical forests.

Except during breeding, tinamous lead a solitary existence. They are considered secretive and, with their cryptic colors, elusive. It is common to hear them but not see them, or to see the rear of one, up ahead on the trail, disappearing into the underbrush.

Breeding
The tinamous employ some unusual mating systems, the most intriguing of which is a kind of *group polyandry* (polyandry being a system in which one female mates with several males during a breeding season). One or more females will mate with a male and lay clutches of eggs in the same nest, for the male to incubate and care for. The females then move on to repeat the process with other males of their choosing. Apparently in all tinamous the male incubates the eggs and leads and defends the young. Nests can hardly be called that; they are simply slight indentations in the ground, hidden in a thicket or at the base of a tree. Up to 12 eggs, deposited by one or more females, are placed in the nest. The male incubates for 19 or 20 days; when the eggs hatch, he leads the troop of tiny tinamous about, defending them from predators. From hatching, the young feed themselves.

Lore and Notes
Outside of protected areas, all tinamous are hunted extensively for food. Tinamou meat is considered tender and tasty, albeit a bit strange-looking; it has been described variously as greenish and transparent.

Status

The tinamous' camouflage coloring and secretive behavior must serve the birds well because, although hunted for food, tinamous presently are able to maintain healthy populations. None of the Central American species is considered vulnerable or threatened. Some of the tinamous are known to be able to move easily from old, uncut forest to *secondary*, recently cut, forest, demonstrating an impressive adaptability that should allow these birds to thrive even amid major habitat alterations such as deforestation. To be sure, some of the tinamous are in trouble, including especially the critically endangered SOLITARY TINAMOU of Argentina and Brazil (CITES Appendix I and USA ESA listed), the MAGDALENA (RED-LEGGED) TINAMOU of Colombia and KALINOWSKI'S TINAMOU of Peru. Unfortunately, dependable information on many other tinamous is scarce, so it is very difficult to to know their statuses accurately.

Profiles

Great Tinamou, *Tinamus major*, Plate 28b
Slaty-breasted Tinamou, *Crypturellus boucardi*, Plate 28c
Little Tinamou, *Crypturellus soui*, Plate 28d

9. Vultures

Birds at the very pinnacle of their profession, eating dead animals, *vultures* are highly conspicuous and among the most frequently seen birds of rural Central America. That they feast on rotting flesh does not reduce the majesty of these large, soaring birds as they circle for hours high over field and forest. The family of American vultures, Cathartidae, has only seven species, all confined to the New World; several are abundant animals but one is close to extinction. They range from southern Canada to Tierra del Fuego, with several of the species sporting wide and overlapping distributions. Four species, the KING, BLACK, TURKEY (Plate 29), and LESSER YELLOW-HEADED VULTURES, occur in Belize and Guatemala. The two largest members of the family are known as *condors*, the CALIFORNIA and ANDEAN CONDORS. Vultures are seen often above both open country and forested areas; the BLACK VULTURE, one of the most frequently encountered birds of tropical America, is very common around garbage dumps. Traditional classifications place the New World vulture family within the avian order Falconiformes, with the hawks, eagles, and falcons, but some biologists believe the group is more closely related to the storks.

Central American vultures are large birds, from 60 to 80 cm (24 to 32 in) long, with wing spans to 1.8 m (6 ft). (The Andean Condor has a wing span of 3 m (10 ft)!). Vultures generally are black or brown, with hooked bills and curious, unfeathered heads whose bare skin is richly colored in red, yellow, or orange. Turkey Vultures, in fact, are named for their red heads, which remind people of turkey heads. The King Vulture, the largest in Central America, departs from the standard color scheme, having a white body, black rump and wing feathers, and multi-colored head. Male and female vultures look alike; males are slightly larger than females.

Natural History

Ecology and Behavior

Vultures are carrion eaters of the first order. Most soar during the day in groups, looking for and, in the case of TURKEY VULTURES, sniffing for, food. (Turkey

Vultures can find carcasses in deep forest and also buried carcasses, strongly implicating smell, as opposed to vision, as the method of discovery.) They can move many miles daily in their search for dead animals. KING and BLACK VULTURES, supplementing their taste for carrion, also occasionally kill animals, usually newborn or those otherwise defenseless. Some of the vultures, especially the Black Vulture, also eat fruit. With their super eyesight, fine-tuned sense of smell, and ability to survey each day great expanses of habitat, vultures are, to paraphrase one ornithologist, amazingly good at locating dead animals. No mammal species specializes in carrion to the degree that vultures do, the reason being, most likely, that no mammal could search such large areas each day. That is, no mammal that ate only carrion could find enough food to survive.

King Vultures are usually seen in pairs or solitarily, as are LESSER YELLOW-HEADED VULTURES, but the other species are more social, roosting and foraging in groups of various sizes. Black Vultures, in particular, often congregate in large numbers at feeding places, and it is common to find a flock of them at any village dump. At small to medium-sized carcasses, there is a definite pecking order among the vultures: Black Vultures are dominant to Turkey Vultures, and can chase them away; several Black Vultures can even chase away a King Vulture, which is the bigger bird. However, in an area with plenty of food, all three species may feed together in temporary harmony. When threatened, vultures may regurgitate partially digested carrion, a strong defense against harassment if ever there was one.

Breeding
Vultures are monogamous breeders. Both sexes incubate the one to three eggs, which are placed on the ground in protected places or on the floor of a cave or tree cavity. Eggs are incubated for 32 to 58 days; both sexes feed the young regurgitated carrion for 2 to 5 months until they can fly. Young vultures at the nest site very rarely become food for other animals, and it has been suggested that the odor of the birds and the site, awash as they are in badly decaying animal flesh, keep predators (and everything else) at bay.

Ecological Interactions
Vultures are abundant and important scavengers around Neotropical towns and villages. Usefully, they help clean up garbage; expert observers have said they "perform at least as much of the Sanitation Department's chores as do its human members" (F. G. Stiles & D. H. Janzen 1983). Scavengers, or *detritus* feeders, are important parts of ecosystems, recycling energy and nutrients back into food webs. Although vultures are an integral part of these systems, most detritus is consumed by small arthropods (insects and the like) and such microorganisms as fungi and bacteria.

BLACK and TURKEY VULTURES roost communally, the two species often together. A common observation has been that once an individual finds a food source, other vultures arrive very rapidly to share the carcass. Biologists strongly suspect that the group roosting and feeding behavior of these birds are related, and that the former increases each individual's food-finding efficiency. In other words, a communal roost serves as an *information center* for finding food. Researchers believe that vultures may locate the probable position of the next day's food while soaring high in the late afternoon, before they return to the roost before sunset. In the morning, the ones that detected potential carcasses set out from the roost to locate the food, with others, less successful the previous day, following in the general direction. Thus, on different days, the birds take turns as leaders and followers, and all benefit from the communal roosting association. Recent research suggests that Black Vultures make more use of roosts as information centers than do Turkey Vultures.

Lore and Notes

Being such large and conspicuous birds, and being carrion-eaters associated with death, guaranteed that vultures would figure prominently in the art and culture of most civilizations. Indeed, descriptions and pictoral renderings of vultures are found in the remains of early Iranian, Mesopotamian, and Egyptian civilizations. In some cases, they are thought to be symbols of death. On the other hand, some good was thought to come from vultures; for instance, their bile was considered a top curative agent in ancient Egypt. Vultures were sacred to Mut, the Egyptian goddess of maternity; having them close by was reputed to ease childbirth. Vultures have also played the role of undertaker in past cultures and still do, to this day. In parts of India, Tibet, and Mongolia, dead people are laid out to be disposed of by vultures.

Europeans first arriving in the New World thought the region's vultures evil – "the sloth, the filth, and the voraciousness of these birds, almost exceeds credibility," wrote one impressionable Englishman in the late 1700s. But the native peoples, especially in hot, humid areas where rotting of corpses occurs quickly, generally thought well of these carrion-eaters. Ancient Mayans called the KING VULTURE "Oc," including it frequently in their artworks. Vulture feathers were used in Mayan headdresses. Mayans apparently believed that vultures, when near death, changed into armadillos; the proof being that both were "bald."

The Mayan legend of how the vulture came to be black and bald and to feed on carrion goes like this: in the old days, vultures were actually handsome, white birds with feathered heads, which ate only the finest fresh meat; they had an ideal life. One day, the vulture family, out soaring in the sun, spied a feast laid out on banquet tables in a forest clearing. They swooped down and ate the splendid food. Unfortunately for the vultures, the food had been set out by nobles as an offering to the gods. The nobles schemed to punish the unknown culprits. They set out another feast in the clearing and hid behind trees with their witch doctors. When the vultures returned for another meal, the nobles and witch doctors raced out from the trees and threw magic powder on the birds. The vultures, in their panic to escape the people, flew straight up and got too close to the sun, scorching their heads, causing their feathers to fall out. In the clouds, the magic powder turned their white plumage to black. When they returned to Earth, the Great Spirit ruled that for their thievery, from that day forward, vultures would eat only carrion (A. L. Bowes 1964).

Status

The four Central American vultures are all somewhat common to very common birds; none is threatened. The only New World vulture in dire trouble is the CALIFORNIA CONDOR (CITES Appendix I and USA ESA listed), which for awhile was extinct in the wild. The main causes of their decline in the 20th century were hunting (they were persecuted especially because ranchers believed they ate newborn cattle and other domesticated animals), their ingestion of poisonous lead shot from the carcasses they fed on, and the thinning of their eggshells owing to the accumulation of organochlorine pesticides (DDT) in their bodies. The last eight free-ranging specimens were caught during the mid-1980s in their southern

Californian haunts for use in captive breeding programs. The total captive population is now more than 100 individuals, and several have been released back into the wild in California and Arizona.

Profiles

Turkey Vulture, *Cathartes aura*, Plate 29a
Black Vulture, *Coragyps atratus*, Plate 29b
King Vulture, *Sarcoramphus papa*, Plate 29c

10. Raptors

Raptor is another name for *bird-of-prey*, birds that make their living hunting, killing, and eating other animals, usually other vertebrates. When one hears the term raptor, one usually thinks of soaring *hawks* that swoop to catch rodents, and of speedy, streamlined *falcons* that snatch small birds out of the air. Although these *are* common forms of raptors, the families of these birds are large, the members' behavior, diverse. The two main raptor families are the Accipitridae, containing the *hawks*, *kites* and *eagles*, and the Falconidae, including the *true falcons*, *forest-falcons*, and *caracaras*. The reasons for classifying the two raptor groups separately mainly have to do with differences in skeletal anatomy and hence, suspected differences in evolutionary history. (Owls, nocturnal birds-of-prey, can also be considered raptors.) Raptors are common and conspicuous animals in Belize and Guatemala and, generally, in the Neotropics. Many are birds of open areas, above which they soar during the day, using the currents of heated air that rise from the sun-warmed ground to support and propel them as they search for meals. But raptors are found in all types of habitats, including within woodlands and closed forests.

The *accipitrids* are a worldwide group of about 200 species; they occur everywhere but Antarctica. Belize and northern Guatemala are home to about 30 species, some of them migratory: 16 hawks, eight kites, five eagles and hawk-eagles. *Falconids* likewise are worldwide in their distribution. There are about 60 species, nine occurring in Belize and northern Guatemala. Some falcons have very broad distributions, with the PEREGRINE FALCON found almost everywhere, that is, its distribution is *cosmopolitan*. Peregrines may have the most extensive natural distribution of any bird.

Raptors vary considerably in size and in patterns of their generally subdued color schemes, but all are similar in overall form – we know them when we see them. They are fierce-looking birds with strong feet, hooked, sharp claws, or *talons*, and strong, hooked and pointed bills. Accipitrids vary in size in Belize and northern Guatemala from a 28-cm-long (11 in) hawk to one-meter-long (40 in) eagles. Females are usually larger than males, in some species noticeably so. Most raptors are variations of gray, brown, black, and white, usually with brown or black spots, streaks, or bars on various parts of their bodies. The plumages of these birds are actually quite beautiful when viewed close-up, which, unfortunately, is difficult to do. Males and females are usually alike in color pattern. Juvenile raptors often spend several years in *subadult* plumages that differ in pattern from those of adults. Many falcons can be distinguished from hawks by their long, pointed wings, which allow the rapid, acrobatic flight for which these birds are justifiably famous.

Natural History

Ecology and Behavior

Raptors are meat-eaters. Most hunt and eat live prey. They usually hunt alone, although, when mated, the mate is often close by. Hawks, kites, and eagles take mainly vertebrate animals, including some larger items such as monkeys, sloths, and birds up to the size of small vultures. Prey is snatched with talons first, and then killed and ripped apart with the bill. Some invertebrate prey is also taken. One species, the SNAIL KITE (Plate 31), specializes almost completely on one kind of freshwater marsh snail, which before eating it daintily removes from the shell with its long, pointed bill.

Falcons are best known for their remarkable eyesight and fast, aerial pursuit and capture of flying birds – they are "birdhawks." Thus, the small AMERICAN KESTREL, a telephone wire bird familiar to many people, is a falcon that formerly was known as the Sparrowhawk; the MERLIN, a slightly larger falcon, was known as the Pigeonhawk. Both of these falcons breed in North America, with some populations migrating south to winter in Central and South America. Most people are familiar with stories of PEREGRINE FALCONS diving through the atmosphere (*stooping*, defined as diving vertically from height to gain speed and force) at speeds approaching 320 kph (200 mph) to stun, grab, or knock from the sky an unsuspecting bird. But some falcons eat more rodents than birds, and some even take insects. One species specializes in taking bats on the wing at dawn and dusk. Forest-falcons are just that, falcons of the inner forest. They perch motionless for long periods on tree branches, waiting to ambush prey like birds and lizards. The LAUGHING FALCON (Plate 30) is a bird of open fields and forest edge that specializes in snakes. Laughing Falcons perch until they spot a likely candidate for dinner, then swoop down fast and hit powerfully, grabbing the reptile and immediately biting off the head – a smart move because these falcons even take highly poisonous prey such as coral snakes. They then fly off to a high perch to feast on the headless serpent.

Many raptors are territorial, a solitary individual or a breeding pair defending an area for feeding and, during the breeding season, for reproduction. Displays that advertise a territory and may be used in courtship consist of spectacular aerial twists, loops, and other acrobatic maneuvers. Although many raptors are common birds, typically they exist at relatively low densities, as is the case for all *top predators* (a predator at the pinnacle of the food chain, preyed upon by no animal). That is, there usually is only enough food to support one or two of a species in a given area. For example, a typical density for a small raptor species, perhaps one that feeds on mice and small lizards, is one individual per square kilometer. A large eagle that feeds on monkeys may be spaced so that a usual density is one individual per thousand square kilometers.

Breeding

Hawk and eagle nests are constructed of sticks that both sexes place in a tree or on a rock ledge. Some nests are lined with leaves. The female incubates the one to six eggs (only one or two in the larger species) for 28 to 49 days and gives food to the nestlings. The male frets about and hunts, bringing food to the nest for the female and for her to provide to the nestlings. Both sexes feed the young when they get a bit older; they can fly at 28 to 120 days of age, depending on species size. After fledging, the young remain with the parents for several more weeks or months until they can hunt on their own. Falcon breeding is similar.

Falcons nest in vegetation, in a rock cavity, or on a ledge; some make a stick nest, others apparently make no construction. Incubation is from 25 to 35 days, performed only by the female in most of the falcons, but by both sexes in the caracaras. In most falcons, the male hunts for and feeds the female during the egg-laying, incubation, and early nestling periods. Male and female feed nestlings, which fledge after 25 to 49 days in the nest. The parents continue to feed the youngsters for several weeks after fledging until they are proficient hunters.

Ecological Interactions
The hunting behavior of falcons has over evolutionary time shaped the behavior of their prey animals. Falcons hit perched or flying birds with their talons, stunning the prey and sometimes killing it outright. An individual bird caught unawares has little chance of escaping the rapid, acrobatic falcons. But birds in groups have two defenses. First, each individual in a group benefits because the group, with so many eyes and ears, is more likely to spot a falcon at a distance than is a lone individual, thus providing all in the group opportunities to watch the predator as it approaches and so evade it. This sort of anti-predation advantage may be why some animals stay in groups. Second, some flocks of small birds, such as starlings, which usually fly in loose formations, immediately tighten their formation upon detecting a flying falcon. The effect is to decrease the distance between each bird, so much so that a falcon flying into the group at a fast speed and trying to take an individual risks injuring itself – the "block" of starlings is almost a solid wall of bird. Biologists believe that the flock tightens when a falcon is detected because the behavior reduces the likelihood of an attack.

SNAIL KITES, which have a broad range from the southeastern USA to the middle of South America, and which are fairly common along waterways in parts of southern Mexico, Belize and northern Guatemala, are an endangered species in the USA. There, also called the Everglades Kite, they occur only over small bits of Florida. During the 1960s, owing to destruction and draining of their marsh habitats, the entire Florida population was believed to number no more than 60 individuals. Snail kites are extremely specialized in their feeding; in fact, they may be *monophagic* – eating only one thing: freshwater apple snails. This high degree of specialization is one of the kite's biggest problems, because periodic droughts lead to very low food availability and, therefore, to crashes in the kite population.

Lore and Notes
Large raptors have doubtless always attracted people's attention, respect, and awe. Wherever eagles occur, they are chronicled in the history of civilizations. Both the ancient Greeks and Romans associated eagles with their gods. Early Anglo-Saxons were known to hang an eagle on the gate of any city they conquered. Some North American Indian tribes and also Australian Aboriginal peoples deified large hawks or eagles. Several states have used likenesses of eagles as national symbols, among them Turkey, Austria, Germany, Poland, Russia, and Mexico. Eagles are popular symbols on regal coats of arms and one of their kind, a fierce-looking fish-eater, was chosen as the emblem of the USA (although, as most USA schoolchildren know, Benjamin Franklin would have preferred that symbol to be the Wild Turkey.)

People have had a close relationship with falcons for thousands of years. Falconry, in which captive falcons are trained to hunt and kill game at a person's command, is a very old sport, with evidence of it being practiced in China 4000 years ago and in Iran 3700 years ago. One of the oldest known books on a sport is *The Art of Falconry*, written by the King of Sicily in 1248. Falconry reached its zenith during medieval times in Europe, when a nobleman's falcons were apparently considered among his most valued possessions. The CRESTED CARACARA is depicted on the national emblem of Mexico (caracaras are falcons with distinctively long legs and unfeathered facial skin; several species are distributed throughout most of Mexico and Central America, but none occurs in Belize or northern Guatemala).

Status

Several hawks and falcons are considered to be threatened or endangered in Belize and Guatemala. Most of these raptors are rare but have extensive distributions, often ranging from Mexico to northern or central South America; some are more numerous in other regions. The HARPY EAGLE, perhaps the world's most powerful eagle, due to hunting is rare over most of its range and is CITES Appendix I and USA ESA listed. The CRESTED EAGLE, SOLITARY EAGLE, and ORANGE-BREASTED FALCON (Plate 30) are all rare in the region, and are CITES Appendix II listed (as are all hawks, kites, eagles, and falcons). Some hawks adapt well to peoples' habitat alterations. A case in point is the common ROADSIDE HAWK (Plate 32). It prefers open habitats and, especially, roadsides. It has expanded its range and numbers in Central America with deforestation and road-building in areas that previously were large tracts of inaccessible closed forest. Conservation measures aimed at raptors are bound to be difficult to formulate and enforce because the birds are often persecuted for a number of reasons (hunting, pet and feather trade, ranchers protecting livestock) and they roam very large areas. Also, some breed and winter on different continents, and thus need to be protected in all parts of their ranges, including along migration routes. Further complicating population assessments and conservation proposals, there are still plenty of Neotropical raptor species about which very little is known. For example, for the approximately 80 species of raptors that breed primarily in Central and South America (excluding the vultures), breeding behavior has not been described for 27 species, nests are unknown for 19 species, as is the typical prey taken by six species.

Profiles

Osprey, *Pandion haliaetus*, Plate 30a
Laughing Falcon, *Herpetotheres cachinnans*, Plate 30b
Collared Forest Falcon, *Micrastur semitorquatus*, Plate 30c
Bat Falcon, *Falco rufigularis*, Plate 30d
Orange-breasted Falcon, *Falco deiroleucus*, Plate 30e
Gray-headed Kite, *Leptodon cayanensis*, Plate 31a
American Swallow-tailed Kite, *Elanoides forficatus*, Plate 31b
Snail Kite, *Rostrhamus sociabilis*, Plate 31c
Plumbeous Kite, *Ictinia plumbea*, Plate 31d
Common Black Hawk, *Buteogallus anthracinus*, Plate 32a
White Hawk, *Leucopternis albicollis*, Plate 32b
Black-collared Hawk, *Busarellus nigricollis*, Plate 32c
Roadside Hawk, *Buteo magnirostris*, Plate 32d

11. Pigeons and Doves

The *pigeon* family is a highly successful group, represented, often in large numbers, almost everywhere on dry land, except for Antarctica and some oceanic islands. Their continued ecological success must be viewed as at least somewhat surprising, because pigeons are largely defenseless creatures and quite edible, regarded as a tasty entrée by human and an array of nonhuman predators. The family, Columbidae, includes approximately 250 species, 16 of which occur in Belize and northern Guatemala. They inhabit almost all kinds of habitats, from semi-deserts, to tropical moist forests, to high-elevation mountainsides. Smaller species generally are called *doves*, larger ones, *pigeons*, but there is a good amount of overlap in name assignments.

All pigeons are generally recognized as such by almost everyone, a legacy of people's familiarity with domestic and feral pigeons. Even small children in zoos, upon encountering an exotic, colorful dove will determine it to be "some kind of pigeon." Pigeons worldwide vary in size from the dimensions of a sparrow to those of a small turkey; the ones in Belize and northern Guatemala range from 15 cm-long (6 in) ground-doves to the 35 cm (14 in) SCALED and RED-BILLED PIGEONS (Plate 33). Doves and pigeons are plump-looking birds with compact bodies, short necks, and small heads. Legs are usually fairly short, except in the ground-dwelling species. Bills are small, straight, and slender. Typically there is a conspicuous patch of naked skin, or *cere*, at the base of the bill, over the nostrils. Although many of the Old World pigeons are easily among the most gaily colored of birds (Asian *fruit doves*, for instance), the New World varieties generally color their soft, dense plumages with understated grays and browns, although a few also have bold patterns of black lines or spots. Many have splotches of iridescence, especially on necks and wings. In the majority of Central American species, male and female are generally alike in size and color, although females are often a bit duller than the males.

Natural History

Ecology and Behavior
Most of the pigeons are at least partly arboreal, but some spend their time in and around cliffs, and still others are primarily ground-dwellers. They eat seeds, ripe and unripe fruit, berries, and the occasional insect, snail, or other small invertebrate. Even those species that spend a lot of time in trees often forage on the ground, moving along the leaf-strewn forest floor, for example, with the head-bobbing walk characteristic of their kind. Owing to their small, weak bills, they eat only what they can swallow whole; "chewing" is accomplished in the *gizzard*, a muscular portion of the stomach in which food is mashed against small pebbles that are eaten by pigeons expressly for this purpose. Pigeons typically are strong, rapid flyers, which, in essence, along with their cryptic color patterns, provide their only defenses against predation. Most pigeons are gregarious to some degree, staying in groups during the nonbreeding portion of the year; some gather into large flocks. Visitors to the Neotropics from North America often are struck by the relative scarcity of sparrows; it is in large part the pigeons of the region that ecologically "replace" sparrows as predominant seed-eaters.

Breeding
Pigeons are monogamous breeders. Some breed solitarily, others in colonies of various sizes. Nests are shallow, open affairs of woven twigs, plant stems, and roots, placed on the ground, on rock ledges, or in shrubs or trees. Reproductive duties are shared by male and female. This includes nest-building, incubating the one or two eggs, and feeding the young, which they do by regurgitating food into

the nestlings' mouths. All pigeons, male and female, feed their young *pigeon milk*, a nutritious fluid produced in the *crop*, an enlargement of the esophagus used for food storage. During the first few days of life, nestlings receive 100% pigeon milk but, as they grow older, they are fed an increasing proportion of regurgitated solid food. Incubation time ranges from 11 to 28 days, depending on species size. Nestlings spend from 11 to 36 days in the nest. Parent pigeons of some species give *distraction displays* when potential predators approach their eggs or young; they feign injury as they move away form the nest, luring the predator away. Most nesting occurs within the period from March through August, although some species breed year round.

Ecological Interactions

The great success of the pigeon family – a worldwide distribution, robust populations, the widespread range and enormous numbers of rock doves (wild, domestic pigeons) – is puzzling to ecologists. At first glance, pigeons have little to recommend them as the fierce competitors any hugely successful group needs to be. They have weak bills and therefore are rather defenseless during fights and ineffectual when trying to stave off nest predators. They are hunted by people for food. In several parts of the world they compete for seeds and fruit with parrots, birds with formidable bills, yet pigeons thrive in these regions and have spread to many more that are parrot-less. To what do pigeons owe their success? First, to reproductive advantage. For birds of their sizes, they have relatively short incubation and nestling periods; consequently, nests are exposed to predators for relatively brief periods and, when nests fail, parents have adequate time to nest again before the season ends. Some species breed more than once per year. Also, the ability of both sexes to produce pigeon milk to feed young may be an advantage over having to forage for particular foods for the young. Second, their ability to capitalize on human alterations of the environment points to a high degree of hardiness and adaptability, valuable traits in a world in which people make changes to habitats faster than most organisms can respond with evolutionary changes of their own.

A general pattern within the pigeon group is that smaller pigeons are usually cryptically colored, whereas larger ones are more often brightly colored. The reason probably has to do with predation pressures: large pigeons are quite a bit safer from such predators as hawks and falcons, and thus have less need of camouflage.

Lore and Notes

Although many pigeons today are very successul animals, some species met extinction within the recent past. There are two particularly famous cases. The DODO was a large, flightless pigeon, the size of turkey, with a large head and strong, robust bill and feet. Dodos lived, until the 17th century, on the island of Mauritius, in the Indian Ocean, east of Madagascar. Reported to be clumsy and stupid (hence the expression, "dumb as a dodo"), but probably just unfamiliar with and unafraid of predatory animals, such as people, they were killed by the thousands by sailors who stopped at the island to stock their ships with food. This caused population numbers to plunge; the birds were then finished off by the pigs, monkeys, and cats introduced by people to the previously predator-free island – animals that ate the Dodos' eggs and young. The only stuffed Dodo in existence was destroyed by fire in Oxford, England, in 1755.

North America's PASSENGER PIGEON, a medium-sized, long-tailed member of the family, suffered extinction because of overhunting and because of its habits of roosting, breeding, and migrating in huge flocks. People were able to kill many thousands of them at a time on the Great Plains in the central part of the USA, shipping the bodies to markets and restaurants in large cities through the mid-1800s. It is estimated that when Europeans first settled in the New World, there were three billion Passenger Pigeons, a population size perhaps never equalled by any other bird, and that they may have accounted for up to 25% or more of the birds in what is now the USA. It took only a bit more than 100 years to kill them all; the last one died in the Cincinnati Zoo in 1914.

The common ROCK DOVE, with which everyone who has visited a city or town is familiar, is a native of the Old World. Domesticated for thousands of years and transported around the world by people, feral populations have colonized all settled and many unsettled areas of the Earth. In the wild, they breed and roost in cliffs and caves. In several large cities of North America, aside from creating problems in parks, plazas, and buildings, pigeons have become the staple prey of Peregrine Falcons. The falcons have been introduced to cities by people seeking to re-establish populations in areas from which they have disappeared. A common if gruesome sight these days for visitors to the observatory at the Sears Tower building in Chicago, for instance, is a Peregrine perched on one of the building's nearby 90th floor corner setbacks, pulling apart its pigeon dinner.

Status

None of the pigeon species that occurs in Belize or northern Guatemala is currently threatened. Several New World pigeons in other regions, however, are now endangered, some critically so. Among these are the RING-TAILED WOOD PIGEON of Jamaica, the PLAIN PIGEON of the Caribbean, the BLUE-EYED and PURPLE-WINGED GROUND DOVES of Brazil and Argentina, the VERACRUZ QUAIL-DOVE of Mexico, and the BLUE-HEADED QUAIL-DOVE of Cuba. The SOCORRO DOVE, which was endemic to small Pacific islands off Mexico's western coast, was last seen in the wild in the 1950s. They were victims of human settlement of the islands, and of the cats people brought along. Today, only about 200 of the doves exist, all in captivity.

Profiles

Pale-vented Pigeon, *Columba cayennensis*, Plate 33a
Scaled Pigeon, *Columba speciosa*, Plate 33b
Red-billed Pigeon, *Columba flavirostris*, Plate 33c
Short-billed Pigeon, *Columba nigrirostris*, Plate 33d
Blue Ground Dove, *Claravis pretiosa*, Plate 34a
Ruddy Ground-dove, *Columbina talpacoti*, Plate 34b
Common Ground-dove, *Columbina passerina*, Plate 34c
White-tipped Dove, *Leptotila verreauxi*, Plate 34d
White-winged Dove, *Zenaida asiatica*, Plate 34e

12. Parrots

Everyone knows *parrots* as caged pets, so discovering them for the first time in their natural surroundings is often a strange but somehow familiar experience (like a dog-owner's first sighting of a wild coyote): one has knowledge and expectations of the birds' behavior and antics in captivity, but how do they act in the wild? Along with toucans, parrots are probably the birds most commonly symbolic of the tropics. The 300+ parrot species that comprise the family Psittacidae (the P is silent; refer to parrots as *psittacids* to impress your friends and tour-guides!) are globally distributed across the tropics, with some species extending into sub-tropical and even temperate zone areas. The family has a particularly diverse and abundant presence in the Neotropical and Australian regions. Ornithologists divide parrots by size: *parrotlets* are small birds (as small as 10 cm, or 4 in) with short tails; *parakeets* are also small, with long or short tails; *parrots* are medium-sized, usually with short tails; and *macaws* are large (up to 1 m, or 40 in) and long-tailed.

Consistent in form and appearance, all parrots are easily recognized as such. They share a group of traits that set them distinctively apart from all other birds. Their typically short neck and compact body yield a form variously described as stocky, chunky, or bulky. All possess a short, hooked bill with a hinge on the upper part that permits great mobility and leverage during feeding. Finally, their legs are short and their feet, with two toes projecting forward and two back, are adapted for powerful grasping and a high degree of dexterity – more so than any other bird. The basic parrot color scheme is green, but some species, such as a few of the macaws, depart from basic in spectacular fashion, with gaudy blues, reds, and yellows. Green parrots feeding quietly amid a tree's high foliage can be diffi-cult to see, even for experienced birdwatchers. Parrots in Central America are most numerous in forested lowland areas. Best views are commonly obtained when flocks fly noisily overhead, when they depart feeding trees, or when a flock is located loafing and squabbling the afternoon away in an isolated, open tree.

Natural History

Ecology and Behavior
Parrots are incredibly noisy, highly social seed and fruit eaters. Some species seem to give their assortment of harsh, screeching squawks during much of the day, whereas others are fairly quiet while feeding. During early mornings and late afternoons, raucous, squawking flocks of parrots characteristically take flight explosively from trees, heading in mornings for feeding areas and later for night roosts, and these are usually the best sighting times. Parrots are almost always encountered in flocks of four or more, and groups of 30+ macaws or 50+ smaller parrots are common. Flocks are usually groups of mated pairs and, with brief observation of behavior, married pairs are often noticeable. Flocks move about seeking fruits and flowers in forests, parkland, and agricultural areas. In flight, parrots are easily identified by their family-specific silhouette: thick bodies and usually long tails, with short, relatively slowly beating wings. Parrots generally are not considered strong flyers, but are certainly fast over the short run. Most do not need to undertake long-distance flights; they are fairly sedentary in their habits, with some regular movements as they follow the seasonal geographic progres-sions of fruit ripening and flower blossoming.

Parrots use their special locomotory talent to clamber methodically through trees in search of fruits and flowers, using their powerful feet to grasp branches and their bills as, essentially, a third foot. Just as caged parrots, they will hang at odd angles and even upside down, the better to reach some delicious morsel. Par-rot feet also function as hands, delicately manipulating food and bringing it to the bill. Parrots feed mostly on fruits and nuts, buds of leaves and flowers, and on flower parts and nectar. They are usually considered frugivores, but careful study reveals that when they attack fruit, it is usually to get at the seeds within. The powerful bill slices open fruit and crushes seeds. As one bird book colorfully put it, "adapted for opening hard nuts, biting chunks out of fruit, and grinding small seeds into meal, the short, thick, hooked parrot bill combines the destructive powers of an ice pick (the sharp-pointed upper mandible), a chisel (the sharp-edged lower mandible), a file (ridged inner surface of the upper mandible), and a vise" (F. G. Stiles & A. F. Skutch 1989). Thick, muscular parrot tongues are also specialized for feeding, used to scoop out pulp from fruit and nectar from flowers.

Breeding

In most of the Central American parrots, the sexes are very similar or identical in appearance; breeding is monogamous and pairing is often for life. Nesting is carried out during the dry season and, for some, into the early wet season. Most species breed in cavities in dead trees, although a few build nests. Macaw nests are almost always placed 30 m (100 ft) or more above the ground. A female parrot lays two to eight eggs, which she incubates alone for 17 to 35 days while being periodically fed regurgitated food by her mate. The helpless young of small parrots are nest-bound for 3 to 4 weeks, those of the huge macaws, 3 to 4 months. Both parents feed nestlings and fledglings.

Ecological Interactions

Many fruit-eating birds are fruit seed dispersers, but apparently not so parrots. Their strong bills crush seeds, and the contents are digested. For example, in one study in southern Central America, an ORANGED-CHINNED PARAKEET was examined after it fed all morning at a fig tree. It had in its digestive tract about 3500 fig seeds, almost all of which were broken, cracked, or already partially digested. Therefore, the main ecological interaction between parrots and at least some fruit trees is that of a seed predator. Because parrots eat fruit and seeds, they are attracted to farms and orchards and in some areas are considered agricultural pests, with implications for their future populations (see below). Macaws and other parrots often congregate at *licks*, exposed riverbank or streamside clay deposits. The clay that is eaten may help detoxify harmful compounds that are consumed in their seed, fruit and leaf diet, or may supply essential minerals that are not provided by a vegetarian diet. Some ecotour destinations are based on lick locations, e.g. in Peru, where visitors reliably find parrots to watch at traditional clay licks.

Lore and Notes

Parrots have been captured for people's pleasure as pets for thousands of years. Greek records exist from 400 BC describing parrot pets. Ancient Romans wrote of training parrots to speak and even of how they acted when drunk! The fascination stems from the birds' bright coloring, their ability to imitate human speech and other sounds, their individualistic personalities (captive parrots definitely like some people while disliking others), and their long lifespans (up to 80 years in captivity). Likewise, parrots have been hunted and killed for food and to protect crops for thousands of years. Some Peruvian Inca pottery shows scenes of parrots eating corn and being scared away from crops. Historically, people have also killed parrots to protect crops – Charles Darwin noted that in Uruguay in the early 1800s, thousands of parakeets were killed to prevent crop damage. Macaws, the largest parrots, are thought to have been raised in the past for food in the West Indies.

Status

About 90 parrot species are considered vulnerable, threatened or endangered worldwide, but only two of the nine species that occur in Belize and northern Guatemala are currently endangered – the SCARLET MACAW (CITES Appendix I listed; Plate 35) and the YELLOW-HEADED PARROT. Scarlet Macaws now range in this region only over southern Belize and the southern Petén. Hunted intensively for the pet trade and for sport, they have been reduced in Belize probably to no more than a few hundred surviving individuals (but the species is more numerous in other parts of its range in Central and northern South America). Many Central American parrot species still enjoy healthy populations and are frequently seen. Unfortunately, however, parrots are subject to three powerful forces that, in combination, take heavy tolls on their numbers: parrots are primarily forest birds, and forests are increasingly under attack by farmers and developers; parrots are considered agricultural pests by farmers and orchardists owing to their seed and fruit eating, and are persecuted for this reason; and parrots are among the world's most popular cage birds. Among the region's species, Scarlet Macaws, MEALY PARROTS (Plate 35), and Yellow-headed Parrots are particularly prized as pets, and nests of these parrots are often robbed of young for local sale as pets or to international dealers. Without fast, additional protections, many Central American parrots will probably soon be threatened.

Profiles

Scarlet Macaw, *Ara macao*, Plate 35a
Mealy Parrot, *Amazona farinosa*, Plate 35b
Red-lored Parrot, *Amazona autumnalis*, Plate 35c
Yellow-lored Parrot, *Amazona xantholora*, Plate 35d
White-fronted Parrot, *Amazona albifrons*, Plate 36a
White-crowned Parrot, *Pionus senilis*, Plate 36b
Brown-hooded Parrot, *Pionopsitta haematotis*, Plate 36c
Olive-throated Parakeet, *Aratinga nana*, Plate 36d

13. Cuckoos and Anis

Many of the *cuckoos* and *anis* ("AH-neez") are physically rather plain but behaviorally rather extraordinary: as a group they employ some of the most bizarre breeding practices known among birds. Cuckoos and anis are both included in the cuckoo family, Cuculidae, which, with a total of about 130 species, enjoys a worldwide distribution in temperate areas and the tropics. Eight species occur in Belize and northern Guatemala. Cuckoos are mainly shy, solitary birds of forests, woodlands, and dense thickets. Anis are the opposite; gregarious animals that spend their time in small flocks in savannahs, brushy scrub, and other open areas, particularly around human habitations. Anis are among those birds that make one wonder where they perched before the advent of fences. A notable *cuculid* relative of the cuckoos and anis is a common ground bird of scrub desert areas of Mexico and southwestern USA, the GREATER ROADRUNNER of cartoon fame.

Most Cuckoos are medium-sized, slender, long-tailed birds. Male and female mostly look alike, attired in plain browns, tans, and grays, often with streaked or spotted patches. Several have alternating white and black bands on their tail undersides. (Many cuckoos of the Old World are more colorful.) They have short legs and bills that curve downwards at the end. Anis are conspicuous medium-sized birds, glossy black all over, with iridescent sheens particularly on the head, neck and breast. Their bills are exceptionally large, with humped or crested upper parts.

Natural History

Ecology and Behavior

Most of the cuckoos are arboreal. They eat insects, apparently having a special fondness for caterpillars. They even safely consume hairy caterpillars, which are avoided by most potential predators because they taste bad or contain sickness-causing noxious compounds. Cuckoos have been observed to snip off one end of the hairy thing, squeeze the body in the bill until the noxious entrails fall out, then swallow the harmless remainder. A few cuckoos, such as the rarely seen PHEASANT CUCKOO, are ground-dwellers, eating insects but also vertebrates such as small lizards and snakes. These large cuckoos typcially follow army ant swarms, picking off prey that rushes from cover to evade the ant hordes.

The highly social anis forage in groups, usually on the ground. Frequently they feed around cattle, grabbing the insects that are flushed out of hiding places by the grazing mammals. They eat mostly bugs, but also a bit of fruit. Anis live in groups of eight to 25 individuals, each group containing two to eight adults and several juveniles. Each group defends a territory from other groups throughout the year. The flock both feeds and breeds within its territory.

Breeding

Cuckoos are known in most parts of the world for being *brood parasites*: they build no nests of their own, and the females lay their eggs in the nests of other species. These other birds often raise the young cuckoos as their own offspring, usually to the significant detriment of their own, often smaller, young. About 50 of the 130 members of the family are brood parasites. Only two of the species in the covered region, STRIPED (Plate 37) and PHEASANT CUCKOOS, breed in this manner. The rest of them are somewhat typically monogamous breeders. The male feeds the female in courtship, especially during her egg-laying period. Both sexes build the plain platform nest that is made of twigs and leaves and placed in a tree or shrub. Both sexes incubate the two to six eggs for about 10 days, and both parents feed the young. In several species, the young hop out of the nest before they have been flight-certified, to spend the several days before they can fly flopping around in the vegetation near the nest, being fed by their parents.

Anis, consistent with their highly social ways, are *communal breeders*. In the most extreme form, all the individuals within the group contribute to a single nest, several females laying eggs in it; up to 29 eggs in one nest have been noted. Many individuals help build the stick nest and feed the young. Although at first glance it would seem as if all benefit by having the group breed together, females contributing eggs to a common nest which all build, defend and tend, actually it is the dominant male and female within each group that gain most. Their eggs go in the nest last, on top of the others that sometimes become buried. Also, some females roll others' eggs out of the nest before they lay their own; thus, it pays to lay last. In some species, several nests are built by pairs within the group's territory. Ani breeding in Central America usually occurs during the wet season, when bugs are most abundant.

Lore and Notes

The name *cuckoo* comes from the calls made by a common member of the family, the EUROPEAN CUCKOO. Many of the parasitic cuckoos lay their eggs in the nests of *host* species that are much smaller than they are. The result is that the host parents often end up bringing food to the nest to feed cuckoo nestlings that are not only much larger than their own offspring (who cannot compete for food against the larger cuckoos and starve), but who are often larger than the parents themselves – a phenomenon that provides a never-ending stream of striking photographs in biology books.

The Mayan folk tale about how the Ani came to have only black feathers is a sad one. It seems the Ani in the past was bright pink. She was very proud of her young nestlings, so when her friend the hawk said he was going off to feed, mother Ani, exaggerating, told him to be sure to avoid the nest of beautiful young birds that was her own. The hawk tried, but when he spied a nest of gawky, ugly little birds, he judged that they could not be the fine-looking youngsters described by the Ani, so he ate them. When the Ani found out what her incorrect description had cost her, she put on black feathers to mourn, and all anis ever since have worn black mourning plumage (A. L. Bowes 1964).

Status
None of cuckoos or anis that occur in Belize or northern Guatemala is currently considered threatened. Some cuckoos of Central America, in fact, actually are increasing in numbers and expanding their ranges because they do well in the forest edge, thicket, and open areas that increasingly are created through deforestation. Two species of New World cuckoos appear to be threatened: the RUFOUS-BREASTED CUCKOO, endemic to the island of Hispaniola, and the BANDED GROUND-CUCKOO of Ecuador and Colombia. Costa Rica's COCOS CUCKOO is considered vulnerable. The reason is that it is endemic to Cocos Island, which is in the Pacific some 800 km (500 miles) from the mainland. Although the precise population size is unknown, species confined to a single small place are always vulnerable, because a single catastrophe there could exterminate the species.

Profiles
Striped Cuckoo, *Tapera naevia*, Plate 37a
Squirrel Cuckoo, *Piaya cayana*, Plate 37b
Groove-billed Ani, *Crotophaga sulcirostris*, Plate 37c
Smooth-billed Ani, *Crotophaga ani*, Plate 37d

14. Owls

Although some *owls* are common Central American birds, they are considered here only briefly because most are active only at night and so are rarely seen. But there are a few exceptions. Most owls are members of the family Strigidae, a worldwide group of about 120 species that lacks representation only in Antarctica and remote oceanic islands. Owls are particularly diverse in the tropics and subtropics; Belize and northern Guatemala have about 10 species. Most people can always identify owls because of several distinctive features: all have large heads with forward-facing eyes, small, hooked bills, plumpish bodies and sharp, hooked claws. Most have short legs and short tails. Owls are clad mostly in mixtures of gray, brown, and black, the result being that they usually are highly camouflaged against a variety of backgrounds. They have very soft feathers. Most are medium-sized birds, but the group includes species that range in length from 15 to 75 cm (6 to 30 in). Males and females generally look alike, although females are a bit larger.

Natural History

Ecology and Behavior

In general, owls occupy a variety of habitats: forests, clearings, fields, grasslands, mountains, marshes. They are considered to be the nocturnal equivalents of the day-active birds-of-prey – the hawks, eagles, and falcons. Most owls hunt at night, taking prey such as small mammals, birds (including smaller owls), and reptiles; smaller owls specialize on insects, earthworms, and other small invertebrates. But some owls hunt at twilight (*crepuscular* activity) and sometimes during the day, including the FERRUGINOUS PYGMY-OWL (Plate 38). Owls hunt by sight and by sound. Their vision is very good in low light, the amount given off by moonlight, for instance; and their hearing is remarkable. They can hear sounds that are much lower in sound intensity (softer) than most other birds, and their ears are positioned on their heads asymmetrically, the better for localizing sounds in space. This means that owls in the darkness can, for example, actually hear small rodents moving about on the forest floor, quickly locate the source of the sound, then swoop and grab. Additionally, owing to their soft, loose feathers, owls' flight is essentially silent, permitting prey little chance of hearing their approach. Owls swallow small prey whole, then instead of digesting or passing the hard bits, they regurgitate bones, feathers, and fur in compact *owl pellets*. These are often found beneath trees or rocks where owls perch and they can be interesting to pull apart to see what an owl has been dining on.

Breeding

Most owls are monogamous breeders. They do not build nests themselves, but either take over nests abandoned by other birds or nest in cavities such as tree or rock holes. Incubation of the one to 10 or more eggs (often two to four) is usually conducted by the female alone for 4 to 5 weeks, but she is fed by her mate. Upon hatching, the female broods the young while the male hunts and brings meals. Young fledge after 4 to 6 weeks in the nest.

Lore and Notes

The forward-facing eyes of owls are a trait shared with only a few other animals: humans, most other primates, and to a degree, the cats. Eyes arranged in this way allow for almost complete binocular vision (one eye sees the same thing as the other), a prerequisite for good depth perception, which, in turn, is important for quickly judging distances when catching prey. On the other hand, owl eyes cannot move much, so owls swivel their heads to look left or right.

Owls have a reputation for fierce, aggressive defense of their young; many a human who ventured too near an owl nest has been attacked and had damage done! Owls through history have been regarded as symbols of wisdom (for instance, in ancient Greece) or of death, darkness, and supernatural evil (the Mesopotamians and the Romans).

Status

Owls in Central America are threatened primarily by forest clearing. However, none of the owls that occurs in Belize or northern Guatemala is officially listed yet as threatened. Most currently threatened owls are Old World species. The endangered Northern Spotted Owl, of which so much is heard in the USA, is a *subspecies* of Spotted Owl; because the other subspecies, the Southern Spotted Owl, which occurs in the southwestern USA and Mexico, is still fairly common, the species as a whole is not presently considered threatened. Trade in owls is severely restricted; the group as a whole is CITES Appendix II listed.

Profiles

Ferruginous Pygmy-owl, *Glaucidium brasilianum*, Plate 38a
Mottled Owl, *Ciccaba virgata*, Plate 38b

15. Goatsuckers

Members of the family of birds known as the *goatsuckers*, or Caprimulgidae, do not actually suck the milk of goats, as legend has it, but they do possess one of the most fanciful of bird names. The *caprimulgids* are a group of about 70 species spread over most of the world's land masses, with the exceptions of northern North America and northern Eurasia, southern South America, and New Zealand. Their closest relatives are probably the owls, and some recent classification schemes place the two in the same avian order. Eight species occur in Belize and northern Guatemala. One of them, the PAURAQUE (POWR-ah-kay) (Plate 38) is an extremely common bird in many regions of the country and the most abundant caprimulgid of Central America. Pauraques, like most caprimulgids, inhabit open areas such as grassland and farmland, thickets, parkland, and forest edge areas.

Goatsuckers have a very characteristic appearance. In the New World most range from 16 to 32 cm (6 to 12 in) in length. They have long, pointed wings, medium or long tails, and big eyes. Their small, stubby bills enclose big, wide mouths that they open in flight to scoop up flying insects. Many species have bristles around the mouth area. With their short legs and weak feet, they are poor walkers – flying is their usual mode of locomotion. The plumage of these birds is uniformly cryptic: mottled, spotted, and barred mixtures of browns, grays, tans, and black. They often have white patches on their wings or tails that can be seen only in flight.

Natural History

Ecology and Behavior

Most caprimulgids are night-active birds, with some, such as the COMMON NIGHTHAWK (familiar to North Americans) and LESSER NIGHTHAWK (Plate 38), becoming active at twilight (*crepuscular* is the term ecologists use for such a habit). They feed on insects, which they catch on the wing, either with repeated forays from perched locations on the ground or on tree branches, or, as is the case with Common and Lesser Nighthawks, with continuous, often circling flight. Caprimulgids usually gather at night near bright lights to feast on the light-drawn insects. Most of these birds are not seen during the day unless they are accidentally flushed from their roosting spots, which are either on the ground or on tree branches on which they perch sideways. Because of their camouflage coloring, they are almost impossible to see when perched.

Breeding

Goatsuckers breed monogamously. No nest is built. Rather, the female lays her one or two eggs on the ground, perhaps in a small depression in the soil under the branches of a tree, or on a rock or sandbar. Around human developments, they are known for placing their eggs on bare, gravelly rooftops. Either the female alone or both sexes incubate (both in the PAURAQUE) for 18 to 20 days, and both parents feed insects to the young. Goatsuckers engage in broken-wing displays if their nest is approached by a predator or a person, which distracts a predator's attention. They flop about on the ground, often with one or both wings held out as if injured, making gargling or hissing sounds, all the while moving away from the nest.

Lore and Notes

Americans tend to call this group either goatsuckers or *nighthawks*, whereas Europeans prefer *nightjars*.

One of the goatsucker family, North America's COMMON POORWILL, may be the only bird known actually to hibernate, as some mammals do, during very cold weather. During their dormant state, poorwills save energy by reducing their metabolic rate and their body temperature, the latter by about 22 °C (40 °F).

Status

None of the Central American goatsuckers is threatened. In the New World, the WHITE-WINGED NIGHTJAR of Brazil and the USA's PUERTO RICAN NIGHTJAR (USA ESA listed) occur in very limited areas and are endangered. The former is known from only a few old specimens and a few modern sightings in Central Brazil. Little is known about the bird, but the area of modern sightings falls within a national park, offering some hope for its survival. The Puerto Rican Nightjar occupies dry forest areas of southwestern Puerto Rico; only several hundred pairs remain.

Profiles

Pauraque, *Nyctidromus albicollis*, Plate 38c
Lesser Nighthawk, *Chordeiles acutipennis*, Plate 38d

16. Swifts and Swallows

Swifts and *swallows*, although not closely related, are remarkably similar in appearance and habit. Most famously, they pursue the same feeding technique – catching insects on the wing during long periods of sustained flight. The swallows (Family Hirundinidae) are a passerine group, 80 species strong, with a worldwide distribution. Nine species occur in Belize and northern Guatemala, but several are present only as over-winter migrants from more northerly breeding areas (for instance, PURPLE MARTIN and TREE, BANK, BARN (Plate 39), and CLIFF SWALLOWS). Swallows are small, streamlined birds, 11.5 to 21.5 cm (4.5 to 8.5 in) in length, with short necks, bills, and legs. They have long, pointed wings and forked tails, plainly adapted for sailing through the air with high maneuverability. Some are covered in shades of blue, green, or violet, but many are gray or brown. The sexes look alike.

Swifts, although superficially resembling swallows are actually only distantly related; they are not even classified with the passerines. The 80 or so species of swifts (Family Apodidae) are, in fact, most closely related to hummingbirds. About five species are found in Belize and northern Guatemala, some very rarely. Swifts, like swallows, are slender, streamlined birds, with long, pointed wings. They are 9 to 25 cm (3.5 to 10 in) long and have very short legs, short tails or long, forked tails, and very small bills. Swifts' tails are stiffened to support the birds as they cling to vertical surfaces. The sexes look alike: sooty-gray or brown, with white, grayish or reddish rumps or flanks. Many are glossily iridescent.

Natural History

Ecology and Behavior

Among the birds, swifts and swallows represent pinnacles of flying prowess and aerial insectivory. It seems as if swifts and swallows fly all day, circling low over water or land, or flying in erratic patterns high overhead, snatching insects from the air. Perpetual flight was in the past so much the popular impression of swifts that it was actually thought that they never landed – that they essentially remained flying throughout most of their lives (indeed, it was long ago believed that they lacked feet; hence the family name, Apodidae, literally, *without feet*). They do land, however, although not often. When they do, they use their clawed feet and stiff tail to cling to and brace themselves against vertical structures. They almost never land on the ground, having trouble launching themselves back into the air from horizontal surfaces. A swift spends more time airborne than any other type of bird, regularly flying all night, and even copulating while in the air (a tricky affair, apparently: male and female are partially in freefall during this activity). Swifts are also aptly named, as they are among the fastest flyers on record.

Swallows also take insects on the wing as they fly back and forth over water and open areas. Some also eat berries. Not quite the terra-phobes that swifts are, swallows land more often, resting usually during the hottest parts of the day. Directly after dawn, however, and at dusk, swallows are always airborne.

Breeding

All swallows are monogamous, many species breeding in dense colonies of several to several thousand nesting pairs. Nests are constructed of plant pieces placed in a tree cavity, burrow, or building, or, alternatively, consist of a mud cup attached to a vertical surface such as a cliff. Both sexes or the female alone incubate the three to seven eggs for 13 to 16 days. Both parents feed nestlings, for 18 to 28 days, until they fledge. Swifts are monogamous and most are colonial breeders, but some species nest solitarily. The sexes share breeding chores. Nests consist of plant pieces, twigs, and feathers glued together with the birds' saliva. One to six-eggs are incubated for 16 to 28 days, with young fledging at 25 to 65 days of age. Most breeding is accomplished from March to August.

Ecological Interactions

Swallows, small, vulnerable lightweights, are often under competitive pressure for breeding space from other hole-nesting species. Starlings and some sparrows, for instance, sometimes try to take over nests built by swallows and, indeed, such nest usurpation appears to be the chief cause for the serious decline in numbers of the GOLDEN SWALLOW in Jamaica.

Some swallows, such as CLIFF SWALLOWS, locate their colonies near to or actually surrounding the cliff-situated nests of large hawks (predatory birds that take mostly rodents), basking in the protection afforded by having a nest close to a fearsome predator.

Because swifts and swallows depend each day on capturing enough insects, their daily habits are largely tied to the prevailing weather. Flying insects are thick in the atmosphere on warm, sunny days, but relatively scarce on cold, wet ones. Therefore, on good days, swallows, for instance, can catch their fill of bugs in only a few hours of flying, virtually anywhere. But on cool, wet days, they may need to forage all day to find enough food, and they tend to do so over water or low to the ground, where under such conditions bugs are more available.

Lore and Notes

Swallows have a long history of association with people. The ancient Greeks believed swallows to be sacred birds probably because they nested in and flew around the great temples. In the New World, owing to their insect-eating habits, they have been popular with people going back to the time of the ancient Mayan civilization. Mayans, it is believed, respected and welcomed swallows because they reduced insect damage to crops. In fact Cozumel (the word refers to swallows), off Mexico's Yucatán Peninsula, is the Island of Swallows. People's alterations of natural habitats, harmful to so many species, are often helpful to swallows, which adopt buildings, bridges, road culverts, roadbanks, and quarry walls as nesting areas. BARN SWALLOWS have for the most part given up nesting in anything other than human-crafted structures. The result of this close association is that, going back as far as ancient Rome, swallows have been considered good luck. Superstitions attached to the relationship abound; for example, it is said that the cows of a farmer who destroys a swallow's nest will give bloody milk. Arrival of the first migratory Barn Swallows in Europe is considered a welcome sign of approaching spring, as is the arrival of CLIFF SWALLOWS at some of California's old Spanish missions.

Although swifts are common birds in many parts of the world, they is much less well known than are swallows, owing to the fact that their pattern of almost perpetual flight hampers detailed observation.

Status

None of the swifts or swallows that breed or winter in Central America is threatened. A few Old World species, from Africa and Asia, are known to be quite rare and are considered threatened; for some others, so little is known that we are uncertain of their populations' sizes or vulnerabilities.

Profiles

White-collared Swift, *Streptoprocne zonaris*, Plate 39a
Vaux's Swift, *Chaetura vauxi*, Plate 39b
Gray-breasted Martin, *Progne chalybea*, Plate 39c
Barn Swallow, *Hirundo rustica*, Plate 39d
Northern Rough-winged Swallow, *Stelgidopteryx serripennis*, Plate 40a
Mangrove Swallow, *Tachycineta albilinea*, Plate 40b

17. Hummingbirds

Hummingbirds are birds of extremes. They are among the most recognized kinds of birds, the smallest of birds, and undoubtedly among the most beautiful, albeit on a minute scale; fittingly, much of their biology is nothing short of amazing. Limited to the New World, the hummingbird family, Trochilidae, contains about 330 species, about 22 of which occur in Belize and northern Guatemala. The variety of forms encompassed by the family, not to mention the brilliant iridescence of most of its members, is indicated in the names attached to some of the different subgroups: In addition to the hummingbirds proper, there are the *emeralds*, *sapphires*, *sunangels*, *sunbeams*, *comets*, *metaltails*, *fairies*, *woodstars*, *woodnymphs*, *pufflegs*, *sabrewings*, *thorntails*, *thornbills*, and *lancebills*. Hummingbirds occupy a broad array of habitat types, from exposed high mountainsides at 4000 m (13,000 ft) to mid-elevation arid areas to sea level tropical forests and mangrove swamps, as long as there are nectar-filled flowers to provide necessary nourishment.

Almost everyone can identify hummingbirds (call them *hummers* to sound like an expert), being familiar with their general appearance and behavior: very small birds, usually gorgeously clad in iridescent metallic greens, reds, violets, and blues, that whiz by us at high speeds, with the smallest among them resembling nothing so much as large flying insects.

Most hummers are in the range of only 6 to 13 cm (2.5 to 5 in) long, although a few of the larger kinds reach 20 cm (8 in), and they tip the scales at an almost imperceptibly low 2 to 9 g (up to about a quarter of an ounce) (most being 3 to 6 grams) – the weight of a large paper-clip! Bill length and shape varies extensively among species, each bill closely adapted to the precise type of flowers from which a species delicately draws its liquid food. Males are usually more colorful than females, and many of them have *gorgets*, bright, glittering throat patches in red, blue, green, or violet. Not all hummers are so vividly outfitted; one group, called *hermits* (because of their solitary ways), are known for dull, greenish-brown and gray plumages. Hummers have tiny legs and feet; in fact, in some classifications they are included with the swifts in the avian order Apodiformes, meaning *those without feet*.

Natural History

Ecology and Behavior

Owing to their many anatomical, behavioral, and ecological specializations, hummingbirds have long attracted the research attention of biologists; the result is that we know quite a bit about them. A hefty fraction of the best studies have taken place in Central America. These highly active, entertaining-to-watch birds are most often studied for one of four aspects of their biology: (1) flying ability, (2) metabolism, (3) feeding ecology, and (4) their aggressive defense of food resources.

(1) Hummers are capable of very rapid, finely controlled, acrobatic flight, more so than any other kind of bird. The bones of their wings have been modified through their evolutionary history to allow for perfect, stationary hovering flight and also for the unique ability to fly *backwards*. Their wings vibrate in a figure eight-like wingstroke at a speed beyond our ability to see each stroke – up to 80 times per second. Because people usually see hummers only during the birds' foraging trips, they often appear never to land, remaining airborne as they zip from flower to flower, hovering briefly to probe and feed at each. But they do perch every now again, providing opportunities to get good looks at them.

(2) Hummingbirds have very fast metabolisms, a necessary condition for small, warm-blooded animals. To pump enough oxygen and nutrient-delivering blood around their little bodies, their hearts beat up to 10 times faster than human hearts – 600 to 1000 times per minute. To obtain sufficient energy to fuel their high metabolism, hummingbirds must eat many times each day. Quick starvation results from an inability to feed regularly and frequently. At night, when they are inactive, they burn much of their available energy reserves and on cold nights, if not for special mechanisms, they would surely starve to death. The chief method to avoid energy depletion on cold nights is to enter into a sleep-like state of *torpor*, during which the body's temperature is lowered to just above that of the outside world, from 17 to 28 °C (30 to 50 °F) below their daytime operating temperatures, saving them enormous amounts of energy. In effect, they put the thermostat down and hibernate overnight.

(3) All hummingbirds are *nectarivores* – they get most of their nourishment from consuming nectar from flowers. They have long, thin bills and specialized tongues to lick nectar from long, thin flower tubes, which they do while hovering. Because nectar is mostly a sugar and water solution, hummingbirds need to obtain additional nutrients, such as proteins, from other sources. Toward this end they also eat the odd insect or spider, which they catch in the air or pluck off spiderwebs. Some ornithologists believe that insects constitute a larger proportion of hummingbird diets than is generally believed, some going so far as to suggest that some species visit flowers more often to catch bugs there than to gather nectar. Recent research in Central America shows that hummers with strongly curved bills (adapted to feed from curved flower nectar tubes) obtain their protein from spiderwebs, hovering while they glean spiders and bugs from the webs; whereas those with straight bills tend to obtain their protein in "flycatching" mode – via aerial capture of flying wasps and flies. The difference makes sense: flycatching with a long, sharply curved bill, we may assume, would be quite difficult.

(4) Many hummers are highly aggressive birds, energetically defending individual flowers or feeding territories from all other hummingbirds, regardless of species. Not all are territorial, however. Some are *trapline* feeders, repeatedly following a regular route around a section of their habitat, checking the same flowers for nectar, which the flowers replenish at intervals. Some traplines cover as much as a kilometer (0.6 miles) of habitat. Whether birds defend territories depends usually on whether it is an economically attractive option. If the costs of defense (including forcefully evicting intruders), in terms of the amount of energy expended, exceed the amount that can be gained from feeding on the territory, or if nectar-producing flowers are super-abundant in the environment, providing sufficient food for all, then owning and defending a territory is not worthwhile.

Predators on hummingbirds include small, agile hawks and falcons and also frogs and large insects, such as praying mantises, which ambush the small birds as they feed at flowers. Another hazard is large spider webs, from which sometimes they cannot extricate themselves.

Breeding

Hummingbirds are polygamous breeders in which females do almost all the work. In some species, a male in his territory advertises for females by singing squeaky songs. A female enters the territory and, following courtship displays, mates. Afterwards, she leaves the territory to nest on her own. Other species are *lek breeders*. In these systems, males gather at traditional, communal mating sites called leks. For instance, a lek may be in a cleared spot in the forest undergrowth. Each of three to 25 males has a small mating territory in the lek, perhaps just a perch on a flower. The males spend hours there each day during the breeding season, advertising for females. Females enter a lek, assess the displaying males, and choose ones to mate with. A male might spend months at the lek, but only have one 15-minute mating interaction with a female; other males may mate with many females in a season. After mating, females leave the lek or territory and build their nests, which are cup-like and made of plant parts, mosses, lichens, feathers, animal hairs, and spider webs. Nests are placed in the small branches of trees, often attached with spider web. The female lays two eggs, incubates them for 15 to 19 days, and feeds regurgitated nectar and insects to her young for 20 to 26 days, until they fledge. Hummers may be found breeding at any time of year, depending on species and geography. Breeding in a particular area often occurs when flowers are most abundant.

Ecological Interactions

The relationship between hummingbirds (nectar consumers) and the flowering plants from which they feed (nectar producers) is mutually beneficial. The birds obtain a high-energy food that is easy to locate and always available because various flowering plant species, as well as groups of flowers on the same plant, open and produce nectar at different times. The flowering plants, in turn, use the tiny birds as other plants use bees – as pollinators. The nectar is produced and released into the part of the flower the hummer feeds from for the sole reason of attracting the birds so that they may accidentally rub up against other parts of the flower (*anthers*) that contain pollen grains. These grains are actually reproductive spores that the flower very much "wants" the bird to pick up on its body and transfer to other plants of the same species during its subsequent foraging, thereby achieving for the flower *cross-pollination* – breeding with another member of its species (many plants also have the ability to pollinate themselves). Flowers that are specialized for hummingbird pollination place nectar in long, thin tubes that fit the shape of the birds' bills and also protect the nectar from foraging insects. Hummingbird-pollinated plants often have red, pink, or orange flowers, colors which render them easily detectable to the birds but, owing to peculiarities of their vision, indistinguishable from the background environment to insects. Furthermore, these flowers are often odorless because birds use colorvision rather than smell to find them (whereas nectar-eating insects, which the plants want to discourage, use odor to find flowers).

Interlopers in this mutualistic interaction are a group of pollen-eating mite species. Mites are minuscule arthropods, allied to the spiders and ticks. Some mites may spend their lives on a single plant, feeding and reproducing, but others, perhaps searching for mates or new sites to colonize, try to reach other plants. Walking to another plant for such a small animal is almost out of the question. What to do? The mites jump onto the bills of hummingbirds when the birds visit flowers and become hitchhikers on the bird, usually holing up in their nostrils. The passengers leap off the bird's bill during a subsequent visit to a plant of the same species that they left, necessary because the mites are specialized for certain plants. Recent research in Central America suggests that the passenger mites monitor the scents of flowers to identify the correct type, to know when to get off the bus.

Lore and Notes

Intriguingly, some hummingbirds are as curious about us as we are of them. A common occurrence while following a trail is to be closely approached by a passing hummingbird, which stops in mid-air to size up the large primate, darts this way and that to view the intruder from all angles, then, its curiosity apparently satisfied, zips off into the forest.

Hummingbirds, as one might expect, have been the object of considerable myth and legend. The Mayan tale of how hummingbirds became so bright and beautiful is that, way back, the Great Spirit created the hummingbird as a tiny, plain-looking, delicate bird with exceptional flying prowess. The plain hummingbird was nonetheless happy with its existence, and privileged to be the only bird permitted to drink the nectar of pretty flowers. When the drably attired hummer planned her marriage, all the other birds of the kingdom, including the motmot and oriole, donated colorful feathers, so that the hummer's bridal gown was glittering and showy. The Great Spirit, pleased with the hummingbird and her gown, ruled that she could wear it forever (A. L. Bowes 1964).

The Aztecs also took note of hummers, adorning their ceremonial clothes with the birds' gaudy, metallic feathers. Several groups of Indians used these feathers in their wedding ornaments. Hummingbird bodies have a long mythical history in Latin America of being imbued with potent powers as love charms. Having a dead hummer in the hand or pocket is thought by some even today to be a sure way to appear irresistible to a member of the opposite sex. Even powdered and minced hummingbird is sold for this purpose.

Status

None of the hummers of Belize or northern Guatemala is currently threatened, but at least 25 species are threatened or considered vulnerable to threat in other regions. Several are endangered, including the ESMERALDAS WOODSTAR of Ecuador, the LITTLE WOODSTAR of Ecuador and Peru, the HONDURAN EMER-ALD of Honduras, the TURQUOISE-THROATED PUFFLEG of Colombia, the BLACK-BREASTED PUFFLEG of Ecuador, and the SHORT-CRESTED COQUETTE of Mexico. All hummers are CITES Appendix II listed.

Profiles

Long-tailed Hermit, *Phaethornis superciliosus*, Plate 40c
Little Hermit, *Phaethornis longuemareus*, Plate 40d
Wedge-tailed Sabrewing, *Campylopterus curvipennis*, Plate 41a
Violet Sabrewing, *Campylopterus hemileucurus*, Plate 41b
White-necked Jacobin, *Florisuga mellivora*, Plate 41c
Green-breasted Mango, *Anthracothorax prevostii*, Plate 41d
Fork-tailed Emerald, *Chlorostilbon canivetti*, Plate 41e
White-bellied Emerald, *Amazilia candida*, Plate 42a
Azure-crowned Hummingbird, *Amazilia cyanocephala*, Plate 42b
Cinnamon Hummingbird, *Amazilia rutila*, Plate 42c
Rufous-tailed Hummingbird, *Amazilia tzacatl*, Plate 42d
Purple-crowned Fairy, *Heliothrix barroti*, Plate 42e

18. Trogons

Although not as familiar to most people as other gaudy birds such as toucans and parrots, *trogons* are generally regarded by wildlife enthusiasts as among the globe's most visually striking, glamorous of birds; as such, visitors to Central America should try hard not to miss them. The trogon family, Trogonidae, inhabits tropical and semi-tropical regions in the Neotropics, Africa, and southern Asia. It consists of about 40 species of colorful, medium-sized birds with compact bodies, short necks and short "chicken-like" bills. Considering that trogons are distributed over three widely separated geographic regions, it is striking that the family's body plan and plumage pattern are so uniform: male trogons are rather consistently described as having metallic or glittering green, blue, or violet heads and chests, with deeply contrasting bright red, yellow, or orange underparts. Females are duller in color, usually with brown or gray heads, but share the males' brightly colored breasts and bellies. The characteristic trogon tail is long and squared-off, with horizontal black and white stripes on the underside. Trogons usually sit erect with their distinctive tails pointing straight to the ground.

One trogon stands out from the flock: the regal-looking RESPLENDENT QUETZAL (Plate 43). Famously described as "the most spectacular bird in the New

World," the quetzal generally resembles other trogons, but the male's emerald-green head is topped by a ridged crest of green feathers and, truly ostentatiously, long green plumes extend half a meter (18 in) or more past the end of the male's typical trogon tail. Seeing a male quetzal gracefully swooping low through a forest, its long, trailing plumes flashing by, is frequently mentioned by bird lovers as a supreme experience.

Natural History

Ecology and Behavior
Although trogons are distributed throughout many Neotropical forests, they are not limited to warm areas: some species, such as the quetzal, inhabit cool cloud forests at elevations up to 3000 m (10,000 ft). One species, the ELEGANT TROGON, ranges northward into southern Arizona (USA). Trogons are generally observed either solitarily or in pairs, and occasionally in small family groups. In spite of their distinctive calls (typically a *cow-cow-cow* call that is one of a tropical forest's characteristic sounds) and brilliant plumages, trogons can be difficult to locate and even to see clearly when spotted perched on a tree branch. This is because, just like green parrots, partly green trogons easily meld into dark green overhead foliage. (Some biologists, in fact, suspect that the flashy hues of forest birds such as trogons, so glaring and conspicuous when the birds are viewed in the open, might actually appear as dull and inconspicuous to potential predators within the dark confines of closed forests.) Trogon behavior is not much help because typically these birds perch for long periods with little moving or vocalizing, the better presumably to keep them off some predator's dinner plans. Trogons are best seen, therefore, when flying. This often occurs in sudden bursts as they flip off the branches on which a moment before they sat motionless, and sally out in undulatory, short flights to snatch succulent insects. Trogons can thus be considered sit-and-wait predators. They also swoop to grab small lizards, frogs, and snails. Trogons are also partial frugivores, taking small fruits from trees while hovering; particular favorites apparently include figs and avocados.

Breeding
Trogons usually breed from March through June. They nest in cavities in dead trees or in structures high up in trees, such as termite or wasp nests (they have been observed "taking over" a wasp nest, carving a nest hole in it and, adding insult to injury, feasting daily on the wasps during nesting!). Generally the trogon female incubates her two or three eggs overnight and the male does duty during the day. Incubation is 17 to 19 days. Young are tended by both parents; fledging is at 14 to 30 days. Quetzal nest holes generally are about 10 m (33 ft) high in trees. Both sexes share nest duties and apparently divide each day into two shifts each at the nest. Quetzals are known to defend exclusive territories around their nest tree that average about 700 m (2300 ft) in diameter.

Lore and Notes
Most trogon lore concentrates, as might be expected, on the RESPLENDENT QUETZAL, which is thought to have been revered by, or even sacred to, local peoples going back to ancient Mayan and Incan times. One legend of indigenous Guatemalans is that the quetzal received its showy plumage during the European conquest of the Americas: "After a particularly gruesome battle, huge flocks of quetzals (which were then only green) flew down to keep a watch over the dead Mayans, thus staining their breasts red" (C. M. Perrins 1985). Another story is that

the Great Spirit of the Mayans decided one day to choose a king of the birds. The various species competed, showing off their beauty, intelligence, strength, knowledge, or artistry. The quetzal initially held back because, although he was ambitious and proud, his plumage was quite plain. An idea came to the quetzal. He convinced his friend, the roadrunner, to lend him some elegant feathers (promising untruthfully to return them later) and, with the new, long, showy tail feathers, was appointed king of the birds (A. L. Bowes 1964). Ancient Mayans used the long quetzal tail plumes for ceremonial head-dresses, feather capes, and artwork. The chief god of the Mayans was *Kukulcan* and the chief god of the Toltecs was *Quetzalcoatl*, both meaning "The Plumed Serpent."

Status

None of the four trogon species that occur in Belize and northern Guatemala is currently endangered. All are fairly common residents of various forest types, although some range over relatively small, local areas. The RESPLENDENT QUETZAL does not occur in Belize or northern Guatemala; where it does occur in southern Mexico and Central America, it is considered endangered (CITES Appendix I and USA ESA listed), primarily owing to destruction of its favored cloud forest habitat. Large tracts of cloud forest continue to be cleared for cattle pasture, agriculture, and logging, especially below 2000 m (6500 ft). Another factor threatening quetzal populations is that local people illegally hunt them with rifles, blowguns, and traps for trade in skins, feathers, and live birds. Because of the quetzal's special prominence as the national bird of Guatemala (depicted on its state seal and on its currency) and as a particularly gorgeous poster animal for conservation efforts, several special reserves have been established for the bird in Guatemala (including the Mario Dary Rivera Quetzal Reserve near Cobán, in the central Guatemalan highlands), and quetzals are specially protected in some of Costa Rica's national parks and reserves. A system of cloud forest reserves stretching from Mexico to Panama is required for complete protection of the quetzal and other higher elevation Central American trogons. Mexico's EARED TROGON also appears on lists of threatened species.

Profiles

Resplendent Quetzal, *Pharomachrus mocinno*, Plate 43a
Slaty-tailed Trogon, *Trogon massena*, Plate 43b
Violaceous Trogon, *Trogon violaceus*, Plate 43c
Collared Trogon, *Trogon collaris*, Plate 43d
Black-headed Trogon, *Trogon melanocephalus*, Plate 43e

19. Jacamars and Puffbirds

Two interesting, closely related families of insect eaters, each represented in the covered region by only one or two species, are the *jacamars* and *puffbirds*. The jacamar family (Galbulidae) includes 16 species, all Neotropical in distribution, and the puffbirds (Family Bucconidae) about 30 species, similarly limited in distribution. Both kinds of birds are typically forest dwellers, usually in warmer, lowland areas. Jacamars are often described by bird experts as resembling glittering, iridescent hummingbirds enlarged to the size of starlings or robins. They are fairly slender, small to medium-sized birds (15 to 31 cm, 6 to 12 in, long), metallic green above and brownish or reddish below, with very long, fine, pointed bills. Most puffbirds are smaller (15 to 24 cm, 6 to 9 in), with distinctively large heads, stout bills with hooked ends, heavy-looking bodies, and loose plumage that produces a chubby, puffy appearance. Puffbirds are not glamorously colored as are the jacamars, being covered in more subdued browns, grays, and whites.

Natural History

Ecology and Behavior

Jacamars are often seen along rivers and in forests and forest clearings, whereas puffbirds are chiefly forest birds. Both eat insects and hunt in the same way. They perch quietly on tree limbs and, spotting a flying insect, dart out suddenly to overtake and snatch it in mid-air, flycatcher-fashion. Jacamars are renowned for their vital, "charged" personality and lifestyle: they sit quietly waiting for a meal to happen by, but they do so very alertly, snapping their heads this way and that as they scan for moving insects. After these birds grab an insect, such as a large butterfly, they often return to their perch, and proceed manically to beat the insect against the perch until wings fall off and the body alone can be swallowed. The jacamar's long, elegant bill may aid the birds in tightly grasping a butterfly's body while its wings flap violently as it attempts escape, and also in holding wasps and other stinging insects at safe distances from vulnerable parts of its body. Other common diet items are beetles, bees and dragonflies.

Jacamars are usually encountered singly. Some of the puffbirds, in contrast, are quite social, often found congregating in groups of up to 10, for example, perched in a row on a branch or telephone wire. Like jacamars, puffbirds sit quietly until they detect a bug, then zip out and grab it. Puffbirds take insects on the wing and, from leaves, such other delicacies as spiders and small frogs and lizards.

Breeding

Jacamars nest in short burrows that they dig in steep hillsides or in river or stream banks. Both parents incubate the two to four eggs, for a total of 20 to 22 days. Young are fed insects by the parents for 19 to 26 days before fledging. Not much is known about breeding of puffbirds, but some of them nest in burrows on the forest floor and some in burrows in arboreal termite nests.

Lore and Notes

"Puffbirds of several kinds have frequently been called 'stupid' ('bobo') because, fearless of man in regions where they have had little experience of him, they often remain perching quietly while one approaches fairly close to them. But this appearance of dull apathy is most deceptive. One need only attempt to study the (puffbird) at its subterranean burrows, using all one's ingenuity to overcome its distrust, to realize what a keen-sighted, wary creature it can be" (A. F. Skutch 1958).

Status

The jacamar and the two puffbirds that occur in Belize and Guatemala are not considered threatened. However, two jacamars, the COPPERY-CHESTED of Colombia and Ecuador and the THREE-TOED of Brazil, are now threatened, and one species of puffbird, known as the LANCEOLATED MONKLET, and which is distributed from Costa Rica to Brazil, is considered near-threatened.

Profiles

Rufous-tailed Jacamar, *Galbula ruficauda*, Plate 44a
White-necked Puffbird, *Bucco macrorhynchos*, Plate 44b
White-whiskered Puffbird, *Malacoptila panamensis*, Plate 44c

20. Kingfishers

Kingfishers are handsome, bright birds most often encountered along rivers and streams or along the seashore. Classified with the motmots in the Order Coraciiformes, the approximately 90 kingfisher species are grouped in three families and range throughout the tropics, with a few of them pushing deeply northward and southward into temperate areas. Only six kingfisher species, all in the Family Cerylidae, reside in the New World; five are found in Belize and Guatemala (one is migratory from North America). They differ in size (see below), from 12 to 40 cm (5 to 16 in), but all are of a similar form: Large heads with very long, robust, straight bills, short necks, short legs, and, for some, highly noticeable crests. The kingfisher color scheme in the New World is also fairly standardized: dark green or blue-gray above, white and/or chestnut-orange below.

Natural History

Ecology and Behavior

New World kingfishers, as the name suggests, are all mainly fish eaters (that is, they are *piscivores*). Usually seen hunting alone, they sit quietly, attentively on a low perch – a tree branch over the water, a bridge spanning a stream – while scanning the water below. When they locate suitable prey, they swoop and dive, plunging head-first into the water (to depths of 60 cm, or 24 in) to seize it. If successful, they quickly emerge from the water, return to the perch, beat the fish against the perch to stun it, then swallow it whole, head first. Thus, kingfishers are sit-and-wait predators of the waterways. They will also, when they see movement below the water, hover over a particular spot before diving in. BELTED KINGFISHERS (Plate 45), migrants that breed to the north and only winter in the covered region, commonly fly out 500 m (a quarter mile) or more from a lake's shore to hover 3 to 15 m (10 to 50 ft) above the water, searching for fish. Kingfisher diets occasionally are supplemented with tadpoles and insects. Kingfishers fly fast and purposefully, usually in straight and level flight, from one perch to another; often they are seen only as flashes of blue or green darting along waterways.

Kingfishers are highly territorial, aggressively defending their territories from other members of their species with noisy, chattering vocalizations, chasing, and fighting. They inhabit mostly lowland forests and waterways, but some range up to elevations of 2500 m (8000 ft).

Breeding

Kingfishers are monogamous breeders that nest in holes. Both members of the pair help defend the territory in which the nest is located, and both take turns digging the 0.75 to 1.5 m (2 to 5 ft) long nest burrow into the soft earth of a river or stream bank. Both parents incubate the three to eight eggs, up to 24 hours at a stretch, for a total of 19 to 26 days. The young are fed increasingly large fish by both parents until they fledge at 25 to 38 days old. Fledglings continue to be fed by the parents for up to 10 weeks. At some point after they are independent, the parents expel the young from the territory. Many young kingfishers apparently die during their first attempts at diving for food. Some have been seen first "practicing" predation by capturing floating leaves and sticks.

Ecological Interactions

Central American kingfishers can be arranged quite nicely by size order, from the largest, the RINGED KINGFISHER (Plate 45), to the smallest, the 12.5 cm (5 in) long AMERICAN PYGMY KINGFISHER (Plate 45). The size order is not accidental: Ecologists believe that such graded variation in size allows all the different kingfisher species to coexist in the same places because, although they are so alike in habits and, especially, in the kinds of foods they eat, they actually avoid serious competition by specializing on eating fish of different sizes. Ringed Kingfishers eat large fish, BELTEDS eat slightly smaller fish, and Pygmys eat tiny fish, tadpoles, and insects. Intriguingly, the larger the species of kingfisher, the higher is the average perch height above the water from which it hunts – from 1.4 m (4 ft) for the smallest species to about 10 m (32 ft) for the largest.

Lore and Notes
Kingfishers are the subject of a particularly rich mythology, a sign of the bird's conspicuousness and its association with water throughout history. In some parts of the world, kingfishers are associated with the biblical Great Flood. It is said that survivors of the flood had no fire and so the kingfisher was chosen to steal fire from the gods. The bird was successful, but during the theft, burned his chest, resulting in the chestnut-orange coloring we see today. According to the ancient Greeks, Zeus was jealous of Alcyone's power over the wind and waves and so killed her husband by destroying his ship with thunder and lightning. "In her grief, Alcyone threw herself into the sea to join her husband, and they both turned immediately into kingfishers. The power that sailors attributed to Alcyone was passed on to the Halcyon Bird, the kingfisher, which was credited with protecting sailors and calming storms" (D. Boag 1982). Halcyon birds were thought to nest 7 days before and 7 days after the winter solstice and these days of peace and calm, necessary to rear the young birds, were referred to as *halcyon* days.

Status
All kingfishers of Belize and Guatemala are moderately to very abundant; none is considered threatened. Some breed quite well in the vicinity of human settlements. Eleven species of kingfishers currently reside on lists of vulnerable or threatened animals, but they are Old World in their distributions, most from Polynesia and the Philippines.

Profiles
Belted Kingfisher, *Ceryle alcyon*, Plate 45b
Ringed Kingfisher, *Ceryle torquata*, Plate 45a
Amazon Kingfisher, *Chloroceryle amazona*, Plate 45c
Green Kingfisher, *Chloroceryle americana*, Plate 45d
American Pygmy Kingfisher, *Chloroceryle aene*, Plate 45e

21. Motmots
Motmots – beautiful kingfisher relatives with several distinctive features and a ridiculous name. The name probably originates with the BLUE-CROWNED MOTMOT (Plate 46), whose common call is *whoot-whoot, whoot-whoot*. Family Momotidae includes only nine species, all limited geographically to the Neotropics. Motmots are mainly residents of low-altitude forests, but occur in other habitats also, such as orchards, tree-lined plantations, suburban parks, and some dryer scrub areas; they are common inhabitants of many archeological ruin sites. Motmots are colorful, slender, small to medium-sized birds, 18 to 48 cm (7 to 19 in) long. They have fairly long, broad, bills that are downcurved at the end; the bills have serrated edges, adapted to grab and hold their animal prey. The most

peculiar motmot feature, however, is the tail: in most motmots, two central feathers of the tail grow much longer than others. Soon, feather barbs near the end of these two feathers drop off, either from the bird's preening or from brushing against tree branches, resulting in short lengths of barbless vane and, below this area, in what is commonly described as a *racquet head* appearance of the feather ends. Male and female motmots are alike in size and coloring. If you get a sufficiently close look, you will discover that motmots are among the most handsome, visually stunning of Central American birds, with their bodies of blended shades of green, black masks and, in some, brilliant blue head patches.

Natural History

Ecology and Behavior

Motmots are predators on insects (particularly beetles, butterflies, dragonflies, and cicadas), spiders, and small frogs, lizards and snakes, which they snatch in the air, off leaves, and from the ground. Typically they perch quietly on tree branches or on telephone wires or fences, sometimes idly swinging their long tails back and forth, until they spy a suitable meal. They then dart quickly, seize the prey, and ferry it back to the perch for munching. If the item is large or struggling – a big beetle, a lizard – the hungry motmot will hold it tight in its serrated bill and whack it noisily against the perch before swallowing it. Motmots are also frugivores, eating small fruits, up to the size of plums, which they collect from trees while hovering. Motmots are never observed in flocks. They are seen either solitarily or in pairs, and may remain in pairs throughout the year (although the sexes may separate during the day to feed). An unusual feature of their behavior is that motmots are usually active well into the twilight, going to sleep later than do most birds.

Breeding

Some courtship activities have been observed, with male and female motmots calling back and forth high up in the trees, and sometimes holding bits of green leaves in their bills. Motmots are burrow nesters, like their kingfisher cousins. Both male and female dig the burrow, often placed in the vertical bank of a river or roadside. Tunnels up to 4 m (13 ft) long have been uncovered, but most are on the order of 1.5 m (5 ft). Both parents incubate the two to four eggs. Young are fed and brooded by male and female for 24 to 30 days, at the end of which the juvenile motmots are well feathered and able to fly from the burrow entrance.

Lore and Notes

"In the wet Caribbean forests of southern Central America, the hollow hooting of RUFOUS MOTMOTS ('hoohoo' or 'hoohoohoo') is one of the characteristic dawn sounds. Until traced to their source – which may take long – the deep, soft, scarcely-birdlike notes create an atmosphere of unfathomable mystery. It is easy to imagine that the ghosts of the vanished aborigines are calling to each other through the dripping woodland" (A. F. Skutch 1971).

"The curious racket-tailed motmots have what I call the most velvety of all bird notes. It is usually a single short *oot*, pitched about five tones below where one can whistle...Most of the natives have sound-names for motmots, and the Maya Indians of Yucatán call the brilliant (Turquoise-browed Motmot) 'Toh,' and, as an appreciation of the interest, he has come to nest and roost familiarly in the age-long deserted ruins of their former glory" (L. A. Fuertes 1914).

One Mayan legend explains both how motmot tails came to have racquet ends and why motmots are burrow nesters. The motmot, with his brilliant coloring and long tail, considered himself a bit above other, less regal-looking birds. When a large storm was brewing and all the birds set to work to prepare to weather the storm and survive, building dams and storing fruits and seeds, the motmot, too pretty and important to be bothered with work, hid in the brush and went to sleep. He did not notice that his long tail stuck out into a trail, where working birds frequently stepped on it, causing barbs to fall out. The storm never materialized and, later, as all the birds gathered to preen in relief, they laughed at the motmot's ruined tail. The embarrassed motmot fled into the dark forest, dug a burrow, and became an underground recluse (A. L. Bowes 1964).

Status

Several motmots, including TODY and KEEL-BILLED MOTMOTS (Plate 46), are rare over parts of their ranges (for example, in Costa Rica), but are not considered threatened owing to their greater abundance in other parts of their ranges. The Keel-billed is on some lists of threatened species, chiefly because its extremely patchy distribution is not understood. That is, Keel-billeds have an extensive range within Central America but they are common only in small, isolated areas within that range, in Mexico, Belize, Guatemala, Nicaragua, and Costa Rica.

Profiles

Tody Motmot, *Hylomanes momotula*, Plate 46a
Blue-crowned Motmot, *Momotus momota*, Plate 46b
Keel-billed Motmot, *Electron carinatum*, Plate 46c

22. Woodpeckers

We are all familiar with *woodpeckers*, at least in name and in their cartoon incarnations. These are industrious, highly specialized birds of the forest – where there are trees in the world, there are woodpeckers (excepting only Australia, the polar regions, and some islands). The group, encompassing 200+ species, from the 9-cm (3.5-in) *piculets* to large woodpeckers up to 50 cm (20 in) long, is contained in the Family Picidae, placed, along with the toucans, jacamars, and puffbirds, in the Order Piciformes. Eleven species of various sizes occur in Belize and northern Guatemala (one, the YELLOW-BELLIED SAPSUCKER, is a North American migrant, present only during winter) and they occupy diverse habitats and employ various feeding methods. Small and medium-sized birds, woodpeckers have strong, straight, chisel-like bills, very long tongues that are barbed and often sticky-coated, and toes that spread widely, firmly anchoring the birds to tree trunks and branches. They come in various shades of olive-green, brown, and black and white, usually with small but conspicuous head or neck patches of red or yellow. Some have red or brown crests. A few woodpeckers are actually quite showy, and some have striking black and white stripes on chest or back. The sexes usually look alike. Because of the tapping sounds they produce as they butt their bills against trees and wooden structures, and owing to their characteristic stance – braced upright on vertical tree trunks – woodpeckers often attract our notice and so are frequently observed forest-dwellers.

Natural History

Ecology and Behavior

Woodpeckers are associated with trees and are adapted to cling to a tree's bark and to move lightly over its surface, searching for insects; they also drill holes in bark and wood into which they insert their long tongues, probing for hidden bugs. They usually move up tree trunks in short steps, using their stiff tail as a prop, or third foot. Woodpeckers eat many kinds of insects that they locate on or in trees, including larval ones. They also are not above a bit of flycatching, taking insects on the wing, and many supplement their diets with fruits, nuts, and nectar. Members of the genus *Melanerpes*, in particular, which includes the BLACK-CHEEKED and GOLDEN-FRONTED WOODPECKERS (Plates 46, 47), also eat a lot of fruit. A few species have ants as a dietary staple. The *sapsuckers*, a type of woodpecker, use their bills to drill small holes in trees that fill with sap, which is then eaten. Some woodpeckers also forage on the ground.

Woodpeckers are monogamous, and some live in large family groups. Tropical woodpeckers usually remain paired throughout the year. They sleep and nest in cavities that they excavate in trees. Woodpeckers hit trees with their bills for three very different reasons: for drilling bark to get at insect food; for excavating holes for roosting and nesting; and for *drumming*, sending signals to other woodpeckers. Thus, one never knows upon first hearing the characteristic drumming sound whether the bird in question is feeding, signalling, or carving a new home. Woodpeckers typically weave up and down as they fly (*undulatory* flight), a behavior suited to make it more difficult for predators to track the birds' movements.

Breeding

A mated male and female woodpecker carve a nesting hole in a tree. Sometimes they line the cavity with wood chips. Both sexes incubate the two to four eggs for 11 to 18 days, males typically taking the entire night shift. Young are fed by both parents for 20 to 35 days until they fledge. Juveniles probably remain with the parents for several months more, or longer in those species in which families of up to 20 individuals associate throughout the year.

Ecological Interactions

The different woodpecker species that live in one region usually are graded in size. There are small, medium (for instance, BLACK-CHEEKED WOODPECKER, Plate 46), and large (PALE-BILLED WOODPECKER, Plate 47) species. The size differences permit coexistence in the same area of such ecologically similar species because birds of various sizes specialize on different foods, thereby reducing negative effects of competition. When there are two or more woodpecker species of about the same size inhabiting the same place, it always appears to be the case that the potential competitors forage in different ways, or for different items – again, eliminating competition that could drive one of the species to extinction in the region over which they overlap.

Woodpeckers as a group have both beneficial and harmful effects on forests. On the one hand, they damage living, dying, and dead trees with their excavations and drilling, but on the other, they consume great quantities of insects, such as *tree borers*, that can themselves significantly damage forests. Because other birds use tree holes for roosting and/or nesting, but do not necessarily or cannot dig holes themselves, sometimes the carpenter-like woodpeckers end up doing the work for them. Many species occupy deserted woodpecker holes. More sinisterly, some birds "parasitize" the woodpecker's work by stealing holes. For instance, COLLARED ARACARIS (Plate 48), medium-sized toucans, have been observed evicting PALE-BILLED WOODPECKERS from their nest holes.

Lore and Notes

In ancient Roman mythology, Saturn's son, Picus, was a god of the forests. The sorceress Circe, attracted to the handsome Picus, courted him, but was rejected. In her wrath, she transformed Picus into a woodpecker, providing the basis for the woodpecker family's name, Picidae. The Mayans of ancient America thought that the woodpecker was a lucky bird, possessor of a lucky green stone that it kept under its wing. The legend was that the luck would be transferred to any person who could find a woodpecker hole and cover it. The bird would excavate a new hole, but that one, too, should be covered. After nine excavations, the woodpecker would drop the charm, allowing the person to claim it (A. L. Bowes 1964). During the height of the Mayan civilization, presumably, there were quite a few highly frustrated woodpeckers.

Woodpeckers damage trees and buildings and also eat fruit from gardens and orchards (especially cherries, apples, pears, and raspberries) and so in some parts of the tropics are considered significant pests and treated as such. The HISPANIOLAN WOODPECKER was routinely killed in the Dominican Republic because of its habits of carving holes in royal palms and boring into woody cacao pods to eat the inner pulp and insects. And, of course, we cannot fail to mention the lovesick NORTHERN FLICKER (a type of woodpecker) in Florida (USA) that continually drilled holes in what the bird must have thought was soft wood, but what was actually the hardened foam protective covering of the about-to-be-launched Space Shuttle's nose cone. The space ship was delayed for several days while ornithologists and technicians figured out how to move the troublesome bird from the area.

Status

None of the woodpeckers of Belize and Guatemela is presently threatened, but several species are noticeably declining as forests continue to be cut. Several woodpeckers appear on lists of endangered animals, including the HELMETED WOODPECKER of South America and the RED-COCKADED WOODPECKER (USA ESA listed) of the southeastern USA. Two of the largest woodpeckers, which survived until several decades ago, are now probably extinct: the USA's IVORY-BILLED WOODPECKER, a victim of the destruction of its old growth river forest habitat, and Mexico's IMPERIAL WOODPECKER, which, at 58 cm (22 in) long, was the largest member of the family.

Profiles

Black-cheeked Woodpecker, *Melanerpes pucherani*, Plate 46d
Golden-fronted Woodpecker, *Melanerpes aurifrons*, Plate 47a
Smoky-brown Woodpecker, *Veniliornis fumigatus*, Plate 47b
Golden-olive Woodpecker, *Piculus rubiginosus*, Plate 47c
Lineated Woodpecker, *Dryocopus lineatus*, Plate 47d
Pale-billed Woodpecker, *Campephilus guatemalensis*, Plate 47e
Acorn Woodpecker, *Melanerpes formicivorus*, Plate 48a

23. Toucans

Spectacular. No other word fits them – *toucans* are spectacular animals. Their shape, brilliant coloring, and tropical quintessence make them one of the most popular "poster animals" for the tropical forests of the Americas and one most visitors want to see. It's hardly surprising, therefore, that the logos of several conservation organizations and tour companies feature toucans. The toucan family, Ramphastidae, is classified with the woodpeckers, and contains about 40 species – the toucans and the usually smaller *toucanets* and *aracaris* (AH-rah-SAH-reez); all are restricted to the American tropics. Three species occur in Belize and Guatemala.

The first sighting of toucans in the wild is always exhilarating – the large size of the bird, the bright colors, the enormous, almost cartoonish bill. Toucans are usually first noticed flying from treetop to treetop in small groups. Your eyes immediately lock onto the flight silhouette; something is different here! As one observer put it, it looks as if the bird is following its own bill in flight (J. C. Kricher 1989). The effect of the bill seeming to lead the bird is that toucans appear unbalanced while flying. The bird's most distinguishing feature, the colorful, disproportionately large bill, is actually light, mostly hollow, and used for cutting down and manipulating the diet staple, tree fruit.

Natural History

Ecology and Behavior
Toucans are gregarious forest birds, usually observed in flocks of three to 12. They follow each other in *strings* from one tree to another, usually staying in the high canopy (a toucan only occasionally flies down to feed at shrubs, or to pluck a snake or a lizard from the forest floor). The birds are playful, grasping each other's bills in apparent contests, and tossing fruit to each other. Toucans are primarily fruit-eaters, preferring the darkest, so ripest, fruit. Their long bill allows them to perch on heavier, stable branches and reach a distance for hanging fruits. They snip the fruit off, hold it at the tip of the bill, and then, with a forward flip of the head, toss the fruit into the air and into their throats. (Seems, we humans think, an inefficient eating method, but the toucans do quite nicely with it.) Toucans also increase their protein intake by consuming the occasional insect, spider, or small reptile, or even bird eggs or nestlings. (I will never forget my surprise when I lifted my binoculars to a toucan high up in an Argentine tree and watched it snatch in its bill a big black tarantula, then hit its bill against a heavy branch, the better to knock the spider senseless, then gulp it down.) Sometimes individual fruit trees are defended by a mated toucan pair from other toucans or from other frugivorous birds – defended by threat displays and even, against other toucans, by bill clashes.

Breeding
Breeding usually is during the dry season. Toucans nest (and some sleep) in tree cavities, either natural ones or those hollowed out by woodpeckers, in either live or dead trees. Nests can be any height above the ground, up to 30 m (100 ft) or more. Both sexes incubate and feed the two to four young. Toucans are apparently monogamous. Some species, such as the COLLARED ARACARI (Plate 48), seem to breed cooperatively; that is, other family members, in addition to the mother and father, help raise the young in a single nest.

Ecological Interactions
Small fruit seeds pass unharmed through toucan digestive tracts and large seeds are regurgitated, also unharmed. Thus, these frugivores aid in the dispersal of tree seeds, and, together with other fruit-eaters, are responsible for the positions of some forest trees. In other words, many forest trees grow not where a parent tree drops its seeds, but where frugivorous birds do so.

Lore and Notes

According to stories and legends, some groups of South American Indians that existed at least until the European conquests (for instance, the U'wa, or Tunebo, of Venezuela and Colombia) recognized frugivorous birds such as toucans to be beneficial dispersers of fruit seeds. To reward the animals, the people left fruit and nuts for them whenever crops were harvested.

Toucan feathers have long been used as ornaments. Alfred Russell Wallace, co-formulator with Darwin of the theory of evolution, visited South America from 1848 to 1852, noting in his journals that dancers in Brazilian villages commonly wore hats with red and yellow toucan feathers.

Toucans are commonly known in many areas of the Neotropics as "Dios te de," (God gives it to you), apparently because the three-syllable call of the large CHESTNUT-MANDIBLED TOUCAN, which occurs from Honduras south to Colombia, sounds like this expression.

Status

Toucans are common residents in the various regions in which they occur, except where there is extensive deforestation. None of the family is currently threatened in Belize and Guatemala. Some toucans, for example the CHESTNUT-MANDIBLED, have suffered substantial population declines in heavily deforested areas of Central America, for instance, in some regions of Panama. Also, some toucan species may be scarce locally due to hunting. Several toucans, including the KEEL-BILLED (Plate 48), are listed by CITES but, rather than being immediately threatened, they are listed because they are considered "look-alikes" of threatened species, and so they need to be monitored during international trade.

Profiles

Collared Aracari, *Pteroglossus torquatus*, Plate 48b
Keel-billed Toucan, *Ramphastos sulfuratus*, Plate 48c
Emerald Toucanet, *Aulacorhynchus prasinus*, Plate 48d

All of the bird families considered below are *passerine* families, or *perching birds*, contained within the Order Passeriformes (see p. 109):

---

24. Woodcreepers

Woodcreepers are small and medium-sized brown birds that pursue a mostly arboreal lifestyle. The family, Dendrocolaptidae, consists of about 50 species, all tree-climbing birds of Central and South America. They are common in wet forest at low and moderate elevations, but also at the forest edge and in semi-open areas. In contrast to many other groups, the woodcreepers, including the nine species that occur in Belize and northern Guatemala, are fairly uniform in size, plumage colors, and natural history. Most are slender birds, 20 to 36 cm (8 to 14 in) in length. The sexes look alike, with plumages mostly of various shades of brown, chestnut, or tan. Many have white patches of varying dimension on breast, head, or back; and most have some spotting, streaking, or banding, particularly on the chest. Woodcreepers resemble woodpeckers to some extent, with longish bills (some strongly curved downwards) and stiff tails that they use to brace themselves against tree trunks. Owing to their physical similarities, the various woodcreepers are often difficult to tell apart, even for experienced birdwatchers. Body size, bill size and shape, and type of streaking are used to distinguish members of the group.

Natural History

Ecology and Behavior
Woodcreepers feed by moving upwards on tree trunks and also horizontally along branches, peering under bark and into moss clumps and epiphytes, using their long bills to probe and snatch prey in tight nooks and crannies. Unlike woodpeckers, they do not dig holes in search of prey. The foraging technique is quite standardized: A woodcreeper flies to the base of a tree and then spirals up the trunk, using its stiff, spiny tail as a third foot to brace itself in a vertical posture against the tree; it checks for prey as it climbs. At the top, the bird flies down to the base of the next tree, and repeats the process. The group is primarily *insectivorous*, but also takes spiders as well as small lizards and amphibians. Many woodcreepers are frequent participants, with antbirds, tanagers, and motmots, among others, in *mixed-species flocks* (see p. 166) that follow swarms of army ants, taking prey that rush out from hiding places to avoid the voracious ants. Woodcreepers are most often observed singly or in pairs, but occasionally in small family groups. They roost in tree crevices or holes.

Breeding
Most Central American woodcreepers breed from March through July. Some practice standard monogamy, with the sexes equally sharing nesting chores, but in some, apparently no real pair-bonds are established and, after mating, females nest alone. Nests are usually tree crevices or holes, but sometimes are established in arboreal termite nests. Parents line nests with wood chips. The two or three eggs are incubated for 17 to 21 days and young fledge 18 to 24 days after hatching.

Ecological Interactions
Quite often, a large number of woodcreeper species coexist in the same local area. The food items they take and their foraging methods are quite similar – which ordinarily should engender much harmful competition among the birds and lead to elimination of the weaker competitors. But the species apparently avoid much direct competition by having sufficiently different body sizes and bill sizes and shapes to support specialization on slightly different prey and foraging on slightly different parts of trees.

Lore and Notes
Some woodcreepers have reputations for being extremely aggressive toward other species, for instance, for harassing and evicting roosting or nesting woodpeckers from tree cavities.

Status
Many woodcreepers are quite abundant in Central America. A few species are uncommon over certain regions, but are not threatened because they are more abundant in other parts of their ranges. One Brazilian species with low population numbers, the MOUSTACHED WOODCREEPER, is considered vulnerable to threat.

Profiles
Tawny-winged Woodcreeper, *Dendrocincla anabatina*, Plate 49a
Wedge-billed Woodcreeper, *Glyphorhynchus spirurus*, Plate 49b

Olivaceous Woodcreeper, *Sittasomus griseicapillus*, Plate 49c
Ivory-billed Woodcreeper, *Xiphorhynchus flavigaster*, Plate 49d

25. Antbirds

Antbirds are small and medium-sized, rather drably attired inhabitants of the lower parts of the forest that have intriguing feeding behavior; unfortunately, owing to their usual behavior of hopping about along the dark forest floor, they are difficult to observe. Antbirds (Family Formicariidae) are active passerines, about 250 species strong, which are confined chiefly to the warm forests and thickets of the Neotropics. The family name refers to the feeding behavior of some of the species, which regularly follow ant swarms, snatching small creatures that leave their hiding places to avoid the predatory ants. Ten species occur in Belize and northern Guatemala.

Antbirds range in size from 8 to 36 cm (3 to 14 in). The smallest are the *antwrens* and *antvireos*, whereas the ones known formally as *antbirds* are mid-sized, and the largest are *antshrikes* and *antthrushes*. In fine detail, these birds are quite varied in appearance and some are boldly patterned, but males mostly appear in understated shades of dark gray, brown, or black, with varying amounts of white on backs, shoulders, or wings. A few species are black and white striped. Female plumage is likewise dull, generally olive, brown, or chestnut. Both sexes in some species have red eyes surrounded by patches of bare skin that are bright blue or other colors.

Natural History

Ecology and Behavior
Antbirds are mostly found at the lower levels of the forest or on the forest floor – they are shade dwellers. Most species practice *insectivory*, although some of the larger ones also eat fruit or small lizards, snakes, and frogs. Some are ant-followers, feeding in *mixed-species flocks* that follow army ants (see below), but others are ground and foliage *gleaners*, many rummaging around on the ground through the leaf litter, tossing dead leaves aside with their bills as they search for insects. When those that follow ants for a living breed, they temporarily cease ant following and establish and defend breeding territories. In some species, family groups remain together, male offspring staying with the parents, even after acquiring mates.

Breeding
Many antbirds appear to mate for life. Courtship feeding occurs in some of these birds, males passing food to females prior to mating. Many antbirds build cup nests out of pieces of plants that they weave together. Nests are usually placed in a fork of branches low in a tree or shrub. Some nest in tree cavities. Male and female share nest-building duty, as well as incubation of the two to three eggs and feeding insects to the young. Incubation is 14 to 20 days and young remain in the nest for nine to 18 days.

Ecological Interactions
Antbirds are participants in two related ecological interactions that facilitate feeding. Some antbirds are "professional" *ant followers* (that is, they do it all the time), such as the BICOLORED ANTBIRD of southern Central America, and some follow army ant swarms occasionally. Because these birds usually refrain from eating the

ants – a high formic acid content makes these insects unpalatable to most – but simply follow swarms of ants, using them to scare food out into the open as hunters use beaters to flush animals from hiding spots, this interaction between birds and bugs is a *commensalism*: one population benefits and the other, the ants, is essentially unaffected by it. Army ant swarms, consisting of from 50,000 to a million tiny carnivores, generally advance across the forest floor with a front that is 3 to 15 m (10 to 50 ft) wide, driving out all animals they encounter; the ants get some and the birds get many of the others.

A second phenomenon, *mixed species flocks* of foragers that roam large territories within the forest, is suspected of being a strong *mutualistic* interaction, in which all participants benefit. Interestingly, we are not sure in this case precisely what those benefits are, but many bird species throughout the tropics participate in such feeding flocks, so benefits to all there must be. Some of the flocks follow army ants, but others do not. Antbirds are regular members of these feeding flocks, with some South American species even appearing to be regular flock "leaders." Other birds join the feeding assemblages occasionally, or for parts of a day – tanagers (frequently), motmots, cuckoos, woodcreepers, ovenbirds. Sometimes upwards of 50 different species are observed moving in a single flock. Individuals tend to remain with the same flock for a year or more, breeding within the flock's territory. These flocks move through forests at a reported typical speed of about 1 km (0.6 mile) every 3 hours, although not in a straight line. A common experience of visitors to tropical forests is that, as they walk along a trail, very few birds are noticed. Suddenly, from nowhere, a large flock appears, birds of many species are everywhere, calling, foraging, fluttering around, flying, moving; then, in a few moments, just as suddenly, they are gone, passed on, and the quiet returns.

As you might expect, to avoid direct competition, the various species within a flock will specialize on feeding in particular places with respect to the flock; in fact, on close examination, the feeding flocks appear to be tightly structured. Some species always forage on or near the ground, others on trees at 2, 5 or 10 m (6, 15, 30 ft) up. Some explore live leaves for bugs, others specialize on dead leaves. Some might make constant, short sallies, flycatching. One species might always be at the flock center, another typically at the flock periphery. Some birds concentrate on catching prey that flushes in response to the flock's whirlwind arrival, while others search the leaf litter. Notice the advantage of this arrangement for an individual bird, as opposed to its joining a single-species flock: Because feeding behavior is usually the same for all members of a species, in a single-species flock an individual needs to compete continually for the same food in the same part of the forest using the same feeding method.

What are the possible benefits of foraging in large flocks of diverse species? First, there is always safety in numbers – more birds means more eyes and ears available to detect dangerous predators, such as falcons or snakes. Also, some of the flock members (often shrike-tanagers and antshrikes), in shifts, seem to serve as *sentinels*, feeding less, keeping alert for danger, and giving alarm calls when predators are detected. It has been noted that some of the flock participants that feed on the forest floor will not even put their head down into the leaf litter unless sentinels are posted. Further, should a predator strike, the likelihood of any one individual flock member being taken is small. Second, there must be some feeding advantage that results from the moving, mixed-species flock – probably the propensity of the rapidly moving flock to flush insects from hiding places, thus making them easier to find for all.

Lore and Notes

The strange compound names of these birds, such as antwrens, antshrikes, and antthrushes, apparently arose because naturalists from outside of the Neotropics who named them could not ascertain local names or believed that local people had no names for these species. Although the birds do not resemble, for example, wrens, shrikes, or thrushes, they were so designated owing to their relative sizes.

Status

None of the antbirds of Belize or Guatemala is presently considered threatened, and many are very common, if difficult to see, residents of various forest areas. About 30 species within the family Formicariidae, mostly Brazilian, are considered vulnerable to threat; at least four species in Brazil are endangered, including the BLACK-HOODED ANTWREN and the FRINGE-BACKED FIRE-EYE.

Profiles

Barred Antshrike, *Thamnophilus doliatus*, Plate 50a
Plain Antvireo, *Dyssithamnus mentalis*, Plate 50b
Black-faced Antthrush, *Formicarius analis*, Plate 50c
Dot-winged Antwren, *Microrhopias quixensis*, Plate 50d
Dusky Antbird, *Cercomacra tyrannina,* Plate 50e

26. Manakins

The *manakins*, Family Pipridae, are a Neotropical group of about 60 species of small, compact, stocky passerine birds, 9 to 19 cm (3.5 to 7.5 in) long, with short tails and bills, and two attention-grabbing features: brightly colored plumages and perhaps the most elaborate courtship displays among birds. Some male manakins are outstandingly beautiful, predominantly glossy black but with brilliant patches of bright orange-red, yellow, or blue on their heads and/or throats. Some have deep blue on their undersides and/or backs. The exotic appearance of male manakins is sometimes enhanced by long, streamer-like tails, up to twice the length of the body, produced by the elongation of two of the central tail feathers. Females, in contrast, are duller and less ornate, usually shades of yellowish olive-green or gray. To accompany the bird's courtship displays, the wing feathers of some species, when moved in certain ways, make whirring or snapping sounds. Only three species occur in Belize and Guatemala.

Natural History

Ecology and Behavior

Manakins are highly active forest birds, chiefly of warmer, lowland areas, although some range up into cloud forests. Residents of the forest understory, they eat mostly small fruits, which they pluck from bushes and trees while in flight, and they also take insects from the foliage. Manakins are fairly social animals when it comes to feeding and other daily activities, but males and females do not pair. They employ a non-monogamous mating system and, in fact, most of our knowledge about manakin behavior concerns their breeding – how females choose males with which to mate and, in particular, male courting techniques. To use the ornithological jargon, manakins are *promiscuous* breeders. No pair-bonds are formed between males and females. Males mate with more than one female and females probably do the same. After mating, females build nests and rear young by themselves. Males, singly or in pairs, during the breeding season stake out display sites on tree branches, in bushes, or on cleared patches of the forest floor, and then spend considerable amounts of time giving lively vocal and visual displays, trying to attract females. An area that contains several of these performance sites is called a *lek*, and thus manakins, along with other birds such as some grouse, some cotingas, and some hummingbirds, are *lekking* breeders.

At the lek, male manakins *dance*, performing elaborate, repetitive, amazingly rapid and acrobatic movements, sometimes making short up and down flights, sometimes rapid slides, twists, and turn-arounds, sometimes hanging upside down on a tree branch while turning rapidly from side to side and making snapping sounds with their wings. The details of a male's dance are *species specific*, that is, different species dance in different ways. Females, attracted to leks by the sounds of male displays and by their memories of lek locations – the same traditional forest sites are used from one year to the next – examine the energetically performing males with a critical eye and then choose the ones they want to mate with, sometimes making the rounds several times before deciding. In a few species, such as southern Guatemala's LONG-TAILED MANAKIN, two and sometimes three males (*duos* and *trios*) join together in a coordinated dance on the same perch. Long-tails in their dance alternate *leapfrog hops* with bouts of slow, *butterfly* flight, and the males jointly give a synchronous call that sounds like "toledo" up to 19 times per minute. A duo may give up to 5000 "toledos" in a single day, apparently alerting passing females that the males are ready to display and mate. In these curious cases, one male is dominant, one subordinate, and only the dominant of the pair eventually gets to mate with interested females. Why the subordinate male appears to help the dominant one obtain matings (are they closely related? Do subordinate males stand to inherit display sites when the dominants die? Do subordinates achieve "stolen" matings with females when the dominants are temporarily distracted?), why the manakins dance at all, and on what basis females choose particular males to become the fathers of their young, are all areas of continuing scientific inquiry.

Breeding
Manakins of various species appear to breed during both wet and dry seasons. Males take no part in nesting. The female builds a shallow cup nest that she weaves into a fork of tree branches, 1 to 15 meters (3 to 50 ft) off the ground. She incubates the 1 to 2 eggs for 17 to 20 days, and rears the nestlings herself, bringing them fruit and insects, for 13 to 20 days.

Ecological Interactions
Manakins, like most birds that use open, cup-like nests, often suffer very high rates of nest destruction. In one small study, only about 7% of eggs survived the incubation stage and hatched. Most nests were lost to predators, for which the suspect list is quite lengthy: ground-dwelling as well as arboreal snakes, birds such as motmots, puffbirds, toucans, and magpie-jays, large arboreal lizards, and mammals such as opossums, monkeys, kinkajous, and coatis.

Largely frugivorous, manakins are important seed dispersers of the fruit tree species from which they feed (see p. 170).

Lore and Notes
Colorful manakin feathers were often used by the indigenous peoples of Central and South America for ornamental purposes, especially for clothing and masks used during dances and solemn festivals.

Status

None of the manakins of Belize and Guatemala is currently considered to be threatened. Several South American species possibly face trouble, including the threatened GOLDEN-CROWNED MANAKIN of Brazil and the BLACK-CAPPED MANAKIN of Argentina and Brazil.

Profiles

White-collared Manakin, *Manacus candei*, Plate 51a
Red-capped Manakin, *Pipra mentalis*, Plate 51b

27. Cotingas

Owing to their variety of shapes, sizes, ecologies, and breeding systems, as well as to their flashy coloring, *cotingas* are usually considered to be among the Neotropic's glamour birds. The family, Cotingidae, is closely allied to the *manakins* and contains about 65 species that live primarily in lowland tropical forests. All observers of these birds stress the group's diversity. The cotingas include tiny, warbler-sized birds and large, crow-sized birds (in fact, the group contains both some of the smallest and largest passerine birds); fruit-and-insect eaters but also some that eat only fruit (which among birds is uncommon); species in which the sexes look alike and many in which males are spectacularly attired in bright spectral colors but females are plain; territorial species that breed monogamously and *lekking* species that breed *promiscuously* (see below); and, without doubt, some of the strangest looking birds of Neotropical forests.

The classification of the cotingas is controversial. If two closely related groups, the *tityras* and *becards*, are included with them, there are a total of about 10 species that occur within Belize and northern Guatemala. Perhaps the only generalizations that apply to all cotingas is that they have short legs and relatively short, rather wide bills, the better to swallow fruits. Males of some of the group are quite ornate, with patches of gaudy plumage in unusual colors. For instance, some of the typical cotingas are lustrous blue and deep purple, and some are all white; others are wholly black, or green and yellow, or largely red or orange or gray. Unusual-looking cotingas include two from southern Central America: the male THREE-WATTLED BELLBIRD, which is brown with a shiny white head and has attached to its bill area three hanging, worm-like, darkly colored wattles; and the BARE-NECKED UMBRELLABIRD, which has an umbrella-shaped black crest.

Natural History

Ecology and Behavior

Cotingas primarily inhabit the high canopy of the forest. They are fruit specialists, a feature of their natural history that has engendered much study. They eat small and medium-sized fruits that they take off trees, often while hovering. Some cotingas, such as the *pihas* and *fruitcrows*, supplement the heavily frugivorous diet with insects taken from the treetop foliage, but others, particularly the *bellbirds*, feed exclusively on fruit – which has both benefits and problems (see below).

Breeding

Some cotingas pair up, defend territories, and breed conventionally in apparent monogamy. But others, such as umbrellabirds and bellbirds, are *lekking* species, in which males individually stake out display trees and repeatedly perform vocal and visual displays to attract females. Females enter display areas (*leks*), assess the jumping and calling males, and choose the ones they wish to mate with. With this type of breeding, females leave after mating and then nest and rear young alone. Cotinga nests, usually placed in trees or bushes, are generally small, open, and inconspicuous, some nest cups being made of loosely arranged twigs, some of mud, and some of pieces of plants. Many species lay only a single egg, some one or two eggs. Incubation is 17 to 28 days and the nestling period is 21 to 44 days, both stages quite long for passerine birds.

Ecological Interactions
A key feature of tropical forests, and of the animal communities that inhabit them, is the large number of birds (cotingas, finches, manakins, parrots, orioles, tanagers, toucans, and trogons make up a partial list) that rely on fruit as a diet staple. Frugivory (fruit-eating) represents a trade, each participant – the fruit-bearing tree and the fruit-eating bird – offering the other something of great value (and therefore it is a kind of *mutualism* – p. 55). The complex web of relationships between avian fruit-eaters and fruit-producing trees is particularly interesting because it nicely demonstrates ecological interactions between plants and animals. Birds benefit greatly from the association because, for several reasons, fruit is an excellent type of food on which to specialize. It is conspicuous, abundant, and, in the tropics, usually available year-round. Also, unlike some other food types, like insects, fruit is easy to find and devour – it rarely hides or resists being eaten. But fruit is not ideal. Problems involved with eating mostly or only fruit include the fact that fruit is relatively low in protein so, for example, nestlings fed only fruit grow very slowly (as is the case in some cotingas). Trees benefit from the relationship by having birds eat, transport, and then drop their seeds far away, thereby achieving efficient, successful reproduction – something well worth their investment in fruit production. Seeds dropped very close to a parent tree must compete with the parent for sun and soil nutrients, and most often do not survive. Seeds dropped at a distance from a parent tree have a much greater chance of survival. Parent trees, therefore, make use of birds as winged, animate, seed *dispersal agents*. Because of the cotingas' feeding specialization on fruit, they are considered to be major dispersers of tree seeds. Owing to their high-canopy habits, the precise fruits cotingas go after often are difficult to determine. They are believed to feed heavily at palms, laurels, and incense trees, and also at, among others, members of the blackberry/raspberry family.

Status
In addition to several threatened and endangered South American species, four Central American cotingas are considered threatened: the BARE-NECKED UMBRELLABIRD, THREE-WATTLED BELLBIRD, YELLOW-BILLED COTINGA, and TURQUOISE COTINGA. The umbrellabird, for instance, is sparsely distributed in several localized areas scattered throughout its range (Costa Rica and Panama) and, often, only a few individuals can be found where it does occur. Leks that have been discovered have contained only three to six displaying males. The prime threat to umbrellabirds and other cotingas is deforestation; a particular problem for the umbrellabird, an *altitudinal migrant*, is that to live and reproduce it requires both highland forest breeding habitat and lowland forest wintering habitat. Thus, for the bird to survive, both types of forests in a single area, together with connecting forest corridors, must be preserved.

The smallest cotinga, the 7.5-cm (3-in) KINGLET CALYPTURA of southeastern Brazil, is either endangered or extinct. There are a few museum specimens taken in the 1800s from near Rio de Janeiro, but no one this century has reported a live sighting of the bird.

Profiles

Rufous Piha, *Lipaugus unirufus*, Plate 51c
Lovely Cotinga, *Cotinga amabilis*, Plate 51d
Masked Tityra, *Tityra semifasciata*, Plate 51e

28. American Flycatchers

The American *flycatchers* comprise a huge group of passerine birds that is broadly distributed over most habitats from Alaska and northern Canada to the southern tip of South America. The flycatcher family, Tyrannidae, is considered among the most diverse of avian groups. With about 380 species, flycatchers usually contribute a hefty percentage of the avian biodiversity in every locale. For instance, it has been calculated that flycatchers make up fully one-tenth of the land bird species in South America, and perhaps one-quarter of Argentinian species. Even in relatively tiny Belize, the group is represented by a healthy contingent of about 50 species.

Flycatchers range in length from 6.5 to 30 cm (2.5 to 12 in). At the smallest extreme are some of the world's tiniest birds, weighing, it is difficult to believe, only some 7 g (a quarter of an ounce). Bills are usually broad and flat, the better to snatch flying bugs from the air. Tail length is variable, but some species have very long, forked tails, which probably aid the birds in their rapid, acrobatic, insect-catching maneuvers. Most flycatchers are dully turned out in shades of gray, brown, and olive-green; many species have some yellow in their plumage, and a relatively few are quite flashily attired in, for example, bright expanses of red or vermilion. One set of frequently seen flycatchers, the best known of which is the GREAT KISKADEE (Plate 52), share a common, bright color scheme, with yellow chests and bellies, and black and white striped heads. A great many of the smaller, drabber flycatchers, clad in olives and browns, are extremely difficult to tell apart in the field, even for experienced birdwatchers. Flycatcher sexes are usually similar in size and coloring.

Natural History

Ecology and Behavior

Flycatchers are common over a large array of different habitat types, from mountainsides high in the Andes and in Belize's Maya Mountains, to lowland moist forests, to treeless plains and grasslands, to marshes and mangrove swamps; they are especially prevalent in rainforests. As their name implies, most flycatchers are *insectivores*, obtaining most of their food by employing the classic flycatching technique: they perch motionless on tree or shrub branches or on fences or telephone wires, then dart out in short, swift flights to snatch from the air insects foolhardy enough to enter their field of vision; they then return time and again to the same perch to repeat the process. Many flycatchers also take insects from foliage as they fly through vegetation, and many supplement their diets with berries and seeds. Some of the larger flycatchers will also take small frogs and lizards, and some, such as the GREAT KISKADEE, consider small fish and tadpoles delicacies to be plucked from shallow edges of lakes and rivers. A few, such as the OCHRE-BELLIED FLYCATCHER (Plate 53), have ceded flycatching to their relatives and now eat only fruit. Almost all of the relatively few flycatchers that have been studied inhabit exclusive territories that mated pairs defend for all or part of the year.

Breeding
Flycatchers are mainly monogamous. Some forest-dwelling species, however, breed *promiscuously*: groups of males call and display repeatedly at traditional courting sites called *leks*, attracting females that approach for mating but then depart to nest and raise young by themselves. Many flycatchers are known for spectacular courtship displays, males showing off to females by engaging in aerial acrobatics, including flips and somersaults. In monogamous species, males may help the females build nests. Some build cup nests, roofed nests, or globular hanging nests placed in trees or shrubs, others construct mud nests that they attach to vertical surfaces such as rock walls, and some nest in holes in trees or rocks. Tropical flycatchers generally lay two eggs that are incubated by the female only for 12 to 23 days; nestlings fledge when 14 to 28 days old.

Ecological Interactions
Some flycatchers show marked alterations in their lifestyles as seasons, locations, and feeding opportunities change. Such ongoing capacity for versatile behavior in response to changing environments is considered a chief underlying cause of the group's great ecological success. An excellent example is the EASTERN KINGBIRD'S drastic changes in behavior between summer and winter. Breeding during summer in North America, these flycatchers are extremely aggressive in defending their territories from birds and other animals, and they feed exclusively at that time on insects. But a change comes over the birds during the winter, as they idle away the months in South America's Amazon Basin. There, Eastern Kingbirds congregate in large, nonterritorial flocks with apparently nomadic existences, and they eat mostly fruit.

Some small flycatchers, known as *tody flycatchers* (Plate 53), construct large, hanging, woven, or *felted*, nests that take up to a month or more to build. These nests tend to hang from slender vines or weak tree branches, providing a degree of safety from climbing nest predators such as snakes and small mammals. Often, however, such efforts are ineffective – nest predation rates are quite high. In response, some of the tody flycatchers purposely build their nests near to colonies of stinging bees, apparently seeking additional protection from predators.

Lore and Notes
Of all the groups of birds, it is probably among the flycatchers that the most undiscovered species remain. This distinction is owing to the group's great diversity, its penetration into essentially all terrestrial habitats, and the inconspicuousness of many of its members. In fact, as people reach previously inaccessible locations – hidden valleys, cloud-draped mountain plateaus – in the remotest parts of South America, hitherto unknown flycatchers are indeed sighted. One species was first identified in 1976 in northern Peru, and another, weighing only 7 g (a quarter of an ounce), was found in southern Peru in 1981. Two more species were first described in the scientific literature in 1997.

Status
The BELTED FLYCATCHER, endemic to southern Mexico and southern Guatemala, is now considered to be threatened. Probably the only other flycatchers in Central America that are near-threatened are the TAWNY-CHESTED

FLYCATCHER of Costa Rica and Nicaragua, and perhaps the COCOS FLY-CATCHER, which is endemic to Costa Rica's Cocos Island. At least six South American species are presently endangered, including especially the very rare ASH-BREASTED TIT-TYRANT, which is confined to small, wooded patches of Peru and adjacent Bolivia.

Profiles

Tropical Kingbird, *Tyrannus melancholicus*, Plate 52a
Great Kiskadee, *Pitangus sulphuratus*, Plate 52b
Boat-billed Flycatcher, *Megarhynchus pitangua*, Plate 52c
Social Flycatcher, *Myiozetetes similis*, Plate 52d
Yellow-bellied Elaenia, *Elaenia flavogaster*, Plate 53a
Ochre-bellied Flycatcher, *Mionectes oleagineus*, Plate 53b
Common Tody Flycatcher, *Todirostrum cinereum*, Plate 53c
Yellow-olive Flycatcher, *Tolmomyias sulphurescens*, Plate 53d
Royal Flycatcher, *Onychorhynchus coronatus*, Plate 54a
Vermilion Flycatcher, *Pyrocephalus rubinus*, Plate 54b
Brown-crested Flycatcher, *Myiarchus tyrannulus*, Plate 54c
Dusky-capped Flycatcher, *Myiarchus tuberculifer*, Plate 54d
Fork-tailed Flycatcher, *Tyrannus savana*, Plate 54e

29. Wrens

Wrens are small brownish passerines with an active, snappish manner and, characteristically, upraised tails. The approximately 60 wren species comprise the family Troglodytidae, a group for the most part confined in distribution to the Western Hemisphere. Among other traits, wrens are renowned for their singing ability, vocal duets, and nesting behavior. They range in length from 10 to 20 cm (4 to 8 in) and usually appear mainly in shades of brown or reddish brown, with smaller bits of gray, tan, black, and white. Some of these birds are tiny, weighing in at less than 15 g, or half an ounce. Wings and tails are frequently embellished with finely barred patterns. Wrens have rather broad, short wings and owing to this, are considered poor flyers. The sexes look alike. Wrens' tails may be the group's most distinguishing feature, much of the time being held stiffly upright, at military attention. Tails are waved back and forth during displays, both those for courtship and aggression.

Natural History

Ecology and Behavior

Wrens are cryptically colored and fairly secretive in their habits as they flip, flutter, hop, and poke around the low levels of the forest, and through thickets, grasslands, and marshes, searching for insects. They are completely insectivorous or nearly so. Often spending the year living in pairs, they defend territories in which during the breeding season they will nest. Some of the larger wrens, such as the BANDED-BACKED WREN (Plate 55), spend their days in pairs or small family flocks, and, owing to their size, are a bit bolder in their movements. After using their nests for breeding, wrens will use them as roosting places – or "dormitories," as one researcher puts it. The vocalizations of wrens have been studied extensively. A pair will call back and forth as they lose sight of each other while foraging in thickets, keeping in contact. In some species, mated pairs sing some of the bird world's most complex duets, male and female rapidly alternating in giving parts of one song (as we think of it), so rapidly and expertly that it actually sounds as if one individual utters the entire sequence. Such duets probably function as "keep-out" signals, warning away from the pair's territory other members of the species, and in maintaining the pair-bond between mated birds. Other wrens, such as North America's WINTER WREN, have amazingly complex songs, long trains of notes in varied sequences up to 10 seconds or more in duration; researchers place these vocalizations at the very pinnacle of bird song complexity.

Breeding
Central America wrens are mainly monogamous, but some breed *cooperatively*, with members of the small family group helping out at the single nest of the parents. Nests, generally of woven grass, are placed in vegetation or in tree cavities. They are small but elaborate nests, roofed, with inconspicuous side entrances. Intriguingly, in some species the male builds many more nests on his territory than his mate (or mates, in polygynous species) can use, apparently as a courtship signal, perhaps as an inducement for a female to stay and mate. Only the female incubates the two to five eggs, for 13 to 19 days. Sometimes she is fed by the male during this period. Nestlings are fed by both parents for 14 to 19 days, until fledging.

Ecological Interactions
Some wrens enjoy a *commensal* relationship with ants. They often place their nests in cactus or acacia (p. 55) plants that serve as residences for ant colonies. The ants do not bother the birds and *vice versa*, yet the birds' nests bask in the ants' formidable protective powers against such possible egg and nestling predators as snakes and small mammals.

Lore and Notes
The HOUSE WREN (Plate 55) has all but abandoned breeding in its forgotten natural haunts and now, quite profitably, associates itself with people. These birds root about near and in human settlements, looking for insects. Nests are often placed in crannies and crevices within buildings or other structures. (Many wrens nest in naturally occurring cavities, hence the family name, Troglodytidae, or *cave dweller*.) The bird has been so successful living with people that it is quite common throughout its range, from Canada to the southern tip of South America.

From European antiquity come tales of the wren being considered among bird-dom's royalty, perhaps even the very King of Birds. One story of how the wren was crowned, likely one of Aesop's famous fables, is that in a contest to prove royal worth, the wily wren flew higher than any other bird by hiding on the back of the ascending eagle, then flying higher itself when the eagle tired.

Status
Most of the nine or so wren species that occur in Belize and northern Guatemala are fairly or very abundant; none is threatened. A few Mexican species are considered vulnerable, owing to small and/or declining populations. Only a few wren species are known to be endangered: Cuba's ZAPATA WREN and Colombia's APOLINAR'S and NICEFORO'S WRENS.

Profiles
Banded-backed Wren, *Campylorhynchus zonatus*, Plate 55a
Spot-breasted Wren, *Thryothorus maculipectus*, Plate 55b
White-breasted Wood-wren, *Henicorhina leucosticta*, Plate 55c
House Wren, *Troglodytes aedon*, Plate 55d

30. Thrushes and Mockingbirds

The more than 300 species of *thrushes* inhabit most terrestrial regions of the world and include some of the most familiar park and garden songbirds. The family, Turdidae, has few defining, common features that set all its members apart from other groups, as perhaps could be expected; so large an assemblage of species is sure to include a significant amount of variation in appearance, ecology, and behavior. Thrushes as a group are tremendously successful birds, especially when they have adapted to living near humans and benefiting from their environmental modifications. Most obviously, on five continents, a thrush is among the most common and recognizable garden birds, including North America's AMERICAN ROBIN, Europe's REDWING and BLACKBIRD, and Central America's CLAY-COLORED ROBIN (Plate 56). Thrushes of the Western Hemisphere are slender-billed birds that range from 12.5 to 31 cm (5 to 12 in) in length. Generally they are not brightly colored; instead, they come in drab browns, grays, brown-reds, olive, and black and white. The sexes are very similar in appearance. During their first year of life, young thrushes are clad in distinctively spotted plumages.

Family Mimidae is a New World group that consists of about 30 species of mid-sized, often slender songbirds, 20 to 32 cm (8 to 13 in) long, with characteristically long tails; they are known variously as *mockingbirds, thrashers,* and *catbirds.* Most are brown or gray with lighter chests, which are often streaked or spotted; within a species, the sexes generally look alike.

Natural History

Ecology and Behavior

Among the thrushes are species that employ a variety of feeding methods and that take several different food types. Many eat fruits, some are primarily insectivorous, and most are at least moderately omnivorous. Although arboreal birds, many thrushes frequently forage on the ground for insects, other arthropods, and, a particular favorite, delicious earthworms. The thrushes associated with gardens and lawns in Central America usually forage like the familiar thrushes from North America or Europe – they hop and walk along the ground, stopping at intervals, cocking their heads to peer downwards. These birds are residents of many kinds of habitats – forest edge, clearings, and other open areas such as shrub areas and grasslands, gardens, parks, suburban lawns, and agricultural areas. Many thrushes are quite social, spending their time during the nonbreeding season in flocks of the same species, feeding and roosting together. Some of the tropical thrushes make seasonal migrations from higher to lower elevations, following abundant food supplies.

Mockingbirds and catbirds are mostly birds of the ground, shrubs, and low trees. They forage on the ground in open areas and gardens for insects and other small invertebrate animals, and also take some fruit. These birds, as a group, are known for their virtuoso singing performances, their highly intriguing ability to closely mimic the songs of other species, and their aggressive territoriality during breeding seasons – many a person who wandered innocently across a mockingbird territory during nesting has been hit on the head by the swooping mockers.

Breeding

Thrushes breed monogamously, male and female together defending exclusive territories during the breeding season; pairs may associate year round. Nests, usually built by the female and placed in tree branches, shrubs, or crevices, are cup-shaped, made of grass, moss, and like materials, and often lined with mud. Two to six (usually two or three) eggs are incubated by the female only for 12 to 14 days. Young are fed by both parents for 12 to 16 days prior to their fledging. Likewise, catbirds and mockingbirds are monogamous. Cup nests are built of sticks and leaves by both sexes or by the female alone; she also incubates the two to five eggs for about 12 days. Young are fed in the nest by both sexes for 11 to 14 days until they fledge.

Lore and Notes

English colonists in the New World gave the AMERICAN ROBIN, a thrush, its name because it resembled England's common ROBIN – both birds have reddish breasts. The New World bird, however, is more closely related to Europe's BLACK-BIRD, also a common garden bird and a true thrush. Not content with incorrectly labeling birds that were new to them with English names, British settlers around the world, homesick, it is thought, imported birds from the British Isles to their new domains so that familiar birds would surround their new homes. The effects on native birds were often disastrous, and European thrushes such as the SONG THRUSH and BLACKBIRD, among many other birds, are now naturalized, dominant citizens of, for instance, Australia and New Zealand.

Status

Although several thrush species and a few members of the mockingbird family in various parts of the world are vulnerable to threat or are now threatened, none of the 12 species that breed or winter in Belize and northern Guatemala is in imminent danger. The BLACK CATBIRD (Plate 56), a slim, iridescent black beach-comber with red eyes, endemic to the Yucatán region, is considered threatened on some of Belize's offshore cayes; its coastal scrub and beach habitat increasingly is used for building purposes. The proposed Siwa-ban Marine Preserve on Caye Caulker would protect the catbird's habitat on that island, which probably supports the largest population of the bird in Belize.

Profiles

Wood Thrush, *Hylocichla mustelina*, Plate 56a
Clay-colored Robin, *Turdus grayi*, Plate 56b
Tropical Mockingbird, *Mimus gilvus*, Plate 56c
Black Catbird, *Melanoptila glabrirostris*, Plate 56d

31. Jays

Jays are members of the Corvidae, a passerine family of a hundred or so species that occurs just about everywhere in the world – or, as ecologists would say, *corvid* distribution is *cosmopolitan*. The group includes the *crows, ravens,* and *magpies.* Although on many continents birds of open habitats, Neotropical jays are primarily woodland or forest birds. Jays, aside from being strikingly handsome birds, are known for their versatility, adaptability, and for their seeming intelligence; in several ways, the group is considered by ornithologists to be the most highly developed of birds. They are also usually quite noisy.

Members of the family range in length from 20 to 71 cm (8 to 28 in), many near the higher end – large for passerine birds. Corvids have robust, fairly long bills and strong legs and feet. Many corvids (crows, ravens, rooks, jackdaws) are all or mostly black, but the jays are different, being attired in bright blues, purples, greens, yellows, and white. American jays tend to be blue, and many have conspicuous crests (like North America's BLUE JAY and STELLER'S JAY). Central America's BROWN JAY (Plate 57) is an exception among Neotropical jays, being plain brown and white and crest-less; owing to this, even researchers who work with the bird affectionately refer to it as the most homely of the group. In corvids, the sexes generally look alike. The COMMON RAVEN is the largest passerine bird, but although its range encompasses several continents, it does not extend to Belize and northern Guatemala.

Natural History

Ecology and Behavior

Jays eat a large variety of foods (and try to eat many others) and so are considered omnivores. They feed on the ground, but also in trees, taking bird eggs and nestlings, carrion, insects (including some in flight), and fruits and nuts. Bright and versatile, they are quick to take advantage of new food sources and to find food in agricultural and other human-altered environments. Jays use their feet to hold food down while tearing it with their bills. Hiding food for later consumption, *caching*, is practiced widely by the group.

Corvids are usually quite social, Central American jays being no exception. BROWN JAYS, for instance, remain all year in small groups of relatives, five to 10 individuals strong, that forage together within a restricted area, or *home range*, and at the appropriate time, breed together on a group-defended territory. They inhabit more open wooded areas, forest edges, fields, plantations, and habitat along waterways and near human settlements. Jays are raucous and noisy, giving varieties of harsh, grating, loud calls (some that sound like *jay*) as the foraging flock straggles from tree to tree.

Breeding

YUCATAN, GREEN, and BROWN JAYS (Plate 57) breed cooperatively. Generally the oldest pair in the group breeds and the other members serve only as *helpers*, assisting in nest construction and feeding the young. Courtship feeding is common, the male feeding the female before and during incubation, which she performs alone. Bulky open nests, constructed primarily of twigs, are placed in trees or rock crevices. Two to seven eggs are incubated for 16 to 21 days, the young then being fed in the nest by parents and helpers for 20 to 24 days.

Ecological Interactions

Jays and other corvids are often scavengers. Other carrion-eating birds exist, such as vultures, but jays and crows and their relatives contribute a good deal to breaking down dead animals so that the nutrients bound up in them are recycled into food webs. (And where there are roads, civic-minded corvids assist highway departments in keeping them clear of automobile-killed animals.) Corvids' omnivory also drives them to be predators on bird nests – generally on species that are smaller than they are, of which there are many. Jays, crows and magpies tear up nests and eat eggs and nestlings. They are considered to be responsible for a significant amount of the nest predation on many songbird species, particularly those with open-cup nests. Owing to their seed caching behavior, jays are important to trees as dispersal agents. In the USA, for example, the BLUE JAY'S acorn burying habit must surely result in the maintenance and spread of oak forests.

Lore and Notes

Although corvids are considered by many to be among the most intelligent of birds, and by ornithologists as among the most highly evolved, folklore is rife with tales of crows, ravens and magpies as symbols of ill-omen. This undoubtedly traces to the group's frequently all-black plumage and habit of eating carrion, both sinister traits. Ravens, in particular, have long been associated in many Northern cultures with evil or death, although these large, powerful birds also figure more benignly in Nordic and Middle Eastern mythology. Several groups of indigenous peoples of northwestern North America consider the COMMON RAVEN sacred and sometimes, indeed, as a god. As for jays themselves, their loud, chattering and scolding voices together with their physical beauty, have sometimes earned for these birds derogatory reputations. In fact, in Shakespearian England, "jay" was a term for a dishonest or loose woman.

Status

Only three corvids, all jays, occur in Belize and northern Guatemala, and all are common or fairly common birds. Many corvids adjust well to people's activities, indeed often expanding their ranges when they can feed on agricultural crops. Two smaller blue jays, DWARF and WHITE-THROATED JAYS, are endemic to small regions of Mexico and are considered endangered; and two island species, the HAWAIIAN and MARIANA CROWS, are now highly endangered (both are USA ESA listed).

Profiles

Brown Jay, *Cyanocorax morio*, Plate 57a
Green Jay, *Cyanocorax yncas*, Plate 57b
Yucatán Jay, *Cyanocorax yucatanicus*, Plate 57c

32. Warblers and Other Small, Flitting Birds

Birdwatchers and perhaps other users of this book realize that there are a large number of tiny birds that flit about trees, shrubs, thickets, and grasslands, birds that go by such names as *vireo, warbler, gnatcatcher, yellowthroat, redstart*. For good reasons, these birds are treated here only lightly. Owing to their sizes and agile natures, they are often difficult to identify, even for journeymen birdwatchers. Although they are beautiful little birds, even experienced birders sometimes despair of trying to differentiate the various species. Also, American warblers are common birds of North America, and so are not in any way exotic to travellers from that continent. In fact, many of the warblers seen in Central America, particularly from November through March, are breeders from North America, escaping the northern cold to winter in the tropics. Warblers are also more important birds in North than in Central America, in the sense that they are often so diverse and numerous in many northern forest habitats that, as a group, they make up more of the birdlife than all other birds combined. But for our purposes here, brief descriptions of a few of these birds will suffice. When one's interest is sufficiently piqued by these tiny birds to warrant further exploration, it is time to consider oneself a birdwatcher and to invest in a professional field guide!

Warblers, gnatcatchers, and the BANANAQUIT (Plate 59) are very small birds that flit and move jauntily about in trees, shrubs, and gardens, for the most part searching for or pursuing their dietary staple, insects. American warblers (Family Parulidae), also known as *wood warblers*, are a group of approximately 110 species, with wide distributions over the New World's forests, fields, marshes, and gardens. About 40 species occur regularly in Belize and northern Guatemala, many of them seasonal migrants from North American breeding sites. Warblers are brightly colored, predominantly yellow or greenish, often mixed with varying amounts of gray, black and white; a few have even more color, with patches of red, orange or blue. Gnatcatchers are members of a large, primarily Old World family, Sylviidae. There are 11 gnatcatcher species, tiny gray birds that flit about in wooded and forest edge areas; three species occur in Belize and northern Guatemala. The Bananaquit, which has been variously lumped into the warbler group, considered a honeycreeper (p. 183), and made the only member of its own subfamily, Coerebinae (its classification is controversial), is a tiny yellow and olive/grayish bird with a broad Neotropical distribution, from southern Mexico and the Caribbean to northern Argentina.

Natural History

Ecology and Behavior
These birds are commonly found in a variety of natural habitats and in gardens and plantations. They forage in lively fashion mainly for insects and spiders; many also pierce berries to drink juice and some partake of nectar from flowers. Many warblers typically join *mixed species feeding flocks* with other small songbirds such as honeycreepers and tanagers. Warblers generally are territorial birds: either during the breeding season (in migratory species) or year-round (in nonmigratory, purely tropical species) a male and a female defend a piece of real estate from other members of the species. Some tropical warblers and gnatcatchers remain paired throughout the year. For the most part, warblers that remain all year in the tropics reside at middle and high elevations, whereas migratory warblers are found at a variety of elevations. Unusual among birds, BANANAQUITS build not only breeding nests, but also lighter, domed *dormitory* nests, which they sleep in individually.

Breeding
Warblers, gnatcatchers, and the BANANAQUIT are monogamous, but partners do not necessarily make equal contributions to breeding efforts. Warblers build open cup or roofed nests in trees or bushes, but sometimes on the ground. Often the female alone builds the nest and incubates the two to three eggs for 14 to 17 days; the male may feed his incubating mate. Young fledge after 8 to 15 days in the nest. Gnatcatchers build cup nests several meters up in trees, weaving together vegetation, moss, and spider web. Both sexes build the nest, incubate the two to three eggs for 13 to 15 days, and feed chicks, which fledge 11 to 14 days after hatching. Both Bananaquit sexes build the round, domed, breeding nest. Only the female incubates the two to three eggs, for 12 to 13 days. Both parents feed the chicks in the nest for 17 to 19 days by regurgitating food to them.

Ecological Interactions
For many years, North American scientists interested in warblers and many other songbirds concentrated their research on the birds' ecology and behavior during breeding, essentially ignoring the fact that the birds spend half of each year wintering in the tropics, many of them in Central America. Now, with the realization that the birds' biology during the nonbreeding season is also important for understanding their lives, their ecology and behavior during the winter have become areas of intense interest. Being addressed in research studies are such questions as: Are species that are territorial during breeding also territorial on their wintering grounds, and if so, in what way? Do individual birds return to the same spot in the tropics each year in winter as they do for nesting during the North American

spring? Do migratory birds compete for food on their wintering grounds with those species that remain all year in the tropics? Are the highly colored plumages of many migratory birds more of use in signalling to other birds on the breeding or wintering grounds?

Status

Only one warbler or gnatcatcher that occurs in Central America is known to be endangered: the GOLDEN-CHEEKED WARBLER (USA ESA listed), which breeds in central Texas but winters in Mexico and Central America. Three other warblers now in trouble (all USA ESA listed) are KIRTLAND'S WARBLER, which breeds in the USA (Michigan) and winters in the Bahamas, BACHMAN'S WARBLER, which breeds in the southeastern USA and winters in Cuba, and SEMPER'S WARBLER, which occurs only on the Caribbean island of St Lucia. Kirtland's Warbler, which nests only in stands of young Jack-pine trees, has been victimized by its own specialization on one type of breeding habitat combined with a shrinking availability of that habitat, by destruction of its wintering habitat, and by BROWN-HEADED COWBIRDS, which lay their eggs in the nests of warblers and other species, reducing their reproductive success (p. 182). It is suspected that mongooses, which were introduced to St Lucia by people and which are predators on bird nests, play a major role in endangering Semper's Warbler, which nests on or near the ground. Several other American warblers are probably now at risk, but there is at present insufficent information about their populations to judge their statuses with any certainty.

Profiles

Mangrove Warbler, *Dendroica petechia*, Plate 58a
Magnolia Warbler, *Dendroica magnolia*, Plate 58b
Grace's Warbler, *Dendroica graciae*, Plate 58c
Rufous-capped Warbler, *Basileuterus rufifrons*, Plate 58d
American Redstart, *Setophaga ruticilla*, Plate 59a
Bananaquit, *Coereba flaveola*, Plate 59b
Blue-gray Gnatcatcher, *Polioptila caerulea*, Plate 59c

33. Blackbirds and Orioles

Diversity is the key to comprehending the American orioles and blackbirds. The passerine family Icteridae includes about 95 species, which partition neatly into very different groups called *blackbirds, caciques (kah-SEE-kays), cowbirds, grackles, meadowlarks, orioles,* and *oropendolas;* they vary extensively in size, coloring, ecology, and behavior. These *icterids* are highly successful and conspicuous birds throughout their range, which encompasses all of North, Central, and South America. Distinguishing this varied assemblage from other birds are a jaunty deportment and a particular feeding method not widely used by other birds, known as *gaping* – a bird places its closed bill into crevices or under leaves, rocks or other objects, then forces the bill open, exposing the previously hidden space to its prying eyes and hunger. Most icterids are tropical in distribution and about 18 species, a few of which are seasonal migrants from the north, occur in Belize and northern Guatemala. The icterid group inhabits marshes and almost all types of terrestrial habitats, and occupies warm lowland areas, middle elevations, as well as colder, mountainous regions. Many of these birds have adapted well to human settlements and are common denizens of gardens, parks, and urban and agricultural areas. The wide ranges of sizes, shapes, colors, mating systems, and breeding behaviors of these birds attract frequent interest from avian researchers.

Grackles, common in city areas, are primarily black birds with slender bills and, usually, long tails. Blackbirds are often marsh-dwellers (the term "blackbirds" is also sometimes used as a synonym for the entire icterid group, as in "the New World Blackbirds"). Orioles are small, bright, often exquisitely marked birds in yellow or orange mixed with black and white, whose preferred habitat is forest. Meadowlarks are yellow, black, and brown grassland birds. Oropendolas are spectacular, larger birds of tropical forests and woodlands that often breed in colonies. Caciques, which also breed in colonies, are smaller, sleeker black birds, frequently with red or yellow rumps and yellow bills. Finally, cowbirds, usually quite inconspicuous in various shades of brown and black, have a dark family (or subfamily) secret – they are *brood parasites*.

Icterids range in length from 15 to 56 cm (6 to 22 in) – medium to fairly large-sized birds. Bills are usually sharply pointed and conical. Black is the predominant plumage color in the group, but many combine it with bright reds, yellows, or oranges. In some species, the sexes are alike (particularly in the tropical species), but in others, females look very different from males, often more cryptically outfitted in browns, grays, or streaked plumage. Pronounced size differences between the sexes, females being smaller, are common; male oropendolas, for instance, may weigh twice as much as females. Bills and eyes are sometimes brightly colored.

Natural History

Ecology and Behavior
Icterids occur in all sorts of habitat types – woodlands, thickets, grassland, marshes, forest edges, and the higher levels of closed forests – but they are especially prevalent in more open areas. Their regular occupation of marshes has always been viewed as interesting, as they are not obviously adapted for living in aquatic environments – they do not have webbed feet, for example, nor are they able to float or dive. They eat a wide variety of foods including insects and other small animals, fruit and seeds. Some are fairly omnivorous, as befitting birds that frequently become scavengers in urban and suburban settings. A common feature of the group is that seed-eaters (*granivores*) during the nonbreeding periods become insect-eaters during breeding, and feed insects to their young. Gaping for food is frequent and will be seen repeatedly if one observes these birds for any length of time. Orioles and caciques join in *mixed-species foraging flocks*; in a single fruit tree one may see two or more oriole species feeding with several species of tanagers, honeycreepers, and others. Caciques often associate with oropendolas, fruitcrows, and other birds in foraging flocks. Outside of the breeding season, icterids, particularly the blackbirds and grackles, typically gather in large, sometimes enormous, flocks that can cause damage to roosting areas and agricultural crops.

Breeding
Icterid species pursue a variety of breeding strategies. Some, such as the orioles, breed in classically monogamous pairs, male and female defending a large territory in which the hanging pouch nest is situated. But others, including many caciques and the oropendolas, nest in colonies. The members of an oropendola colony weave large, bag-like or pouch-like nests that hang from the ends of tree

branches, many on the same tree. In a rare form of non-monogamous breeding, three to 10 male MONTEZUMA'S OROPENDOLAS (Plate 60) establish a colony in a tree (often an isolated one) and defend a group of 10 to 30 females that will mate and nest in the colony. The males engage in fighting and aggressive displays, competing among themselves to mate with the females. Detailed observations show that the most dominant males (the *alpha* animals) in each colony, usually heavier males, obtain up to 90% of all matings, and therefore, are the fathers of most of a colony's young. Caciques, also with pouch-like nests, breed either solitarily in the forest or in colonies. In one study it was noted that each cacique in a colony tries to locate its nest toward the center of the colony, presumably because there is less of a chance of suffering nest predation at the colony's center. Perhaps most intriguing to scientists that study mating systems is that some very closely related icterid species have very different mating systems and breeding behaviors.

Icterid nests range from hanging pouches woven from grasses and other plant materials to open cups lined with mud to roofed nests built on the ground, hidden in meadow grass. Nests are almost always built by females. The female also incubates the two to three eggs, for 11 to 14 days, while the male guards the nest. Nestlings are fed for 10 to 30 days either by both parents (monogamous species) or primarily by the female (polygamous species).

Most of the cowbirds are brood parasites, building no nests themselves. Rather, females, after mating with one or more males, lay their eggs, up to 14 or more per season, in the nests of other species – other icterids as well as other birds – and let *host* species raise their young (see below).

Ecological Interactions

As are many *cuckoo* species, especially those of the Old World, five of the six species of cowbirds are brood parasites – including North America's BROWN-HEADED COWBIRD and Central America's GIANT and BRONZED COWBIRDS (Plate 60). In these species, a female, the parasite, lays eggs in the nests of other species, the hosts, and her young are raised by the foster parents. Some of the cowbirds specialize on icterine hosts – the Giant Cowbird parasitizes only caciques and oropendolas. Some host species have evolved the abilities to recognize cowbird eggs and eject them from their nests, but others have not. The cowbirds benefit from the interaction by being freed from defending a nesting territory and from nest-building and tending chores – what must amount to significant savings of energy and also decreased exposure to predators. The host species suffer reproductive harm because a female cowbird often ejects a host egg when she lays her own (when the nest is left unguarded). Also, more often than not, the cowbird's young are larger than the host's own, and are thus able to outcompete them for food brought to the nest by the adult birds. The host's own young often starve or are significantly weakened. Because of these harmful effects, the very successful cowbirds are believed to be responsible for severe population declines in North America of several species of small passerine birds. Because one population in these interactions benefits and one is harmed, the relationships between cowbirds and their hosts is *parasitic* – social parasitism in this case. How can brood parasitic behavior arise? Evolutionary biologists posit that one way would be if, long ago, some female cowbirds that built nests had their nests destroyed mid-way through their laying period. With an egg to lay but no nest in which to place it, females in this situation may have deposited the eggs in the nests of other species, which subsequently raised the cowbird young.

Breeding colonies of caciques and oropendolas are often located in trees that contain or are near large bee or wasp nests. The wasps or bees swarm in large numbers around the birds' nests. Apparently the birds benefit from this close association because the aggressiveness the stinging insects show toward animals that try to raid the birds' hanging nests offers a measure of protection.

Status

The icterid group includes some of the most abundant birds of the Western Hemisphere, such as RED-WINGED BLACKBIRDS (Plate 61) and COMMON GRACKLES. Some of the Neotropical orioles, such as the YELLOW-TAILED ORIOLE (Plate 62d) have been severely reduced in numbers because they are hunted as prized cage birds. Several icterids are now endangered: Puerto Rico's YELLOW-SHOULDERED BLACKBIRD (USA ESA listed), Brazil's FORBE'S BLACK-BIRD, and Martinique's MARTINIQUE ORIOLE. A few others in South America are in serious trouble from combinations of habitat destruction, brood parasitism, and the pet trade.

Profiles

Eastern Meadowlark, *Sturnella magna*, Plate 59d
Great-tailed Grackle, *Quiscalus mexicanus*, Plate 60a
Montezuma's Oropendola, *Psarocolius montezuma*, Plate 60b
Bronzed Cowbird, *Molothrus aeneus*, Plate 60c
Giant Cowbird, *Scaphidura oryzivora*, Plate 60d
Melodious Blackbird, *Dives dives*, Plate 61a
Yellow-billed Cacique, *Amblycercus holosericeus*, Plate 61b
Red-winged Blackbird, *Agelaius phoeniceus*, Plate 61c
Baltimore Oriole, *Icterus galbula*, Plate 61d
Hooded Oriole, *Icterus cucullatus igneus*, Plate 62a
Black-cowled Oriole, *Icterus dominicensis*, Plate 62b
Yellow-backed Oriole, *Icterus chrysater*, Plate 62c
Yellow-tailed Oriole, *Icterus mesomelas*, Plate 62d

34. Tanagers

Tanagers comprise a large New World group of beautifully colored, small passerine birds, most of which are limited to tropical areas. They are among the tropics' most common and visible birds, primarily owing to their habit of associating in *mixed-species flocks* that gather in the open, often near human habitation, to feed in fruit trees, and they are a treat to watch. All told, there are some 230 species of tanagers (Family Thraupidae), the group including the typical *tanagers*, the *honeycreepers*, and the *euphonias*; about 25 species occur in Belize and northern Guatemala. Some of the tanagers migrate north or south to breed in temperate areas of North and South America (four breed in the USA, including the WESTERN TANAGER, among the most colorful of North American birds). Tanagers inhabit all forested and shrubby areas of the American tropics, over a wide range of elevations, and are particularly numerous in wet forests and forest edge areas. Not devotees of the dark forest interior, they prefer the lighter, upper levels of the forest canopy and more open areas; some prefer low, brushy habitat.

Tanagers vary in length from 9 to 28 cm (3.5 to 11 in), with most concentrated near the smaller end of the range. They are compact birds with fairly short, thick bills and short to medium-long tails. Tanagers' outstanding physical attribute is their bright coloring – they are strikingly marked with patches of color that traverse the entire spectrum, rendering the group among the most fabulously attired of birds. It has been said of the typical tanagers (genus *Tangara*) that they must "exhaust the color patterns possible on sparrow-sized birds" (F. G. Stiles and A. F. Skutch 1989). Yellows, reds, blues and greens predominate, although a relatively few species buck the trend and appear in plain blacks, browns, or grays. The sexes usually look alike. Euphonias are small, stout tanagers, whose appearances, all species being slightly different, revolve around a common theme: blue-black above, with yellow foreheads, breasts, and bellies. Honeycreepers are also usually brilliantly colored.

Natural History

Ecology and Behavior
Most tanager species associate in mixed-species tanager flocks usually together with other types of birds; finding five or more tanager species in a single group is common. A mixed flock will settle in a tree full of ripe fruit and enjoy a meal. These flocks move through forests or more open areas, searching for fruit-laden trees. Although tanagers mostly eat fruit, some also take insects from foliage or even out of the air. And although most species are arboreal, a few are specialized ground foragers, taking seeds and bugs. Tanagers usually go after small fruits that can be swallowed whole, such as berries, plucking the fruit while perched. After plucking it, a tanager rotates the fruit a bit in its bill, then mashes it and swallows. (Ecologists divide frugivorous birds into *mashers*, such as tanagers, and *gulpers*, such as trogons and toucans, which swallow fruit whole and intact.) One explanation is that mashing permits the bird to enjoy the sweet juice prior to swallowing the rest of the fruit. This fits with the idea that mashers select fruit based partially on taste, whereas gulpers, which swallow intact fruit, do not (D. J. Levey et al. 1994).

Some tanagers, such as the *ant-tanagers*, are frequent members of mixed-species flocks (along with antbirds, woodcreepers and others) that spend their days following army ant swarms, feeding on insects that rush from cover at the approach of the devastating ants (see p. 166). Euphonias specialize on mistletoe berries, but eat other fruits and some insects as well. The honeycreepers are tanagers that are specialized for nectar feeding, their bills and tongues modified to punch holes in flower bottoms and suck out nectar; they also feed on some fruits and insects.

Some tanagers are altitudinal migrants, seasonally moving to higher or lower elevation habitats.

Breeding
Most tanagers appear to breed monogamously, although a number of bigamists have been noted (BLUE-GRAY and SCARLET-RUMPED TANAGERS, Plates 63, 66, among them). Breeding is usually concentrated during the transition from dry to wet season, when fruit and insects are most plentiful. In many species, male and female stay paired throughout the year. Males of many species give food to females in *nuptial feeding*, and during courtship displays make sure that potential mates see their brightly colored patches. Either the female alone or the pair builds a cup nest in a tree or shrub. Two eggs are incubated by the female only for 12 to 18 days and young are fed by both parents for 12 to 18 days prior to their

fledging. A pair of tiny euphonias build a nest with a roof and a side entrance, often within a bromeliad plant.

Ecological Interactions
Tanagers, as mashing frugivores, sometimes drop the largest seeds from the fruits they consume before swallowing but, nonetheless, many seeds are ingested; consequently, these birds are active seed dispersers. Some ecologists believe tanagers to be among the most common dispersers of tropical trees and shrubs, that is, they are responsible for dropping the seeds that grow into the trees and shrubs that populate the areas they inhabit. Euphonias, for example, are crucial for the mistletoe life cycle because, after eating the berries, they deposit their seed-bearing droppings on tree branches, where the seeds germinate, the mistletoe plants starting out there as epiphytes.

Lore and Notes
The word *tanager* comes from the Brazilian Tupi Indian word *tangara*, which is also used as the genus name for a group of tanagers.

Status
The only endangered tanager in Belize or Guatemala is the AZURE-RUMPED TANAGER, an uncommon bird that occurs only in very limited regions of southern Guatemala and adjacent Mexico. The only other endangered Central American tanager is Costa Rica's BLACK-CHEEKED ANT-TANAGER; it is fairly rare and it is thought that it soon might be found only in very small parts of the country. Fortunately, despite being among tropical America's most beautiful birds, tanagers are not favorites of the international pet trade, probably because they have never been popularized as cage birds outside their native regions. However, several of the euphonias, such as the BLUE-HOODED EUPHONIA, are increasingly scarce and the reason may be that, although they are not hunted for the international trade, they *are* prized as cage birds within Central American countries. Several of South America's tanagers, especially in Brazil, are considered threatened or endangered, primarily owing to habitat loss.

Profiles
Golden-hooded Tanager, *Tangara larvata*, Plate 63a
Blue-gray Tanager, *Thraupis episcopus*, Plate 63b
Red-legged Honeycreeper, *Cyanerpes cyaneus*, Plate 63c
Green Honeycreeper, *Chlorophanes spiza*, Plate 63d
Olive-backed Euphonia, *Euphonia gouldi*, Plate 64a
Scrub Euphonia, *Euphonia affinis*, Plate 64b
Yellow-throated Euphonia, *Euphonia hirundinacea*, Plate 64c
Gray-headed Tanager, *Eucometis penicillata*, Plate 64d
Red-crowned Ant-tanager, *Habia rubica*, Plate 65a
Red-throated Ant-tanager, *Habia fuscicauda*, Plate 65b
Hepatic Tanager, *Piranga flava figlina*, Plate 65c
Summer Tanager, *Piranga rubra*, Plate 65d
Yellow-winged Tanager, *Thraupis abbas*, Plate 66a
White-winged Tanager, *Piranga leucoptera*, Plate 66b
Crimson-collared Tanager, *Ramphocelus sanguinolentus*, Plate 66c
Scarlet-rumped Tanager, *Ramphocelus passerinii*, Plate 66d

35. Sparrows and Grosbeaks

The *sparrows* and *grosbeaks* are large, diverse groups, totaling about 320 species, that include some of Central America's most common and visible passerine birds. The groups' classification is continually revised, but here we can consider them to be separate families: the sparrows, *seedeaters*, *towhees* and *grassquits* in Family Emberizidae, and the grosbeaks, *saltators*, and *buntings* in Family Cardinalidae. The groups are almost *cosmopolitan* in distribution in the New World, meaning representatives occur just about everywhere, in all kinds of habitats and climates, from Alaska and northern Canada south to Tierra del Fuego. In fact, one species, the SNOW BUNTING, a small black and white bird, breeds farther north than any other land bird, in northern Alaska, Canada, and Greenland.

Sparrows and grosbeaks are generally small birds, 9 to 22 cm (3.5 to 9 in) in length, with relatively short, thick, conical bills that are specialized to crush and open seeds. In some species, the upper and lower halves of the bill can be moved from side-to-side, the better to manipulate small seeds. Sparrows have relatively large feet that they use in scratching the ground to find seeds. Coloring varies greatly within the group but the plumage of most is dull brown or grayish, with many sporting streaked backs. The sexes generally look alike.

Natural History

Ecology and Behavior

Sparrows and grosbeaks are mostly seed eaters, although many are considered almost omnivorous and even those that specialize on seeds for much of the year often feed insects to their young. Some species also eat fruit. These birds mainly inhabit open areas such as grassland, parkland, brushy areas, and forest edge. They are birds of thickets, bushes, and grasses, foraging mostly on the ground or at low levels in bushes or trees. Because many species spend large amounts of time in thickets and brushy areas, they can be quite inconspicuous.

Most species are strongly territorial, a mated pair aggressively excluding other members of the species from sharply defined areas. In the typical sparrows, pairs often stay together all year; other species within the group often travel in small family groups. Sometimes, territories are defended all year round and almost all available habitat in a region is divided into territories. The result is that those individuals that do not own territories must live furtively on defended territories, always trying to avoid the dominant territory owner, retreating when chased, and waiting for the day when the owner is injured or dies and the territory can be taken over. Only when one of these *floaters* ascends in the hierarchy to territory ownership status can he begin to breed. In species that have this kind of territorial system, the floater individuals that live secretly on other individual's territories, waiting and watching, were termed by their discoverer an avian *underworld*, and the name has stuck.

Whereas in North America sparrows constitute perhaps the most important group of seed-eating birds, they are less dominant in the Neotropics. Other groups of birds, such as pigeons, occupy more of the seed-eating "niche" in Central American countries than do sparrows and, as a consequence, one encounters sparrows much more often in North than in Central America.

Breeding

Most sparrows and grosbeaks are monogamous breeders. The female of the pair usually builds a cup-shaped or, more often in the tropics, a domed nest, from grasses, fine roots and perhaps mosses and lichens. Nests are concealed on the ground or low in a shrub or tree. The female alone incubates two to three eggs, for 12 to 14 days. Both male and female feed nestlings, which fledge after 10 to 15 days in the nest.

Ecological Interactions

HOUSE SPARROWS, which occur in southern Belize and southern Guatemala, are small gray, brown, and black birds that currently enjoy an almost worldwide distribution, living very successfully in close association with humans. Nests are often placed in buildings. Formally, however, this bird is not a New World sparrow at all, but a member of an Old World family, the Passeridae; until recently, it was restricted to the Eastern Hemisphere. How and why these sparrows arrived in the West, and the unintended consequences of their arrival, is a cautionary tale of human interference in the natural distribution of animals. European settlers brought House Sparrows and other garden birds, such as starlings, to North America and released them, so that the animals around their new homes in the New World would resemble the animals they remembered from their old homes, an ocean away. A small number of House Sparrows released on the East Coast of the USA in the 1800s spread to the north, west, and south, and, after rapidly colonizing all of North America, are still spreading. House Sparrows reached Central America in the mid-twentieth century and are now successfully ensconced there in most urban and suburban areas, where they compete for food with native sparrows. Species such as the House Sparrow that, owing to people's machinations, are now distributed outside of their natural ranges are said to be *introduced*, as opposed to naturally occurring species, which are termed *indigenous* or *native*. A species that spreads far beyond its original distribution, whether aided by people or not, is called, in ecological terms, an *invader*.

Lore and Notes

In addition to their reputation for ecological success, the New World sparrows are known especially as a group that is the subject of frequent scientific research, and therefore as one that has contributed substantially to many areas of our knowledge about birds. For instance, studies of North America's SONG SPARROW and the Neotropic's RUFOUS-COLLARED SPARROW provided the basis for much of the information we have about avian territoriality and many other kinds of behavior. Also, the WHITE-CROWNED SPARROW has been the species of choice for many researchers for over 30 years for investigations of bird physiology and the relationships between ecology and physiology.

Status

None of Central America's sparrows and grosbeaks is currently considered threatened. Many are among the most abundant and frequently observed birds in the areas that they inhabit. A few sparrows of Mexico and South America are threatened or endangered, as are a few sparrow subspecies in the USA.

Profiles

Buff-throated Saltator, *Saltator maximus*, Plate 67a
Grayish Saltator, *Saltator coerulescens grandis*, Plate 67b
Black-headed Saltator, *Saltator atriceps atriceps*, Plate 67c

Black-faced Grosbeak, *Caryothraustes poliogaster*, Plate 67d
Blue-black Grosbeak, *Cyanocompsa cyanoides*, Plate 68a
Orange-billed Sparrow, *Arremon aurantiirostris*, Plate 68b
Green-backed Sparrow, *Arremonops chloronotus*, Plate 68c
Blue-black Grassquit, *Volatinia jacarina*, Plate 68d
Variable Seedeater, *Sporophila aurita*, Plate 69a
White-collared Seedeater, *Sporophila torqueola moreletti*, Plate 69b
Rusty Sparrow, *Aimophila rufescens pyrgatoides*, Plate 69c
Chipping Sparrow, *Spizella passerina*, Plate 69d

Environmental Close-up 3
Coffee Crops and Conservation

Modern agriculture, although somewhat necessary for the continuation of human life on Earth, has its drawbacks. Aside from afflicting ecosystems with pesticides and chemical fertilizers (*agrochemicals*), pollution, and massive soil erosion, the basic disruption is that large tracts of natural habitats are cleared of native vegetation and replaced with one or a few crop plant species. Such wholesale habitat alteration is bound to cause significant problems for wildlife adapted to the natural vegetation. Harmful effects of modern farming may be reduced by employing techniques of *sustainable agriculture*, a phrase used with increasing frequency by environmentalists and others concerned with the future condition of the Earth's habitats. The phrase means farming in ways that are economically profitable for the local economy yet not ecologically harmful; using techniques, in other words, that will not lead to significant ecosystem damage or to decline in biodiversity. Researchers are finding more and more ways that environmentally harmful farming practices can be altered to make them more "eco-friendly." Perhaps the most internationally publicized case concerns the modest brown coffee bean.

Coffee crops can be grown on plantations in environmentally damaging or environmentally enhancing (*green*) ways. Traditional coffee crops over much of Central America were grown on small family farms where low coffee plants thrived beneath a canopy of taller trees, which provided shade as well as protective ground mulch. The trees selected to shade the coffee were often themselves productive: species that increased soil nutrients like nitrogen, food-producing fruit trees, or timber/fuel-wood trees. (Some coffee was also grown using *rustic* methods: by placing coffee plants under natural forest canopy after first clearing away the understory vegetation.) When large corporations went into the coffee business, they increased yields by switching to *sun coffee*, growing coffee plants alone on large plantations, using fertilizers and pesticides extensively to do for their crop what shade trees formerly did. With smaller coffee plants packed closely together, and with chemical fertilizers, sun coffee can produce up to three times as much coffee as shade plants in the same space. Now many growers, large and small, produce sun coffee. Unfortunately, monotonous rows of low coffee plants make a poor habitat for animal life, especially birds. The drive to get large companies to produce only *shade-grown coffee* is concerned with having them add canopy trees to their plantations, thus improving the coffee's taste (as some insist), decreasing the amounts of chemicals needed, and, not incidentally, greatly enhancing the habitat for wildlife use. You might not think that simply planting shade trees above coffee plants would make much of a difference, but it does! It turns out that plantations with trees and understory crop plants provide habitats sufficiently complex to attract abundant wildlife, particularly migratory birds.

Ecological researchers are beginning to look closely at the relationship between declining populations of migratory songbirds in North America and changes in agricultural practices in Latin America and the Caribbean over the past few decades. *Neotropical migrants* are songbirds that migrate each year between breeding areas in the north temperate zone and wintering areas in Central and South America. (In fact, about 335 of the 650 or so bird species that occur regularly in the USA and Canada migrate in this way.) During the last 25 years, many species of these small birds have shown significant declines in the sizes of their populations; in some, the rate of decline is still accelerating. For instance, surveys of breeding birds each spring and summer in the USA indicate that some species of warblers have suffered declines of about 40%, as have some species of orioles and sparrows. (But some very recent studies conclude that when total songbird numbers are considered over large sections of North America, many species have actually been stable or even increasing in population size during the past few decades.) Ecologists who study these birds have pretty much concluded that the chief culprit behind most of the population crashes is loss of forest habitat to development, including loss of breeding sites in North America, loss of migratory stop-over habitat, and loss of wintering habitat in the Neotropics. Recently, a fourth kind of habitat loss was added to the list: the switch to sun coffee from shade coffee, and the accompanying loss of tree plantation habitat for the little migrants.

Many Neotropical migrants originally wintered in forest habitats, but as forests were cut for development and agriculture, the birds increasingly switched their wintering sites to plantations with trees, such as the traditional coffee farms. In fact, in some regions of Latin America, tree plantations comprise essentially the only surviving forest-like habitat. Ecologists term these kinds of places *refugia* – the last remaining patches of naturalistic habitat in which wildlife under siege can seek refuge. In southern Mexico, researchers found that many migrants even seemed to prefer coffee plantations over native forest – often finding more species among plantations' trees than in nearby forests. Likewise, a study in Guatemala found about twice as many bird species using shade coffee farms as were using sun coffee farms. In fact, the usual relationship is that the more recent the farming methods used on a plantation, the fewer bird species found there. The tree plantations also apparently provide good habitat for many other kinds of animals – especially abundant are snakes, bats, monkeys, and opossums, and insect biodiverity is high. (In fact, one theory of why so many birds seem to prefer shade coffee farms to forests is the great abundance of insect food available on the farms, particularly cicadas.) Now these last refuges of the migrant birds and other animals are increasingly transformed to tree-less sun coffee plantations. As of the mid-1990s, it was estimated that at least half of Latin America's coffee production was sun coffee.

It seems that, from a conservation stand-point, shade-grown coffee is the way to go. Fortunately, there is an incentive for companies to produce shade-grown coffee: they can advertise it as such and, hence, charge more for it. Many surveys have demonstrated that consumers in export countries are willing to pay a premium price for green products such as shade-grown coffee. As this book is written, popular calls for shade-grown coffee, reported in the media, are becoming more frequent. Also, some environmental groups have begun their own certification processes. They give an "Eco-OK" seal of approval to particular coffee brands that they feel meet green criteria, such as the coffee being grown beneath a splendid green canopy of native trees.

Chapter 8

MAMMALS

- *Introduction*
- *Features of Tropical Mammals*
- *Seeing Mammals in Belize and Guatemala*
- *Family Profiles*
- *Environmental Close-up 4*
  The Belize Zoo and Tropical Education Center

Introduction

Leafing through this book, the reader will have noticed the profiles of many more birds than mammals. This may at first seem discriminatory, especially when it is recalled that many people themselves are mammals and, owing to that direct kinship, are probably keenly interested and motivated to see and learn about mammals. Are not mammals as good as birds? Why not include more of them? There are several reasons for the discrepancy – good biological reasons. One is that, even though the tropics generally have more species of mammals than temperate or arctic regions, the total number of mammal species worldwide, and the number in any region, is less than the number of birds. In fact, there are in total only about 4000 mammal species, compared with 9000 birds, and the relative difference is reflected in the fauna of Belize and northern Guatemala. But the more compelling reason not to include more mammals in a book on commonly sighted wildlife, is that, even in regions sporting high degrees of mammalian diversity, mammals are relatively rarely seen – especially by short-term visitors. Most mammals lack that basic protection from predators that birds possess, the power of flight. Consequently, mammals being considered delicious fare by any number of predatory beasts (eaten in good numbers by reptiles, birds, other mammals, and even the odd amphibian), most are active nocturnally, or, if day active, are highly secretive. Birds often show themselves with abandon, mammals do not. Exceptions are those mammals that are beyond the pale of predation – huge mammals and fierce ones. But there are no elephants or giraffes in Belize and Guatemala, nor prides of lions. Another exception is monkeys. They are fairly large and primarily arboreal, which keeps them safe from a number of kinds of predators, and thus permits them to be noisy and conspicuous.

A final reason for not including more mammals in the book is that about half of those occurring in the covered region are bats, for the most part nocturnal animals that, even if spotted, are very difficult for anyone other than experts to identify to species.

General Characteristics

If birds are feathered vertebrates, mammals are hairy ones. The group first arose, so fossils tell us, approximately 245 million years ago, splitting off from the primitive reptiles during the late Triassic Period of the Mesozoic Era, before the birds did the same. Four main traits distinguish mammals and confer upon them great advantage over other types of animals that allowed them in the past to prosper and spread, and continue to this day to benefit them: hair on their bodies which insulates them from cold and otherwise protects from environmental stresses; milk production for the young, freeing mothers from having to search for specific foods for their offspring; the bearing of live young instead of eggs, allowing breeding females to be mobile and, hence, safer than if they had to sit on eggs for several weeks; and advanced brains, with obvious enhancing effects on many aspects of animal lives.

Classification of Mammals

Mammals are quite variable in size and form, many being highly adapted – changed through evolution – to specialized habitats and lifestyles: bats specialized to fly, marine mammals specialized for their aquatic world, etc. The smallest mammals are the *shrews*, tiny insect eaters that weigh as little as 2.5 g (a tenth of an ounce). The largest are the *whales*, weighing in at up to 160,000 kg (350,000 lb, half the weight of a loaded Boeing 747) – as far as anyone knows, the largest animals ever.

Mammals are divided into three major groups, primarily according to reproductive methods. The *Monotremes* are an ancient group that actually lays eggs and still retains some other reptile-like characteristics. Only three species survive, the platypus and two species of spiny anteaters; they are fairly common inhabitants of Australia and New Guinea. The *Marsupials* give birth to live young that are relatively undeveloped. When born, the young crawl along mom's fur into her *pouch*, where they find milk supplies and finish their development. There are about 240 marsupial species, including kangaroos, koalas, wombats, and opossums; they are limited in distribution to Australia and the Neotropics (the industrious but road-accident-prone VIRGINIA OPOSSUM (Plate 70) also inhabits much of Mexico and the USA). The majority of mammal species are *Eutherians*, or *true* mammals. These animals are distinguished from the other groups by having a *placenta*, which connects a mother to her developing offspring, allowing for long internal development. This trait, which allows embryos to develop to a fairly mature form in safety, and for the female to be mobile until birth, has allowed the true mammals to be rather successful, becoming, in effect, the dominant vertebrates on land for millions of years. The true mammals include those with which most people are intimately familiar: rodents, rabbits, cats, dogs, bats, primates, elephants, horses, whales – everything from house mice to ecotravellers.

The 4000 species of living mammals are divided into about 20 orders and 115 families. Approximately 150 species occur in Belize and northern Guatemala and, again, half of those are bats.

Features of Tropical Mammals

There are several important features of tropical mammals and their habitats that differentiate them from temperate zone mammals. First, tropical mammals face different environmental stresses than do temperate zone mammals, and respond to stresses in different ways. Many temperate zone mammals, of course, must endure cold winters, snow, and low winter food supplies. Many of them respond with *hibernation*, staying more or less dormant for several months until conditions improve. Tropical mammals do not encounter extreme cold or snow, but they face dry seasons, up to 5 months long, that sometimes severely reduce food supplies. But for some surprising reasons, they cannot alleviate this stress by hibernating, waiting for the rainy season to arrive and increase food supplies. When a mammal in Canada or Alaska hibernates, so too do most of its predators. This is not the case in the tropics. A mammal sleeping away the dry season in a burrow would be easy prey to snakes and other predators. Moreover, a big danger to sleeping mammals would be... army ants! These voracious insects are very common in the tropics and would quickly eat a sleeping mouse or squirrel. Also, external parasites, such as ticks and mites, which are inactive in extreme cold, would continue to be very active on sleeping tropical mammals, sucking blood and doing considerable damage. Last, the great energy reserves needed to be able to sleep for an extended period through warm weather may be more than any mammal can physically accumulate. Therefore, tropical mammals need to stay active throughout the year. One way they counter the dry season's reduction in their normal foods is to switch food types seasonally. For instance, some rodents that eat mostly insects during the rainy season switch to seeds during the dry; some bats that feed on insects switch to dry-season fruits. (D. H. Janzen & D. E. Wilson 1983)

The abundance of tropical fruit brings up another interesting difference between temperate and tropical mammals: a surprising number of tropical mammals eat a lot of fruit, even among the *carnivore* group, which, as its name implies, should be eating meat. All the carnivores in Belize and Guatemala, save the PUMA and NEOTROPICAL OTTER (Plate 76, 77), are known to eat fruit – the dogs, cats, raccoons, weasels – and some seem to prefer it. Upon reflection, it makes sense that these mammals should consume fruit. Fruit is very abundant in the tropics, available all year, and, at least when it is ripe, easily digested by mammalian digestive systems. A consequence of such *frugivory* (fruit-eating) is that many mammals have become, together with frugivorous birds, major dispersal agents of fruit seeds, which they spit out or which travel unharmed through their digestive tracts. These mammals, therefore, spread fruit tree seeds as they travel, seeds that eventually germinate and become trees. Some biologists believe that, even though the carnivores plainly are specialized for hunting down, killing, and eating animal prey, it is possible that fruit was always a major part of their diet. (D. H. Janzen & D. E. Wilson 1983)

Finally, there are some differences in the *kinds* of mammals inhabiting tropical and temperate regions. For instance, bears are nowhere to be found in Belize and Guatemala (in fact, there is only a single Neotropical bear species, distributed sparsely from Panama to northern South America), nor are most social rodents like beavers and prairie dogs. Rabbits are few in number of species and usually in their abundances, also. On the other hand, some groups occur solely in the tropics or do fabulously there. There are about 50 species of New World monkeys, all of which occur in tropical areas (but only two occur in Belize and northern Guatemala). Arboreal mammals such as monkeys and procyonids (raccoon relatives) are plentiful in tropical forests probably because there is a rich, resource-filled, dense canopy to occupy and feed in. Also, the closed canopy blocks light to the ground, which only allows an undergrowth that is sparse and poor in resources, and consequently permits few opportunities for mammals to live and feed there. Bats thrive in the tropics, being very successful both in terms of number of species and in their abundances. Seven families of bats probably occur in Belize and northern Guatemala, including more than 70 species; only 4 families and 40 species occur in the entire USA. While all the North American bats are insect eaters, the Neotropical bats are quite varied in lifestyle, among them being fruit-eaters, nectar-eaters, and even a few that consume animals or their blood. (D. H. Janzen & D. E. Wilson 1983)

The social and breeding behaviors of various mammals are quite diverse. Some are predominantly solitary animals, males and females coming together occasionally only to mate. Others live in family groups. Some are rigorously territorial, others are not. Details on social and breeding behavior are provided within the individual family descriptions that follow.

Seeing Mammals in Belize and Guatemala

No doubt about it, mammals are tough. One can go for two weeks in the Neotropics and, if in the wrong places at the wrong times, see very few of them. A lot of luck is involved – a tapir, a small herd of peccaries, a porcupine happens to cross the trail just a bit ahead of you. Or you will be out birdwatching along a gravel road in the pre-dawn grayness when (as happened once to me) a small anteater, a NORTHERN TAMANDUA (Plate 73), will stroll slowly out of the forest, almost bump into your legs, detour around you, and walk back into the forest. I offer three pieces of mammal-spotting advice. First, if you have time and are a patient sort, stake out a likely looking spot near a stream or watering hole, be quiet, and wait to see what approaches. Second, try taking strolls very early in the morning; at this time, many nocturnal mammals are quickly scurrying to their day shelters. Third, although only for the stout-hearted, try searching with a flashlight at night around field stations, campgrounds, or forest lodges. After scanning the ground (for safety's sake as well as for mammals), shine the light toward the middle regions of trees and look for bright, shiny eyes reflecting the light. You will certainly stumble across some kind of mammal or another; then it is simply a matter of whether you scare them more than they scare you.

Some mammals, of course, are reliably seen. Monkeys, for instance, are commonly seen by visitors to the Community Baboon Sanctuary, the Lamanai Archeological Park, and Tikal National Park. Coatis, in the raccoon family, are seen eventually by almost everyone who travels to national parks and wildlife reserves. Banish all thoughts right now of ever encountering *El Tigre*, the Jaguar; even where their populations are still healthy, such as at Cockscomb Basin Wildlife Sanctuary (the Jaguar Sanctuary), they are sighted by visitors only occasionally.

Family Profiles

1. Opossums

Marsupials are an ancient group, preceding in evolution the development of the *true*, or *placental*, mammals, which eventually replaced the less advanced marsupials over most parts of the terrestrial world. Marsupials alive today in the Australian and Neotropical regions therefore are remnants of an earlier time when the group's distribution spanned the Earth. Of the eight living families of marsupials, only three occur in the New World, and only one, the *opossums*, occurs in Belize and Guatemala. That family, Didelphidae, is distributed widely over the northern Neotropics (with one member, the VIRGINIA OPOSSUM (Plate 70), reaching deeply northwards into the USA). Eight species represent the family in Belize and northern Guatemala. They are a diverse group, occupying essentially all of the countrys' habitats except high mountain areas. Some, such as the Virginia Opossum, are abundant and frequently sighted, while others are more obscure.

All opossums are basically alike in body plan, although species vary considerably in size. Their general appearance probably has not changed much during the past 40 to 65 million years. As one nature writer put it, the opossums scurrying around today are much the same as the ones dinosaurs encountered (J. C. Kricher 1989). Basically, these mammals look like rats, albeit in the case of some, such as the Virginia Opossum, like large rats. Their distinguishing features are a long, hairless tail, which is *prehensile* (that is, opossums can wrap it around a tree branch and hang from it), and large, hairless ears. Females in most of the opossums have pouches for their young on their abdomens, but a few groups of species do not. Opossum hindfeet have five digits each, one digit acting as an opposable thumb. The hindfeet of the WATER OPOSSUM (Plate 70) are webbed. The Virginia Opossum, one of the region's largest, grows to nearly a meter (3 ft) in length, if the long tail is included. A large adult of the species can weigh up to 4 kg (9 lb), but most weigh 1 to 2.5 kg (2 to 5 lb). Similar in size and general appearance is the more infrequently encountered COMMON OPOSSUM. (The two large opossums, Virginia and Common, occur together over much of Central America; the Virginia ranges from there north to the USA and the Common ranges from there south to South America.) Some of the species are much smaller, the MEXICAN MOUSE OPOSSUM, for instance, being only 25 to 30 cm (10 to 12 in) in length, tail included, and weighing only 100 grams (4 oz). Opossums come in a narrow range of colors – shades of gray, brown, and black. Male and female opossums generally look alike, but males are usually larger than females of the same age.

Natural History

Ecology and Behavior

Most opossums are night-active *omnivores*, although some also can be seen during the day. Their reputation is that they will eat, or at least try to eat, almost anything they stumble across or can catch; mostly they take fruit, eggs, and invertebrate and small vertebrate animals. The VIRGINIA OPOSSUM forages mainly at night, often along ponds and streams, sometimes covering more than a kilometer per night within its home range, the area within which it lives and seeks food. Opossums that have been studied are not territorial – they do not defend part or all of their home ranges from others of their species. Some opossums forage mainly on the ground, but most are good climbers and are able to forage also in trees and shrubs; and some species are chiefly arboreal. After a night's foraging, an opossum spends the daylight hours in a cave, a rock crevice, or a cavity in a tree or log. Most opossums are unsociable animals, usually observed singly. The exception is during the breeding season, when males seek and court females, and two or more may be seen together.

Predators on opossums include owls, snakes, and carnivorous mammals. Some opossums apparently are somewhat immune to the venom of many poisonous snakes. The response of the COMMON OPOSSUM to threat by a predator is to hiss, growl, snap its mouth, move its body from side to side, and finally, to lunge and bite. They often try to climb to escape. The VIRGINIA OPOSSUM is famous for faking death ("playing possum") when threatened, but that behavior is rare or absent in the Common Opossum and others.

Breeding
Female opossums give birth only 12 to 14 days after mating. The young that leave the reproductive tract are only about one cm (half an inch) long and weigh less than half a gram. These tiny opossums, barely embryos, climb unassisted along the mother's fur and into her pouch. There they grasp a nipple in their mouth. The nipple swells, essentially attaching the young; they remain there, attached, for about 2 months. Usually more young are born (up to 20) than make it to the pouch and attach correctly. In studies, 6 young, on average, are found in females' pouches (which have up to 13 nipples). Following the pouch phase, the female continues to nurse her young for another month or more, often in a nest she constructs of leaves and grass in a tree cavity or burrow.

Ecological Interactions
The VIRGINIA and COMMON OPOSSUMS have what can be considered commensal relationships (p. 55) with people. Throughout Central America, populations of these mammals are concentrated around human settlements, particularly around garbage dumps, where they feed. They also partake of fruit crops and attack farmyard birds. Consequently, opossums are more likely to be seen near towns or villages than in uninhabited areas. Of course, these opossums pay a price for the easy food – their pictures are commonly found in the dictionary under "roadkill."

Lore and Notes
COMMON OPOSSUMS are known as foul-smelling beasts. Their reputation probably stems from the fact that they apparently enjoy rolling about in fresh animal droppings. Also, when handled, they employ some unattractive defense mechanisms – tending to squirt urine and defecate.

Status
None of the region's opossum species is considered threatened or endangered, although one, the WATER OPOSSUM, is fairly rare. VIRGINIA OPOSSUM is hunted for food in some areas. COMMON and VIRGINIA OPOSSUMS are sometimes killed intentionally near human settlements to protect fruit crops and poultry, and unintentionally but abundantly, by cars.

Profiles
Virginia Opossum, *Didelphis virginiana*, Plate 70a
Central American Woolly Opossum, *Caluromys derbianus*, Plate 70b

Water Opossum, *Chironectes minimus*, Plate 70c
Gray Four-eyed Opossum, *Philander opossum*, Plate 70d

2. Bats

Of all the kinds of mammals, perhaps we can comprehend the lives, can mentally put ourselves into the skins, of nonhuman primates (monkeys and apes) best, and of *bats*, least. That is, monkeys, owing to their similarities to people, are somewhat known to us, familiar in a way, but bats are at the other extreme: foreign, exotic, mysterious. The reasons for their foreignness are several. Bats, like birds, engage in sustained, powered flight – the only mammals to do so ("rats with wings," in the memorable phrasing of a female acquaintance). Bats are active purely at night – every single species. Bats navigate the night atmosphere chiefly by "sonar," or *echolocation*: not by sight or smell but by broadcasting ultrasonic sounds – extremely high-pitched chirps and clicks – and then gaining information about their environment by "reading" the echos. Although foreign to people's primate sensibilities, bats, precisely because their lives are so very different from our own, are increasingly of interest to us. In the past, of course, bats' exotic behavior, particularly their nocturnal habits, engendered in most societies not ecological curiosity but fear and superstition.

Bats are flying mammals that occupy the night. They are widely distributed, inhabiting most of the world's tropical and temperate regions, excepting some oceanic islands. With a total of about 980 species, bats are second in diversity among mammals only to rodents. Ecologically, they can be thought of as nighttime equivalents of birds, which dominate the daytime skies. Bats of the Neotropics, although often hard to see and, in most cases, difficult for anyone other than experts to identify, are tremendously important mammals, and that is why they are treated here. Their diversity and numbers tell the story: 39% of all Neotropical mammal species are bats, and there are usually as many species of bats in a Neotropical forest than of all other mammal species combined. Researchers estimate that most of the mammalian biomass (the total amount of living tissue, by weight) in any given Neotropical region resides in bats. Of the 150 or so species of mammals that occur in Belize and northern Guatemala, about half are bats. Some of the more common and more interesting bats are profiled here.

Bats have true wings, consisting of thin, strong, highly elastic membranes that extend from the sides of the body and legs to cover and be supported by the elongated fingers of the arms. (The name of the order of bats, Chiroptera, refers to the wings: *chiro*, meaning hand, and *ptera*, wing.) Other distinctive anatomical features include bodies covered with silky, longish hair; toes with sharp, curved claws that allow the bats to hang upside down and are used by some to catch food; scent glands that produce strong, musky odors; and, in many, very odd-shaped folds of skin on their noses (noseleaves) and prominent ears that aid in echolocation. Like birds, bats' bodies have been modified through evolution to conform to the needs of energy-demanding flight: they have relatively large hearts, low body weights, and fast metabolisms.

Bats, although they come in a variety of sizes, are sufficiently standardized in form such that all species are easily recognized by everyone as bats. Females in most species are larger than males, although there are exceptions, such as the NECTAR BAT (Plate 72), in which males are larger. Because few people get near enough to resting or flying bats to examine them closely, I describe the forms of individual species only in the plate section. It will suffice to say that the bats under our consideration here range from tiny, 5-g (less than a quarter of an ounce) bats with 5-cm (2 in) wing spans (the HAIRY-LEGGED BAT; Plate 72) to one of the New World's larger bats, which weighs up to 95 g (a fifth of a pound) and has a wing span greater than 60 cm (2 ft) – the WOOLLY FALSE VAMPIRE BAT; Plate 71).

Natural History

Ecology and Behavior

Neotropical bats are renowned for their insect-eating ways. Indeed, most species specialize on insects. They use their sonar not just to navigate the night but to detect insects, which they catch on the wing, pick off leaves, or scoop off the ground. Bats use several methods to catch flying insects. Small insects may be captured directly in the mouth; some bats use their wings as nets and spoons to trap insects and pull them to their mouth; and others scoop bugs into the fold of skin membrane that connects their tail and legs, then somersault in mid-air to move the catch to their mouth. Small bugs are eaten immediately on the wing, while larger ones, such as large beetles, are taken to a perch and dismembered. Not all species, however, are insectivores. Neotropical bats have also expanded ecologically into a variety of other feeding *niches*: some specialize in eating fruit, feeding on nectar and pollen at flowers, preying on vertebrates such as frogs or birds, eating fish, or even, in the case of the COMMON VAMPIRE BAT (Plate 71), sipping blood.

Bats spend the daylight hours in day roosts, usually tree cavities, shady sides of trees, caves, rock crevices, or, these days, in buildings or under bridges. Some bats make their own individual roosting sites in trees by biting leaves so that they fold over, making small *tents* that shelter them from predators as well as from the elements. More than one species of bat may inhabit the same roost, although some species will associate only with their own kind. For most species, the normal resting position in a roost is hanging by their feet, head downwards, which makes taking flight as easy as letting go and spreading their wings. Many bats leave roosts around dusk, then move to foraging sites at various distances from the roost. Night activity patterns vary, perhaps serving to reduce food competition among species. Some tend to fly and forage intensely in the early evening, become less active in the middle of the night, then resume intense foraging near dawn; others are relatively inactive early in the evening, but more active later on. Bats do not fly continuously after leaving their day roosts, but group together at a *night roost*, a tree for instance, where they rest and bring food. Fruit-eaters do not rest in the tree at which they have discovered ripe fruit, where predators might find them, but make several trips per night from the fruit tree to their night roost. Bats are highly social animals, roosting and often foraging in groups.

Most of the species described below are common representatives of groups of bats, each of which differs anatomically, ecologically, and behaviorally.

GREATER WHITE-LINED BAT (Plate 72). These tiny animals are one of the most frequently encountered bats of lowland rainforests. By day they roost in groups of five to 50 in hollow trees or caves, rocks, or buildings; they are often seen under overhangs at ecotourist facilities. They leave roosts just before dark to commence their insect foraging, which they do under the forest canopy, usually within 300 m (1000 ft) of their roosts. Individual males defend territories in the day roosts, and they have harems of up to nine females each. After birth, a mother carries her pup each night from the day roost and leaves it in a hiding place while she forages. Pups can fly at about 2 weeks old, but continue to nurse for several months.

FISHING BAT (Plate 71). Relatively large bats, Fishing Bats roost in hollow trees and buildings near fresh- or salt-water. They have very large hind feet and claws that they use to pull fish, crustaceans, and insects from the water's surface. These bats fly low over still water, using their sonar to detect the ripples of a fish just beneath or breaking the water's surface. Grabbing the fish with their claws, they then move it to their mouth, land, hang upside down, and feast.

WOOLLY FALSE VAMPIRE BAT (Plate 71). These are fairly large bats that inhabit forest regions, particularly evergreen rainforests, from southern Mexico to Brazil. They roost in small groups in caves or hollow trees and logs. They take insects, some fruit, and, being one of only a few carnivorous New World bats, vertebrates such as lizards, birds, and, in particular, small rodents such as mice. The bat's name refers to the dense fur covering its body, and to the fact that, in the past, large bats such as this one were often mistaken for vampire bats.

NECTAR BAT (Plate 72). These are small bats that can hover for a few seconds at flowers to take pollen or nectar; however, most of their omnivorous diet consists of fruit and insects. They roost in large groups in both dry and wet forest habitats. Young use their teeth to cling to their mothers' fur after birth, being carried along during foraging trips; pups can fly on their own at about a month old.

SHORT-TAILED FRUIT BAT (Plate 72). These are small, very common bats that live in large groups, up to several hundred, usually in caves or tree cavities. They are primarily fruit-eaters, but also seasonally visit flowers for nectar. Usually they pick fruit from a tree, then return to a night roost to consume it. After giving birth, females carry their young for a week or two during their nightly foraging; older young are left in the day roost. Because of their abundance and frugivory, these bats are important dispersers of tree seeds in Neotropical forests.

JAMAICAN FRUIT-EATING BAT (Plate 71). A medium-sized fruit-eater of wet and dry forests, these bats also take insects and pollen from flowers. They pluck fruit and carry it to a night roost 25 to 200 m (80 to 650 ft) away to eat it. Observers estimate that every night each bat carries away from trees more than its own weight in fruit. Jamaican Fruit Bats roost in caves, hollow trees, or in foliage. Breeding is apparently polygynous (a single male mates with several females), because small roosts are always found to contain one male plus several females (up to 11) and their dependent young.

COMMON VAMPIRE BAT (Plate 71). Vampire bats are the only mammals that feed exclusively on blood; the only true mammal parasites. Day roosts are in hollow trees and caves. At night vampires fly out, using both vision (they have larger eyes and better vision than most bats) and sonar to find victims, usually large mammals. They not only fly well, they are also agile walkers, runners, and hoppers, of great assistance in perching on, feeding on, and avoiding swats by their prey. They use their sharp incisor teeth to bite the awake or sleeping animal, often on the neck, and remove a tiny piece of flesh. An anti-clotting agent in the bat's saliva keeps the small wound oozing blood. The vampire laps up the oozing blood –it does not suck it out. The feeding is reported to be painless (we won't ask how researchers know this, but, with a shudder, we can guess). Because blood is such a nutritious food, these bats need only about 15 ml (a half ounce) a day. Vampires breed at any time of the year; young are fed blood from the mother's mouth for several months until they can get their own.

SUCKER-FOOTED BAT (Plate 72). These tiny bats have circular adhesive cups on their thumbs and feet. They roost most commonly in small family groups (two to nine) in rolled up banana or Heliconia leaves or fronds. The "sucker" cups adhere to the leaves. Interestingly, unlike most bats, the Sucker-foots roost head upwards. When in a few days the leaf matures and unfurls, the family must seek a new home. They are common in lowland rain forests and gardens and often can be spotted by peering up into banana or palm fronds.

HAIRY-LEGGED BAT (Plate 72). This species is a common representative in Belize and Guatemala of the genus *Myotis*, the *little brown bats*, which are distributed widely over the Neotropics and, indeed, much of the world. *Myotis* bats roost in large groups in hollow trees, rock crevices, and buildings; males usually roost separately from females and their young. At sunset they leave the roost in search of flying insects, and return just before dawn. Young are carried by the mother for a few days after birth, but are then left behind with other young in the roost when the female leaves to forage. Pups can fly at about 3 weeks of age, are weaned at 5 to 6 weeks, and are reproductively mature at only 4 months.

BLACK MASTIFF BAT (Plate 71). These smallish bats are common inhabitants of low elevation rainforests from Mexico to northern Argentina. They roost, often in groups of 50 to 100, in hollow trees and rocky areas. They are also common in towns and villages, where they roost in buildings. Food consists mainly of insects.

Breeding

Bat mating systems are diverse, various species employing monogamy (one male and one female breed together), polygyny (one male and several females), and promiscuity (males and females both mate with more than one individual); the breeding behavior of many species has yet to be studied in detail. Some Central American bats breed at particular times of the year, but others have no regular breeding seasons. Most bats produce a single pup at a time.

Ecological Interactions

Bats are beneficial to forests and to people in a number of ways. Many Neotropical plants have bats, instead of bees or birds, as their main pollinators. These species generally have flowers that open at night and are white, making them easy for bats to find. They also give off a pungent aroma that bats can home in on. Nectar-feeding bats use long tongues to poke into flowers to feed on nectar – a sugary solution – and pollen. As a bat brushes against a flower, pollen adheres to its body, and is then carried to other plants, where it falls and leads to cross-pollination. Fruit-eating bats, owing to their high numbers, are important seed dispersers, helping to regenerate forests by transporting and dropping fruit seeds onto the forest floor. Also, particularly helpful to humans, bats each night consume enormous numbers of annoying insects.

Bats eat a variety of vertebrate animals; unfortunately for some of them they play right into the bat's hands...uh, feet. Some bats that specialize on eating frogs, it has been discovered, can home in on the calls that male frogs give to attract mates. These frogs are truly in a bind: if they call, they may attract a deadly predator; if they do not, they will lack for female company. Some types of bat prey, on the other hand, have developed anti-bat tactics. Several groups of moth species, for instance, can sense the ultrasonic chirps of some echolocating insectivorous bats; when they do, they react immediately by flying erratically or diving down into vegetation, decreasing the success of the foraging bats. Some moths even make their own clicking sounds, which apparently confuse the bats, causing them to break off approaches. The interaction of bats and their prey animals is an active field of animal behavior research because the predators and the prey have both developed varieties of tactics to try to outmaneuver or outwit the other.

Relatively little is known about which predators prey on bats. The list however, includes birds of prey (owls, hawks), snakes, other mammals such as opossums, cats, and (yes) people, and even other bats. Some monkeys actually hunt tent-roosting bats that they find in tree leaves. Tiny bats, such as the 5-g (a fifth of an ounce) HAIRY-LEGGED BAT, are even captured by large spiders and cockroaches. Bats, logically, are usually captured in or near their roosts, where predators can reliably find and corner them. One strong indication that predation is a real concern to bats is that many species reduce their flying in bright moonlight. Bats showing this "lunar phobia" include the JAMAICAN FRUIT-EATING BAT and SHORT-TAILED FRUIT BAT. Others, like the very small GREATER WHITE-LINED BAT, do not decrease their activity levels under full moons.

Lore and Notes

Bats have frightened people for a long time. The result, of course, is that there is a large body of folklore that portrays bats as evil, associated with or incarnations of death, devils, witches, or vampires. Undeniably, it was bats' alien lives – their activity in the darkness, flying ability, and strange form – and people's ignorance of bats, that were the sources of these myriad superstitions. Many cultures, worldwide, have evil bat legends, from Japan and the Philippines, to Europe, the Middle East, and Central and South America. Even the Australian Aborigines were not immune. One of their legends concerning the origin of death features a large bat that guarded the entrance to a cave: the first man and woman on Earth were warned to stay away from the bat. The woman, curious, approached the bat, which grew frightened and flew off (notice how women are always the bad guys in these stories?). The cave housed Death, which, with its bat guard gone, escaped into the world, with chronic, fatal consequences for people.

Many ancient legends tell of how bats came to be creatures of the night. But the association of bats with vampires – blood-sucking monsters – may have originated in recent times with Bram Stoker, the English author who in 1897 wrote *Dracula* (the title character, a vampire, could metamorphose into a bat). Vampire bats are native only to the Neotropics. Stoker may have heard stories of their blood-lapping ways from travellers, and for his book, melded the behavior of these bats with legends of vampires from India and from Slavic Gypsy culture. Although not all New World cultures imparted evil reputations to bats, it is not surprising, given the presence of vampire bats, that some did. The Mayans, for instance, associated bats with darkness and death; there was a "bat world," a part of the underworld ruled by a bat god, through which dead people had to pass. Some groups in what is now Guatemala apparently worshipped and greatly feared a bat-god named Camazotz.

Speaking of vampire bats: these bats presumably are much more numerous today than in the distant past. Before the introduction of domesticated animals to the Neotropics, vampires would have had to seek blood meals exclusively from mammals such as deer and peccaries; now they have, over large parts of their range, herds of large domesticated animals to feed on. In fact, examinations of blood meals reveal that vampire bats in settled areas feed almost exclusively on ranch and farm animals – cattle, horses, poultry, etc. By the way, vampire bats rarely attack people, although it is not unheard of. In some regions, they may transmit rabies.

Status

Determining the statuses of bat populations is difficult because of their nocturnal behavior and habit of roosting in places that are hard to census. With some exceptions, all that is known for most Neotropical species is that they are common or not common, widely or narrowly distributed. Some species are known from only a few museum specimens, or from their discovery in a single cave, but that does not mean that there are not healthy but largely hidden wild populations. Over the past few years biologists in Belize have been trying to catalog bat species there by recording and analyzing their ultrasonic sonar chirps, which differ among species. In this way, eventually the biologists will be able to identify the bat species present in any area without actually catching bats; all they will need to do is record the chirps at night and then let a computer analyze the tape to identify all bat species that contributed sounds.

Because many forest bats roost in hollow trees, deforestation is obviously a primary threat. For example, the HONDURAN WHITE BAT, a tiny fruit-eater, is now apparently limited to the Caribbean lowlands of southern Central America, and is threatened by further habitat loss. All of the bats profiled here are common. Many bat populations in temperate regions in Europe and the USA are known to be declining and under continued threat by a number of agricultural, forestry, and architectural practices (about five bat species or subspecies of the continental USA are endangered, USA ESA listed). Traditional roost sites have been lost on large scales by mining and quarrying, by the destruction of old buildings, and by changing architectural styles that eliminate many building overhangs, church belfries, etc. Many forestry practices advocate the removal of hollow, dead trees, which frequently provide bats with roosting space. Additionally, farm pesticides are ingested by insects, which are then eaten by bats, leading to death or reduced reproductive success.

Profiles

Fishing Bat, *Noctilio leporinus*, Plate 71a
Woolly False Vampire Bat, *Chrotopterus auritus*, Plate 71b
Jamaican Fruit-eating Bat, *Artibeus jamaicensis*, Plate 71c
Common Vampire Bat, *Desmodus rotundus*, Plate 71d
Black Mastiff Bat, *Molossus ater*, Plate 71e
Greater White-lined Bat, *Saccopteryx bilineata*, Plate 72a
Nectar Bat, *Glossophaga soricina,*, Plate 72b
Short-tailed Fruit Bat, *Carollia perspicillata*, Plate 72c
Sucker-footed Bat, *Thyroptera tricolor*, Plate 72d
Hairy-legged Bat, *Myotis keaysi*, Plate 72e

3. Primates

People's reactions to *monkeys* are interesting. All people, it seems, find monkeys striking, even transfixing, when first encountered, but then responses diverge. Many people adore the little primates and can watch them for hours, whether it be in the wild or at zoos. But others, myself included, find them a bit, for want of a better word, unalluring; we are slightly uncomfortable around them. What is so intriguing is that it is probably the same characteristic of monkeys that both so attracts and repels people, and that is their quasi-humanness. Whether or not we acknowledge it consciously, it is doubtless this trait that is the source of all the attention and importance attached to monkeys and apes. They look like us, and, truth be told, they act like us, in a startlingly large number of ways. Aristotle, 2300 years ago, noted similarities between human and nonhuman primates, and Linnaeus, the Swedish originator of our current system for classifying plants and animals, working more than 100 years pre-Darwin, classed people together in the same group with monkeys. Therefore, even before Darwin's ideas provided a possible mechanism for people and monkeys to be distantly related, we strongly suspected there was a link; the resemblance was too close to be accidental. Given this bond between people and other primates, it is not surprising that visitors to parts of the world that support nonhuman primates are eager to see them and very curious about their lives. Belize and northern Guatemala provide homes for two species of monkeys, one of them still sufficiently abundant in protected areas to be readily located and observed.

Primates are distinguished by several anatomical and ecological traits. They are primarily arboreal animals. Most are fairly large, very smart, and highly social – they live in permanent social groups. Most have five very flexible fingers and toes per limb. Primates' eyes are in the front of the skull, facing forward (eyes in the front instead of on the sides of the head are required for binocular vision and good depth perception, without which swinging about in trees would be an extremely hazardous and problematic affair), and primates have, for their sizes, relatively large brains. Female primates give birth usually to a single, very helpless infant.

Primates are distributed mainly throughout the globe's tropical areas and many sub-tropical ones, save for the Australian region. They are divided into four groups: (1) *Prosimians* include several families of primitive primates from the Old World. They look the least like people, are mainly small and nocturnal, and include lemurs, lorises, galago (bushbaby), and tarsiers. (2) *Old World Monkeys* (family Cercopithecidae) include baboons, mandrills, and various monkeys such as rhesus and proboscis monkeys. (3) *New World Monkeys* (family Cebidae) include many kinds of monkeys and the tiny marmosets. (4) The *Hominoidea* contains the gibbons, orangutans, chimpanzees, gorillas, and ecotravellers.

New World monkeys, in general, have short muzzles and flat, unfurred faces, short necks, long limbs, and long tails that are often used as fifth limbs for climbing about in trees. They are day-active animals that spend most of their time in trees, usually coming to the ground only to cross treeless space that they cannot traverse within the forest canopy. About 40 species of New World Monkeys are distributed from southern Mexico to northern Argentina; only two occur within the region covered in this book. Several species of *howler monkeys*, named for the tremendous roaring calls they give at dawn and dusk, occur from Central America to northern South America. The YUCATAN BLACK HOWLER (Plate 73) is a large monkey, weighing between 5 to 7 kg (11 to 16 lb); howlers, in fact, are among the New World's largest monkeys. They are all black with longish hair; males are larger than females. *Spider monkeys*, named for their long, slender limbs, range from southern Mexico to Brazil's lower Amazon region. The CENTRAL AMERICAN SPIDER MONKEY (Plate 73), like the howler, is also large, and weighs up to 8 kg (17 lb). It has a strong, *prehensile* tail and long, thin limbs. Coat color is variable – black, brown, or reddish, with lighter underparts and a light, unfurred facial mask and muzzle. A third species, the MANTLED HOWLER

MONKEY, which ranges over much of Central America save for the Yucatán region, may occur along Belize's southern border with Guatemala.

Natural History

Ecology and Behavior

Howler Monkeys. Howlers inhabit a variety of forest habitat types, but apparently prefer lowland wet evergreen forests. The YUCATAN BLACK HOWLER occurs only in southern Mexico, Guatemela, and Belize, mostly below about 300 m (1000 ft) in elevation, and they seem to prefer to live along rivers and streams. They are highly arboreal and rarely come to the ground; typically they spend most of their time in the upper reaches of the forest. In contrast to many other New World monkeys, howlers are relatively slow-moving and more deliberate in their travels. They eat fruit and a lot of leafy material; in fact, in one study, leaves comprised 64% of their diet, fruit and flowers, 31%. Owing to their specialization on a super-abundant food resource – leaves – the home range of a troop need not be very large. At Belize's Community Baboon Sanctuary, howler territories average about 5 to 6 ha, or 12 to 15 acres. Most troops in Belize and northern Guatemala contain between about four and 10 individuals, usually an adult male plus females and associated young. Slow-moving and often quiet, howlers can go unnoticed by people on trails passing directly below them. They are most assuredly not inconspicuous, however, when the males let loose with their amazing roaring vocalizations (females also roar occasionally). Their very loud, piercing choruses of roars, at dawn, during late afternoon, and, frequently, during heavy rain, are a characteristic and wonderful part of the rainforest environment. (The initial response of a newcomer to the Neotropics, upon being awakened in the morning by howling howlers, is sure to be "Now what the heck is THAT?".) These vocalizations are probably used by the howlers to communicate with other troops, to advertise their locations and to defend them; although troops of these monkeys do not maintain exclusive territories, they do appear to defend current feeding sites. The males' howling can be heard easily at 3 km (1.8 miles) away in a forest or 5 km (3 miles) away across water.

Spider Monkeys. Spider monkeys are found in Central American rainforests and deciduous forests at a wide range of elevations. They are extremely arboreal, rarely descending to the ground. They stay mostly within a forest's upper canopy, moving quickly through trees using their fully prehensile tail as a fifth limb to climb, swing, and hang. Spider monkeys eat ripe fruit, young leaves, and flowers. Troops in Panama were observed to feed on 80% fruit and 20% leaves and other plant materials. During the day, troops, varying in size from two to 25 or more (groups of 100 or more have been reported), range over wide swaths of forest, but stay within a home range of 2.5 to 4.0 square km (1 or 2 square miles). Troops usually consist of an adult male and several females and their dependent offspring. Spider monkeys are commonly observed in small groups, often two animals, but frequently they are members of a larger troop; the troop breaks up daily into small foraging parties, then coalesces each evening at a mutual sleeping tree. Spider monkeys are usually seen only in more remote parts of Belize. They require large tracts of undisturbed forest (as opposed to the howlers, which can live in disturbed forests near human settlements), and their populations never rebounded strongly after an outbreak of yellow fever during the early 1950s severely reduced their numbers. They are somewhat more common in northern Guatemala, for instance, in Tikal National Park.

Breeding

Female monkeys in Central America usually produce a single young that is born furred and with its eyes open. In the YUCATAN BLACK HOWLER, females reach sexual maturity usually at 4 to 5 years of age, and males at 6 to 8. Birth occurs following pregnancy of about 6 months. At 3 months, youngsters begin making brief trips away from their mothers, but until a year old, they continue to spend most of their time on their mother's back; they are nursed until they are 10 to 12 months old. Howlers have survived in the wild for up to 20 years. CENTRAL AMERICAN SPIDER MONKEYS appear to have no regular breeding seasons. Females reach sexual maturity at about 4 years old (males at about 5), then give birth every 2 to 4 years after pregnancies of about 7.5 months. Young, which weigh about 500 g (1 lb) at birth, are carried by the mother for up to 10 months and are nursed for up to a year. Upon reaching sexual maturity, young females leave their troops to find mates in other troops; males remain with their birth troop. Spider monkeys have lived for 33 years in captivity.

Ecological Interactions

A variety of predatory animals prey on Central America's monkeys, including Boa Constrictors (Plate 14), birds of prey such as eagles, arboreal cats such as Jaguarundi and Margay (Plate 75), and people. Spider and howler monkeys attain a degree of safety because they are fairly large. Other causes of death are disease (for instance, many monkey populations in Belize crashed during the 1950s because of an outbreak of yellow fever) and parasite infestations, such as that by *botflies*. Botflies lay their eggs on mosquitos, monkeys being exposed when infected mosquitos land on them to feed. Botfly larvae burrow into a monkey's skin, move into the bloodstream, and often find their way to the neck region. Many howlers, for instance, are observed to have severe botfly infestations of their necks, seen as swollen lumps and the holes created when adult botflies emerge from the monkey's body. In one Panamanian study, members of a howler population were found each to have an average of two to five botfly parasites; several monkeys in the study died, apparently of high levels of botfly infestation.

Monkeys are especially crucial elements of rainforest ecosystems because they are seed dispersers for many hundreds of plant species, particularly of the larger canopy trees. Mammals transport seeds that stick to their fur from the producing tree to the places where the seeds eventually fall off. Mammals that are *frugivores* (fruit-eaters) also carry fruit away from a tree, then eat the soft parts and drop the seeds, which may later germinate; or they eat the fruit whole and transport the seeds in their digestive tracts. The seeds eventually fall, unharmed, to the ground and germinate. Monkeys, it turns out, are major seed dispersers. For example, in Panama, where they were studied, a troop of *capuchin monkeys* was estimated to disperse each day more than 300,000 tiny seeds of a single tree species; up to two-thirds of the seeds that passed through the monkeys' digestive systems later germinated (a proportion that was actually higher than seeds that made it to the ground without passing through an animal gut).

Lore and Notes

Although humans cut down forests, destroying the habitats which howler monkeys need to live, and, in many regions, hunt and eat howler monkeys, biologists working at Belize's Community Baboon Sanctuary have discovered that not all the interactions between humans and YUCATAN BLACK HOWLERS are so negative. In fact, it turns out that the two species, people and howlers, agree on the importance of several tree species, such as chicle (p. 51) and breadfruit. People, from the time of the ancient Mayans, usually did not, and still do not, cut these trees owing to their economic importance; the howlers also use these trees – as main providers of food.

People hunt monkeys for reasons other than food and the pet trade. Many monkey body parts – meat, blood, bones – in various regions of the world are believed to have effective medicinal or aphrodisiac value. Some monkeys are killed to be used as bait, for instance, in the Amazon Basin to lure large cats into traps. Monkeys are also killed for their skins and other body parts, which are made into ornaments. Last, some monkeys, including the New World's capuchins, are killed as crop pests.

A cautionary note: wildlife guides sometimes are able to find quiet howler monkeys by locating their droppings beneath trees. But ecotravellers be warned – these monkeys have reputations for sending their droppings downwards, directly toward the heads of people standing below them.

Status

All New World Monkeys are listed in CITES Appendix I or II as endangered species (I) or species that, although they may not be currently threatened, need to be highly regulated in trade or they could soon become threatened (II). The main menaces to monkeys are deforestation – elimination of their natural habitats – and poaching for trade and meat. The larger monkeys especially – spiders, howlers – are often hunted for their meat, and therefore are usually rare near human settlements. (Those who eat monkeys claim that spider monkey is best.) The YUCATAN BLACK HOWLER is listed by the USA ESA as threatened, and the CENTRAL AMERICAN SPIDER MONKEY is listed as endangered (in some countries). Large expanses of protected forest are the basic requirement for continued survival of Central America's monkey populations.

Profiles

Yucatán Black Howler Monkey, *Alouatta pigra*, Plate 73a
Central American Spider Monkey, *Ateles geoffroyi*, Plate 73b

4. Anteaters and Armadillos

Anteaters and *armadillos*, together with *sloths*, comprise a group of very different and different-looking mammals that, somewhat surprisingly, are closely related. The group they belong to is the Order Edentata, meaning, literally, *without teeth*. Since all but the anteaters have some teeth, the name is a misnomer. The *edentates* are New World mammals specialized to eat ants and termites, or to eat leaves high in the forest canopy. Although the edentates might look and behave differently, they are grouped together because they share certain skeletal features and aspects of their circulatory and reproductive systems that indicate close relationships. Because anteaters and sloths are unique and found only in the tropical and semi-tropical forests of Central and South America, they are perhaps the quintessential mammals of the region, the way that toucans and parrots are quintessential Neotropical birds.

Anteaters. The anteater family, Myrmecophagidae, has four species, all restricted to Neotropical forests. Two of the species occur in Belize and northern Guatemala: the NORTHERN TAMANDUA and the very small SILKY ANTEATER (Plate 73). Because the latter species is a nocturnal tree-dweller, only the Northern Tamandua is likely to be seen. Fairly common inhabitants of rainforests, they have long cone-shaped snouts, large hooked claws on each front foot, noticeable ears, and a conspicuously dense coat of yellowish or brownish hair, with black on the belly and sides (a black *vest*, biologists say). Tamanduas weigh between 3 and 6 kg (6 to 13 lb). The anteater shape is unmistakable, and once you've studied a picture, you'll know one when you see one.

Armadillos. Armadillos are strange ground-dwelling mammals that, probably owing to the armor plating on their backs, are ecologically quite successful. The family, Dasypodidae, contains about 20 species that are distributed from the southern tip of South America to the central USA. Only one species occurs in the covered region, the NINE-BANDED ARMADILLO (Plate 73). These armadillos, which weigh from 3 to 4 kg (6 to 9 lb), are grayish or yellowish with many cross-wise plates of hard, horn-like material on their backs (bony plates underlie the outer horny covering). The plating produces a look that makes them unmistakable.

Sloths. What can one say? There is nothing else like a sloth. They vaguely resemble monkeys with longish, stiff hair, but their slow-motion lifestyle is the very antithesis of the primates' hyperkinetic life. There are two families of sloths, the two-toed and three-toed varieties, distinguished by the number of claws per foot. Sloths are active either nocturnally or both during the day and at night. They spend almost all their time in trees, feeding on leaves. None of the five Neotropical sloth species makes it as far north as Guatemala or Belize.

Natural History

Ecology and Behavior

Anteaters. Anteaters are mammals highly specialized to feed on ants and termites; some also dabble in bees. From an anteater's point of view, the main thing about these social insects is that they live in large colonies, so that finding one often means finding thousands. The anteaters' strong, sharp, front claws are put to use digging into ant colonies in or on the ground, and into termite nests in trees (the very abundant, dark, globular, often basket-ball sized *termitaries* attached to the trunks and branches of tropical trees); their long, thin snouts are used to get down into the excavation, and their extremely long tongues, coated with a special sticky saliva, are used to extract the little bugs. Anteaters have prehensile tails for hanging about and moving in trees, allowing them to get to hard-to-reach termite nests. Particular about their food, anteaters don't generally go after army ants or large, stinging ants that might do them harm. Tamanduas rest in hollow trees or other holes during midday, but are otherwise active, including nocturnally. They forage both on the ground and in trees, usually solitarily. Each individual's home range, the area in which it lives and seeks food, averages about 70 hectares (170 acres). Anteaters are fairly slow-moving animals and their metabolic rates low because, although ants and termites are plentiful and easy to find, they don't provide a high nutrition, high energy diet.

Armadillos. Some armadillos feed mainly on ants and termites, but the NINE-BANDED ARMADILLO is more omnivorous, eating many kinds of insects, small vertebrates, and also some plant parts. These armadillos, as is characteristic of their kind, have long claws for digging for food and for digging burrows. Usually they spend the day foraging alone, but several family members may share the same sleeping burrow. They are generally slow-moving creatures that, if not for their armor plating, would be easy prey for predators. When attacked, they curl up into a ball so that their armor faces the attacker, their soft abdomen protected at the center of the ball. Few natural predators can harm them. However, like opossums, they are frequently hit on roads by automobiles. Nine-banded armadillos can be found anywhere in the forest, but are more common in drier areas.

Breeding
Female anteaters bear one offspring at a time, and lavish attention on it. At first the newborn is placed in a secure location, such as in a tree cavity, and the mother returns to it at intervals to nurse. Later, when it is old enough, the youngster rides on the mother's back. After several months, when the young is about half the mother's size, the two part ways. Breeding may be at any time of year. Female armadillos, after 70-day pregnancies, produce several young at a time, usually four. For some unknown reason, each litter of armadillo young arises from a single fertilized egg so that if a female has four young, they are always identical quadruplets.

Ecological Interactions
The theory of the ecological niche suggests that two or more species that are virtually identical in their lifestyles and resource use cannot coexist within the same habitat or, at least, not for long. Competition among the species for resources will eventually drive the poorer competitors to extinction. If true, how do several species of anteater all occur in the same tropical forest? After all, they all eat ants and termites. Ecologists believe that the SILKY and GIANT ANTEATERS (a very large, rare species that occurs in South and southern Central America), and the NORTHERN TAMANDUA, coexist in some of the same places because they are different sizes and, although they eat the same food, their activity patterns differ sufficiently so as to reduce competition. For instance, Silky Anteaters are strictly nocturnal, but Giant Anteaters and Tamandua are also active during the day. The Silky is arboreal, the Giant is ground-dwelling, and Tamandua are both.

Lore and Notes
People, it seems, have always had trouble deciding precisely what an armadillo is. Linnaeus, the Swedish botanist who originated our current method of scientifically naming organisms, came up with the armadillo genus name *Dasypus*, a term he derived from the Greek for *rabbit*. It seems Linnaeus was trying to incorporate into the scientific name the Aztec word for armadillo, which was *azotochtli*, and which translates as *turtle-rabbit*. Arguments went on for years in the Texas (USA) State Legislature over whether to name the armadillo as the state mammal; some legislators apparently balked at the idea because they felt that armadillos, instead of being pure mammals, might be crosses between mammals and reptiles.

Status
Overall, the edentate mammals are not doing badly, but all suffer population declines from habitat destruction. One problem in trying to determine the status of their populations is that many are nocturnal and some of the armadillos spend most of their time in burrows. The result is that nobody really knows the real health of some populations. The GIANT ANTEATER (CITES Appendix II listed) has been rare in southern Central America for over 100 years, and may be extinct now in most of the region. It is fairly common only on the savannahs of Venezuela and Colombia. NORTHERN TAMANDUA (CITES Appendix III listed by Guatemala) are found throughout Belize and northern Guatemala but, outside of

protected areas, they are sometimes killed as pests by locals. The SILKY ANTEATER is thought to be fairly common, but because their populations naturally are sparse and also because they are so difficult to spot, good information on them is lacking. Armadillos are common in Belize, Guatemala, and other parts of their ranges, but because they are hunted for meat, their populations are often sparse around heavily settled areas. NINE-BANDED ARMADILLOS may be one of the most abundant mammals of Central American forests. In South America, the GIANT ARMADILLO, which weighs up to 30 kg (65 lb) and is killed for meat, is now endangered (CITES Appendix I and USA ESA listed) from overhunting.

Profiles

Nine-banded Armadillo, *Dasypus novemcinctus*, Plate 73c
Silky Anteater, *Cyclopes didactylus*, Plate 73d
Northern Tamandua, *Tamandua mexicana*, Plate 73e

5. Rodents

Ecotravellers discover among *rodents* an ecological paradox: although by far the most diverse and successful of the mammals, rodents are, with a few obvious exceptions in any region, relatively inconspicuous and rarely encountered. The number of living rodent species globally approaches 1750, fully 43% of the approximately 4050 known mammalian species. Probably in every region of the world save Antarctica, rodents – including the mice, rats, squirrels, chipmunks, marmots, gophers, beaver, and porcupines – are the most abundant land mammals. More individual rodents are estimated to be alive at any one time than individuals of all other types of mammals combined. Rodents' near-invisibility to people, particularly in the Neotropics, derives from the facts that most rodents are very small, most are secretive or nocturnal, and many live out their lives in subterranean burrows. That most rodents are rarely encountered, of course, many people do not consider much of a hardship.

Rodent ecological success is related to their efficient, specialized teeth and associated jaw muscles, and to their broad, nearly omnivorous diets. Rodents are characterized by having four large incisor teeth, one pair front-and-center in the upper jaw, one pair in the lower (other teeth, separated from the incisors, are located farther back in the mouth). With these strong, sharp, chisel-like front teeth, rodents "make their living": gnawing (*rodent* is from the Latin *rodere*, to gnaw), cutting, and slicing vegetation, fruit, and nuts, killing and eating small animals, digging burrows, and even, in the case of beaver, imitating lumberjacks.

Rodents are distributed throughout the world except for Antarctica and some Arctic islands. The Neotropics contain some of the largest and most interesting of the world's rodents. About 30 species occur in Belize and Guatemala. Only a few of these are commonly spotted by visitors and so warrant coverage here – a few squirrels, a porcupine, and two larger rodent representatives, the PACA and CENTRAL AMERICAN AGOUTI (Plate 74). Squirrels are members of the family Sciuridae, a worldwide group of more than 350 species that occurs on all continents except Australia and Antarctica. The family includes ground, tree, and flying squirrels. Only three or four species occur in Belize and northern Guatemala. The family Erethizontidae contains the 15 species of New World porcupines, which are distributed throughout the Americas except for the southern third of South America. A single species is native to the covered region. Last, two families that are restricted to tropical America contain a few large, common rodents: Family Agoutidae contains the Paca, and family Dasyproctidae includes the Agouti.

Most of the world's rodents are small mouse-like or rat-like mammals that weigh less than a kilogram (2.2 lb); they range, however, from tiny pygmy mice that weigh only a few grams to South America's pig-like CAPYBARA, behemoths at up to 50 kg (110 lb). The two common tree squirrels of Belize and northern Guatemala are DEPPE'S and YUCATAN SQUIRRELS (Plate 74), which are moderate-sized squirrels with short ears and long, moderately bushy tails. Porcupines generally are fairly large, heavyset rodents, but the MEXICAN HAIRY PORCUPINE (Plate 74) is a relatively small, thin member of the group, weighing between 1.5 and 2.5 kg (3.3 to 5.5 lb). Its body is covered with long, dark hair that covers most of its spines. It has short limbs, a longish prehensile tail, small eyes, mostly hidden ears, and a hairless snout. AGOUTI and PACA are large, almost pig-like rodents, usually brownish, with long legs, short hair, and squirrel-like heads. Paca weigh up to 10 kg (22 lb), twice the weight of an Agouti. Males are slightly larger than females.

Natural History

Ecology and Behavior
DEPPE'S and YUCATAN SQUIRRELS are day-active tree squirrels, generally seen in trees and, occasionally, foraging on the ground. Deppe's Squirrel, usually encountered moving about tree branches and vines in forests at various elevations, eats berries, acorns, and fungi. The larger Yucatán Squirrel, more restricted to lower elevation forests and semi-open areas with trees, eats flowers and fruit. MEXICAN HAIRY PORCUPINES are solitary, nocturnal animals, almost always found in trees. They move slowly along branches, using their prehensile tail as a fifth limb, to feed on leaves, green tree shoots, and fruit. During the day they sleep in tree cavities or on branches hidden amid dense vegetation. They are found mostly in higher-elevation forests.

PACA are usually active only at night, foraging for fruit, nuts, seeds, and vegetation. Along with AGOUTI, they can sit up on their hind legs and eat, holding their food with their front paws, much like a squirrel or rat. They sleep away daylight hours in burrows. Several observers have noted that Paca, if startled or threatened, will freeze, and, if chased, will dive into nearby water, around which they are usually found. The smaller Agouti are naturally day-active, but have become increasingly nocturnal in their habits in areas where they are intensively hunted. Agouti mainly eat seeds and fruit, but also flowers, vegetation, and insects. Both Paca and Agouti appear to live in monogamous pairs on territories, although male and female tend to forage alone. When threatened or startled, Agoutis usually run, giving warning calls or barks as they go, presumably to warn nearby relatives of danger. Agouti and Paca, large and tasty, are preyed on by a variety of mammals and reptiles, including large snakes and such carnivores as Jaguarundi (Plate 75).

Breeding
Relatively little is known of the breeding behavior of most Neotropical tree squirrels and of many other rodents. Tree squirrel nests consist of a bed of leaves placed in a tree cavity or a ball of leaves on a branch or in a tangle of vegetation. One to three (usually two) young are born per litter. Young born blind and naked about 40 days after mating occurs, stay in the nest for at least 6 weeks, and nurse for 8

to 10 weeks. Mexican Hairy Porcupines have one to three young per litter. Pregnancies are relatively long, and, as a result, the young are *precocial* – born with eyes open and in an advanced state. They are therefore mobile and quickly able to follow the mother. Agouti and Paca also have precocial young, usually in litters of one or two. A day after their birth, a mother Agouti leads her young to a burrow where they hide, and to which she returns each day to feed them. Pregnancy durations for Agouti and Paca are 115 to 120 days.

Ecological Interactions
Rodents are important ecologically primarily because of their great abundance. They are so common that they make up a large proportion of the diets of many carnivores. For instance, in a recent study of Jaguars (Plate 76) in Costa Rica, it was discovered that rodents were the third most frequent prey of the large cats, after sloths and iguanas. In turn, rodents, owing to their ubiquitousness and numbers, are themselves important predators on seeds and fruit. That is, they eat seeds and seed-containing fruit, digesting or damaging the seeds, rendering them useless to the plants that produced them for reproduction. Of course, not every seed is damaged (some fall to the ground as rodents eat, others pass unscathed through their digestive tracts), and so rodents, at least occasionally, also act as seed dispersers. Burrowing is another aspect of rodent behavior that has significant ecological implications because of the sheer numbers of individuals that participate. When so many animals move soil around (rats and mice, especially), the effect is that over several years the entire topsoil of an area is turned, keeping soil loose and aerated, and therefore more suitable for plant growth.

Lore and Notes
Through the animals' constant gnawing, rodents' chisel-like incisors wear down rapidly. Fortunately for the rodents, their incisors, owing to some ingenious anatomy and physiology, continue to grow throughout their lives, unlike those of most other mammals.

Contrary to folk wisdom, porcupines cannot "throw" their quills, or spines, at people or predators. Rather, the spines detach quite easily when touched, such that a predator snatching a porcupine in its mouth will be impaled with spines and hence, rendered very unhappy. The spines have barbed ends, like fishhooks, which anchor them securely into the offending predator.

PACA meat is considered to be among the most superior of wild meats, because it is tasty, tender, and lacks much of an odor; as such, when it can be purchased, it is very expensive. Both Agouti and Paca are favorite game animals throughout their ranges.

Status
The YUCATAN SQUIRREL is a common, widespread species, and although hunted for meat in some areas, is not presently threatened. DEPPE'S SQUIRREL is now threatened in Costa Rica owing to deforestation (CITES Appendix III listed). The precise status of MEXICAN HAIRY PORCUPINE populations is unknown, but they are thought to be secure. The same is true for many other species of New World porcupines – little is known about them, but most appear not to be presently threatened. These nocturnal rodents are hunted for meat in some areas. One species, southeastern Brazil's BRISTLE-SPINED PORCUPINE, is now highly endangered (USA ESA listed). PACA are hunted for meat throughout their broad geographic range, but, although scarce in heavily hunted areas, they are secretive

enough and broadly enough distributed over Central and South America to still maintain many healthy populations. There are still good populations of CENTRAL AMERICAN AGOUTI in relatively undisturbed regions of Belize and northern Guatemala.

Profiles

Deppe's Squirrel, *Sciurus deppei*, Plate 74a
Yucatán Squirrel, *Sciuris yucatanensis*, Plate 74b
Mexican Hairy Porcupine, *Sphiggurus mexicanus*, Plate 74c
Paca, *Agouti paca*, Plate 74d
Central American Agouti, *Dasyprocta punctata*, Plate 74e

6. Carnivores

Carnivores are the ferocious mammals – the cat that sleeps on your pillow, the dog that takes table scraps from your hand – that are specialized to kill and eat other vertebrate animals. Four families within the Order Carnivora have representatives in Belize and Guatemala: *felids* (cats), *canids* (dogs), *procyonids* (raccoons), and *mustelids* (weasel-like things). They have in common that they are primarily ground-dwelling animals and have teeth customized to grasp, rip, and tear flesh – witness their large, cone-shaped canines. Most are meat-eaters, but many are at least somewhat omnivorous, taking fruits and other plant materials. Only one wild member of the dog family, Canidae, occurs in the covered region, the GRAY FOX (Plate 75); because this is a common mammal that ranges into North America, it is pictured but not detailed here. In total there are about 37 species of cat, Family Felidae, with representatives inhabiting all continents but Australia and Antarctica. Because all six species that occur in Central America are fairly rare, most to the point of being endangered, and because of their mainly nocturnal habits, seeing even a single wild cat is an infrequent occurrence on any brief trip. More than likely, all that will be observed of cats are traces; some tracks in the mud near a stream or scratch marks on a tree trunk or log.

All of the cats are easily recognized as such. They come in two varieties – spotted and not spotted. The four spotted species generally are yellowish, tan, or cinnamon on top and white below, with black spots and stripes on their heads, bodies, and legs. The smallest is the ONCILLA, or LITTLE SPOTTED CAT, which is the size of a small house cat, and occurs only in southern Central America and southwards. Next in size is the MARGAY (Plate 75), which is the size of a large house cat, weighing 3 to 5 kg (6 to 11 lb). OCELOTS (Plate 75) are the size of medium-sized dogs and weigh 7 to 14 kg (15 to 30 lb). Last, the JAGUAR (Plate 76) is the largest New World cat and the region's largest carnivore, sometimes nearly 2 m (6.5 ft) long and weighing between 60 and 120 kg (130 to 260 lb). The two unspotted cats are the mid-sized JAGUARUNDI (Plate 75), which is blackish, brown, gray, or reddish, and the PUMA (Plate 76), or MOUNTAIN LION, which is tan or grayish and almost as large as the Jaguar. Female cats often are smaller than males, up to a third smaller in the Jaguar.

The mustelid family is comprised of about 70 species of small and medium-sized, slender-bodied carnivores that are distributed globally except for Australia and Antarctica. Included in the family are the weasels, skunks, mink, otters, and badgers, animals that occupy diverse habitats, including, in the case of otters, the water. Mustelids generally have long, thin bodies, short legs, long tails, and soft, dense fur. Six species probably occur in Belize and Guatemala, but all are wary animals that, except for the occasional skunk, are not commonly sighted. The TAYRA (TIE-rah) (Plate 77) is a medium-sized, mink-like animal, being long and slender and mostly black or brown; they weigh up to 5 kg (11 lb). STRIPED HOG-NOSED SKUNKS (Plate 76) weigh about 4 kg (9 lb) and are black with white stripes. NEOTROPICAL OTTERS (Plate 77) are short-legged and brownish, usually weighing about 11 kg (25 lb). Males are larger than females in many mustelid species.

The raccoons, or Family Procyonidae, are a New World group of about 15 species (for several reasons, the Asian pandas were thought until recently to be procyonids). This is a very successful group of small and medium-sized mammals that occupy a range of habitats, usually where there are trees. Four species occur in Belize and Guatemala, but two are rarely seen. The more visible ones are the NORTHERN RACCOON and the WHITE-NOSED COATI (kah-WAH-tee) (Plate 78). In general, procyonids have long, pointed muzzles, short legs, and long tails that more often than not are noticeably ringed. Northern Raccoons (3 to 6 kg, 6 to 13 lb) are brownish or grayish with black-tipped outer hairs that produce a salt-and-pepper look. They have strongly banded tails and a distinguishing black face mask that surrounds their eyes. Coatis (4 to 5 kg, 9 to 11 lb), brown or reddish with dark face masks, are more slender than raccoons and have very long, banded tails that, like a cat, they hold erect as they walk. As with the felids and mustelids, male procyonids are often a bit larger than females.

Natural History

Ecology and Behavior
Felids. The cats are finely adapted to be predators on vertebrate animals. Hunting methods are extremely similar among the various species. Cats do not run to chase prey for long distances. Rather, they slowly stalk their prey or wait in ambush, then capture the prey after pouncing on it or after a very brief, fast chase. Biologists are often impressed by the consistency in the manner that cats kill their prey. Almost always it is with a sharp bite to the neck or head, breaking the neck or crushing the skull. Retractile claws, in addition to their use in grabbing and holding prey, give cats good abilities to climb trees, and some of them are partially arboreal animals, foraging and even sleeping in trees. Aside from some highly social large cats of Africa, most cats are solitary animals, foraging alone, individuals coming together only to mate. Some species are territorial but in others individuals overlap in the areas in which they hunt. Cats, especially those of rainforests, are often nocturnal, but some are also active by day. When inactive, they shelter in rock crevices or burrows dug by other animals. Cats are the most carnivorous of the carnivores; their diets are more centered on meat than any of the other families. Little is known of the natural history of forest-dwelling ONCILLAS; they eat birds and small rodents. MARGAYS are mostly arboreal forest cats; they forage in trees for rodents and birds. OCELOTS eat rodents, snakes, lizards, and birds. They are probably more common than Oncillas and Margays and, although quite secretive, they are the most frequently seen of the spotted cats. Active mainly at night, they often spend daylight hours asleep in trees. JAGUARS can be active day or night. These cats inhabit low and middle elevation forests, hunting for large prey such as peccary and deer, but also monkeys, birds, lizards, even caiman. Studied at Belize's Cockscomb Basin Wildlife Sanctuary, male Jaguars were active at night and had overlapping home ranges of 28 to 40 square km (11 to 15 square miles). When hunting was good, a Jaguar would

often stay in the same small area for up to 2 weeks. Prey taken was mostly armadillo, paca, and brocket deer. JAGUARUNDI are both day and night active, and are seen fairly frequently in forests. They eat small rodents, rabbits, and birds. PUMA occupy various habitat types and prey on deer and other large mammals. They are rare in Central America, the total population of the region probably no more than a few hundred.

Mustelids. Most of the mustelids are strongly carnivorous, although some, such as the ones detailed below, eat a number of other foods. These are powerful animals, sometimes capable of killing prey as large as, or even larger than themselves. Like the cats, they kill with swift crushing bites to the head or neck. TAYRAS are tree climbers, active both day and night. Singly or sometimes in pairs or family groups, they search the ground and in trees for a variety of foods – fruit, bird eggs or nestlings, lizards, rodents, rabbits, and insects. Skunks occupy many kinds of habitats, although they avoid dense forest. They are active only at dusk and during the night, when they forage, usually solitarily. Skunks root about a good deal in the leaf litter and soil, looking for insects, snails, and small vertebrates such as rodents, lizards and perhaps snakes; occasionally they take fruit, and some species consume a good amount of vegetation. Skunks, having their spray defenses (see below), usually move quite leisurely, apparently knowing that they are well protected from most predators. NEOTROPICAL OTTERS forage alone or in pairs. They are active both during the day and at night, hunting in streams, rivers, and ponds for fish and crustaceans such as crayfish. Although otters always remain in or near the water, they spend their inactive time in burrows on land. Adapted for moving swiftly and smoothly through water, they move on land awkwardly, with a duck-like waddle.

Procyonids. The distinctive ecological and behavioral traits of the procyonids are that (1) although classified as carnivores, they are omnivorous, (2) they are mostly nocturnal in their activities (except for the coati), and that (3) as a group, they have a great propensity to climb trees. NORTHERN RACCOONS forage either singly or in small groups composed of a mother and her young. They eat fruit and all sorts of small animals, both vertebrates and invertebrates, not to mention garbage around human settlements. Exhibiting a high degree of manual dexterity and sensitivity of their "fingers," raccoons actually search for food in ponds and streams by lowering only their front paws into the water and feeling for frogs, crabs, crayfish, etc. When not active, Raccoons seek shelter in burrows or in tree or rock crevices. WHITE-NOSED COATIS are known for their daylight activity and for the fact that, unlike others of the family, they are quite social. They usually group together in small bands, most commonly several adult females and their young. Occasionally coatis are seen in groups of 50 or more. Males tend to be solitary animals, joining a female band only for several weeks during the breeding season. Coatis are as comfortable foraging in trees as they are on the ground; they search for fruit, lizards, mice, insects and, in the great raccoon tradition, they are also denizens of trash heaps. KINKAJOUS (Plate 78) spend most of their time in trees, foraging for fruits and arboreal vertebrates. Alone among the procyonids, their tail is fully prehensile, permitting them to grasp branches with it and hang upside down. Kinkajous are nocturnal, and relatively little is known of their behavior in the wild. With a flashlight, they can often be spotted moving about tree branches at night, making squeaking sounds; several are often found feeding together in a single tree. CACOMISTLES (Plate 78) are nocturnal tree-climbers that feed mainly on fruit and insects. Adult procyonids probably have a relatively low rate of predation, but their enemies would include boas, raptors, cats, and Tayras.

Breeding

Felids. Male and female cats of the Neotropics come together only to mate; the female bears and raises her young alone. She gives birth in a den fashioned from a burrow, rock cave, or tree cavity. The young are sheltered in the den while the female forages; she returns periodically to nurse and bring the kittens prey to eat. Most of the cats have one or two young at a time, although PUMA and JAGUAR may have up to four. Pregnancy is about 75 days in the smaller cats, about 100 in the large ones. Juvenile Jaguars remain with their mother for up to 18 months, learning to be efficient hunters, before they go off on their own.

Mustelids. Female mustelids give birth in dens under rocks or in crevices, or in burrows under trees. Pregnancy for TAYRA, skunk, and otter usually lasts about 60 to 70 days. Tayra produce an average of two young per litter, skunk, two to five, and otter, two or three. As is true for many of the carnivores, mustelid young are born blind and helpless.

Procyonids. In all the Central American procyonids, females raise young without help from males. Young are born in nests made in trees (NORTHERN RACCOONS in North America also give birth in rock crevices and in tree cavities). Duration of pregnancy varies from about 65 days in raccoons, to 75 days in WHITE-NOSED COATIS, to about 115 days in KINKAJOUS. Raccoons have three to seven young per litter; coatis, one to five young, and Kinkajous, always only one.

Ecological Interactions

The six species of Central American cats are quite alike in form and behavior. Therefore, according to ecological theory, they should compete strongly for the same resources, competition that if unchecked, should drive some of the species to extinction. But are all the cats really so similar? One major difference is size. ONCILLA are very small, MARGAY a bit bigger, and JAGUARUNDI larger than that. OCELOT are next in size. The two large cats, PUMA and JAGUAR, are somwhat similar in size, but Puma live in more diverse habitats than do Jaguar. Prey the animals take also varies. The smallest cats take small rodents and birds, the medium-sized cats take larger rodents and birds, and the large cats take larger prey such as large mammals. Biologists believe that these kinds of differences among similar species permit sufficient "ecological separation" to allow somewhat peaceful coexistence.

Lore and Notes

JAGUAR rarely attack people, who normally are given a wide berth; these cats tend to run away quickly when spotted. Recently there have been widely circulated reports of PUMA attacking people in the USA, but this seems more due to people moving to live in prime Puma habitat, which is increasingly limited, than to a desire on the cat's part for human prey. Large cats in Central America are sometimes seen walking at night along forest trails or roads. General advice if you happen to stumble across one: do not run because that often stimulates a cat to chase. Face the cat, make yourself large by raising your arms, and make as much loud noise as you can.

Based on the excavated artworks of ancient Mayan and Aztec civilizations of Mexico and Central and South America, it is clear that felids in general, and especially the Jaguar, held important positions in the religious beliefs and cultures of these peoples. It is not hard to imagine why the Jaguar would occupy a central place in such cultures: the cat is a large, aggressive predator, a lone hunter, a night stalker with superior senses, one of the few competitors with people for larger prey animals such as deer. The Jaguar in ancient art was usually associated with kings, shamans, and warfare. The supreme Aztec god, Tezcatlipoca, in fact, appeared in one guise as a Jaguar.

Mustelids have a strong, characteristic odor, *musk*, that is produced by secretions from scent glands around their backsides. The secretions are used to communicate with other members of the species and to mark habitats, presumably also for signalling. In skunks, these glands produce particularly strong, foulsmelling fluids that with startling good aim can be violently squirted in a jet at potential predators. The fluids are not toxic, cannot cause blindness as is sometimes commonly believed, but they can cause temporary, severe irritation of eyes and nose. Predators that approach a skunk once rarely repeat the exercise.

One facet of mustelid natural history that is particularly helpful to people, though not universally appreciated, is that these carnivores eat a staggering number of rodents. For instance, it has been calculated that weasels each year in New York State eat some 60 million mice and millions of rats. In fact, in the past TAYRA were kept as pets in parts of South America to protect homes and belongings from rodents.

Sometimes the name *coatimundi* is used for a coati, but the longer term is often incorrect. "Coati" is an Indian name for the species. "Coati-mundi" apparently was used by Indians to refer to solitary coatis (usually males, because females travel in groups). Thus, coatimundi is not really a synonym for coati.

Status

All of the Neotropical cats are now threatened or actually endangered. Their forest habitats are increasingly cleared for agricultural purposes, they were, and still are to a limited extent, hunted for their skins, and large cats are killed as potential predators on livestock and pets. The five species profiled here are all CITES Appendix I and USA ESA listed, although the JAGUARUNDI and PUMA are listed for only parts of their ranges. Jaguar still roam more remote parts of Belize and northern Guatemala. Estimates are that there are between 600 and 2000 adults in Belize. The Cockscomb Basin Wildlife Sanctuary was established in southern Belize specifically to preserve habitat for the healthy Jaguar population that occurs there.

Many mustelids in the past were trapped intensively for their fur, which is often soft, dense, and glossy, just the ticket, in fact, to create coats of otter or weasel, mink or marten, sable or fisher. River otters, although still widespread in the Americas, are sufficiently rare to be considered endangered (CITES I and USA ESA listed). Skunks are common, their populations healthy, and TAYRA are common animals that usually do well even where people disturb their natural habitats. Another Central American mustelid, the GRISON (Plate 77), a grayish and black weasel-like animal, is fairly uncommon throughout its range. None of the procyonids of Belize or Guatemala is currently threatened.

Profiles

Gray Fox, *Urocyon cinereoargenteus*, Plate 75a
Jaguarundi, *Herpailurus yaguarondi*, Plate 75b
Ocelot, *Leopardus pardalis*, Plate 75c
Margay, *Leopardus wiedii*, Plate 75d

Puma, *Puma concolor*, Plate 76a
Jaguar, *Panthera onca*, Plate 76b
Striped Hog-nosed Skunk, *Conepatus semistriatus*, Plate 76c
Southern Spotted Skunk, *Spilogale putorius*, Plate 76d

Tayra, *Eira barbara*, Plate 77a
Neotropical Otter, *Lontra longicaudis*, Plate 77b
Grison, *Galictis vittata*, Plate 77c
Long-tailed Weasel, *Mustela frenata*, Plate 77d

Northern Raccoon, *Procyon lotor*, Plate 78a
White-nosed Coati, *Nasua narica*, Plate 78b
Kinkajou, *Potos flavus*, Plate 78c
Cacomistle, *Bassariscus sumichrasti*, Plate 78d

7. Peccaries and Deer

Peccaries and *deer* are the two Neotropical representatives of the Artiodactyla, the globally distributed order of hoofed mammals (ungulates) that have an even number of toes on each foot. (The Perissodactyla are ungulates with odd numbers of toes; p. 219.) Other artiodactyls are pigs, hippos, giraffes, antelope, bison, buffalo, cattle, gazelles, goats, and sheep. In general, the group is specialized to feed on leaves, grass, and fallen fruit. The truth be told, peccaries look like mid-sized pigs; and deer are self-explanatory. Three peccary species comprise the Family Tayassuidae. They are confined in their distributions to the Neotropics, although one species pushes northwards into the southwestern USA; two species, the COLLARED and WHITE-LIPPED PECCARIES (Plate 79), occur in Belize and Guatemala. Collared Peccaries are more abundant than the White-lipped, occur in more habitats, and are seen more frequently. Collareds are found in rainforests, deciduous forests, and areas of scattered trees and shrubs, including agricultural areas (where they raid crops). White-lippeds are denizens only of rainforests. The two deer species that occur in the region, WHITE-TAILED and RED BROCKET DEER (Plate 79) are members of the Family Cervidae, which is 36 species strong and distributed almost worldwide.

Peccaries are small to medium-sized hog-like animals covered with coarse longish hair, with slender legs, large heads, small ears, and short tails. They have enlarged, sharp and pointed, tusk-like canine teeth. The Collared Peccary is the smaller of the two species, adults typically weighing between 17 and 30 kg (35 to 75 lb). They come in black or gray as adults, with a band of lighter-colored hair at the neck that furnishes their name; youngsters are reddish-brown or buff-colored. The White-lipped Peccary, so named for the white patch of hair on its chin, weighs from 25 to 40 kg (55 to 85 lb). Deer are large mammals, reddish, brown, or gray. They have long, thin legs, short tails, and big ears. Males have antlers that they shed each year and regrow. White-tailed Deer have white markings around their eyes, on their muzzles, and, appropriately, on their tails. Central American White-tailed Deer (30 to 50 kg, 65 to 110 lb) are, in general, slightly larger than Red Brocket Deer (24 to 48 kg, 50 to 100 lb), but usually smaller, by a third to a half, than members of their species in the USA and Canada. Very young deer are usually spotted with white.

Natural History

Ecology and Behavior

Peccaries are day-active, highly social animals, rarely encountered singly. COL-LARED PECCARIES travel in small groups of 3 to 25 or so, most frequently 6 to 9; WHITE-LIPPED herds generally are larger, often 50 to 100 or more (smaller groups occur where they are heavily hunted). Peccaries travel single file along narrow forest paths, spreading out when good foraging sites are found. These animals are omnivores, but mainly they dig into the ground with their snouts, "rooting" for vegetation. They feed on roots, underground stems, and bulbs, but also leaves, fruit (especially the White-lipped), insects, and even small vertebrates that they stumble across. Because White-lipped Peccaries are larger than Collareds and travel in larger groups, they need to wander long distances each day to locate enough food. Like pigs, peccaries wallow in mud and shallow water, and there is usually a wallowing spot within their home ranges, the area within which a group lives and forages. During dry seasons, peccaries may gather in large numbers near lakes or streams. Because peccaries are hunted by people, they are usually quiet, wary, and therefore, sometimes hard to notice or approach. Peccaries are preyed upon by large snakes such as boas (Plate 14), and probably by Puma and Jaguar (Plate 76).

Deer are *browsers* and *grazers*, that is, they eat leaves and twigs from trees and shrubs that they can reach from the ground (browsing), and grass (grazing). The RED BROCKET DEER, in particular, also eats fruit and flowers, chiefly those that have already fallen to the ground. WHITE-TAILED DEER inhabit open places and forest edge areas, rarely dense forest, whereas the Red Brocket Deer is a forest species that wanders through trailless terrain. The large, branched antlers of male White-tails make moving through dense forest a dubious business; male Red Brockets, on the other hand, have short, spike-like, rearwards-curving antlers – plainly better for maneuvering in their dense jungle habitats. Both White-tails and Red Brockets are active during daylight hours and also often at night; Red Brocket Deer are most commonly seen during early mornings and at dusk. White-tails travel either solitarily or in small groups, whereas Red Brockets are almost always solitary. Deer are *cud-chewers*. After foraging and filling a special chamber of their stomach, they find a sheltered area, rest, regurgitate the meal into their mouths and chew it well so that it can be digested. Predators on deer include the big cats – Puma and Jaguar; eagles may take young fawns.

Breeding

Female peccaries have either one or two young at a time, born 4 to 5 months after mating. The young are precocial, meaning that they can walk and follow their mother within a few days of birth. Deer, likewise, give birth to one or two young that, within a week or two, can follow the mother. Until that time, they stay in a sheltered spot while their mother forages, returning at intervals to nurse them.

Lore and Notes

Both species of peccary enjoy reputations for aggressiveness toward humans, but experts agree that the reputation is exaggerated. There are stories of herds panicking at the approach of people, stampeding, even chasing people. These are large enough beasts, with sufficiently large and sharp canine teeth, to do damage. If you spot peccaries, err on the side of caution; watch them from afar and leave them alone. Be quiet and they might take no notice of you; their vision apparently is poor. If you are charged, a rapid retreat into a tree could be a wise move.

When a WHITE-TAILED DEER spots a predator or person that has not yet spotted it, the deer slinks away with its head and tail down, the white patch under the tail concealed. But when the deer is alarmed – it spots a predator stalking it or hears a sudden noise – it bounds off with its tail raised, its white rump and white tail bottom exposed, almost like a white flag. Animal behaviorists believe that the white is a signal to the deer's party, relatives likely to be among them, that a potential predator has been spotted and that they should flee.

The Collared Peccary ranges northwards to the USA's Arizona, New Mexico, and Texas, where it is known locally simply as the PECCARY, or JAVELINA.

Status

Peccaries were hunted for food and hides long before the arrival of Europeans to the New World, and such hunting continues. COLLARED PECCARIES, listed in CITES Appendix II, are still locally common in protected, wilderness, and more rural areas. WHITE-LIPPED PECCARIES, also CITES Appendix II listed, are less common, and less is known about their populations; they may soon be threatened. Deer are likewise hunted for meat, skins, and sport. Deer range widely in Belize and Guatemala but, due to hunting pressures, they are numerous only in the protected environs of national parks and wildlife preserves. RED BROCKET DEER employ excellent anti-hunting tactics, being solitary animals that keep to dense forests. Both deer species profiled here are CITES Appendix III listed by Guatemala.

Profiles

Collared Peccary, *Tayassu tajacu*, Plate 79a
White-lipped Peccary, *Tayassu pecari*, Plate 79b
White-tailed Deer, *Odocoileus virginianus*, Plate 79c
Red Brocket Deer, *Mazama americana*, Plate 79d

8. Tapir

Tapirs (TAE-peers) are small, funny-looking relatives of the horse and rhinoceros and the only members of that group to occur naturally in the New World. (Horses were brought from Asia by people.) Tapirs, horses, and rhinos belong to an order of mammals called the Perissodactyla, which refers to the fact that all of its members have an odd number of toes on each foot. Only four species of tapir comprise the family Tapiridae, three residing in the Neotropics and one in Asia. BAIRD'S TAPIR (Plate 80) is the only one to occur in Belize and Guatemala, and it is now fairly rare; owing to its scarcity, spotting it is often a priority for visitors eager to see mammalian wildlife. This tapir used to be common in many habitats, including grassy swamps, rainforests, forested hillsides, and flooded grasslands. Now it is found only in small numbers, and then only where it is protected from hunting, mainly in national parks and wildlife sanctuaries.

Baird's Tapir is the largest of the Neotropical tapirs, and a substantial animal; stocky and up to 2 m (6 ft) long, with short legs and a long snout somewhat reminiscent of a horse's. Weighing between 150 and 300 kg (330 to 660 lb), it has the distinction of being Central America's largest native terrestrial mammal. Tapirs have short, sparse hair – from a distance they appear almost hairless – and short tails. The long snout, or *proboscis*, consists of an enlarged, elongated upper lip. Tapirs are blackish to dark- or reddish-brown in color. Youngsters have a characteristic lighter brown coloring with white or yellowish spots and stripes.

Natural History

Ecology and Behavior

Tapirs are mainly nocturnal, but are also seen foraging during daylight hours. They are herbivores, feasting on leaves, twigs, grass, fruit, and perhaps some seeds. As *browsers*, they walk along, stopping occasionally to munch on low plants. Apparently tapirs are very particular about the types of plants they consume, relying at least partially on a highly developed sense of smell to choose the right stuff; their vision is quite poor. In one study conducted in western Belize, many more tapirs were sighted in open habitats such as partially logged forests than in dense, virgin, unlogged forests, apparently because many of the tapirs' preferred food plants grow more densely in open habitats. The distinctive tapir snout is used both to shovel food into the mouth and to reach food that the tongue and teeth cannot. Tapirs are not very social; they are usually encountered in ones or twos; for instance, a female and her young. These mammals have a strong affinity for water and are excellent swimmers; if they are disturbed, they often seek refuge in the water. Usually there is a bathing and wallowing site within their home range, the area within which they live and forage; sometimes tapirs sleep in the water.

Breeding

Relatively little is known about breeding in wild tapirs. A single offspring is born to a female BAIRD'S TAPIR 13 months after mating. At first, the youngster stays in a secluded spot while its mother forages elsewhere and periodically returns to nurse. After 10 days or so, the youngster can follow the mother, and stays with her for up to a year. When it is about two-thirds the mother's size, it goes its separate way. Mothers are reputed to attack people that threaten their dependent young.

Ecological Interactions

At least two researchers have noted that tapirs, which can become infested with blood-sucking, disease-carrying ticks, have let other mammals – a coati in one case, a tame peccary in the other – approach them and pick and eat the ticks on their bodies. If this occurs regularly, it is a *mutualistic* association: tapirs obviously benefit because they are freed temporarily from the harmful ticks, and the tick-eaters receive the nutritional value of the bloodsuckers (yech!).

Lore and Notes

BAIRD'S TAPIR is Belize's national animal, and the species is given prominent display and much attention at the Belize Zoo (p. 224).

Status

Because it is hunted for meat, and also owing to deforestation, BAIRD'S TAPIR is now rare and considered an endangered species, listed by both CITES Appendix I and USA ESA. Tapirs are rarely seen because of their low population sizes, because they are active mostly at night, and because, owing to hunting, they are very shy and cautious animals.

Profile

Baird's Tapir, *Tapirus bairdii*, Plate 80a

9. Marine Mammals

Two kinds of large marine mammals, *manatees* and *dolphins*, occur in Belizean waters and both are seen fairly frequently. Manatees, or *sea cows*, are heavy-bodied, slow-moving mammals that inhabit Belize's offshore areas, especially around river mouths, coastal lagoons, and certain of the cayes, particularly those off Belize City. The WEST INDIAN MANATEE (Plate 80) is one of four species placed within the Order Sirenia (along with African and South American manatee species, and an Australian member of the group, known as the DUGONG). The group is actually related more closely to elephants than to the whales and dolphins or to the seals and walruses. One subgroup of the West Indian Manatee occurs in the coastal waters of the southeastern USA, especially Florida's, and the other subgroup ranges throughout the Caribbean and along the eastern coast of Mexico and Central America, and the northern coast of South America. Manatees vaguely resemble walruses, but without the tusks. They are large, gray, cylindrical animals, tapered at the front and back. The hands are modified into flippers and the tail is a single, flattened fluke, or paddle. Manatees have thick, rough, mostly hairless skin, with some bristles near the mouth. Some grow to 3.5 m (11.5 ft) long and weigh up to 1000 kg (2200 lb).

Dolphins are smaller members of the Order Cetacea, which also includes whales and porpoises. The approximately 75 species of *cetaceans* occur throughout the world's oceans and some of the smaller dolphins also inhabit larger rivers and estuaries in Asia, Africa, and South America. Whether a given cetacean species is called a whale or a dolphin has to do with length: whales generally are at least 4.5 to 6 m (15 to 20 ft) long, while dolphins and porpoises are smaller. The differences between dolphins and porpoises? Dolphins have a beak-type nose and mouth, a backwards-curving dorsal fin, and sharp, pointed teeth; porpoises are more blunt-nosed with a triangular dorsal fin and blunt teeth. The two most commonly seen dolphins (family Delphinidae) in coastal Belize are the ATLANTIC SPOTTED and BOTTLE-NOSED DOLPHINS (Plate 80), members of dolphin groups that are distributed throughout the world's tropical seas. These dolphins are cigar-shaped, long and thin, and tapered at the ends. They have smooth, hairless skin and prominent beaks and dorsal fins. Their front limbs have been modified into paddles, they have no rear limbs, and the tail is flattened to form two rear paddles. Atlantic Spotted Dolphins are 1.2 to 3 m (4 to 10 ft) long, gray to black, with pale spots on their bodies; Bottle-nosed Dolphins are grayish or dark blue, 1.8 to 3.6 m (6 to 12 ft) long, with a distinctively rounded forehead. (The largest member of the dolphin family is the KILLER WHALE, *Orcinus orca*; males grow to 9.5 m (31 ft) long, and weigh as much as 7000 kg (15,400 lb).)

Natural History

Ecology and Behavior

Manatees are considered semi-social: Most often they are seen as solitary animals or female and calf pairs, moving slowly through the water, grazing on aquatic plants; at other times, groups congregate. The reasons for the groups are not always clear. In colder regions, manatees in winter sometimes associate in large groups in warm-water areas, such as near power-plant water outflows. Manatees, usually active both day and night, are the only aquatic mammals to be completely herbivorous. They feed on submerged, floating, and shoreline vegetation such as sea grasses, mangrove leaves, and water hyacinths. They remain underwater foraging for periods of up to 15 minutes before surfacing to breathe.

Because BOTTLE-NOSED DOLPHINS were the first to be kept in captivity for long periods (they are the species often seen in aquarium shows), and because they are often found close to shore and so are easily observed, more is known of their biology than of other species; spotted dolphins apparently lead lives that are very similar to those of Bottle-nosed Dolphins. Although sometimes found as solitary animals, these dolphins usually stay in groups, sometimes of up to a thousand or more. Large groups apparently consist of many smaller groups of about two to six individuals, which usually are quite stable in membership for several years. There are dominance hierarchies within groups, the largest male usually being top dolphin. Large schools are believed to aid the dolphins in searching for and catching food, and to decrease the likelihood of the dolphins themselves becoming food. They eat primarily fish and squid, which they catch by making shallow dives into the water. They are fast swimmers, routinely jumping clear of the water when feeding or travelling. Dolphins use sounds as well as visual displays and touching to signal each other underwater; they also use sound for *echolocation*, like bats, for underwater navigation. Dolphins are considered highly intelligent and sometimes develop close affinities with people.

Breeding
Little is known about manatee courtship and mating in the wild. Adult males have been observed bumping and pushing each other, apparently in competition for females. Females give birth usually to a single calf after pregnancies of 12 to 13 months. Calves, at birth about 30 kg (66 lb) in weight and 1.2 m (4 ft) in length, stay with their mother for 1 to 2 years. Manatees apparently do not reach sexual maturity for at least 5 or 6 years, when they are about 2.7 m (9 ft) long. In Florida, breeding occurs year round, although newborns are more often spotted in spring and summer.

Dolphins usually produce a single young after pregnancies of about 12 months. When born, dolphins are about a meter (3 ft) long. The mating systems of dolphins in the wild are not well known, for the obvious reason that it is difficult to observe underwater courtship and mating behaviors; that males and females look much alike complicates observation.

Lore and Notes
Although manatees, as endangered marine mammals, are not as well known today as their more celebrated cousins, the whales and dolphins, they have a long history of interactions with people. For instance, it is generally believed that legends of *mermaids* – beings half woman, half fish – arose with manatees, although the resemblance to human females is difficult to discern. The order of manatees, Sirenia, is named for these legendary female "sirens." Even Columbus referred to manatees in his ships' logs, supposedly complaining that the New World mermaids were not as attractive as their advance billing. Ancient Mayans hunted and ate manatees, as evidenced by the frequent renderings of the bulky sea creatures in their artworks. One species of manatee, the STELLER'S SEA COW, which reached 8 m (26 ft) in length and 6000 kg (13,000 lb) in weight, and that lived in the shallow, cold waters of the Bering Sea, was hunted to extinction in about 1770, less than 30 years after being first discovered.

Dolphins' intelligence and friendliness toward people have inspired artists and authors for thousands of years. Images of dolphins appear frequently on artworks and coins from at least 3500 years ago, and from both ancient Greece and Rome. Aristotle, 2300 years ago, noted that dolphins were mammals, not fish, and remarked on their intelligence and gentle personalities. Many other ancient writings tell stories of close relationships between people and dolphins. These animals are considered the only group, aside from humans, that regularly assists members of other species that are in distress (although house cats have been known to assist small birds and rodents by putting them out of their misery). There have been many reports of dolphins supporting on the water's surface injured members of their own and other dolphin species, as well as helping people in the same way.

BOTTLE-NOSED DOLPHINS, among other claims to fame, were perhaps the first species, during the 1970s, to be studied using photographs that allowed biologists to track and study individual animals. In this case, close photos of dorsal fins permitted researchers to identify individuals and follow their activities for extended periods. This method of photographic identification is now widely used to study the long-term behavior and movements of such other animals as whales, elephants, and lions.

Status

The WEST INDIAN MANATEE is considered endangered, listed by both CITES Appendix I and USA ESA; there is also a Florida law protecting manatees that declares the state a manatee sanctuary. In fact, all species of manatees and dugongs are threatened or endangered. The main threats to these animals are hunting – they are still taken in some parts of the world for meat, oil, and their skin – and collisions with boats and motorboat propellers. Unfortunately, the shallow, warm waters that manatees prefer are also usually the main sites people use for fishing, boating, tourism, and coastal development, so collisions are frequent. Even where manatees are strictly protected, conservation and population recovery is hampered owing to the lack of scientific information about their ecology and behavior in the wild, and by their slow breeding rate. Belize, its long coast providing excellent habitat for the West Indian Manatee, is considered one of the last, best hopes for the species.

Both BOTTLE-NOSED and ATLANTIC SPOTTED DOLPHINS are CITES Appendix II listed as species not currently threatened but certainly vulnerable if protective measures are not taken. Spotted dolphins (genus *Stenella*) are among the dolphins most frequently caught accidentally in the nets of tuna fisherman, and hundreds of thousands have been killed in that way. Dolphins in some regions of the world are also sometimes killed by fishermen who consider them to be competitors for valuable fish, or to be used as bait – for instance, for crab fishing.

Profiles

West Indian Manatee, *Trichechus manatus*, Plate 80b
Atlantic Spotted Dolphin, *Stenella frontalis*, Plate 80c
Bottle-nosed Dolphin, *Tursiops truncatus*, Plate 80d

Environmental Close-up 4
The Belize Zoo and Tropical Education Center

Perhaps 50 km (30 miles) west of Belize City, along the main highway, tucked among the tall trees of the tropical savannah, sits a small zoo. You might chance upon it, visit for an hour or two, enjoy the 30-odd exhibits with more than 100 animals, stroll the pleasant, winding walkways, read the hand-lettered explanatory signs in local lingo, and leave, without ever recognizing the place for what it really is: a center for Belize's conservation efforts. The Belize Zoo (open every day from 9:30 am or so to about 4:30 pm, phone: 081-3004), which opened in 1983 and significantly enlarged and improved in 1991, plays a leading national role in wildlife and habitat conservation, and, especially, in education and research in these fields.

The zoo itself is very nice with a cozy, small-operation atmosphere; it offers a pleasant couple of hours to anyone, whether Belizean or foreign visitor jaded from visits to large, modern zoos. In fact, I would recommend a visit to the zoo as a first Belize stop to anyone interested in animals but unfamiliar with Central American wildlife; the place provides a good introduction to many of the region's larger animals. Along the zoo's walkways are naturalistic enclosures that provide good viewing of, among other things, monkeys, big cats and other carnivores, peccaries, deer, some larger birds such as vultures, macaws, and toucans, as well as some reptiles. All are native to Belize, and all the animals were either donated to or born in the zoo – none was captured expressly for exhibition there. Veteran zoo-goers know that inhabitants of many zoos appear dull, lethargic, or neurotic. In contrast, many of the animals at the Belize zoo appear healthy, energetic, and well cared for. Somewhat mysteriously, this may be the only zoo I've seen where many of the animals actually come to the edge of their enclosures to greet people. The last time I was there, even a mid-sized Boa Constrictor saw fit to uncoil itself and approach me, probably to get a better look at the strange beast with legs.

But the Belize Zoo represents much more than simple, good recreation. Even the story of its unique development is interesting, the stuff of many newspaper feature articles. The story centers on the zoo's director and driving force, Sharon Matola. Ask knowledgeable people inside or outside the country about wildlife or conservation in Belize, and Matola's name quickly crops up, followed usually by adjectives such as "energetic" and "impressive." The fairy-tale-like zoo story goes like this: Matola, a native of Maryland, USA, had a varied background, having served in the US Air Force, acquired some graduate training in the biological sciences, and worked in a Mexican travelling circus. Hired by a film director to care for about 20 Belizean animals – mostly monkeys and big cats – that were to star in a nature film, Matola found herself responsible for the menagerie when the filming ended. Instead of releasing the semi-tamed animals to a probable quick death, or putting them to sleep, Matola put signs on the cages and opened a zoo. Probably because Belize had no other zoo and local people were curious about the animals around them that few saw in the wild, the zoo quickly attained modest success. Matola set about raising funds to improve the zoo, calling on businesspeople, diplomats, and environmental organizations such as Wildlife Preservation Trust International. She talked; people with money listened. By 1991, with design expertise donated by a North American firm, some exhibit construction donated by British Army troops who train in Belize, and funds given by, among many others, world-famous entertainers, the improved facility could open. The new zoo attracts many people and has grown along with Belize ecotourism. About 30,000 people visit the zoo annually, fully a third of those being kids.

The Belize Zoo is now a vital part of Belize's environmental and conservation movements. Therefore, education is a primary mission of the zoo because people are more likely to want to preserve their natural habitats and wildlife if they know about them and about the dangers they face. To this end, the educational signs around the zoo and its outreach programs are aimed mostly at local people and, especially, at kids. All school classes in Belize are invited to visit the zoo for free. The kids are particularly drawn to the featured tapir exhibit; in fact April, the zoo's first tapir, has become a minor national celebrity whose birthday is widely acclaimed. A friendly, motivated zoo staff, all Belizeans, includes wildlife specialists who travel to Belize's schools and villages to give slide shows on the zoo, wildlife, and conservation. Sharon Matola, in addition to her other activities, has authored some popular children's books that feature the zoo's animals. As an example of the zoo's influence, manatee (p. 221) conservation is generally considered to be making good progress in Belize primarily because of the zoo's education programs on the manatees' behalf.

To further its educational objectives, the zoo also operates the Tropical Education Center, located just across the main highway from the zoo. Here, with grants from the MacArthur Foundation, the zoo has established a field station dedicated to local tropical natural history. There are trails through the savannah habitat and a bird observation deck overlooking a small marsh/pond area. The complex includes a visitor-center building with a large classroom, a small library, staff offices and research space, and kitchen and sleeping space for a dozen or so. The station is visited by local school groups but is also utilized by researchers and travelling classes from North American colleges. The list of species recorded on the extensive property includes about 20 bats, 24 amphibians, 54 reptiles, and about 150 birds. Contact the zoo to inquire about the possibility of visiting the Tropical Education Center (PO Box 1781, Belize City, Belize; tel/fax: 501-8-13004).

The zoo also conducts zoo-related research, such as programs in captive breeding of local birds and reptiles. In addition, the zoo is involved with exploring some of Belize's wilderness regions, with an eye toward cataloging the country's plants and animals. Determining the diversity and abundance of organisms in a region is an important first step in deciding which areas require special conservation attention. For example, zoo personnel were involved in ecological explorations and assessments in 1990 and 1993 of the Columbia River Forest Reserve in southern Belize. To facilitate its educational and research roles, zoo staff, with financial backing from organizations such as the World Wildlife Fund, write and publish books on local wildlife – a good example is *A Field Guide to the Snakes of Belize*, by Tony Garel and Sharon Matola; the books are for sale at the zoo and other sites in Belize.

If you have the time during your trip, visit the Belize Zoo: it's a truly interesting place and an organization doing important work.

Chapter 9

MARINE LIFE
(By Briana Timmerman and Brian Helmuth)

- *The Barrier Reef Ecosystem*
  Coral Reef Communities
  Coral Biology
  Common Reef Animals
- *Mangrove Swamps*
- *Diving in Belize*

A wildlife guide to Belize would be incomplete without a section on marine animals because a sizable fraction of visitors to the country don snorkels or scuba gear to peer under the tropical waters. In what follows you will find a brief introduction to Belize's marine environments and to the organisms most people see on their dives. Color illustrations of many of the most common marine animals will be found in Plates 81–104.

The Barrier Reef Ecosystem

Like its terrestrial counterpart, perhaps the most striking aspect of the underwater environment of Belize is the diversity of habitats that it supports. From mangrove roots draped with colorful invertebrate animals and algae, to ancient coral heads playing host to myriad other creatures, to mainland deltas and lagoons harboring occasional manatees (Plate 80), this small country boasts a remarkable diversity of underwater habitats.

Stretching 250 km (155 miles) from Belize's border with Mexico in the north to its coastal intersection with Guatemala in the south, Belize's barrier reef is the second longest continuous reef in the world, after Australia's Great Barrier Reef. The reef complex, basically a shallow underwater platform 10 to 30 km (6 to 18 miles) wide, creates a variety of habitats and supports not only coral reefs but also the offshore cayes and mangrove lagoons scattered along its length. The barrier reef roughly parallels the coast of Belize beginning with the northernmost portion at Ambergris Caye (Map 2, p. 9), which lies only a few hundred meters offshore. But the reef gradually moves away from the mainland as you progress down the coast; the southernmost cayes occur more than 40 km (25 miles) from the mainland. Between the reef complex and the mainland lies a relatively shallow lagoon, which consists predominantly of sand flats. These areas often support eel grass beds and are punctuated by small patch reefs typically containing large mounding corals. Mangrove swamps, a hallmark of coastal tropical waters, are common both along the mainland shore and on the offshore reef platform. To a large extent it is the physical structure and complexity of the coral reefs and mangrove swamps that are responsible for creating habitat for the myriad organisms that form the underwater community.

Coral Reef Communities

Except for large *pelagic* predators (open ocean animals such as sharks), everything that lives on a coral reef requires a place to live, a substrate, or base, which is solid enough to resist the shifting sands and ever-present forces of waves and currents. Tiny organisms called *reef-building corals*, or *hermatypic corals*, form the foundation of tropical reef communities because they create the habitat that is used by other reef dwellers such as algae, fish, and invertebrates. The most defining characteristic of a reef is its ability to withstand wave motion. *Stony corals* secrete a skeleton of calcium carbonate (limestone) that extends as the coral grows in much the same way that trees form growth rings, and is fairly resistant to the rigors of moving water. Many large mounding corals seen while diving in Belize, such as *brain corals* (Plate 99), have been growing continuously for at least 100 years. These large coral colonies, however, are frequently dislodged and damaged during intense storms and hurricanes. Once dislodged, these enormous coral heads can act as "bowling balls," causing extensive destruction as they bounce around the reef. Some corals, such as the staghorn coral *Acropora cervicornis* (Plate 98), can reproduce when broken, and small fragments fortunate enough to settle onto bare substrate can re-attach and grow. Coral fragments from most other species, however, die after being broken off, and are eventually pulverized into coral sand.

Coral reefs are able to resist wave action not only by the strength of the coral skeletons, but also by the combined effects of other species living within the matrix of the coral reef. Newly settling coral larvae most commonly inhabit the surfaces of corals that have previously died. In this way, over centuries of time, layer upon layer of dead coral form a support structure for the thin layer of living coral tissue that inhabits the reef's uppermost surface. In between the cracks and crevices of the living and dead coral, *sponges* and *encrusting algae*, among other organisms, continually break down and cement the coral pieces, effectively binding the reef together. In Belize, one of the most dominant corals is the lettuce coral, *Agaricia tenuifolia* (Plate 98). Growing in large aggregations, or *buttresses*, often several meters long, *A. tenuifolia* most commonly grows as rows of fairly short (10 cm, or 4 in, tall) blades, and ranges in color from light tan and green to deep red. A cosmopolitan species, aggregations can be found from just subsurface to depths of 25 m (80 ft) or more. It has been suggested that by growing in these large aggregations, corals of this species reduce the chances of being broken by wave action by reducing drag and increasing attachment to the substrate.

Despite the slow but inexorable march of coral growth, coral reefs are by no means static and, in fact, an intriguing story has begun to unfold on Belize's barrier reef. Currently, lettuce coral, *Agaricia tenuifolia*, is by far the most common coral on Belize's reef complex. Recently, scientists working under the auspices of the Smithsonian Institution's facility on Carrie Bow Caye collected core samples through the layers of dead coral underlying the living reef. Surprisingly, they found that until only a decade ago, the staghorn coral *Acropora cervicornis* outnumbered any other single species at between 3 and 15 m (10 to 50 ft) water depth on the reef. The lettuce corals, so common today, covered only 10% of the substrate in previous generations. Furthermore, reef cores from Channel Caye indicated that lettuce corals have not been dominant on Belizean reefs for the last 3800 years. The mass mortality of staghorn coral after 1986 was most likely caused by White Band Disease, a bacterial infection which appears as a white band that expands across a coral, leaving dead tissue in its wake. With the decline of staghorn coral, new substrate was available on the reef and the lettuce coral exploded into abundance. Thus, the reef environment which is seen today in Belize is in some sense very new – "new paint on an old canvas".

Coral Biology

Corals, despite their plant-like appearance, are actually *colonies* of individual animals (called *polyps*) each only a few millimeters (a tiny fraction of an inch) across. Polyps are produced as clones, so that all members of a colony are genetically identical, and share common digestive and nervous systems. Each polyp is a bag-shaped body with a ring of tentacles around the edge which are extended into the water to capture prey (Plate 98e). Each tentacle is equipped with a battery of small, harpoon-like *nematocysts* which discharge upon contact. In general, nematocysts are only potent enough to catch tiny invertebrate animals. Some species of corals, however, such as fire corals (*Millepora* sp., Plate 98), which despite their name are not true corals but belong to a related group, *hydroids*), contain nematocysts that have a strong enough sting to be really rather unpleasant to unprotected human skin. Fire corals are a soft golden color and range in shape from pronounced vertical blades to encrusting forms which follow the contour of the substrate. *Millepora* is fairly ubiquitous on the Belizean barrier reef, and can be found everywhere from the shallows around cayes to depths of 40 m (130 ft) on the fore reef slope (the outer, seaward section of the barrier reef). A thin wetsuit, or long-sleeved shirt, running tights, and thin gardening gloves can help reduce accidental contact. People seem to vary in the severity of their response to fire corals, and the application of meat tenderizer or baking soda to the rash following the dive can help to reduce the pain.

Divers are always warned to avoid touching any coral, however, and while fear of rashes is definitely part of the reason, the more important motivation is protection of the coral. Despite their hardy appearance, coral skeletons provide little protection against contact, as much of a coral's living tissue is exposed to the outside world. Each polyp basically sits atop a raised section of skeleton called a *corallite*, and can withdraw into this recess when disturbed, affording it some protection against predators. However, each polyp in its corallite is also connected to all neighboring polyps by a very thin (2 cells thick) layer of tissue, which at all times remains exposed to the outside environment. While this design is great for allowing corals to cover large surface areas without the need to expend a lot of precious resources, it makes corals very susceptible to damage because the thin tissue layer is so easily crushed against the hard skeleton.

While the damage to coral reefs by divers can be extensive, an even more immediate danger facing coral reefs worldwide is *bleaching*, and while corals in

Belize have been less affected than those in many other Caribbean countries, recent evidence suggests that this problem is beginning to occur here as well. Much of the color in many corals is actually the product of symbiotic one-celled brown algae (called *zooxanthellae*) which live inside the cells of the coral tissue. Like plants, zooxanthellae use solar energy to produce carbohydrates. The coral host then uses materials leaked from the algae as a readily available, internal food source. In return, these tiny brown plants have access to nutrients in the form of animal wastes from the coral. A bleached coral appears ghostly white because it has lost its zooxanthellae, and often dies following such a bleaching event. Recent research suggests that bleaching is caused by a range of factors, such as increased water temperature and changes in salinity, pollution, and ultraviolet (UV) radiation, although the exact mechanisms are still under investigation.

Corals vary in their dependence on zooxanthellae, and while some species may rely almost exclusively on energy extracted from their algae, others may to a large extent depend on food captured from the surrounding water. While some species extend their tentacles during both day and night, others remain closed during the day, and feed only at night when small zooplankton (minuscule invertebrate water animals) rise to the shallows of the reef. Research into basic coral biology needs to continue because of coral's obvious importance to reef ecosystems, and because of the recent mysterious increase in coral reef bleaching and diseases.

Common Reef Animals

The coral community of Belize is similar to those of other parts of the Caribbean, but in recent years has been spared the devastating hurricanes which have plagued many of the more easterly reefs. Belize is certainly not immune to the pressures of overfishing and truly large fish are now rare, but large (2 m, or 6.5 ft, diameter) spotted eagle rays (Plate 97) and barracuda (Plate 83) are still fairly common, and the former are often encountered flying over the ridgetops of the outer fore reef slopes. Large nurse sharks (Plate 97) are occasionally seen resting on sand patches in shallows and, as sharks go, are relatively safe. Hammerhead sharks (Plate 97), more unpredictable in their behavior toward divers, are sometimes encountered swimming in schools on offshore cayes. Other large creatures found in Belizean waters include manatee (Plate 80) in the river deltas of the mainland, several species of dolphins (Plate 80) and porpoises, and even the occasional sea turtle (Plate 10).

While seeing some of these large, impressive animals is an easy way to make any dive memorable, most of what is seen diving and snorkeling consists of smaller fish and invertebrates. Several species of large angelfish (Plate 81) live on the barrier reef, and parrotfish (Plate 91) are commonly seen munching away on corals. In fact, much of the sand in the reef environment is created as fish crunch, scrape, and otherwise break up coral into small bits. Many of the fish, corals, and other invertebrates seen while snorkeling or diving off Belize are illustrated in Plates 81 to 104.

In addition to the lettuce and staghorn corals (Plate 98) previously described, there are over 40 other species of corals encountered in most forereef environments (the outer, seaward section of the barrier reef). Two species of star coral, *Montastrea annularis* and *Montastrea cavernosa* (Plate 98), are commonly encountered over a fairly wide depth range. Corallites (raised sections of carbonate skeleton into which the polyps withdraw) are round and evenly distributed on the surface of the coral, and are much larger in *Montastrea cavernosa*. Polyps are usually retracted into the corallites during the day and extend at night as a means of capturing prey (Plate 98). Colonies are generally brownish to light tan in color, and range in shape from flowing, encrusting forms to large boulders. In addition, colonies of *Montastrea annularis* can form large pillars, often with a bumpy appearance. *Montastrea cavernosa* can be extremely aggressive towards other adjacent coral colonies, producing large, modified tentacles which hammer the competitor with batteries of nematocysts. Often these aggressive zones are made conspicuous by a region of dead tissue on the losing coral, and a whitish, puffy appearance on the edge of the aggressor. While several species of coral use similar methods, fights are especially obvious when they involve this large-polyped species.

Colonies of elkhorn coral, *Acropora palmata* (Plate 98), a much more robust relative of the fragile staghorn coral, grow in shallower sections of the reef, although its abundance has been declining in recent years. True to its name, colonies appear as large, flat branches which resemble the horns of a moose or elk. Colonies can range up to 3 m (10 ft) or more in length and 3 to 4 m (10 to 13 ft) in diameter. Often, fire worms, *Hermodice* (Plate 100), are encountered eating the tissue from the growing tips of staghorn coral, popsicle-style.

Soft corals, or *gorgonians*, are close relatives of the stony corals, and are found in many parts of the reef and in lagoon environments. Unlike the stony corals, the polyps of gorgonians are supported by a flexible skeleton of protein embedded with tiny skeletal elements called *sclerites*. At least 35 species are encountered in Belize, including the sea rods *Plexaura* and *Plexaurella* (Plate 100), which appear highly branched and can reach heights of 2 m (6.5 ft). Large purplish sea fans, *Gorgonia* (Plate 100), are also common, and can been seen swaying back and forth in wave surges. Colonies of the soft corals *Erythropodium* (Plate 99) and *Briareum* (Plate 99) are both bright purple, but appear more brown when their tentacles are extended. Both are common as encrusting forms, although *Briareum* more frequently grows as erect, unbranched rods, lending it the common name "sea finger." Colonies of *Briareum*, along with sea fans are the favorite prey item of flamingo tongue cowries, *Cyphoma* (Plate 101). Recent evidence suggests that *Briareum* colonies damaged by predation often respond by producing more sclerites at their growing tips, reducing the effectiveness of future predators. This ability to survive the predation of one section of the colony, and then to respond in other parts of the colony, is termed a *plastic* response, and may in part account for the success of corals and other colonial invertebrates.

Several large, barrel-shaped sponges are common on deeper portions of the reef, including purple loggerhead sponges (Plate 103), *Spheciospongia*, and giant barrel sponges (Plate 103), *Xestospongia*, which can be over a century old. Composed mostly of fibrous tissue, sponges are supported by small skeletal rods called *spicules*, similar to the sclerites of soft corals. In addition to providing support against wave action, spicules discourage predation by some would-be predators, although many fish and turtles are capable of dealing with the spicules. Many sponges also contain toxins, and several have small fiberglass-like spicules which are capable of damaging human skin. Sponges actively filter and eat bacteria-sized particles from the surrounding water, and so to a large extent are responsible for the clear waters of tropical reefs.

Mangrove Swamps

Although most people envision coral reefs and sandy beaches when they think of Belize's underwater environment, another hallmark of tropical coastal environments is the mangrove swamp, a zone where the terrestrial environment meets the underwater world in a dense tangle of life. Typically, mangrove swamps are divided into two categories depending on their proximity to shore. *Oceanic mangroves*, which live atop the offshore reef platform, live at the edge of the marine environment, and often lead to the formation of cayes through their ability to trap and retain sediment. In several instances their removal from offshore sites has led to almost the complete breaking down of former islands. *Mainland mangroves*, situated on the mainland along the coast, must contend with both saltwater and freshwater running off of the land. Both mangrove types support rich invertebrate and fish communities on their roots, which drape into the ocean. Many species of sponges, sea squirts (tiny marine animals often attached to the substrate as adults; Plate 103a) and even several species of corals flourish in these environments, and mangrove roots serve as nurseries for a host of organisms. Most offshore mangrove swamps encircle small lagoons of relatively still, high nutrient, low visibility water. A common inhabitant of these lagoons is the jelly *Cassiopea* (Plate 104). Like corals, these jellies maintain symbiotic algae in their tissues, and although mobile, are most commonly encountered sitting upside down on the bottoms of mangrove lagoons.

Although we are just now beginning to understand the complex interactions that drive these communities, recent work in Belize has suggested that although similar in some respects, each mangrove lagoon is in many senses a unique environment, each one different from the next. A good overview of these communities was written by K. Rützler and I. Feller for *Scientific American* (vol. 274, no. 3, 1996), and can be read at your local library.

Diving in Belize

As in any part of the world, it is best to know something of the reputation of a dive operation before signing on for a day of diving. There are many excellent, conscientious dive operators in Belize, including some former fishermen on the outer cayes. Unfortunately, as everywhere else in the world, there are also some shady, less-than-safe operators out there as well. A few well formulated questions regarding dive plans and emergency procedures can be quite revealing. Keep in mind that dive sites are often an hour or more from shore, and several hours from the nearest recompression chamber. As elsewhere, most sights of interest are in relatively shallow water; diving deep not only severely curtails bottom time but also can increase risks of decompression sickness. Similarly, be sure to take an occasional day off when diving on multiple days. While this advice holds true in any situation, the remote location of many sites in Belize calls for even more caution than usual. The Divers Alert Network, a non-profit organization devoted to diver safety worldwide, not only maintains a 24-hour referral system in case of a diving accident (919-684-4326, emergencies only) but also provides very affordable diving and snorkeling insurance, and can assist in evacuation to the United

States in case of emergencies (call membership services at 800-446-2671).

While Belizean waters are fairly warm in spring and summer (25–30 °C, 75–86 °F), a light wetsuit can ward off cold from extended dives and snorkels, and provides an excellent barrier against inevitable bumps and scrapes. Water currents can vary from nonexistent to very strong, as can wave action on the fore reef. Because diving in Belize often involves fairly long boat rides, be sure to bring plenty of sunblock, a long-sleeved shirt, and plenty of drinking water. Except following storms, water clarity on the offshore cayes is excellent, and can exceed 75 m (250 ft). A small flashlight can be useful for examining overhangs and crevices, and serves to bring out colors of fish and invertebrates.

IDENTIFICATION PLATES

Plates 1–104

Abbreviations on the Identification Plates are as follows:

M;   male
F;   female
IM;   immature

The species pictured on any one plate are usually the correct size relative to each other, but sometimes this was impossible to accomplish.

Plate 1a

Mexican Caecilian
Dermophis mexicanus
Dos Cabezas = two heads
ID: Wormlike, limbless, long (to 60 cm, 23 in) and wide (to 2.5 cm, 1 in); head triangular and a bit flattened; small eyes covered by skin; body encircled by ringed creases; gray, purplish, or blackish back; lighter underneath.

HABITAT: Low elevation wet forests and warm, moist places (under leaves, garbage piles) in other habitats; found on or under the ground.

DISTRICTS: TOL, PET

Plate 1b

Mexican Salamander (also called Mexican Mushroom-tongue Salamander)
Bolitoglossa mexicana
Galliwasp (Belize)
Salamandra
ID: Small reddish brown or red-orange salamander with irregular darker spots and blotches; sides usually brownish; some with two stripes running along back; webbed feet; to 7.5 cm (3 in) plus tail.

HABITAT: Low and middle elevation wet forests; found in trees, vegetation (often in bromeliad epiphytes), on ground, and under rocks and logs.

DISTRICTS: STN, CAYO, TOL, PET

Plate 1c

Rufescent Salamander (also called Northern Banana Salamander)
Bolitoglossa rufescens
Galliwasp (Belize)
Salamandra
ID: Very small, slender salamander with large eyes and webbed feet; many are brown with darker sides and stomach; others are light tan with darker spots; to 3.5 cm (1.5 in) plus tail.

HABITAT: Low and middle elevation wet forests; found in trees, often in bromeliad epiphytes, banana leaves; nocturnal.

DISTRICTS: STN, CAYO, TOL, PET

Plate 1d

Marine Toad (also called Cane Toad, Giant Toad)
Bufo marinus
Sapo Grande, Sapo Gigante = giant toad
ID: A large, warted, ugly toad; large, triangular glands on each side of the head behind brown eyes; females are mottled, combinations of dusky brown, tan, and chocolate; males generally are uniformly brown; to 20 cm (8 in).

HABITAT: Low and middle elevation forests; found in open and semi-open areas, often in and around buildings.

DISTRICTS: COR, ORW, BEL, STN, CAYO, TOL, PET

Plate I 235

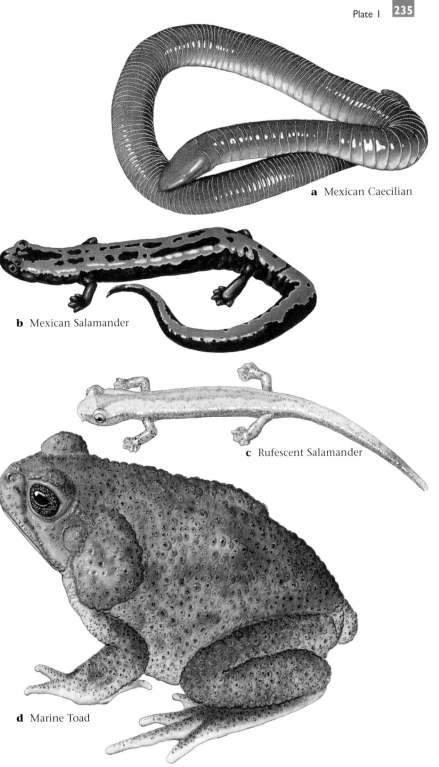

a Mexican Caecilian

b Mexican Salamander

c Rufescent Salamander

d Marine Toad

Plate 2a
Gulf Coast Toad
Bufo valliceps
Sapo Común = common toad
Sapo = toad
ID: Mid-sized gray, brown, olive, yellowish, or reddish orange toad with darker blotches; short legs; rough, warty skin; small ridges on head near eyes; to 10 cm (4 in).

HABITAT: Low and middle elevation forests and more open sites such as grasslands, agricultural areas; found on ground and under rocks, logs.

DISTRICTS: COR, ORW, BEL, STN, CAYO, TOL, PET

Plate 2b
Rainforest Toad
Bufo cambelli
Sapo = toad
ID: Mid-sized toad similar in appearance to Gulf Coast Toad (Plate 2a) but with smoother skin and longer legs; also lacks the small ridges on head; to 10 cm (4 in).

HABITAT: Low and middle elevation forests; found on ground.

DISTRICTS: TOL (POSSIBLY OCCURS IN OTHER DISTRICTS AS WELL – CAYO, STN, PET)

Plate 2c
Mexican Burrowing Toad
Rhinophrynus dorsalis
Sapo Borracho = drunk toad
ID: Medium-sized, odd-looking frog described as resembling a blob of jelly; smooth, moist skin of the back is gray, reddish-brown, dark brown, or purplish black, with red, orange, or yellow lines and spots; often there is a single line down the center of the back; small eyes; fat legs; inflates like blowfish when scared; to 7 cm (2.8 in).

HABITAT: Lowland drier forests and wet pastures, fields; found on and under the ground.

DISTRICTS: COR, ORW, BEL, STN, CAYO, TOL, PET

Plate 2d
Broad-headed Rainfrog
Eleutherodactylus laticeps
Rana = frog
ID: Striking, mid-sized brown frog, sometimes with dark bars or spots, with dark face mask; some have light stripe down back; to 9 cm (3.5 in).

HABITAT: Low and middle elevation forests; found on ground.

DISTRICTS: STN, CAYO, TOL, PET

Plate 2 237

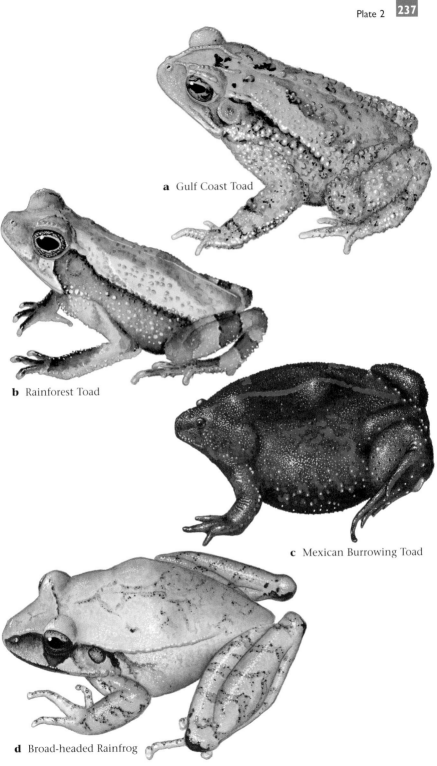

a Gulf Coast Toad

b Rainforest Toad

c Mexican Burrowing Toad

d Broad-headed Rainfrog

Plate 3a

Maya Rainfrog (also called Chac's Rainfrog, Izabal Robber Frog)
Eleutherodactylus chac
Rana = frog

ID: Small, slender, tan, brown, yellowish, or grayish frog with darker markings and dark face mask; many have dark bars on limbs, and some have light stripe down back; toes partially webbed; red eyes; to 4 cm (1.5 in).

HABITAT: Low and middle elevation forests; found on ground.

DISTRICTS: STN, CAYO, TOL

Plate 3b

Central American Rainfrog (also called Rugulose Rainfrog)
Eleutherodactylus rugulosus
Rana = frog

ID: Mid-sized brown, reddish brown, or grayish frog with darker blotches; most have light stripe down back; many have dark bars on lips, limbs; very little webbing between toes; rough-looking (rugulose) skin; to 9 cm (3.5 in).

HABITAT: Low and middle elevation forests; found on ground and low vegetation, often near streams.

DISTRICTS: STN, CAYO, TOL, PET

Plate 3c

Black-backed Frog (also called Sabinal Frog)
Leptodactylus melanonotus
Rana = frog

ID: Small, stocky, dark brown or grayish frog with darker markings and large triangular patch on head between eyes; skin with small warts; to 4 cm (1.5 in).

HABITAT: Low and middle elevation forests and more open areas; found near streams and ponds, and in marshes, wet pastures.

DISTRICTS: COR, ORW, BEL, STN, CAYO, TOL, PET

Plate 3d

Tungara Frog (also called Mudpuddle Frog, Foam Toad)
Physalaemus pustulosus
Rana = frog

ID: Small brownish frog with very rough (pustular) skin; resembles a toad, but lacks a toad's big glands on the head behind the eyes; to 3.5 cm (1.5 in).

HABITAT: Low and middle elevation forests, grasslands, pastures; found on the ground or under leaf litter.

DISTRICTS: COR, ORW, PET

Plate 3   239

a Maya Rainfrog

b Central American Rainfrog

c Black-backed Frog

d Tungara Frog

Plate 4a

Red-eyed Leaf Frog (also called Red-eyed Treefrog)
Agalychnis callidryas
Rana Verde = green frog
Rana Arbórea, Rana de Arbol = treefrog

ID: Largish treefrog, with large toes with considerable webbing; colors vary, but often has a pale or dark green back, sometimes with white or yellow spots; top of the thigh is green; blue-purple patches on rear of limbs; vertical bars on sides; often, hands and feet are orange; ruby red eyes; to 7 cm (3 in).

HABITAT: Lowland wet forests; found in trees, small pools, swamps; nocturnal.

DISTRICTS: COR, ORW, BEL, STN, CAYO, TOL, PET

Plate 4b

Morelet's Leaf Frog (also called Morelet's Treefrog)
Agalychnis moreletti
Rana Arbórea, Rana de Arbol = treefrog

ID: Largish treefrog, with large toes with some webbing; light or dark green back, sometimes with white or yellow spots; inner surfaces of limbs and some toes orange; large, dark eyes; to 8 cm (3 in).

HABITAT: Middle elevation wet forests; found in trees, ponds, small pools.

DISTRICTS: CAYO, TOL, PET

Plate 4c

Bromeliad Treefrog
Hyla bromeliacia
Rana = frog

ID: Small tan, light brown, or reddish brown frog often with tiny dark flecks; toes partially webbed; translucent stomach with internal organs visible; large eyes; to 3.5 cm (1.5 in).

HABITAT: Middle elevation wet forests; found in trees, particularly in bromeliad epiphytes and banana leaves.

DISTRICTS: TOL

Plate 4d

Variegated Treefrog (also called Hourglass Treefrog)
Hyla ebraccata
Rana = frog

ID: Small frog with a short, blunt snout, yellowish tan or yellow back with or without large dark brown splotches; often with large hourglass-shaped mark on back; others with spots; yellowish thighs; often, dark bands on legs; in some, dark stripes start at the snout and run along both sides; webbed toes; to 3.5 cm (1.5 in).

HABITAT: Low and some middle elevation forests; usually found on understory shrubs or in or near forest pools.

DISTRICTS: ORW, BEL, STN, CAYO, TOL, PET

Plate 4 **241**

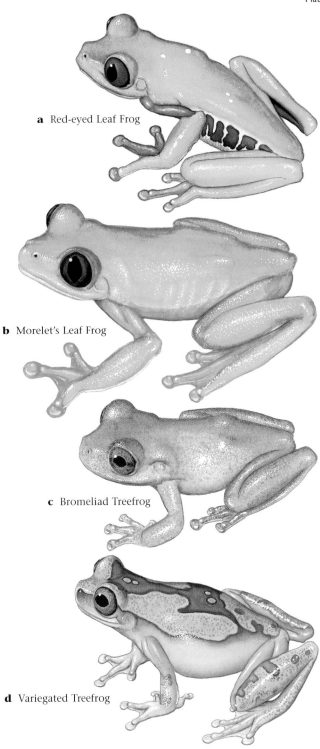

a Red-eyed Leaf Frog

b Morelet's Leaf Frog

c Bromeliad Treefrog

d Variegated Treefrog

Plate 5a

Red-footed Treefrog (also called Mahogany Treefrog, Loquacious Treefrog)
Hyla loquax
Rana = frog

ID: Mid-sized cream-colored, light brown, reddish brown, or grayish frog (more tan or yellowish at night) with brown bars or spots on limbs; some reddish webbing on toes and red on rear of thighs; to 5 cm (2 in).

HABITAT: Low and middle elevation forests and more open areas such as forest edges; found in trees or in or near ponds.

DISTRICTS: COR, ORW, BEL, STN, CAYO, TOL, PET

Plate 5b

Yellow Treefrog (also called Small-headed Treefrog)
Hyla microcephala
Rana Arborícola
Rana de Arbol = treefrog
Ranita = little frog

ID: Small yellowish, orangish, tan, or light brown frog with darker (often X-shaped) markings; yellowish throat; smooth skin; partially webbed toes; to about 4 cm (1.5 in).

HABITAT: Low elevation forest edges and more open areas – roadsides, ditches, wet pastures, etc.; often found in or near pools and puddles.

DISTRICTS: COR, ORW, BEL, STN, CAYO, TOL, PET

Plate 5c

Cricket Treefrog (also called Painted Treefrog)
Hyla picta
Ranita = little frog

ID: Tiny yellowish, cream, or olive-brown frog with darker spots on back; a light (or light and dark) stripe runs through each eye and along sides; large eyes; smooth skin; partial webbing on toes; to 2.5 cm (1 in).

HABITAT: Low and middle elevation forests, forest edges, and more open areas such as roadside ditches, wet pastures; found on vegetation or in or near pools or ponds.

DISTRICTS: COR, ORW, BEL, STN, CAYO, TOL, PET

Plate 5d

Pepper Treefrog (also called Veined Treefrog)
Phrynohyas venulosa
Rana Arbórea, Rana de Arbol = treefrog
Quech

ID: Largish, very rough-skinned frog; brown, cream, or tan with darker blotches; large eyes; partially webbed toes with large end disks; to 10 cm (4 in).

HABITAT: Low and middle elevation forests and more open areas such as forest edges, savannah, wet pastures and around human settlements; found in trees or on ground near water.

DISTRICTS: COR, ORW, BEL, STN, CAYO, TOL, PET

Note: This species produces noxious skin secretions.

Plate 5 **243**

a Red-footed Treefrog

b Yellow Treefrog

c Cricket Treefrog

d Pepper Treefrog

Plate 6a

Stauffer's Treefrog
Scinax staufferi
Rana de Arbol = treefrog

ID: Small gray, grayish brown, or tan frog with darker bars or irregular stripes; many have a dark spot between eyes; longish, pointed snout; big eyes; toes but not fingers webbed; to about 4 cm (1.5 in).

HABITAT: Low and middle elevation open wooded areas such as forest edges and tree plantations, and open areas such as savannah, wet pastures, and around human settlements; found in trees, particularly in bromeliad epiphytes and banana leaves, or in or near pools and ponds.

DISTRICTS: COR, ORW, BEL, STN, CAYO, TOL, PET

Plate 6b

Mexican Treefrog
Smilisca baudinii
Rana Arbórea, Rana de Arbol = treefrog

ID: Largish treefrog with short, bluntly rounded snout; pale green, tan, or brown above with darker blotches; limbs marked with dark bands; dark eye bar; often, vertical dark bars on upper lip; to 7 cm (2.75 in).

HABITAT: Low and middle elevation wet forests and drier areas; found in trees, low vegetation, and near standing water.

DISTRICTS: COR, ORW, BEL, STN, CAYO, TOL, PET

Plate 6c

Blue-spotted Treefrog (also called Blue-Spotted Mexican Treefrog)
Smilisca cyanosticta

ID: Largish tan or green frog, some with darker blotches; dark bars occasionally on limbs; light lip stripe and often, dark stripe through eye; light blue or green spots on rear of thighs; webbed toes; to 7 cm (2.75 in).

HABITAT: Middle elevation forests; found in trees and in pools and ponds.

DISTRICTS: STN, CAYO, TOL, PET

Plate 6d

Casque-headed Treefrog (also called Yucatecan Shovel-headed Treefrog)
Triprion petasatus

ID: Largish olive, brown, or grayish frog with darker markings; head distinctively bony and triangular; large eyes; to about 7 cm (2.75 in).

HABITAT: Low and middle elevation drier forests and more open sites such as forest edges and savannah; found in trees, other vegetation, and around pools, ponds.

DISTRICTS: COR, ORW, BEL, CAYO, PET

Plate 6 245

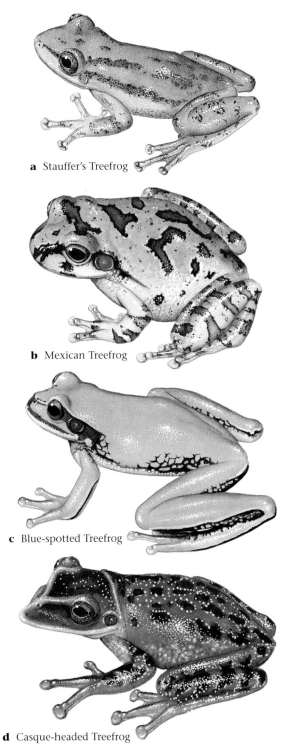

a Stauffer's Treefrog

b Mexican Treefrog

c Blue-spotted Treefrog

d Casque-headed Treefrog

Plate 7a

Rainforest Frog (also called Vaillant's Frog)
Rana vaillanti
Rana = frog

ID: A large frog with greenish head and shoulders; body and limbs shading to brown, bronze, or grayish with black flecks; sides sometimes gray or gray-brown with black spots; dark bars on rear legs; toes fully webbed; to 12 cm (4.75 in).

HABITAT: Low and middle elevation forests; found in quiet water of rivers and streams, and in ponds and lakes near shore.

DISTRICTS: COR, ORW, BEL, STN, CAYO, TOL, PET

Plate 7b

Julian's Frog (also called Maya Mountains Frog)
Rana juliani
Rana = frog

ID: Large brown, tan, or olive frog with darker markings; head area often green; sides usually darker than back; dark bars on rear limbs; light stripe along upper lip; to about 10 cm (4 in).

HABITAT: Low and middle elevation forests; found in fast-flowing rocky streams.

DISTRICTS: STN, CAYO, TOL

Plate 7c

Rio Grande Leopard Frog (also called Rio Grande Frog)
Rana berlandieri
Rana = frog

ID: Large tan, brown, or green/olive frog with dark circles and ovals on back; limbs with dark bands or spots; light stripe often runs through eye and down back; to about 11 cm (4.25 in).

HABITAT: Low, middle, and some higher elevation wet forests; found in and along rivers and streams, ponds, small pools, marshes.

DISTRICTS: COR, ORW, BEL, STN, CAYO, TOL, PET

Plate 7d

Fleischmann's Glass Frog (also called Mexican Glass Frog)
Hyalinobatrachium fleischmanni
Ranita Verde = little green frog

ID: Tiny translucent frog with a rounded snout; lime green with yellow spots and yellowish hands; organs/bones visible through abdominal skin; to 3 cm (1 in).

HABITAT: Low, middle and some higher elevation wet forests; found in vegetation along rivers and streams.

DISTRICTS: BEL, STN, CAYO, TOL, PET

Plate 7e

Sheep Frog
Hypopachus variolosus
Rana Ovejera = sheep frog

ID: Small, squat, gray-brown or reddish brown frog with darker markings on sides and limbs; a light thin line runs from snout along center of back; often, a light line runs from eye to throat; to 4.5 cm (1.75 in).

HABITAT: Low and middle elevation forests and more open sites such as forest edges; found on or under ground, under leaf litter, beneath rocks, logs, and on roads after rains.

DISTRICTS: COR, ORW, BEL, STN, CAYO, PET

Plate 7 247

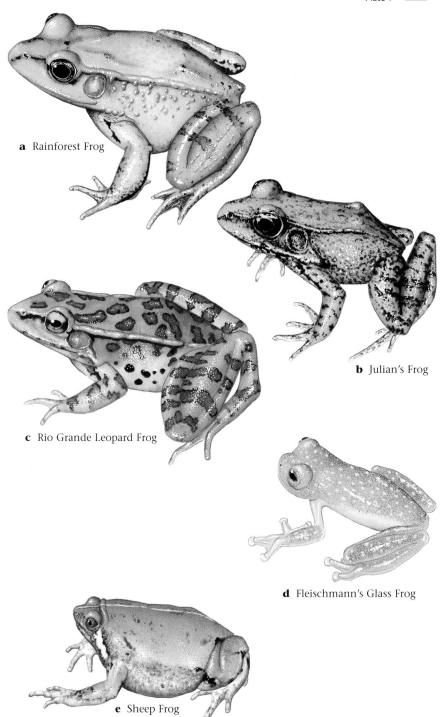

a Rainforest Frog

b Julian's Frog

c Rio Grande Leopard Frog

d Fleischmann's Glass Frog

e Sheep Frog

Plate 8a

American Crocodile
Crocodylus acutus
Alligator (Belize)
Agarei (Belize)
Cocodrilo Amarillo = yellow crocodile
ID: Large grayish, brown, or olive crocodile, to as long as 7 m (21 ft), but most are much smaller; individuals longer than 4 m (13 ft) are rare. Youngsters may show dark bands on back and tail. Distinguished from Morelet's Crocodile by (1) generally larger size; (2) narrower snout; and (3) typical habitat/locations.

HABITAT: Coastal lowlands and islands, in brackish or freshwater; found in or near swamps, mangrove swamps, estuaries, larger rivers.

DISTRICTS: CAYE, PET

Note: This species listed as endangered, CITES Appendix I and USA ESA.

Plate 8b

Morelet's Crocodile
Crocodylus moreleti
Alligator (Belize)
Agarei (Belize)
Cocodrilo Pardo = brown crocodile
Cocodrilo de Pantano = swamp crocodile
ID: Dark brown or blackish crocodile with broad snout; to about 4 m (13 ft), but most are less than 2.5 m (8 ft). Youngsters are lighter colored, olive or yellowish, with dark bands on body and tail. Distinguished from American Crocodile by (1) generally smaller size; (2) broader snout; and (3) typical habitat/locations.

HABITAT: Prefers inland lakes, ponds, lagoons, swamps, slow-moving rivers.

DISTRICTS: COR, ORW, BEL, STN, CAYO, PET

Note: This species listed as endangered, CITES Appendix I and USA ESA.

Plate 8c

Central American River Turtle
Dermatemys mawii
Hickatee (Belize)
Tortuga Blanca = white turtle
ID: Large brown or olive turtle with broad, smooth-appearing top shell; several small plates on each side between top and bottom shells; small, flat head; webbed toes; to about 60 cm (2 ft).

HABITAT: Lowland rivers, larger streams, and freshwater lagoons.

DISTRICTS: COR, ORW, BEL, CAYO, TOL, PET

Note: This species listed as endangered, USA ESA, and by CITES Appendix II.

Plate 8d

Furrowed Wood Turtle (also called Black-bellied Turtle)
Rhinoclemmys areolata
Blackbelly (Belize)
Aragagao (Belize)
Panza Negra = blackbelly
Mojina
ID: Mid-sized tan, olive-brown, or blackish turtle, often with yellow markings; fairly high top shell; small head and long neck with red or yellow markings; yellow bottom shell; toes partially webbed; to about 20 cm (8 in).

HABITAT: Low elevation forests and more open areas such as savannahs and marshes; found on the ground.

DISTRICTS: COR, ORW, BEL, STN, CAYO, TOL, PET

Plate 8 **249**

a American Crocodile

b Morelet's Crocodile

c Central American River Turtle

d Furrowed Wood Turtle

Plate 9a

Common Slider (also called Sun Turtle, Ornate Terrapin)
Trachemys scripta
Bokatura (Belize)
Wayamu (Belize)

ID: Large olive or brown turtle with yellowish and dark markings; limbs and head brown or green with yellowish or orange stripes; large head; webbed toes; to 60 cm (2 ft), but most are smaller.

HABITAT: Low and middle elevation forests and more open areas; found in or near rivers, streams, lakes, or ponds.

DISTRICTS: COR, ORW, BEL, STN, CAYO, TOL, CAYE, PET

Plate 9b

Snapping Turtle
Chelydra serpentina
Tortuga Lagarto = alligator turtle
Sambodanga

ID: A large, mean aquatic turtle; brown, tan, olive, or blackish back often caked with mud or aquatic vegetation; usually three ridges of sharp bumps along back; underneath yellow to tan; very large head with scales on its side and back; neck with pointed bumps; tail as long as shell; to 45 cm (18 in), but most are smaller.

HABITAT: Fresh and brackish water at low elevations; found in marshes, ponds, lakes, streams, rivers with abundant aquatic vegetation.

DISTRICTS: TOL, PET

Plate 9c

Tabasco Mud Turtle
Kinosternon acutum
Pochitoque

ID: Mid-sized brown or blackish turtle with darker seams; fairly high top shell; bottom shell yellowish with dark seams; head and limbs yellowish or grayish with dark markings and, often, red or yellow markings; male only with long tail and hooked "beak" on head; female with short tail; to 12 cm (5 in).

HABITAT: Low elevation forests and more open areas such as savannahs; found in or near lakes, streams, forest pools.

DISTRICTS: COR, ORW, BEL, STN, CAYO, PET

Plate 9d

White-lipped Mud Turtle (also called White-faced Mud Turtle)
Kinosternon leucostomum
Swanka (Belize)
Tortuga de los Pantanos = swamp turtle
Pochitoque

ID: A mid-sized dark brown or blackish turtle; head brown with whitish jaws, sometimes with dark markings; a yellowish stripe on each side of the head from eye to neck; underneath yellow with darker seams; to 18 cm (7 in).

HABITAT: Low and some middle elevation forests and more open areas; found in quiet water with abundant vegetation in marshes, swamps, streams, rivers, ponds; also terrestrial.

DISTRICTS: COR, ORW, BEL, STN, CAYO, TOL, PET

Plate 9e

Scorpion Mud Turtle (also called Red-cheeked Mud Turtle)
Kinosternon scorpioides

ID: Mid-sized brown, tan, or yellowish turtle with fairly high top shell; brown head with reddish spots on sides; bottom shell yellowish with dark seams; male only with hooked upper jaw and long tail; female with short tail; to 18 cm (7 in).

HABITAT: Low elevation lakes, ponds, streams, rivers.

DISTRICTS: COR, ORW, BEL, STN, CAYO, PET

Plate 9 251

a Common Slider

b Snapping Turtle

c Tabasco Mud Turtle

d White-lipped Mud Turtle

e Scorpion Mud Turtle

Plate 10a

Green Sea Turtle
Chelonia mydas
Carey (Belize)

ID: A medium to large sea turtle with black, gray, greenish, or brown heart-shaped back, often with bold spots or streaks; yellowish white underneath; males' front legs each have one large, curved claw; name refers to greenish body fat; to 1.5 m (5 ft).

HABITAT: Ocean waters off mainland coast and cayes; feeds in shallow water; lays eggs on beaches.

DISTRICTS: COR, BEL, STN, TOL, CAYE

Note: This species listed as endangered, CITES Appendix I and USA ESA.

Plate 10b

Hawksbill Sea Turtle
Eretmochelys imbricata

ID: A small to mid-sized sea turtle; shield-shaped back mainly dark greenish brown; yellow underneath; head scales brown or black; jaws yellowish with dark markings; chin and throat yellow; two claws on each front leg; narrow head and tapering hooked "beak" give the species its name; to 90 cm (35 in).

HABITAT: Feeds in clear, shallow ocean water near rocks and reefs, and also in shallow bays, estuaries, and lagoons; lays eggs on beaches.

DISTRICTS: COR, BEL, STN, TOL, CAYE

Note: This species listed as endangered, CITES Appendix I and USA ESA.

Plate 10c

Loggerhead Sea Turtle
Caretta caretta

ID: Large brown or reddish brown sea turtle with heart-shaped top shell; tan or yellowish markings on plates at edge of top shell; head and limbs brownish with yellow or tan markings; bottom shell yellowish; to 2 m (6.5 ft).

HABITAT: Feeds often in shallow coastal areas and bays, occasionally wandering up larger rivers; lays eggs on beaches.

DISTRICTS: COR, BEL, STN, TOL, CAYE

Note: This species listed as endangered, CITES Appendix I, and as threatened, USA ESA.

Plate 10d

Leatherback Sea Turtle
Dermochelys coriacea
Trunk Back (Belize)

ID: Largest of the world's sea turtles, to lengths of 2.4 m (7.8 ft) and weights of 550+ kg (1200+ lb). Back is black or brown, smooth, covered with a continuous layer of black, often white-spattered, leathery skin (instead of the hardened plates of other sea turtles); seven ridges along back running front to rear; no claws on limbs; no scales on skin except in youngsters; front limbs up to 1 m (3 ft) long.

HABITAT: An open-ocean turtle, but occasionally feeds in shallow water of bays and estuaries; lays eggs on beaches.

DISTRICTS: COR, BEL, STN, TOL, CAYE

Note: This species listed as endangered, CITES Appendix I and USA ESA.

Plate 10 253

a Green Sea Turtle

b Hawksbill Sea Turtle

c Loggerhead Sea Turtle

d Leatherback Sea Turtle

Plate 11a

Mussurana
Clelia clelia
Zopilota = vulture (Belize)
Zumbadora = buzzer

ID: A large, uniformly colored, bluish black, brown, or grayish snake, to 2.5 m (8 ft); youngsters are bright red or pink with black and yellow heads.

HABITAT: Low and middle elevation forests and more open areas; found on the ground; active day and night.

DISTRICTS: BEL, STN, CAYO, PET

Note: This species regulated for conservation purposes; CITES Appendix II listed.

Plate 11b

Brown Racer
Dryadophis melanolomus
Dryad Snake (Belize)
Zumbadora = buzzer

ID: Mid-sized tan or brown snake with black edging around scales; dark brown head; yellowish or cream lips and chin; to 1.2 m (4 ft).

HABITAT: Low and middle elevation forests and more open sites such as forest edges, savannahs; found on the ground; day-active.

DISTRICTS: COR, ORW, BEL, STN, CAYO, TOL, PET

Plate 11c

Indigo Snake (also called Black-tailed Indigo)
Drymarchon corais
Blacktail (Belize)
Cola Negra = blacktail

ID: A large, long snake, beige, brown, reddish tan, or olive; last third of body darker; often has noticeable black lines radiating under eye and a short black bar just behind and to the side of the head; black eyes; to 3 m (10 ft).

HABITAT: Low and middle elevation forests and more open areas such as savannahs, agricultural sites; found on ground, along riverbeds, or in swamps, marshes; also climbs low plants; day-active.

DISTRICTS: COR, ORW, BEL, STN, CAYO, TOL, PET

Plate 11d

Speckled Racer (also called Guinea Hen Snake)
Drymobius margaritiferus
Ranera = frog-eater
Petatilla

ID: A black or green snake spotted all over with yellow, orange, or bluish dots; head black, often with yellow markings; eyes black; to about 1.2 m (4 ft).

HABITAT: Low and middle elevation forests and more open areas; terrestrial, often found in thickets and near water; day-active.

DISTRICTS: COR, ORW, BEL, STN, CAYO, TOL, PET

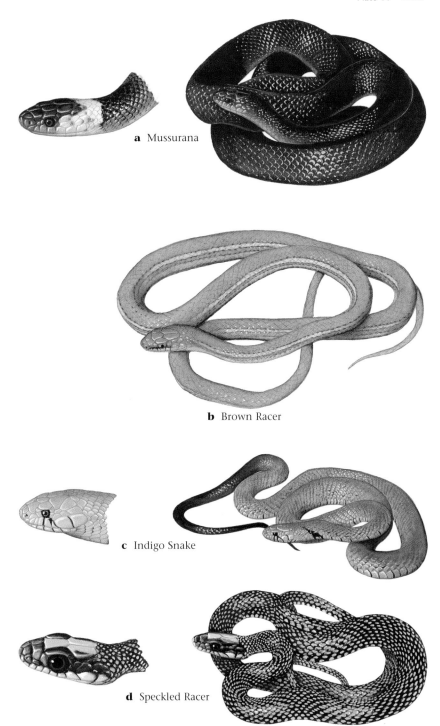

Plate 11 255

a Mussurana

b Brown Racer

c Indigo Snake

d Speckled Racer

Plate 12a

Blunt-headed Tree Snake (also called Chunk-headed Snake, Brown Blunt-headed Vine Snake)
Imantodes cenchoa
Cohune Ridge Tommygoff (Belize)
Bejuquilla = little vine snake
Cordelilla Manchada = little spotted cord

ID: Small, very slim snake, tan or light brown with wide dark brown bands; thin neck but noticeably wide, squarish head; very large, bulging eyes; body compressed side-to-side; to 1 m (3 ft).

HABITAT: Low and middle elevation forests; arboreal, usually found in small, outer branches of shrubs and trees; mostly nocturnal.

DISTRICTS: COR, ORW, BEL, STN, CAYO, TOL, PET

Plate 12b

Green Tree Snake
Leptophis ahaetulla
Green Tommygoff (Belize)
Green Parrot Snake (Belize)
Culebra Lora = parrot snake

ID: A slender snake, bright green on top; belly ranges from lighter green to whitish; large yellow and black eyes; to 2.2 m (7 ft).

HABITAT: Low and middle elevation forests and more open sites such as forest edges, clearings; found on ground and in small trees and shrubs, usually near water; day-active.

DISTRICTS: ORW, BEL, STN, CAYO, TOL, PET

Plate 12c

Green-headed Tree Snake (also called Mexican Green Tree Snake)
Leptophis mexicanus
Greenhead (Belize)
Bejuquillo = vine snake

ID: Mid-sized slender snake with brown and green back; striking, long green head with black stripe through eye; whitish lips, chin, and stomach; to 1.5 m (5 ft).

HABITAT: Low and middle elevation forest edges and savannahs; found in trees and shrubs; day-active.

DISTRICTS: COR, ORW, BEL, STN, CAYO, TOL, CAYE, PET

Plate 12d

Neotropical Vine Snake (also called Brown Vine Snake, Mexican Vine Snake)
Oxybelis aeneus
Ti-tie Snake (Belize)
Bejuquilla Parda = little brown vine snake

ID: A very slender snake with a slim elongated head that comes to blunt point; brown, reddish brown, or grayish, sometimes with small dark spots; sides of head and under head yellowish or whitish; black eye stripe; to 1.5 m (5 ft).

HABITAT: Low and middle elevation forests and forest edges; arboreal; day-active.

DISTRICTS: ORW, BEL, STN, CAYO, TOL, PET

Plate 12e

Green Vine Snake
Oxybelis fulgidus
Bejuquilla Verde = little green vine snake
Culebra Verde Arbórea = green tree snake

ID: Largish slender green snake with lighter green chin; some with darker eyestripe; belly lighter green or yellowish, often with two light stripes running length of body; pointed head; to 2 m (6.5 ft).

HABITAT: Low and middle elevation forests and forest edges; arboreal; day-active.

DISTRICTS: COR, ORW, BEL, STN, CAYO, TOL, PET

Plate 12 257

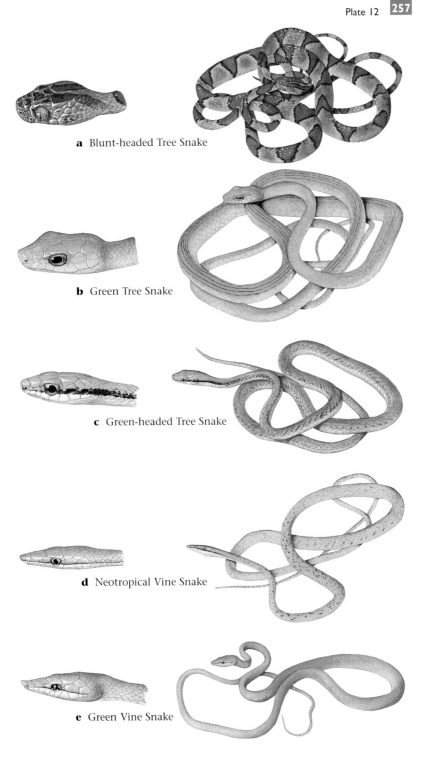

a Blunt-headed Tree Snake

b Green Tree Snake

c Green-headed Tree Snake

d Neotropical Vine Snake

e Green Vine Snake

Plate 13 (*See also*: Colubrid snakes, p. 89)

Plate 13a

Cat-eyed Snake (also called Rainforest Cat-eyed Snake)
Leptodeira frenata
Cohune Ridge Tommygoff (Belize)

ID: Mid-sized brown snake, sometimes a bit pinkish, with darker blotches; broad, flat, brown head with darker stripe behind eye; tan or cream chin; to 65 cm (2 ft).

HABITAT: Low and middle elevation forests and more open areas; found on the ground and in trees; nocturnal.

DISTRICTS: COR, ORW, BEL, STN, CAYO, TOL, PET

Plate 13b

Tropical Rat Snake
Spilotes pullatus
Bocatora Clapansaya (Belize)
Thunder and Lightning Snake (Belize)
Culebra Mica = monkey snake

ID: A mid-sized snake, variable in color, but often shiny black with yellow markings and bands; chin whitish and black; yellow under head and extending rearwards, changing to a black belly; large brown/black eyes; to 2.2 m (7.2 ft).

HABITAT: Low and middle elevation forests, forest edges, brushy woodland, savannahs, open areas around settlements; arboreal and terrestrial; often found near water.

DISTRICTS: COR, ORW, BEL, STN, CAYO, TOL, PET

Plate 13c

Red Coffee Snake (also called Redback Coffee Snake)
Ninia sebae
Bead and Coral (Belize)

ID: Small red snake with black head; yellowish "collar" followed by wide black band; often, a few narrow black markings or bands on back; cream or grayish belly; a coral snake mimic (see p. 95); to 30 cm (1 ft).

HABITAT: Low and middle elevation forests and more open sites such as savannahs, agricultural areas; found on the ground; nocturnal.

DISTRICTS: COR, ORW, BEL, STN, CAYO, TOL, PET

Plate 13d

Neckband Snake (also called Shovel-toothed Snake)
Scaphiodontophis annulatus
Double Snake (Belize)

ID: A small, thickish snake with two forms: in one, rings of dull red, yellow, and black run down the entire body; in the other, the rings cover only the first third of the body, with the remainder being solid light brown or olive; a coral snake mimic (see p. 95); to 60 cm (2 ft).

HABITAT: Low and middle elevation wet forests; terrestrial; often found on or under leaf litter, in rocky areas, or near streams or swamps.

DISTRICTS: ORW, BEL, STN, CAYO, TOL, PET

Plate 13   259

a Cat-eyed Snake

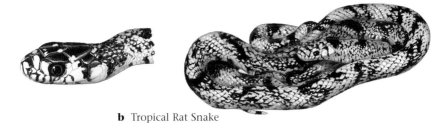

b Tropical Rat Snake

c Red Coffee Snake

d Neckband Snake

Plate 14a

Tropical Kingsnake (also called
Tropical Milk Snake)
Lampropeltis triangulum
Bead and Coral (Belize)
Coral (Belize)
Coralillo Falso = false coral snake

ID: A mid-sized snake with repeated pattern of
red, black, and yellow/orange rings, with red the
widest and yellow/orange the narrowest; a coral
snake mimic (see p. 95); to 1.7 m (5.5 ft).

HABITAT: Low, middle, and higher-elevation wet
forests; moutainsides, hillsides, agricultural areas;
found on the ground, often concealed in leaf litter.

DISTRICTS: ORW, STN, CAYO, TOL, PET

Plate 14b

Coral Snake (also called Many-ringed
Coral Snake)
Micrurus diastema
Bead and Coral (Belize)
Coral
Coralillo = little coral

ID: Smallish snake with red, yellow, and black
rings; red rings have black spots or markings;
front part of head usually black; yellowish lips,
chin; to 85 cm (34 in).

HABITAT: Low and middle elevation forests and
most other areas; terrestrial; active day or night.

DISTRICTS: COR, ORW, BEL, STN, CAYO, TOL, PET

Plate 14c

Boa Constrictor (also called Imperial
Boa)
Boa constrictor
Wowla (Belize)
Boa

ID: A large, shiny, handsome snake with a long
triangular head, often with a single stripe along its
top, and dark eyestripes; tan, brown, or grayish
body with dark blotches; the tail, often with
browns, reds, and yellows, is usually brighter and
more colorful than the body; to 3 m (10 ft).

HABITAT: Low and middle elevation forests and
more open areas; found on the ground or in
vegetation, trees, especially near human
settlements.

DISTRICTS: COR, ORW, BEL, STN, CAYO, TOL,
CAYE, PET

Note: This species regulated for conservation
purposes, CITES Appendix II listed.

Plate 14d

Tropical Rattlesnake
Crotalus durissus
Rattlesnake (Belize)
Cascabel = rattlesnake

ID: A stout brown or gray rattlesnake with a
triangular head; body with a pattern of dark
triangles or diamonds; two stripes run from the
top of the head along the neck; a noticeable ridge
runs along the middle of the back; tail rattle; to
1.8 m (6 ft).

HABITAT: Low and middle elevation forests and
more open sites such as forest clearings,
savannahs, dry grasslands; found on the ground
or in rock crevices.

DISTRICTS: COR, ORW, BEL, STN, CAYO, TOL, PET

Plate 14 **261**

a Tropical Kingsnake

b Coral Snake

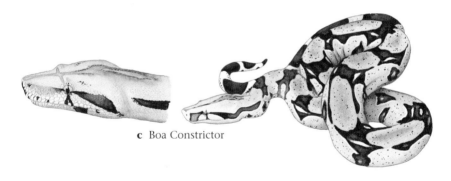

c Boa Constrictor

d Tropical Rattlesnake

Plate 15a

Fer-de-lance (also called Terciopelo)
Bothrops asper
Yellow-jaw Tommygoff (Belize)
Cantil Devanador

ID: A large, fairly slender snake with a triangular head; brown, tan, or gray back covered with a series of beige and brown or black triangles on each side (when viewed from above the series of triangles can resemble hourglass figures or X's); dark stripe on each side of head behind eye; yellowish under head; youngsters with yellowish tail tip; to 2.5 m (8 ft).

HABITAT: Low and middle elevation forests and open areas; somewhat arboreal as juveniles, terrestrial as adults.

DISTRICTS: COR, ORW, BEL, STN, CAYO, TOL, PET

Plate 15b

Eyelash Viper (also called Eyelash Palm Pit-viper, Palm Viper)
Bothriechis schlegelii
Green Tommygoff (Belize)
Víbora de Árbol = tree viper

ID: A slender snake with triangular head; individuals of different colors may occur in the same area, but most are green or grayish green with brown, tan, or rust-colored markings on head and body; dark stripe behind eye; two or three horny, spine-like scales jut out over each eye (the "eyelashes"); small eyes; to 85 cm (33 in).

HABITAT: Low and middle elevation forests; arboreal, often hanging from vegetation with prehensile tail; nocturnal.

DISTRICTS: ORW, CAYO, PET

Plate 15c

Jumping Viper (also called Jumping Pit-viper)
Atropoides nummifer
Jumping Tommygoff (Belize)
Brazo de Piedra = rock-arm

ID: A thickset, stocky pit-viper with a triangular brown head and dark eye stripes; tan, light brown, or grayish brown body with dark brown or black blotches; the name refers to its rumored ability to launch itself and strike at long distance, but usually only over about half its body length; to 80 cm (32 in).

HABITAT: Low and middle elevation forests; found on the ground, but also low in trees.

DISTRICTS: STN, CAYO, TOL, PET

Plate 15d

Rainforest Hognosed Pit-viper (also called Rainforest Hognosed Viper)
Porthidium nasutum
Tommygoff (Belize)
Xalpate de Palo

ID: A small, stocky pit-viper; tip of snout of rounded triangular head is strongly upturned, providing the basis for the name; tan, brown, grayish-, or yellowish brown, often with triangular or rectangular light or dark blotches; dark head often with light stripe behind or below eye; to 60 cm (2 ft).

HABITAT: Low and middle elevation wet forests; prefers open areas, clearings; often found near logs, stumps, litter piles.

DISTRICTS: CAYO, TOL, PET

Plate 15 **263**

a Fer-de-lance

b Eyelash Viper

c Jumping Viper

d Rainforest Hognosed Pit-viper

Plate 16a

Yucatán Banded Gecko
Coleonyx elegans

ID: Large gecko with blackish, whitish, and brown bands and blotches; some have light and dark stripes down back; adults with blotched sides, youngsters with more solid brown sides; to 11 cm (4.5 in), plus tail.

HABITAT: Low elevation forests; found on ground, in rotting logs, around archeological ruins.

DISTRICTS: COR, ORW, BEL, STN, CAYO, TOL, PET

Plate 16b

Yellowbelly Gecko (also called Leaf-toed Gecko)
Phyllodactylus tuberculosus
Mangrove Gecko (Belize)

ID: Mid-sized gecko with oval snout; head widens behind eyes; distinct neck; light brown, tan, or grayish with spots; darker markings on head, sides, legs; often, dark bars on tail; smaller and larger bumps ("tubercles") along back, the larger ones arranged in distinct rows; to 6.5 cm (2.5 in), plus tail.

HABITAT: Low elevation coastal areas and cayes; found on rocks and ground, especially near human settlements, and in buildings; mostly nocturnal.

DISTRICTS: BEL, STN, CAYE

Plate 16c

Dwarf Gecko (also called Least Gecko)
Sphaerodactylus glaucus
Escorpión = scorpion

ID: Tiny tan or grayish spotted house gecko; often with dark spot on neck and two spots at start of tail; to 3 cm (1.2 in), plus tail.

HABITATS: Low and middle elevations, regionwide; found in buildings, trees, on ground, and under leaf litter.

DISTRICTS: COR, ORW, BEL, STN, CAYO, TOL, CAYE, PET

Plate 16d

Central American Smooth Gecko (also called Turnip-tail Gecko)
Thecadactylus rapicaudus
Turnip Tail (Belize)
Escorpión = scorpion

ID: A large gecko with triangular head, distinct from neck; brown, tan, or gray with darker blotches or bands; often, black eyestripe running to shoulder; various kinds of scales on body; partly webbed hands and feet; newly grown tails (see p. 104) often greatly enlarged (the "turnip") and lighter in color than body; to 11 cm (4.5 in), plus tail.

HABITAT: Low and middle elevation forests; found on rocks and trees near human settlements, around Mayan ruins, sometimes in buildings.

DISTRICTS: ORW, CAYO, TOL, PET

Plate 16 **265**

a Yucatán Banded Gecko

b Yellowbelly Gecko

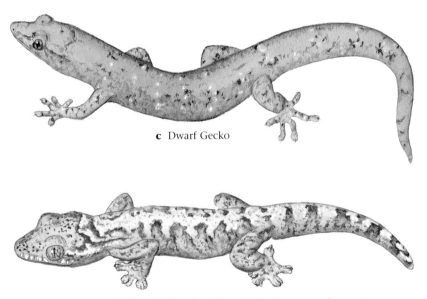

c Dwarf Gecko

d Central American Smooth Gecko

Plate 17a

Green Iguana (also called Common Iguana)
Iguana iguana
Bamboo Chicken (Belize)
Wayamaga (Belize)

ID: Very large lizard with a tall crest (consisting of long, sickle-shaped scales) running from neck to tail; short head with prominent eye and large circular scale (larger than eye) at angle of the jaw; large dewlap (throat sac); greenish, brown, or gray with wavy black bands on body and tail; often some orange on head, body; to 1.8 m (6 ft), including very long tail.

HABITAT: Low elevation forests and forest edges; found on ground and in trees, often along streams, rivers, lakes; sometimes on sunny, leafy branches as high as 20 m (65 ft).

DISTRICTS: ORW, BEL, STN, CAYO, TOL, CAYE, PET

Note: This species regulated for conservation purposes, CITES Appendix II listed.

Plate 17b

Striped Basilisk (also called Jesus Christ Lizard, Brown Basilisk)
Basiliscus vittatus
Cock Lizard (Belize)
Cock Malakka (Belize)
Jesucristo = Jesus Christ lizard
Lagartija = lizard

ID: Medium to large brown or olive lizard with dark cross bands along body, often a light stripe along lips and sides, and large, continuous crest along the head, back, and tail (much less prominent in females and young; small ones are good at running quickly across the surface of water (see p. 100), providing the irreverent name; to about 80 cm (32 in), including tail.

HABITAT: Low and middle elevations, region-wide; found especially along streams and bodies of water; terrestrial but also climbs trees, low vegetation.

DISTRICTS: COR, ORW, BEL, STN, CAYO, TOL, CAYE, PET

Plate 17c

Spiny-tailed Iguana (also called Ctenosaur, Black Iguana)
Ctenosaura similis
Wish-willy (Belize)
Garrobo

ID: Large lizard with a tan, olive, olive-brown, or grayish body with dark cross-wise bands; banded limbs; pale brown, weakly banded tail with circular rows of scales; back often with red/orange spots; old males have short crest of vertical scales along back; to 1.2 m (4 ft), including tail.

HABITAT: Low and middle elevation open areas, particularly around human settlements and beaches; found on the ground, in trees, on buildings and archeological ruins; day-active.

DISTRICTS: COR, ORW, BEL, STN, CAYO, CAYE, PET

Plate 17d

Big-headed Anole
Anolis capito

ID: Mid-sized tan, brown, or greenish brown lizard with spots, streaks, bars, and/or mottling; distinct neck; some females with wide light or light and dark stripes down back; to about 10 cm (4 in), plus very long tail.

HABITAT: Low and middle elevation wet forests; found on trees and ground; day-active.

DISTRICTS: ORW, BEL, STN, CAYO, TOL, PET

Plate 17 267

a Green Iguana

b Striped Basilisk

c Spiny-tailed Iguana

d Big-headed Anole

Plate 18a

Lesser Scaly Anole
Anolis uniformis

ID: Small, stout-bodied lizard; tan, brown, or brownish olive with wide bronze stripe running down back; male dewlap (throat sac) reddish or purple with blue spot; to 4 cm (1.5 in), plus tail.

HABITAT: Low elevation wet forests; found on the ground and low on tree trunks; day-active.

DISTRICTS: STN, CAYO, TOL, PET

Plate 18b

Brown Anole
Anolis sagrei
Hu Wa (Belize)
Cock Maklala (Belize)

ID: Mid-sized grayish or brown lizard with darker or lighter spots, bars, or V-shaped markings; some females with light stripe down back; male dewlap (throat sac) orangish; to 7 cm (2.75 in), plus tail.

HABITAT: Low elevations, usually around human settlements; found on fences, rock walls, buildings.

DISTRICTS: COR, ORW, BEL, STN, CAYO, TOL, CAYE

Plate 18c

Silky Anole
Anolis sericeus

ID: Small brown or gray lizard with darker markings; narrow head; some females with light stripe down back; male dewlap (throat sac) red or orangish with bluish spot; to about 5 cm (2 in), plus long tail.

HABITAT: Low and middle elevation open sites such as forest edges, savannahs, agricultural areas, roadsides; found on low vegetation and ground; often align themselves on blade of grass when startled.

DISTRICTS: COR, ORW, BEL, STN, CAYO, TOL, PET

Plate 18d

Yellow-spotted Spiny Lizard
Sceloporus chrysostictus

ID: Small gray, brown, or tan lizard with two rows of bars or V-shapes along back; males often with two light stripes down back and dark sides; to about 6 cm (2.5 in), plus tail.

HABITAT: Low elevation forest edges and other open areas; found on ground on rocks, logs, roadsides, etc.; day-active.

DISTRICTS: COR, ORW, BEL, CAYO, CAYE, PET

Plate 18   269

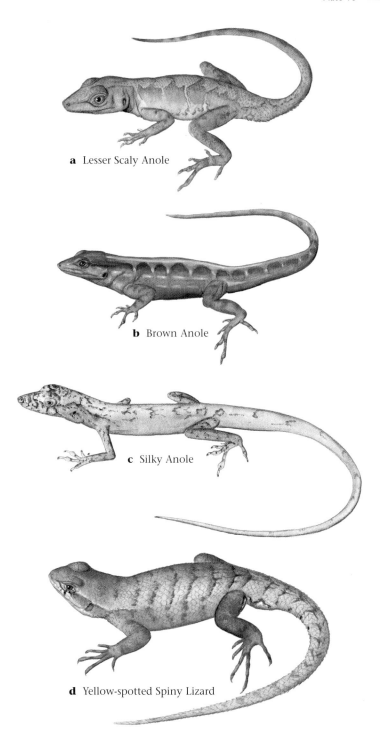

a Lesser Scaly Anole

b Brown Anole

c Silky Anole

d Yellow-spotted Spiny Lizard

Plate 19a

Ground Skink (also called Brown
Forest Skink, Litter Skink)
Sphenomorphus cherriei
Galliwasp (Belize)

ID: Small lizard with longish head, body, and tail;
short legs; shiny bronze/brown back with dark
spots; sides darker; dark eyestripes extend along
neck to body; to 6.5 cm (2.5 in), plus tail.

HABITAT: Low and middle elevation wet forests
and forest edges, tree groves, and other open
areas; usually found on the ground, in leaf litter;
day-active.

DISTRICTS: ORW, BEL, STN, CAYO, TOL, PET

Plate 19b

Shiny Skink (also called Striped Skink,
Central American Mubuya)
Mabuya brachypoda (also called
Mabuya unimarginata)
Snake Waiting Boy (Belize)

ID: Mid-sized shiny brown lizard; dark stripe
along each side, with light stripe below and
sometimes also above the dark stripe; narrow
head; short legs; to about 8 cm (3 in), plus tail.

HABITAT: Low and middle elevations; prefers
more open sites such as forest edges, savannahs,
and near human settlements; found on ground and
in trees.

DISTRICTS: COR, ORW, BEL, STN, CAYO, TOL,
CAYE, PET

Plate 19c

Central American Whiptail (also
called Central American Ameiva)
Ameiva festiva

ID: A mid-sized lizard, olive, gray, or brown with a
conspicuous yellow, whitish, or bluish stripe down
center of back; white or bluish dashes or dots
along sides; youngsters with blue tail; to 12 cm (5
in), plus tail.

HABITAT: Low and middle elevation wet forests;
found on the ground or in low vegetation.

DISTRICTS: STN, CAYO, TOL, PET

Plate 19d

Barred Whiptail (also called Rainbow
Ameiva)
Ameiva undulata

ID: Mid-sized brown or greenish brown lizard
with dark spots; sides dark brown sometimes with
vertical green-blue bars; breeding males with
bright yellowish, green, or orange face; to 10 cm
(4 in), plus tail.

HABITAT: Low and middle elevation forest edges
and other open sites; found on ground in leaf
litter; also in thickets, agricultural areas,
roadsides.

DISTRICTS: COR, ORW, BEL, STN, CAYO, TOL,
CAYE, PET

Plate 19e

Cozumel Whiptail (also called Cozumel
Racerunner)
Cnemidophorus cozumelae

ID: Mid-sized slender tan, brownish, or gray
lizard; several light stripes run along each side; to
about 8 cm (3 in), plus tail.

HABITAT: Low elevation open areas such as
savannahs, beaches, roadsides; found on ground;
day-active.

DISTRICTS: ORW, BEL, TOL, PET

Plate 19   271

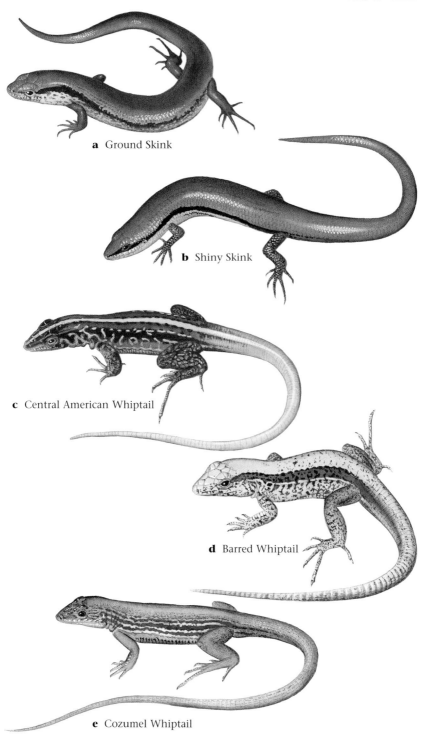

a Ground Skink

b Shiny Skink

c Central American Whiptail

d Barred Whiptail

e Cozumel Whiptail

Plate 20a

Brown Booby
Sula leucogaster
Alcatraz Pardo = brown gannet
Boba Parda = brown stupid bird
ID: A mid-sized seabird with brown back, brown neck, white belly, and yellowish, cone-shaped, sharply pointed bill; pointed wings; to 66 cm (26 in); wingspan to 1.4 m (4.7 ft).

HABITAT: Coastal; found around seashores and islands.

DISTRICTS: COR, BEL, STN, TOL, CAYE

Plate 20b

Magnificent Frigatebird
Fregata magnificens
Fragata Pelágica = pelagic frigatebird
Rabihorcado
ID: Large black seabird with long, narrow, pointed wings; long, forked tail; long gray bill with down-curved tip; male with reddish throat patch; female with white belly; immature bird has white head and belly; to 90 cm (3 ft); wingspan to 2 m (6 ft).

HABITAT: Coastal; found around seashores and islands; often seen soaring high over coastal areas.

DISTRICTS: COR, BEL, STN, TOL, CAYE

Plate 20c

Laughing Gull
Larus atricilla
Gaviota Gritóna = shouting gull
Gaviota Risueña = smiling gull
ID: Smallish seabird, white with grayish back and upper wings; white ring around eye; reddish gray bill; adults during breeding have black heads and reddish bills; 40 cm (16 in); wingspan to 1 m (3.3 ft).

HABITAT: Marine and freshwater; found along shores, beaches, islands; also seen inland on and near mudflats, river outlets, lake edges.

DISTRICTS: COR, ORW, BEL, STN, CAYO, TOL, CAYE, PET

Plate 20d

Royal Tern
Sterna maxima
Golondrina de Mar = sea swallow
ID: Largish white seabird with black head top; grayish wings; orange bill; black feet; forked tail; breeding adults (shown flying) have black head with noticeable crest; to 48 cm (19 in); wingspan to 1 m (3.3 ft).

HABITAT: Marine and freshwater; found along shores, beaches, islands; also seen inland near river outlets, lake edges.

DISTRICTS: COR, ORW, BEL, STN, CAYO, TOL, CAYE, PET

Plate 20e

Brown Pelican
Pelecanus occidentalis
Pelícano Pardo = brown pelican
ID: Large brownish seabird with blackish (during breeding) or white (nonbreeding) neck; very long bill with large throat pouch; head yellowish and bill reddish during breeding; immature bird is overall brown with lighter belly; to 1 m (3.3 ft); wingspan to 2.1 m (7 ft).

HABITAT: Coastal; found along shores, beaches, islands; occasionally inland.

DISTRICTS: COR, ORW, BEL, STN, CAYO, TOL, CAYE, PET

Note: This species endangered over parts of its range, USA ESA listed.

Plate 20 **273**

a Brown Booby

b Magnificent Frigatebird

d Royal Tern

c Laughing Gull

e Brown Pelican

Plate 21a

Olivaceous Cormorant (also called Neotropic Cormorant)
Phalacrocorax brasilianus
Cormorán = cormorant
Malache

ID: A blackish or brownish mid-sized waterbird with brownish yellow facial skin and gray or black bill with down-curved tip, and long tail; 64 cm (2 ft); wingspan to 1 m (3.3 ft).

HABITAT: Found in and around lakes, rivers, lagoons, and near shore in the Caribbean; often seen in rivers and lakes diving for fish.

DISTRICTS: COR, ORW, BEL, STN, CAYO, TOL, PET

Plate 21b

Anhinga
Anhinga anhinga
Snake Bird (Belize)
Pato Aguja = needle duck

ID: Large black waterbird with long, sharply pointed bill; silvery-white streaks on wings; black (males) or buffy-brown (females) neck and head; to 90 cm (3 ft); wingspan to 1.1 m (3.8 ft).

HABITAT: Found in and around lakes, rivers, lagoons, and marshes; often seen swimming with only head and neck above water, or perched with wings spread to dry.

DISTRICTS: COR, ORW, BEL, STN, CAYO, TOL, CAYE, PET

Plate 21c

Jabiru Stork
Jabiru mycteria
Fillymingo (Belize)
Turk (Belize)
Jabirú or Cigüeño Jabirú

ID: A very large white, wading bird with black head and huge black bill; reddish area at bottom of neck; to 1.4 m (4.5 ft) tall; wingspan to 2.3 m (7.5 ft).

HABITAT: Aquatic habitats in only a few lowland areas; found around streams, rivers, ponds, lakes, but most often in marshes.

DISTRICTS: COR, BEL, STN, TOL, PET

Plate 21d

Wood Stork
Mycteria americana
John Crow Culu (Belize)
Cigüeñón = big stork
Garzón Pulido = polished heron

ID: Large white wading bird with black head, neck, and bill; black shows under wings in flight; to 1.1 m (3.5 ft) tall; wingspan to 1.5 m (5 ft).

HABITAT: Aquatic habitats in some lowland areas; found around streams, rivers, ponds, lakes, but most often in marshes, including saltwater marshes.

DISTRICTS: COR, ORW, BEL, STN, PET

Plate 21 275

a Olivaceous Cormorant

M

F

c Jabiru Stork

b Anhinga

d Wood Stork

Plate 22a

Roseate Spoonbill
Ajaia ajaja
Espátula Rosada = pink spatula
Ibis Espátula = spatula ibis
ID: A large pink or light red wading bird with white neck and large spoon-shaped bill; immature bird is whitish to slightly pink; to 80 cm (32 in); wingspan to 1.3 m (4.2 ft).

HABITAT: Lowland aquatic sites; found around ponds, lakes, marshes, including saltwater marshes.

DISTRICTS: COR, BEL, STN, TOL, CAYE

Plate 22b

White Ibis
Eudocimus albus
Ibis Blanco = white ibis
ID: Large white wading bird with thin, downward-curved, red bill and red legs; black wing tips noticeable in flight; immature bird is brownish; to 62 cm (2 ft); wingspan to 97 cm (38 in).

HABITAT: Lowland aquatic sites; found along shorelines, beaches, mangroves, streams and rivers, ponds, lakes, and marshes.

DISTRICTS: COR, ORW, BEL, STN, CAYE

Plate 22c

Boat-billed Heron
Cochlearius cochlearius
Cooper (Belize)
Garza Cucharón = scoop or ladle heron
Garza Pico de Zapato = shoe-bill heron
ID: Medium-sized grayish heron with large head and very large, broad bill; head top and crest black; belly rusty brown; immature bird has less black and more brown; to 50 cm (20 in).

HABITAT: Aquatic sites; found in or near marshes, swamps, rivers, mangroves, often perched in trees.

DISTRICTS: COR, ORW, BEL, STN, CAYE, PET

Plate 22d

Bare-throated Tiger Heron
Tigrisoma mexicanum
Garza Tigre = tiger heron
ID: Large brownish heron with fine black stripes on neck, back and sides; black and gray head; yellow throat; immature bird is more chestnut-brown, has brown and black mottled wings, and lacks gray and black on head; to 80 cm (32 in).

HABITAT: Aquatic sites; found along coasts and inland around marshes, lakes, ponds, rivers.

DISTRICTS: COR, ORW, BEL, STN, CAYO, TOL, CAYE, PET

Plate 22 277

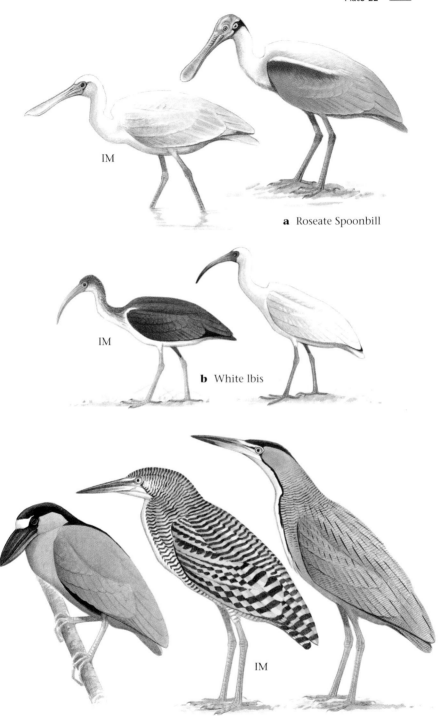

IM

a Roseate Spoonbill

IM

b White Ibis

IM

c Boat-billed Heron　　　　**d** Bare-throated Tiger Heron

Plate 23a

Little Blue Heron
Egretta caerulea
Gaulin (Belize)
Garcita Azul = little blue heron
Garza Gris = gray heron
ID: Medium-sized blue-gray heron with purplish or brownish red head and neck and grayish bill; legs vary in color but often grayish or black; immature white with dark-tipped bill, lighter-colored legs; to 66 cm (26 in); wingspan to 1 m (3.3 ft).

HABITAT: Aquatic sites; found in coastal areas and in or near ponds, rivers, marshes, mangroves.

DISTRICTS: COR, ORW, BEL, STN, CAYO, TOL, CAYE, PET

Plate 23b

Tricolored Heron
Egretta tricolor
Gaulin (Belize)
Garceta Tricolor = tricolored heron
ID: Medium-sized gray or bluish gray heron with brownish purple neck and chest; white throat and belly; yellowish or grayish bill; yellowish legs; 66 cm (26 in); wingspan to 91 cm (3 ft).

HABITAT: Aquatic sites; found in coastal areas and in or near ponds, rivers, marshes, mangroves.

DISTRICTS: COR, ORW, BEL, STN, CAYO, TOL, CAYE, PET

Plate 23c

Snowy Egret
Egretta thula
Gaulin (Belize)
Garceta Nevada = snowy egret
Garcita Blanca = white egret
ID: Medium-sized all-white heron with black bill and legs; immature bird is similar but back of legs yellowish green and with some gray on bill; to 64 cm (25 in); wingspan to 1 m (3.3 ft).

HABITAT: Aquatic sites; found in coastal areas and in or near ponds, rivers, marshes.

DISTRICTS: COR, ORW, BEL, STN, CAYO, TOL, CAYE, PET

Plate 23d

Cattle Egret
Bubulcus ibis
Gaulin (Belize)
Garza Ganadera, Garcilla Bueyera = cattle egret
ID: A smaller, white heron with thickish neck, yellow bill and dark legs; yellowish buff color during breeding on head, chest, and back; bill and legs reddish during breeding; immature bird is white with yellowish bill; 50 cm (20 in); wingspan to 91 cm (3 ft).

HABITAT: Low and middle elevation agricultural areas; found foraging in fields or following tractors; also marshes.

DISTRICTS: COR, ORW, BEL, STN, CAYO, TOL, CAYE, PET

Plate 23e

Great Egret
Casmerodius albus
Gaulin (Belize)
Garza Real = royal egret
Garzón Blanco = white egret
Garceta Grande = big egret
ID: Large all-white heron with yellow bill and dark legs; 1 m (3.3 ft); wingspan to 1.3 m (4.3 ft).

HABITAT: Aquatic sites; found along coasts and inland around marshes, lakes, ponds, rivers.

DISTRICTS: COR, ORW, BEL, STN, CAYO, TOL, CAYE, PET

Plate 23 **279**

a Little Blue Heron

IM

IM

d Cattle Egret

e Great Egret

b Tricolored Heron

c Snowy Egret

IM

Plate 24a

Green Heron
Butorides striatus
Garcita Verde = little green heron
ID: Small heron with grayish green back; maroon or reddish brown neck; black on top of head; yellowish orange legs; immature bird is darker and heavily streaked; to 45 cm (18 in); wingspan to 60 cm (2 ft).

HABITAT: Aquatic sites; found along coasts in mangroves and inland around marshes, lakes, ponds, rivers.

DISTRICTS: COR, ORW, BEL, STN, CAYO, TOL, CAYE, PET

Plate 24b

Yellow-crowned Night-Heron
Nycticorax violaceus
Garza de Noche de Corona Amarilla = yellow-crowned night-heron
ID: Small gray heron with big black head; white forehead, head top, and behind eye; thick black bill; yellow legs; immature bird has brown streaks; to 60 cm (2 ft); wingspan to 1.1 m (3.5 ft).

HABITAT: Aquatic sites; found especially in and near mangroves, mudflats, riversides.

DISTRICTS: COR, ORW, BEL, STN, CAYO, TOL, CAYE, PET

Plate 24c

Ruddy Crake
Laterallus ruber
Gallinita Colorada = little reddish hen
Gallineta (or Gallina) Enana = dwarf hen
Polluela Colorada = small red hen
ID: Small reddish or reddish brown, chicken-like bird with gray head; black bill; olive-gray legs; to 16 cm (6.5 in).

HABITAT: Lowland forests and savannahs; found in marshes, wet fields and pastures, roadside ditches.

DISTRICTS: COR, ORW, BEL, STN, CAYO, TOL, PET

Plate 24d

Gray-necked Wood-rail
Aramides cajanea
Top-na-chick (Belize)
Rascón Cuelligris = gray-necked rail
Gallineta = little hen
ID: Mid-sized marsh bird with gray head and neck; yellowish bill; olive/brownish back; reddish brown chest; long, reddish legs; to 40 cm (16 in).

HABITAT: Low and middle elevation forests; found in wet forest areas and around streams, rivers, marshes, mangroves.

DISTRICTS: COR, ORW, BEL, STN, CAYO, TOL, PET

Plate 24e

Purple Gallinule
Porphyrula martinica
Gallareta (or Gallineta) Morada = purple hen
Gallineta de Pecho Morado = purple-chested hen
ID: Striking mid-sized wading bird with bluish violet head, neck, and chest; green wings; red and yellow bill; light blue forehead; yellow legs; immature bird is light brown with greenish wings; to 40 cm (16 in).

HABITAT: Aquatic sites; found in marshes and along lake and pond shores.

DISTRICTS: COR, ORW, BEL, STN, CAYO, TOL, PET

Plate 24   281

a Green Heron

c Ruddy Crake

d Gray-necked Wood-rail

b Yellow-crowned Night-Heron

IM

e Purple Gallinule

Plate 25a

Northern Jacana
Jacana spinosa
Georgie Bull (Belize)
Jacana Centroamericana = Central
American jacana
Gallito de Pantano = little marsh
rooster
ID: Smallish wading bird with black head, neck, and chest; bright brown wings, back, and belly; yellow bill and forehead; greenish legs and very long toes; yellow under wings seen in flight; immature bird is brown with white chest/belly and black eyestripe; to 25 cm (10 in).

HABITAT: Low and middle elevations; found in rivers, ponds, marshes, wet fields.

DISTRICTS: COR, ORW, BEL, STN, CAYO, TOL, PET

Plate 25b

Sungrebe
Heliornis fulica
Pájaro Cantil = cantil (snake) bird
ID: Smallish duck-like bird, brownish olive and white, with black and white stripes on head and neck; longish tail; straight, nonduckish bill; to 30 cm (1 ft).

HABITAT: Low elevation forests; found in and along wooded streams and rivers, often in brushy areas.

DISTRICTS: COR, ORW, BEL, STN, CAYO, TOL, PET

Plate 25c

Black-bellied Whistling Duck
Dendrocygna autumnalis
Pijiji Aliblanco = white-winged pijiji
ID: Slender, medium-sized duck, rust-colored with black belly; bill and feet red; immature dull brown with grayish belly and dark bill; to 51 cm (20 in).

HABITAT: Aquatic sites; found in ponds, lakes, marshes, wet grassy areas.

DISTRICTS: COR, ORW, BEL, STN, CAYO, TOL, PET

Plate 25d

Muscovy Duck
Cairina moschata
Pato Real = royal duck
ID: Large, chunky duck, mostly black with greenish gloss, and with white wing patches; male with feathered head crest and red "warts" on face; female lacks red warts, is a bit smaller and has a smaller crest; immature bird is brownish; to 85 cm (34 in).

HABITAT: Lowland forests; found in mangroves, wooded streams, rivers, and swamps.

DISTRICTS: COR, ORW, BEL, STN, CAYO, TOL, PET

Plate 25e

Black-necked Stilt
Himantopus mexicanus
Cigüeñuela Cuellinegra = little black-necked stork
Soldadito = little soldier
ID: Mid-sized, slender white and black marsh bird with long pink legs and long, thin, straight black bill; to 38 cm (15 in).

HABITAT: Low elevation aquatic sites; found in ponds, lagoons, estuaries, mudflats.

DISTRICTS: COR, ORW, BEL, STN, CAYO, TOL, CAYE, PET

Plate 25 283

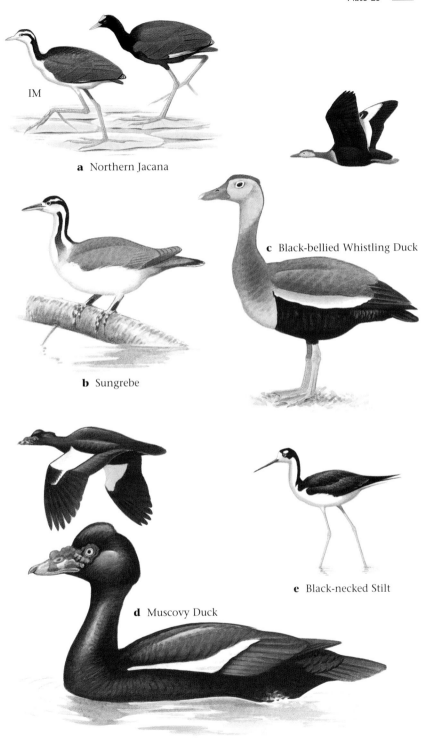

a Northern Jacana

b Sungrebe

c Black-bellied Whistling Duck

d Muscovy Duck

e Black-necked Stilt

IM

Plate 26a

Spotted Sandpiper
Actitis macularia
Shaky Batty (Belize)
Playerito Alzacolita = beach tail-raiser
Andarríos Maculado = spotted river
walker

ID: Small brownish shorebird; white chest and belly, spotted with black during breeding; whitish eyestripe; straight brownish bill; yellowish legs; to 20 cm (8 in).

HABITAT: Aquatic habitats at low and middle elevations; found along ocean shores and around lakes, ponds, rivers; also mangroves, marshes.

DISTRICTS: COR, ORW, BEL, STN, CAYO, TOL, CAYE, PET

Note: This species is a nonbreeding seasonal migrant.

Plate 26b

Sanderling
Calidris alba
Playerito (or Playero) Arenero = beach
sand-dweller

ID: Small light gray shorebird with darker shoulder area and white head, chest and belly; straight black bill; black legs; to 20 cm (8 in).

HABITAT: Seashores; found on sandy shorelines and mudflats.

DISTRICTS: COR, BEL, STN, TOL, CAYE

Note: This species is a nonbreeding seasonal migrant.

Plate 26c

Black-bellied Plover
Pluvialis squatarola
Chorlito Gris = gray plover

ID: Medium-sized brown, grayish, and white shorebird; grayish brown chest mixed with white; white belly; black bars on tail; short black bill; gray legs; black throat and chest during breeding; 30 cm (12 in).

HABITAT: Coastal areas; found on beaches, mudflats, mangroves; occasionally along rivers near coast.

DISTRICTS: COR, BEL, STN, TOL, CAYE

Note: This species is a nonbreeding seasonal migrant.

Plate 26d

Whimbrel
Numenius phaeopus
Zarapito Trinador = warbling zarapito

ID: Large gray-brown shorebird with black striped head and long, black bill that turns downward; to 45 cm (18 in).

HABITAT: Coastal areas; found along sandy and rocky beaches, on mudflats; occasionally along rivers near coast.

DISTRICTS: COR, BEL, STN, TOL, CAYE

Plate 26e

Limpkin
Aramus guarauna
Totolaca
Correa (or Carao)

ID: Largish brown marsh bird with white streaking; long, straight, yellowish or pink/orange bill; gray legs; to 64 cm (25 in).

HABITAT: Lowland aquatic sites; found in rivers, ponds, marshes, swamps, mangroves.

DISTRICTS: COR, ORW, BEL, STN, CAYO, TOL, PET

Plate 26 **285**

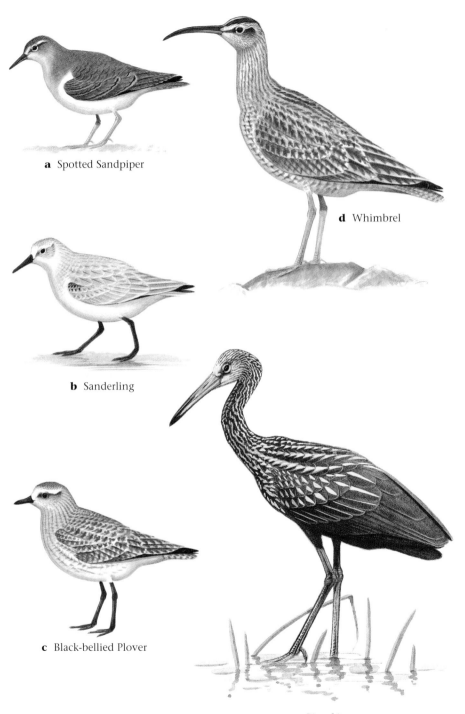

a Spotted Sandpiper

b Sanderling

c Black-bellied Plover

d Whimbrel

e Limpkin

Plate 27a

Plain Chachalaca
Ortalis vetula
Cockrico (Belize)
Chachalaca Común = common chachalaca

ID: Largish olive bird with small gray head and reddish throat; dark tail with light tip; blackish bill; to 53 cm (21 in).

HABITAT: Low and middle elevation forests; found in trees in more open forests, forest edges, and savannahs.

DISTRICTS: COR, ORW, BEL, STN, CAYO, TOL, PET

Note: This species regulated in Guatemala for conservation purposes, CITES Appendix III listed.

Plate 27b

Crested Guan
Penelope purpurascens
Quam (Belize)
Pava Cojolita = little lame guan
Cojolita

ID: Large, turkey-like brown bird with crest on head; red throat sac; white spots/streaks on chest; reddish legs; to 90 cm (3 ft).

HABITAT: Low and middle elevation forests; found in canopy or on ground.

DISTRICTS: COR, ORW, STN, CAYO, TOL, PET

Plate 27c

Great Curassow
Crax rubra
Hocofaisán = pheasant
Pajuil

ID: Very large chicken-like bird with conspicuous, curly head crest and long tail; male is black with white belly and has yellow "knob" on bill; female is mostly brownish or reddish brown with white and black barred head; to 91 cm (3 ft).

HABITAT: Low and middle elevation forests; found walking on ground in forest interior and at forest edges.

DISTRICTS: COR, ORW, STN, CAYO, TOL, PET

Note: This species regulated in Guatemala, Honduras, and Costa Rica for conservation purposes, CITES Appendix III listed.

Plate 27d

Black-throated Bobwhite (also called Yucatán Bobwhite)
Colinus nigrogularis
Codorniz-cotui Yucateca
Codorniz = quail

ID: Small, brownish chicken-like bird with striking black and white scalloped pattern on chest/belly; male with black and white head stripes, black throat; female with buffy/tan eyestripe and throat; to 20 cm (8 in).

HABITAT: Low and middle elevation open sites such as brushy fields and woodlands, clearings, savannahs.

DISTRICTS: BEL, STN, CAYO, PET

Plate 27   287

a Plain Chachalaca

d Black-throated Bobwhite

F

M

b Crested Guan

c Great Curassow

F

M

Plate 28a

Ocellated Turkey
Agriocharis ocellata
Guajolote Ocelado (or Pavo Ocelado) =
ocellated turkey
Pavo del Petén = Petén turkey
ID: Large, metallic blue-green chicken-like bird
with bare skin blue head with reddish warts;
grayish tail with large blue and copper spots;
female duller overall and without head warts; to
1 m (3.3 ft).

HABITAT: Low and middle elevation forests; found
in more open sites such as forest edges, brushy
and overgrown fields.

DISTRICTS: COR, ORW, BEL, CAYO, PET
Note: This species considered near-threatened in
Belize and Guatemala; CITES Appendix III listed
for Guatemala.

Plate 28b

Great Tinamou
Tinamus major
Partridge (Belize)
Tinamú Grande (or Tinamú Mayor) =
great tinamou
Mancolola Grande = great mancolola
ID: Large, thick-set bird, olive-brownish with
darker bars; gray legs; very small tail; slender bill;
to 45 cm (18 in).

HABITAT: Low and middle elevation wet forests;
found usually on the ground, but rests in trees.

DISTRICTS: COR, ORW, BEL, STN, CAYO, TOL, PET

Plate 28c

Slaty-breasted Tinamou
Crypturellus boucardi
Tinamú Jamuey = jamuey tinamou
Mancolola Morena = brown mancolola
ID: Mid-sized, thick-set bird with dark gray head
and chest, brownish back and wings; white throat;
red legs; very small tail; slender bill; female with
light brown/buffy wing bars; to 28 cm (11 in).

HABITAT: Low elevation wet forests; found on
ground.

DISTRICTS: COR, ORW, BEL, STN, CAYO, TOL, PET

Plate 28d

Little Tinamou
Crypturellus soui
Tinamú Menor = small tinamou
Mancolola Enana = dwarf mancolola
ID: Smallish thick-set bird, dark brownish with
gray head; paler, reddish brown chest/belly;
whitish throat; almost no tail; to 23 cm (9 in).

HABITAT: Low and middle elevation forests and
forest edges; found on ground.

DISTRICTS: COR, ORW, BEL, STN, CAYO, TOL, PET

Plate 28 **289**

a Ocellated Turkey

d Little Tinamou

b Great Tinamou

M

F

c Slaty-breasted Tinamou

Plate 29a

Turkey Vulture
Cathartes aura
John Crow (Belize)
Zopilote = vulture
Viuda = widow

ID: Large black bird with featherless red head and neck, whitish bill, and yellowish, flesh, or light red legs; underside of wing in flight is black in front, grayish behind; wings held in shallow V during soaring flight; to 80 cm (32 in); wingspan to 1.8 m (5.8 ft).

HABITAT: Found region-wide; usually seen in the air, circling above open areas and many other habitats.

DISTRICTS: COR, ORW, BEL, STN, CAYO, TOL, CAYE, PET

Plate 29b

Black Vulture
Coragyps atratus
John Crow (Belize)
Zopilote Negro = black vulture
Carroñero Común = common carrion-eater

ID: Large black bird with featherless black head and neck; whitish legs; underside of wing in flight shows a whitish area near wingtip; wings held flat out during soaring flight; to 66 cm (26 in); wingspan to 1.4 m (4.8 ft).

HABITAT: Found region-wide; usually spotted in the air, circling above villages, towns, garbage dumps, other open areas.

DISTRICTS: COR, ORW, BEL, STN, CAYO, TOL, CAYE, PET

Plate 29c

King Vulture
Sarcoramphus papa
King John Crow (Belize)
Zopilote Rey = king vulture
Carroñero Rey = king carrion-eater

ID: Large white bird with featherless multi-colored head, black wings, gray neck, orange bill; underside of wing in flight is white in front, black behind; to 81 cm (32 in); wingspan to 2 m (6.5 ft).

HABITAT: Found region-wide; usually seen in the air, circling above forested or partly wooded areas.

DISTRICTS: COR, ORW, BEL, STN, CAYO, TOL, PET

Plate 29 291

a Turkey Vulture

b Black Vulture

c King Vulture

Plate 30a

Osprey
Pandion haliaetus
Aguila Pescadora = fishing eagle
ID: Large brownish bird with white head; dark stripe through eye; gray legs; wing in flight has backward "bend;" underside of wing white with darker stripes and markings; to 60 cm (2 ft); wingspan to 1.8 m (6 ft).

HABITAT: Low and middle elevations; seen flying or perched in trees near water – ocean shores, mangroves, ponds, lakes.

DISTRICTS: COR, ORW, BEL, STN, CAYO, TOL, CAYE, PET

Plate 30b

Laughing Falcon
Herpetotheres cachinnans
Halcón Guaco = guaco falcon
Vaquero = cowboy
ID: Largish brown bird-of-prey with tawny or buffy head, chest, and belly; black mask around eyes; black tail with light bars; dark, hooked bill; to 55 cm (22 in); wingspan to 94 cm (37 in).

HABITAT: Low elevation open and semi-open areas; found in forest edge areas, grasslands, agricultural areas.

DISTRICTS: COR, ORW, BEL, STN, CAYO, TOL, PET

Plate 30c

Collared Forest Falcon
Micrastur semitorquatus
Halcón de Monte Collarejo = collared forest falcon
Gavilán de Collar = collared hawk
ID: Largish bird-of-prey with dark, hooked bill, long, yellowish legs, and dark tail with light bars. Two forms: light form has black back and wings, white or tawny chest and belly, white face; dark form is mostly blackish, often with chest and belly barred with white or light brown; to 61 cm (24 in); wingspan to 94 cm (37 in).

HABITAT: Low and middle elevation wooded areas; found in forest interiors and edges.

DISTRICTS: COR, ORW, BEL, STN, CAYO, TOL, PET

Plate 30d

Bat Falcon
Falco rufigularis
Lion Hawk (Belize)
Halcón Enano = dwarf falcon
Halcón Caza Murcielagos = bat-hunting falcon
ID: Mid-sized blackish bird-of-prey with fine barring on belly and under wings; white throat, side of neck, chest; reddish brown lower belly; yellow legs; to 28 cm (11 in); wingspan to 73 cm (29 in).

HABITAT: Low and middle elevations; found in semi-open sites such as forest edges, clearings, town parks.

DISTRICTS: COR, ORW, BEL, STN, CAYO, TOL, PET

Plate 30e

Orange-breasted Falcon
Falco deiroleucus
Halcón Pechirrufo = reddish-brown-breasted falcon
Halcón de Pecho Anaranjado = orange-breasted falcon
ID: Mid-sized blackish bird-of-prey with reddish brown chest; white throat; fine barring on belly and under wings; reddish brown lower belly; yellow eye-ring and legs; to 40 cm (16 in); wingspan to 90 cm (35 in).

HABITAT: Low and middle elevation forests; found in semi-open sites such as forest edges and near cliffs.

DISTRICTS: COR, ORW, STN, CAYO, TOL, PET

Note: This species is threatened in Guatemala and probably in Belize.

Plate 30

a Osprey

b Laughing Falcon

d Bat Falcon

e Orange-breasted
Falcon

c Collared Forest Falcon

Plate 31a

Gray-headed Kite
Leptodon cayanensis
Gavilán Cabecigris = gray-headed kite

ID: Largish white and black bird-of-prey with gray head; black above, white below; underside of wing in flight is black in front, black with gray bars behind; tail with light and dark bars; dark, hooked bill; grayish legs; to 53 cm (21 in); wingspan to 1.1 m (3.6 ft).

HABITAT: Low elevation wooded areas; found in forest edge areas and along wooded waterways, mangroves

DISTRICTS: COR, ORW, STN, CAYO, TOL, PET

Plate 31b

American Swallow-tailed Kite
Elanoides forficatus
Gavilán Tijereta = scissor hawk
Elanio Tijereta

ID: Largish white and black bird-of-prey with black, deeply forked tail; underside of wing in flight is white in front, black behind; to 60 cm (2 ft); wingspan to 1.3 m (4.4 ft).

HABITAT: Low and middle elevations; often seen soaring over forested areas and near water.

DISTRICTS: COR, ORW, BEL, STN, CAYO, TOL, PET

Plate 31c

Snail Kite
Rostrhamus sociabilis
Gavilán Caracolero = snail-eater hawk

ID: Largish bird-of-prey with black and white barred tail; long, fine, down-curved hook on bill; male black with red skin at base of bill and reddish legs; female dark brown with light face, orange/yellow skin at base of bill, dark eye-stripe, brown streaked chest/belly, orange legs; to 51 cm (20 in); wingspan to 1.2 m (3.8 ft).

HABITAT: Low elevation aquatic sites; found in and along waterways, lakes, marshes.

DISTRICTS: COR, ORW, BEL, STN, CAYO, TOL, PET

Plate 31d

Plumbeous Kite
Ictinia plumbea
Gavilán Plomizo = lead-colored hawk

ID: Mid-sized blackish bird-of-prey with gray head, chest, and belly; reddish brown patch under wing; bottom of tail with black and white bars; red eyes; reddish or yellowish legs; to 37 cm (14 in); wingspan to 94 cm (37 in).

HABITAT: Low and middle elevation forests and forest edges; often found near water.

DISTRICTS: COR, ORW, BEL, STN, CAYO, TOL, PET

Plate 31 295

a Gray-headed Kite

M

c Snail Kite

F

b American Swallow-
tailed Kite

d Plumbeous Kite

Plate 32a

Common Black Hawk
Buteogallus anthracinus
Gavilán Cangrejero = crab hawk

ID: Large, mostly black bird-of-prey with dark, hooked bill, yellow legs; shortish black tail with wide white bar; 56 cm (22 in); wingspan to 1.3 m (4.2 ft).

HABITAT: Low and middle elevation forests, forest edges; found often in trees near water – ocean shores, rivers, streams, marshes, mangroves.

DISTRICTS: COR, ORW, BEL, STN, CAYO, TOL, CAYE, PET

Plate 32b

White Hawk
Leucopternis albicollis
Gavilán Blanco = white hawk
Aguililla Blanca = little white eagle

ID: Large white bird-of-prey with black on wings and black bar on tail; yellow legs; underside of wing in flight is white with black edge; to 58 cm (23 in); wingspan to 1.3 m (4.3 ft).

HABITAT: Low and middle elevations; found in forested and forest edge areas.

DISTRICTS: ORW, STN, CAYO, TOL, PET

Plate 32c

Black-collared Hawk
Busarellus nigricollis
Chestnut Hawk (Belize)
Gavilán Pescador = fishing hawk
Gavilán Cuellinegro = black-collared hawk

ID: Large reddish brown bird-of-prey with whitish head; black chest band; tail with black and brown bars; underside of wing in flight is brown with black tip; to 53 cm (21 in); wingspan to 1.3 m (4.3 ft).

HABITAT: Low and middle elevation forests, forest edges; usually found near water – marshes, swamps, lagoons, lakes, rivers, mangroves.

DISTRICTS: COR, ORW, BEL, STN, CAYO, TOL, PET

Plate 32d

Roadside Hawk
Buteo magnirostris
Gavilán de los Caminos = road hawk
Gavilán Chapulinero = grasshopper hawk

ID: Mid-sized brown or brownish gray bird-of-prey with grayish head and chest; gray and brown barred belly; tail with light and dark bars; yellow legs; to 40 cm (16 in); wingspan to 78 cm (31 in).

HABITAT: Low and middle elevations; found in open wooded areas, grasslands, forest edges, agricultural areas, roadsides.

DISTRICTS: COR, ORW, BEL, STN, CAYO, TOL, CAYE, PET

Plate 32 **297**

a Common Black Hawk

b White Hawk

c Black-collared Hawk

d Roadside Hawk

Plate 33a

Pale-vented Pigeon
Columba cayennensis
Paloma Vientre-claro = light-bellied pigeon
Paloma Piquinegra = black-billed pigeon
ID: Large purplish pigeon with gray head and brownish wings; back of neck iridescent green; whitish chin and belly; red eyes; black bill; to 33 cm (13 in).

HABITAT: Low elevation open wooded sites, forest edges, savannahs, tree plantations; found in trees, shrubs.

DISTRICTS: COR, ORW, BEL, STN, CAYO, TOL, PET

Plate 33b

Scaled Pigeon
Columba speciosa
Paloma Escamosa = scaly pigeon
ID: Large reddish brown pigeon with bold dark (purple, green, or blackish) scaling on neck, back, and chest; belly light with light scaling; red bill with light tip; red eye-ring; female duller; to 33 cm (13 in).

HABITAT: Low and middle elevation forests and more open areas such as forest edges, clearings; found in trees.

DISTRICTS: COR, ORW, BEL, STN, CAYO, TOL, PET

Plate 33c

Red-billed Pigeon
Columba flavirostris
Paloma Piquirroja = red-billed pigeon
Paloma Morada = purple pigeon
ID: Large, dark reddish purplish pigeon with brown back; gray belly and tail; whitish and red bill; reddish legs; to 33 cm (13 in).

HABITAT: Low and middle elevations; found in open wooded areas, forest edge, clearings, grassland, agricultural areas.

DISTRICTS: COR, ORW, BEL, STN, CAYO, TOL, PET

Plate 33d

Short-billed Pigeon
Columba nigrirostris
Paloma Piquicorta = short-billed pigeon
ID: Mid-sized purplish brown or ruddy brown pigeon with short, black bill; reddish legs; 27 cm (11 in).

HABITAT: Low and middle elevation forests; found in trees or on ground in more open areas such as forest edges and clearings.

DISTRICTS: COR, ORW, BEL, STN, CAYO, TOL, PET

Plate 33 299

a Pale-vented Pigeon

c Red-billed Pigeon

b Scaled Pigeon

d Short-billed Pigeon

Plate 34a

Blue Ground-dove
Claravis pretiosa
Turtle Dove (Belize)
Tórtola Azul = blue turtle dove
Tortolita Celeste = little blue turtle dove
ID: Smallish dove with yellowish bill; male bluish gray with lighter face, chest, and belly; dark spots and bars on wings; sides of tail black; female brownish with reddish brown bars on wings; to 20 cm (8 in).

HABITAT: Low and middle elevation forest edges, open woodlands, pastures, fields; found usually on the ground.

DISTRICTS: COR, ORW, BEL, STN, CAYO, TOL, PET

Plate 34b

Ruddy Ground-dove
Columbina talpacoti
Turtle Dove (Belize)
Tórtola Rojiza = reddish turtle dove
ID: Smallish dove with yellow or brown bill; male reddish brown with gray head; black spots on wings; female duller, less reddish; 17 cm (7 in).

HABITAT: Low and middle elevations; found usually on ground in open areas – pastures, fields, woodland clearings.

DISTRICTS: COR, ORW, BEL, STN, CAYO, TOL, PET

Plate 34c

Common Ground-dove
Columbina passerina
Turtle Dove (Belize)
Tórtola Común = common turtle dove
ID: Small dove with reddish or yellowish bill with dark tip; male gray with black "scaling" on neck and chest, black spots on wings, reddish tinge on underparts; female brownish with less scaling; black spots on wings; 16 cm (6.5 in).

HABITAT: Coastal cayes and occasionally on mainland coast; found usually on ground in open and semi-open areas.

DISTRICTS: CAYE

Plate 34d

White-tipped Dove
Leptotila verreauxi
Paloma Rabiblanca = white-tailed dove
ID: Mid-sized dove with gray or grayish brown head; brown back and wings; lighter-colored face; pinkish or violet tinge to head and chest; tail dark with white edging at end; reddish skin around eye; black bill; male with iridescent sheen on neck; to 28 cm (11 in).

HABITAT: Low and middle elevation forests; found usually on ground in open areas such as agricultural sites, gardens, open woodlands, forest edges.

DISTRICTS: COR, ORW, BEL, STN, CAYO, PET

Plate 34e

White-winged Dove
Zenaida asiatica
Paloma Aliblanca = white-winged dove
ID: Mid-sized brownish dove with black spot on side of face below blue-ringed eye; grayish belly; white bar on wing, seen mostly in flight; sides of tail tipped with white; male with iridescent sheen on neck; to 28 cm (11 in).

HABITAT: Low elevation forests and coastal areas, including cayes; found on ground or in trees/shrubs in more open areas, such as pastures, open woodlands, forest edges.

DISTRICTS: COR, ORW, BEL, STN, CAYO, CAYE

Plate 34 301

M

b Ruddy Ground-dove

F

a Blue Ground-dove

c Common Ground-dove

d White-tipped Dove

e White-winged Dove

Plate 35 (*See also*: Parrots, p. 138)

Plate 35a

Scarlet Macaw
Ara macao
Guacamaya Roja = red macaw
ID: Very large, long-tailed red parrot; big patches of yellow on wings and blue on wings and tail; to 91 cm (3 ft).

HABITAT: Lowland wet forests; usually found high in tree canopy in wooded and forest edge areas, often near water.

DISTRICTS: TOL, PET

Note: This species is endangered, CITES Appendix I listed.

Plate 35b

Mealy Parrot
Amazona farinosa
Loro Grande de Cabeza Azul = big blue-headed parrot
ID: Large green parrot with blue tinge on top of head; touches of red and blue on wings, seen mostly in flight; end of tail lighter green or yellowish; whitish eye-ring; to 40 cm (16 in).

HABITAT: Low elevation forests; found in tree canopy in wooded areas, forest edges, tree plantations.

DISTRICTS: COR, ORW, BEL, STN, CAYO, TOL, PET

Plate 35c

Red-lored Parrot
Amazona autumnalis
Loro Frentirrojo = red-forehead parrot
Loro Cariamarillo = yellow-faced parrot
ID: Mid-sized green parrot with red forehead and blue tinge on head feathers; often some yellow on face; red and blue patches on wings, seen mostly in flight; to 34 cm (13 in).

HABITAT: Low and middle elevation forests; found in tree canopy in wooded and semi-open areas, forest edges, tree plantations.

DISTRICTS: COR, ORW, BEL, STN, CAYO, TOL, PET

Plate 35d

Yellow-lored Parrot (also called Yucatán Parrot)
Amazona xantholora
Loro Yucateco = Yucatán parrot
ID: Mid-sized green parrot; male with white forehead, small yellow patch behind bill, red eye-ring, red and blue patches on wings seen mostly in flight; female bluish on top of head, small yellow patch behind bill, inconspicuous red and green eye-ring, only blue patches on wings; to 28 cm (11 in).

HABITAT: Low elevation forests and forest edges; seen in trees and flying low over forest.

DISTRICTS: COR, ORW, BEL

Plate 35   303

c Red-lored Parrot

a Scarlet Macaw

b Mealy Parrot

F

M

d Yellow-lored Parrot

Plate 36a

White-fronted Parrot
Amazona albifrons
Loro Frentiblanco = white-fronted parrot

ID: Mid-sized green parrot with red on face, including around eyes; white forehead; blue at top of head; red and blue patches on wings, seen mostly in flight; to 28 cm (11 in).

HABITAT: Low and middle elevation forests, forest edges, and other semi-open sites, and mangroves; seen in tree canopy and flying low over forest.

DISTRICTS: COR, ORW, BEL, STN, CAYO, TOL, PET

Plate 36b

White-crowned Parrot
Pionus senilis
Loro Coroniblanco = white-crowned parrot
Perico Cabeza Blanca = white-headed parakeet

ID: A smallish, dark green parrot with white forehead and white throat; blue or greenish blue head and upper breast; brownish or bronze shoulder patches; blue under wings and red under tail, seen in flight; to 25 cm (10 in).

HABITAT: Low and middle elevation forests, forest edges, and other semi-open sites; seen in tree canopy and flying low over forests.

DISTRICTS: COR, ORW, BEL, STN, CAYO, TOL, PET

Plate 36c

Brown-hooded Parrot
Pionopsitta haematotis
Loro Cabecipardo = brown-headed parrot

ID: A small green parrot with brownish head, neck, and chest; dark face; red spot on side of head; red and blue patches on wings, seen in flight; to 22 cm (8.5 in).

HABITAT: Lowland wet forests; found in tree canopy in wooded areas and forest edges.

DISTRICTS: COR, ORW, BEL, STN, CAYO, TOL, PET

Plate 36d

Olive-throated Parakeet (also called Aztec Parakeet)
Aratinga nana
Keetie (Belize)
Perico Pechisucio = dirty-chested parakeet
Perico Grande = big parakeet

ID: Small green parrot with olive or brownish chest/belly; blue patches on wings; yellow underneath tail; white eye-ring; to 23 cm (9 in).

HABITAT: Low and middle elevation forests, forest edges, tree plantations, and other semi-open sites; seen in tree canopy and flying low over forests.

DISTRICTS: COR, ORW, BEL, STN, CAYO, TOL, PET

Plate 36   305

a White-fronted Parrot

c Brown-hooded Parrot

d Olive-throated Parakeet

b White-crowned Parrot

Plate 37a

Striped Cuckoo
Tapera naevia
Cuclillo Listado = striped cuckoo
ID: Mid-sized brown bird with short bushy crest; black-striped brown back; whitish to light brownish chest; smallish down-curved bill; to 30 cm (12 in).

HABITAT: Low elevation wet forests, especially in more open sites such as forest edges, tree plantations, scrub areas; found in trees and on the ground, often near water.

DISTRICTS: COR, ORW, STN, CAYO, TOL, PET

Plate 37b

Squirrel Cuckoo
Piaya cayana
Pequam (Belize)
Cuco Ardilla = squirrel cuckoo
Piscoy
ID: Large reddish-brown bird with grayish belly; long tail with alternating bars of black and white on its underside; to 48 cm (19 in).

HABITAT: Low and middle elevation forests, and more open sites such as forest edges, tree plantations.

DISTRICTS: COR, ORW, BEL, STN, CAYO, TOL, PET

Plate 37c

Groove-billed Ani
Crotophaga sulcirostris
Cowboy (Belize)
Garrapatero = tick-eater
Pijuy
ID: A mid-sized all black bird with relatively huge, humped bill with conspicuous ridges; iridescent sheen on head, breast; long tail; to 33 cm (13 in).

HABITAT: Low and middle elevations; found in small flocks in more open habitats such as scrub and open wooded areas, fields, pastures, and other agricultural sites.

DISTRICTS: COR, ORW, BEL, STN, CAYO, TOL, CAYE, PET

Plate 37d

Smooth-billed Ani
Crotophaga ani
Cowboy (Belize)
ID: A mid-sized dull black bird with relatively huge, humped bill and long tail; iridescent sheen on head, neck, breast; to 35 cm (14 in).

HABITAT: Occurs on several cayes off the Belize coast in open habitats.

DISTRICTS: CAYE

Plate 37 **307**

a Striped Cuckoo

b Squirrel Cuckoo

c Groove-billed Ani

d Smooth-billed Ani

Plate 38a

Ferruginous Pygmy-owl
Glaucidium brasilianum
Lechucita Listada = little striped screech owl
Tecolotito Listado = little striped owl

ID: A small grayish brown or reddish brown owl with white streaks on chest, belly; fine white streaks on head; brown or black tail with paler bars; black spot on side of neck; to 18 cm (7 in).

HABITAT: Low and middle elevations; found in wooded areas, as well as in semi-open sites such as forest edges, grassland areas with trees, and agricultural areas with trees; day-active.

DISTRICTS: COR, ORW, BEL, STN, CAYO, TOL, PET

Plate 38b

Mottled Owl
Ciccaba virgata
Búho Café (or Lechuza Café) = brown owl
Búho Tropical = tropical owl

ID: Mid-sized brownish or grayish owl with lighter bars/streaks; whitish eyebrows; whitish or buffy/yellowish throat and chest with darker mottling; streaked belly; to 38 cm (15 in).

HABITAT: Low and middle elevation forests and semi-open sites such as forest edges, tree plantations; nocturnal.

DISTRICTS: COR, ORW, BEL, STN, CAYO, TOL, PET

Plate 38c

Pauraque
Nyctidromus albicollis
Tapacaminos Pucuyo = road-blocker pucuyo
Pucuyo

ID: Mid-sized brown bird with fine brown mottling and black spots or streaks; whitish band on throat; light brown chest/belly with fine black bars; longish tail with white sides; white or light-colored band on wings, seen in flight; to 28 cm (11 in).

HABITAT: Low and middle elevation sites; found resting on the ground during the day in shady spots in grasslands, pastures, open woodlands, forest edges; nocturnal.

DISTRICTS: COR, ORW, BEL, STN, CAYO, TOL, CAYE, PET

Plate 38d

Lesser Nighthawk
Chordeiles acutipennis
Tapacaminos Menor = lesser road-blocker

ID: Mid-sized gray-brown bird with light and dark brown and black markings; horizontal whitish bar on throat; light brown chest/belly with fine black bars; white or light-colored band on wings, seen in flight; male has white band on tail; to 23 cm (9 in).

HABITAT: Low elevation forests and more open sites, often near water; forest edges, mangroves, beaches; found on the ground or on low tree branches; nocturnal.

DISTRICTS: COR, ORW, BEL, STN, CAYO, TOL, CAYE, PET

Plate 38 309

a Ferruginous Pygmy-owl

b Mottled Owl

c Pauraque

d Lesser Nighthawk

Plate 39a

White-collared Swift
Streptoprocne zonaris
Vencejo Collarejo = collared swift
Vencejo = swift

ID: Mid-sized black bird (for a swift, fairly large) with white ring encircling neck; squarish or slightly notched tail; long, slender, swept-back wings; to 21 cm (8.5 in).

HABITAT: Low and middle elevations; seen flying above all types of habitats; flies continuously.

DISTRICTS: COR, ORW, BEL, STN, CAYO, TOL, PET

Plate 39b

Vaux's Swift
Chaetura vauxi
Vencejo Alirrápido = fast-winged swift
Vencejo Común = common swift

ID: Small, mostly blackish swift with slightly lighter chest and gray throat; very short tail; relatively short wings; to 11 cm (4.5 in).

HABITAT: Low and middle elevations; seen flying above all types of habitats; flies continuously.

DISTRICTS: COR, ORW, BEL, STN, CAYO, TOL, PET

Plate 39c

Gray-breasted Martin
Progne chalybea
Golodrina Urbana = urban swallow
Golodrina Gris = gray swallow
Martín Pechigrís = gray-breasted martin

ID: Small, glossy dark blue and blackish bird with brownish gray throat, chest; whitish belly; forked tail; female duller with less blue; to 18 cm (7 in).

HABITAT: Low and middle elevation forests and more open areas such as forest edges, clearings, bridges, human settlements; seen flying or perched on wires, bridges, other structures.

DISTRICTS: COR, ORW, BEL, STN, CAYO, TOL, PET

Plate 39d

Barn Swallow
Hirundo rustica
Golondrina Tijereta = scissor swallow

ID: Small, slender, dark blue bird with narrow, swept-back wings and deeply forked tail; reddish brown forehead, throat, and chest; light brown or tawny belly; thin dark band across chest; to 17 cm (6.5 in).

HABITAT: Low and middle elevations, particularly along coasts; often seen flying low over open areas – fields, pastures, lawns, waterways.

DISTRICTS: COR, ORW, BEL, STN, CAYO, TOL, CAYE, PET

Note: This species is a nonbreeding seasonal migrant.

Plate 39 **311**

c Gray-breasted Martin

a White-collared Swift

b Vaux's Swift

d Barn Swallow

Plate 40a

Northern Rough-winged Swallow
Stelgidopteryx serripennis
Golodrina Alirrasposa Norteña = northern rough-winged swallow
ID: Small brownish bird with darker wings and tail; light brown throat, chest; whitish belly; slightly notched tail; to 13 cm (5 in).

HABITAT: Low and middle elevation open areas, especially near waterways, roads.

DISTRICTS: COR, ORW, BEL, STN, CAYO, TOL, CAYE, PET

Plate 40b

Mangrove Swallow
Tachycineta albilinea
Golondrina Manglera = mangrove swallow
ID: Small glossy dark green bird with dark wings and short, dark, notched tail; narrow white line over eye; white chest, belly, and rump; to 12 cm (4.5 in).

HABITAT: Low elevations; seen flying over aquatic sites – rivers, large streams, ponds, lakes, lagoons, marshes, wet pastures.

DISTRICTS: COR, ORW, BEL, STN, CAYO, TOL, CAYE, PET

Plate 40c

Long-tailed Hermit
Phaethornis superciliosus
Ermitaño Colilargo = long-tailed hermit
Ermitaño Común = common hermit
Chupaflor de Cola Larga = long-tailed hummingbird
ID: Fairly large brownish or greenish brown hummingbird with long, white-tipped tail and very long, down-curved bill; black and light-colored eye-stripes; light brown to gray-brown chest/belly; to 16 cm (6.5 in).

HABITAT: Low elevation forests; found around flowers in the forest interior and at forest edges, particularly near waterways.

DISTRICTS: COR, ORW, BEL, STN, CAYO, TOL, PET

Plate 40d

Little Hermit
Phaethornis longuemareus
Ermitaño Enano = dwarf hermit
Chupaflor Ocrillo = ochre hummingbird
ID: Small brownish or greenish brown hummingbird with down-curved bill; black and light facial stripes; cinnamon chest/belly; tail brownish with light tip; 9 cm (3.5 in).

HABITAT: Low and middle elevation forests; found near flowers in the forest interior and forest edge areas, particularly near watercourses; also in gardens.

DISTRICTS: COR, ORW, BEL, STN, CAYO, TOL, PET

Plate 40　313

a Northern Rough-winged Swallow

c Long-tailed Hermit

d Little Hermit

b Mangrove Swallow

Plate 41a

Wedge-tailed Sabrewing
Campylopterus curvipennis
Chupaflor Gritón = shouting
hummingbird

ID: Largish green hummingbird with long, slightly down-curved bill; violet forehead; grayish face, chest, belly; long greenish tail with dark edges; female with white tail tips; to 13 cm (5 in).

HABITAT: Low elevation forests and forest edges; found near flowers.

DISTRICTS: COR, ORW, STN, CAYO, TOL, PET

Plate 41b

Violet Sabrewing
Campylopterus hemileucurus
Ala de Sable Violáceo = violet
sabrewing
Chupaflor Morado = purple
hummingbird

ID: A large hummingbird with down-curved bill and white patches at end of tail; male with blue violet head/chest/belly, dark green back, dark wings; female with blue violet throat, gray chest/belly; to 15 cm (6 in).

HABITAT: Low and middle elevation wet forests; found near flowers in forest interior and more open sites at forest edges, tree plantations.

DISTRICTS: STN, CAYO, TOL

Plate 41c

White-necked Jacobin
Florisuga mellivora
Chupaflor Coliblanco = white-necked
hummingbird
Jacobino Nuquiblanco = white-necked
jacobin

ID: Mid-sized bluish green hummingbird with fairly short, straight bill; male with bluish head and chest, white back-of-neck and belly, white tail; female lacks blue head and white neck but has light green scalloped chest, green tail with some white feather tips; to 12 cm (4.5 in).

HABITAT: Low and middle elevation forests; found usually in more open areas such as forest edges, plantations.

DISTRICTS: ORW, BEL, STN, CAYO, TOL, PET

Plate 41d

Green-breasted Mango
Anthracothorax prevostii
Mango Pechiverde = green-chested
mango
Chupaflor Pechiverde = green-chested
hummingbird

ID: Mid-sized green hummingbird with down-curved bill; male with black throat, bluish center of chest; reddish/purplish tail; female with white throat/chest with dark/greenish central stripe, green and blackish tail with white tip; to 12 cm (4.5 in).

HABITAT: Low and middle elevations; found in semi-open sites such as forest edges, clearings, savannahs, plantations.

DISTRICTS: COR, ORW, BEL, STN, CAYO, TOL, CAYE, PET

Plate 41e

Fork-tailed Emerald
Chlorostilbon canivetti
Chupaflor Esmeralda = emerald
hummingbird
Chupaflor Tijereta = scissors
hummingbird

ID: Small green hummingbird with straight bill; male with dark, deeply forked tail; female with white stripe behind eye, pale grayish chest/belly, dark, slightly forked tail with some white feather tips; to 9 cm (3.5 in).

HABITAT: Low elevation semi-open sites such as open brushy woodlands, forest edges, clearings.

DISTRICTS: COR, ORW, BEL, STN, CAYO, TOL, CAYE, PET

Plate 41 315

d Green-breasted Mango

a Wedge-tailed Sabrewing

b Violet Sabrewing

F

M

c White-necked Jacobin

e Fork-tailed Emerald

Plate 42a

White-bellied Emerald
Amazilia candida
Esmeralda Vientre-blanca = white-bellied emerald
Chupaflor Cándido = candid hummingbird
ID: Small green hummingbird with straight reddish bill with dark tip; white chest/belly; greenish or brownish tail with some gray feather tips; to 9 cm (3.5 in).
HABITAT: Low elevation forests and forest edges.

DISTRICTS: COR, ORW, STN, CAYO, TOL, PET

Plate 42b

Azure-crowned Hummingbird
Amazilia cyanocephala
Chupaflor Cabeciazul = blue-headed hummingbird
ID: Mid-sized green hummingbird with straight reddish bill with dark tip; blue/turquoise head top; white chest/belly; brownish green lower back and tail; to 12 cm (4.5 in).
HABITAT: Low and middle elevation forests and semi-open areas such as forest edges, savannahs.

DISTRICTS: BEL, STN, CAYO, PET

Plate 42c

Cinnamon Hummingbird
Amazilia rutila
Chupaflor Canelo = cinnamon hummingbird
Chupaflor Rojizo = reddish hummingbird
ID: Mid-sized green hummingbird with cinnamon chest/belly, straight bill, and reddish brown tail; to 10 cm (4 in).
HABITAT: Low elevation coastal areas; found near flowers in mangrove forests and more open sites – forest edges, brushy areas.

DISTRICTS: COR, BEL, STN, CAYE

Plate 42d

Rufous-tailed Hummingbird
Amazilia tzacatl
Chupaflor Colirrufo = rufous-tailed hummingbird
ID: Mid-sized green hummingbird with grayish belly and reddish brown squared or slightly notched tail; straight red and black bill; to 10 cm (4 in).
HABITAT: Low and middle elevations; found near flowers in forest interior and more open sites – forest edges, scrub areas, gardens, plantations.

DISTRICTS: COR, ORW, BEL, STN, CAYO, TOL, PET

Plate 42e

Purple-crowned Fairy
Heliothrix barroti
Chupaflor Enmascarado = masked hummingbird
Chupaflor de Pecho Blanco = white-chested hummingbird
ID: Largish green hummingbird with straight bill, white chest/belly, long white-edged tail; male with violet forehead and black eyestripe ending with small violet patch; female lacks violet; to 13 cm (5 in).
HABITAT: Lowland wet forests and forest edges.

DISTRICTS: STN, CAYO, TOL, PET

Plate 42 317

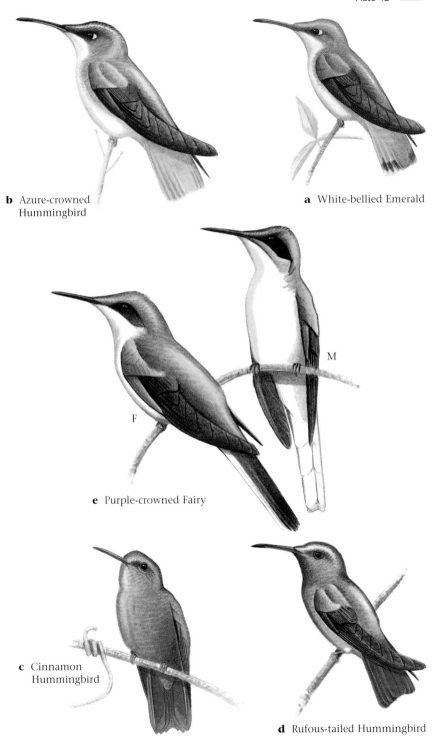

b Azure-crowned
Hummingbird

a White-bellied Emerald

e Purple-crowned Fairy

F

M

c Cinnamon
Hummingbird

d Rufous-tailed Hummingbird

Plate 43a

Resplendent Quetzal
Pharomachrus mocinno
Feníx del Bosque = forest phoenix
Quetzal

ID: Male is unmistakable: a large bright green bird with red belly, green crest on head, white underneath tail, yellow bill, and a few extremely long tail feathers (streamers); female, lacking streamers, is duller green with brown-gray chest, red belly, white and black barred tail; to 38 cm (15 in), plus long tail streamers.

HABITAT: High elevation wet forests; found in tree canopy in forest interior and forest edge areas.

DISTRICTS: Southern Guatemala highlands

Note: This species is endangered, CITES Appendix I and USA ESA listed.

Plate 43b

Slaty-tailed Trogon
Trogon massena
Ramatutu (Belize)
Trogón Colioscuro = dark-tailed trogon
Trogón Gigante = giant trogon
Aurora Grande = big aurora

ID: Male is largish green bird with red belly, red/orange eye-ring and bill, and gray-black under tail; female is mostly gray with red belly and two-toned bill: black above, reddish below; to 35 cm (14 in).

HABITAT: Low elevation wet forests; found in tree canopy in forest interior and semi-open sites such as forest edges, tree plantations.

DISTRICTS: ORW, STN, CAYO, TOL, PET

Plate 43c

Violaceous Trogon
Trogon violaceus
Ramatutu (Belize)
Trogón Violáceo = violaceous trogon
Trogón Pechiamarillo Colibarrado = yellow-chested bar-tailed trogon
Aurora de Pecho Violeta = violet-chested aurora

ID: Mid-sized bird with yellow belly, dark bill, black and white barred tail; male with black and dark blue/violet head and chest, greenish back, yellow eye-ring; female with gray head, back, and chest, white eye-ring; to 24 cm (9.5 in).

HABITAT: Low elevation forests; found in tree canopy in forest interior and in more open areas such as clearings, forest edges, mangroves, tree plantations, near streams and rivers.

DISTRICTS: COR, ORW, BEL, STN, CAYO, TOL, PET

Plate 43d

Collared Trogon
Trogon collaris
Ramatutu (Belize)
Trogón Collarejo = collared trogon
Aurora de Cola Rayada = striped-tailed aurora

ID: Mid-sized bird with red belly, narrow white chest band, dark wings, black and white barred tail, yellowish bill; male with green head, blackish face and throat; female with brownish head, white eye-ring; to 28 cm (11 in).

HABITAT: Low and middle elevation forests; found in tree canopy.

DISTRICTS: COR, ORW, STN, CAYO, TOL, PET

Plate 43e

Black-headed Trogon
Trogon melanocephalus
Ramatutu (Belize)
Trogón Cabecinegro = black-headed trogon
Aurora de Pecho Gris = gray-chested aurora

ID: Mid-sized bird with yellow belly, black/gray head and chest, pale bluish eye-ring, dark bill, and large white patches on black tail; male with greenish back and blue rump; female with grayish back; to 27 cm (10.5 in).

HABITAT: Low and middle elevation semi-open sites; found in tree canopy in forest edges, tree plantations, mangroves.

DISTRICTS: COR, ORW, BEL, STN, CAYO, TOL, PET

Plate 43   319

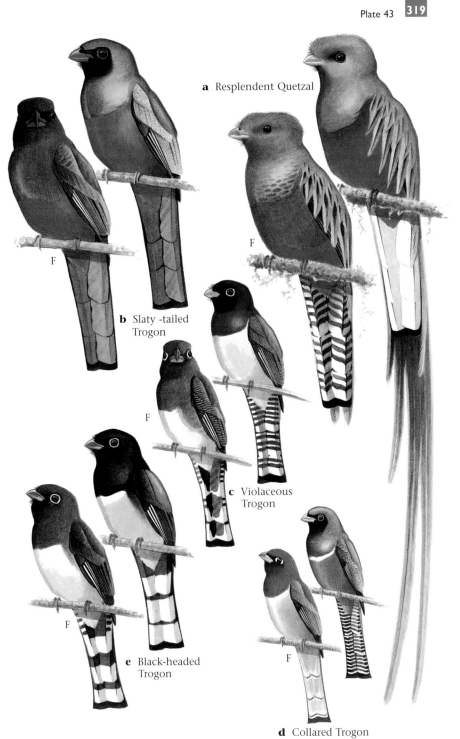

a Resplendent Quetzal

F

F

b Slaty-tailed Trogon

c Violaceous Trogon

e Black-headed Trogon

F

d Collared Trogon

Plate 44a

Rufous-tailed Jacamar
Galbula ruficauda
Jacamar Rabirrufo = rufous-tailed jacamar
Pico Largo = long bill

ID: Slender, bright green bird with long tail and long, straight, stiletto bill; reddish brown belly and underside of tail; wide green bar across chest; male with white throat, female with light brown/tan throat; to 23 cm (9 in).

HABITAT: Low elevation sites; found in more open wooded areas such as tree plantations, forest edges, along rivers and streams.

DISTRICTS: COR, ORW, STN, CAYO, TOL, PET

Plate 44b

White-necked Puffbird
Bucco macrorhynchos
Pájaro Collarejo = necklace bird

ID: Mid-sized, heavy-looking black and white bird with biggish head and thick, black bill; white forehead, throat, and belly; black bar across chest; black on top of head; black wings and tail; to 25 cm (10 in).

HABITAT: Low elevation forests; found in tree canopy in more open sites such as forest edges, clearings, along waterways.

DISTRICTS: COR, ORW, BEL, STN, CAYO, TOL, PET

Plate 44c

White-whiskered Puffbird
Malacoptila panamensis
Pájaro Barbón = bearded bird

ID: Smallish, puffy-looking brown bird with streaked chest/belly; whitish throat; fine light brown spots/streaks on head; largish bill, dark above, lighter below; female similar to male, but darker brown; to 19 cm (7.5 in).

HABITAT: Low and middle elevation wet forests; found in forest interior and along forest edges, tree plantations.

DISTRICTS: STN, CAYO, TOL, PET

Plate 44 321

F   M

a Rufous-tailed Jacamar

b White-necked Puffbird

M

F

c White-whiskered Puffbird

Plate 45a

Ringed Kingfisher
Ceryle torquata
Martín Pescador Collarejo = necklace
martin fisher
Martín Pescador Grande = big martin
fisher
ID: Large blue-gray bird with ragged head crest,
brownish belly, white neck-band and throat, and
large, heavy bill; female with bluish bar across
chest; to 40 cm (16 in).

HABITAT: Low elevation aquatic sites; found
along streams, rivers, lakes, ponds, lagoons,
estuaries, mangroves.

DISTRICTS: COR, ORW, BEL, STN, CAYO, TOL, PET

Plate 45b

Belted Kingfisher
Ceryle alcyon
Martín Pescador Norteño = northern
martin fisher
Pescador Norteño = northern fisher
ID: Largish blue-gray bird with ragged head crest,
white belly, white neck-band and throat, bluish
bar across chest, and large, heavy bill; female has
reddish brown bar across belly; to 33 cm (13 in).

HABITAT: Low elevation aquatic sites; found
along shoreline, streams, rivers, lakes, ponds,
lagoons.

DISTRICTS: COR, ORW, BEL, STN, CAYO, TOL,
CAYE, PET
Note: This species is a nonbreeding seasonal
migrant.

Plate 45c

Amazon Kingfisher
Chloroceryle amazona
Martín Pescador Amazónico = Amazon
martin fisher
Martín Pescador Mediano = medium
martin fisher
ID: Mid-sized green and white bird with long,
heavy bill; conspicuous green head crest; white
belly, white neck-band and throat; male has wide
reddish brown bar across chest; to 28 cm (11 in).

HABITAT: Low elevation aquatic sites; found
along rivers, larger streams, lakes, mangroves.

DISTRICTS: COR, ORW, BEL, STN, CAYO, TOL, PET

Plate 45d

Green Kingfisher
Chloroceryle americana
Martín Pescador Verde = green martin
fisher
Martín Pescador Menor = smaller
martin fisher
ID: Smallish green and white bird with long,
heavy bill; white belly, white neck-band and
throat; male with wide reddish brown bar across
chest; female with greenish bands across chest;
smaller than Amazon Kingfisher, with less
conspicuous head crest; to 20 cm (8 in).

HABITAT: Low and middle elevation aquatic
sites; found along shoreline, rivers, larger
streams, lakes, ponds, lagoons.

DISTRICTS: COR, ORW, BEL, STN, CAYO, TOL, PET

Plate 45e

American Pygmy Kingfisher
Chloroceryle aene
Martín Pescador Enano = dwarf martin
fisher
Martincito Pescador = little martin
fisher
ID: Small green and reddish brown bird with long,
heavy bill; reddish brown neck-band, throat, and
chest; white lower belly; female with dark
greenish bar across chest; to 13 cm (5 in).

HABITAT: Low and middle elevation aquatic sites;
found along small forest streams, ponds, pools,
swamps.

DISTRICTS: COR, ORW, BEL, STN, CAYO, TOL, PET

Plate 45 **323**

a Ringed Kingfisher

F

b Belted Kingfisher

F

c Amazon Kingfisher

F

d Green Kingfisher

F

e American Pygmy Kingfisher

F

F

Plate 46a

Tody Motmot
Hylomanes momotula
Momoto Enano (or Tolobojo Enano) =
dwarf motmot

ID: Small green bird with darker green wings and tail; reddish brown head top; small turquoise spot above eye; black stripe behind eye; whitish stripes on throat; light green chest; whitish belly; to 18 cm (7 in).

HABITAT: Low and middle elevation forests; found in tree canopy.

DISTRICTS: COR, ORW, STN, CAYO, TOL, PET

Plate 46b

Blue-crowned Motmot
Momotus momota
Good Cook (Belize)
Momoto Mayor = large motmot
Tolobojo

ID: Large green bird with red eyes and long tail; black facial mask with blue edging; longish down-curved bill; blue on head; bluish green throat; greenish to greenish brown chest and belly; small dark spot on chest; tail usually with "tennis racket" ends; to 41 cm (16 in).

HABITAT: Low and middle elevation forests; found in forest interior and in more open areas such as forest edges, tree plantations, gardens, and along watercourses.

DISTRICTS: COR, ORW, BEL, STN, CAYO, TOL, PET

Plate 46c

Keel-billed Motmot
Electron carinatum
Momoto Piquiancho (or Tolobojo Pico
Ancho) = broad-billed motmot

ID: Mid-sized greenish bird with turquoise stripe above eye; black eye mask; reddish brown forehead; turquoise chin; lighter green chest/belly; small black spot on chest; tail usually with "tennis racket" ends; to 32 cm (12.5 in).

HABITAT: Low elevation wet forests; found in tree canopy.

DISTRICTS: STN, CAYO, TOL, PET

Plate 46d

Black-cheeked Woodpecker
Melanerpes pucherani
Carpintero Carinegro = black-faced
woodpecker
Carpintero Selvático = jungle
woodpecker

ID: Smallish black and white barred bird with light grayish or olive chest; reddish belly; yellow forehead; red at back of neck and top of head, black eye mask with white patch behind eye; longish, straight bill; female only has gray head top with black patch; to 19 cm (7.5 in).

HABITAT: Low and middle elevation wet forests; found in tree canopy in open, wooded sites such as forest edges, clearings, tree plantations.

DISTRICTS: ORW, STN, CAYO, TOL, PET

Plate 46 **325**

c Keel-billed
Motmot

a Tody
Motmot

b Blue-crowned
Motmot

F

M

d Black-cheeked
Woodpecker

Plate 47a

Golden-fronted Woodpecker
Melanerpes aurifrons
Carpenter (Belize)
Carpintero Frentidorado = golden-fronted woodpecker
Cheje Común = common cheje

ID: Mid-sized black and white finely barred bird with grayish face, throat, chest; some red on belly; small red patch on forehead; male with red on head top and back of neck; female with red on back of neck; to 25 cm (10 in).

HABITAT: Low and middle elevation semi-open sites such as forest edges, tree plantations, shady gardens.

DISTRICTS: COR, ORW, BEL, STN, CAYO, TOL, CAYE, PET

Plate 47b

Smoky-brown Woodpecker
Veniliornis fumigatus
Carpintero Café = brown woodpecker
Carpintero Atabacado = tobacco-colored woodpecker

ID: Small brownish bird with darker wings and tail; dark gray throat; black bill; male with some red on head top; female with dark brown head top; to 15 cm (6 in).

HABITAT: Low elevation forests and more open sites such as forest edges, tree plantations.

DISTRICTS: COR, ORW, BEL, STN, CAYO, TOL, PET

Plate 47c

Golden-olive Woodpecker
Piculus rubiginosus
Carpintero Verde = green woodpecker

ID: Mid-sized olive-green bird with finely barred yellow and olive chest; gray head top; yellowish/buffy facial area; male with red back of neck and facial stripe; female lacks red facial stripe; to 22 cm (8.5 in).

HABITAT: Low and middle elevation forests and more open sites such as forest edges, tree plantations.

DISTRICTS: COR, ORW, BEL, STN, CAYO, TOL, PET

Plate 47d

Lineated Woodpecker
Dryocopus lineatus
Father Red-cap (Belize)
Carpintero Lineado = lineated woodpecker

ID: Large black bird with red crest on head; whitish stripe runs from edge of bill down along neck; two whitish stripes on back; light-colored, barred lower chest/belly; male has small red stripe on side of throat; female has black forehead; to 34 cm (13.5 in).

HABITAT: Low and middle elevation forests; found in tree canopy in open, wooded sites such as forest edges and clearings.

DISTRICTS: COR, ORW, BEL, STN, CAYO, TOL, PET

Plate 47e

Pale-billed Woodpecker
Campephilus guatemalensis
Father Red-cap (Belize)
Carpintera Grande Cabecirroja = large red-headed woodpecker

ID: Large black bird with red head and crest; two whitish stripes on back form V; light-colored, barred lower chest/belly; female has black at front of crest; to 37 cm (14.5 in).

HABITAT: Low and middle elevation forests; found in tree canopy in open, wooded sites such as forest edges and clearings, tree plantations, along rivers and streams.

DISTRICTS: COR, ORW, STN, CAYO, TOL, PET

Plate 47 327

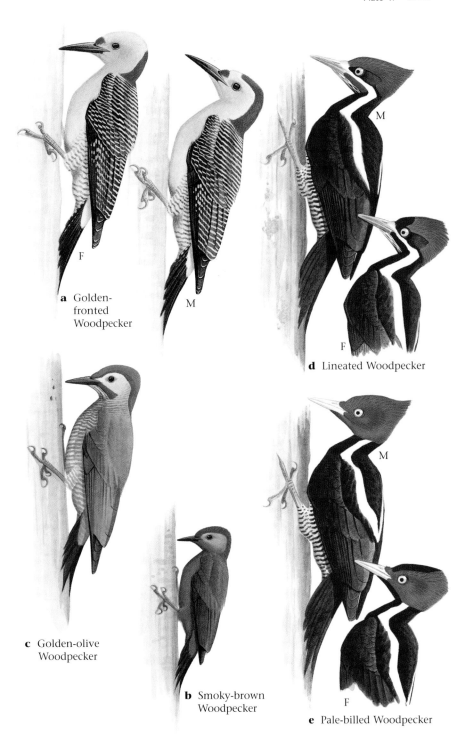

a Golden-fronted Woodpecker

d Lineated Woodpecker

c Golden-olive Woodpecker

b Smoky-brown Woodpecker

e Pale-billed Woodpecker

Plate 48a

Acorn Woodpecker
Melanerpes formicivorus
Carpintero Careto = masked woodpecker

ID: Mid-sized black and white bird with longish black bill; red on head top; white forehead; white eye-ring on black facial area; black chin; whitish throat; female with less red on top of head; to 23 cm (9 in).

HABITAT: Low and middle elevation oak and pine-oak forests and savannahs.

DISTRICTS: ORW, BEL, STN, CAYO, PET

Plate 48b

Collared Aracari
Pteroglossus torquatus
Tucancillo Collarejo = little necklace toucan
Cucharón

ID: Large black bird with huge bill light above, dark below; yellow lower chest/belly with red markings and central black spot; red skin around eye; to 41 cm (16 in).

HABITAT: Low elevation forests; found in tree canopy in more open habitats such as forest edges, tree plantations, along rivers and streams.

DISTRICTS: COR, ORW, BEL, STN, CAYO, TOL, PET

Plate 48c

Keel-billed Toucan
Ramphastos sulfuratus
Bill Bird (Belize)
Tucán Piquiverde = green-billed toucan
Pito Real

ID: A large, mostly black bird with yellow face and chest, yellowish green skin around eye, and that amazing, rainbow-colored (green-orange-blue) toucan's bill; to 56 cm (22 in).

HABITAT: Low and middle elevation forests; found in tree canopy in more open habitats such as forest edges, tree plantations, along rivers and streams.

DISTRICTS: COR, ORW, BEL, STN, CAYO, TOL, PET

Plate 48d

Emerald Toucanet
Aulacorhynchus prasinus
Tucancillo Verde = little green toucan
Pico de Nabaja = razor blade bill

ID: Large green bird with blue throat; tail green above, brown below; large bill yellow above, black below; to 35 cm (14 in).

HABITAT: Low and middle elevation wet forests; found in tree canopy in forest interior, forest edges, clearings, tree plantations.

DISTRICTS: ORW, BEL, STN, CAYO, TOL, PET

Plate 48

a Acorn Woodpecker

b Collared Aracari

c Keel-billed Toucan

d Emerald Toucanet

Plate 49a

Tawny-winged Woodcreeper
Dendrocincla anabatina
Trepapalo Alifajeado = striped-winged tree-climber
Trepador Coliliso = smooth-tailed woodcreeper

ID: Small brown bird with buffy/tan throat; reddish brown wings and tail; light stripe above eye; straight gray bill; to 19 cm (7.5 in).

HABITAT: Low and middle elevation forests; found climbing up tree trunks in forest interior.

DISTRICTS: COR, ORW, BEL, STN, CAYO, TOL, PET

Plate 49b

Wedge-billed Woodcreeper
Glyphorhynchus spirurus
Trepadorcito Pico de Cuña = wedge-billed woodcreeper
Trepador Piquicorto = short-billed woodcreeper

ID: Small brown bird with shortish, wedge-shaped black bill; light stripe above eye; other light streaks and spots on head; tan/buffy throat; light streaks/spots on brown chest; 15 cm (6 in).

HABITAT: Low elevation wet forests; found climbing up tree trunks in forest interior and in more open sites such as forest edges, tree plantations.

DISTRICTS: ORW, STN, CAYO, TOL, PET

Plate 49c

Olivaceous Woodcreeper
Sittasomus griseicapillus
Trepadorcito Aceitunado = olivaceous woodcreeper

ID: Small reddish brown bird with gray head and chest; dark, slender, straight bill; to 15 cm (6 in).

HABITAT: Low and middle elevation forests; found climbing up tree trunks in forest interior and in more open sites such as forest edges, tree plantations.

DISTRICTS: COR, ORW, BEL, STN, CAYO, TOL, PET

Plate 49d

Ivory-billed Woodcreeper
Xiphorhynchus flavigaster
Trepador Dorsirrayado Mayor = larger lined-back woodcreeper
Trepador Goteado = dripped woodcreeper
Trepador Pico Ebúrnea

ID: Mid-sized brownish bird with bold buffy streaks on head, back, chest; reddish brown wings, tail; tan/buffy throat; long pale bill; to 25 cm (10 in).

HABITAT: Low elevation forests; found climbing up tree trunks in forest interior and in more open sites such as forest edges, tree plantations, mangroves.

DISTRICTS: COR, ORW, BEL, STN, CAYO, TOL, PET

Plate 49 **331**

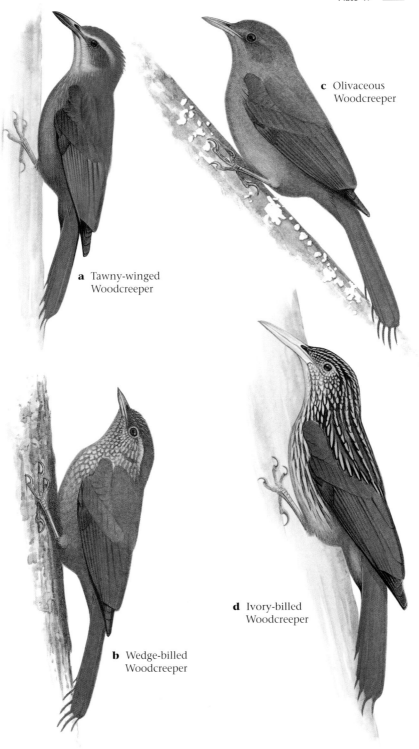

c Olivaceous
Woodcreeper

a Tawny-winged
Woodcreeper

b Wedge-billed
Woodcreeper

d Ivory-billed
Woodcreeper

Plate 50a

Barred Antshrike
Thamnophilus doliatus
Batará Barrada = barred batará
Pájaro Hormiguero Rayado = striped
anteater bird

ID: Male is a small white-and-black barred bird with a mostly black head crest; female is reddish brown with black streaks on face, buffy throat, and light brown chest/belly; 17 cm (6.5 in).

HABITAT: Low and middle elevation forests; found usually on the ground in open areas such as thickets but also in the forest interior.

DISTRICTS: COR, ORW, BEL, STN, CAYO, TOL, PET

Plate 50b

Plain Antvireo
Dyssithamnus mentalis
Matagusano = worm-killer
Pájaro Hormiguero = anteater bird
Buruiara Pequeña

ID: Small bird with dark, heavy, slightly hooked bill; male is olive/grayish with dark gray head, light gray throat/chest, yellowish belly, white wing bars; female is olive/brownish with reddish brown head, light gray throat, whitish eye-ring; to 11 cm (4.5 in).

HABITAT: Low and middle elevation wet forest; found low in trees.

DISTRICTS: STN, CAYO, TOL, PET

Plate 50c

Black-faced Antthrush
Formicarius analis
Hormiguero Gallito = little rooster
anteater

ID: Mid-sized dark or olive-brown bird with black cheeks and throat; grayish chest and belly; small amount of pale bluish skin around eye; long legs, short tail; to 18 cm (7 in).

HABITAT: Low and middle elevation forests; found in forest interior or edge, on or near the ground.

DISTRICTS: COR, ORW, BEL, STN, CAYO, TOL, PET

Plate 50d

Dot-winged Antwren
Microrhopias quixensis
Hormiguerito Alipunteado = little dot-
winged anteater
Motorralero

ID: Small black bird with white spots and bar on wing, white tail tips; male is almost all black; female more grayish with reddish brown chest and belly; 11 cm (4.5 in).

HABITAT: Low elevation wet forests; found foraging on or near the ground in forest interior and more open sites such as forest edges, tree plantations, thickets.

DISTRICTS: COR, ORW, BEL, STN, CAYO, TOL, PET

Plate 50e

Dusky Antbird
Cercomacra tyrannina
Hormiguero Marañero = thicket
anteater
Pájaro Hormiguero = anteater bird

ID: Small bird with dark, slender bill and longish tail; male is blackish/gray with white wing bars; female is brownish/olive with reddish brown or tawny chest/belly and inconspicuous light eye-ring; to 14 cm (5.5 in).

HABITAT: Low and middle elevation forests and forest edges; found low in trees and in thickets.

DISTRICTS: COR, ORW, BEL, STN, CAYO, TOL, PET

Plate 50 **333**

a Barred Antshrike

b Plain Antvireo

d Dotted-winged Antwren

e Dusky Antbird

c Black-faced Antthrush

Plate 51a

White-collared Manakin
Manacus candei
Saltarín Cuelliblanco = white-necked jumper

ID: Female is a small olive-green bird with yellowish belly, orange legs, and small dark bill; male is black on wings and top of head; black band across back; white throat, chest, and upper back; olive-green rump; yellow belly; orange legs; small black bill; to 11 cm (4.5 in).

HABITAT: Low elevation wet forests; found in trees and thickets in more open wooded habitats – forest edges, tree plantations, along watercourses.

DISTRICTS: COR, ORW, BEL, STN, CAYO, TOL, PET

Plate 51b

Red-capped Manakin
Pipra mentalis
Saltarín Cabecirrojo = red-headed jumper
Pipra Cabecirroja = red-headed pipra
Sargento = sergeant

ID: Female is small olive-green bird with lighter belly, brownish legs and small brownish bill; male is black with red head and yellow thighs; 10 cm (4 in).

HABITAT: Low elevation wet forests; found in trees in forest interior and in more open sites such as forest edges, clearings.

DISTRICTS: COR, ORW, BEL, STN, CAYO, TOL, PET

Plate 51c

Rufous Piha
Lipaugus unirufus
Piha Rufa = rufous piha
Guardabosque Rufo = rufous forest-ranger

ID: Mid-sized reddish brown bird with dark, fairly thick bill, slightly paler throat, and grayish legs; to 25 cm (10 in).

HABITAT: Low elevation wet forests; found in tree canopy and lower, usually in more open sites such as forest edges and clearings.

DISTRICTS: ORW, BEL, STN, CAYO, TOL, PET

Plate 51d

Lovely Cotinga
Cotinga amabilis
Cotinga Linda = lovely cotinga

ID: Mid-sized bird with smallish dark bill; male is bright blue with purple throat and chest, blue band across chest, blackish wings and tail edges; female is gray-brown with scaled pattern; whitish chest/belly with brownish spots; brown wings and tail; to 19 cm (7.5 in).

HABITAT: Low elevation forests and semi-open sites such as forest edges, shady clearings; found in tree canopy.

DISTRICTS: ORW, BEL, STN, CAYO, TOL, PET

Plate 51e

Masked Tityra
Tityra semifasciata
Titira Enmascarada = masked tityra
Torrejo

ID: Mid-sized gray bird with black-tipped red bill, red skin around eye, broad black wing bar and tail; male with black on chin, forehead, and behind eye; white chest/belly; female is gray-brown with whitish throat and gray chest/belly; to 23 cm (9 in).

HABITAT: Low elevation forests; found in tree canopy, usually in more open sites such as forest edges, clearings, tree plantations, along waterways.

DISTRICTS: COR, ORW, BEL, STN, CAYO, TOL, CAYE, PET

Plate 51 335

a White-collared Manakin

M

F

b Red-capped Manakin

M

F

c Rufous Piha

M

d Lovely Cotinga

F

e Masked Tityra

F

M

Plate 52a

Tropical Kingbird
Tyrannus melancholicus
Tirano Tropical = tropical tyrant
Chatilla Tropical

ID: Mid-sized olive-colored bird with gray head; whitish throat; dark wings and dark notched tail; dark bar through eye; yellow belly; reddish patch on top of head usually concealed; to 23 cm (9 in).

HABITAT: Low and middle elevation sites; found in trees in open wooded areas such as forest edges and tree plantations, and also in more open areas such as grasslands, pastures and other agricultural sites, beach areas, and near human settlements.

DISTRICTS: COR, ORW, BEL, STN, CAYO, TOL, PET

Plate 52b

Great Kiskadee
Pitangus sulphuratus
Luis Bienteveo Grande = big Luis good-to-see
Mosquero Grande = big fly-eater
Kiscadí

ID: Mid-sized olive brown bird with reddish-brown wings and bright yellow chest/belly; black and white head; yellow patch on top of head usually concealed; white throat; to 25 cm (10 in).

HABITAT: Low and middle elevations; found in trees in more open sites such as grasslands, pastures, forest edges, gardens, and along waterways.

DISTRICTS: COR, ORW, BEL, STN, CAYO, TOL, CAYE, PET

Plate 52c

Boat-billed Flycatcher
Megarhynchus pitangua
Mosquerón Picudo = sharp-billed fly-eater

ID: Mid-sized olive or olive brown bird with bright yellow chest/belly; black and white head; yellow or orange patch on top of head usually concealed; white throat; distinguished from Great Kiskadee by wing color and larger bill; to 24 cm (9.5 in).

HABITAT: Low and middle elevations; found in tree canopy in wooded areas and more open sites such as forest edges, tree plantations, gardens, and along waterways.

DISTRICTS: COR, ORW, BEL, STN, CAYO, TOL, PET

Plate 52d

Social Flycatcher
Myiozetetes similis
Mosquero Coronicolorado = red-crowned fly-eater

ID: Smallish olive or olive brown bird with dark gray/blackish and white head; dark eye mask; reddish patch on top of head usually concealed; white throat; bright yellow chest/belly; very small black bill; to 18 cm (7 in).

HABITAT: Low and middle elevation sites; found in trees in more open areas such as grasslands, pastures and agricultural sites, forest edges, along rivers and lakes, gardens.

DISTRICTS: COR, ORW, BEL, STN, CAYO, TOL, CAYE, PET

Plate 52 337

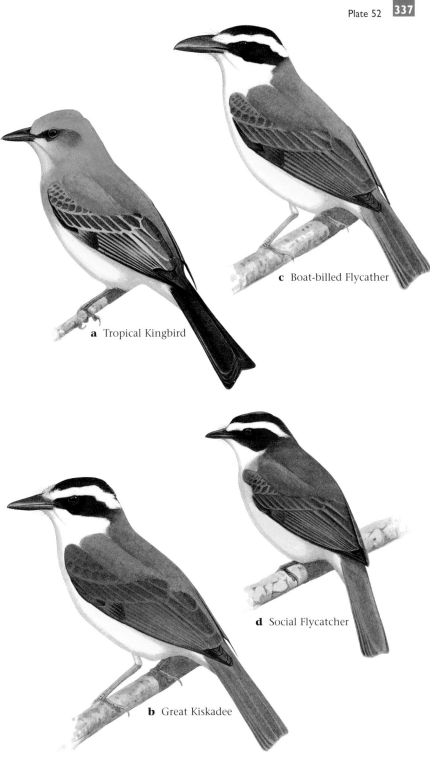

a Tropical Kingbird

c Boat-billed Flycather

d Social Flycatcher

b Great Kiskadee

Plate 53a

Yellow-bellied Elaenia
Elaenia flavogaster
Elainia Vientriamarillo = yellow-bellied elaenia

ID: Small greenish-olive or brownish-olive bird with bushy crest; darker wings, tail; light wing bars; grayish throat, chest; yellowish belly; to 15 cm (6 in).

HABITAT: Low and middle elevation semi-open areas such as forest edges, tree plantations, shady gardens; found in bushes and trees.

DISTRICTS: COR, ORW, BEL, STN, CAYO, TOL, CAYE, PET

Plate 53b

Ochre-bellied Flycatcher
Mionectes oleagineus
Mosquero Vientre-ocre = ochre-bellied fly-eater
Mosquero Ocrillo = ochre fly-eater

ID: Small olive-greenish bird with slightly darker wings and tail; orangy-yellow belly; 13 cm (5 in).

HABITAT: Low and middle elevation forests; found in forest interior and in semi-open sites such as forest edges, clearings, tree plantations.

DISTRICTS: COR, ORW, BEL, STN, CAYO, TOL, PET

Plate 53c

Common Tody Flycatcher
Todirostrum cinereum
Titirijí Común

ID: Very small bird with black head, greenish gray back, black and yellow wings, black tail with white tip, yellow chest/belly, pale yellow eyes; 10 cm (4 in).

HABITAT: Low elevation forest edges, tree plantations, mangroves, shady gardens; found in trees and bushes.

DISTRICTS: COR, ORW, BEL, STN, CAYO, TOL, CAYE, PET

Plate 53d

Yellow-olive Flycatcher
Tolmomyias sulphurescens
Piquichato sulfuroso = yellow flatbill
Mosquero Pico Plano = flat-billed fly-eater

ID: Small greenish olive bird with gray head, light gray throat, yellowish olive chest, and yellow belly; broad, flat bill; pale eye with light eye-ring; bill black above, light below; to 13 cm (5 in).

HABITAT: Low elevation forests and more open sites such as forest edges, tree plantations, clearings; found in tree canopy.

DISTRICTS: COR, ORW, BEL, STN, CAYO, TOL, PET

Plate 53   339

a Yellow-bellied Elaenia

c Common Tody Flycatcher

d Yellow-olive Flycatcher

b Ochre-bellied Flycatcher

Plate 54a

Royal Flycatcher
Onychorhynchus coronatus
Mosquero Real = royal fly-eater
Mosquero Resplendor = resplendent
fly-eater

ID: Small, slender brownish bird with long reddish-brown tail, whitish throat, and buffy-brown chest/belly; light spots on wings; long, flat bill is dark above, light below; large red (male) or orangish (female) crest usually concealed; to 17 cm (6.5 in).

HABITAT: Low and middle elevation forests, often near rivers and streams; found low in trees.

DISTRICTS: COR, ORW, BEL, STN, CAYO, TOL, PET

Plate 54b

Vermilion Flycatcher
Pyrocephalus rubinus
Mosquero Colorado = red fly-eater
Cardenalito = little cardinal

ID: Male is small red bird with blackish brown back, wings, tail, and eye-mask; female is grayish to grayish brown with light throat and chest with darker streaks; pinkish belly; pale eye-stripe; to 14 cm (5.5 in).

HABITAT: Low elevation semi-open and open sites such as agricultural areas, shady gardens, human settlements with scattered trees.

DISTRICTS: COR, ORW, BEL, STN, CAYO, PET

Plate 54c

Brown-crested Flycatcher
Myiarchus tyrannulus
Mosquero Copetón = big-crested
fly-eater

ID: Mid-sized grayish olive or grayish brown bird with bushy head crest, gray throat and chest, yellowish belly; to 21 cm (8.5 in).

HABITAT: Low and middle elevations; found in more open habitats such as forest edges, along waterways, open plantations and gardens.

DISTRICTS: COR, ORW, BEL, STN, CAYO, TOL, PET

Plate 54d

Dusky-capped Flycatcher
Myiarchus tuberculifer
Copetón Crestioscuro = dusky-capped
big crest
Mosquero Común = common fly-eater

ID: Smallish olive or brownish olive bird with very dark/blackish head, gray throat/chest, yellow belly; wings and tail brown or grayish brown; to 18 cm (7 in).

HABITAT: Low and middle elevation forests; prefers more open parts of forests – edges, clearings, tree plantations, along waterways.

DISTRICTS: COR, ORW, BEL, STN, CAYO, TOL, PET

Plate 54e

Fork-tailed Flycatcher
Tyrannus savana
Mosquero Tijereta = little scissor fly-eater

ID: Smallish gray-backed bird with black head, blackish or dark brown wings, white chest/belly, and very long, black tail; to 18 cm (7 in) plus long outer tail feathers (longer in male).

HABITAT: Low and middle elevation semi-open and open sites with scattered trees and bushes such as savannahs, grasslands.

DISTRICTS: ORW, BEL, STN, CAYO, PET

Plate 54 **341**

b Vermilion Flycatcher

M

F

c Brown-crested Flycatcher

e Fork-tailed Flycatcher

d Dusky-capped Flycatcher

a Royal Flycatcher

M

F

Plate 55a

Banded-backed Wren
Campylorhynchus zonatus
Chinchivirín Dorsilistado = striped-
backed chinchivirín
Carrasquita = little rattle
ID: Small black-and-whitish-barred bird (fairly
large, however, for a wren) with white
throat/chest with dark spots; light brown belly;
light stripe above eye; thin bill grayish above,
brownish below; to 19 cm (7.5 in).

HABITAT: Low and middle elevation wet forests;
prefers more open sites such as forest edges,
clearings, tree plantations, along waterways,
vegetation around human settlements.

DISTRICTS: STN, CAYO, TOL, PET

Plate 55b

Spot-breasted Wren
Thryothorus maculipectus
Katy-yu-baby-di-cry (Belize)
Chinchivirín Pinto = spotted
chinchivirín
Troglodita Pechimanchado = spot-
breasted wren
ID: Small brown bird with whitish chest/belly with
black spots; brown tail with black bars; light and
dark striped face; 13 cm (5 in).

HABITAT: Low and middle elevation forests and
semi-open areas such as forest edges, tree
plantations.

DISTRICTS: COR, ORW, BEL, STN, CAYO, TOL, PET

Plate 55c

White-breasted Wood-wren
Henicorhina leucosticta
Chinchivirín Pechiblanco = white-
breasted chinchivirín
Chinchivirín Cantor = singing
chinchivirín
ID: Small brown bird with streaked black, dark
brown, and white head, white throat/chest,
tawny/light brown belly, black-barred wings, and
short, black-barred tail; 10 cm (4 in).

HABITAT: Low and middle elevation forests; found
low in trees in forest interior and more open areas
such as forest edges, tree plantations.

DISTRICTS: COR, ORW, BEL, STN, CAYO, TOL, PET

Plate 55d

House Wren
Troglodytes aedon
Cucarachero Común = common
cockroach-eater
ID: A small brown bird with black-barred wings
and tail; lighter brown chest/belly; pale stripe
above eye; 11 cm (4.5 in).

HABITAT: Low elevations; found mostly around
houses and other structures, and open habitats
such as pastures and low scrub.

DISTRICTS: COR, ORW, BEL, STN, CAYO, TOL, PET

Plate 55 343

a Banded-backed Wren

b Spot-breasted Wren

c White-breasted Wood-wren

d House Wren

Plate 56a

Wood Thrush
Hylocichla mustelina
Zorzal Maculado = spotted thrush
Tordo Pinto = spotted thrush
ID: Mid-sized brown bird with reddish brown head; chest/belly white with black spots; white eye-ring; white and dark streaks on side of head; bill dark above, light below; to 19 cm (7.5 in).

HABITAT: Low elevation forests and forest edges; found low in trees and on ground.

DISTRICTS: COR, ORW, BEL, STN, CAYO, TOL, CAYE, PET

Note: This species is a nonbreeding seasonal migrant.

Plate 56b

Clay-colored Robin
Turdus grayi
Cusco (Belize)
Zorzal Pardo = brown thrush
ID: Mid-sized brownish bird with lighter brown/tawny chest and belly, dark-streaked throat, yellowish bill, flesh-colored legs; to 25 cm (10 in).

HABITAT: Low and middle elevations; inhabits open and semi-open areas such as forest edges, tree plantations, pastures, agricultural sites, gardens, lawns.

DISTRICTS: COR, ORW, BEL, STN, CAYO, TOL, PET

Plate 56c

Tropical Mockingbird
Mimus gilvus
Mímido Tropical = tropical mimic
Sinsontle Tropical = tropical mockingbird
ID: Mid-sized gray bird with whitish chest/belly; black wings with white bars, long dark tail with white edges; yellowish eye; to 25 cm (10 in).

HABITAT: Low and middle elevation open and semi-open areas with scattered bushes and trees, especially roadsides, gardens; found on telephone wires, in bushes, trees, and on ground.

DISTRICTS: COR, ORW, BEL, STN, CAYO, CAYE

Plate 56d

Black Catbird
Melanoptila glabrirostris
Siwa-ban (Belize)
Mímido Negro = black mimic
Pájaro-gato Negro = black catbird
ID: Mid-sized glossy black bird with dark reddish eyes; slender black bill; black legs; to 20 cm (8 in).

HABITAT: Low elevation semi-open wooded sites such as forest edges, wooded thickets, woodlands adjacent to beaches.

DISTRICTS: COR, BEL, CAYE, PET

Plate 56 345

a Wood Thrush

c Tropical Mockingbird

b Clay-colored Robin

d Black Catbird

Plate 57a

Brown Jay
Cyanocorax morio
Urraca Chillona = screaming magpie
Chara Papán = foolish jay
Pea
ID: Large dark brown bird with whitish lower chest and belly; tail partially white-tipped; large black bill; to 40 cm (16 in).

HABITAT: Low and middle elevations; found in tree canopy in open wooded sites such as forest edges, tree plantations, near human settlements.

DISTRICTS: COR, ORW, BEL, STN, CAYO, TOL, PET

Plate 57b

Green Jay
Cyanocorax yncas
Chara Verde = green jay
ID: Largish green bird with blue and black head, yellow chest/belly; blue-green tail with yellow edges; yellowish eyes; to 30 cm (12 in).

HABITAT: Low and middle elevation forests and semi-open sites such as forest edges, tree plantations.

DISTRICTS: COR, ORW, BEL, STN, CAYO, TOL, PET

Plate 57c

Yucatán Jay
Cyanocorax yucatanicus
Chara Yucateca = Yucatán jay
Chara de Negro y Azul = black and blue jay
ID: Largish turquoise-blue bird with black head, chest, and belly; yellow legs; youngsters just out of nest are white with blue wings; to 33 cm (13 in).

HABITAT: Low elevation forests and semi-open sites such as forest edges, tree plantations.

DISTRICTS: COR, ORW, BEL, CAYE, PET

Plate 57 347

a Brown Jay

b Green Jay

c Yucatán Jay

Plate 58a

Mangrove Warbler
Dendroica petechia
Chipe Manglera = mangrove chipe
Chipe Amarilla = yellow chipe
Reinita Manglera = little mangrove queen

ID: Small greenish olive bird with yellow chest/belly, light brown legs; male with reddish brown chest streaks and head; female sometimes with reddish brown tinge on head top and few chest streaks; to 13 cm (5 in).

HABITAT: Coastal; found in mangroves, brushy woodlands, scrubby areas.

DISTRICTS: COR, BEL, STN, TOL, CAYE

Plate 58b

Magnolia Warbler
Dendroica magnolia
Chipe Colifaja = band-tail chipe
Chipe Pechirayado = lined-breasted chipe

ID: Small olive-green bird with black streaks on back; gray head; black tail; yellowish chest/belly with dark spots/streaks; white eye-ring; to 11.5 cm (4.5 in).

HABITAT: Low and middle elevation forests and semi-open sites such as forest edges, tree plantations; found in tree canopy.

DISTRICTS: COR, ORW, BEL, STN, CAYO, TOL, PET

Note: This species is a nonbreeding seasonal migrant.

Plate 58c

Grace's Warbler
Dendroica graciae
Chipe de Grace = Grace's chipe

ID: Small bluish gray bird with yellow throat/chest; yellow eye-stripe and small yellow patch under eye; white belly with black streaks on side; 13 cm (5 in).

HABITAT: Middle elevation pine-oak forests.

DISTRICTS: BEL, STN, CAYO

Plate 58d

Rufous-capped Warbler
Basileuterus rufifrons
Chipe Cabecirrufa = rufous-capped chipe

ID: Small greenish olive bird with reddish brown head with white and black eye-stripes; gray neck; yellow chest/belly; 13 cm (5 in).

HABITAT: Low and middle elevations; prefers semi-open sites such as forest edges, thickets, and scrubby areas with scattered trees.

DISTRICTS: STN, CAYO, TOL

Plate 58 349

a Mangrove
Warble

F

M

c Grace´s Warbler

F

b Magnolia
Warbler

M

d Rufous-capped Warbler

Plate 59a

American Redstart
Setophaga ruticilla
Pavito Migratorio = little migratory turkey
Pavito Naranja = little orange turkey
Rey Chipe = king chipe
ID: Male is small black bird with whitish belly; orange on sides of chest, on wing bars, and on sides of tail; female is olive-grayish with whitish throat and eye-ring; yellow on sides of chest, on wingbars, and on sides of tail; to 13 cm (5 in).

HABITAT: Low and middle elevation forests and semi-open sites such as forest edges, light woodlands, scrubby areas with scattered trees.

DISTRICTS: COR, ORW, BEL, STN, CAYO, TOL, CAYE, PET

Note: This species is a nonbreeding seasonal migrant.

Plate 59b

Bananaquit
Coereba flaveola
Reinita Amarilla = little yellow queen
Reinita Común = little common queen
Pajarito Amarillo = little yellow bird
ID: Very small olive grayish bird with white eye-stripe, gray throat, yellow chest/belly, and short, pointed, down-curved black bill; 10 cm (4 in).

HABITAT: Low and middle elevation forests; found in tree canopy in more open wooded sites such as forest edges, gardens, plantations.

DISTRICTS: COR, ORW, BEL, STN, CAYO, TOL, CAYE, PET

Plate 59c

Blue-gray Gnatcatcher
Polioptila caerulea
Perlita Grisilla = little grayish pearl
ID: Very small bluish gray bird with whitish chest/belly; black tail with white edges; white eye-ring; male often with black stripe above eye; to 10 cm (4 in).

HABITAT: Low and middle elevation forests and semi-open sites such as forest edges, open woodlands, scrubby areas with scattered trees.

DISTRICTS: COR, ORW, BEL, STN, CAYO, TOL, PET

Plate 59d

Eastern Meadowlark
Sturnella magna
Peruchío
ID: Mid-sized chunky brownish bird with lighter and darker streaks; black head stripes; yellow eye-stripe; yellow chest/belly with black chest band; short brown tail with white edges; longish dark bill; female a bit duller than male; to 23 cm (9 in).

HABITAT: Low and middle elevation open sites such as agricultural areas and grasslands.

DISTRICTS: ORW, BEL, STN, CAYO, PET

Plate 59 **351**

a American Redstart

F

M

c Blue-gray
Gnatcatcher

b Bananaqit

d Eastern Meadowlark

Plate 60a

Great-tailed Grackle
Quiscalus mexicanus
Clarinero = clarion-player
Zanate Mayor = large zanate
ID: Male is largish black bird with purple gloss, especially on head and back, long black tail that folds to V-shape, large black bill, yellowish eye; female is brownish with darker wings and lighter eye-stripe, yellowish eye, black bill; male to 43 cm (17 in); female to 33 cm (13 in).

HABITAT: Low and middle elevations; found in almost all open and semi-open habitats such as open woodlands, tree plantations, gardens, grasslands, pastures, roadsides.

DISTRICTS: COR, ORW, BEL, STN, CAYO, TOL, CAYE, PET

Plate 60b

Montezuma's Oropendola
Psarocolius montezuma
Yellowtail (Belize)
Oropéndola Gigante (or Mayor) = giant (or large) oropendola
ID: Large brown bird with black head and chest; yellow-edged tail; large black bill with orange tip; blue patch under eye; to 50 cm (20 in); male larger than female.

HABITAT: Low elevations; found in tree canopy in forest interior and in more open areas such as forest edges, clearings, tree plantations.

DISTRICTS: COR, ORW, STN, CAYO, TOL, PET

Plate 60c

Bronzed Cowbird
Molothrus aeneus
Vaquero Ojirrojo = red-eyed cowboy
ID: Mid-sized blackish bird with greenish, bluish, or bronze gloss, black bill, red eyes; female is duller, browner; male especially has conspicuous area of raised feathers on back of neck; to 20 cm (8 in).

HABITAT: Low and middle elevation open and semi-open sites including open woodlands, agricultural areas, along roads, in town parks, near human settlements.

DISTRICTS: COR, ORW, BEL, STN, CAYO, TOL, CAYE, PET

Plate 60d

Giant Cowbird
Scaphidura oryzivora
Vaquero Grande (or Vaquero Gigante) = big cowboy
ID: Largish all black bird with purple or blue gloss, red eyes, thick, pointed bill; male especially has conspicuous area of raised feathers on back of neck; female is a bit smaller and a bit duller; to 33 cm (13 in).

HABITAT: Low elevation open and semi-open sites including forest edges and agricultural areas.

DISTRICTS: COR, ORW, BEL, STN, CAYO, TOL, PET

Plate 60 353

a Great-tailed Grackle

F

M

b Montezuma's Oropendola

F

c Bronzed Cowbird

M

d Giant Cowbird

Plate 61a

Melodious Blackbird
Dives dives
Tordo Cantor = singing thrush
ID: Mid-sized all black bird with bluish gloss, pointed black bill, black eyes; female is a bit smaller and a bit duller; to 28 cm (11 in).

HABITAT: Low and middle elevation open and semi-open sites with scattered trees such as forest edges, open woodlands, tree plantations.

DISTRICTS: COR, ORW, BEL, STN, CAYO, TOL, PET

Plate 61b

Yellow-billed Cacique
Amblycercus holosericeus
Piquiamarillo = yellow-bill
Cacique Piquiclaro = light-billed cacique
ID: Mid-sized all black bird with pointed yellow bill and yellow eyes; to 24 cm (9.5 in).

HABITAT: Low elevations; found low in thickets with scattered trees and in open wooded areas such as forest edges and trees near water.

DISTRICTS: COR, ORW, BEL, STN, CAYO, TOL, CAYE, PET

Plate 61c

Red-winged Blackbird
Agelaius phoeniceus
Tordo Capitán = captain thrush
Tordo Alirrojo = red-winged thrush
ID: Male is mid-sized all black bird with red shoulder patches that can be covered; female is smaller, streaked-brown bird with whitsh/buffy eye-stripe, whitish/buffy chest with dark streaks; to 24 cm (9.5 in).

HABITAT: Low elevation marshes and other open sites such as fields, agricultural areas; often found near water.

DISTRICTS: COR, ORW, BEL, STN, PET

Plate 61d

Baltimore Oriole
Icterus galbula
Bolsero Norteño = northern oriole
Chorcho Amarillo = yellow chorcho
ID: Male is smallish orange bird with black head and wings; black tail edged with orange; female is orangish olive with blackish wings and pale orange chest/belly; 19 cm (7.5 in).

HABITAT: Low and middle elevations; found in tree canopy and shrubs in semi-open sites such as forest edges, tree plantations, gardens.

DISTRICTS: COR, ORW, BEL, STN, CAYO, TOL, CAYE, PET

Note: This species is a nonbreeding seasonal migrant.

Plate 61   355

a Melodious Blackbird

F

M

c Red-winged Blackbird

b Yellow-billed Cacique

F

M

d Baltimore Oriole

Plate 62a

Hooded Oriole
Icterus cucullatus igneus
Bolsero Cuculado = cuculado oriole
ID: Male is smallish orange bird with black back, throat, mid-chest patch, and eye-mask; black wings with white bars; black tail; slender, slightly down-curved blackish bill; female is yellowish olive with darker wings and yellow chest/belly; to 19 cm (7.5 in).

HABITAT: Low elevation open and semi-open sites with scattered trees and bushes such as forest edges, open woodlands, tree plantations.

DISTRICTS: COR, ORW, BEL, CAYE

Plate 62b

Black-cowled Oriole
Icterus dominicensis
Bolsero de Capa Negra = black-capped oriole
Chorcho de Cabeza Negra = black-headed chorcho
ID: Mid-sized yellow bird with black head, chest, wings, and tail; yellow shoulder patches can be almost covered; small, pointed, slightly down-curved blackish bill; female resembles male or has olive-yellow head top and back; to 20 cm (8 in).

HABITAT: Low and middle elevation forests and more open areas such as forest edges, clearings, tree plantations.

DISTRICTS: COR, ORW, BEL, STN, CAYO, TOL, PET

Plate 62c

Yellow-backed Oriole
Icterus chrysater
Bolsero Dorsidorado = golden-backed oriole
Bolsero Dorsigualdo
Chiltote
ID: Mid-sized yellow bird with black throat, center of chest, and facial area around eyes; black wings and tail; smallish, straight, pointed, blackish bill; female a bit darker; to 23 cm (9 in).

HABITAT: Low and middle elevations; found in more open wooded areas such as forest edges, clearings, tree plantations.

DISTRICTS: COR, ORW, BEL, STN, CAYO, CAYE, PET

Plate 62d

Yellow-tailed Oriole
Icterus mesomelas
Bolsero Coliamarillo = yellow-tailed oriole
ID: Mid-sized yellow bird with black throat, center of chest, and facial area below eyes; black wings with yellow shoulder stripe; black tail with yellow edges; very slightly down-curved, pointed, blackish bill; to 23 cm (9 in).

HABITAT: Low elevation forests and forest edges; often found low in brushy areas and thickets.

DISTRICTS: COR, ORW, BEL, STN, CAYO, TOL, PET

Plate 62   357

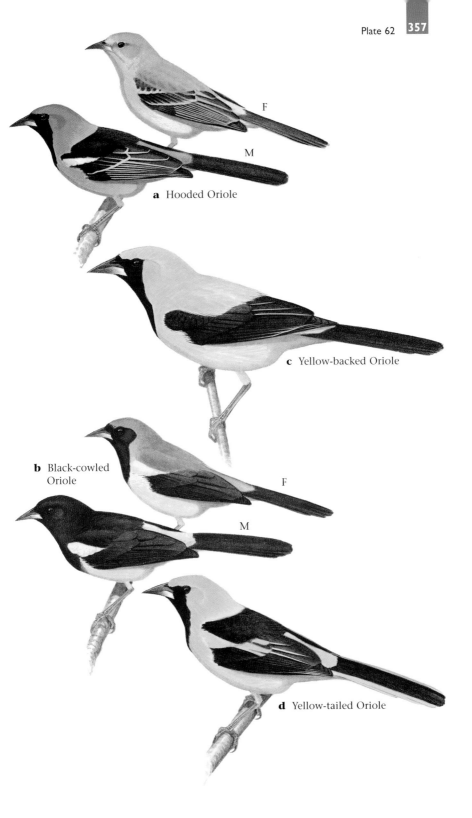

a Hooded Oriole — F, M

c Yellow-backed Oriole

b Black-cowled Oriole — F, M

d Yellow-tailed Oriole

Plate 63a

Golden-hooded Tanager
Tangara larvata
Tángara Careta de Oro = golden-masked tanager
Quintrique Careto
ID: Small black bird with yellowish head; black on chin and around eye; bluish face, shoulders, rump; white belly; female's head greenish yellow often with dark spots; 13 cm (5 in).

HABITAT: Low and middle elevation forests; found in tree canopy in forest interior and semi-open sites such as forest edges, clearings, shady gardens.

DISTRICTS: ORW, STN, CAYO, TOL, PET

Plate 63c

Red-legged Honeycreeper
Cyanerpes cyaneus
Mielero Patirrojo = red-legged honey-eater
ID: Male is small blue bird with black back, wings, tail, and eye-stripe; turquoise head top; red legs; longish, thin, down-curved bill; female is green with light eye-stripe; yellowish green chest/belly; 12 cm (4.75 in).

HABITAT: Low and middle elevation forests; found in tree canopy usually in more open sites such as forest edges, tree plantations, gardens, along waterways.

DISTRICTS: COR, ORW, BEL, STN, CAYO, TOL, PET

Plate 63b

Blue-gray Tanager
Thraupis episcopus
Tángara Azuligris = blue-gray tanager
Pito
ID: Small pale blue-gray bird, darker on back, with darker blue wings and tail; small dark bill; female duller; to 16 cm (6.5 in).

HABITAT: Low elevation open and semi-open sites; found in forest edges, tree plantations, and in trees and shrubs in human settlements, town parks.

DISTRICTS: COR, ORW, BEL, STN, CAYO, TOL, PET

Plate 63d

Green Honeycreeper
Chlorophanes spiza
Mielero Verde = green honey-eater
ID: Male is small green bird with black head, black and yellowish down-curved bill, red eyes; female is paler green with even lighter chest/belly; 14 cm (5.5 in).

HABITAT: Low and middle elevation wet forests; found in tree canopy in forest interior and in more open sites such as trees and shrubs at forest edges, clearings, shady gardens.

DISTRICTS: ORW, STN, CAYO, TOL, PET

Plate 63 359

a Golden-hooded Tanager

F

M

c Red-legged Honeycreeper

F

b Blue-gray Tanager

d Green Honeycreeper

M

F

Plate 64a

Olive-backed Euphonia
Euphonia gouldi
Eufonia Olivácea = olive euphonia
Calandrita Selvática = forest lark
Fruterito Aceitunado = little olive fruit-eater
ID: Very small greenish olive bird; male with brownish belly and yellow forehead; female with yellowish olive belly and reddish brown forehead; 10 cm (4 in).

HABITAT: Low and middle elevations; found in tree canopy in forest interior and more open sites such as forest edges, tree plantations, and along rivers and streams.

DISTRICTS: COR, ORW, STN, CAYO, TOL, PET

Plate 64b

Scrub Euphonia
Euphonia affinis
Eufonia Gorjinegra = black-throated euphonia
Fruterito Gargantinegro = black-throated fruit-eater
ID: Male is very small bluish black bird with black throat, yellow forehead, and yellow chest/belly; female is olive greenish with lighter green-to-yellowish chest/belly, grayish on head top; 10 cm (4 in).

HABITAT: Low and middle elevations; found in tree canopy in semi-open sites such as forest edges, trees along waterways, and in open habitats with scattered trees.

DISTRICTS: COR, ORW, STN, CAYO, TOL, PET

Plate 64c

Yellow-throated Euphonia
Euphonia hirundinacea
Eufonia Gorjiamarilla = yellow-throated euphonia
Calandrita de Garganta Amarilla = yellow-thoated lark
ID: Male is very small bluish black bird with yellow forehead and yellow throat, chest, and belly; female is greenish olive with grayish chest/belly and yellowish sides; 11 cm (4.5 in).

HABITAT: Low and middle elevations; found in tree canopy in forests and semi-open sites such as forest edges, clearings, tree plantations.

DISTRICTS: COR, ORW, BEL, STN, CAYO, TOL, PET

Plate 64d

Gray-headed Tanager
Eucometis penicillata
Tángara Cabecigris = gray-headed tanager
Hormiguero de Cabeza Gris = gray-headed ant-eater
ID: Smallish olive-green bird with gray, slightly ruffled or bushy head and yellow chest/belly; black bill; flesh-colored legs; to 18 cm (7 in).

HABITAT: Low elevation forests; found low in trees, often near ground.

DISTRICTS: COR, ORW, STN, CAYO, TOL, PET

Plate 64

a Olive-backed
Euphonia

F

c Yellow-throated Euphonia

F

b Scrub Euphonia

d Gray-headed Tanager

Plate 65a

Red-crowned Ant-tanager
Habia rubica
Tángara-hormiguera Coronirroja = red-crowned ant-eater tanager
Hormiguero Matorralero = thicket ant-eater

ID: Male is mid-sized dark red bird with reddish gray belly; bright red patch with black borders on head top usually concealed; blackish bill; brownish legs; female is olive-brownish with lighter chest/belly and usually concealed yellowish/tawny patch on head top; to 20 cm (8 in).

HABITAT: Low and middle elevation forests; found in trees and thickets.

DISTRICTS: COR, ORW, STN, CAYO, TOL, PET

Plate 65b

Red-throated Ant-tanager
Habia fuscicauda
Tángara-hormiguera Gorjirroja = red-throated ant-eater tanager
Hormiguero de Garganta Rosada = rose-throated ant-eater

ID: Male is mid-sized dark red bird with bright red throat, paler red belly; bright red patch on head top usually concealed; very dark between eye and black bill; brownish legs; female is dark reddish brown with paler chest/belly and yellowish throat; to 21 cm (8.5 in).

HABITAT: Low and middle elevation forests and more open sites such as forest edges; often found in thickets and low in trees.

DISTRICTS: COR, ORW, BEL, STN, CAYO, TOL, PET

Plate 65c

Hepatic Tanager
Piranga flava figlina
Quitrique de los Altiplanos = high plateau quitrique
Tángara Encinera = oak tanager

ID: Male is mid-sized dark red bird with lighter red chest/belly; dark gray bill, legs; small light patch behind eye; female is olive-greenish with olive-yellowish chest belly; to 20 cm (8 in).

HABITAT: Low and middle elevation pine-oak and pine forests and savannahs.

DISTRICTS: ORW, BEL, STN, CAYO

Plate 65d

Summer Tanager
Piranga rubra
Tángara Roja = red tanager
Quitrique Colorado (or Rojo) = red quitrique

ID: Male is mid-sized bright red bird with slightly darker back and wings; yellowish beige bill; gray legs; female is yellowish olive with yellow chest/belly; to 20 cm (8 in).

HABITAT: Low and middle elevation forests and more open woodlands, tree plantations, forest edges.

DISTRICTS: COR, ORW, BEL, STN, CAYO, TOL, CAYE, PET

Note: This species is a nonbreeding seasonal migrant.

Plate 65   363

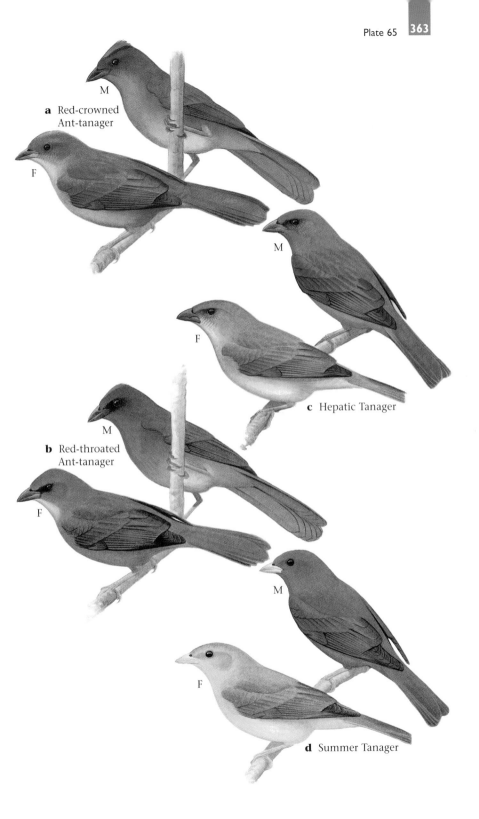

a Red-crowned
Ant-tanager

M

F

M

F

c Hepatic Tanager

b Red-throated
Ant-tanager

M

F

M

F

d Summer Tanager

Plate 66a

Yellow-winged Tanager
Thraupis abbas
Azulejo Buscahigo = bluish fig-searcher
Tángara Aliamarilla = yellow-winged tanager

ID: Smallish bird with bluish/lavender head, grayish olive chest/belly; black wings with yellow patches; black tail; small black bill; to 18 cm (7 in).

HABITAT: Low elevation open wooded sites such as forest edges, tree plantations, gardens.

DISTRICTS: COR, ORW, BEL, STN, CAYO, TOL, PET

Plate 66b

White-winged Tanager
Piranga leucoptera
Tángara Aliblanca = white-winged tanager
Quitrique de Alas Listadas = striped-wing quitrique
Cardenalito = little cardinal

ID: Male is small red bird with black eye-mask, black tail, and black wings with two white bars; female is olive/yellowish with yellow chest/belly, dark tail, and grayish wings with two white bars; to 14 cm (5.5 in).

HABITAT: Low and middle elevation forests and forest edges, clearings, tree plantations; found in tree canopy.

DISTRICTS: ORW, STN, CAYO, TOL, PET

Plate 66c

Crimson-collared Tanager
Ramphocelus sanguinolentus
Tángara Cuellirroja = red-collared tanager
Rojinegro = red-black

ID: Smallish black bird with red neck, chest, and head top, and red at base of tail; pale bluish white or silvery white bill; to 19 cm (7.5 in).

HABITAT: Low and middle elevation forests and forest edges; found in tree canopy.

DISTRICTS: ORW, BEL, STN, CAYO, TOL, PET

Plate 66d

Scarlet-rumped Tanager
Ramphocelus passerinii
Tángara Terciopelo = velvet tanager
Terciopelo = velvet

ID: Male is smallish black bird with red rump and light gray or pale blue bill with dark tip; female is brownish or olive with grayish head, and orangish/tawny rump, chest, and belly; to 18 cm (7 in).

HABITAT: Low elevation thickets and open wooded areas such as forest edges, tree plantations; also found in trees and shrubs in gardens.

DISTRICTS: ORW, BEL, STN, CAYO, TOL, PET

Plate 66 **365**

a Yellow-winged Tanager

c Crimson-collared Tanager

F

M

d Scarlet-rumped Tanager

M

F

b White-winged Tanager

Plate 67a

Buff-throated Saltator
Saltator maximus
Saltador Garganticanelo = cinnamon-
throated saltator

ID: Mid-sized olive-green bird with whitish chin
and tan/buffy throat with black border; grayish
face and belly; white eye-stripe; short, thick, black
bill; 22 cm (8.5 in).

HABITAT: Low elevations; found in forests and
semi-open sites such as forest edges, shady
gardens, tree plantations.

DISTRICTS: COR, ORW, BEL, STN, CAYO, TOL, PET

Plate 67b

Grayish Saltator
Saltator coerulescens grandis
Saltador Gris = gray saltator

ID: Mid-sized olive-gray bird with grayish brown
to light brown chest/belly; whitish throat with black borders; brownish tail;
short, thick, black bill; to 23 cm (9 in).

HABITAT: Low elevations; found in semi-open
and open sites such as forest edges, tree
plantations, parks, gardens.

DISTRICTS: COR, ORW, BEL, STN, CAYO, TOL, PET

Plate 67c

Black-headed Saltator
Saltator atriceps atriceps
Saltador Cabecinegro = black-headed
saltator
Chinchigorrión

ID: Mid-sized olive-green bird with blackish head;
white eye-stripe; white throat with black borders;
gray lower chest and belly; short, thick, black bill;
to 27 cm (10.5 in).

HABITAT: Low and middle elevation forest edges
and more open sites such as thickets, brushy
pastures.

DISTRICTS: COR, ORW, BEL, STN, CAYO, TOL, PET

Plate 67d

Black-faced Grosbeak
Caryothraustes poliogaster
Picogrueso Carinegro = black-faced
grosbeak
Picogrueso Enmascarado = masked
grosbeak
Semillero Aceitunado = olive
seedeater

ID: Smallish olive-green bird with yellowish head
and chest; black face; grayish belly; short, thick,
black bill; to 18 cm (7 in).

HABITAT: Low and middle elevation forests; found
in tree canopy in forest interior and more open
sites such as forest eges, clearings, tree
plantations.

DISTRICTS: COR, ORW, BEL, STN, CAYO, TOL, PET

Plate 67   **367**

a Buff-throated Saltator

b Grayish Saltator

d Black-faced Grosbeak

c Black-headed
Saltator

Plate 68a

Blue-black Grosbeak
Cyanocompsa cyanoides
Picogrueso Negro Azulado = blue-black grosbeak
Picogrueso Negro = black grosbeak
Realejo Negro = black royal

ID: Male is smallish dark blue-black bird with heavy dark bill; female is dark brown with slightly lighter chest/belly; to 18 cm (7 in).

HABITAT: Low and middle elevation forest edges, clearings, agricultural fields adjacent to woodlands.

DISTRICTS: COR, ORW, BEL, STN, CAYO, TOL, PET

Plate 68b

Orange-billed Sparrow
Arremon aurantiirostris
Pico de Oro = golden bill
Saltón Piquidorado = golden-billed hopper

ID: Small olive-green bird with black, white, and gray striped head, white throat, black chest, whitish belly; grayish sides; small orange bill; 16 cm (6.5 in).

HABITAT: Low and middle elevation wet forests; found on ground and low in brush in forest interior and more open sites such as forest edges, thickets.

DISTRICTS: BEL, STN, CAYO, TOL, PET

Plate 68c

Green-backed Sparrow
Arremonops chloronotus
Gorrión Dorsiverde = green-backed sparrow
Talero = whip

ID: Small olive-green bird with black and gray striped head; gray chest; whitish throat, belly; small dark bill; flesh-colored legs; 15 cm (6 in).

HABITAT: Low and middle elevation forests and forest edges; found on or near the ground.

DISTRICTS: COR, ORW, BEL, STN, CAYO, TOL, PET

Plate 68d

Blue-black Grassquit
Volatinia jacarina
Semillero Negro Azulado = blue-black seedeater
Jaulín Negro Azulado = blue-black jaulín

ID: Male is small blue-black bird with smallish black bill and gray legs; outside breeding season male is brown with blue-black wings and tail and has light chest with dark spots; female is brownish with light brown chest/belly with dark streaks; 10 cm (4 in).

HABITAT: Low and middle elevation open and semi-open areas including brushy agricultural fields and pastures, roadsides.

DISTRICTS: COR, ORW, BEL, STN, CAYO, TOL, PET

Plate 68 369

a Blue-black Grosbeak

F

M

c Green-backed Sparrow

b Orange-billed Sparrow

F

M

M

d Blue-black Grassquit

Plate 69a

Variable Seedeater
Sporophila aurita
Jaulín Negro = black jaulín
Semillero Variable = variable seedeater

ID: Male is small black bird with white patch on wings; small black bill; dark gray legs; female is brownish olive with lighter chest/belly and grayish bill; to 11 cm (4.25 in).

HABITAT: Low and middle elevations; found on or near ground in more open habitats, including forest edges, grasslands, pastures, gardens, roadsides.

DISTRICTS: BEL, STN, CAYO, TOL

Plate 69b

White-collared Seedeater
Sporophila torqueola moreletti
Ricey (Belize)
Semillero Collarejo = collared seedeater
Jaulín de Collar = collared jaulín

ID: Male is small black bird with white neck and throat; whitish belly and rump; black wings with white bars; black chest band; small black bill; outside breeding season male is olive-brownish with black wings and tail, light brown chest/belly; female is olive-brownish with brown wings and tail, light brown/buffy chest/belly, and brownish bill; to 11 cm (4.5 in).

HABITAT: Low and middle elevations; found on or near ground in more open habitats, including brushy forest edges, pastures, gardens, roadsides, marshes.

DISTRICTS: COR, ORW, BEL, STN, CAYO, TOL, CAYE, PET

Plate 69c

Rusty Sparrow
Aimophila rufescens pyrgatoides
Sabanero Rojizo = reddish savannah sparrow

ID: Smallish brown bird with black-streaked back; reddish brown on head top; gray neck and facial area; white bar above eye; dark eye-stripe and whitish throat with two black stripes; grayish brown chest/belly; bill black above, gray below; to 19 cm (7.5 in).

HABITAT: Low and middle elevation forest edges, clearings, brushy areas with scattered trees and bushes.

DISTRICTS: CAYO, PET

Plate 69d

Chipping Sparrow
Spizella passerina
Gorrión Cejiblanco = white eye-browed sparrow
Semillero = seedeater

ID: Small brown bird with black streaks; reddish brown head top with black and gray streaks; black eye-stripe below lighter stripe; grayish facial area and chest; whitish throat and belly; brownish wings with light wing bars; bill black (breeding) or lighter-colored; to 14 cm (5.5 in).

HABITAT: Low and middle elevation semi-open woodlands, brushy areas with scattered trees and bushes.

DISTRICTS: STN, CAYO, TOL, CAYE, PET

Plate 69 **371**

a Variable Seedeater

M

F

d Chipping Sparrow

c Rusty Sparrow

F

M

Non-breeding Male

b White-collared Seedeater Seedeater

Plate 70a

Virginia Opossum
Didelphis virginiana
Black-eared Opossum (Belize)
Possum (Belize)
Zorro = fox

ID: A large opossum with yellowish face; blackish or gray back; black ears; whitish cheek area; to 46 cm (18 in), plus long, almost hairless tail. (Common Opossum, *Didelphis marsupialis*, is also fairly common in the region; it closely resembles Virginia Opossum but has yellowish or darker cheeks.)

HABITAT: Regionwide, in trees and on the ground; common near human settlements; nocturnal.

DISTRICTS: COR, ORW, BEL, STN, CAYO, TOL, PET

Plate 70b

Central American Woolly Opossum
Caluromys derbianus

ID: A smaller, very furry opossum, reddish brown with a grayish face; dark stripe from nose to forehead; gray patch on back; light-colored front feet; last half of tail is hairless; to 30 cm (12 in), plus long tail.

HABITAT: Low and middle elevation wet and dry forests, tree plantations; nocturnal; arboreal.

DISTRICTS: COR, ORW, BEL, STN, CAYO, TOL, PET

Plate 70c

Water Opossum
Chironectes minimus
Yapok (Belize)
Water Dog (Belize)

ID: A smaller opossum with webbed toes on rear feet; gray back with broad black/brown bands and a black stripe down its center; head blackish; cheeks and throat whitish; to 30 cm (12 in), plus tail.

HABITAT: Regionwide in both wet and dry forests and cleared areas; found in water or on ground along fast-flowing watercourses; nocturnal.

DISTRICTS: COR, ORW, BEL, STN, CAYO, TOL, PET

Plate 70d

Gray Four-eyed Opossum
Philander opossum

ID: Smaller opossum with gray back and lighter-colored throat, chest, and belly; black face mask; black on top of head; a white mark above each eye; to 33 cm (13 in), plus hairless tail.

HABITAT: Low and middle elevation forests, plantations and other agricultural areas; prefers dense vegetation near water; nocturnal; found in trees and on the ground.

DISTRICTS: COR, ORW, BEL, STN, CAYO, TOL, PET

Plate 70 **373**

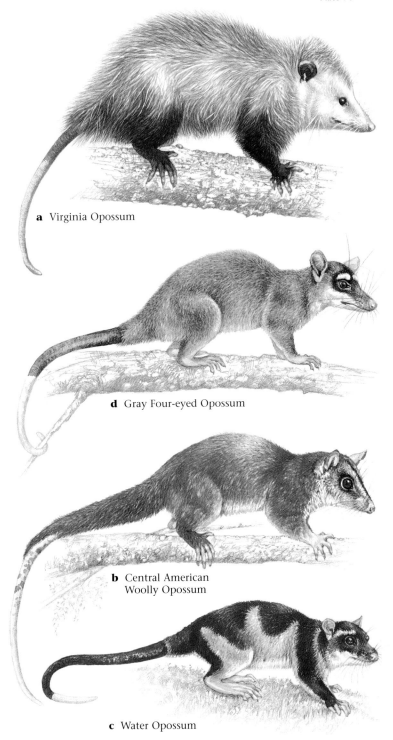

a Virginia Opossum

d Gray Four-eyed Opossum

b Central American
Woolly Opossum

c Water Opossum

Plate 71a

Fishing Bat (also called Greater Bulldog Bat)
Noctilio leporinus
Rat-bats (Belize)
Murciélago Pescador = fishing bat

ID: A large brown or reddish bat; usually one light stripe on back; forward-pointing ears; lips split in the middle, with drooping folds of skin, like a bulldog; no noseleaf; head and body length to 10 cm (4 in), plus tail; wing span to 60 cm (2 ft).

HABITAT: Lowland forests, pastures, plantations, near water; roosts in hollow trees, caves; forages over water for small fish.

DISTRICTS: COR, ORW, BEL, STN, CAYO, TOL, PET

Plate 71b

Woolly False Vampire Bat
Chrotopterus auritus
Rat-bats (Belize)
Murciélago = bat

ID: A large grayish brown bat with long fur, very large ears, largish noseleaf, and white wingtips; head and body length to 11 cm (4 in); little or no tail.

HABITAT: Low and middle elevation wet and dry forests, plantations; roosts in hollow trees, caves.

DISTRICTS: COR, ORW, BEL, STN, CAYO, TOL, PET

Plate 71c

Jamaican Fruit-eating Bat
Artibeus jamaicensis
Rat-bats (Belize)
Murciélago Come Frutas = fruit-eating bat

ID: A large, stout-bodied bat, black, brown, or grayish; large head usually with light stripes on face; short, broad snout with spear-shaped noseleaf; V-shaped row of small bumps on chin; head and body length to 10 cm (4 in); wingspan to 40 cm (16 in).

HABITAT: Low and middle elevation wet and dry forests, gardens, plantations; roosts in caves, hollow trees, under palm leaves; feeds on fruit.

DISTRICTS: COR, ORW, BEL, STN, CAYO, TOL, PET

Plate 71d

Common Vampire Bat
Desmodus rotundus
Rat-bats (Belize)
Vampiro = vampire

ID: A mid-sized, dark brown bat with shiny fur; tips of hair on back often silvery white; short snout with U-shaped, fleshy, skin folds; large, sharp middle incisor and canine teeth; triangular, pointed ears; no tail; head and body length to 9 cm (3.5 in).

HABITAT: Low and middle elevation wet and dry forests, clearings, farm areas; roosts in trees, caves; nocturnal; often flies along riverbeds.

DISTRICTS: COR, ORW, BEL, STN, CAYO, TOL, PET

Plate 71e

Black Mastiff Bat
Molossus ater
Rat-bats (Belize)
Murciélago = bat

ID: Mid-sized black or dark brown bat with black wings, short fur; no noseleaf; low, rounded ears; hairy feet; head and body length to 9 cm (3.5 in), plus longish, naked tail.

HABITAT: Lowland wet and dry forests and around human settlements; roosts in trees, rock crevices, buildings.

DISTRICTS: COR, ORW, BEL, STN, CAYO, TOL, PET

Plate 71 | 375

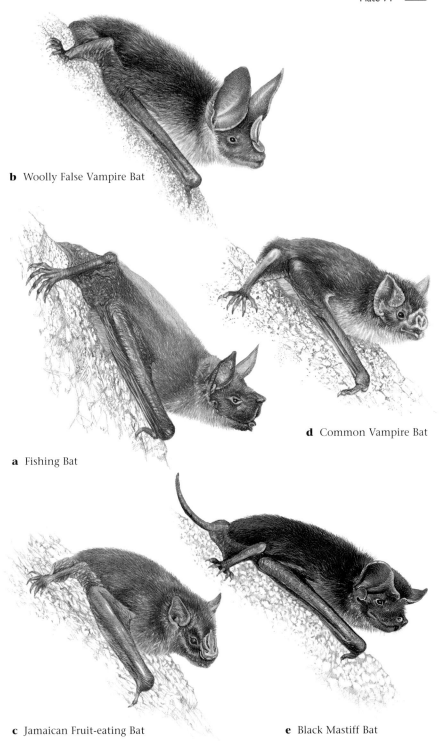

b Woolly False Vampire Bat

a Fishing Bat

d Common Vampire Bat

c Jamaican Fruit-eating Bat

e Black Mastiff Bat

Plate 72a

Greater White-lined Bat (also called White-lined Sac-winged Bat)
Saccopteryx bilineata
Rat-bats (Belize)
Murciélago de Saco = sac bat

ID: Small, dark, brown to black bat with two white lines running along back; grayish belly; head and body length to 5.5 cm (2 in), plus short tail.

HABITAT: Lowland forests, gardens, pastures; roosts in hollow trees, caves, also buildings, under roofs; forages at dusk, often near water.

DISTRICTS: COR, ORW, BEL, STN, CAYO, TOL, PET

Plate 72b

Nectar Bat (also called Common Long-tongued Bat)
Glossophaga soricina
Rat-bats (Belize)
Murciélago = bat

ID: A small brown or gray bat with a long snout; small, spear-shaped noseleaf; short, blunt ears; lower lip with a V-shaped notch lined with small bumps; head and body length to 6.5 cm (2.5 in), plus short tail; wingspan to 28 cm (11 in).

HABITAT: Low and middle elevation wet and dry forests and open areas; roosts in caves, trees, bridges, buildings; forages within forest but also in open areas, dry stream beds, plantations, farms; hovers at flowers to feed on nectar.

DISTRICTS: COR, ORW, BEL, STN, CAYO, TOL, PET

Plate 72c

Short-tailed Fruit Bat (also called Seba's Short-tailed Bat)
Carollia perspicillata
Rat-bats (Belize)
Murciélago = bat

ID: A small brown or gray bat with short, narrow snout with relatively large, spear-shaped noseleaf; small warts on chin; triangular, pointed ears; head and body length to 6.5 cm (2.5 in).

HABITAT: Low and middle elevation forests, gardens, agricultural areas; roosts in trees, caves, riverbanks, buildings; prefers moist areas; feeds at fruit sources, flowers (especially at the piper plant's candle-like flowers).

DISTRICTS: COR, ORW, BEL, STN, CAYO, TOL, PET

Plate 72d

Sucker-footed Bat (also called Disc-winged Bat)
Thyroptera tricolor
Rat-bats (Belize)
Murciélago de Ventosas = sucker-footed bat

ID: A tiny brown bat with white or yellowish belly; short, narrow snout without noseleaf; triangular, pointed ears; fleshy sucker disks near ankles and thumbs for attaching to leaves; head and body length to 4.5 cm (2 in), plus tail.

HABITAT: Low elevation wet forests, gardens, farm areas; nocturnal; roosts in rolled up Heliconia and banana leaves.

DISTRICTS: COR, ORW, BEL, STN, CAYO, TOL, PET

Plate 72e

Hairy-legged Bat
Myotis keaysi
Rat-bats (Belize)
Murciélago = bat

ID: Tiny dark brown bat with paler underparts; small pointed snout without noseleaf; triangular, pointed ears; head and body length to 5 cm (2 in), plus tail.

HABITAT: Low and middle elevation forests, gardens, parks, agricultural sites; roosts in trees, rock crevices, buildings.

DISTRICTS: COR, ORW, BEL, STN, CAYO, TOL, PET

Plate 72 377

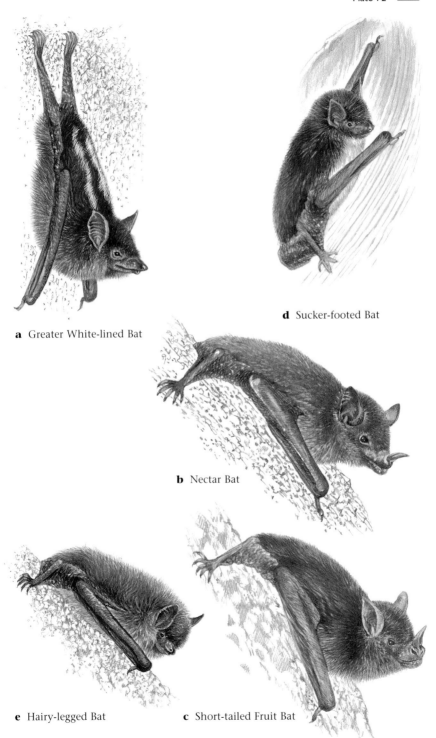

a Greater White-lined Bat

d Sucker-footed Bat

b Nectar Bat

e Hairy-legged Bat

c Short-tailed Fruit Bat

Plate 73a

Yucatán Black Howler Monkey
Alouatta pigra
Baboon (Belize)
Mono Aullador = howling monkey
Zaraguate

ID: Large, long-haired, all-black monkey; to 55 cm (22 in), plus long prehensile tail; males larger than females.

HABITAT: Lowland wet and dry forests; arboreal, usually in upper reaches of trees.

DISTRICTS: ORW, BEL, STN, CAYO, TOL, PET
Note: This species listed as endangered, CITES Appendix I and USA ESA.

Plate 73b

Central American Spider Monkey (also called Geoffroy's Spider Monkey)
Ateles geoffroyi
Monkey (Belize)
Mono Araña = spider monkey

ID: A large monkey, brown, chestnut, or silvery; lighter-colored belly; dark or black lower legs, feet, hands, and forearms; pale skin around eyes and nose; to 63 cm (25 in), plus long prehensile tail.

HABITAT: Low and middle elevation wet and dry forests; arboreal.

DISTRICTS: ORW, CAYO, TOL, PET
Note: This species listed as endangered, CITES Appendix I and USA ESA.

Plate 73c

Nine-banded Armadillo
Dasypus novemcinctus
Dilly (Belize)
Armado = armoured one
Armadillo

ID: Gray to yellowish body; hairless back consisting of hard, bony plates; about 9 movable bands in midsection; long snout; large ears; scales on head, legs; to 57 cm (22 in), plus long, ringed tail.

HABITAT: Forests, scrub areas, thickets, and grasslands; nocturnal; terrestrial.

DISTRICTS: COR, ORW, BEL, STN, CAYO, TOL, PET

Plate 73d

Silky Anteater (also called Pygmy Anteater)
Cyclopes didactylus
Hormiguero Dorado = golden anteater

ID: Small anteater with gray, brownish, or yellowish dense, silky fur; darker on top, with a dark line running from top of head along the back; to 18 cm (7 in), plus thick prehensile tail as long as or longer than body.

HABITAT: Low and middle elevation wet forests; nocturnal; arboreal; especially found among vines and thin tree branches.

DISTRICTS: COR, ORW, BEL, STN, CAYO, TOL, PET

Plate 73e

Northern Tamandua
Tamandua mexicana
Ant Bear (Belize)
Oso Hormiguero = anteater bear

ID: Mid-sized anteater with snout, pointed snout; brown or yellowish head and legs with a black "vest" on belly and back that encircles body; 47 to 77 cm (18 to 30 in) long, plus tail as long as body; last section of tail is bare.

HABITAT: Low and middle elevation forests, and more open sites such as forest edges, tree plantations; active day and night; found in trees and on the ground.

DISTRICTS: COR, ORW, BEL, STN, CAYO, TOL, PET
Note: This species regulated for conservation purposes in Guatemala, CITES Appendix III listed.

Plate 73 379

e Northern Tamandua

a Yucatán Black Howler Monkey

b Central American Spider Monkey

d Silky Anteater   **c** Nine-banded Armadillo

380 Plate 74 (*See also*: Rodents, p. 409)

Plate 74a
Deppe's Squirrel
Sciurus deppei
Ardilla Montañera = mountain squirrel

ID: Small brownish or grayish squirrel with grizzled appearance; gray front legs and shoulders; black and white "frosted" tail; to 22 cm (9 in), plus 19 cm (7 in) tail.

HABITAT: Low, middle, and higher-elevation forests; found in trees and on the ground.

DISTRICTS: COR, ORW, BEL, STN, CAYO, TOL, PET

Plate 74b
Yucatán Squirrel
Sciuris yucatanensis
Ardilla = squirrel

ID: Blackish or grayish squirrel with grizzled appearance; black and white "frosted" tail; dark or gray feet; to 26 cm (10 in), plus 23 cm (9 in) tail.

HABITAT: Lowland wet and dry forests, tree plantations; arboreal.

DISTRICTS: COR, ORW, BEL, STN, CAYO, TOL, PET

Plate 74c
Mexican Hairy Porcupine (also called Prehensile-tailed Porcupine)
Sphiggurus mexicanus (formerly *Coendou mexicanus*)
Puercoespín = porcupine

ID: Small brown or black porcupine with long prehensile tail bare at the end; spines ("quills") are largely hidden by long, soft hair; usually 30 to 40 cm (12 to 16 in), plus tail.

HABITAT: Low, middle, and some higher-elevation forests and more open areas; nocturnal; mostly arboreal but also found on the ground.

DISTRICTS: COR, ORW, BEL, STN, CAYO, TOL, PET

Plate 74d
Paca
Agouti paca
Gibnut (Belize)
Tepezcuintle

ID: Large, pig-like rodent; brown or blackish with horizontal rows of whitish spots on sides; 60 to 80 cm (24 to 31 in), plus tiny tail.

HABITAT: Low and middle elevation wet forests and drier areas near water; nocturnal; found on the ground.

DISTRICTS: COR, ORW, BEL, STN, CAYO, TOL, PET

Plate 74e
Central American Agouti
Dasyprocta punctata
Bush-rabbit (Belize)
Indian Rabbit (Belize)
Guatusa

ID: Large, pig-like rodent; reddish brown, brown, or blackish back and sides; 40 to 62 cm (16 to 24 in), plus tiny tail.

HABITAT: Low and middle elevation forests, plantations, gardens; diurnal; found on the ground.

DISTRICTS: COR, ORW, BEL, STN, CAYO, TOL, PET

Plate 74   381

a Deppe's Squirrel

b Yucatán Squirrel

c Mexican Hairy Porcupine

e Central American Agouti

d Paca

Plate 75a

Gray Fox
Urocyon cinereoargenteus
Zorro Gris = gray fox
ID: Small, silver-gray, dog-like mammal, with reddish ears and shoulders; to 52 to 64 cm (20 to 24 in), plus tail.

HABITAT: Low and middle elevation forests and more open areas, especially forest edges; active day or night; often seen during early morning; found on ground and in trees.

DISTRICTS: COR, ORW, BEL, STN, CAYO, TOL, PET

Plate 75b

Jaguarundi
Herpailurus yaguarondi
Halari (Belize)
Yaguarundi/Jaguarundi
ID: Smallish to mid-sized slender cat without spots; gray, brown, or reddish; 50 to 65+ cm (20 to 25+ in), plus long tail.

HABITAT: Wet and dry forests, regionwide; active day or night; usually seen on the ground, but also climbs.

DISTRICTS: COR, ORW, BEL, STN, CAYO, TOL, PET
Note: This species listed as endangered, CITES Appendix I and USA ESA.

Plate 75c

Ocelot
Leopardus pardalis
Tiger Cat (Belize)
Ocelote = ocelot
ID: Medium-sized yellow/tawny cat with black spots and lines; tail shorter than rear leg; to 70 to 85 cm (28 to 34 in), plus tail.

HABITAT: Low and middle elevation wet and dry forests and more open sites such as forest edges and scrub areas; mostly nocturnal; found on the ground or in trees (where it sleeps).

DISTRICTS: COR, ORW, BEL, STN, CAYO, TOL, PET
Note: This species listed as endangered, CITES Appendix I and USA ESA.

Plate 75d

Margay
Leopardus wiedii
Tiger Cat (Belize)
Tigrillo = little tiger
ID: Small to mid-sized yellowish, tawny, or brownish-gray cat with black spots and lines; tail longer than rear leg; to 50 to 70 cm (20 to 28 in), plus tail.

HABITAT: Low and middle elevation forests, regionwide; nocturnal; found mostly in trees but also on the ground.

DISTRICTS: ORW, STN, CAYO, TOL, PET
Note: This species listed as endangered, CITES Appendix I and USA ESA.

Plate 75   383

a Gray Fox

b Jaguarundi

d Margay

c Ocelot

Plate 76a

Puma
Puma concolor
Red Tiger (Belize)
León del Monte, León de Montaña = mountain lion
León Colorado = red lion
ID: A large cat, brownish, reddish-brown, or tawny; white throat and around mouth; 0.9 to 1.5 m (3 to 5 ft), plus long, dark-tipped tail.

HABITAT: Low, middle, and higher-elevation forests and more open sites, such as forest edges, scrub areas.

DISTRICTS: STN, CAYO, TOL, PET
Note: This species is threatened throughout its range, USA ESA listed.

Plate 76b

Jaguar
Panthera onca
Tiger (Belize)
Tigre = tiger
ID: A large or very large cat, yellowish/tawny with black spots; to 1.1 to 1. 8 m (3.5 to 6 ft), plus tail; you will know it when you see it.

HABITAT: Low and middle elevation forests and semi-open areas, regionwide; active day or night.

DISTRICTS: COR, ORW, STN, CAYO, TOL, PET
Note: This species listed as endangered, CITES Appendix I and USA ESA.

Plate 76c

Striped Hog-nosed Skunk
Conepatus semistriatus
Polecat (Belize)
Zorrillo = skunk
ID: Black or brown skunk with wide white stripe on top of head and neck, dividing to 2 white stripes along back; bushy white tail; 30 to 49 cm (12 to 19 in), plus tail.

HABITAT: Found regionwide in most forests but more usually in cleared areas, gardens, agricultural areas; nocturnal; found on the ground.

DISTRICTS: COR, ORW, BEL, STN, CAYO, TOL, PET

Plate 76d

Southern Spotted Skunk
Spilogale putorius
Zorrillo = skunk
ID: Smallish black skunk with white stripes on back and sides, white spots on rump, white mark on forehead; to 33 cm (13 in) plus black/white, long-haired tail.

HABITAT: Low and middle elevations; prefers open woodlands, forest edges, rocky and scrub areas; found on the ground and in trees.

DISTRICTS: COR, ORW, BEL, STN, CAYO, TOL, PET

Plate 76 385

c Striped Hog-nosed Skunk

d Southern Spotted Skunk

b Jaguar

a Puma

Plate 77a

Tayra
Eira barbara
Bush-dog (Belize)
Cabeza de Viejo = old man's head
Gato de Monte = mountain cat
ID: Medium-sized weasel-like mammal, resembling a large mink; black or brown body; tan, brown, or yellowish head and neck; often a large yellowish spot on throat/chest; to 52 to 70 cm (20 to 28 in), plus long, densely furred tail.

HABITAT: Wet forests, drier areas, gardens, and agricultural sites; day- and dusk-active; found in trees or on the ground.

DISTRICTS: ORW, STN, CAYO, TOL, PET

Plate 77b

Neotropical Otter (also called River Otter)
Lutra longicaudis
Water Dog (Belize)
Perro de Agua = water dog
Lobito de Río = little river wolf
ID: Short-legged, short-haired brown mammal with whitish throat and belly; first half of tail very thick; webbed feet; 45 to 75 cm (18 to 30 in) long, plus tail.

HABITAT: Found in and around rivers and streams, regionwide; active day and night.

DISTRICTS: ORW, BEL, STN, CAYO, TOL, PET

Note: This species listed as endangered, CITES Appendix I and USA ESA.

Plate 77c

Grison (also called Huron)
Galictis vittata
Bush Dog (Belize)
Hurón
ID: A weasel-like mammal with short legs; grayish or "grizzled" above and on sides; black muzzle, throat, chest, and limbs; 45 to 55 cm (18 to 21 in), plus short tail.

HABITAT: Low and middle elevation forests, especially near waterways, regionwide; night- and morning-active; found on the ground.

DISTRICTS: COR, ORW, BEL, STN, CAYO, TOL, PET

Plate 77d

Long-tailed Weasel
Mustela frenata
Comadreja = weasel
ID: Smallish brown weasel with cream-colored throat, chest, and belly; white stripe through eye area; tip of tail black; 18 to 30 cm (7 to 12 in), plus tail.

HABITAT: Low, middle, and higher-elevation forests, drier cleared areas, and agricultural areas, regionwide; active day or night; usually found on the ground but also climbs.

DISTRICTS: COR, ORW, BEL, STN, CAYO, TOL, PET

Plate 77 **387**

a Tayra

b Neotropical Otter

c Grison

d Long-tailed Weasel

Plate 78a

Northern Raccoon
Procyon lotor
Mapache = raccoon

ID: Gray-black back with "grizzled" appearance; whitish face with black mask; gray forearms and thighs; light gray/white feet; pointed muzzle; 45 to 64 cm (18 to 25 in), plus ringed tail.

HABITAT: Low and middle elevation forests and open areas, often near water; nocturnal; found on the ground and in trees.

DISTRICTS: COR, ORW, BEL, STN, CAYO, TOL, PET

Plate 78b

White-nosed Coati
Nasua narica
Quash (Belize)
Pizote

ID: Light-, dark-, or reddish-brown raccoon-like mammal with grayish or yellowish shoulders; white muzzle, chin, and throat; 45 to 70 cm (18 to 27 in), plus very long, faintly ringed tail.

HABITAT: Low and middle elevation wet and dry forests and forest edge areas, regionwide; day active; found on the ground and in trees.

DISTRICTS: COR, ORW, BEL, STN, CAYO, TOL, PET

Plate 78c

Kinkajou
Potos flavus
Nightwalker (Belize)
Mico León = lion monkey

ID: Grayish or reddish brown short-haired mammal, sometimes with a darker stripe along back; roundish head with short muzzle; short legs; 40 to 55 cm (16 to 22 in), plus very long, prehensile tail.

HABITAT: Low and middle elevation forests, tree plantations; nocturnal; found in trees.

DISTRICTS: COR, ORW, BEL, STN, CAYO, TOL, PET

Plate 78d

Cacomistle
Bassariscus sumichrasti
Ring-tail Cat (Belize)

ID: A light brown or tawny-brown densely furred mammal with dark stripe down back; dark facial mask surrounding yellowish or whitish rings around eyes; dark lower legs and feet; 39 to 47 cm (15 to 18 in), plus long, bushy, ringed tail.

HABITAT: Low and middle elevation forests; nocturnal; found in middle and upper levels of trees.

DISTRICTS: STN, CAYO, TOL, PET

Plate 78 **389**

d Cacomistle

c Kinkajou

a Northern Raccoon

b White-nosed Coati

Plate 79a

Collared Peccary
Tayassu tajacu
Pecari
Saíno

ID: Gray or blackish pig-like mammal with long, coarse hair; white or yellowish "collar" around shoulders; to 80 to 92 cm (31 to 36 in).

HABITAT: Low and middle elevation wet and dry forests, agricultural areas, regionwide; day active.

DISTRICTS: COR, ORW, BEL, STN, CAYO, TOL, PET
Note: This species regulated for conservation purposes, CITES Appendix II listed.

Plate 79b

White-lipped Peccary
Tayassu pecari
Warree (Belize)
Puerco de Monte = mountain pig

ID: Black or brown pig-like mammal with long, coarse hair; white lower cheek and throat; to 92 to 110 cm (36 to 43 in).

HABITAT: Low and middle elevation wet and dry forests; day active.

DISTRICTS: ORW, STN, CAYO, TOL, PET
Note: This species regulated for conservation purposes, CITES Appendix II listed.

Plate 79c

White-tailed Deer
Odocoileus virginianus
Savanna Deer (Belize)
Venado = deer

ID: Mid-sized light-, dark-, or grayish brown deer with white belly, white under tail, and, often, white chin/throat; males with branched antlers; 1 to 1.8 m (3 to 6 ft) long; about 1 m (3 ft) high at shoulders.

HABITAT: Low, middle, and higher-elevation forest edges and more open areas, such as pastures and grasslands; active day or night.

DISTRICTS: COR, ORW, BEL, STN, CAYO, TOL, PET
Note: This species regulated in Guatemala for conservation purposes, CITES Appendix III listed.

Plate 79d

Red Brocket Deer
Mazama americana
Antelope (Belize)
Venado Colorado = red deer

ID: Small reddish or reddish brown deer with dark brown head and neck, and brownish belly; white under tail; males with small, straight antlers; 1 to 1.4 m (3.4 to 4.6 ft); 70 cm (28 in) high at shoulders.

HABITAT: Low and middle elevation wet forests, forest edge areas, and plantations; active day or night.

DISTRICTS: STN, CAYO, TOL, PET
Note: This species regulated in Guatemala for conservation purposes, CITES Appendix III listed.

Plate 79   391

a Collared Peccary

b White-lipped Peccary

d Red Brocket Deer

c White-tailed Deer

Plate 80a

Baird's Tapir
Tapirus bairdii
Mountain Cow (Belize)
Danta

ID: Large mammal, brownish, black, or grayish, with short, often sparse hair; lighter colored throat and chest; vaguely horse-like head with large, hanging upper lip, or "proboscis;" to 1.8 to 2.0 m (5.8 to 6.5 ft); weight to 200+ kg (440+ lb).

HABITAT: Low, middle, and higher-elevation wet forests and swampy areas; active day or night; found on land or in shallow water.

DISTRICTS: ORW, STN, CAYO, TOL, PET

Note: This species listed as endangered, CITES Appendix I and USA ESA.

Plate 80b

West Indian Manatee (also called Caribbean Manatee)
Trichechus manatus
Sea Cow (Belize)
Vaca Marina = sea cow
Manatí

ID: Very large, hairless, gray aquatic mammal; paddle-like front limbs, each with three nails; to 4.5 m (14.5 ft).

HABITAT: Shallow coastal areas, especially around some offshore cayes, and coastal lagoons, estuaries.

DISTRICTS: COR, BEL, STN, TOL, CAYE

Note: This species listed as endangered, CITES Appendix I and USA ESA.

Plate 80c

Atlantic Spotted Dolphin
Stenella frontalis
Delfín = dolphin
Pampas

ID: Gray or blackish dolphin with pronounced beak; pale spots on body; underparts lighter; dorsal fin about 25 cm (10 in) high; 1.5 to 3 m (5 to 10 ft) long.

HABITAT: Coastal and offshore areas.

DISTRICTS: COR, BEL, STN, TOL, CAYE

Plate 80d

Bottle-nosed Dolphin
Tursiops truncatus
Delfín = dolphin
Pampas

ID: Gray or slaty-blue dolphin with pronounced beak; flippers and flukes often darker; underparts lighter; dorsal fin about 25 cm (10 in) high; 1.8 to 3.5 m (6 to 11 ft) long.

HABITAT: Coastal areas, bays and lagoons, and offshore areas.

DISTRICTS: COR, BEL, STN, TOL, CAYE

Plate 80 393

a Baird's Tapir

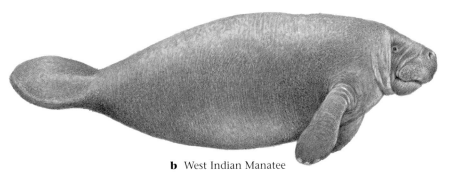

b West Indian Manatee

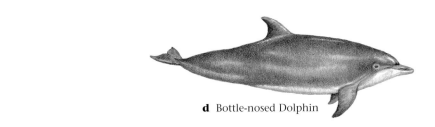

d Bottle-nosed Dolphin

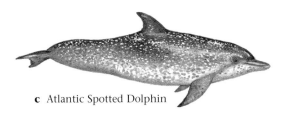

c Atlantic Spotted Dolphin

Lengths given for each fish are "standard lengths," the distance from the front of the mouth to the point where the tail appears to join the body; that is, tails are not included in the measurement.

Text by Richard Francis.

Plate 81a
Reef Butterflyfish
Chaetodon sedentarius
Closely related to the angelfishes, butterflyfishes are also generally monogamous. This species is fairly common and prefers the tops of coral reefs where it can be easily observed, usually in pairs. Very attractive, but not flashy by butterflyfish standards, look for the vertical black bar through the eye. Like many members of its family, the reef butterflyfish eats live coral. (to 16 cm, 6 in)

Plate 81b
Spotfin Butterflyfish
Chaetodon ocellatus
This beauty is named for the small black spot on the trailing edge of its dorsal fin. Its snow-white body is fringed by bright yellow dorsal and anal fins. The vertical black stripe that runs through the eye probably serves to deceive predators as to which end is the head. Usually found in pairs cruising over the top of the reef. The best way to get close is to place yourself in their line of travel. They will move away when approached. (to 20 cm, 8 in)

Plate 81c
Longsnout Butterflyfish
Chaetodon aculeatus
This is a rather shy fish, and unlike most butterflyfishes, tends to be solitary. This fish prefers somewhat deeper water than snorkelers typically explore, and is best observed on SCUBA. As its common name indicates, this species has an elongated snout, which facilitates deep coral probing. The color of this species typically ranges from olive to dusky. (to 10 cm, 4 in)

Plate 81d
Queen Angelfish
Holocanthus ciliaris
One of the most spectacular fishes in the Caribbean. This rather shy angelfish must be approached slowly. It is fairly common in the protected reefs preferred by snorkelers, where it can be seen poking around coral heads looking for various invertebrates to eat. These fish are highly territorial and usually occur in pairs. (to 45 cm, 18 in)

Plate 81e
French Angelfish
Pomacanthus paru
Another large angelfish that can be distinguished from the gray angel by the yellow highlights on its scales. It resembles the Gray Angelfish in both habits and temperament. If you are above them, they will turn toward the horizontal to better keep an eye on you. (to 35 cm, 14 in)

Plate 81f
Gray Angelfish
Pomacanthus arcuatus
These large angelfish are quite curious and may approach if you remain still. They mate for life and once formed, a pair is rarely separated by more than a few meters. They consume a variety of invertebrates and are quite active during the day. Much less shy than Queen Angelfish. (to 50 cm, 20 in)

Plate 81   **395**

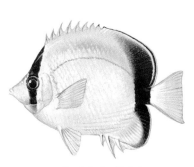

a Reef Butterflyfish

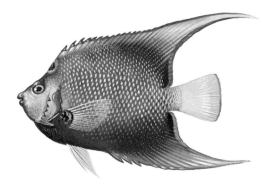

d Queen Angelfish

b Spotfin Butterflyfish

e French Angelfish

c Longsnout Butterflyfish

f Gray Angelfish

Plate 82a

Rock Beauty
Holocanthus tricolor

This is a common but fairly shy species. They patrol well-defined territories on the reef. The quiet snorkeler will be rewarded by the sight of this striking fish. Yellow areas in the front and tail sections are separated by a large area of black. Also notice the blue highlights around the eye. Juveniles are bright yellow with a blue-ringed black bulls-eye on the body toward the tail. (to 20 cm, 8 in)

Plate 82b

Blue Tang
Acanthurus coeruleus

This is one of the surgeonfishes, as indicated by the scalpel-like protrusion near the base of the tail, which is deployed in aggressive encounters. Individuals can rapidly change color from a deep purple to powder blue. Abundant and usually in fairly large groups that move restlessly along reef tops grazing on algae. (to 23 cm, 9 in)

Plate 82c

Ocean Surgeonfish
Acanthurus bahianus

This species is also a color-changer (from dark brown to bluish gray). Fairly common and generally found in loose aggregations, along with Blue Tangs and Doctorfish. Grazers, they are approachable but tend to keep a minimum distance from divers. (to 35 cm, 14 in)

Plate 82d

Doctorfish
Acanthurus chirurgus

Very similar in appearance and habits to the Ocean Surgeonfish. They can be distinguished by their vertical body bars, which, however, can be quite faint. This is one of the most abundant shallow water species. (to 25 cm, 10 in)

Plate 82e

Bar Jack (also called Skipjack)
Caranx ruber

A fast-moving predator that courses over the reefs in groups of variable size. Bar jacks can make surprisingly close passes and you may be lucky enough to find yourself in the middle of a swirling school. This species can be distinguished from other jacks by its black stripe, bordered by bright blue, running from its dorsal fin through the bottom half of the tail. (to 60 cm, 24 in)

Plate 82f

Horse-eye Jack (also called Bigeye Jack, Horse-eye Trevally)
Caranx latus

Another common jack found in open water over reefs, usually in small schools. More skittish than Bar Jacks, the snorkeler will usually only get a brief glimpse of these fast-moving fish. Distinguished by their yellow tails and large eyes. (to 75 cm, 29 in)

Plate 82 397

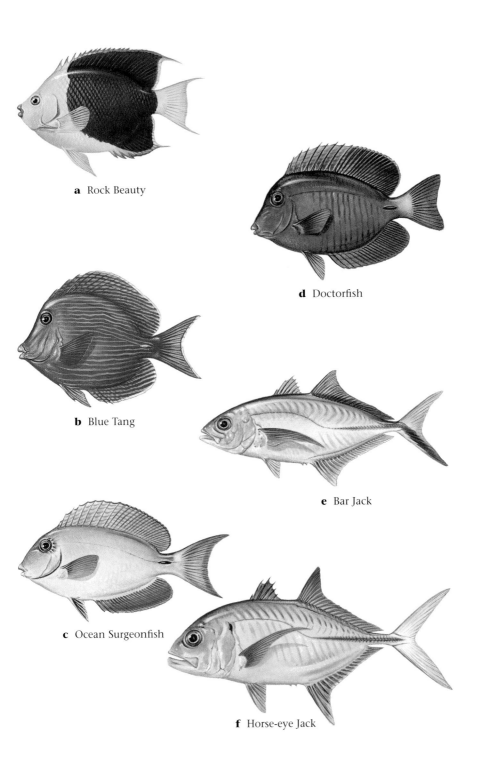

a Rock Beauty

d Doctorfish

b Blue Tang

e Bar Jack

c Ocean Surgeonfish

f Horse-eye Jack

Plate 83a
Houndfish
Tylosurus crocodilus
This species belongs to the needlefish family, of which it is the largest. They are typically found in shallow water over turtle grass beds or small patch reefs, where they tend to drift just below the surface. A favorite food item for Brown Pelicans in the Belize area. They are fairly shy and not easy to see from below. (to 1.5 m, 5 ft)

Plate 83b
Great Barracuda
Sphyraena barracuda
This consummate predator has an impressive array of teeth which it displays while slowly opening and closing its mouth (to assist respiration). Not dangerous, but they can be disconcertingly curious. They may even follow you around the reef. Barracudas exhibit an economy of movement, generally drifting, but capable of rapid bursts should prey approach. (to 2 m, 6.5 ft)

Plate 83c
Bonefish
Albula vulpes
One of the species most prized by sports-fisherpersons. When feeding, usually found in shallow flats on a rising tide, in the vicinity of mangroves. Tend to prefer the coral rubble when they are not feeding. Bonefish are common but very shy; they must be approached slowly. Not colorful, they are silvery with no characteristic markings. Forked tails and an underslung jaw, somewhat like freshwater suckers. (to 1 m, 3.3 ft)

Plate 83d
Common Snook
Centropomus undecimalis
Another prized sportfish, look for them near mangroves along the mainland coastline. Wary, but not as shy as Bonefish; they can be approached. Snook have a characteristic black line running through the middle of their bodies. The shape of their head is rather unique, like a shallow slide. (to 1.4 m, 4.5 ft)

Plate 83e
White Mullet
Mugil curema
These common fish are found in shallow, open water over sand or other soft bottom habitats. They feed on tiny animals found on bottom detritus or sea grasses. This species has a characteristic black spot at the base of the pectoral fin and very large scales. (to 38 cm, 15 in)

Plate 83f
Bermuda Chub
Kyphosus sectatrix
This common species swims in loose schools over reefs, sometimes quite near the surface. Chubs have a characteristic oval shape, silvery body, and dusky-colored fins. (to 76 cm, 30 in)

Plate 83   399

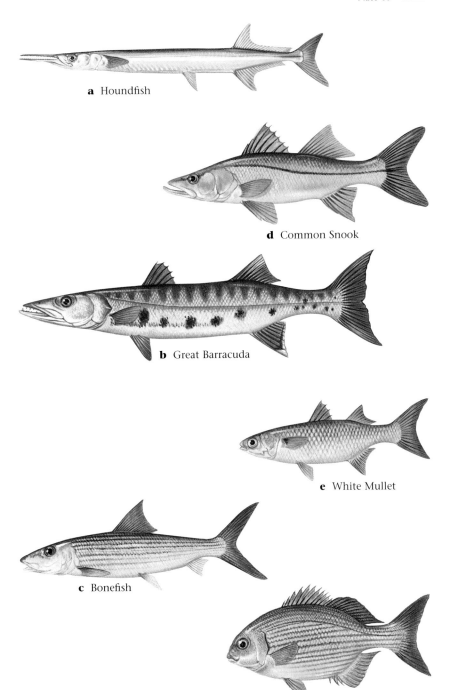

a Houndfish

d Common Snook

b Great Barracuda

e White Mullet

c Bonefish

f Bermuda Chub

Plate 84a

French Grunt
Haemulon flavolineatum
Grunts are named for the characteristic sound they make by grinding teeth-like structures in their throats. They are an important group of predators throughout the Caribbean and closely related to snappers. Grunts are found on reefs, sandy areas and seagrass beds. The French grunt is one of the common species in this part of the Caribbean. Wavy blue horizontal lines on a yellow body are characteristic. Look for them under ledges. (to 30 cm, 12 in)

Plate 84b

White Grunt
Haemulon plumieri
This grunt species is distinguished by the checkered pattern of blue and yellow on its body, as well as the parallel blue and yellow lines on its long head. Like many grunt species, white grunts seem to drift in groups of variable size; they retreat to cover when approached. (to 45 cm, 18 in)

Plate 84c

Blue-striped Grunt
Haemulon sciurus
This striking fish has bright blue stripes on a golden-yellow body. Also note the dark dorsal fin and tail. This is one of the most wary of the grunt species; patience and slow movements are required in order to approach. (to 45 cm, 18 in)

Plate 84d

Spanish Grunt
Haemulon macrostomum
This species is not so common as other grunts in the Belize reefs. A prominent black stripe runs through the eye to the base of the tail. The body is generally silvery and the fins have yellow borders. (to 43 cm, 17 in)

Plate 84e

Sailor's Choice
Haemulon parra
This handsome grunt has a silvery body with dark highlights. Its fins are quite dusky. They drift in small schools over and between reefs. (to 40 cm, 16 in)

Plate 84f

Margate
Haemulon album
This gray grunt prefers the sand flats between reef patches. Behaviorally a typical grunt; fairly wary but sometimes curious, they tend to drift passively, either alone or in small groups. (to 60 cm, 24 in)

Plate 84   401

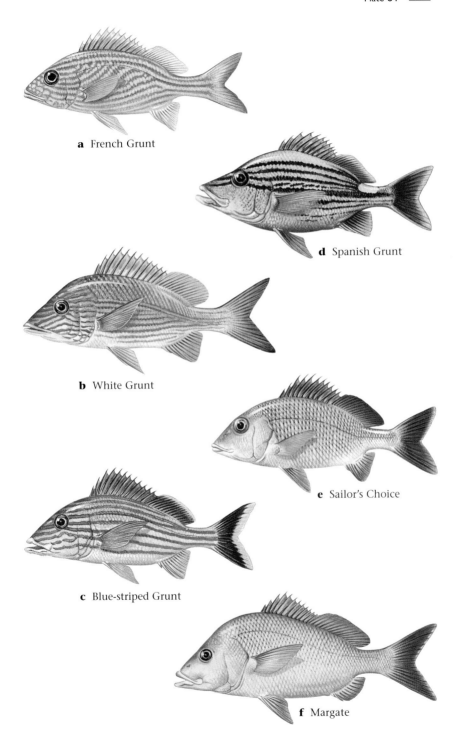

a French Grunt

d Spanish Grunt

b White Grunt

e Sailor's Choice

c Blue-striped Grunt

f Margate

Plate 85a

Atlantic Spadefish
Chaetodipterus faber
You will not confuse this fish with any other.
Laterally compressed like a pompano, this species
gets its name from its supposed resemblance to a
suit of playing cards. The body is silver with dark
vertical bars which may, however, rapidly fade.
They occur in slow-moving schools and are fairly
approachable. (to 91 cm, 36 in)

Plate 85b

Porkfish
Anisotremus virginicus
This is one of the more abundant species in the
Caribbean, and a favorite for snorkelers. Bright
yellow lateral stripes behind two striking vertical
black bands distinguish this beautiful grunt. As an
added bonus, they are quite easy to approach. (to
40 cm, 16 in)

Plate 85c

Mutton Snapper
Lutjanus analis
Most snappers are favorite food fishes for
humans, which tends to make them wary. In
protected areas though, they can be approached.
Look for them in caves and deep crevices. This
species has quite variable coloration, from silver
to reddish-brown, but almost always with a black
spot near midbody. (to 75 cm, 30 in)

Plate 85d

Cubera Snapper
Lutjanus cyanopterus
Difficult to distinguish from other snappers, but
with relatively thick lips. This is an extremely shy
species. (to 1.5 m, 5 ft)

Plate 85e

Mahogany Snapper
Lutjanus mahogoni
One of the smaller snappers, their scales usually
have a reddish tinge and more distinct red
borders around the fins. They drift in small groups
near cover. (to 38 cm, 15 in)

Plate 85f

Schoolmaster
Lutjanus apodus
This snapper usually occurs in loose schools
drifting above the reef. They are quite common
but not easy to approach. The body is generally
silver and the fins are yellow. (to 60 cm, 24 in)

Plate 85   403

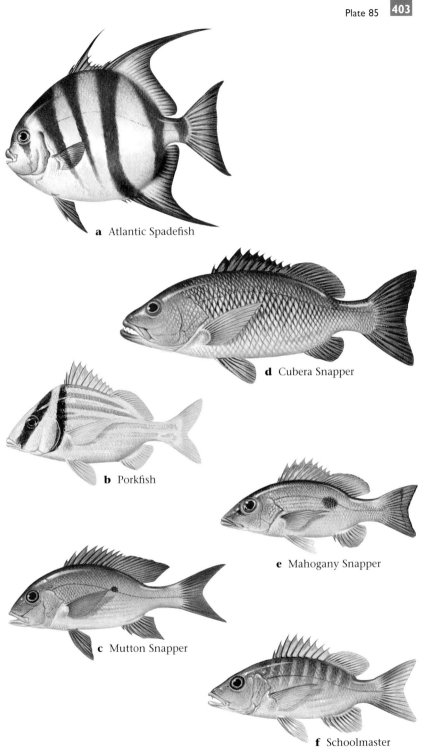

a Atlantic Spadefish

d Cubera Snapper

b Porkfish

e Mahogany Snapper

c Mutton Snapper

f Schoolmaster

Plate 86a
Longfin Damselfish
Stegastes diencaeus
The damselfishes are among the most
entertaining coral reef inhabitants. Highly
territorial and aggressive, especially during the
breeding season when the males are tending the
eggs. Though diminutive, they will even attack
divers, which can be quite comical. This species
is dusky brown throughout and is distinguished by
its relatively long dorsal and anal fins. The
juveniles of this, and most other damselfishes,
differ markedly from adults in coloration. In this
species the juveniles are yellow with distinctive
blue stripes dorsally and a prominent blue-ringed
black spot near the base of the dorsal fin. (to
13 cm, 5 in)

Plate 86b
Dusky Damselfish
Stegastes fuscus
Very similar to the Longfin Damsel but with
shorter and more rounded fins. Juveniles are
bluish with a bright orange swath running from
the snout to the middle of the dorsal fin. (to 15
cm, 6 in)

Plate 86c
Threespot Damselfish
Stegastes planifrons
The adults are a fairly bland dusky color but with
a small yellow crescent above the eye. Juveniles
(shown) are bright yellow with a black spot near
the base of the dorsal fin. Another pugnacious
species that is extremely active and bold. (to
13 cm, 5 in)

Plate 86d
Cocoa Damselfish
Stegastes variabilis
The adults of this species can be hard to
distinguish from other damsels, but look for a dark
spot at the base of the tail. Juveniles (shown) are
blue above the eye and yellow below. Not as
aggressive as most damsels. (to 13 cm, 5 in)

Plate 86e
Beaugregory
Stegastes leucostictus
This damsel prefers coral rubble and sandy areas,
and like cocoa damsels, is relatively
unaggressive. It is not shy, however. Adults are
distinguished from other damsels, such as Longfin
and Dusky, by their yellowish-tinged fins.
Juveniles (shown) closely resemble cocoa
damsels. (to 10 cm, 4 in)

Plate 86f
Bicolor Damselfish
Stegastes partitus
This species defends smaller territories than most
damsels. They are aggressive but channel it
toward fishes of about the same size. This
species is easy to identify, with its body divided
between a black fore-region and a white rear.
Juveniles have a lesser black area and a bright
yellow triangular swath originating beneath the
chin. (to 10 cm, 4 in)

Plate 86 405

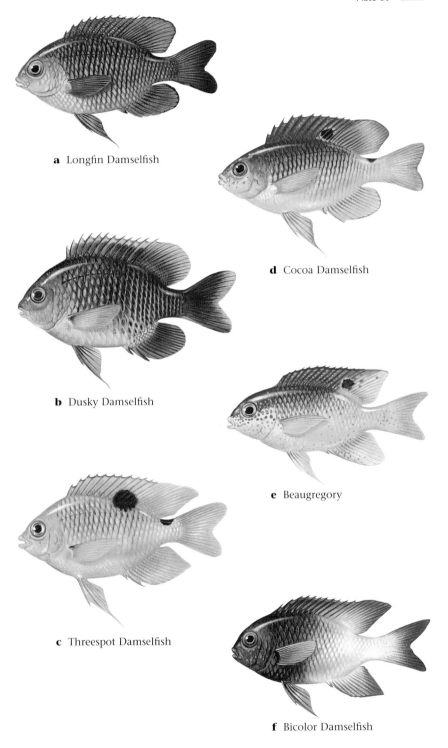

a Longfin Damselfish

d Cocoa Damselfish

b Dusky Damselfish

e Beaugregory

c Threespot Damselfish

f Bicolor Damselfish

Plate 87a
Yellowtail Snapper
Ocyurus chrysurus
This abundant species is much more streamlined than most snappers. A distinctive yellow line runs from behind the eye to the base of the tail, which is also yellow. They swim above the reefs in loose schools, and are much less wary than most snappers. (to 75 cm, 30 in)

Plate 87b
Yellowtail Damselfish
Microspathodon chrysurus
Large by damselfish standards, this species has a distinctive yellow tail. The juveniles are spectacular in bright light; their dark blue bodies are covered with electric blue dots. Be aware that the juveniles prefer to hang around skin-irritating fire coral. (to 21 cm, 8 in)

Plate 87c
Sergeant Major
Abudefduf saxatilis
Probably the most common damselfish, it can be easily distinguished by its five vertical black bars on a silvery gray body. Juveniles have more yellow tones, and the adult males turn dark purplish-blue when guarding eggs. They prefer to remain higher above the reefs than most damsels and usually occur in loose aggregations. (to 15 cm, 6 in)

Plate 87d
Blue Chromis
Chromis cyanea
This brilliant blue damsel with a black nape is extremely abundant in midwater, often in very large groups. The tail is very deeply forked. They are most common slightly below typical snorkeling depths, but look for them over drop-offs. (to 13 cm, 5 in)

Plate 87e
Brown Chromis (also called Yellow-edge Chromis)
Chromis multilineata
Generally tan or brownish gray with a characteristic black spot at the base of the pectoral fin. The deeply forked tail often has black borders. Similar in habits to the Blue Chromis, with which it often schools. (to 16 cm, 6 in)

Plate 87f
Purple Reeffish (also called Purple Chromis)
Chromis scotti
Not so much purple as varying shades of blue. The juveniles (shown) are a very deep and bright blue. This is a deeper water species that is best observed on SCUBA. They occur in small groups near the bottom of deep reefs. (to 10 cm, 4 in)

Plate 87 **407**

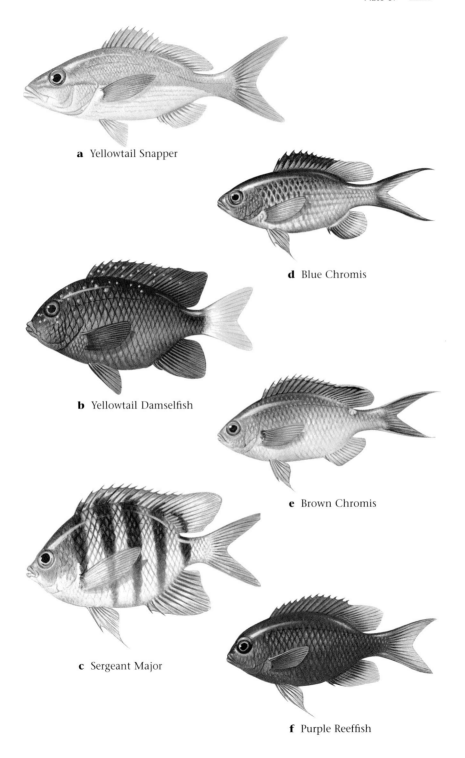

a Yellowtail Snapper

d Blue Chromis

b Yellowtail Damselfish

e Brown Chromis

c Sergeant Major

f Purple Reeffish

Plate 88a

Barred Hamlet
Hypoplectrus puella

All hamlets are true hermaphrodites. Their fascinating mating behavior, known as egg-trading, involves the alternate release of eggs and sperm with their partner. This species has brown bars of varying width, interspersed with whitish areas. Bright blue vertical lines on the head. Perhaps the most common hamlet, they prefer the bottom of shallow reefs. All hamlets exhibit an interesting mixture of wariness and curiosity. (to 13 cm, 5 in)

Plate 88b

Indigo Hamlet
Hypoplectrus indigo

Indigo blue bars separated by white bars make this species easy to identify. All hamlets exhibit essentially the same behavior. Belize is a particularly good area to see a variety of these species. (to 13 cm, 5 in)

Plate 88c

Shy Hamlet
Hypoplectrus guttavarius

The name implies that this species is particularly reclusive, although I have not found this to be the case. Sometimes it is very curious. Much of the body is brown to blackish, but head and chest yellowish, as well as all fins. Bright blue lines on snout. (to 13 cm, 5 in)

Plate 88d

Golden Hamlet
Hypoplectrus gummigutta

Yellow body with striking blue and black markings on face. Occurs in deeper water than most hamlets. (to 13 cm, 5 in)

Plate 88e

Yellowtail Hamlet
Hypoplectrus chlorurus

The body of this species often appears black but is actually a dark blue or dark brown. The yellow tail is what distinguishes it from other hamlets. (to 13 cm, 5 in)

Plate 88f

Black Hamlet
Hypoplectrus nigricans

The entire body is black to bluish brown. Probably the least shy of the hamlets. (to 13 cm, 5 in)

Plate 88 409

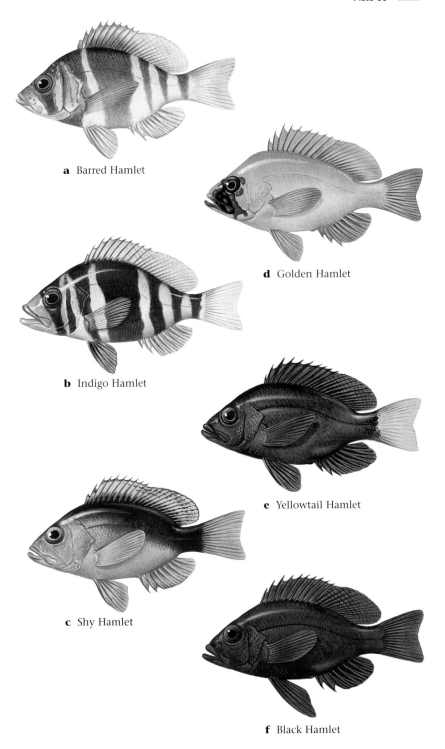

a Barred Hamlet

d Golden Hamlet

b Indigo Hamlet

e Yellowtail Hamlet

c Shy Hamlet

f Black Hamlet

Plate 89a

Blue Hamlet
Hypoplectrus gemma
Iridescent blue body often with darker eye. This beautiful species stays close to the bottom and will remain motionless for long periods while being observed. (to 13 cm, 5 in)

Plate 89b

Masked Hamlet
Hypoplectrus sp.
This very handsome hamlet has a taupe-colored body and an upside-down triangular black stripe below the eye, from whence its name derives. Some scientists consider all hamlets to be variants of a single species and ichthyologists have not yet bothered to provide a species name for this one, but its color pattern is consistent over a broad geographic range. (to 13 cm, 5 in)

Plate 89c

Jewfish
Epinephelus itajara
The largest grouper in the Caribbean, this species is severely threatened by overfishing, particularly spearfishing. Its appearance is variable but always splotched or mottled. Shy in unprotected areas, but much less so where protected. They spend much of the day inside caves or other protected areas. Groupers, as well as the hamlets, are seabasses of the family Serranidae. Many are suspected to be serial hermaphrodites that are female while young and small, then turn to male when larger. In some of the largest groupers the reverse transition is thought to occur. (to 2.4 m, 7.8 ft)

Plate 89d

Nassau Grouper
Epinephelus striatus
Another grouper threatened by overfishing. This species has five distinctive brown stripes on its body, but it can change color from a very pale hue to virtually black. A somewhat steeper forehead than most groupers. You can often find them resting on the bottom. (to 1.2 m, 4 ft)

Plate 89e

Yellowfin Grouper
Mycteroperca venenosa
Many groupers exhibit different color phases. This one varies from black to bright red and white. The only constants are the yellow edges on the pectoral fins and the black fringe at the end of the tail. This is a mid-size grouper, often found resting on sand. It prefers reef-tops near drop-offs. (to 90 cm, 35 in)

Plate 89f

Tiger Grouper
Mycteroperca tigris
Another mid-sized grouper with highly variable coloration. The juveniles are usually yellow with brown bars. (to 1 m, 3.3 ft)

Plate 89 411

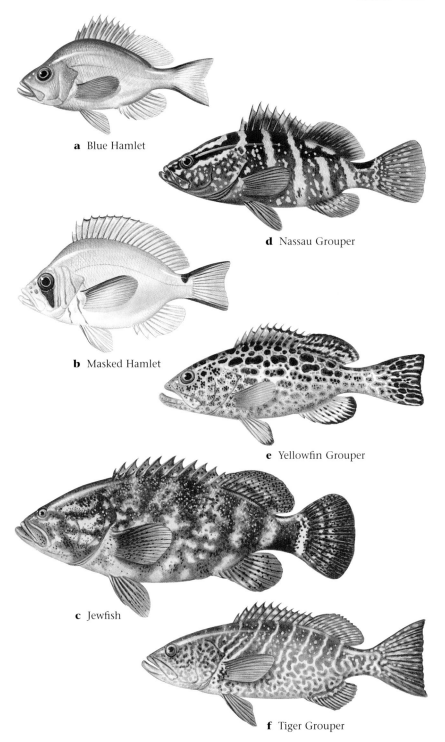

a Blue Hamlet

b Masked Hamlet

c Jewfish

d Nassau Grouper

e Yellowfin Grouper

f Tiger Grouper

Plate 90a

Graysby

Epinephelus cruentatus

This small grouper is one of the most common in the Belize area. It can quickly change color. Look for the three distinctive black spots at the base of the dorsal fin. (to 35 cm, 14 in)

Plate 90b

Red Hind

Epinephelus guttatus

A fairly common small grouper with red spots over a white background. They can be found at a variety of depths, including shallow reef patches. (to 67 cm, 26 in)

Plate 90c

Coney

Epinephelus fulvus

This common small grouper exhibits a wide range of color patterns. All individuals have at least a few small spots. They can be quite curious and are more social than most groupers. (to 41 cm, 16 in)

Plate 90d

Tobaccofish

Serranus tabacarius

This small seabass can be found in very shallow water and is not at all shy. Common in the Belize region where it prefers areas of coral rubble. Tends to hover near the bottom. The common name derives from the horizontal midbody band, which someone, who must have been smoking something else, thought was the shade of tobacco. (to 18 cm, 7 in)

Plate 90e

Creole-fish

Paranthias furcifer

This member of the seabass family is one of the more common fish in the Caribbean. They occur in large schools that hover above deeper reefs. Coloration is variable, but often with a purplish hue. Look for the bright red area at the base of the pectoral fin and three spots along the back. (to 38 cm, 15 in)

Plate 90f

Fairy Basslet (also called Royal Gramma)

Gramma loreto

This beautiful little fish is quite common but wary, and tends to retreat into cracks and crevices when approached. Be patient though, and it will reappear. The purple head region and yellow tail region are about equally divided. (to 8 cm, 3 in)

Plate 90 413

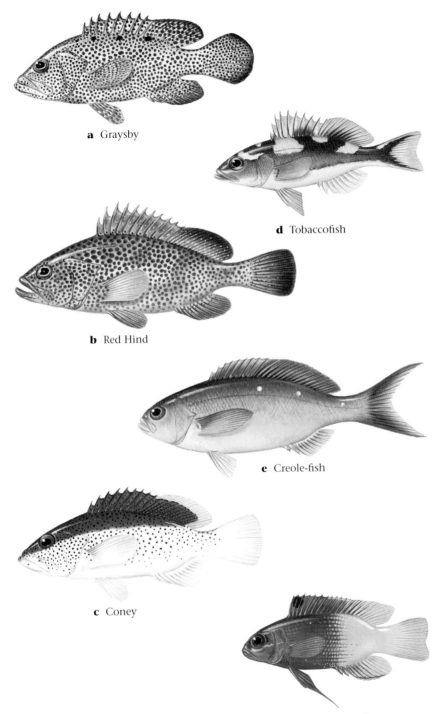

a Graysby

d Tobaccofish

b Red Hind

e Creole-fish

c Coney

f Fairy Basslet

Plate 91a

Blue Parrotfish
Scarus coeruleus

Parrotfishes are unique grazers. They feed primarily on algae from rocks and coral, and can munch the hard corals with their powerful beak-like mouth. Watch for the wispy white clouds of coral dust that they occasionally void. Parrotfishes are female-to-male sex changers but with a twist. Some males (initial phase males) are born that way, and have a completely different reproductive strategy than the large (terminal phase) males. The latter are solitary and territorial, while the initial phase males tend to congregate with females. Identifying parrotfishes is tricky because of the different color phases associated with their development. Terminal phase males are easiest to identify and it is from their coloration that the common names usually derive. In this species, however, all phases come in beautiful shades of blue, from light to quite dark. Terminal phase males have a squared-off head. This is one of the largest parrotfish species. (to 90 cm, 35 in)

Plate 91b

Midnight Parrotfish
Scarus coelestinus

All phases of this species are midnight blue, with brighter blue splashes around the head. Not wary, but will not allow close approach. Parrotfishes tend to be quite active and stop only to scrape algae off coral. This is one of the larger parrotfish species. (to 76 cm, 30 in)

Plate 91c

Queen Parrotfish
Scarus vetula

A medium-sized parrotfish, similar in habits to the Midnight Parrotfish. Terminal phase males have blue-green bodies with striking blue and green markings around the mouth. (to 61 cm, 24 in)

Plate 91d

Stoplight Parrotfish
Scarus viride

One of the more common parrotfishes in the Belize area. This mid-sized species is distinguished by a characteristic yellow spot on the upper part of the gill-cover. Also look for the crescent-shaped tail. (to 50 cm, 20 in)

Plate 91e

Hogfish
Lachnolaimus maximus

This species belongs to the wrasse family, close relatives of parrotfishes. A favorite food fish wherever it occurs, they are wary wherever spearfishing is allowed, but can become quite tame where protected. Most wrasses exhibit the complicated reproductive strategy typical of parrotfishes, as well as various developmental color phases. This species has only one male type, which has an off-white, grayish, or reddish brown body, with a black swath over the head. When erected, the dorsal fin has a dramatic appearance, with several long spines in front. (to 91 cm, 36 in)

Plate 91f

Spanish Hogfish
Bodianus rufus

One of the few wrasse species without distinct color phases, this common species is constantly on the move and quite easy to approach. A large purple area on the upper half of the body behind the head is characteristic. (to 40 cm, 16 in)

Plate 91 415

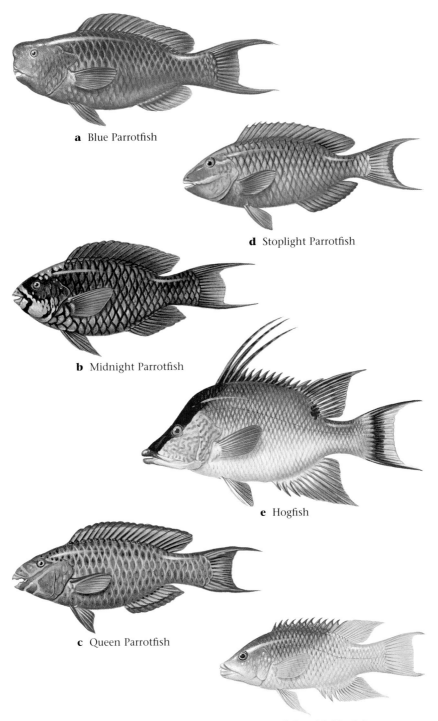

a Blue Parrotfish

d Stoplight Parrotfish

b Midnight Parrotfish

e Hogfish

c Queen Parrotfish

f Spanish Hogfish

Plate 92a
Creole Wrasse
Clepticus parrae
This wrasse is one of the most abundant fishes in the Caribbean. They prefer the open water over the top of deep reefs where they occur in large groups, often in the afternoon forming long stream-like schools over the drop-offs. Another wrasse without distinct color phases, the snout area is usually dark purple and the front half of the body dark blue to slate. Older individuals show more yellow and red in the tail region. (to 30 cm, 12 in)

Plate 92b
Yellowhead Wrasse
Halichoeres garnoti
This species exhibits several distinct developmental color phases. Terminal phase males have the yellow head and forebody for which the species is named, and a dark vertical bar at midbody. Initial phase males and females have a dusky back and yellow mid-region. Juveniles are bright yellow with bright blue horizontal stripe. (to 18 cm, 7 in)

Plate 92c
Bluehead Wrasse
Thalassoma bifasciatum
This common wrasse is easy to observe on shallow reefs. Terminal phase males have the bright blue head for which the species is named. Initial phase males and females have a dusky blue color with irregular white stripes. Juveniles have variable color patterns and may act as cleaners – small fish that remove external parasites and dead scales from the bodies of large fish. (to 18 cm, 7 in)

Plate 92d
Slippery Dick
Halichoeres bivittatus
This very common species can be found on reefs as well as adjacent sandy areas and turtle grass patches. Terminal phase males are various shades of green with a darker horizontal stripe at midbody. As to the meaning of the common name, don't ask. (to 20 cm, 8 in)

Plate 92e
Squirrelfish
Holocentrus ascensionis
Members of the squirrelfish family are most active at night. By day, you can observe them in protected areas such as rock crevices and inside large barrel sponges preferably in shallow patch reefs. They are not shy and allow close observation. This species is red with white patches and, as do all members of the family, has very large eyes. (to 30 cm, 12 in)

Plate 92f
Blackbar Soldierfish
Myripristis jacobis
This member of the squirrelfish family can often be found in caves or other dark recesses swimming upside down. They can be quite curious and approachable. The body is bright red, with a black stripe behind the gill-cover. (to 20 cm, 8 in)

Plate 92 **417**

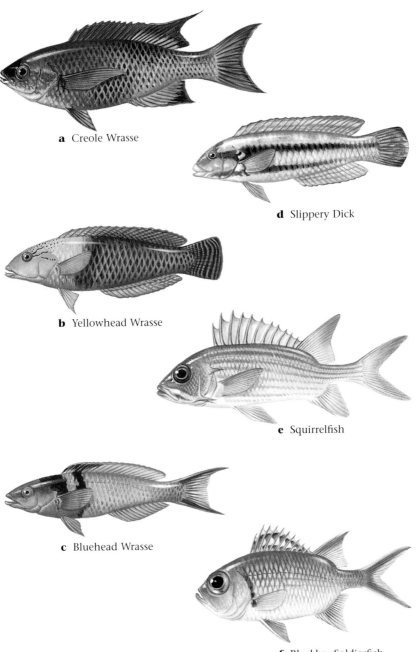

a Creole Wrasse

d Slippery Dick

b Yellowhead Wrasse

e Squirrelfish

c Bluehead Wrasse

f Blackbar Soldierfish

Plate 93a
Glasseye Snapper
Priacanthus cruentatus
Another nocturnal species that can be observed by day in its hideouts. Their coloration is variable but they usually have silver bars on the back. Unlike other "bigeyes" in the area, they prefer shallow reefs. (to 33 cm, 13 in)

Plate 93b
Bigeye
Priacanthus arenatus
This species is best observed on SCUBA because it prefers deep reefs where it drifts in small groups. The body is a uniform but variable shade of red. (to 30 cm, 12 in)

Plate 93c
Flamefish
Apogon maculatus
One of the cardinalfishes, this species is active at night. By day they can be found in various dark places in a variety of habitats, including reefs and docks. One of the species most often seen on night dives. Body color is salmon to bright red; distinctive features are small white lines above and below eye and a black spot behind eye. (to 11 cm, 4 in)

Plate 93d
Neon Goby
Gobiosoma oceanops
Gobies constitute the largest family of fishes, indeed, the largest vertebrate family, yet only the careful observer will be able to enjoy these diminutive fishes. This common goby often acts as a cleaner. They often establish cleaning stations at which several congregate waiting for clients. This is a very attractive fish with its black body bisected by an electric blue horizontal stripe. (to 5 cm, 2 in)

Plate 93e
Yellowline Goby
Gobiosoma horsti
This species is much shyer than the neon goby. Usually found near sponges on reefs of medium depth. It has a black body and a yellow horizontal stripe running from head to tail, including the top of the eye. (to 4 cm, 1.5 in)

Plate 93f
Cleaning Goby
Gobiosoma genie
As its common name suggests, this species is one of the so-called "cleaner fishes." They congregate at established cleaning stations waiting for clients. As is typical of gobies that clean other fishes, this species is bold and approachable. The upper body is dark with a bright yellow V on the snout which is continuous with two paler body stripes. (to 4 cm, 1.5 in)

Plate 93   **419**

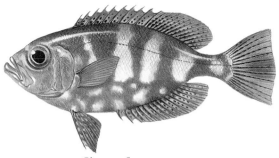

a Glasseye Snapper

d Neon Goby

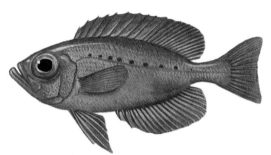

b Bigeye

e Yellowline Goby

c Flamefish

f Cleaning Goby

Plate 94a

Rusty Goby (also called Sharknose Goby)
Priolepis hipoliti

The unusual feature of this goby is that it can often be found perched upside down on the roofs of small clefts in reefs or under boulders. This goby is fairly approachable. It has bright orange spots on the dorsal, tail, and anal fins, as well as several dusky body bars. (to 4 cm, 1.5 in)

Plate 94b

Redlip Blenny
Ophioblennius atlanticus

Large, by blenny standards, members of this species are also full of personality. They typically sit on an exposed perch, ever watchful for territorial intrusions. Their prominent eyes, which move independently of one another, allow them to monitor events in all compass directions. Their coloration varies from gray to reddish brown; the head is usually darker and redder than the rest of the body. The head looks almost flat in profile. (to 12 cm, 5 in)

Plate 94c

Yellowhead Jawfish
Opistognathus aurifrons

These inhabitants of the sand and coral rubble are fun to watch. They typically excavate burrows in the sand and line the entrance with small bits of coral, which tend to migrate from one burrow to another, as they are perpetually stealing their neighbors' goods. They look like small eels, especially when only the upper half of the body is extended above the surface. The body is pale and the head a very pale yellow. (to 10 cm, 4 in)

Plate 94d

Peacock Flounder
Bothus lunatus

This flatfish is most active at night. By day you will see them only if you happen to swim close enough to cause them to swim away; otherwise their camouflage is quite effective. This species also prefers sandy areas or coral rubble. The species is named for the striking blue spots on the body and fins. (to 39 cm, 15 in)

Plate 94e

Splendid Toadfish (also called Coral Toadfish)
Sanopus splendidus

This spectacular fish seems to be endemic to Cozumel Island, Mexico. The flattened head is especially striking with its densely packed black and white stripes. The ventral fins are entirely yellow, the rest of the fins have an attractive yellow border. Also look for the very prominent barbels around the mouth. This is a shy species, most likely to be found in crevices and other dark recesses, where it is supported by its pectoral fins. (to 20 cm, 8 in)

Plate 94f

Sand Diver
Synodus intermedius

This common reef inhabitant belongs to the lizardfish family. They often lie half buried in the sand, which along with their camouflaged coloration both protects them from predators and allows them to dart out and grab unwary prey. They exhibit a mottled reddish-brown coloration but they can change hue to blend with the background. (to 45 cm, 18 in)

Plate 94 421

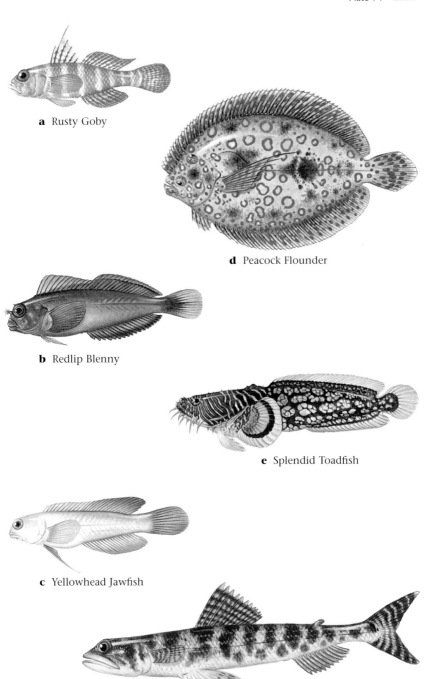

a Rusty Goby

d Peacock Flounder

b Redlip Blenny

e Splendid Toadfish

c Yellowhead Jawfish

f Sand Diver

Plate 95a

Trumpetfish
Aulostomus maculatus

One of the more distinctively shaped reef creatures, this elongate fish actually looks more like a soprano saxaphone than a trumpet. They are usually seen drifting with their head down, which may serve as a sort of camouflage, especially in grass beds or among some gorgonians. They will not tolerate a direct approach but these curious creatures may approach you if you don't flail around too much. (to 1 m, 3.3 ft)

Plate 95b

Sand Tilefish
Malacanthus plumieri

Look for these fish in sandy areas, where their large, inverted, conical burrow entrances are easy to spot. This is a fairly shy species and will retreat to the burrow when approached too closely. But if you are patient, they will eventually emerge and hover over the burrow by undulating their long dorsal and anal fins. (to 60 cm, 24 in)

Plate 95c

Porcupinefish
Diodon hystrix

This member of the puffer family will inflate its body dramatically when threatened, its sharp spines becoming erect during the process. This obviously makes them less easy to swallow for any would-be predator. It does not facilitate movement, however, and they can look quite comical when attempting to swim away in this state, furiously beating their pectoral fins. During the day they occupy various recesses. But you can often spot their head peering outward, and they can then be approached quite closely. (to 90 cm, 35 in)

Plate 95d

Smooth Trunkfish
Lactophrys triqueter

Like puffers, trunkfish manage to negotiate the reefs using their pectoral fins almost exclusively. This species is not wary and allows the diver fairly close inspection. Aside from its peculiar shape and small mouth with those seemingly kissable lips, notice the bulbous eyes, which seem to rotate in various directions like radar dishes. The smooth trunkfish has a dark body with numerous white spots throughout. These spots thin somewhat behind the pectoral fin in older fish and honeycomb markings appear. (to 30 cm, 12 in)

Plate 95e

Queen Triggerfish
Balistes vetula

This is one of the most strikingly beautiful species on the reef. Background body coloration is various shades of purple, blue, turquoise and green, and the head is usually lighter, tending toward yellow; but these fish can rapidly darken or lighten. Irregular black lines radiate from the eye and two striking blue lines run above the mouth. Triggerfish move about primarily by means of the coordinated action of their dorsal and anal fins. Queen Triggers prefer reef tops and coral rubble. This species is fairly shy but your patience will be rewarded. (to 60 cm, 24 in)

Plate 95f

Ocean Triggerfish
Canthidermis sufflamen

This is more of an open water species, most frequently observed near drop-offs. However, during the nesting season, they can be found in sandy areas between reef patches. Males create large depressions into which the female lays her eggs, which the male then guards until hatching. This species is almost entirely gray but with a prominent black spot at the base of the pectoral fin. (to 65 cm, 26 in)

Plate 95   423

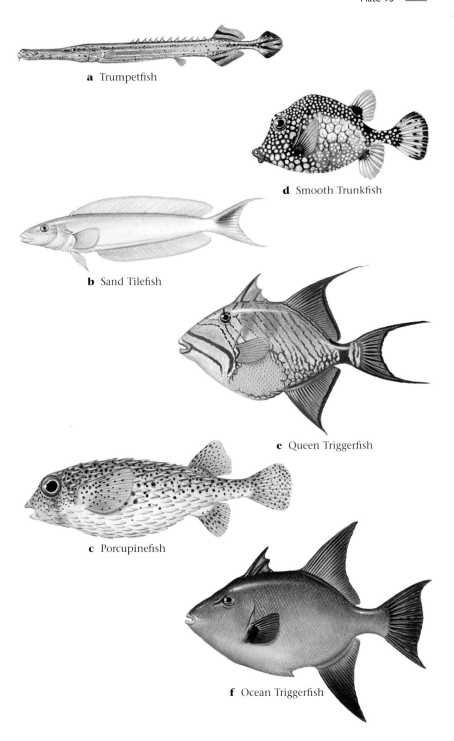

a Trumpetfish

d Smooth Trunkfish

b Sand Tilefish

e Queen Triggerfish

c Porcupinefish

f Ocean Triggerfish

Plate 96a
Black Durgeon
Melichthys niger
One of the more social members of the triggerfish family, this species occurs in groups of variable size, sometimes quite large. Quite common and easy to observe at a distance, they usually do not permit close inspection. Their body is black and fins blacker, but with prominent pale blue lines beneath dorsal and anal fins. (to 50 cm, 20 in)

Plate 96b
Scrawled Filefish
Aluterus scriptus
This very odd-looking fish always seems to have a disheveled appearance because its tail is usually limp. The body coloration is usually a shade of yellow-green, and covered with blue and black spots. Fairly common, they drift over the reefs, seemingly without aid of their fins, until they are approached; they then retreat but again without much exertion. These fish are loners. (to 1.1 m, 3.6 ft)

Plate 96c
Yellow Goatfish
Mulloidichthys martinicus
Goatfish look very much like freshwater catfish, primarily because of their barbels under the lower jaw. Goatfish prefer sandy areas where they can be found, usually in small groups, busily probing the bottom for food. This species has a silvery white body with a yellow midbody stripe. The tail is also yellow. This is one of the more approachable species and it can be found in quite shallow water. (to 40 cm, 16 in)

Plate 96d
Spotted Drum
Equetus punctatus
This handsome fish can be found in protected areas of the reef, under ledges or in various nooks and crannies, where they rest by day. Drums are most active at night. The Spotted Drum and the similar Jackknife Fish have an unusual dorsal fin that is extremely long and directed upward with a slight curve. Striking black and white stripes on the body, and black back and tail with white spots. Quite unafraid, they will allow close inspection if you approach slowly. (to 25 cm, 10 in)

Plate 96e
Green Moray
Gymnothorax funebris
Largest of the morays, this species occurs in diverse habitats and is fairly common, even in shallow water. Morays rest by day in crevices with only their head protruding. They open and close their jaws in order to breathe, exposing their teeth. Though they look menacing, they are actually quite docile and retreat deeper into the reef when approached. They quickly become tame, however, and can be observed quite closely in some protected areas. All morays are active at night. (to 2.4 m, 8 ft)

Plate 96f
Spotted Moray
Gymnothorax moringa
This species is much smaller than the green moray. They prefer shallow reefs with abundant rubble, where they can be observed resting by day, head protruding from their refuge. This species is more speckled than spotted, seemingly splattered by black paint. (to 1.2 m, 4 ft)

Plate 96 **425**

a Black Durgeon

d Spotted Drum

b Scrawled Filefish

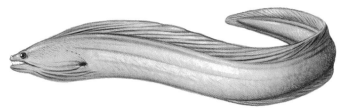

e Green Moray

c Yellow Goatfish

f Spotted Moary

Plate 97a

Goldentail Moray
Gymnothorax miliaris

Tiny yellow spots over a dark background distinguish this species from other morays. They prefer shallow to mid-depth reefs and are fairly common. (to 60 cm, 32 in)

Plate 97b

Nurse Shark
Ginglymostoma cirratum

This is the shark species you are most likely to observe. Nurse sharks are quite sluggish by shark standards, spending much of their time resting on the bottom. But they do reach impressive sizes and if one happens to swim by, your heart rate will increase. Nurse sharks seem to be missing the bottom half of the tail. Their heads are also larger than those of most sharks. (to 4.2 m, 14 ft)

Plate 97c

Bull Shark
Carcharhinus leucas

This is the most heavy-bodied of the requiem sharks. Bulls prefer inshore waters and some even migrate hundreds of miles up rivers into freshwater lakes, most notably in Nicaragua. Though fairly common, they are rarely seen. I once watched from shore while a large bull shark approached to within 3 m (10 ft) of a group of snorkelers who, nonetheless, remained unaware of its presence. This species should be treated with utmost respect. (to 3.5 m, 11.5 ft)

Plate 97d

Hammerhead Shark (also called Smooth Hammerhead)
Sphyrna zygaena

This species spends most of its time in open water, but they do cruise the reefs on occasion, especially at night. The bizarre head with eyes stuck at each end ensure that this shark will not be confused with any other. They reach impressive sizes and, though quite wary, should be treated with care. (to 3.5 m, 11.5 ft)

Plate 97e

Southern Stingray
Dasyatis americana

This common species prefers sandy areas where it lies buried to varying degrees. The name derives from the venomous spine near the base of the tail, contact with which can be exquisitely painful. Because they prefer shallow water, they are a factor to consider while wading in sandy areas. They are quite unafraid and will not move unless you are almost on top of them. (to 1.5 m, 5 ft)

Plate 97f

Spotted Eagle Ray
Aetobatus narinari

This common and quite handsome species prefers to stay well up in the water column, where it seems to fly through the water with its considerable wing-like fins. These rays have venomous spines but do not pose any threat to divers. They are quite wary, in fact, and best observed by staying motionless. They often leap out of the water for unknown reasons, and the sound they make upon re-entry is an impressive clap. (to 2.3 m, 7.5 ft)

Plate 97 **427**

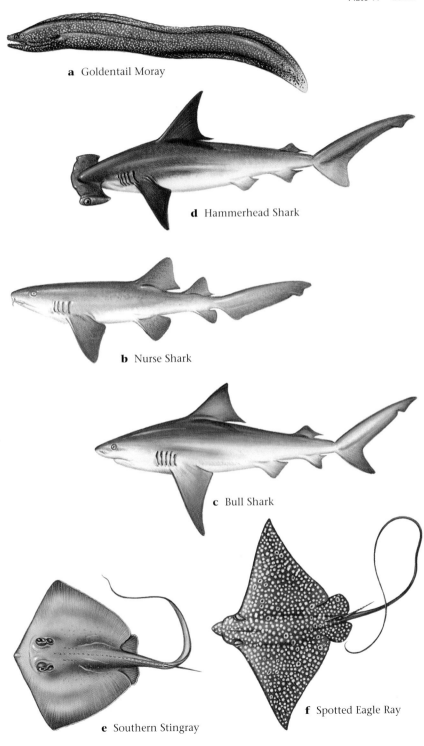

a Goldentail Moray

d Hammerhead Shark

b Nurse Shark

c Bull Shark

e Southern Stingray

f Spotted Eagle Ray

Plate 98a

Staghorn Coral
Acropora cervicornis

One of the fastest growing coral species, it prefers shallow, calm water. Forms dense tangles of branches in which only the outer tips are alive. Staghorn coral is fragile and subject to storm damage, but it recovers more quickly than most corals due to rapid growth rate.

Plate 98b

Elkhorn Coral
Acropora palmata

Another fast-growing species, it prefers shallow areas with good water movement and wave action. This coral can cover vast areas of shallow bottom, and it is one of the characteristic species living on the shallow fringing reefs off Belize's cayes. The branches are flattened like moosehorns.

Plate 98c

Lettuce Coral (also called Thin Leaf Coral)
Agaricia tenuifolia

This is one of the plate or sheet corals, but in contrast to most species, the "leaves" are positioned vertically and resemble leafy lettuce. Parallel wavy ridges run across each leaf. The color varies from gray to brown, sometimes with tints of blue or green. Can form large colonies in shallow water with plenty of wave action. Its crevices often harbor small fish and invertebrates such as brittle stars, urchins, and shrimp.

Plate 98d

Fire Coral
Millepora alcicornis

Fire corals are named for their skin-irritating capacity. They can cause welts and swelling in sensitive people, although the effect is usually of short duration. Pictured here is the branching species of fire coral but they can become encrusting on certain substrates. They tend to be brownish-orange but the color is variable. This species prefers deeper, calmer water than other fire corals.

Plate 98e

Large Star Coral
Montastrea cavernosa

This species forms very large coral heads in the form of mounds or domes. The polyps look like small blisters of variable hue when retracted. Like many coral species, the polyps are active at night and retracted by day. This species is found in a wide variety of reef habitats.

Plate 98f

Common Star Coral (also called Boulder Star Coral)
Montastrea annularis

This species is common in a variety of reef environments. There are several distinct forms that some consider to be separate species. The most spectacular form, sometimes called mountainous star coral, has irregular pillars and bumps.

Plate 98 **429**

a Staghorn Coral

d Fire Coral

b Elkhorn Coral

e Large Star Coral

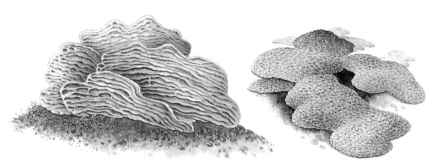

c Lettuce Coral

f Common Star Coral

Plate 99a

Porous Coral (also called Finger Coral)
Porites sp.

Stubby, smooth branches with blunt tips. The coralites are embedded, giving the branches a smooth appearance when the polyps are retracted. However during the day, the polyps are often extended, in which case the branches have a fuzzy appearance. Can be found in most reef environments.

Plate 99b

Common Brain Coral (also called Smooth or Symmetrical Brain Coral)
Diploria strigosa

A favorite subject for macro-photography because of the numerous wavy ridges that look something like the outside of a human brain. The effect is especially pronounced in the varieties that form rounded heads.

Plate 99c

Flower Coral
Eusmilia fastigiata

This beauty is another favorite of photographers. The coralites are often iridescent greenish-blue, with a lot of space between each. They form small round heads from which the polyps seem to emerge from a central core, somewhat like a hydrangea. The tentacles are extended only at night. This species is found in several reef environments but prefers protected areas.

Plate 99d

Encrusting Gorgonian (a soft coral)
Erythropodium caribaeorum

Colonies form mats which, when the polyps are retracted, are smooth, like oozing leather. When the polyps are extended, they look like dense, fine hair and move in unison with the currents. This species prefers protected shallow reefs.

Plate 99e

Corky Sea Finger (a soft coral)
Briareum sp.

Colonies of this soft coral consist of several (or a single) cylindrical columns arising from a common base. When the polyps are retracted, the columns are reddish-purple and smooth; when the polyps are extended, the rods look like they are covered with yellow-greenish or brownish hairs. This species prefers shallow and calm areas.

Plate 99f

Swollen Knob Candelabrum (a soft coral gorgonian)
Eunicea sp.

This species forms relatively compact colonies with thick branches. It prefers turbulent, shallow water and requires a hard substrate.

Plate 99 431

a Porous Coral

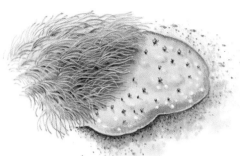

d Encrusting Gorgonian

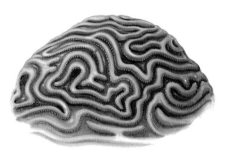

b Common Brain Coral

e Corky Sea Finger

c Flower Coral

f Swollen Knob Candelabrum

Plate 100a

Common Sea Fan (a soft coral gorgonian)
Gorgonia ventalina

This, and other closely related species of sea fans, are one of the more characteristic sights on a Belizean reef. The colonies form large, flat, fan-like structures that grow on a single plane. Upon close inspection, you will find an intricate vein-like network of branches, emerging from several large veins or branches. Usually a shade of purple, but sometimes yellow. This species prefers shallow reefs with clear water.

Plate 100b

Black Sea Rod
Plexaura sp.

This species forms bushy colonies that grow in one plane. The stalks are black, which contrasts with the yellowish brown polyps. It prefers patch reefs in clear water.

Plate 100c

Split-Pore Sea Rod
Plexaurella sp.

Named for the slit-like – as opposed to round or oval – openings that are evident when the polyps are retracted. The structure of the colony can often resemble organ-pipe cactus. This species is common in clear water environments, often in quite shallow areas. Shown with polyps retracted and extended.

Plate 100d

Magnificent Feather Duster
Sebellastarte sp.

This marine worm is the largest of the feather dusters. Most of the worm is hidden from view; only the highly modified head region is visible, most notably the feather appendages that function both for capturing food and as gills for respiration. It will quickly retract when approached too closely. Once it retracts, remain motionless and it may slowly re-emerge. These worms inhabit a wide variety of environments, from patch reefs to pilings.

Plate 100e

Christmas Tree Worm
Spirobranchus giganteus

These worms somewhat resemble the feather dusters but they belong to a separate family, the members of which construct calcareous tubes. The head appendages spiral around a single central core. Their color is variable but usually includes some red or orange with white highlights. They prefer to construct their tubes on living coral but they are not picky as to the type of coral or reef.

Plate 100f

Bearded Fire Worm
Hermodice sp.

This is a fairly active species that often forages in the open. It is covered with tufts of white bristles, interspersed with red gill filaments. Do not touch! The bristles contain a toxin that causes an unpleasant burning sensation, and sometimes a painful wound. When they are disturbed, they will display their bristles by way of warning. This species has branched and bushy appendages on the head that look somewhat beard-like. They can be found in a variety of habitats, including reefs, rubble, and grass beds.

Plate 100   433

a Common Sea Fan

d Magnificent Feather Duster

b Black Sea Rod

e Christmas Tree Worm

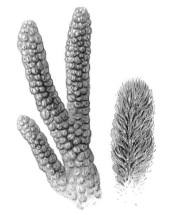

c Split-Pore Sea Rod

f Bearded Fire Worm

Plate 101a
Spiny Lobster
Panulirus sp.
This lobster can reach impressive sizes in areas where it is not hunted. The carapace is brown to tan with two horn-like projections above the eye. Their very long antennae often project from their hiding places and they always seem to be moving. Being a favorite food item for humans, they are understandably wary and will retreat deeper into their refuges when approached, but will remain facing you. In protected areas they are quite common on the reef.

Plate 101b
Banded Shrimp
Stenopus hispidus
This attractive crustacean seems to be all appendages. Its skinny body and claws are covered with red and white bands. This is one of the cleaning shrimps, and it hangs out at the openings of sponges, waving its antennae to attract its fish clients. They are not particularly wary but will retreat into a protective recess when approached closely. However, they have been known to clean the hands of divers when extended slowly.

Plate 101c
Queen Conch
Strombus gigas
This huge gastropod was once very common throughout the Caribbean; now its numbers are greatly reduced owing to overfishing, at least in shallow waters. The shells grow in a conical spiral with the outer lip flaring outward. The shell is various shades of orange but often obscured by algae and other encrustations. The snail itself is mottled gray. Its eyes are set at the ends of very long eye stalks. These conchs prefer sandy areas or grass beds between reef patches.

Plate 101d
Flamingo Tongue (also called Flamingo Tongue Cowrie)
Cyphoma gibbosum
At first glance this appears to be a nudibranch (sea slug) but the creamy white surface covered with orange spots is actually the snail's mantle covering a cowry-shaped shell. The shell can be seen only when the snail retracts its mantle. Most often seen on the gorgonians, including sea fans, upon which they feed. Quite common and found in a variety of shallow water habitats.

Plate 101e
Reef Squid
Sepioteuthis sepioidea
One of the most fascinating reef creatures, and the only squid that frequents the reefs. These are intelligent and curious creatures. If you remain motionless or swim toward them at an oblique angle, they will allow you to approach closely. Sometimes they will follow divers from a safe distance, observing you with those very large eyes. They will retreat if approached directly, and if they really feel threatened, they will turn on their jet propulsion and disappear in an eyeblink.

Plate 101f
Golden Crinoid
Davidaster sp.
Crinoids, or feather stars, are related to sea stars and sea urchins, though at first glance they look like some kind of gorgonian. They comprise the most ancient group of echinoderms. They have five arms that branch one or more times, so that the terminal arms are always a multiple of five. Each arm has numerous appendages extending laterally to give them their feathery appearance. The arms are used to gather small food particles. Though they appear to be fastened to one spot for life, they can move short distances while some species can even swim. This species has 20 feathery arms that are usually yellow-gold to orange in color. The body is usually concealed in a recess of some sort. This species is common but usually occurs below snorkeling depths.

Plate 101 **435**

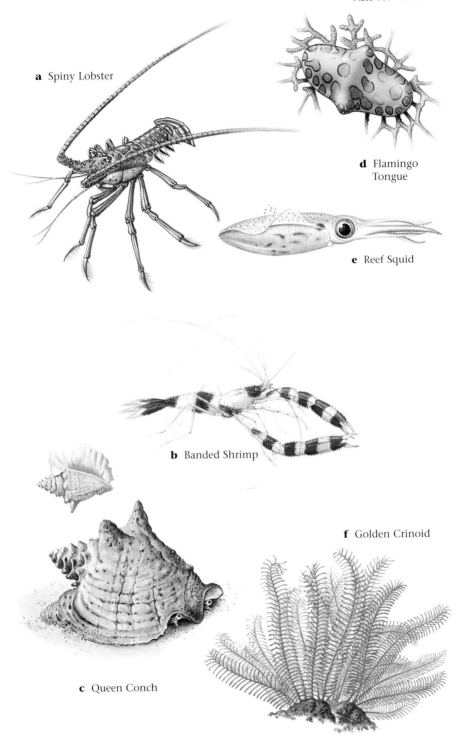

a Spiny Lobster

d Flamingo Tongue

e Reef Squid

b Banded Shrimp

f Golden Crinoid

c Queen Conch

Plate 102a

Blunt-Spined Brittle Star
Ophiocoma sp.

Brittle stars are echinoderm relatives of sea stars and sea urchins. They always have five arms emerging from a small central disk. During the day you will find them hiding under rocks and crevices; at night, they are active and can move with surprising speed. Their arms break off quite easily, the attribute for which they are named, but the arms regenerate. This species is one of the more common in shallow water. Generally brown to black with blunt spines on the exposed parts of its arms.

Plate 102b

Giant Basket Star
Astrophyton sp.

Basket stars are closely related to brittle stars; their five main arms branch many times giving the appearance of tentacles with a perm. During the day they curl up in a tight ball, usually on a gorgonian. At night, the arms unfurl and are directed toward the current, forming a sort of net by which they capture their planktonic prey. This species is a common reef inhabitant, generally colored orange to brown.

Plate 102c

Cushion Sea Star
Oreaster sp.

Sea stars are the most familiar echinoderms but they are not a particularly prominent component of the Caribbean reefs. This sea star has five short, thick arms. The color is usually some shade of orange to brown, with the dorsal spines forming a net-like pattern. They are common in sand flats and grass beds.

Plate 102d

Variegated Sea Urchin
Lytechinus sp.

Sea urchins are grazers. Their mouths are on the underside and the spines function to protect these otherwise vulnerable creatures. Urchins are a common cause of injury, because their spines, should they penetrate the skin, are difficult to remove. This beautiful species has short spines and well-defined grooves between plates. Coloration is variable, but usually white or some shade of green. Often camouflaged with sea grass or other debris. Look for them over grass beds or on reefs.

Plate 102e

Long-Spined Sea Urchin
Diadema sp.

Formerly abundant throughout the Caribbean, but has experienced a dramatic die-back. This species is one of the main sources of injury for unwary bathers and snorkelers. The long spines easily puncture the skin, often causing infection. This species is typically black. It is found in all habitats.

Plate 102f

Donkey Dung Sea Cucumber
Holothuria mexicana

The common name says it all concerning the outward appearance of this common sea cucumber. Unlike most echinoderms, sea cucumbers lack either spines or arms. They are shaped like a bloated caterpillar and are usually spotted moving slowly over sandy areas between reef patches. Seemingly defenseless, many species contain skin toxins to deter would-be predators.

Plate 102 437

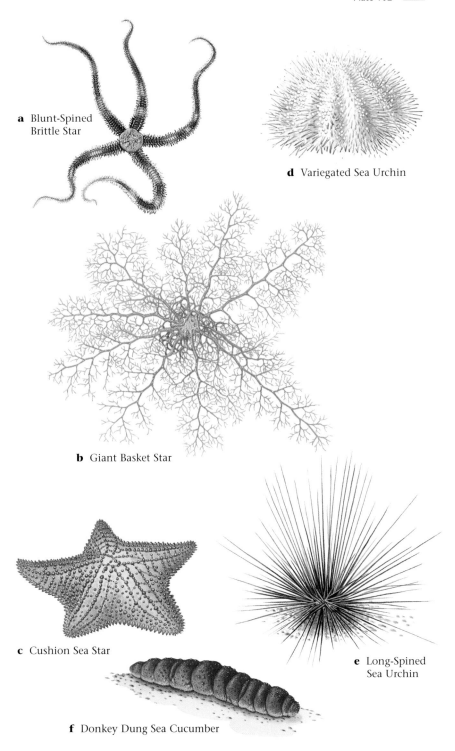

a Blunt-Spined Brittle Star

d Variegated Sea Urchin

b Giant Basket Star

c Cushion Sea Star

e Long-Spined Sea Urchin

f Donkey Dung Sea Cucumber

Plate 103a

Bulb Tunicate
Clavelina sp.

Tunicates, or sea squirts, are among the most abundant marine creatures, and certainly among the least recognized. They are often mistaken for sponges, but they are more closely related to you and me. This is easiest to discern in the larval phase during which they look very much like tadpoles. Pelagic tunicates remain free-swimming for life, but most species settle out and metamorphose into the sponge-like creatures we observe attached to various substrates on the reef. This attractive species is one of the compound tunicates, in which a number of individuals are joined at the base and share a common excurrent siphon. Purplish-blue varieties, known as blue bells, are particularly attractive.

Plate 103b

Sponge
Tethya sp.

Sponges are the most primitive multi-cellular animals and are an extremely important component of the reef community. They come in a dizzying variety of sizes and shapes. Sponges can be distinguished from non-sponges, such as tunicates, by their large excurrent openings through which they expel the water taken in while filter feeding.

Plate 103c

Branching Vase Sponge
Agelas sp.

This attractive species is common on fairly shallow reefs. Typically there are clusters of up to 30 tubes, each with numerous conical projections. The color varies from lavender to gray. Search this sponge's surface for brittle stars.

Plate 103d

Loggerhead Sponge
Spheciospongia sp.

This species is one of the barrel sponges, large squat creatures with a large central depression. It is often host to shrimps and others that dwell in the canals. Also check the depression for small fish.

Plate 103e

Giant Barrel Sponge
Xestospongia muta

These are some of the most spectacular creatures to be found anywhere on the reef. This species grows at depths that require SCUBA. They can grow to over 2 m (6 ft) in diameter and their central depression is large enough to contain a diver, but do not enter as these are fragile creatures that easily break. Large specimens may be over 100 years old!

Plate 103f

Yellow Tube Sponge
Aplysina sp.

This attractive sponge forms clusters of yellow tubes that are joined at the base. This is a soft sponge but don't squeeze it unless you don't mind a purple stain that will last for days. This sponge prefers open water reefs and reef walls. Look for gobies and other small fishes inside the tubes.

Plate 103   **439**

a Bulb Tunicate

d Loggerhead Sponge

b Sponge

e Giant Barrel Sponge

c Branching Vase Sponge

f Yellow Tube Sponge

Plate 104a
Feather Hydroid
Gymnangium longicauda

Hydroids are related to corals, gorgonians, and anemones, as well as jellyfishes. In fact, during the medusa stage of their life cycle, they are hard to distinguish from jellyfishes. You are most likely to observe their sessile (non-moving) stage, however, in which they have a fern-like appearance. Each hydroid is actually a colony of numerous individuals. This species is fairly common throughout the Caribbean on the top of reefs where there is some current. Do not touch, as they contain toxins irritating to the skin.

Plate 104b
Moon Jelly
Aurelia sp.

Jellies belong to a large group of animals known as cnidarians, which also includes coral, gorgonians, hydroids, and anemones, all of which possess a specialized structure, known as a nematocyst, which is a hook-like barb for injecting toxins. All cnidarians have a medusa stage in which the animal is free-swimming but only the jellies spend most of their lives in this mode. This is one of the more common species in the Caribbean; you are most likely to find them drifting near the surface over the reefs. The moon jelly is almost transparent; the four-leaf clover structure near the top is the reproductive organs.

Plate 104c
Upsidedown Jelly
Cassiopea sp.

This common inhabitant of lagoons and quiet sand flats has a flattened bell and typically orients with arms and tentacles facing upward, hence the name. They have symbiotic single-celled algae from which they derive some of their nourishment. Sometimes they can be observed lying upside down on the bottom, which is thought to facilitate the algae's growth. The closely related Mangrove Upsidedown Jelly is often abundant, not surprisingly, among mangroves.

Plate 104d
Giant Anemone
Condylactis gigantea

Anemones comprise another distinct group of cnidarians; they are very familiar to inhabitants of temperate regions. This species is the largest in the Caribbean and can be distinguished by the distinct swelling at the tip of each tentacle. The main body is usually hidden with only the tentacles visible. Several species of shrimp, including cleaner shrimp, frequently use this anemone for refuge, as do some blennies.

Plate 104e
Turtle Grass
Thalassia testudium

This shallow-water grass grows on sandy areas, forming beds that can cover large areas. This is a flowering plant, though its pale greenish-white flowers are not obvious. Individual blades are flat with rounded tips. Turtle grass beds are an important habitat for many small fishes and invertebrates, and well worth exploring.

Plate 104 **441**

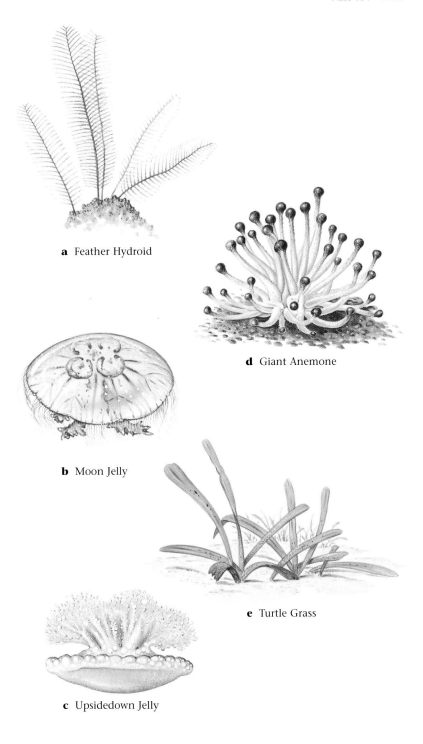

a Feather Hydroid

d Giant Anemone

b Moon Jelly

e Turtle Grass

c Upsidedown Jelly

HABITAT PHOTOS

1 Pine and palm savannah, an open, strangely attractive habitat, Rio Bravo Conservation Area, Orange Walk District, Belize.

2 Butterfly Falls, Mountain Pine Ridge Forest Reserve, Cayo District, Belize.

3 Trail on the property of the Hidden Valley Inn, Mountain Pine Ridge Forest Reserve, Cayo District, Belize.

4 Crooked Tree Lagoon, Crooked Tree Wildlife Sanctuary, Belize District, Belize. At certain times of the year, a great place for marsh and water birds.

5 Coastal marsh, south of Dangriga, Stann Creek District, Belize. Wet, grassy fields, as far as the eye can see.

6 The sand walkways along the shore on laid-back Caye Caulker, Belize.

7 Jeep-track through tropical pine forest, Mountain Pine Ridge Forest Reserve, Cayo District, Belize. Some of the most beautiful forest habitats seen anywhere are found in this region.

8 Along the New River, on the boat trip to Lamanai Archaeological Reserve, Orange Walk District, Belize.

9 Pimenta palms with fan-like fronds line the New River, on the boat trip to Lamanai Archaeological Reserve, Orange Walk District, Belize.

10 Ancient ruins excavated from the tropical forest, Lamanai Archaeological Reserve, Orange Walk District, Belize.

11 Jeep-track through cut lowland tropical forest, Monkey Bay Wildlife Sanctuary and Nature Reserve, Cayo District, Belize.

12 Blue Creek, running through the middle of Blue Creek Field Station, Toledo District; Belize, remote and rustic.

13 Buttressed tree in a clearing on the path into the Tikal archaeological ruins, Tikal National Park, Petén, Guatemala.

14 Waterfall and pool, Cockscomb Basin Wildlife Sanctuary (the Jaguar Sanctuary), Stann Creek District, Belize. Stunning trails in a remote setting, and the chance to see El Tigre.

15 Trail between ruins, Tikal National Park, Petén, Guatemala. Trails here are stunning, the wildlife, wonderful; an incomparable site.

16 Excellent birding and lizard-hunting habitat, Tikal archaeological ruins, Tikal National Park, Petén, Guatemala. Visitors interested in subjects other than plants and animals, such as ancient civilizations, may also find much to admire in the park.

17 Towering lowland tropical forest along the Passion River, on the boat trip to El Ceibal Archaeological Park, Petén, Guatemala.

18 Trail through the tropical forest at El Ceibal Archaeological Park, Petén, Guatemala.

19 Excavated ruins in a remote, park-like setting, surrounded by tropical forest; E l Ceibal Archaeological Park, Petén, Guatemala.

20 The view of Lake Petén Itza from one of the look-outs at Cerro Cahui Nature Reserve, Petén, Guatemala.

REFERENCES

Boag, D. 1982. *The Kingfisher*. Blandford Press, Poole, UK.

Bowes, A. L. 1964. *Birds of the Mayas*. West-of-the-Wind Publications, Big Moose, NY.

Emmons, L. H. 1997. *Neotropical Rainforest Mammals: A Field Guide, 2nd ed.* University of Chicago Press, Chicago.

Fuertes, L. A. 1914. Impressions of the voices of tropical birds. *Bird Lore* 16: 342–349.

Greene, H. W. 1997. *Snakes: The Evolution of Mystery in Nature*. University of California Press, Berkeley.

Greene, H. W. & R. L. Seib. 1983. *Micrurus nigrocinctus* (Coral Snake). In: *Costa Rican Natural History*, D. H. Janzen, ed. University of Chicago Press, Chicago, pp. 406–408.

Hairston, N. G. 1994. *Vertebrate Zoology: An Experimental Field Approach*. Cambridge University Press, Cambridge.

Howell, S. N. G. & S. Webb. 1995. *A Guide to the Birds of Mexico and Northern Central America*. Oxford University Press, New York.

Janzen, D. H. 1983. *Costa Rican Natural History*. University of Chicago Press, Chicago. (an edited work with many contributors)

Janzen, D. H. & D. E. Wilson. 1983. Mammals. In: *Costa Rican Natural History*, D. H. Janzen, ed. University of Chicago Press, Chicago, pp. 426–442.

Kricher, J. C. 1989. *A Neotropical Companion: An Introduction to the Animals, Plants, and Ecosystems of the New World Tropics*. Princeton University Press, Princeton, NJ.

Lee, J. C. 1996. *The Amphibians and Reptiles of the Yucatán Peninsula*. Cornell University Press, Ithaca, New York.

Levey, D. J., T. C. Moremond, & J. S. Denslow. 1994. Frugivory: An overview. In: *La Selva: Ecology and Natural History of a Neotropical Rain Forest*, L. A. McDade, K. S. Bawa, H. A. Hespenheide, & G. S. Hartshorn, eds. University of Chicago Press, Chicago, pp. 282–298.

Perrins, C. M. 1985. Trogons. In: *The Encyclopedia of Birds*, C. M. Perrins & A. L. A. Middleton, eds. Facts on File Publications, New York.

Peterson, C. R., A. R. Gibson, & M. E. Dorcas. 1993. Snake thermal ecology. In: *Snakes: Ecology and Behavior*, R. A. Seigel & J. T. Collins, eds. McGraw-Hill, New York, pp. 241–314.

Pough, F. H., J. B. Heiser, & W. N. McFarland. 1996. *Vertebrate Life*. Prentice Hall, Upper Saddle River, NJ.

Primack, R. B. 1993. *Essentials of Conservation Biology*. Sinauer Associates, Sunderland, MA.

Skutch, A. F. 1958. Life history of the White-whiskered Soft-wing *Malacoptila panamensis. Ibis* 100: 209–231.

Skutch, A. F. 1971. Life history of the Broad-billed Motmot, with notes on the Rufous Motmot. *Wilson Bulletin* 83: 74–94.

Stiles, F. G. & D. H. Janzen. 1983. *Cathartes aura* (Turkey Vulture). In: *Costa Rican Natural History*, D. H. Janzen, ed. University of Chicago Press, Chicago, pp. 560–562.

Stiles, F. G. & A. F. Skutch. 1989. *A Field Guide to the Birds of Costa Rica*. Cornell Univeristy Press, Ithaca, NY.

Strauch, J. G. 1983. *Calidris alba* (Sanderling). In: *Costa Rican Natural History*, D. H. Janzen, ed. University of Chicago Press, Chicago, pp. 556–557.

Zug, G. 1983. *Bufo marinus* (Marine Toad). In: *Costa Rican Natural History*, D. H. Janzen, ed. University of Chicago Press, Chicago, pp. 386–387.

SPECIES INDEX

GENERAL INDEX

trogons 152
vultures 129
see also cryptic coloration
colubrid snakes 89–93
Colubridae 90
Columbia River Forest Reserve (Belize)
9, 42–3
Columbidae 136
comets (hummingbirds) 148
commensalism 55
antbirds 166
opossums 196
wrens 174
communal breeders, cuckoos as 142
communal roosting of vultures 131
Community Baboon Sanctuary (Belize)
9–11, 38–9, 47–8, 82, 194, 204–5
competition 55
condors 129
Consejo Nacional de Areas Protegidas
(CONAP, Guatemala) 50–1
Conservation International 51
Convention on International Trade in
Endangered Species (CITES) 60
cooperative breeding in birds 110, 174
Coraciiformes 156
Coral Cay Conservation Ltd. 48
coral reef communities 227–8
coral snakes 94, 95, 97
corallite 228
corals 227–9
cormorants 43, 114, 116
Corozal District (Belize) 9, 29–30, 37,
61
Corvidae 176
cosmopolitan species 59
cotingas 110, 169–71
Cotingidae 169
cowbirds 180, 181, 182
Cracidae 125
cracids 126
crepuscular species 59
crocodiles 81, 83–6
crocodilians 83–6
Crooked Tree Wildlife Sanctuary (Belize)
9, 10, 11, 38, 47, 48, 82
crows 1763
cryptic coloration
amphibians 65
geckos 98
goatsuckers 145
reptiles 82
tinamous 128–9
cuckoos 45, 141–3
Cuculidae 141

cuculids 141
cud-chewing, in deer 218
curassows 125–7
cursorial species 59

dabbler ducks 121
darters 116
Dasypodidae 207
Dasyproctidae 210
deciduous forests 29
deer 13, 34, 37, 40, 42, 50, 217–19
defense mechanisms
color schemes in snakes 96
distraction displays of pigeons 137
opossums 196
poisons in amphibians 105–6
poisons in reptiles 106–7
salamanders 67
toads 68
deforestation 46
Delphinidae 221
Dendrocolaptidae 163
detritivores 59
dewlap 126
Didelphidae 195
distraction displays of pigeons 137
distribution 56
diurnal species 59
diver ducks 121
dogs 212
dolphins 221–3, 229
Doubloon Bank Caye 43
doves 135–8
drumming, by woodpeckers 160
ducks 121–3
Dugong 221, 223

eagles 132
echolocation of bats 197
ecological interactions 54–6, 59
ecological niches
bats 198
ecology 54–6
ecotourism
benefits 3–5
ethics 3–5
history 2–3
importance of 1–2
Edentata 206
edentates 206
egrets 43, 117–19
El Mirador National Park (Guatemala)
52, 53
El Pilar Archaeological Reserve (Belize)
42